1 & 2 TIMOTHY AND TITUS

Raymond F. Collins

1 & 2 TIMOTHY AND TITUS

A Commentary

Westminster John Knox Press
LOUISVILLE • LONDON

© 2002 Raymond F. Collins

Book design by Jennifer K. Cox

First edition
Published by Westminster John Knox Press
Louisville, Kentucky

This book is printed on acid-free paper that meets the American National Standards Institute Z39.48 standard. ∞

PRINTED IN THE UNITED STATES OF AMERICA

02 03 04 05 06 07 08 09 10 11 — 10 9 8 7 6 5 4 3 2 1

Cataloging-in-Publication Data can be obtained from the Library of Congress.
ISBN 0-664-22247-1

In Grateful Memory
of
Oscar R. Ferland
and
Arthur A. Sullivan
Devoted Pastors and Preachers

CONTENTS

PREFACE

The Pastoral Epistles constitute an exercise in carrying on the tradition of Paul the apostle. These texts in the form of letters are an abiding witness to the pioneering effort of an anonymous author who sought to convey the apostle's message to people of a later generation. Similarly, this commentary on the Pastoral Epistles represents a pioneering effort and an attempt to carry on the tradition. It launches the New Testament Library commentary series, seeking to carry on the work of those who published the Old Testament Library and the various monographs of the companion New Testament Library. For this writer, participation in this new endeavor has been simultaneously exciting, challenging, and rewarding.

The commentary strives to carry on the tradition of the Pastoral Epistles. It attempts to interpret for people of a new time these ancient texts and the tradition to which they attest. With this as its goal, the volume attempts to show how the author of these epistles reached back to Paul, interpreting his message anew. In doing so, the author employed the idiom of the Hellenistic world and alluded to the practices of a developing rabbinic Judaism. As witness to the world in which the author wrote his epistles, this commentary sets before the reader various Hellenistic and Jewish texts. I hope these references will challenge the reader of this commentary to use the idiom and practices of our times to interpret once again the tradition of Paul the apostle.

Reflecting on Paul, the author of the Pastorals mentions many people associated with Paul in the exercise of his ministry. Some of the names that appear in the epistles belong to otherwise anonymous individuals; other names are those of individuals who are relatively well known. Many people have been associated with me in the writing of this commentary. Most of them remain anonymous. To all of them, I am grateful. For more than forty years they have contributed to my understanding of the Pauline tradition and have helped me, in turn, to interpret that tradition for others.

Of the many individuals who have contributed in a special way to this effort to interpret the Pauline tradition, there are a few I would like to mention by name. First of all, I would like to thank Frank Matera and Beverly Roberts

Gaventa, who encouraged me to undertake this work. Their kind words led me to repeated contacts with C. Clifton Black and Carey C. Newman, respectively, my academic editor and a member of the NTL editorial board, and the series editor for Westminster John Knox Press. It was a great pleasure to work with Clift and Carey in this pioneering effort. I am grateful for all their work and their encouragement. I can only hope that their personal investment in this project will be well rewarded by those who will use this commentary and the volumes yet to be published in this series.

The author of the Pastorals describes Paul, who, in the waning moments of his life, requested books and especially the parchments (2 Tim. 4:13). As this volume was reaching its final stages, I too needed a few books and an occasional article. I am grateful to those who provided them to me, especially Reimund Bieringer, Pieter de Villiers, Jack Dick, Florence Morgan Gillman, and Veronica Koperski. I am also grateful to those former students, especially John Barba, Ireneusz Ekiert, Mary Elizabeth Kenel, Maureen Roan, and Paul Williamson, who read earlier versions of the manuscript. Their observations, probing questions, and helpful suggestions have contributed substantially to my work.

Unlike those Hellenistic authors who dictated their letters to faithful scribes, I had no scribe to assist me in the production of this manuscript. I was blessed, however, in having the help of Ms. Joan V. Fricot, lecturer in English at Johnson and Wales University. Her discerning eye allowed me to avoid many grammatical errors and more than one confusing statement. May this printed volume serve as a token of my gratitude.

The Pastorals proclaim that the apostle Paul passed the mantle of his ministry to his faithful sons in faith, Timothy and Titus. As this project was coming to its close, I often reflected on my recent association with James Rhodes. Like Paul and Timothy (2 Tim. 1:5), Jim and I share a common heritage. For four years, Jim toiled as my research assistant, closely following my teaching, my way of life, my purpose, my faith, my patience, my love, my steadfastness, my persecutions, and my suffering (2 Tim. 3:10–11). I trust that he has learned as much from me as I have learned from him. I am grateful to him for all that he did to bring this book into existence. As he is about to embark on his own academic career, I acknowledge him as a faithful and competent coworker.

For the most part, the Pastoral Epistles look ahead to the continuation of Paul's ministry. They are not, however, devoid of memory (2 Tim. 1:3–6). My own memory has provided inspiration and energy for this commentary on the Pastorals. I have the heartfelt memory of two Roman Catholic priests who have gone before me to receive the crown of righteousness (2 Tim. 4:8). These devoted pastors, Oscar R. Ferland (d. 1998) and Arthur A. Sullivan (d. 2000), manifested their abiding love for the word of God when they zealously proclaimed in the household of God the mystery with which all believers agree (1 Tim. 3:15). My life has been enriched by the friendship of Oscar and Arthur. My work, once supported by their encouragement, is now inspired by their memory. To them this book is dedicated. May it provide the kind of tribute that each of them so richly deserves.

ACKNOWLEDGMENTS

Citations of the biblical texts follow the New Revised Standard Version. Citations of the Old Testament Apocrypha are taken from *The Old Testament Pseudepigrapha,* edited by James H. Charlesworth (2 vols.; Garden City, N.Y.: Doubleday, 1983–1985). Citations of the *Acts of Paul* are taken from *New Testament Apocrypha,* vol. 2, edited by W. Schneemelcher, translated by R. McL. Wilson (London: Lutterworth; Phildelphia: Westminster, 1965). Citations of classical authors are taken from the editions of the Loeb Classical Library (Cambridge, Mass.: Harvard University Press).

ABBREVIATIONS

Most of these abbreviations are those found in *The SBL Handbook of Style: For Ancient Near Eastern, Biblical, and Early Christian Studies* (Peabody, Mass.: Hendrickson, 1999).

AB	Anchor Bible
AnBib	Analecta biblica
ANF	*Ante-Nicene Fathers*
ANRW	*Aufstieg und Niedergang der römischen Welt: Geschichte und Kultur Roms im Spiegel der neueren Forschung.* Edited by H. Temporini and W. Haase, Berlin, 1972–
ANTC	Abingdon New Testament Commentaries
APB	*Acta Patristica et Byzantina*
AUSS	*Andrews University Seminary Studies*
AV	Authorized Version
BAGD	Bauer, W., W. F. Arndt, F. W. Gingrich, and F. W. Danker. *Greek-English Lexicon of the New Testament and Other Early Christian Literature.* Chicago, 1957
BDF	Blass, F., A. Debrunner, and R. W. Funk. *A Greek Grammar of the New Testament and Other Early Christian Literature.* Chicago, 1961
BETL	Bibliotheca ephemeridum theologicarum lovaniensium
BGU	*Aegyptische Urkunden aus den Königlichen Staatlichen Museen zu Berlin, Griechische Urkunden.* 15 vols. Berlin, 1895–1983
Bib	*Biblica*
BJRL	*Bulletin of the John Rylands University Library of Manchester*
BJS	Brown Judaic Studies
BNTC	Black's New Testament Commentaries
BR	*Biblical Research*
BSac	*Bibliotheca sacra*
BTB	*Biblical Theology Bulletin*
BZ	*Biblische Zeitschrift*

BZNW	Beihefte zur Zeitschrift für die neutestamentliche Wissenschaft
CBQ	*Catholic Biblical Quarterly*
CEV	Contemporary English Version
EBib	*Etudes bibliques*
EDNT	*Exegetical Dictionary of the New Testament*. Edited by H. Balz, G. Schneider. ET. Grand Rapids, 1990–1993
EKKNT	Evangelisch-katholischer Kommentar zum Neuen Testament
EncJud	*Encyclopaedia Judaica*. 16 vols. Jerusalem, 1972
EncRel	*Encyclopedia of Religion*. 16 vols. New York, 1987
ETL	*Ephemerides theologicae lovanienses*
ETS	Erfurter theologische Studien
EvQ	*Evangelical Quarterly*
ExpTim	*Expository Times*
FNT	*Filologia neotestamentaria*
FRLANT	Forschungen zur Religion und Literatur des Alten und Neuen Testaments
GNS	*Good News Studies*
GNT	*Greek New Testament*. Edited by B. Aland, et al. 4th ed. Stuttgart, 1993
Gn. Vat	*Gnomologium Vaticanum e codice Vaticano Graeco 743*. Edited by L. Sternbach. Berlin, 1963.
HBT	*Horizons in Biblical Theology*
HTKNT	Herders theologischer Kommentar zum Neuen Testament
HUT	Hermeneutische Untersuchungen Zur Theologie
ICC	International Critical Commentary
ITQ	*Irish Theological Quarterly*
JB	Jerusalem Bible
JBL	*Journal of Biblical Literature*
JETS	*Journal of the Evangelical Theological Society*
JSNT	*Journal for the Study of the New Testament*
JSNTSup	Journal for the Study of the New Testament: Supplement Series
JSOT	*Journal for the Study of the Old Testament*
LS	*Louvain Studies*
LTP	*Laval théologique et philosophique*
LXX	Septuagint
MAL	Middle Assyrian Laws
MAMA	*Monumenta Asiae Minoris Antiqua*. Manchester and London, 1928–1993
MM	Moulton, J. H. and G. Milligan, *The Vocabulary of the Greek New Testament*. London, 1930. Reprint, Peabody, Mass., 1997
MNTC	Moffatt New Testament Commentary

MTS	Münchener Theologische Studien
NCB	New Century Bible
NIGTC	New International Greek Testament Commentary
NIV	New International Version
NJBC	*The New Jerome Biblical Commentary.* Edited by R. E. Brown, et al. Englewood Cliffs, N.J., 1990
NRSV	New Revised Standard Version
NTD	Das Neue Testament Deutsch
NTL	New Testament Library
NTS	*New Testament Studies*
NTT	*Norsk Teologisk Tidsskrift*
NTTS	New Testament Tools and Studies
OTL	Old Testament Library
PG	Patrologia graeca [=Patrologiae cursus completus: Series graeca]. Edited by J.-P. Migne. 162 vols. Paris, 1857–1886
PL	Patrologia latina [=Patrologiae cursus completus: Series latina]. Edited by J.-P. Migne. 217 vols. Paris, 1844–1864
RB	*Revue biblique*
REB	Revised English Bible
RNAB	New American Bible, revised edition
RNT	Regensburger Neues Testament
RST	Regensburger Studien zur Theologie
RSV	Revised Standard Version
RThom	*Revue thomiste*
SB	Sources bibliques
SBFLA	*Studii biblici Franciscani liber annus*
SBLDS	Society of Biblical Literature Dissertation Series
SBLSBS	Society of Biblical Literature Sources for Biblical Study
SBLSP	*Society of Biblical Literature Seminar Papers*
SBT	Studies in Biblical Theology
SEÅ	*Svensk exegetisk årsbok*
SIG	*Sylloge inscriptionum graecarum.* Edited by W. Dittenberger. 4 vols. 3d ed. Leipzig, 1915–1924
SNTSMS	Society for New Testament Studies Monograph Series
ST	*Studia theologica*
SVF	*Stoicorum veterum fragmenta.* H. von Arnim. 4 vols. Leipzig, 1903–1924
TDNT	*Theological Dictionary of the New Testament.* Edited by G. Kittel and G. Friedrich. Translated by G. W. Bromiley. 10 vols. Grand Rapids, 1964–1976
THKNT	Theologischer Handkommentar zum Neuen Testament

TLNT	*Theological Lexicon of the New Testament*. C. Spicq. Translated and edited by J. D. Ernest. 3 vols. Peabody, Mass., 1994
TTJ	*Trinity Theological Journal*
TynBul	*Tyndale Bulletin*
TZ	*Theologische Zeitschrift*
WUNT	Wissenschaftliche Untersuchungen zum Neuen Testament
ZBKNT	Zürcher Bibelkommentar, Neues Testament
ZNW	*Zeitschrift für die neutestamentliche Wissenschaft und die Kunde der älteren Kirche*

BIBLIOGRAPHY

1. Commentaries

Barrett, C. K. *The Pastoral Epistles in the New English Bible.* New Clarendon Bible. Oxford: Clarendon, 1963.

Bassler, Jouette M. *1 Timothy, 2 Timothy, Titus.* ANTC. Nashville: Abingdon, 1996.

Brox, Norbert. *Die Pastoralbriefe.* RNT 7/2. 4th ed. Regensburg: Pustet, 1969.

Davies, Margaret. *The Pastoral Epistles.* New Testament Guide. Sheffield: JSOT Press, 1996.

Dibelius, Martin, and Hans Conzelmann. *The Pastoral Epistles.* Hermeneia. Philadelphia: Fortress, 1972.

Dornier, P. *Les Épitres pastorales.* SB. Paris: Gabalda, 1969.

Fee, Gordon D. *1 and 2 Timothy, Titus.* Rev. ed. Peabody, Mass.: Hendrickson, 1988.

Hanson, Anthony Tyrell. *The Pastoral Epistles.* NCB. Grand Rapids: Eerdmans; London: Oliphants, 1982.

Hasler, Victor. *Die Briefe an Timotheus und Titus.* ZBKNT 12. Zurich: Theologischer Verlag, 1978.

Holtz, Gottfried. *Die Pastoralbriefe.* THKNT 13. Berlin: Evangelische Verlagsanstalt, 1965.

Holtzmann, Heinrich Julius. *Die Pastoralbriefe kritisch und exegetisch behandelt.* Leipzig: Engelmann, 1880.

Jeremias, Joachim. *Die Briefe an Timotheus und Titus.* NTD 9. Göttingen: Vandenhoeck & Ruprecht, 1981.

Johnson, Luke Timothy. *The First and Second Letters to Timothy.* AB 35A. New York: Doubleday, 2001.

———. *Letters to Paul's Delegates: 1 Timothy, 2 Timothy, Titus.* New Testament in Context. Valley Forge, Pa.: Trinity Press International, 1996.

Kelly, J. N. D. *A Commentary on the Pastoral Epistles.* BNTC. London: Black, 1963.

Knight, George W., III. *Commentary on the Pastoral Epistles.* NIGTC. Grand Rapids: Eerdmans; Carlisle, England: Paternoster, 1992.

Marshall, I. Howard. *The Pastoral Epistles.* ICC. Edinburgh: T. & T. Clark, 1999.

Oberlinner, Lorenz. *Die Pastoralbriefe.* HTKNT 11/2. Freiburg: Herder, 1994–1996. Vol. 1, *Kommentar zum 1. Timotheusbrief,* 1994; vol. 2, *Kommentar zum 2. Timotheusbrief,* 1995; vol. 3, *Kommentar zur Titusbrief,* 1996.

Oden, Thomas C. *First and Second Timothy and Titus.* Interpretation. Louisville, Ky.: John Knox, 1989.

Quinn, J. D. and W. C. Wacker, *The First and Second Letters to Timothy.* Eerdmans Critical Commentary. Grand Rapids: Eerdmans, 2000.

Quinn, Jerome D. *The Letter to Titus.* AB 35. New York: Doubleday, 1990.

Roloff, Jürgen. *Der Erste Brief an Timotheus.* EKKNT 15. Zurich: Benziger; Neukirchen-Vluyn: Neukirchener, 1988.

Scott, E. F. *The Pastoral Epistles.* MNTC. London: Hodder & Stoughton, 1936.

Spicq, Ceslas. *Saint Paul. Les Épitres pastorales. EBib.* 4th. ed. 2 vols. Paris: Gabalda, 1969.

Towner, Philip H. *1–2 Timothy and Titus.* Downers Grove, Ill.: InterVarsity Press, 1994.

2. Monographs and Important Articles

Aageson, James W. "2 Timothy and Its Theology: In Search of a Theological Pattern." *SBLSP* (1997) 692–714.

Ascough, R. S. *What Are They Saying about the Formation of Pauline Churches?* Mahwah, N.J.: Paulist Press, 1998.

Bauckham, Richard J. "Pseudo-Apostolic Letters." *JBL* 107 (1988): 469–94.

Baum, Armin Daniel. *Pseudepigraphie und literarische Fälschung im frühen Christentum.* WUNT 2/138. Tübingen: Mohr (Siebeck), 2001.

Baumert, Norbert. *Woman and Man in Paul: Overcoming a Misunderstanding.* Collegeville, Minn.: Liturgical Press, 1996.

Berge, Paul Stanton. "'Our Great God and Savior': A Study of *SOTER* as a Christological Title in Titus 2:11–14." Th.D. diss., Union Theological Seminary in Virginia, 1973.

Bligh, Malcolm C. "Seventeen Verses Written for Timothy (2 Tim 4:6–22)." *ExpTim* 109 (1998): 364–69.

Brenk, Frederick E. "Old Wineskins Recycled: *AUTARKEIA* in I Timothy 6.5–10." *FNT* 3 (1990): 39–51.

Brown, Raymond E. *The Churches the Apostles Left Behind.* New York: Paulist Press, 1984.

Bush, Peter G. "A Note on the Structure of 1 Timothy." *NTS* 36 (1990): 152–56.

Campbell, R. A. "*Kai malista oikeiōn*—A New Look at 1 Timothy 5,8." *NTS* 41 (1995): 157–60.

Cipriani, Settimio. "La dottrina del 'depositum' nelle letter pastorali." *Studiorum Paulinorum Congresus Internationalis Catholicus 1961*, vol. 2. AnBib 18. Rome: Pontifical Biblical Institute, 1963.

Collins, Raymond F. "The Case of a Wandering Doxology: Rom 16:25–27." In *New Testament Textual Criticism and Exegesis*, edited by Adelbert Denaux. BETL 161. Louvain: Leuven University Press and Peeters, 2002.

———. "The Image of Paul in the Pastorals." *LTP* 31 (1975): 147–73.

———. "The Pastoral Epistles" in *Letters That Paul Did Not Write: The Epistle to the Hebrews and the Pauline Pseudepigrapha*. GNS 28. Wilmington, Del.: Glazier, 1988.

———. *Sexual Ethics and the New Testament: Behavior and Belief*. Companions to the New Testament. New York: Crossroad, 2000.

———. "The Theology of the Epistle to Titus." *ETL* 76 (2000): 56–72.

Cuss, Dominique. *Imperial Cult and Honorary Terms in the New Testament*. Paradosis 23. Fribourg: Fribourg University Press, 1974.

Dehandschuter, Boudewijn. "*Mēketi hydropotei*: Some Notes on the Patristic Exegesis of 1 Timothy 5:23." *LS* 20 (1995): 265–70.

De Villiers, Pieter G. R. "The Vice of Conceit in 1 Timothy: A Study in the Ethics of the New Testament within Its Graeco-Roman Context." *APB* 7 (1996): 37–67.

Donelson, Lewis R. *Pseudepigraphy and Ethical Argument in the Pastoral Epistles*. HUT 22. Tübingen: Mohr (Siebeck), 1986.

———. "Studying Paul: 2 Timothy as Reminiscence." *SBLSP* (1997): 715–31.

Duff, Jeremy. "P[46] and the Pastorals: A Misleading Comparison." *NTS* 44 (1988): 578–90.

Dupont, Jacques. *Syn Christôi. L'union avec le Christ suivant saint Paul*. Bruges: Desclée, 1952.

Elliott, J. K. *The Greek Text of the Epistles to Timothy and Titus*. Studies and Documents 36. Salt Lake City: University of Utah Press, 1968.

Fee, Gordon D. "Toward a Theology of 2 Timothy—From a Pauline Perspective." *SBLSP* (1997): 732–49.

Fiore, Benjamin. *The Function of Personal Example in the Socratic and Pastoral Epistles*. AnBib 105. Rome: Pontifical Biblical Institute, 1986.

Gillman, Florence M. *Women Who Knew Paul*. Zaccheus Studies: New Testament. Collegeville, Minn.: Liturgical Press, 1992.

Gineste, B. "*Ésan gar proeôrakotes*' (Acts 21,29): Trophime a-t-il été 'vu' à Jersusalem?" *RThom* 95 (1995): 251–72.

Goodwin, Mark J. "The Pauline Background of the Living God as Interpretive Context for 1 Timothy 4.10." *JSNT* 61 (1996): 65–85.

Guerra, Anthony J. "The One God Topos in *Spec. Leg. 1.52*." SBLSP (1990): 148–57.

Gutierrez, Pedro. *La paternité spirituelle selon saint Paul. EBib.* Paris: Gabalda, 1968.

Hanson, A. T. *Studies in the Pastoral Epistles.* London: SPCK, 1968.

Harding, Mark. *Tradition and Rhetoric in the Pastoral Epistles.* Studies in Biblical Literature 3. New York: Peter Lang, 1988.

———. *What Are They Saying about the Pastoral Epistles?* Mahwah, N.J.: Paulist Press, 2001.

Harrill, J. Albert. "The Vice of Slave Dealers in Greco-Roman Society: The Use of a Topos in 1 Timothy 1:10." *JBL* 118 (1999): 97–122.

Harrison, P. N. "Important Hypotheses Reconsidered, III. The Authorship of the Pastoral Epistles." *ExpTim* 67 (1955/56): 77–81.

———. "The Pastoral Epistles and Duncan's Ephesians Theory." *NTS* 2 (1956): 250–61. (Cf. *Paulines and Pastorals.* London: Villiers, 1964, 106–28.)

———. *The Problem of the Pastoral Epistles.* Oxford: Humphrey Milford and Oxford University Press, 1921.

Hasler, Victor. "Epiphanie und Christologie in den Pastoralbriefen." *TZ* 33 (1977): 193–209.

Hegermann, H. "Der geschichtliche Ort der Pastoralbriefe." In *Theologische Versuche,* vol. 2, edited by J. Rogge et al. Berlin: 1970, 47–64.

Holmes, J. M. *Text in a Whirlwind: A Critique of Four Exegetical Devices at 1 Timothy 2.9–15.* JSNTSup 196. Sheffield: Sheffield Academic Press, 2000.

Horrell, David G. "From *adelphoi* to *oikos theou*": Social Transformation in Pauline Christianity." *JBL* 120 (2001): 293–311.

Huston, C. R. "Was Timothy Timid? On the Rhetoric of Fearlessness (1 Corinthians 16:10–11) and Cowardice (2 Timothy 1:7)." *BR* 42 (1997): 58–73.

Jaubert, Annie. "L'image de la colonne (1 Tim 3,15)." *Studiorum Paulinorum Congresus Internationalis Catholicus 1961,* vol. 2. AnBib 18. Rome: Pontifical Biblical Institute, 1963.

Jeffers, James S. "The Influence of the Roman Family and Social Structures on Early Christianity in Rome." *SBLSP* (1988): 370–84.

Jervis, L. Ann. "Paul the Poet in First Timothy 1:11–17; 2:3b–7; 3:14–16." *CBQ* 61 (1999): 695–712.

Johnson, Luke T. "The New Testament's Anti-Jewish Slander and the Conventions of Ancient Polemic." *JBL* 108 (1989): 419–41.

Karris, Robert J. "The Background and the Significance of the Polemic of the Pastoral Epistles." *JBL* 92 (1973): 549–64.

Käsemann, Ernst. "Das Formular eine neutestamentliche Ordinationsparänese." In *Neutestamentliche Studien für Rudolf Bultmann zu seinem 70. Geburtstag am 20. August 1954,* edited by Walter Eltester. BZNW 21. Berlin: Töpelmann, 1954.

Kidd, Reggie M. *Wealth and Beneficence in the Pastoral Epistles: A "Bourgeois" Form of Early Christianity?* SBLDS 122. Atlanta: Scholars Press, 1990.

Kimberley, David R. "1 Tim 2:15: A Possible Understanding of a Difficult Text." *JETS* 35 (1992): 481–86.

Köstenberger, Andreas J., Thomas R. Schreiner, and H. Scott Baldwin, eds. *Women in the Church: A Fresh Analysis of 1 Timothy 2:9–15.* Grand Rapids: Baker, 1995.

Kroeger, Catherine C. "Women in the Church: A Classicist's View of 1 Tim 2:11–15." *Journal of Biblical Equality* 1 (1989): 3–31.

Kroeger, Richard C., Catherine C. Kroeger. *I Suffer Not a Woman: Rethinking 1 Timothy 2:11–14 in Light of Ancient Evidence.* Grand Rapids: Baker, 1992.

Kurz, William S. "Luke 22:14–38 and Greco-Roman and Biblical Farewell Addresses." *JBL* 104 (1985): 251–68.

Läger, K. *Die Christologie der Pastoralbriefe.* Hamburger Theologische Studien 12. Münster: Lit, 1996.

Lau, Andrew Y. *Manifest in Flesh: The Epiphany Christology of the Pastoral Epistles.* WUNT 2/86. Tübingen: Mohr, 1996.

Lemaire, André. "Pastoral Epistles: Redaction and Theology." *BTB* 2 (1972): 25–42.

Lohfink, Gerhard. "Paulinische Theologie in der Rezeption der Pastoralbriefe." In *Paulus in den neutestamentliche Spätschriften,* edited by Karl Kertelege. Freiburg: Herder, 1981.

Low, M. "Can Women Teach? A Consideration of Arguments from Tim. 2:11–15," *TTJ* 3 (1994): 99–123.

Lülsdorff, Raimund. "EKLEKTOI AGGELOI. Anmerkungen zu einer untergegangenen Amtsbezeichnung," *BZ* 36 (1992): 104–8.

Malherbe, Abraham J. *Ancient Epistolary Theorists.* SBLSBS 19. Atlanta: Scholars Press, 1988.

Mappes, David A. "The Discipline of a Sinning Elder." *BSac* 154 (1997): 333–43.

———. "The 'Laying on of Hands' of Elders." *BSac* 154 (1997): 493–97.

Matera, Frank J. *New Testament Ethics: The Legacy of Jesus and Paul.* Louisville, Ky.: John Knox, 1996, 229–47.

McNamara, Martin. *The New Testament and the Palestinian Targum to the Pentateuch.* AnBib 27. Rome: Pontifical Biblical Institute, 1966.

Miller, James D. *The Pastoral Letters as Composite Documents.* SNTSMS 93. Cambridge: Cambridge University Press, 1997.

Mullins, T. Y. "A Comparison between 2 Timothy and the Book of Acts." *AUSS* 31 (1993): 199–203.

Murphy-O'Connor, Jerome. "Redactional Angels in 1 Tim 3,16." *RB* 91 (1984): 178–87.

———. "2 Timothy Contrasted with 1 Timothy and Titus." *RB* 98 (1991): 403–18.

Oberlinner, Lorenz. "Die 'Epiphaneia' des Heilswillens Gottes in Christus Jesus: Zur Grundstruktur der Christologie der Pastoralbriefe." *ZNW* 71 (1980): 192–213.

Osborne, R. E. "St. Paul's Silent Years." *JBL* 84 (1965): 59–65.

Page, Sydney. "Marital Expectations of Church Leaders in the Pastoral Epistles." *JSNT* 50 (1993): 105–20.

Pax, Elpidius. *EPIPHANEIA: Ein religionsgeschichtlicher Beitrag zur biblischen Theologie.* MTS 1/10. Munich: Zink, 1955.

Perriman, Andrew C. "What Eve Did, What Women Shouldn't Do: The Meaning of *authenteō* in 1 Timothy 2:12." *TynBul* 44 (1993): 129–42.

Prior, Michael. *Paul the Letter-Writer and the Second Letter to Timothy.* JSNTSup 23. Sheffield: Sheffield Academic Press, 1989.

Redalié, Yann. *Paul après Paul: Le temps, le salut, la moral selon les épîtres à Timotheé et à Tite.* Le monde de la Bible 31. Geneva: Labor et Fides, 1994.

Rogers, P. V. "The Pastoral Epistles as Deutero-Pauline." *ITQ* 45 (1978): 248–60.

Roloff, Jürgen. *Apostolat-Verkündigung-Kirche. Ursprung, Inhalt und Funktion des kirchlichen Apostelamtes nach Paulus, Lukas und den Pastoralbriefen.* Gütersloh: Gerd Mohn, 1965.

Schenk, Wolfgang. "Die Briefe an Timotheus I und II und an Titus (Pastoralbriefe) in der neueren Forschung (1945–1985)." *ANRW* II, 25, 4 (1987): 3404–431.

Schnider, Franz, and Werner Stenger. *Studien zum neutestamentlichen Briefformular.* NTTS 11. Leiden: Brill, 1987.

Schöllgen, G. "Die *diplē timē* von 1 Tim 5,17." *ZNW* 80 (1989): 232–39.

Spicq, Ceslas. "1 Timothée 5:23." In *Mélanges offerts au Professeur Franz-J. Leenhardt.* Geneva: Labor & Fides, 1968.

Stettler, Hanna. *Die Christologie der Pastoralbriefe.* WUNT 2/105. Tübingen: Mohr, 1998.

Stenger, Werner. *Die Christushymnus 1 Tim 3,16. Eine strukturanalytische Untersuchung.* RST 6. Frankfurt: Lang, 1977.

Stiefel, Jennifer H. "Women Deacons in 1 Timothy: A Linguistic and Literary Look at 'Women Likewise . . .' (1 Tim 3.11)." *NTS* 37 (1995): 442–57.

Testa, E. "L'inno sul 'sacramentum pietatis' (1 Tim 3,16)." *SBFLA* 46 (1996): 87–100.

Thurston, Bonnie B. *The Widows: A Women's Ministry in the Early Church.* Minneapolis: Fortress, 1989.

Tollefson, Kenneth D. "Titus: Epistle of Religious Revitalization." *BTB* 30 (2000): 145–57.

Towner, Philip H. *The Goal of Our Instruction: The Structure of Theology and Ethics in the Pastoral Epistles.* JSNTSup 34. Sheffield: JSOT Press, 1989.

———. "The Portrait of Paul and the Theology of 2 Timothy: The Closing Chapter of the Pauline Story." *HBT* 21 (1999): 151–70.

———. "The Present Age in the Eschatology of the Pastoral Epistles." *NTS* 32 (1986): 427–88.

Trummer, Peter. *Die Paulustradition der Pastoralbriefe*. Frankfurt: Peter Lang, 1978.

Tsuji, M. "Zwischen Ideal und Realität: Zu den Witwen in 1 Tim 5.3–16." *NTS* 47 (2001): 92–104.

Valler, Shulamit. *Women and Womanhood in the Talmud*. BJS 321. Providence, R.I.: Brown University Press, 1999.

Verner, David C. *The Household of God: The Social World of the Pastoral Epistles*. SBLDS 71. Chico, Calif.: Scholars Press, 1983.

Von Campenhausen, Hans. "Polykarp von Smyrna und die Pastoralbriefe." In *Aus der Frühzeit des Christentums: Studien zur Kirchengeschichte des ersten und zeiten Jahrhunderts*. Tübingen: Mohr (Siebeck), 1963.

Von Lips, H. *Glaube, Gemeinde, Amt. Zum Verständnis der Ordination in den Pastoralbriefen*. FRLANT 122. Göttingen: Vandenhoeck & Ruprecht, 1979.

Weima, Jeffrey A. D. *Neglected Endings: The Significance of the Pauline Letter Closings*. JSNTSup 101. Sheffield: Sheffield Academic Press, 1994.

Williams, David J. *Paul's Metaphors: Their Context and Character*. Peabody, Mass.: Hendrickson, 1999.

Wilson, Stephen G. *Luke and the Pastoral Epistles*. London: SPCK, 1979.

Wolter, Michel. *Die Pastoralbriefe als Paulustradition*. FRLANT 146. Göttingen: Vandenhoeck & Ruprecht, 1988.

Young, Frances. "The Pastoral Letters and the Ethics of Reading." *JSNT* 45 (1992): 105–20. Reprinted, Stanley E. Porter and Craig A. Evans, eds., *The Pauline Writings*. Biblical Seminar 34. Sheffield: Sheffield Academic Press, 1995.

———. *The Theology of the Pastoral Letters*. New Testament Theology. Cambridge: Cambridge University Press, 1994.

INTRODUCTION
TO THE PASTORAL EPISTLES

In the New Testament canon, the epistles to Timothy and Titus appear after Paul's letters to the seven churches and before the letter to Philemon. Thomas Aquinas, the thirteenth-century Dominican theologian, described the First Epistle to Timothy as being "virtually a pastoral rule" (*quasi regula pastoralis*, *In omnes S. Pauli Apostoli epistolas commentaria*, at 1 Tim. 1:4.). At the beginning of the eighteenth century (1703), D. N. Bardot described it as a "pastoral letter" (*Pastoral-Brief*). In 1753 Paul Anton published the first of his two "Exegetical Essays on the Pastoral Epistles of Paul to Timothy and Titus" in Halle. The second essay was published in 1755. Since then the New Testament's Epistles to Timothy and its Epistle to Titus have been known as the Pastoral Epistles.

Second Century Witnesses

The oldest extant text containing any part of the Pastorals is a fragment of a single page of a papyrus codex (P^{32})[1] that probably originated in Oxyrhynchus, Egypt. Presently located in the John Rylands University Library, Manchester, England, the papyrus has a partial text of Titus 1:11–15 on one side and of 2:3–8 on the other. Scholars have generally dated this bit of parchment to about 200 C.E., but the similarity of its calligraphy with that of P. Oxy. 656, containing texts from Genesis, has led a number of recent scholars to suggest that the text was probably copied in the late second century.

A turn-of-the-third-century papyrus (P^{46}) sometimes thought to have contained the "canon" of Paul's letters to the churches, does not contain the Pastoral Letters. Neither does the fourth-century Codex Vaticanus, generally considered one of the most reliable manuscripts of the New Testament, contain these texts. Although P^{46} and the Vaticanus do not contain the Pastorals, the epistles were well known in the early church. The 1975 edition of the *Biblia*

---

1. Among extant New Testament papyri only P^{32} and P^{61} contain any portion of the Pastoral Epistles. P^{61}, a late seventh or early eighth-century papyrus, contains a fragmentary text of Titus 3:1–5, 8–11, 14–15.

Patristica cites about 450 second-century references to these epistles. Polycarp's Letter to the Philippians, probably to be dated to about 120, appears to contain many references to the epistles.[2] During the second century there was even some controversy about the authority of the Pastorals. Tertullian reports that Marcion excluded all three epistles from his bowdlerized canon (*Adversus Marcionem* 5:21 [PL 2.524]). Jerome says that Tatian accepted Titus but not the epistles to Timothy (*Prologue to Titus* [PL 26.556]).

It may have been that the Pastoral Epistles circulated during the second century in a small codex containing Paul's personal letters to his coworkers Timothy, Titus, and Philemon. Were this assumption able to be proven, it might explain the omission of the texts from P[46] and the Vaticanus. These four texts are generally considered to have been written by Paul to an individual. A closer reading of each of the texts suggests otherwise. Philemon was written to Philemon, Apphia, Archippus, and the church that gathered in Philemon's house (Phlm. 1–2). The final greeting of each of the Pastoral Epistles suggests that they were intended for a community, not just for the church leader to whom they are addressed (1 Tim. 6:21; 2 Tim. 4:22; Titus 3:15).

The Pastorals, Different from Other Epistles

The Epistles to Timothy and Titus are rather different from the Letter to Philemon. The latter is clearly a personal letter with a single major purpose, namely, the plea that Paul makes on behalf of the slave Onesimus. The Pastoral Epistles are much longer than Philemon; their vocabulary, style, and subject matter set them apart from the short letter to Philemon.

These same features distinguish the Pastoral Epistles from the collection of seven letters generally attributed to Paul himself: Romans, 1–2 Corinthians, Galatians, Philippians, 1 Thessalonians, and Philemon. Of the 850 or so different Greek words used in the Pastorals, not counting the names of persons and places, almost one third do not appear in the seven undisputed Pauline letters. Much of the non-Pauline vocabulary appears in late first-century and early second-century Hellenistic literature, including some early Christian literature. The fact that some of this phraseology is found in Luke-Acts has led some scholars to see a Lukan hand in the redaction of the Pastorals. Some of the personal and geographic names found in the Pastorals are also found in Luke-Acts.

On the other hand, some of Paul's most common phrases and some features of his style are missing from the Pastorals. Some of the more important terms

---

2. See K. Berding, "Polycarp of Smyrna's View of the Authorship of 1 and 2 Timothy," *VC* 53 (1999): 349–60; Paul Hartog, *Polycarp and the New Testament,* WUNT 2/134 (Tübingen: Mohr Siebeck, 2001).

in Paul's theological vocabulary, "body" (*sōma*), for example, are not to be found.[3] The title "Lord" is not a particularly striking element in the Pastorals' Christology even though it is the apostle's preferred christological title. "Righteousness" (*dikaiosynē*) has nuances different from those that the word has in Romans and Galatians. Paul's characteristic "in Christ" (*en Christō*) formula has a different theological connotation in the Pastorals. As used by the apostle, the phrase is to be understood almost in a mystical sense. When the phrase appears in the Pastorals, the phrase means little more than does the adjective "Christian."

The style of the Pastorals is more ponderous and pedantic than the free-flowing epistolary style of Paul. Their style is sometimes periodic with a good use of subordinate clauses and a wide variety of tenses. At other times, the heavy style of the Pastorals is exceedingly complex, with the result that the style of several long sentences is a veritable syntactic maze. In any event, the texts were clearly intended to be read aloud. Several of their stylistic features (asyndeton and polysyndeton, alliteration, assonance, and paronomasia, repetition and rhyme) were intended to increase the rhetorical impact of an oral text that sounded well.

The Matter of Authenticity

Early in the nineteenth century, the lexical and stylistic peculiarities of the Pastoral Epistles led some scholars to question their authenticity. One of the first to raise questions about 1 Timothy was J. E. C. Schmidt, who in 1804/5 published a *Historical-Critical Introduction to the New Testament*. Schmidt held that the vocabulary of this epistle makes it highly unlikely that it was written by the same person who wrote 2 Timothy and Titus. If these two were by Paul, 1 Timothy was not.

In 1807 Friedrich Schleiermacher's study of the vocabulary of 1 Timothy led him to conclude that an author later than Paul borrowed linguistic elements from 2 Timothy and Titus to write 1 Timothy. His systematic examination of the epistle also noted that the biographical information contained in the text was inconsistent with what was otherwise known about Paul. Meanwhile, Edward Evanson (1805) accepted Paul's authorship of both 1 and 2 Timothy but expressed reservations about the authenticity of Titus.

From these early nineteenth-century works, a consensus of critical German scholarship began to emerge, which held the position that none of the Pastorals had been written by Paul. Johann Gottfried Eichorn's *Introduction to the New*

---

3. John A. T. Robinson opined that "the omission of the word [*sōma*] from the Pastorals seems as decisive an argument against their Pauline authorship . . . as any that can be advanced." See J. A. T. Robinson, *The Body: A Study in Pauline Theology*, SBT 5 (London: SCM Press, 1952), 10.

Testament (1812) was one of the first German introductions to deny Pauline authorship of all three epistles. Ferdinand Christian Baur's 1835 publication of *Die sogenannten Pastoralbriefe des Apostels Paulus aufs neue kritisch untersucht* (*The So-called Pastoral Epistles of the Apostle Paul, a New Critical Study* [1835]) added a new element to the discussion. Baur contended that the similarities between the positions attacked by the Pastorals and the Gnostic heresy so vigorously combatted by Irenaeus were sufficient to type the Pastorals as an early second-century response to this Christian heresy. Thereafter, the classic German introductions to the New Testament generally proposed that the Pastorals had not been written by Paul. Thus, Heinrich Julius Holtzmann's introduction (1885), offering a precis of nineteenth-century critical scholarship, opted for a non-Pauline authorship of these epistles.

A large number of conservative scholars dealt with the issues raised by the nineteenth century's critical analysis of the Pastorals by suggesting that these epistles were written by one of Paul's scribes. To its own stylized question about the authenticity of the epistles—"Whether the difficulties commonly advanced . . . in any way weaken the opinion which holds as ratified and certain the genuineness of the Pastoral Epistles?"—the Roman Pontifical Biblical Commission responded with a dismissive negative (June 12, 1913). Nevertheless, the issues were on the table and continued to be discussed.

By the end of the twentieth century New Testament scholarship was virtually unanimous in affirming that the Pastoral Epistles were written some time after Paul's death. Scholars who held this opinion continued to cite the stylistic and lexical issues, the theological views, the biographical data, and the skeletal elements of church structure that emerge from critical study of the epistles. As always, some scholars dissent from the consensus view. Thus, George W. Knight (1992) and Luke Timothy Johnson (1996, 2001) continue to maintain Pauline authorship.

At times, 2 Timothy appears to be a case apart in the discussion about the authenticity of the Pastoral Epistles. Most scholars consider it to be an anonymous composition, the latest of the Pastorals and one of the latest New Testament texts. Michael Prior (1989) and Jerome Murphy-O'Connor (1991,[4] 1996), however, hold that 2 Timothy was written by the apostle himself shortly before—perhaps just a few days before—his death. Some scholars take exception to the general consensus on the composition of the Pastorals by resorting to a fragment hypothesis for the composition of 2 Timothy. They agree the epistle was not written by Paul but hold that an anonymous compiler who had access to authentic notes written by Paul incorporated these fragments into his own work.

That hypothesis is generally associated with the name of P. N. Harrison,

---

4. Jerome Murphy-O'Connor, *Paul: A Critical Life* (Oxford: Clarendon Press, 1996) 357–59.

whose work *The Problem of the Pastoral Epistles* (1921) was to become the focal point of the twentieth-century discussion of the fragment hypothesis. Harrison's theorizing was preceded by various nineteenth-century scholars[5] who doubted the Pauline authorship of 2 Timothy, yet entertained the possibility that it contained some authentic material. Harrison hypothesized that extant 2 Timothy includes fragments of four letters that had been written by Paul himself. From a first letter written from Macedonia would have come 2 Tim. 4:13–15, 20, 21a; from a second, written from Caesarea, 2 Tim. 4:16–18a[b?]; from a third, written after Paul had been recalled to Rome, 2 Tim. 4:9–12, 22b; from a fourth, written in Rome, perhaps on the day of his death, 2 Tim. 1:16–18; 3:10–11; 4:1–2a, 5b; 4:6–8, 18b–19, 21b–22a. In addition, Harrison claimed that much of 2 Timothy 1 was what he called "a cento of phrases culled from the ten Paulines." Harrison mentioned a fifth fragmentary source of the Pastorals that contained extant Titus 3:12–15.

Notwithstanding some criticism of the theory and Harrison's own modification of his ideas (1955, 1956, 1964), Harrison's views were substantially endorsed by C. K. Barrett (1963) and R. E. Osborne (1965).[6] In the modified version of his theory, Harrison continued to maintain that Titus 3:12–15 was originally an independent fragment composed in Macedonia. His revised version held that extant 2 Timothy incorporates fragments from two of Paul's own notes, one sent from Nicopolis in 56 C.E. (= 2 Tim. 4:9–15, 20–21a, 22b), the other sent from Rome in 60 C.E. (= 2 Tim. 1:16–18; 3:10–11; 4:1–2a, 5b–8, 16–19, 21b–22a).

In 1997 James Miller proposed that two Pauline notes comprised the original and authentic core of 2 Timothy. Second Timothy "A," a personal note to Timothy, would have been preserved by Paul's early disciples because of its record of Paul's final days and its moving farewell testimony. This note would have included extant 2 Tim. 1:1–2, (3–5?), 15–18; 4:6–8, 22a. The second note, 2 Timothy "B," would have included 2 Tim. 4:9–21 and 22b (see Miller 147–51). In 1998 Malcolm Bligh suggested that 2 Tim. 4:6–22 was originally part of a note written by Paul in Asia. The apostle had suffered because of Alexander's testimony (see 2 Tim. 4:14–15). Shortly thereafter Paul addressed a note to Timothy but never sent it because he realized that he could borrow a cloak for the winter and obtain parchments from Christians in nearby Colossae!

---

5. Carl Clemen outlined this discussion, beginning in 1836, in an 1894 monograph on the composition of the New Testament epistles.

6. This was the same year that C. F. D. Moule highlighted the improbability of some of the presuppositions of the theory, especially the idea that Paul wrote a series of independent notes that were kept by their recipients and found by a later author who then incorporated them into his own work. See C. F. D. Moule, "The Problem of the Pastoral Epistles: A Reappraisal," *BJRL* 47 (1965): 430–52.

Literary Form

Each of the Pastoral Epistles is in the form of a letter written by Paul to a coworker and apostle (see 1 Thess. 2:7). Both Timothy and Titus had been sent by Paul to communities that Paul had evangelized. Circumstances suggested that a return visit was warranted, but Paul himself was not able to return to these communities. Characteristic epistolary salutations at the beginning and end of each text clearly type each of them as a letter (1 Tim. 1:1–2; 6:21b; 2 Tim. 1:1–2; 4:19–22; Titus 1:1–4; 3:15).

None of the Pastorals clearly corresponds to any one of the epistolary genres identified by the later Hellenistic literary theorists, Pseudo-Demetrius and Pseudo-Libanius. First Timothy and Titus have a similar literary form and both give instructions on church order and address personal exhortation to their respective recipients. In giving instruction on what is to be done and including some hortatory material, the form of these two epistles is similar to that of a Hellenistic papyrus from Egypt, Tebtunis Papyrus 703.[7] In this papyrus, a Ptolemaic official gives instruction to an *oikonomos*, presumably some kind of civic administrator or a manager, on matters pertaining to agriculture, transportation, finances, and government monopolies. Some few lines of the papyrus speak of the personal qualities of the manager and his exemplary behavior. Many of the qualities cited in the papyrus appear in the hortatory material of 1 Timothy and Titus. Johnson (*First and Second Letters*, 139–42) identifies the papyrus as an example of a *mandata principis*, "the commandments of a ruler," letter and assigns both 1 Timothy and Titus to this category. Unfortunately, few examples of such an epistolary type are to be found among the fifty thousand or so extant papyri, and the verses that are truly parallel with 1 Timothy and Titus are relatively few.

The Hellenistic world has also left a legacy of a few testamentary letters. For the most part, these letters deal with bequests, creditors and debtors, and the freeing of slaves.[8] Among these testamentary letters, Socratic Epistles 6 and 27 manifest a hortatory intent, as does 2 Timothy, which is largely concerned with Timothy's succession to the ministry of the dying Paul. As is the case with the *mandata principis* letters, there are too few testamentary letters with a clear hortatory purpose to speak of a literary genre to which 2 Timothy can readily be assigned.

As far as the body of each of the Pastoral Letters is concerned, the material contained in 1 Timothy and Titus is similar to later documents on church order, especially the early second-century *Didache*, the third-century *Didascalia Apostolorum*, the turn-of-the-century *Apostolic Church Order*, the fourth-century

---

7. See A. S. Hunt and J. G. Smyly, *The Tebtunis Papyri* (London: Oxford University Press, 1933), 66–73.

8. See Wilhelm Crönert, *Kolotes und Menedemos. Studien zur Palaeographie und Papyruskunde* 6 (Leipzig: Eduard Avenarius, 1906), 81–87.

Apostolic Constitutions, and the fifth-century *Testamentum Domini*. The material contained in the body of 2 Timothy is of a different sort. With its many "reminiscences" of the life of Paul, its rereading of older traditions, and its concern for Timothy's ministry, the body of this epistle is reminiscent of Jewish and early Christian testamentary literature, to which the *Testaments of the Twelve Patriarchs* and the farewell discourses of Luke 22:25–38, John 13–16, and Acts 20:18–35 belong. Their respective kinship with documents on church order (1 Timothy, Titus) and testamentary literature (2 Timothy) helps to explain the disparate material that they contain. Neither documents on church order nor testamentary texts are truly original compositions. Each of the genres is characterized by its reliance on preexistent material, not all of which is documentary although some of it may be.

In no case can any one of the Pastoral Epistles be considered a truly personal letter. The final words of each of the epistles show that they were directed to an audience larger than the named addressee. The absence of a wish for good health further militates against the possibility that these epistles are truly personal letters. Moreover, the epistolary salutations are far more developed than would be the salutation of a personal note from Paul to one or the other of his close companions and coworkers. A comparison of 1 Tim. 1:1–2; 2 Tim. 1:1–2; and Titus 1:1–4 with Phlm. 1–3 establishes the point. The opening salutations of the Pastoral Epistles are clearly rhetorical ploys intended to establish the authority of the apostle Paul in whose name the directives contained in the body of the letters are promulgated. This is particularly the case with Titus 1:1–4, whose solemnity is such that some commentators claim that it was composed as an introduction to the entire three-letter corpus.

The arguments against Pauline authorship of the Pastoral Epistles that have been advanced and refined during the past two centuries cumulatively raise serious doubts about the authenticity of these texts. Considerations of style and vocabulary,[9] of content and theology, of incipient church order, and of consistency with the Pauline profile established by the undisputed letters and the data supplied by the Acts of the Apostles establish the inauthenticity of these texts beyond all reasonable doubt. The testamentary nature of 2 Timothy suggests that the epistle was not composed by Paul. Extant Hellenistic testamentary letters are a kind of epistolary final will and testament bearing upon the posthumous disposition of one's assets. In contrast, Jewish and Christian testamentary texts, from Deuteronomy to the Johannine farewell discourses, were not composed by those to whom they are attributed.

The pseudepigraphic nature of Judeo-Christian testamentary texts indicates that Jews and early Christians were not averse to accepting pseudepigraphic

---

9. This would include statistical studies of their use of particles, prepositions, conjunctions, and adverbs.

material. In fact, a substantial portion of the Bible's prophetic books and a still larger portion of the wisdom literature was not composed by those to whom it is attributed. This is also the case with apocalyptic literature, both biblical and apocryphal. Of considerable importance in the community's acceptance of these pseudepigraphic texts—albeit less so in the case of apocalyptic literature whose predictive element relies on the naming of an authentic figure in the past—is the authority of religious figure to whom the texts are attributed and the conviction that what is attributed to that authority is a faithful updating of the tradition. The content, not the literary attribution, was the decisive factor in evaluating the "authenticity" of the message.

The idiom and imagery of the Pastoral Epistles identify them as Hellenistic compositions. In that world, some philosophers and orators considered the noble falsehood as an acceptable rhetorical tool (see e.g., Plato, *Republic* 2.282c–283a; Cicero, *Brutus* 11.42). The phenomenon of pseudepigraphic letters was well known. Some of them were written for the pseudepigrapher's self-serving purposes or to discredit the one to whom they were attributed. Others were written to honor the memory of a past teacher or to show that his teaching was relevant for a later generation. The second-century C.E. neo-Platonic philosopher Porphyry acknowledged that of Pythagoras's 280 works, eighty were written by Pythagoras himself. Tertullian admitted that what "disciples publish should be regarded as their master's work" (*Against Marcion* 4.5 [PL 2.567]).

The Pastoral Epistles emerged from the confluence of the Judeo-Christian tradition with the Hellenistic world. Their ostensible epistolary format derives from a desire to engage a tradition that derives from Paul with the circumstances that obtained a few generations later. In the churches of the Roman province of Asia, of which Ephesus was the capital, Paul was singularly acknowledged as the apostle par excellence. He himself had chosen to compensate for his absence through emissaries and letters. Revering the memory of Paul[10] and intending to actualize his teaching, an anonymous author invoked his authority in composing the Pastoral Epistles.

His choice of the epistolary genre owed to the legacy of the letter-writing Paul. The author's adaptation of disparate materials to an epistolary format gave his work historical verisimilitude as the work of Paul himself. He embedded a thanksgiving period in two of the epistles (1 Tim. 1:12–17; 2 Tim. 1:3–5) and elements of the Pauline travelogue and final greetings in the other (Titus 3:12–15). His epistolary salutations enhanced the rhetorical force of the memory of Paul in such a way that the directives contained in the Pastorals were promulgated, as it were, in the name of Paul. The anonymous author, identified as

---

10. Elements of an emerging Pauline hagiography are to be found in the Pastorals, especially in 2 Timothy.

"the Pastor" in this commentary, stands under and invokes the authority of Paul. The search for the identity of the real author is a useful quest that satisfies the demands of modern historical inquiry.[11] The Pastor, however, wanted the readers of his epistles not to think about his own authority but rather to respond to his appeal in the name of Paul.

Related Issues

Given the manifest similarities of vocabulary, style, and theology among the three letters that comprise the small corpus, it is reasonable to assume that a single author wrote all three Pastoral Epistles. Some of their most characteristic features—including their similar use of the epistolary form, the designation of their recipients as Paul's sons, the theological significance of the title "Savior," the "faithful saying" formula, the appearance (*epiphaneia*) motif, the ecclesial use of household imagery, the manifest paraenetic intent, the use of catalogs of virtues and vices—are found in all three epistles notwithstanding the different literary forms of the texts and some variation[12] in the use of common motifs.

The pseudonymous nature of the Pastoral Epistles suggests that they were composed some time after the death of Paul. The testamentary nature of 2 Timothy appears to confirm this hypothesis. Given the absence of any information that can be verified from other sources and the Pastor's use of stock rhetoric and traditional literary forms, it is virtually impossible to determine the date of composition of the Pastoral Epistles. They are post-Pauline; their language is the common language of late first- and early second-century Hellenistic authors; they reflect an ecclesial situation in which the communities for which they were written were trying to find a niche in the Greco-Roman world; and their eschatology has lost its urgency because the expectation of an imminent Parousia has long since waned. These considerations suggest that the Pastorals were probably composed toward the end of the first century sometime after 80 C.E.

11. In 1830 Heinrich August Schott tentatively proposed that Luke was the real author of the Pastorals. In various ways this possibility has been proposed by a number of more recent authors, including August Strobel, "Schreiben des Lukas? Zum spachlichen Problem der Pastoralbriefe," *NTS* 15 (1969): 191–210; Stephen G. Wilson, *Luke and the Pastoral Epistles* (London: SPCK, 1969); Jerome D. Quinn, "The Last Volume of Luke: The Relation of Luke-Acts and the PE," *Perspectives on Luke-Acts*, ed. Charles Talbert (Macon, Ga.: Mercer University Press, 1978), 62–75; and C. F. D. Moule, *Essays in New Testament Interpretation* (Cambridge: Cambridge University Press, 1982), 113–32.

12. Despite the similarities, there are significant differences between 2 Timothy and the epistles that deal with church order. Some of these differences do not depend on their different subjects and literary genres. Jerome Murphy-O'Connor has identified more than thirty differences between 2 Timothy and the other Pastorals. See "2 Timothy Contrasted with 1 Timothy and Titus," *RB* 98 (1991): 403–18.

Timothy and Titus had been Paul's coworkers some thirty or more years earlier. We do not have any reliable information about the deaths of either of these important figures who had enabled Paul to extend his ministry and pastoral care. If for no other reason than that the average life expectancy was about forty,[13] it is all but certain that each of them had died well before the turn of the century. Hence, the Pastoral Epistles should probably be considered as doubly pseudonymous.[14] The name of the recipient as well as the name of the author are literary fictions. Timothy and Titus lent their names to the Pastor's work because they represented Paul's apostolic presence.

The order in which the three epistles appear in the New Testament follows the stylometric principle. First Timothy is longer than 2 Timothy; hence, it precedes 2 Timothy in the New Testament. Because Titus is shorter than 1 Timothy,[15] it finds its place in the canon after the epistles to Timothy. The canonical sequence of the three texts does not depend on the chronological order of their composition. Both the Canon of Muratori and the Ambrosiaster arrange the three epistles in a sequence that differs from the canonical order, namely, Titus, 1 Timothy, 2 Timothy. The elements of church order suggested in Titus are not as developed as are those of 1 Timothy. Thus, it is reasonable to argue that Titus was composed before 1 Timothy.

It is more difficult to situate 2 Timothy within the relative sequence of the three epistles. As a reflective reminiscence on Paul's lifework and his death, 2 Timothy may have been the last of the epistles to have been composed. On the other hand, providing testimony to the importance of that ministry and to the necessity of carrying on the ministry, it may be that 2 Timothy was the first of the Pastorals to have been composed. In any case, it is virtually certain that the epistles were not composed in the order in which they now appear in the New Testament.

Why the Pastor composed two letters to Timothy and one letter to Titus and why he attached their names to these particular epistles remain puzzling questions. That he composed epistles in the name of coworkers who represented Paul's apostolic presence is understandable. Timothy, who had worked with Paul in Asia, Achaia, and Macedonia, was the best known of Paul's companions. An Asian by birth and associated with Paul's ministry in Asia Minor, Timothy represents Paul's presence in the churches of Asia Minor. First Timothy 1:3 locates his work in Ephesus, the capital of the province of Asia. From that metropolitan center, the directives of 1 Timothy could spread throughout the area.

13. Forty years is the generally accepted estimate of life expectancy in the Greco-Roman world. After forty-nine years of age, a man was considered to be elderly; beyond fifty-six he was regarded as old (see Philo, *Creation* 105).

14. See Schnider and Stenger 104–7.

15. The Letter to Philemon is shorter still; hence its place in the canon after the epistles to Timothy and Titus.

The Pastor's choice of Crete and of Titus as Paul's representative on Crete (Titus 1:5) for the shorter letter on church order is even more puzzling, especially if it were written before 1 Timothy. The Pastor has exploited traditions associated with Crete and seemingly alludes to the Jewish presence on the island (Titus 1:12–14). Quinn has suggested that Titus is concerned with the updating of Jewish-Christian congregations and 1 Timothy with Gentile-Christian congregations (see Quinn 16–17; etc.). This is not, however, self-evident. Perhaps one can suggest that directives spelled out in Titus were intended for a less fully developed church community than those of 1 Timothy and that the Pastor's choice of an insular setting was a creative narrative element. This insular setting was further enhanced by the choice of Titus, who was associated with Paul's ministry in the port city of Corinth and who is urged in the epistle to join Paul in the port city of Nicopolis (Titus 3:12).

Engaged Teaching

Guided by considerations of the genre of the Pastoral Epistles and of their pseudepigraphic character, a first reading shows that they have moved some steps beyond Paul's initial proclamation of the gospel and the Spirit-guided communities that he left behind. Taken together, they show a concern for normative formulation of the gospel message, the organization of ecclesial communities, apostolic tradition, and acceptable patterns of behavior to be lived by believers living in the Hellenistic world.

On the horizon of the Pastor's paraenesis, or moral exhortation, are the errors that he seeks to explain and the false teachers whom he seeks to delegitimize. His explanation is both theological and logical. The appearance on the scene of malevolent teachers who lead believers astray is a sign of the final times. As such, they are virtually inevitable (1 Tim. 4:2; 6:3–5; 2 Tim. 3:1–7; 12–13; 4:3–4). The Pastor urges those for whom he is writing to shun these teachers, their teaching, and the various forms of their deviant behavior. The members of the community should not be surprised or overwhelmed by these false teachers and the errors, both doctrinal and behavioral, that they promote. Paul had to deal with false teachers (1 Tim. 1:19–20) and so did Moses before him (2 Tim. 3:8).

Apart from his affirmation of the goodness of God's creation as a rebuttal to those who inhibit marriage and promote dietary abstinence (1 Tim. 4:3–4), the Pastor does not deal directly with the errors on the horizon. He would rather dismiss them as the work of those with seared consciences (1 Tim. 4:2; see Titus 1:15) who have missed the mark of faith (1 Tim. 1:6; 6:21; 2 Tim. 2:18). The Pastor's broadsides make it difficult for a contemporary reader of the gospel to ascertain with any precision the nature and source of the errors with which he is concerned.

To some extent, the errors involve a misreading of the law (1 Tim. 1:7; see Titus 1:14), a misunderstanding of the resurrection (2 Tim. 2:18), an elite sectarianism (1 Tim. 2:1–6), and the worship of divinized emperors (1 Tim. 6:15–16). It is difficult to conceive that this variety of errors comes from a single source, whether in the form of Gnosticism,[16] Judaizing intrusion, or some other form. It is therefore misleading to speak of the Pastor's "opponents" as if they were some well-defined group. It rather seems to be the case that the Pastor wants to put the community on guard against various kinds of error, no matter what their source.

A second reading of the Pastoral Epistles reveals the Pastor's profound engagement with the world in which he and his audience live. Inspired by tradition, he is concerned with effective pastoral ministry. His epistles are themselves an exercise in pastoral ministry. They present a vision of faith, of the Christian life, and of the assembly of believers that would be relevant and effective in the late first century.

A second reading of the Pastoral Epistles shows also that the author's work is profoundly theological. Professing faith in one God and one mediator (1 Tim. 2:5; see 1 Tim. 6:15–16) and promoting the use of the Scriptures (2 Tim. 3:15–17), the Pastor proclaims the paschal mystery in confession (2 Tim. 2:8) and in hymn (1 Tim. 3:16). While these elements are the hallmark of Christian faith, the Pastoral Epistles demonstrate a manifest concern to proclaim the gospel message in the language of late first-century Hellenism. This concern is evident in the way that the Pastor exploits the title of Savior (e.g., 1 Tim. 1:1) and his use of the epiphany motif (e.g., 1 Tim. 6:14) It is equally apparent when the Pastor speaks about the gospel message as sound teaching (e.g., 1 Tim. 1:10). What the Pastor has done is to develop a new and engaged theological idiom for traditional belief.

Sound teaching should lead to appropriate and consistent behavior. In the Decalogue (Exod. 20:2–17; Deut. 5:6–21) and the twofold love command (Matt. 22:37–39; Mark 12:29–31; Luke 10:27), the tradition to which the Pastor is heir proclaims that faith in God is to be accompanied by proper behavior. The Pastor cites neither the Ten Commandments nor Jesus' teaching on love. Instead, he promotes the moral values of the Hellenistic world and uses the paraenetic idiom of his day for this purpose. His paraenesis uses example, employs the

---

16. The discovery of the Nag Hammadi manuscripts in December 1945 has enabled scholars to have a better understanding of late first- and early second-century currents of philosophico-religious thought than was previously possible. Hence, Baur's contention that the Pastorals were composed in opposition to a gnostic heresy has been virtually abandoned in recent discussion about the authenticity of the texts. Various sources, including Paul's First Letter to the Corinthians, show that first-century Hellenistic culture evidenced a fascination with various kinds of knowledge (*gnōsis*), but this was far from the reality of any well-defined and systematized Gnosticism.

agon ("struggle") motif, incorporates catalogs of virtues and vices and household codes, and urges that acceptable moral values be taught. The paraenesis addresses people of different gender, age, and state in life.

For many a contemporary reader, the Pastor's acceptance of the moral values of his world appears to be overly accommodating (1 Tim. 2:11–12; Titus 2:9–10). The Pastor, however, seeks to find a faith-based rationale for his paraenesis (1 Tim. 2:13–3:1; Titus 2:10) and is not uncritical of some societal views (1 Tim. 6:5–10). Elements of a Judeo-Christian anthropology undergird the Pastor's contemporary paraenesis. The epiphany motif enables him to speak of behavior in this life in the light of an expectation of the appearance of the just judge and the great God, our Savior (2 Tim. 4:8; Titus 2:11–13).

A second reading of the Pastoral Epistles also shows that the Pastor's vision of the church was very practical and that it was expressed in the language of first-century Hellenism. Those for whom the Pastor was writing were living at a time when believers were no longer participants in an enthusiastic movement. Rather, they lived in the relatively stable Greco-Roman world, whose rulers were responsible for the general well-being of society within which believers had to find their niche (1 Tim. 2:1–2). Now that the expectation of an imminent Parousia was no longer theirs, believers were constrained to organize themselves. The Pastorals provide evidence of the early church's transition from movement to organization.

The Pastor's use of the image of the Greco-Roman household is key to the organizational structure that he proposes (1 Tim. 3:15; see 2 Tim. 2:20–21). Overseers and servers ensure the management and good function of the house of God. These individuals are to be qualified for their functions, even scrutinized to ensure that they are so qualified (1 Tim. 3:10), and they must enjoy a good reputation (1 Tim. 3:7; see Titus 2:7–8). They are to be properly supported and their rights respected (1 Tim. 5:17–19). Faithful widows without other means of support are to be supported, but they too must meet certain conditions and enjoy a good reputation (1 Tim. 5:3–10).

The Pastorals contain allusions to a ritual of washing, the sign of rebirth and renewal (Titus 3:5), and to the designation of successors-in-ministry through the ritual imposition of hands (1 Tim. 4:14; 2 Tim. 1:6). They say something about the community's worship (1 Tim. 2:1–10), echoing its use of hymn (1 Tim. 3:16; 2 Tim. 2:11–12; Titus 2:14; 3:4–7), confession (1 Tim. 3:16), and creed (2 Tim. 2:8). Finally, the Pastoral Epistles provide a portrait of a founding father (1 Tim. 1:12–16; 2 Tim. 3:10–11), a revered figure from the past by whom they are inspired and whose disciples they profess to be.

This commentary seeks not only to engage the reader with the text of the Pastorals but also to engage the reader with the Pastor's effort to find idioms capable of interpreting the tradition in contemporary terms,[17] to speak of the everyday life and ethical striving of the believer in the language of Hellenistic philosophy and culture,[18] and to find structures and rituals that would provide it with identity, continuity, and permanence in the Greco-Roman world. In doing so, this commentary hopes to help the reader engage traditional faith, ethical teaching, and ecclesial structure in the language of today, contemporary culture, and structures that maintain identity and functional unity while adapting to an ever-changing world.

17. This commentary offers an original translation of the Pastoral Epistles. Other biblical citations are cited according to the NRSV.

18. Classical texts are cited according to the translation provided in the pertinent volumes of the Loeb Classical Library.

1 TIMOTHY

INTRODUCTION

The First Epistle to Timothy, much longer than either of the other two Pastoral Epistles, is ostensibly a letter addressed by Paul, whose apostolate stems from the authority of God and Christ Jesus, to Timothy, his true son in the faith. Immediately after the epistolary greeting, Timothy is described as having been left behind in Ephesus as Paul's delegate to the capital of the Roman province of Asia, where he is to give the word to unidentified persons who are teaching falsely. This verse (1:3) is an implicit statement of purpose, suggesting that the epistle has been written to give Timothy guidance in what and how he should confront those false teachers.

Apart from the epistolary greeting and an apparently misplaced thanksgiving period (1:12–17), 1 Timothy is innocent of typical epistolary conventions. It comes to an abrupt close with an exceptionally terse farewell, a simple "Grace be with you" (6:21b). The epistle lacks the sort of greetings typically found at the end of a Hellenistic letter, greetings such as Paul regularly includes in his letters. This is particularly puzzling insofar as Paul spent a substantial part of his apostolic career in Ephesus—more than two years according to Luke's computation (see Acts 19:8–10; 20:31). True, the epistle is ostensibly addressed only to Timothy (1:2), and Timothy is directly addressed in 1:18 and 6:20[1] (see 6:11), but the final greeting, "Grace be with you," is in the plural. Coupled with the formality of Paul's description of himself in 1:1 in a letter to his true "son," these features render the epistolary character of the text somewhat suspect.

As is the case with many of the New Testament's epistolary texts, a number of different scribal "postscripts" have been added to the text at various points in time. Two of the oldest manuscripts (ℵ and A) identify the epistle as "To Timothy *A*," distinguishing it from 2 Timothy and suggesting that its text was longer than that of 2 Timothy. Several manuscripts identify the epistle as having been written in Laodicea, a city in Asia Minor's Lycus Valley. Others identify its place of origin as Nicopolis, Macedonia, or Athens. These appended notes indicate that, although the church's tradition from the time of Polycarp of

---

1. Once the name of the recipient has been mentioned in the salutation, Hellenistic letters do not normally cite the name again.

Smyrna was unanimous in accepting the Pauline authorship of the epistle, uncertainty reigned over the precise circumstances of its composition.

According to the epistle, Timothy has been mandated by Paul to remain in Ephesus in order to confront false teachers with heartfelt love, a good conscience, and an authentic faith (1:3–5). These troublesome people purported to be teachers of the law but did not understand what they were talking about (1:6), with the result that they were expositing myth and idle speculation rather than God's plan of salvation known in faith (1:4–6). Correcting their erroneous view of the law, the Pastor affirms the utility of the law, specifying that it identifies forms of behavior that must be avoided (see Rom. 7:7). Avoiding the nonsense that comes from these false teachers, Timothy is urged to propose the authentic faith, namely, God's plan of salvation (1:4), sound teaching (1:10), and the glorious gospel entrusted to Paul (1:11).

In 4:1–5 the Pastor returns to the subject of false teachers. His epistle shows no sign of eschatological urgency; nevertheless, it uses an apocalyptic scheme of history that projects the error that Timothy is to confront as a manifestation of an expected onslaught of penultimate evil. This pernicious and widespread error is attributed to demonic influence. False teachers are said to be led astray by deceitful spirits and demonic teaching (4:1). Their error is particularly manifest in an undue asceticism. They forbid marriage and enjoin abstinence from certain foods. By doing so, they denigrate God, who has created all things as good. The practice of this kind of asceticism denies the goodness of God. Timothy's teaching stands in sharp contrast with the erroneous opinions of these false teachers. His teaching is good; it is the message of faith. Their teaching is relegated to the level of "old wives' tales" and impious speech (4:7).

In 1 Timothy 6 the Pastor comes back yet again to the issue of false teaching. That teaching is opposed to the sound words of our Lord Jesus Christ and teaching that leads to godliness (6:3–10). The Pastor treats false teachers with utter disdain (6:4–5), saying that they are deprived of the truth, are puffed up, have corrupt minds, understand nothing, and are prone to useless disputes. In this final exposition on false teachers, the Pastor says that their error is surely one that will cause them trouble. In one of his polemical broadsides he describes their deviance as manifest in a false understanding of godliness that places undue emphasis on money. Saying that "money is a root of all kinds of evil" (6:10) and that it leads people into the snare of temptation and utter destruction, the Pastor rejects their error out of hand.

Just as false teaching leads to the perversion and the destruction of moral values, the sound teaching offered by Timothy leads to ethically correct behavior. To an undue desire for wealth is opposed the Pastor's version of the Stoic virtue of self-sufficiency. His reference to people having nothing when they come into this world and again having nothing when they leave this world (6:7) reminds the audience that the Pastor's moral vision is rooted in a "theology of creation."

The idea that God is the creator of sex and food enables the Pastor to reject an asceticism that denigrates the goods of creation (4:4–5). Earlier in the epistle, the Pastor's respect for the order of creation allowed him to recall the biblical story of Adam and Eve as he urged women to be open to childbearing (2:13–15).

Although generally rooted in an understanding of creation, the description of the ethical life provided by the Pastor has a decidedly Hellenistic tone. He insists on the virtues of godliness, self-sufficiency, and moderation. He uses lists of virtues and catalogs of vices and household codes in promoting the kind of behavior that he considers to be appropriate for a person of faith.

His use of household codes suggests that the Pastor is keen on order within the community: those in authority enabling people to live quietly, slaves obeying masters, wives not lording over their husbands, and Christian family members assuming their family responsibilities. The Pastor's plea for social order evokes comparison with the Stoics' "logical ethic," behavior according to *logos*, the reasoned order of the universe. The Pastor's concern for order within the community inspires his various statements on church order, the second major concern of this epistle.

One expression of his concern for church order is the way that he describes the community as it comes together for worship, a topic briefly addressed in 2:8–10. In 5:20–25 he has something to say about the penitential discipline of the church. What he has to say about widows in 5:3–16 is yet another indication of his concern for the good order of the community. Instead of grouping all widows into a single category, the Pastor identifies three groups of widows. He distinguishes "real widows," who have no one to provide for them, from widows who have living descendants who should be able to provide for their care. Both groups are distinguished in turn from young widows, who are urged to remarry and attend to their family responsibilities.

The most striking feature of the Pastor's desire for order within the Christian community is his use of the image of the house of God to describe the church. The model enables him to distinguish the overseer from servers and to spell out the personal characteristics expected of both an overseer and of those who serve (3:1–13). The Pastor suggests that household management is the task of the overseer, but he does not spell out the responsibilities of servers, including women servers (see 3:11). Finally, the Pastor says a few words about elders, especially those who have a ministry of word and teaching (5:17–19).

A cursory reading of 1 Timothy gives the reader the impression that the Pastor flits from one topic to another without any order or overarching concerns. This would be a false impression. The epistle should be viewed as a mosaic in which the motifs of sound teaching and church order are set before the reader's eyes. These are highlighted in chiaroscuro fashion. The dark side with which they contrast is false teaching and socially disruptive behavior. The highlighted areas and the dark areas are internally coherent. The church is the bulwark of the truth; false teaching leads to immoral and socially disruptive behavior. By its attribution to Paul, the entire mosaic is brought under the aegis of Paul's apostolic authority. The enforcement of its provisions is left to Timothy, Paul's plenipotentiary delegate.

Outline

The Salutation
1 Timothy 1:1–2

Hellenistic letters began in a stylized fashion so that the reader who unrolled the scroll would immediately become aware of the identity of the sender as well as of the identity of the intended recipient. The function of the traditional Hellenistic salutation, following an "*X* to *Y*" pattern, was the same as that of the envelope and formal opening that are part of our contemporary epistolary style. Contemporary English language usage dictates that a letter should begin "Dear *Z*." Hellenistic letters began not with an expression of endearment—often a mere formality in modern usage—but with a greeting.

The Pauline epistolary tradition witnesses to an expansion of all three elements—the designation of the sender, the designation of the recipient, and the greeting—in the Hellenistic epistolary scheme for greetings. In his first letter, 1 Thessalonians, Paul identified the senders and the recipients in simple fashion. Thereafter he added an *intitulatio* to his self-designation as well as to the designation of his recipients. The *intitulatio* is the "title" appended to the author's name in Hellenistic letters. In a fashion analogous to the signature block of a contemporary letter, the epistolary title justifies the claim that the letter-writer is about to make on the recipients of the letter. Rhetorically, the title of a Hellenistic letter is an important element in the author's *ethos* appeal, that is, the attempt to persuade not on the inherent basis of the argument itself (*logos*) or on the advantage to the audience (*pathos*) but rather on the authority of the person from whom it comes.

The greeting in 1 Thess. 1:1 echoes the greeting exchanged in Christian assemblies in much the same fashion as the Hebrew epistolary "shalom" echoed the traditional greeting exchanged between people as they met. After his first letter, Paul expanded his epistolary greeting so that "grace to you and peace from God our Father and the Lord Jesus Christ" became the standard greeting in Paul's later correspondence. In 1:2 the Pastor further expands the apostle's epistolary greeting.

1:1 Paul, apostle of Christ Jesus according to the command of God our Savior and of Christ Jesus our hope, 2 to Timothy, true son in faith: grace, mercy, and peace from God the Father and Christ Jesus our Lord.

[1:1] Each of the Pastoral Epistles opens with an epistolary greeting within the Pauline tradition. In each of them Paul is alone presented as the sender of the letter (cf. 1 Cor. 1:1; 2 Cor. 1:1; Phil. 1:1; 1 Thess. 1:1; Phlm. 1). In each of the two missives to Timothy, Paul is designated as "apostle[2] of Christ Jesus" (*Paulos apostolos Christou Iēsou*). Within the Pastor's circles, the apostle Paul is not simply *an* apostle; he is *the* apostle of Christ Jesus.

The Pastor considers that Paul has been designated apostle according to the command of God our Savior and of Christ Jesus our hope. The parallel construction of the *nomina sacra* indicates that both "God" and "Christ Jesus" have the force of a proper name. In 1 Timothy as in 2 Timothy, "Christ" normally precedes "Jesus."[3] The epithet "Christ" is nominal, part of a name, rather than titulary, as if the Pastor were highlighting the messianic character of Jesus. A single command comes from God and Christ Jesus, as if the two were acting in consort. The identity of both God and Christ Jesus is specified by means of an appositive that highlights the respective relationships between God and Christ Jesus and the community for which the epistle is intended. These appositives may be taken in a still broader sense as indicative of the relationships between God and Christ Jesus and the broader community of Pauline Christians. First Timothy 4:10 designates the living God as the savior of all people, especially of those who believe. The Pastor's use of these appositives serves not only to designate the relationship of God and of Christ Jesus with the community; it also implies that the command addressed to Paul was for the purpose of our salvation and our hope. As a divine functionary, the apostle himself is involved in the realization of our salvation and our hope.

God is designated as Savior three times in this epistle (1:1; 2:3; 4:10). The author of 1 Timothy does not use the term "Savior" of Christ Jesus. In the complex epistolary title provided for the apostle, the Pastor attributes the epithet "our hope" to Christ Jesus. The identification of the living God as "Savior" (*sōtēr*) in 1:1 speaks of the God of the Jewish tradition in terms that would be readily understood in the Hellenistic world. Hellenists called a number of different deities, especially divinized emperors, "Savior" insofar as they were deemed to have rescued their devotees from all sorts of evil, even death. By affirming that God is "our Savior," the Pastor implicitly affirms that for the members of the Pauline community there is no Savior other than "the living God" (3:15; 4:10; see 6:13; see also Excursus 9). From the outset of the missive the reader knows that the God of whom the Pastor writes (1:2, 4, 11, 17; 2:3, 5; 3:5, 15 [2x], 16; 4:3, 4, 5, 10; 5:4, 5, 21; 6:1, 11, 13, 17) is the God of Jewish monotheism (1:17; 2:5).

Hope and salvation go hand in hand. The word "hope" points to the eschatological dimension of salvation. The traditional biblical idea that God is our

2. The Greek text omits the definite article. This construction, an anarthrous appositive, is permissible in the formal context of an epistle such as this (BAGD 268.2).

3. See 1:1 [2x], 2, 12, 14, 15, 16; 2:5; 3:13; 4:6; 5:21; 6:13; 2 Tim. 1:1 [2x], 2, 9, 10, 13; 2:1, 3, 10; 3:12, 15; 4:1. The only exceptions to the general sequence "Christ Jesus" are 6:3, 14, and 2 Tim. 2:8. In these three instances, "Jesus Christ" is a rehearsal of earlier Pauline tradition, the full christological title in 6:3, 14, and a creedal formula in 2 Tim. 2:8.

Savior, the object of the hope of his people, is reflected in 1 Tim. 4:10 and 5:5. The Pastor's designation of Christ Jesus as "our hope" (see Titus 2:13; 3:7; cf. Titus 1:2 and Col. 1:27, where Christ is called "the hope of glory") suggests that one's hope in God our Savior is realized through Christ Jesus. The Pastor does not possess a Trinitarian theology—that would be a much later development in the history of Christianity—but he does share with his readers the conviction that the salvation that they hope to receive from God is mediated through Christ Jesus (see 2:5). In the writings of Ignatius of Antioch, composed under the influence of Paul within but a few years of the writing of 1 Timothy, Jesus Christ is similarly designated as "our hope" (Ign. *Magn.* 11:1) or "our common hope" (Ign. *Eph.* 21:2; *Phld.* 11:2 see *Phld.* 5.1:2). In Polycarp's letter to the Philippians, "our hope" is identified as Christ Jesus (Pol. *Phil.* 8:1).

Within the Pastorals, use of the "hope" word group (the root *elpi-*) is found only in 1 Timothy and Titus. Surprisingly, it does not appear in 2 Timothy, a reflection on Paul's ministry. In 1 Timothy the Pastor employs the verb *elpizō*, "hope," four times (3:14; 4:10; 5:5; 6:17), once in a secular sense (3:14). The noun *elpis*, "hope," appears only here in 1 Timothy, but it is found three times in Titus (1:2; 2:13; 3:7). The passages in Titus make it clear that within the Pastor's circles God was considered to be the ground (Titus 1:2) and the object of hope (Titus 2:13; cf. 1 Tim. 4:10; 5:5; 6:17), which was fulfilled in the gift of eternal life (Titus 3:7). With the exception of 1:1, 1 Timothy presents God as the object of hope in a much more focused manner than does Titus. In 1 Timothy, God is the object of hope insofar as he is the Savior of all people (*sōtēr pantōn anthrōpōn*, 4:10). Real widows (5:5) and all people who live in the present age (6:17) are expected to live with their hope centered on God.

In the salutation of 1 Timothy, the Pastor departs from what will become in this epistle a theocentric focus in talking about Christian hope. The binomial expression "God our Savior and . . . Christ Jesus our hope" suggests, nonetheless, that God is the ground and source of the Christian hope of which Christ Jesus is the object. The relationship to which this epistolary expression points is clarified in the epistle to Titus. That source affirms that God is Savior (Titus 2:10) insofar as he is faithful to his promise (Titus 1:2). God's saving beneficence is manifest in the double appearance of Christ Jesus, who gave himself for us, redeemed us, and formed us as a chosen people (Titus 2:14; see further Excursus 9). We are not saved because of any righteous works that have been done. Rather, we have been saved because of the mercy of God (see 2:3–6). Salvation is mediated to us through God's Spirit in baptism, a rebirth and renewal (Titus 3:4–6). Baptism establishes us as legitimate heirs who can expect eternal life (Titus 3:7), a gift to be received at the time of the second appearance of Christ Jesus (Titus 2:11–14).

[2] The Pastor completes the salutation in customary Hellenistic epistolary fashion with the name of the person to whom the epistle is being sent and a greeting. These elements of the Pastor's salutation recur in 2 Tim. 1:2 in the

same fashion, except that in 2 Timothy Paul's disciple is called a "beloved" son (*agapētō*), whereas in 1 Timothy he is described as a "true" son (*gnēsiō*; cf. Titus 1:4). The difference most probably owes to the different literary genres of the two texts. On reading 1 Timothy the reader becomes aware that the epistle expresses a mandate to Timothy to develop and fulfill Paul's mission. Timothy is to establish order in the community and deal with the source of errors that might lead it to deviate from the faith. From this perspective, the designation of Timothy as "true," that is, as legitimate and faithful, is appropriate to the purpose of the epistle. Timothy is, as it were, an authentic heir who will carry on the Pauline legacy.

On reading 2 Timothy, the reader becomes aware that the epistle is a reflection on Paul's ministry in the guise of a farewell and goodbye. In such a context, the designation of Timothy as "beloved" is most appropriate. The literary genre of the Epistle to Titus, on the other hand, is similar to that of 1 Timothy. In this epistle, Titus is called a "true" son (Titus 1:4). The Pastor indicates that a common faith is the norm of the legitimacy of Titus's relationship with Paul (*kata koinēn pistin*). The more terse expression "in faith" (*en pistei*) fulfills a similar function in 1 Timothy 1:2.

The Law
1 Timothy 1:3–11

Hellenistic letters frequently add some expression of gratitude to the deity before entering into the real body of the letter. The Pastor has deferred his thanksgiving (1:12) so as to convey an exhortation. By so doing he has indicated that his missive is not to be construed as a typical friendly letter of the era. His use of a *parakaleō* formula, an exhortation, indicates that this missive is about serious business. The epistolary usage of such a formula was found in diplomatic letters in which a delegated authority was conveying authoritative directions to his superior's subordinates.

In this case the order is given to Timothy (*se*, "you" in the singular, v. 3) to exercise pastoral responsibility by assuring that "some people" (*tisin*) within the Ephesian community not teach falsely and not engage in idle speculation. The Pastor does not tell his readers who those "some people" are. Throughout the epistle the Pastor continues to refer to these people in the same anonymous fashion. Presumably the intended recipients of the missive would know who they are. The Pastor's references to numerous genealogies and would-be teachers of the law as he begins his missive suggest that "some people" are in fact Jewish Christians beholden to the law. This would seem all the more probable insofar as the Pastor carefully articulates the purpose of the law. Timothy, Paul's delegate in Ephesus, is reminded that he is to deal with these "some people" in diplomatic fashion. The goal of his instruction must be a pure heart, a good conscience, and an authentic faith.

1:3 I exhort you, as[a] I did when I was making my way into Macedonia, to remain in Ephesus in order to give the word to some not to teach falsely 4 and not to attend to myths and untold genealogies that give rise to useless speculation[b] rather than to God's plan of salvation[c] in faith. 5 The purpose of this word is love from a pure heart, a good conscience, and an authentic faith. 6 Having missed the mark,[d] some of them have turned away toward idle talk. 7 They want to be teachers of the law but they do not understand the things that they are saying or the people[e] about whom they are making assertions.

8 For we know that the law is good if anyone lives in accordance with the law, 9 seeing that the law is established for the lawless and the unruly, the godless and sinners, the unrighteous and the impious, killers of fathers and mothers, murderers, 10 the sexually immoral, active homosexuals, kidnappers, liars, perjurers, and anything else that is opposed to sound teaching 11 according to the glorious gospel of the blessed God, which has been entrusted to me.

a. Verses 3–4 form an incomplete sentence in Greek. "As" (*kathōs*) is the first word of the sentence and qualifies the verb "exhort," thus, "as I exhorted you." Either the Pastor forgot to complete his thought or he wanted to say that the epistle is a kind of follow-up to his earlier exhortation.

b. Most of the ancient manuscripts read "debates" (*zētēseis*). "Useless speculation" (*ekzētēseis*) is found in ℵ, A, 0150, and a small number of minuscules. "Useless speculation" is a rare word, found only in Christian writings. On the basis of the principle that the more difficult reading (*lectio difficilior*) is to be preferred, it is more likely to be original.

c. "God's plan of salvation," literally, "household management" (*oikonomian*) is found in the vast majority of ancient manuscripts. Other readings are found in D and Irenaeus. D reads "building" (*oikodomēn*; see 3:15), a reading supported by the Syriac and some Old Latin versions. Irenaeus reads *oikodomian*, another word for "building."

d. In the Greek text, vv. 5–7 are a single sentence.

e. The Pastor's *tinōn* is in a genitive plural form that is either masculine or neuter. Thus, it can be rendered as "the people" or "the things."

[1:3–4] After the opening salutation, the body of the epistle begins with an exhortation that sets the tone of the entire document. The verb *parekalesa*, "I exhorted," is a technical term employed in Hellenistic diplomatic correspondence to express tactfully orders an envoy is conveying on behalf of a higher authority. In the case of 1 Timothy, the envoy is the legendary Paul, who has been effectively designated as the envoy of Christ Jesus according to the command of

God himself (1:1). Paul himself was occasionally prone to anacoloutha, that is, using run-on phrases without the proper conjunctions, but the construction of this initial exhortation with its numerous asides and appendages is singularly confusing (BDF 467). The author has tried to say too much with too few words.

The first injunction is clear: "remain in Ephesus." Verse 3 presents Paul as a man on the move, an envoy of Christ who is on his way to Macedonia. Paul first visited Macedonia during the second missionary voyage (Acts 16:6–13). According to Luke's account of the visit, Timothy had been with Paul when the apostle evangelized Philippi and Thessalonica, respectively one of the leading cities of the Roman province of Macedonia and the capital of the province (Acts 16:1–17:9; cf. Phil. 1:1; 1 Thess. 1:1). Paul's abiding concern for those whom he had evangelized is evident in the fact that he wrote letters to these communities after he had moved on to another locale. When circumstances prevented Paul from making another visit to Thessalonica during the second missionary voyage, he sent Timothy in his stead to strengthen and encourage the Thessalonians.

During the third missionary voyage, Ephesus served as the center of Paul's missionary activity. Paul spent some three years working in and from the Asian capital (Acts 20:31). Then his concern for the Macedonian churches and the unsettled situation in Ephesus (Acts 20:1) prompted him to return to Macedonia (Acts 20:1–6; cf. 2 Cor. 2:12–13). According to Luke, Timothy accompanied Paul during this trip to Macedonia (Acts 20:4). Paul confirms that Timothy was with him at the time by mentioning Timothy in the salutation of his Second Letter to the Corinthians (2 Cor. 1:1), written after Paul had arrived in Macedonia. The Pastor's references to Ephesus and Macedonia reflect the memory of Paul's evangelization in these places as well as the fact that Timothy had been associated with the apostle in both his Asian and his Macedonian missionary activities.

When the Pastor speaks about Paul's leaving Timothy behind in Ephesus, he is suggesting that there was yet another visit by Paul to Macedonia after his stay in Ephesus and that Paul would not have been accompanied by Timothy during this new trip to Macedonia. The Pastor's suggestion of this new trip to Macedonia is confirmed neither by Paul's own letters nor by the account in Acts. Earlier generations of scholarship (see Eusebius, *Ecclesiastical History* 2.22), taking the Pauline authorship of the Pastorals for granted and trying to harmonize their "information" with information from Acts,[4] assumed that Paul was released from house arrest in Rome (see Acts 28:30–31; 2 Tim. 4:16–17) and later made a fourth missionary trip through Asia and Macedonia.

The Pastor may not have been familiar with Luke's account. If he were, he may have been an early witness to the tradition that Paul had been released from Roman custody; if he were not, he may have been building on local tradition

---

4. The difficulties of correlating information in the Pastorals with information supplied by Acts is one of the reasons why contemporary scholarship rejects the Pauline authorship of the Pastorals.

that placed Timothy in Ephesus. Indicating that Paul had virtually commanded Timothy to stay behind in Ephesus, he evokes Paul's abiding pastoral concern for that church. Timothy's mandate is focused. He is charged with giving the word (*parangeilēs*) to some, obviously the teachers or would-be teachers of the community, that they are not "to teach falsely" (*mē heterodidaskalein*), a word that appears here for the first time in Greek literature. The Pastor explains what he means. Timothy is specifically exhorted to tell these teachers to stay away from the myths and genealogies that give rise to useless speculation.

Of itself, a "myth" (*mythos*) is anything that is said. From the early fifth century B.C.E. onward the term generally had the connotation of a fabricated story. Some stories were didactic by nature, as were the fables of Aesop. Others were traditional stories about the gods, used to explain historical and cosmic reality. By the Hellenistic era, authors such as Strabo, Diodorus Siculus, and Plutarch distinguished reality from what the "myths" had to say. Plutarch, Paul's contemporary, described the myth as a "useless fabrication" (*plasma kenon, Obsolescence of Oracles* 46, *Moralia* 435 D), while the principal Hellenistic Jewish writers of the time, Philo and Josephus, described myths as "error" (*planē*).

The Pastor shares this negative understanding of myth. He speaks of it in terms of "untold genealogies that give rise to useless speculation." The language is unusual; the key words are rarely used in the New Testament. "Useless speculation" (*ekzēteseis*) and "untold" (*aperantois*) are found only here; "genealogies" (*genealogiais*) only here and in Titus 3:9; and "myth" (*mythois*), here, in 4:7, and in 2 Tim. 4:4; Titus 1:14; and 2 Pet. 1:16. In the Pastor's circles this last term may have been used to describe elements of Jewish lore (haggadah) that Christians of the Pauline persuasion deemed useless (see Titus 3:9).

Those to whom Timothy is to give the word are presented as preferring these myths and genealogies to the divine training that is in faith. "Training" (*oikonomian*), literally, "household management," is the work of the *oikonomos*, the steward. It belongs to the *oik-* word group that Paul and his heirs so often used of the church and its organization. Its presence in 1:4 is somewhat bizarre, as the manuscript tradition attests. BAGD 558.3, citing Clement of Alexandria, renders the phrase *oikonomian theou* as "divine training." It may, however, be preferable to take the phrase in the sense of God's management plan, the plan of salvation. This plan is worked out in the faith of the community; its contours are known in faith. Those whom Timothy is to confront are teachers and would-be teachers who replace authentic concern for God's plan of salvation with various sorts of useless speculation.

[5–7] Before he describes further those to whom Timothy is to address the admonition, the Pastor reminds Timothy that its purpose (*telos*) is not to emphasize the authority of Timothy. Timothy's goal must be the love that proceeds from a pure heart, a good conscience, and an authentic faith. This triad is unique in the New Testament. It consists of an element of Semitic anthropology, an element of moral philosophy, and an element of Christian faith. The accumulation of the three elements can be taken simply as an example of rhetorical repetition for the sake of emphasis, but it may be preferable to see in the author's unique phrase an example of a stylistic feature of the Pastorals, namely, the interpretive triad. This kind of triad is one in which the central element is explained by the encompassing elements. The interpretive triad in 1:4 is somewhat different from other interpretive triads in the Pastorals in that the phrasing of the central element, "good conscience" (*syneidēseōs agathēs*), comes from the Hellenistic culture in which the readers of the epistle are living. The interpretive phrases come from the religious environment in which the document is to be situated, the first from traditional Judaism, the latter from the author's Christian heritage.

Seneca's Stoic idea of the moral conscience is well attested by his writings (*Happy Life* 20.3–5, *Tranquility of Mind* 3.4, *Epistle* 43.4–5). The Pastor's Greek term *syneidēsis*, analogous to Seneca's *conscientiae*, was of relatively recent vintage when he wrote. Philo wrote about the pure conscience (*Special Laws* 1.203). He had also written that God's servant (*doulos theou*, cf. Titus 1:1) can praise God "when he has been purified from his sins and judges that he loves his master from his conscience" (*Heir* 7, my translation). A good conscience is essentially an indication of moral integrity. A person with a good conscience knows that he or she is pursuing the good.

The "pure heart" (*katharas kardias*) is an expression that reflects Semitic anthropology. The heart, the Hebrew *lēb*, is an instance of synecdoche, the use of the part for the whole. The "heart" represents the whole human person to the depth of his or her being. The prophets (e.g., Jer. 11:20; 17:10; 20:12) and the psalmist (Ps. 17:3; 19:14; 26:2; 44:21; 51:6, 10, 17; 73:1; 139:23) repeatedly state that only God can plumb the depths of the human heart. The pure heart is a heart that is totally turned toward God. God is the sole focus of that person's being (cf. Matt. 5:8).

On the other hand, the expression "genuine faith" (*pisteōs anypokritou*) derives from the Pastor's own moderated Paulinism. "Faith" is a key element in Pauline theology. The apostle often writes about faith to speak of the believer's relationship with God. "Genuine" is a biblical term, first attested in two passages in the book of Wisdom (Wis. 5:18; 18:15) and in six passages of the New Testament, including two passages in the Pastorals where it is used to qualify "faith" (1:5; cf. 2 Tim. 1:5; Rom. 12:9; 2 Cor. 6:6; Jas. 3:17; 1 Pet. 1:22). "A 'sincere' faith," writes Spicq, "is faith that includes intellectual orthodoxy, pious conduct, faithfulness, and loyalty in keeping obligations" (*TLNT* 1.135).

The confused syntax of verses 3–4 continues in verses 6–7. Grammatically, verses 6–7 are part of a single sentence that beings in verse 5. However, the relative phrase "some of whom" (*hōn tines*), with which verse 6 begins, refers back to the "some" (*tisin*) of verse 3. Those to whom Timothy's word is to be addressed are people who have missed the mark. They are off-target and have missed the point. The metaphor, using a verb (*astochēsantes*) found only in the Pastorals (1:6; 6:21; 2 Tim. 2:18; cf. *2 Clem.* 17:7), is striking insofar as the most common word for "sin" in the Hebrew Bible is *ḥāṭā'*, a word that essentially means "miss the mark." The verb was occasionally used, even in the Bible, to describe someone who had missed a target, as, for instance, a stone thrower (Judg. 20:16). Having gone astray, "some" engage in word games, idle talk (*mataiologian*). Titus 1:10 uses a related term to speak derisively of "people of the circumcision."

In the Pastor's circles, Jews engaged in the interpretation of the Torah were considered to be speaking gibberish. The author characterizes them as would-be teachers of the law who do not know what they are talking about. The term *nomodidaskaloi*, "teachers of the law," was apparently first used by Christian writers. Luke used the expression to identify Gamaliel (Acts 5:34) and others among the Pharisees (Luke 5:17). Use of the term exposes the contrast between Jewish teachers and Christian teachers, among whom Christ is the *didaskalos*, the teacher, par excellence (e.g., Luke 2:46; 3:12). The Pastor speaks of those who "want to be" teachers of the law. His nuanced language suggests that they are making pretensions about being teachers of the law but have not really achieved that status. They understand neither what they are saying nor the persons about whom they are speaking.[5] With this double characterization, the author may be referring to what would later be called Jewish halakah and Jewish haggadah, the interpretation of Jewish law and the interpretation of the Jewish story.[6]

[8–11] In an aside, the Pastor offers a reflection on the law. He describes it as good but with a proviso: that one live in accordance with the law (*ean tis autō nomimōs chrētai*; see Josephus, *Ant.* 16.2.3 §27). The tense of the verb, a present subjunctive, suggests a reference to future conduct along with some hesitancy as to whether a person can actually live in full accord with the law. The apostle himself had affirmed that everyone has sinned including those under the law (Rom. 2:12; 3:23). Explaining that all have sinned, including those of the circumcision who are bound to follow the law (cf. Gal. 3:22; 5:3; 6:13), Paul had stated that Jewish teachers did the same wicked things that Gentiles did (Rom. 1:29–2:1). They dared to teach others even as they themselves violated the precepts of the law (Rom. 2:17–23) and were prone to the same vices as the Gentiles were.

For Paul, the law is not sinful in itself. Rather, the law makes sin known; it identifies evil behavior as a violation of God's covenant with his people (Rom. 7:7, 13). In making his argument that all people are sinners, Paul used a classic list of vices to focus on the sinfulness of Gentiles (Rom. 1:29–31) and a

---

5. The preposition *tinōn* can be masculine or neuter.
6. 1 Tim. 2:13–15 offers an example of the Pastor's own use of the tradition of halakah. 2 Tim. 3:8 employs Jewish haggadah.

reference to the Decalogue to point to the sin of Jews (Rom. 2:21b–22a; see Exod. 20:14–15; Deut. 5:18–19). The Pastor makes use of each of these classical literary forms in describing those for whom the law was set down, those whose evil conduct is made manifest in the law.

Ostensibly, the Pastor has employed a catalog of vices. His list mentions fourteen vices in addition to the et cetera clause on which it ends. On closer analysis, the organization of the vices on his list is determined by the order of the precepts of the Decalogue. This Jewish-Christian approach to the Hellenistic vice list is likewise found in Matthew, who similarly arranged a list of vices according to the order of the Ten Commandments (Matt. 15:19; cf. Mark 7:21–22). Within Judaism the Ten Commandments had an important function in liturgy and catechetics, as the Nash papyrus, various tefillin (small leather boxes containing scriptural passages and worn on the arm during prayer) from Qumran, and rabbinic citations (*m. Tamid* 5:1; *y. Ber.* 1:5) show so well. In Matthew's Sermon on the Mount, Jesus is presented as a good Jewish teacher who explains that the Decalogue's prohibition of murder, adultery, and false witness entails more than these three vices narrowly understood. The Pastor's organization of the fourteen vices reflects the Jewish catechetical notion that the ban on murder, adultery, kidnapping, and false witness goes beyond the letter of the law. The law reveals social evil to be sinful.

The catalog of vices was a well-known literary form in the Greco-Roman world (see Excursus 2). Pseudo-Aristotle, Dio Chrysostom, Diogenes Laertius, Lucian, Onasander, and Seneca are just a few of the ancient authors who used such lists. Typically, such lists were used to describe the wanton life led by the masses or given individuals. The lists were rhetorical devices used to denigrate opponents as irrational and thoroughly reprobate. Many of the vices found in the Pastor's catalog are similar to those found in Pollux's *Onomasticon* (see 6.151). In this second-century C.E. work, a kind of rhetorical handbook and encyclopedia, Pollux castigates the tax collector with a long list of thirty-three vices. In act 1, scene 3 of Plautus's *Pseudolus,* the pandering Ballio is accused of everything on the Pastor's list with three exceptions: being unruly, a murderer, and a kidnapper.

The classic catalogs of vices could contain any number of vices. Short lists contained three, four or, more typically, five vices. A very long list—146 vices in all—appears in Philo's *Sacrifices of Abel and Cain* 32. Philo prefixes his long list by saying "the pleasure-lover will be all these things." Among the more than twenty lists of vices in the New Testament,[7] the Pastor's array of fourteen is one of the longest.

---

7. See Matt. 15:19; Mark 7:21–22; Rom. 1:29–31; 13:13; 1 Cor. 5:10–11; 6:9–10; 2 Cor. 12:20–21; Gal. 5:19–21; Eph. 4:31; 5:3–5; Col. 3:5–8; 1 Tim. 6:4–5; 2 Tim. 3:2–5; Titus 1:7; 3:3; 1 Pet. 2:1; 4:3; 2 Pet. 2:1; Rev. 9:21; 21:8; 22:15.

Items in a classic catalog of vices are sometimes listed in the form of adjectives; at other times they appear as verbs or as nouns, either abstract (evil) or personal (evildoers).

The Pastor's list consists of four pairs of personal nouns and six individual categories of evildoers. Arrangement in pairs is a classic literary technique used for the sake of clarity. Use of this technique contributes to the rhetorical force of the Pastor's list of vices. Ultimately, the persuasive use of a list of vices is created by the cumulative effect of the entire list. Thus, it is often quite useless to try to distinguish one vice from another. Classical authors frequently include synonyms in their lists; at other times the meaning of various terms overlap. The rhetorical function of this device is not achieved by the specificity of various vices; rather, it is fulfilled by creating in the reader the impression of wanton behavior and general viciousness.

Some rhetors enhanced the force of their rhetoric by omitting conjunctions. Apart from the four pairs of vices, the Pastor too avoids the use of conjunctions, thus making his point all the more forcefully. Rhetorically, the cumulative effect of the Pastor's list is increased by the Pastor's use of assonance, specifically, the repeated sound of an initial "a." Each of the first five vices is designated by a word beginning with alpha (*anomois, anypotaktois, asebesi, [h]amartōlois, anosiois*).

As is the case with any use of a literary form by an author, the author shapes the use of the form so that it is relevant to the situation at hand (see the emphasis on sexual vices and their association with idolatry in 1 Cor. 5:11; 6:9–10). Thus, the first vice on the Pastor's list, "lawless" (*anomois*), is a standard feature in catalogs of vices, but its presence at the head of the Pastor's list may reflect his problem with would-be teachers of the law. This vice does not appear on the long list in Philo, but it is first on the Pastor's much shorter list. He has made his point: the law has been established for those without the law, the lawless (*a-nomois*, with a privative alpha, equivalent to the English language prefix "non" or "un"). Paired with the lawless are the "unruly" (*anypotaktois*), a term that appears in the New Testament as an intensification (1 Tim. 1:9; Titus 1:6, 10; Heb. 2:8) of a more common word (*ataktos*, see 1 Thess. 5:14; cf. 2 Thess. 3:6, 7, 11) that appears on Philo's list. The unruly person is one whose behavior is markedly antisocial.

The "godless and sinners" make up the Pastor's second pair of vices. "Godless" (*a-sebesi*) is one of the vices cited by Philo. This classical term describes those who lack godliness (*eusebeia*). Godliness is a common goal of those who strive to lead a good life. Striving for godliness is an important aspect of the Pastor's moral exhortation. He distinguishes real godliness from the godliness that others might pursue (see Excursus 7). On the Pastor's list, "sinners" (*hamartōlois*) appear alongside the "impious." "Sinners" do not appear on Philo's list. The term is, however, commonly used in the New Testament even though it appears only twice in the Pastorals (1:9, 15). Its presence in the Pastor's list may well reflect the Pastor's own dependence on the Pauline tradition. Paul's Letter to the Romans has much to say about sin. Sin, reckoned according to the law, is the lot of every human being (Rom. 5:12–13). Christ died for sinners (Rom. 5:8), of whom the Pastor presents Paul as a primary example.

The "unrighteous" and the "impious" constitute the Pastor's third pair. Both "unrighteous" (*anosiois*) and "impious" (*bebēlois*) are among the vices listed by Philo. Taken together, the pair of vices may be a summary reference to the first precepts of the Decalogue. The person who is "unrighteous" (*an-[h]osios*) is one who is not righteous (*hosios*). Hellenistic Jewish literature often contrasts the unrighteous (*anosios*) with the "righteous" or "justified" (*dikaios*), a cipher for Jews who are in a right relationship with God and with one another (Wis. 12:4; 2 Macc. 7:34; 8:32; 4 Macc. 12:11; *Ep. Arist.* 289; Josephus, *Jewish War* 6.8.4§399; *Against Apion* 2.25§201).[8] In ancient religious literature, "godless" is a technical term used to describe that which is not sacred, that is, the nonreligious or even irreligious. Thus, the term means profane in the sense of being available for common use and not fit for sacred use. The term was not used in ordinary parlance, but it frequently occurs in the Greek Bible. Philo uses it to describe the prostitute who is "profane in body and soul" (*Special Laws* 1.102). A prostitute's wages were not acceptable as a temple offering. Priests were not allowed to marry a prostitute or a divorced woman (Lev. 21:7).

With his fourth pair of vices the Pastor begins to shift his emphasis from a person's relationship to God to people's relationship with one another. His list continues with "killers of fathers and mothers" (*patrolōais kai mētrolōais*). Neither term appears elsewhere in the New Testament. For a Jew, killing either of one's parents was a particularly egregious form of dishonor to father and mother (see Exod. 21:15, 17). Marcus Aurelius, a Stoic, considered the killing of one's own father to be one of the worst of moral failures (*Meditations* 6.34).

To the mention of those who kill either of their parents, the Pastor adds those who are murderers (*androphonois*). As did Plato (*Phaedo* 114a), 2 Macc. 9:28 (see 4 Macc. 9:15) uses the Greek term in the generic sense of "murderer," but it was used by Pindar in specific reference to women who kill their own husbands (*Pythian Odes* 4.252). Having spoken about murder and some of its most egregious forms, the Pastor writes about human sexuality, as did the Decalogue after its prohibition of murder. The vice that appears most often in the New Testament's catalog of vices is that of the "sexually immoral" (*pornois*). This general term covers a wide range of human sexual behavior, including anything and everything that is contrary to social mores.

8. This is all the more striking in that Greek has antonyms for both *anosios* and *dikaios*. These are respectively *hosios* and *adikos*.

The Pastor then adds a specific sexual vice, "active homosexuals" (*arseno-koitais*). The term was apparently coined by Paul (1 Cor. 6:9) in reference to the kind of male homosexual activity proscribed by Lev. 18:22. Jewish men were enjoined from having sexual relations with other men as part of the strict code of sexual mores that distinguished Jewish men from Egyptians and Canaanites (see *Ep. Arist.* 152). Paul shared the traditional Jewish view that acts of homosexuality among men were the result of idolatry (Rom. 1:18–27; 1 Cor. 6:9). For Jews, such sexual activity was deemed to be a particularly egregious form of sexual immorality. It violated the principle of demarcation that pervaded the traditional ethos, Jew and Gentile, clean and unclean, male and female. Jews were expected to act like Jews, men were expected to act like men, and so forth.

The next vice on the list, "kidnappers" (*andrapodistais*), literally, "those who reduce men to servitude," was a term used by Plato and Aristotle. The word describes those who had "stolen" persons. In the Hellenistic world, "kidnappers" or "slave-traders" was a term of opprobrium. Their willingness to enslave free people, to exploit them sexually, whether they be young males or females, and to flout the Aedilician Edict (the law on selling slaves and beasts of burden) was legendary—if not always a matter of fact in a particular instance. Philostratus included kidnappers on a vice list along with adulterers, the sexually immoral, clothes-stealers, and pickpockets, all of whom he compared to rabble (*Life of Apollonius of Tyana* 4.22)

In the Jewish tradition, kidnapping was considered to be a serious violation of the precept of the Decalogue, "you shall not steal" (*lō' tignōb*, Exod. 20:15; Deut. 5:19; cf. *b. Sanh.* 86a). Writing about this commandment, Philo explains the malice of kidnapping: "Everyone who is inspired with a zeal for virtue is severe of temper and absolutely implacable against men-stealers [*kata andrapodistōn*], who for the sake of a most unrighteous profit do not shrink from reducing to slavery those who not only are freemen by birth but are of the same nature as themselves" (*Special Laws* 4.14). He considered death to be the appropriate penalty for such a crime (see *Special Laws* 4.19).

The verb in the Hebrew text of the Decalogue (*gānab*, "steal") can have either a person (see Deut. 24:7) or a thing as its object; its underlying nuance suggests the use of stealth or force. Originally the precept referred to kidnapping; in the course of time it came to be understood in reference to any kind of stealing. The *Mekhilta of Rabbi Ishmael*, Rabbi Ishmael being a disciple of Rabbi Akiva, the great second-century C.E. rabbi, held that the precept of the Decalogue must refer to kidnapping (*Ba-Hodesh* 8:5). The hermeneutical principle of *davar ha-lamed me-inyano*, inferring the meaning of a passage from its context, led him to conclude that "you shall not steal" really means "you shall not kidnap." In the Torah, kidnapping was a capital offense (see Exod. 21:16; Deut. 24:7), but stealing an animal or something else was not. Sandwiched between two capital crimes, murder and adultery, the Decalogue's "you shall not steal" prohibits another capital offense.

The final group of malefactors on the Pastor's list are liars and perjurers. As was the case with his citation of sexual immorality, the Pastor first names the generic vice, liars (*pseustais*), and then an example of what Jews considered to be a most egregious instance of that vice, namely, perjury (*epiorkois*; see Matt. 5:33–37). A verb related to this noun occurs in Matthew's account of Jesus' explanation of some precepts of the Decalogue (Matt. 5:33). The Jews considered perjury to be a particularly serious offense against Yahweh (see Exod. 20:16; Lev. 19:12; Num. 30:3; Deut. 5:20). Perjury aggravates the offense of speaking unjustly about another (see Philo, *Special Laws* 4.48). It attempts to manipulate God—"you shall not make wrongful use of the name of the Lord your God" (Exod. 20:7; Deut. 5:11)—in an unjust situation.

The et cetera phrase with which the Pastor concludes his list reminds the reader of a similar usage by Paul (Gal. 5:21), suggesting that vice lists were not intended to be all-inclusive. His reference to sound teaching and to the gospel provides a Christian focus for this otherwise Hellenistic Jewish list. According to the Pastor, the law has been established for those who oppose sound teaching (see Titus 1:9; 2:1). That teaching is qualified as being in accordance with the gospel of the blessed God. In effect, sound teaching is an explanation of that gospel. The qualifying phrases used by the Pastor in speaking about the gospel declare what the gospel means to him. The gospel was entrusted to Paul (see 1 Thess. 2:4). Ultimately, sound teaching is defined by the Pauline gospel of God (see p. 95). The Pastor describes the gospel as glorious, literally, "the gospel of glory."[9]

The Pauline gospel proclaims the "blessed" God. This adjective was typically used to describe humans who were blessed by God, who were fortunate because of the gifts that they received from God (Matt. 5:3–12; Luke 6:20b–23). The Pastor, however, uses "blessed" as an epithet for the only God (6:15). Doing so, he speaks as did Hellenistic Jews who used the language of Hellenism to express their Jewish faith. Thus, Philo wrote, "God alone is happy and blessed, exempt from all evil, filled with perfect forms of good, or rather, if the real truth be told, himself the good, who showers the particular goods on heaven and earth" (*Special Laws* 2.53) and that God is the "Imperishable Blessed One" (*Unchangeableness of God* 26).

Hellenistic Judaism's use of "blessed" to describe God is derived from the Greeks. Aristotle, for example, affirmed that the gods enjoy "supreme felicity [*makarios*] and happiness" and that the activity of the gods is transcendent in blessedness (*makariotēti, Nicomachean Ethics* 10.8.7). He went on to affirm

9. This is an instance of what is sometimes called a Hebrew genitive, that is, a noun used in place of an adjective, in keeping with Semitic syntax.

that "the whole of the life of the gods is blessed, and that of humans insofar as it contains some likeness to the divine activity" (10.8.8). Philo shared the notion that it is only in relationship to God that other things can be called blessed: "The good and beautiful things in the world could never have been what they are, save that they were made in the image of the archetype, which is truly good and beautiful, even the uncreated, the blessed, the imperishable" (*makarion kai aphtharton, Cherubim* 86; see *Gaius* 5).

By writing about the blessed God and the good news that had been entrusted to Paul, the Pastor concludes the first hortatory section of this epistle (1:3–11) on a positive note. The rest of the pericope is not as optimistic. It serves as a reminder that Timothy should not even begin to think that he might be able to fulfill his ministry without encountering any difficulties. He must confront the intellectual opposition of false teaching and the practical opposition of various forms of egregiously inappropriate behavior. Let him be forewarned!

The Thanksgiving
1 Timothy 1:12–17

Typically an epistolary thanksgiving appears immediately after the formal salutation of the Hellenistic letter. Paul regularly follows Hellenistic practice (Rom. 1:8; 1 Cor. 1:4; Phil. 1:3; 1 Thess. 1:2; Phlm. 4; cf. Col. 1:3; 2 Thess. 1:3). The Pastor, however, departs from the style of the classic Hellenistic letter. His thanksgiving occurs only after he has given an explanation of why the letter has been written. His thanksgiving is also different from the typically Pauline letter in that it presents a lengthy description of the apostle himself. Paul's own thanksgivings are expressions of gratitude to God for the faith and love of the community to which he is writing. Rhetorically the Pauline thanksgivings serve as a kind of *pathos* argument. They are a *captatio benevolentiae*, an appeal to the goodwill of Paul's correspondents. Serving to reinforce the image and authority of the purported letter writer (1:1), the thanksgiving of 1 Timothy reinforces the *ethos* appeal of the Pastor's missive.

1:12 I thank the one who has empowered me, Christ Jesus our Lord, because having appointed me for ministry he has kept me faithful, 13 who previously had been a blasphemer, persecutor, and an insolent person, but I have received mercy because in my ignorance I did what I did with a lack of faith; 14 and the favor of our Lord superabounded with faith and that love which is in Christ Jesus. 15 This is a trustworthy[a] saying, worthy of full acceptance: Christ Jesus came into the world to save sinners, among whom I am a prime example. 16 But because of this I have received

mercy so that in me first Christ Jesus would display forbearance as an
example for those who would come to believe in him unto eternal life. 17
To the King of the ages, the incorruptible and invisible one, the only[b]
God, be honor and glory unto the ages of ages. Amen.

a. Some witnesses to the Western textual tradition read *humanus*, reflecting a Greek
anthrōpinos, "human." All extant Greek witnesses read *pistos*, "faithful."

b. Some manuscripts add "wise" (*sophō*) to the list of divine attributes: Ψ, the Byzantine manuscripts, and the Textus Receptus, reflected by the AV. The addition may result
from the influence of Rom. 16:27.

[1:12–13] The Pastor's thanksgiving is unlike the typical Pauline thanksgiving in three respects. First, the thanksgiving formula is not Paul's characteristic "I give thanks" (*eucharistō*, (Rom. 1:8; 1 Cor. 1:4; Phil. 1:3; Phlm. 4;
the plural is used in 1 Thess. 1:2). Rather, the Pastor uses a stilted *charin echō*,
"I have thanks," "I am grateful," that may reflect a Latin form, *gratias ago*.

Second, the thanksgiving is addressed to Christ Jesus rather than to God. The
descriptive formula, namely the title "Christ" followed by the personal name
Jesus, appeared three times in the epistolary salutation (cf. 6:3, 14). The Pastor's addition of "our Lord" to the title and name (see 1:2) reminds the audience that it is the Lord who empowered Paul (see 2 Tim. 4:17). The Lord gave
the strength needed for the proclamation of the gospel, whose power resides not
in the human words of the apostle but in the gospel message itself.

The epithet "our Lord" was very important within Pauline communities. It
calls to mind that Jesus had been raised from among the dead and intimates that
he will come as Lord at the Parousia. The presence of these words enhances the
ethos appeal of the Pastor's composition. It was none other than "the Lord" himself, that is, one who has supreme authority, who positioned and empowered
Paul. Second Timothy 2:1–2 reflects the idea that Timothy was similarly
empowered by the grace of Christ Jesus to continue the apostle's work.

A third difference between the Pastor's thanksgiving and those of Paul is that
this thanksgiving is an expression of gratitude by "Paul" for what the Lord has
done for him (see Rom. 7:25, similarly an interjected thanksgiving). Typically
Paul's thanksgivings focus on what has happened in a community to which the
gospel had been preached. The Pastor says that the reason he gives thanks is that
the Lord kept Paul faithful (see 1 Cor. 15:10–11). This is somewhat surprising.
Paul who has been kept faithful is a Paul who previously had been anything but
faithful. He did what he did with no faith (*en apistia*, v. 13). He had been a blasphemer, a persecutor, and a violent person. This faithless person was appointed
for ministry (*themenos eis diakonian*). The term *diakonia*, literally, "service,"
became a technical term for ministry within the Christian community. Of itself,
the term evokes the image of a servant. The Pastor places the image before the
congregation as he begins to paint his portrait of Paul. Paul has been appointed

to serve, not to lord it over the flock (see Luke 22:24–27). Elsewhere the image will be set before Timothy as an example to be followed (see 2 Tim. 4:5).

The Pastor's portrait of Paul uses a "once-now" scheme often employed in Hellenistic rhetoric. By means of this technique the Pastor allows his readers to think of the "conversion" of Paul in a way that the apostle himself did not. The apostle willingly admitted that he had persecuted (*diōkō*) the church of God (1 Cor. 15:9; Gal. 1:13; Phil. 3:6; see Acts 22:4–5; 26:11). His persecution of the church was in fact legendary (Gal. 1:23; Acts 8:1–3; 9:5). In the undisputed Pauline letters,[10] however, Paul did not call himself specifically a "persecutor" (*diōktēn*).

Neither did Paul call himself a "blasphemer" (*blasphēmon*) or a "violent person" (*hybristēn*; see Rom. 1:30). He used neither of the verbs related to these terms to describe what he had done. Luke, however, does describe Paul as having violently persecuted the church (Acts 8:1–3). The Pastor also casts Paul in the role of a persecutor of the church. Using an interpretive triad, the Pastor explains the implications of his description of Paul as a persecutor. "Persecutor" is the central element in the triad, with "blasphemer" and "violent person" the interpretive elements. Paul's persecution of the church was blasphemy against God and violence against God's people. Paul is, in fact, a prime example of a blasphemer, persecutor of the church, and violent person. Paul is not only a sinner; he is also a prime example of what it means to be a sinner (1:15c). He has not only sinned; he has committed the most egregious of sins, a sin that would have merited death by stoning under traditional Jewish law (see Lev. 24:16; cf. 1 Kgs. 21:13). Paul had violently persecuted the church of God. By so doing, Paul had effectively spoken against God. Through his action he had denied what God had done (through Christ Jesus) for his people.

The Pastor continues to speak of the apostle in a way that would be unfamiliar to those who had read the apostle's letters. He describes Paul as having been ignorant and lacking in faith. Paul did not possess the full knowledge of the truth that was the hallmark of the community's faith. In the Pastor's portrayal of Paul these negative traits, ignorance and lack of faith, offer a kind of excuse for the egregious offense that Paul had committed in persecuting the church: What Paul did had been done in ignorance (*agnoōn*). Paul did not condone the ignorance of the Gentiles (Rom. 1:20–21; see, however, Acts 17:30), let alone pass off his own persecution of the church as coming from ignorance.

The Hebrew Scriptures make a distinction between sins committed out of ignorance (*kata agnoian*, Lev. 22:14; see Lev. 5:18; *akousiōs*, cf. e.g., Num. 15:22–29) and those committed maliciously. The latter are described in a biblical idiom as sins committed high handedly (*en cheiri hyperēphanias*, Num.

---

10. That is, Romans, 1–2 Corinthians, Galatians, Philippians, 1 Thessalonians, and Philemon.

15:30). It is possible to atone for the former but not for the latter. The book of
Numbers explains:

> An individual who sins unintentionally shall present a female goat a year old for
> a sin offering. And the priest shall make atonement before the LORD for the one
> who commits an error, when it is unintentional, to make atonement for the per-
> son, who then shall be forgiven. For both the native among the Israelites and the
> alien residing among them—you shall have the same law for anyone who acts in
> error. But whoever acts high-handedly, whether a native or an alien, affronts the
> LORD, and shall be cut off from among the people. Because of having despised
> the word of the LORD and broken his commandment, such a person shall be utterly
> cut off and bear the guilt. (Num. 15:27–31)

Even though Paul had blasphemed, the Pastor deems that he had sinned out of
ignorance. It was possible for the apostle's sin to be atoned for and for him to
be forgiven.

Having stated that Paul had acted in ignorance, the Pastor explains that
Paul's blasphemy was also due to his lack of faith (*en apistia*). This is one of
Paul's own ideas. In the Letter to the Romans, Paul explains that some among
the Israelites were lacking in faith. If, however, they turn from their lack of faith,
it is possible for them to be grafted onto and share "the rich root of the olive
tree" (see Rom. 3:3; 11:20, 23). Abraham, however, our father in faith, had no
lack of belief, as his faith grew strong and he gave glory to God (Rom. 4:20).
In effect, using the apostle's notion of the lack of faith as a paradigm, the Pastor describes Paul as a typical Jew. Paul lacked in faith but was nonetheless able
to come to faith because the Lord had mercy on him (*ēleēthēn*, a divine passive[11]) and filled him with faith and love.

The notion of faith echoes throughout the Pastor's description of Paul's conversion. The Pastor uses the *pist-* root seven times in all: 1:12, 13, 14, 15, 16,
19 [2x]. Paul was lacking in faith (*en apistia*, 1:13). The faithful word (*pistos
ho logos*, 1:15) is that Christ Jesus came into the world to save sinners. Paul
was a sinner, but the Lord had mercy on him and filled him with faith (*meta pisteōs*, 1:14) and kept him faithful (*piston*, 1:12). Likewise Timothy has faith
(*pistin*, 1:19), but there are some who have abandoned the faith (*pistin*, 1:19)
and allowed themselves to become shipwrecked.

[14] Speaking about faith, the Pastor uses the "once-now" scheme to good
advantage as he contrasts the man whose faith was deficient with the man whose
faith now superabounds. Paul's extraordinary faith and love are a result of the

---

11. In New Testament Greek, the passive voice of a verb is often used to avoid mention of the
name of God. It is God's activity that is implied in statements such as "hallowed be [*hagiasthētō*]
your name" (Matt. 6:9) and "he was raised [*egēgertai*] on the third day" (1 Cor. 15:4). The usage
reflects earlier Aramaic practice.

Lord's favor, the Lord's good grace. In fact, the Lord's favor was almost too much. Paul was keenly aware that God's grace was with him (1 Cor. 15:10). He writes about grace abounding (note the verb "abound" in Rom. 5:20; 6:1; 2 Cor. 4:15). In the emerging hagiographic image of Paul that dominated the Pastor's circles, the Pastor now affirms that grace "superabounded" (*hyperepleonasen*, a neologism) in Paul. The simple verb *pleonazō*, "abound," by itself has the connotation of abundance, more than enough. The prefix *hyper* adds an additional nuance to "more"; the Lord's grace is more than more than enough. The Lord's superabundant grace was active with "faith and that love which is in Christ Jesus." This phrase recurs in 2 Tim. 1:13, where it encapsulates a summary description of the Christian life, as it does here (see 2:15; cf. 4:12; 6:11; 2 Tim. 2:22; Titus 2:2).

The grace that overflowed in Paul with faith and love was from "our Lord" (*tou kyriou hēmōn*). The terminology is characteristic of 1 Timothy. Five times he writes about Christ as "our Lord" (1:2, 12, 14; 6:3, 14). In 6:15 he uses the phrase "Lord of lords" to refer to Christ as the greatest of lords. The title "Lord" is regularly used of Christ in 2 Timothy (16 times), but it is not to be found in Titus. More often than not, 2 Timothy cites the title without any further qualification, whereas 1 Timothy always adds some additional nuance to the epithet. Only twice does 2 Timothy specify that the Lord is "our" Lord (1:2, 8). In addition, the citations of Num. 16:5 and Isa. 52:11 in 2 Tim. 2:19 use the title in reference to God. This usage of the Greek Bible, in which "Lord" regularly renders the Hebrew "Yahweh," is indicative of the practice of Hellenistic Judaism to identify the God of Abraham, Isaac, and Jacob as "Lord."

[15] The affirmation that Christ Jesus came into the world to save sinners has several characteristics that allow it to be identified as a creedal statement developed by the early church. The *hoti* ("that") clause has a formal introduction, similar to the *hoti* clauses employed by the apostle, and is introduced by "we believe" (*pisteuomen*). The *hoti* (represented by a colon in my translation) is a recitative *hoti* meaning "that," not a causal *hoti* meaning "because." The verb "come" (*erchomai*) is a common word, one of the words most frequently used in the New Testament. In the Gospels, a first-person singular form of the verb appears in a number of "I have come" statements attributed to Jesus (see e.g., Mark 1:38; John 18:37). These sayings appear to be the result of early Christian reflection on the mission of Jesus[12] and suggest that the verb "come" affected a particular theological significance in the parlance of the early church. It was a technical term used to designate the mission of Jesus.

With the exception of 1 Tim. 6:7 and Rom. 5:12, the phrase "to come into the world" is used in the New Testament only of the mission of Jesus. "Into the

---

12. See Rudolf Bultmann, *The History of the Synoptic Tradition* (Oxford: Basil Blackwell, 1963) 152–56.

world" is typically a Johannine phrase, found fourteen times in the Gospel and three times in the epistles. In the Johannine tradition, the most characteristic affirmations about the mission of Jesus are that Jesus/the light "came into the world" (*erchomenos eis ton kosmon*; John 6:14; 9:39; 11:27; 16:28; 18:37; with *phōs*, "light": 1:9; 3:19; 12:46) or that he was "sent into the world" by the Father (John 3:17; 10:36; 17:18 [2x][13]; see John 8:26; 1 John 4:9). With one exception (John 16:21), the phrase "into the world" is always used in reference to the mission of Jesus. Hebrews 10:5 also uses the phrase "to come into the world" of the mission of Jesus, as does the Pastor's creed.

The creedal formula affirms that Jesus came into the world "to save sinners" (*hamartōlous sōsai*). First Timothy 1:15 is the only occurrence of this phrase in the New Testament. The verb occurs most often within the Synoptics, where it has reference to physical healing. In the Pauline and deuteropauline writings, "to save" is used of God's salvation. Thus, the Pastor affirms that God is the one who saves (2:15; 4:16; cf. 2 Tim. 1:9; Titus 3:5). This goes along with his characterization of God as "Savior" (*Sōter*, 1:1; 2:3; 4:10). First Timothy does not call Jesus the Savior, yet such usage was common in his circles (see 2 Tim. 1:10; Titus 1:4; 2:13; 3:6). The Pastor's creedal formula nonetheless affirms that Christ Jesus "saves." The Pastor's use of the verb "to save" (*sōzō*) in reference to both God and Christ Jesus provides additional evidence that his circles spoke about both God and Christ using salvation language.

The formal introduction to the Pastor's creedal statement has a familiar ring: It is a trustworthy saying (see 3:1; 2 Tim. 2:11; Titus 3:8). In this phrase, the word "trustworthy" means "reliable." Any saying that can be described as "trustworthy" is one that can be believed and deserves to be believed; the verb "to believe" (*pisteuein*) contains the same root as "trustworthy" (*pistos*). The Pastor's creedal affirmation is trustworthy and deserving of belief because it expresses traditional Christian faith. Its terminology may be different from that of traditional creedal formulae used by Paul, but its basic content is the same.

The Pastor accentuates the trustworthy nature of the creedal statement in 1:15 by adding "worthy of full acceptance" to the familiar "trustworthy saying." Within the Pastorals this additional qualification is found only in 1 Tim. 1:15 and 4:9. The language is that of late *koine*. "Acceptance" evokes the idea of favorable reception. Appended to a "trustworthy" formula that suggests what has been said is believable and to be believed, the added phrase indicates that the creedal words should be warmly received by the audience. The Pastor's "full" (*pasēs*) adds a note of intensity to Hellenism's formula of approval.

As a kind of postscript to the creedal formula, in order to apply it to Paul, the Pastor adds that Paul is the first of sinners (*hōn prōtos eimi egō*, literally, "of

---

13. The second occurrence is a reference to Jesus' analogous sending of his disciples into the world.

whom I am the first"). By his persecution of the church, Paul became a prime example of what it means to be a sinner. By describing Paul as a "sinner," the Pastor associates Paul with the sinners (1:9) for whom the law was established. Consequently, Paul can be an example for would-be teachers of the law. They too can have a conversion. The way in which the Pastor subtly provides Paul as a model for would-be teachers of the law is but one example of the way that the Pastor identifies Paul as a model to be followed.

His description of Paul as the "first" of sinners creates a bit of paronomasia (the repetitive use of a word or word root for rhetorical effect), which provides sonorous and literary unity to his portrayal of Paul. His use of the numerical adjective also adds considerably to his rhetorical argument. "First" (*prōtos*) hearkens back to the "previously" (*proteron*) of verse 13 and looks ahead to the "first" (*prōtos*) in verse 16. The author effectively establishes a contrast between Paul as a prime example of what it means to be a sinner and Paul as a prime example of what it means to receive mercy from God through Jesus Christ. Not only has the Pastor used an effective rhetorical scheme, "once-now," to highlight his portrayal of Paul and his articulation of the common faith of the church, he has also used his literary skill to good effect with his array of literary and rhetorical devices.

Excursus 1: "This Is a Trustworthy Saying"

In 1 Tim. 1:12–17 the Pastor offers a reflection on "Paul's" spiritual autobiography. He highlights Paul's conversion from being a sinner of the first order to one who has been entrusted with the gospel and has become a model for all believers. The Pastor's gratitude for Paul's conversion has been expressed by his incorporating this autobiographical reminiscence withinthe epistle's thanksgiving section. It is the primary object of the author's thanksgiving.

Embedded within his reflection on Paul is a statement with a decidedly formulaic ring: "This is a trustworthy saying, worthy of full acceptance" (1 Tim. 1:15). This is the first of five such statements in the Pastoral Epistles. The formula appears in both a longer (1 Tim. 1:15; 4:9) and a shorter form (1 Tim. 3:1; 2 Tim. 2:11; Titus 3:8).

From a form-critical perspective, the words stand out. They have no parallel in the undisputed Pauline letters, but their use allows the Pastor to move from the subject of Paul's conversion (1:15) to the traditional notion that God desires the salvation of sinners (4:10). In 1:15 the Pastor relates salvation to the coming of Christ Jesus into the world: "Christ Jesus came into the world to save sinners." These words have the ring of a creedal formula. They do not, however, explicitly cite the death and/or resurrection of Jesus, the object of most Pauline creedal fragments (e.g., 1 Cor. 15:3–5; 1 Thess. 1:10; 4:14; 5:10), nor are they introduced by some form of the verb "believe." The formula, "This is a trustworthy saying, worthy of full acceptance" (*pistos ho logos kai pasēs apodochēs axios*), appears to stand in the stead of the more traditional "believe that."

In 4:9 the formula again interrupts the flow of the Pastor's argument, just as it does in 1:12–17. The passage in which the formula occurs (4:7b–10) exploits the Hellenistic agon motif to describe the human struggle for the achievement of godliness. As the description is developed, the Pastor says "Godliness is beneficial for everything. It bears the promise of life in the present and of life to come" (1 Tim. 4:8b–c). He then adds "This is a trustworthy saying, worthy of full acceptance." The appendage reprises the seven words of 1 Tim. 1:15 in exactly the same order. The formula interrupts the flow of the Pastor's argument and is alien to the context, the agon motif, in which it appears. In both 1:15 and 4:9 the formula is linked to a saying that tersely expresses a basic religious tenet: "Christ Jesus came into the world to save sinners" and "Godliness is beneficial for everything. It bears the promise of life in the present and of life to come." Such characteristics identify the predicate "This is a trustworthy saying, worthy of full acceptance" as a literary formula, a stylized seal of approval.

A short version of the formula "This is a trustworthy saying" (*pistos ho logos*) occurs in 1 Tim. 3:1a. The words are nestled between a topos on women (2:11–15) and a topos on overseers (3:1b–7). Once again, the words clearly interrupt the flow of the Pastor's thought. He is in the middle of developing a series of reflections on various groups within the community. The style and vocabulary of the formula are alien to the context. The expression produces a startling break in the Pastor's exposition. In this respect, the words are used in a fashion similar to that of the longer formula of 1 Tim. 1:15 and 4:9. The same three words, *pistos ho logos*, also appear in this short version in 2 Tim. 2:11 and Titus 3:8. Identical wording and similar function identify the expression as a literary formula. Its formulaic nature is enhanced by its terse use of a predicate construction, omitting the verb "to be."

In 1 Tim. 1:15 the long formula precedes a common affirmation of the early church's faith, albeit with a Johannine ring, "Christ Jesus came into the world to save sinners" (1 Tim. 1:15b). In 1 Tim. 4:9 the formula is appended to the words, "Godliness is beneficial for everything. It bears the promise of life in the present and of life to come" (1 Tim. 4:8b–c). These affirmations, to which the long formula of approval is linked, are religious axioms whose authority within the community is thereby endorsed.

In 1 Tim. 3:1 the short version of the formula is appended to a midrash on the Genesis stories of Adam and Eve (Gen. 2:18–3:13). In 2 Tim. 2:11 the short formula introduces hymnic material that appears to be a reworking of a portion of Paul's baptismal catechesis (Rom. 6:8): "For if we die together, we shall also live together. If we endure, we shall also reign together. If we deny [him], he shall deny us. If we are unfaithful, he remains faithful, for he cannot deny himself" (2 Tim. 2:11b–13). In Titus 3:8 the short formula appears after a tersely expressed formulation on baptism and salvation: "According to his mercy, he saved us through the washing of rebirth and renewal by the Holy Spirit, which he poured out on us profusely through Jesus Christ, our Savior, so that, justified by his grace, we may become heirs according to the hope of eternal life" (Titus 3:5b–7).

"This is a trustworthy saying" is sometimes used as a formula of endorsement, that is, when it follows the material to which it is joined. The long formula is used in this way in 1 Tim. 4:9; the short formula is so used in 1 Tim. 3:1 and Titus 3:8. In this posterior position, the formula functions as a kind of "Amen," affirming the reliability of what has been said and the consent of whoever says, "This is a trustworthy saying." The sayings to which the formula is appended are "trustworthy" (*pistos*) because they can be believed and ought to be believed. The sayings are reliable because the believer can base his or her entire life and hope on such affirmations of faith. What is being affirmed is the traditional faith of the church on Adam and Eve, the Christian life, salvation, and baptism.

When it precedes the traditional material with which it is linked, the formula functions as an invitation to belief. This is the case with the long formula in 1 Tim. 1:15 and the short formula in 2 Tim. 2:11. Use of the formula suggests that the words that follow are words the members of the community are to believe and on which they are to base their lives. They are to express that belief in the way that they live, just like Paul, the first of sinners, who was then called to be an apostle and an example for others who follow him in faith (1 Tim. 1:15–16). In 2 Tim. 2:11 the short formula introduces what seems to be a baptismal hymn. It is, nonetheless, noteworthy that the formula appears just after the author has presented Paul's life and sufferings as important for the salvation of God's chosen ones (2 Tim. 2:9b–10).

The words of the trustworthy sayings are messages of faith, creedal cameos. In the Pastoral Epistles the sayings function in much the same way as do the creedal formulae of Paul's letters and the creeds of the later church. The leader of the community, the overseer, is to maintain these trustworthy sayings so that he can encourage the community and confront its opponents (Titus 1:9). Confirmation of the creedal nature of the faithful sayings can be found in the confessional "that" (*hoti*), which introduces the words "Christ Jesus came into the world to save sinners" in 1 Tim. 1:15. The verse could be translated, "This is a faithful saying, worthy of full acceptance, that Christ Jesus came into the world to save sinners." It may have been that the community responded "Amen!" or even repeated *pistos ho logos*, "This is a trustworthy saying" after hearing a formulation of faith introduced by "This is a trustworthy saying."

In some of the cases, the formula of trustworthiness is used with wording so terse that the words to which the formula is attached appear to have been a fixed formulation themselves. In this kind of formulation, they could easily be transmitted from one person to another, one church to another, and from generation to generation within the church (1 Tim. 1:15; 2 Tim. 2:11–13) or society (1 Tim. 4:9). In other instances the ideas endorsed may be traditional, but their formulation derives from the author. This would be the case in 1 Tim. 3:1 and Titus 3:8, two instances of the Pastorals' use of the shorter formula. In such instances the community is invited to accept the authority of the Pastor as a reliable interpreter of tradition.

Used either to introduce or to ratify a traditional formula of faith, the formula functioned in much the same way as did the Hebrew "Amen." In Jewish culture, as both the canonical New Testament and the Qumran scrolls evidence, "Amen" was sometimes used to highlight the importance of a statement to follow or as an affirmation of the reliability of what had just been said. The single "Amen" of Jesus' discourse in the Synoptic Gospels (e.g., Matt 5:18) and the double "Amen" of some of his discourse in the Fourth Gospel (e.g., John 1:51) are examples of the introductory use of "Amen." The book of Revelation provides evidence of "Amen," even a double "Amen" used as a response (Rev. 1:6; 7:12) or acclamation of affirmation (Rev. 5:14; 19:4; 22:20). Revelation 7:12 suggests that "Amen" was sometimes used both to introduce and to confirm, while Rev. 1:7 provides evidence that the confirmatory "Amen" was sometimes duplicated. In the Pastor's community, "This is a trustworthy saying" appears to have been used in much the same way.

What then do the words of the long formula "worthy of full acceptance" add to the familiar "This is a trustworthy saying"? The additional wording appears only in 1 Tim. 1:15 and 4:9, the only passages in the New Testament where the word "acceptance" is used. Hellenistic writers used the phrase "worthy of acceptance" to suggest that particular persons or things were particularly worthy of approbation or admiration. Hierocles used the expression "worthy of much acceptance" (*pollēs axion apodochēs*; see Stobaeus, *Anthology* 4.27.20) to describe some laws. Ultimately, what "worthy of full acceptance" adds to "trustworthy" is repetition for the sake of emphasis, much as the author of the book of Revelation uses *nai*, "yea" or "verily," in addition to the "Amen" of Rev. 1.

[16] Having used the "once-now" scheme to good effect by writing about the blasphemer who received mercy (v. 13a–b) and the faithless one who superabounded in faith (vv. 13c–14), the Pastor completes the third unit of the scheme by portraying the one who had been the first of sinners as an example for believers. His description of Paul as a sinner (v. 15) uses a comprehensive theological term to sum up the earlier description of Paul as a blasphemer, persecutor, and insolent person (v. 13a). The expression, "have received mercy" (*eleēthēn*, v. 16) reprises the terminology of verse 13b. In effect, the Pastor has arranged his portrayal of Paul in a chiastic *a-b-a'* structure. The encompassing elements speak of Paul the sinner who has received mercy. The central element and focus of the chiasm portrays Paul as the one without faith who now superabounds in faith by the grace of the Lord. The now-element of the third unit (1:16) explains why it is that Paul has received mercy, the focus of the first now-element (1:13b).

The words "because of this" refer to what the Pastor has just affirmed, namely, that Christ Jesus came into the world to save sinners, of whom Paul was a prime example. Once a sinner, Paul received mercy. Paul was the recipient of mercy so that he might serve as an example for those who would come to believe. This is the only time that the New Testament uses the word "example" (*hypotypōsin*) to speak of a person who serves as a model for others (see 2 Tim. 1:13). The Pastor's hagiographic intent is manifest in what he has written about Paul in this verse. His singular focus on Paul as an example for believers is a key element in the Pastorals' portrait of the apostle (see Collins, "Image of Paul"). The reader would hear in the words "come to believe" (*tōn mellontōn pisteuein*) an echo of a call to conversion, the invitation to belief.

The communities that Paul had evangelized would know him as a person who had come to believe. He himself would deny that he had been the first to come to faith (Rom. 16:7). Now the Pastor portrays Paul as someone who came to believe even though he had been a sinner, in fact, an egregious sinner. He was someone in whom Jesus Christ had provided a demonstration of forbearance (*makrothymian*) for the benefit of those who would come to believe. Belief in Christ Jesus brings with it a promise of eternal life, the object of Christian hope (see 6:12 and the commentary on Titus 1:2). Paul is a model of this faith. On two occasions Paul had exhorted the Corinthians to follow his example (1 Cor. 4:16; 11:1; see Phil. 3:17; 1 Thess. 1:6). In the Pastorals, the imitation of Paul has become a significant motif (see, e.g., 2 Tim. 3:10–11; 4:7–8). Hagiographic interests are at work in the Pastoral's portrait of Paul. His is an example for the community to follow; memory of his sufferings can encourage them to be steadfast even as they encounter difficulties for the sake of the gospel.

[17] The Pastor concludes the epistle's thanksgiving period with a doxology. Another doxology is found toward the end of the epistle (6:16). The pair of doxologies form a loose inclusio that encompasses the core of the document. This core consists of community regulations. The doxologies are the theological bookends that provide a framework for these regulations.

This doxology in verse 17 is the longest of the three doxologies in the Pastoral Epistles (see 6:16; 2 Tim. 4:18). The classic New Testament doxology consists of four elements: the object of praise, an expression of praise, an indication of time, and a confirmatory response (e.g., Rom. 16:27; see Collins, "Case of a Wandering Doxology"). All four characteristic elements are found in the Pastor's doxology. As is usually the case with post-Pauline New Testament doxologies, the expression of the constitutive elements in the Pastor's doxology has been expanded and the formula of address considerably so.

This epistolary thanksgiving has been addressed to Christ Jesus (1:12). The concluding doxology is addressed to the King of the ages, the incorruptible and invisible one, the only God. The idea that the God of Israel is King of the ages (*basilei tōn aiōnōn*) evokes the biblical and Christian tradition of God as king, celebrated in the familiar phrase, the "kingdom of God." Paul rarely writes about the kingdom of God. He does so, however, in the First Letter to the Corinthians (4:20; 6:9, 10; 15:24, 50) and once each in the letters to the Galatians and Romans (Gal. 5:21; Rom. 14:17). The latter treats several issues relating to God's chosen people and traditional Jewish faith and practice. In both 1 Corinthians and Galatians, Paul uses the biblical phrase "kingdom of God" in an exclusion formula that sanctions a catalog of vices (see 1 Cor. 6:9, 10; Gal. 5:21).

The doxology's proclamation that God is King of the ages identifies God as superior to the emperor or any human ruler whose reign is limited to just one age (see 6:15). The abstract adjectives used to characterize the King of the ages—"incorruptible," "invisible," and "only"—come from the language of Greek philosophical reflection. In their abstraction (see Philo, *Abel and Cain* 101) these terms differ radically from the Bible's anthropomorphic portrayal of

God. The first two epithets begin with a privative alpha. God is not corruptible (*a-phthartō*); God is not seen (*a-(h)oratō*). "Incorruptible" affirms that God does not belong to the realm of flesh (*sarx*; see 3:16). The Bible usually describes this quality of God in positive terms: God lives from age to age, God is spirit, and so forth. The idea that God cannot be seen is central to the Jewish idea of God (see 6:16; Exod. 33:20; John 1:18). Once again, the Bible describes God's lack of visibility in positive terms. It speaks of God's "glory," God's "weightiness," a notion to which later Jewish tradition added the nuance of luminosity. Moses heard the Lord speak but did not see God.

Every day in the recitation of the Shema, the pious Jew proclaimed, "The LORD is our God, the LORD alone" (Deut. 6:4). A note in the Jewish Publication Society's translation of the Bible[14] relies on Rashbam and Ibn Ezra as authorities in support of the reading "alone" in Deut. 6:4. It notes, however, that for others the verse should be rendered "the LORD is one." This would be consistent with the Greek Bible's rendition of the phrase: *kyrios ho theos hēmōn kyrios Eis esti.* "Alone" (cf. Rom. 16:27) speaks of the exclusivity of God, and "one" speaks of of God's uniqueness, the covenant's fundamental tenet. After its accumulation of divine epithets and attributes, the doxology identifies the object of the prayer of praise as God.

Within the Pauline tradition, "God" is almost always a proper noun designating the God of Israel. It is virtually the name of God. In expressing praise to God, the Pastor begins with a doublet; he offers "honor and glory" to God. The language is performative. By pronouncing the doxology, the worshiper *gives* honor and glory to God. *Doxa*, the Greek word from which the name of the genre derives, is found in all the New Testament doxologies save one (6:16). In the New Testament, "honor" and "glory" are often paired together (Rom. 2:7, 10; Heb. 2:7, 9; 1 Pet. 1:7; 2 Pet. 1:17; Rev. 4:9, 11; 5:12, 13; 21:26; cf. Rev. 7:12). Only the Pastor, however, uses the paired terms in a doxology.

The doxology of verse 17 concludes in traditional fashion with a temporal phrase and a choral response. The temporal phrase, "unto the ages of ages" (*eis tous aiōnas tōn aiōnōn*, with a Hebrew genitive, a construction in which a noun replaces an adjective), is the common language of New Testament doxologies (1:17; 2 Tim. 4:18; Gal. 1:5; Phil. 4:20; Heb. 13:21; 1 Pet. 4:11; 5:11 [some mss.]; Rev. 1:6; 5:13; 7:12). The phrase proclaims that God who lives and reigns for ever and ever (Rev. 1:18; 4:9, 10; 10:6; 11:15; 15:7; cf. 14:11; 19:3; 20:10; 22:5) is to be praised for ever and ever.

The doxology's choral response, "Amen," expresses public affirmation of what had just been pronounced. The presence of "Amen" confirms the liturgi-

---

14. *Tanakh: The Holy Scriptures: The New JPS Translation according to the Traditional Hebrew Text* (Philadelphia: Jewish Publication Society, 1988), 284*b*.

cal origins of the New Testament doxology. "Amen" was the congregation's response to each of the three parts of the Aaronic blessing (Num. 6:24–26) pronounced in the synagogue (cf. 1QS 2:10).

Prior Examples
1 Timothy 1:18–20

Having concluded his portrayal of Paul, a model of conversion to the faith, with an encomium, the Pastor turns his attention once again to the apologetic role that Timothy is to play in the community. He is to persevere in dealing with those who have turned from the faith (1:3–4). Having cited the apostle as a model of one who lacked faith and then, by God's mercy, came to faith, the Pastor cites the names of Hymenaeus and Alexander as two intractable individuals with whom Paul had to deal. For the Pastor, Paul is not only a model of conversion to the faith, he is also a model of the pastor who must deal with the recalcitrant.

> 1:18 I am explaining this message to you, Timothy, my son, in accordance with the prophecies previously directed to you so that you might fight the good fight with them, 19 having faith and a good conscience. Some people[a] have moved away from these and have become shipwrecked. 20 Among them are Hymenaeus and Alexander, whom I have handed over to Satan so that they might learn not to blaspheme.

a. Verses 18–20 are a single sentence in Greek.

[1:18–19a] The reference to Timothy, Paul's son in faith (1:2), in verse 18 marks a departure from the epistolary style of the times. In the Hellenistic world, the names of the senders and recipients of letters usually are found only in the opening and closing of the letter, that is, in the salutation and in the greetings and an occasional note added in the hand of the letter writer, who would have dictated his correspondence to a scribe. A formal address to Timothy at this juncture serves to highlight the seriousness of the challenge that he is facing. He must be steadfast in dealing with the difficult members in the community. In this, as a good son (see John 5:19b–20), he is to follow the example of his father Paul. The pronoun "my" is not in the Greek text but is implicit as the pseudonymous Paul addresses Timothy as his son. Within the Pastorals the designation "son" recalls the rabbinic ethos according to which the father transmits traditional lore to his son. Whether that son is his biological offspring or not matters little in the use of the epithet. The son, having learned from his father, is capable of assuming the responsibilities of the father.

The Pastor explains why he told Timothy the things that had just been said. The verb that he has chosen (*paratithemai*) means to lay out something before someone else, thus, "to explain." Williams, however, noting its relationship with *parathēkē* (1 Tim. 6:20; 2 Tim. 1:12, 14), suggests "to deposit" as the real meaning of the verb (Williams 186, 192n57). The Pastor sums up what has been said as "this message" (*tautēn tēn parangelian*). The phrase makes use of a word group (*parangel-*) that within the Pastorals is used only in 1 Timothy.[15] Essentially the word group refers to passing along a message received. In the Hellenistic world it was often used with the connotation of a command. Thus, it is often found in literature that has reference to the military (1 Macc. 5:58; 2 Macc. 5:25; 13:10; Onasander, *General* 25; *P. Oslo* 84.15; *P. Oxy.* 1411.16; 2268.5). The use of this word group in 1:18 indicates that an order, an authoritative challenge, has been addressed to Timothy.

Paul's challenge to Timothy has a norm and a purpose. It is to be undertaken in accordance with the prophecies previously directed to him (*kata tas proagousas epi se prophēteias*). Prophecy, that which is uttered by God's spokespersons, is a charism, the only charism that appears on all four of Paul's lists of spiritual gifts (Rom. 12:6; 1 Cor. 12:10, 28, 29; see 1 Cor. 13:2; 14:6, 22). The Pastor uses the word "prophecy" only twice, each time in conjunction with a chain of tradition that extends from Paul to Timothy (1:18; 4:14). As Timothy takes on a portion of the ministry entrusted to Paul, he is to fulfill his task under the guidance of the word of God spoken in prophecy.

The purpose of the mandate given to Timothy is that he might fight the good fight (see 6:12; 2 Tim. 4:7, where the image appears with the *agōn-* root). The military metaphor, using the *strat-* root, "to fight as a soldier," is an expression of the agon motif used by Paul and his disciples in reference to the gospel (1 Cor. 9:7; 2 Cor. 10:3–4; Phlm. 2; 2 Tim. 2:4). Paul himself tended to use this military metaphor in reference to conflictual situations. As athletes who must strive to attain victory in games and as soldiers who must strive to attain victory in warfare, so the evangelist must strive to proclaim the gospel, notwithstanding the cost or the difficulty. Timothy is to carry the aforementioned prophecies as his weaponry (see 2 Cor. 10:4) or armor (Williams 243n143; see 1 Thess. 5:8).

As had been the case in 1:3–7, the syntax of this pericope is chaotic as a result of the Pastor's insertions and appended clauses. Grammarians might well speak of "having faith and a good conscience" (*echōn pistin kai agathēn syneidēsin*) as a dangling modifier. The phrase qualifies the implied subject of

15. The noun in 1:5, 18; the verb in 1:3; 4:11; 5:7; 6:13, 17.

the verb "fight," yet it is placed after the object in order to provide a ready referent for the relative clauses that follow (1:19b–20). Timothy is to go into battle with faith and a good conscience (see 1:5). The parallelism between the two words in the compound object of "having" suggests that both words have an objective meaning. Since the word "faith" appears without a qualifier (see "authentic" in 1:5), the nuance might be that of "fidelity" rather than that of "doctrinal content."

[**19b–20**] The faith and good conscience of Timothy as he is about to joust on behalf of the gospel message create a contrast between him and those who have rejected faith and good conscience. These people are designated simply as "some" people (*tines*). The usage is characteristic of 1 Timothy. An anonymous "some" is the author's consistent designation of those who have departed from the gospel message and are creating difficulties for his community (1:3, 6, 19; 4:1; 5:15, 24; 6:10, 21; cf. "someone" [*tis*] in 1:8; 5:8; 6:3).

Mixing his metaphors, as the apostle himself was wont to do—Paul had spoken of himself and his fellow evangelists as infants, nursing mothers, and fathers in 1 Thess. 2:8–12—the Pastor describes in nautical terms those with whom Timothy is to fight. In the New Testament, the verb "to be shipwrecked" (*enauagēsan*; see 2 Cor. 11:25) is used in a metaphorical sense only in 1:19. However, the verb is often used metaphorically in the Septuagint and was well-known within the Hellenistic world where it was used by Demosthenes, Josephus (*Ant.* 5.183; 12.355), and others (see Philo, *Change of Names* 215). The verb translated as "moved away" (*apōsamenoi*) appears elsewhere in the Pauline corpus only in a citation of Ps. 93:14 (LXX) to refer to God's having abandoned his people (Rom. 11:1–2). Associated with nautical imagery, the verb may have retained something of its etymological meaning, "push away," with the meaning "push off" as from shore or a dock. Timothy is charged with being a good soldier; the anonymous "some" are rash sailors.

Although the difficult persons with whom Timothy must deal are left in anonymity, the Pastor cites the names of two individuals with whom the apostle had to deal. The Pastor's use of a "historical" example is a familiar ploy in Hellenistic rhetoric, one frequently used in the moral epistles of the late first century C.E. The Pastor cites Hymenaeus and Alexander as examples for Timothy to beware. Hymenaeus is a figure whose existence and participation in a first-century Christian community is not otherwise attested apart from a passage in which someone named Hymenaeus appears alongside Philetus as an example of individuals who denied the resurrection from the dead (2 Tim. 2:17).

An individual named Alexander appears in two other legendary sources of material about Paul. In 2 Tim. 4:14 a coppersmith named Alexander is said to

have done much evil against Paul and to have spoken out against the Pauline
message. "Paul" expected him to suffer at the hand of divine vengeance. The
late second-century C.E. *Acts of Paul* (3.26–36) tells the story of a man named
Alexander, a Syrian Antiochene, who creates difficulties for one of Paul's
disciples, a woman named Thecla. Having fallen in love with her, Alexander
attempts to gain her affection by bribing Paul with money and gifts. The apostle refuses the bribe, claiming to have no information about the woman.
Thereupon Alexander attempts to take her by force, but she tears his robe and
pulls the crown from his head. He takes her before the governor, who con-
demns Thecla to die at the mouths of lions and bears. With the gracious protection of Tryphaena and a miraculous taming of a lioness, she is saved.
Alexander then succeeds in having her sent to the bulls. Once again Thecla
miraculously escapes, whereupon Alexander, fearing the emperor, asks that
Thecla be set free. In addition to its mention of a man named Alexander, this
tale can serve as an illustration of the various legends that developed around
the figure of the apostle in the early church. In some ways these legends are
a kind of early Christian haggadah, the evolving narratives that sustain a faith
community in the course of its history in a way similar to the way that traditional Jewish haggadah has sustained the Jewish people over the course of the
centuries.

The Pastor says that Paul punished the two rebellious individuals,
Hymenaeus and Alexander, by handing them over to Satan so that they would
learn not to speak against God's word, the Pauline message. The expression,
"handed over to Satan so that . . ." (*paredōka tō Satana hina . . .*) has been taken
over from 1 Cor. 5:5. In that letter, the expression describes the temporal punishment to be administered to a man guilty of incest so that he might change his
ways. The expression derives from the judicial sphere. The verb "to hand over"
(*paradidōmi*) was commonly used in reference to a person's being remanded,
"handed over," for some sort of punishment (see, e.g., Antiphon, *Prosecution
for Poisoning* 20; Isocrates, *Orations* 17.15; Demosthenes, *Against Stephanus
I* 45.61; Mark 1:14; 9:31; Acts 8:3; 12:4).

The idea of handing someone over to Satan, God's agent in judicial administration, goes back to Job 2:6. An expression similar to that used by Paul and
the Pastor is found in a fourth-century C.E. papyrus: "Demon of the dead, I
deliver so and so to you so that . . ." (*ekudaimōn . . . paradidōmi . . . hopōs*; F.
G. Kenyon and H. I. Bell, *Greek Papyri in the British Museum* [London:
Trustees of the British Museum London] vol. 1, 1898, 75). Punishment is to be
inflicted on Hymenaeus and Alexander, who have so disastrously veered from
the faith, but hope remains that they may learn their lesson. They must learn not
to speak against God. Encouraging Timothy to deal effectively with recalcitrants from the faith, the Pastor offers Paul's way of dealing with obstinate people as an example for his "son" to follow.

Instruction on Prayer
1 Timothy 2:1–7

The Pastor's instruction on prayer contains one of the richest theological passages in the Pastoral corpus. The instruction itself is rather simple. The Pastor urges that various forms of prayer be offered on behalf of kings and those in authority. Such prayers are to be offered for the sake of the common good. Prayers are to be offered for those who rule so that those who are ruled can live serenely, fulfilling their religious and social obligations as best they can.

The Pastor's defense of this form of prayer to God is most likely motivated by an apologetic intent. The kinds of prayers that were offered on behalf of authorities in the Hellenistic world were tainted by idolatry. These prayers sometimes allowed emperors themselves to be acknowledged as gods, as they often were from the time of Augustus. The Pastor wants the congregation to understand that idol and emperor worship is deviant and to be avoided but that nonetheless prayer should be offered on behalf of those in authority so that those under authority can live in peace (see Rom. 13:1–7; 1 Pet. 2:13–17). His reflection on prayer leads the Pastor to identify God as Savior. God, not the emperor, is the Savior. For the Pastor, God is Savior of all people. The God to whom the prayer of believers is addressed is not the Savior of one or another city or nation. The God in whom Christians believe is the Savior of all people. The Pastor explains God's universal will of salvation with a focus on the specific role of Christ Jesus within the universal plan of salvation and the unique role of the apostle Paul within that plan of salvation.

2:1 Therefore I urge you, first of all, to offer petitions, prayers, invocations, and thanksgivings for all people, 2 for kings and for all who are in authority so that we might live a peaceful and quiet life in all godliness and dignity. 3 This is good and acceptable before our Savior, God, 4 who wills that all people be saved and come to the full knowledge of truth. 5 For there is one God and one intermediary between God and humans, the human being, Christ Jesus, 6 who gave himself as a ransom for all, testimony at the appropriate time.[a] 7 For this I have been appointed herald and apostle—I am speaking[b] the truth, I am not lying—the teacher of the Gentiles in faith[c] and truth.

a. The manuscript tradition attests to various attempts to clarify the grammar of the phrase "testimony at the appropriate time" (*to martyrion kairois idiois*). Thus, a corrector of the Sinaiticus (ℵ) prefixed the phrase with *kai*, "and," so that Jesus gave both himself and testimony. Several manuscripts add a clarifying *edothē* so that the phrase reads, "testimony was given at the appropriate time."

b. Reading *legō en Christō*, "I am speaking in Christ," most of the manuscripts belonging to the Byzantine text type and a few other ancient manuscripts provide the oath with a specifically Christian formulation. This Christian formulation probably derives from scribal dependence on Rom. 9:1. Minuscule 1319 makes the Christian formulation conformable with the style of 1 Timothy by reading *en Christ Iēsou*.

c. The Codex Sinaiticus reads "knowledge" (*gnōsei*) rather than "faith" (*pistei*).

[2:1–2] Having completed the deferred epistolary thanksgiving, the Pastor begins the body of his epistle with "I urge you" (*parakalō*; "you" is not found in the Greek but must be supplied in view of the use of the infinitive, "to do" [*poieisthai*]). This formula was often found in Hellenistic diplomatic letters sent by authorities to those under their control, "urging" them to do something. Given the nature of those documents, what the inferiors were urged to do was obey what was in fact a tactfully phrased order.

The inferential *oun*, "therefore," and the Pastor's "first of all" (*prōton*) suggest that if Timothy is to achieve the purpose for which he was to remain in Ephesus, primarily to stem the tide of false teaching in the community, he had to pray for the stability of the social order. The use of various synonyms from the lexicography of prayer is an example of the literary device of *repetitio*. These synonyms emphasize Timothy's obligation and suggest that Christian prayer includes a variety of forms. The primary import of the literary device lies in its cumulative effect. As a result, the individual prayer forms suggested by the Pastor's list are less important than the fact that the Pastor urges Timothy to pray in the best way possible. His prayer should include petitions (*deēseis*), prayers (*proseuchas*, the most common New Testament word for prayer), invocation (*enteuxeis*), and thanksgiving (*eucharistias*). In 4:4–5 the Pastor offers his audience some idea of how he understands the latter two forms.

The Pastor urges that prayers be offered on behalf of everyone (*hyper pantōn anthrōpōn*). Many commentators read this as if it were directed against a gnosticizing tendency within the Pastor's community. Gnostics would be inclined to pray for those with knowledge (*gnōsis*) but not for those who were outside the circles of the elite. Given the context, it may be that the primary reference of the phrase is to those with whom Timothy and the community are engaged in some kind of struggle. Timothy had been exhorted to take them to task and to correct their mistaken notion of the law (1:3–11). Paul had been presented as an example of someone who took decisive action in dealing with recalcitrants (1:18–20).

In a Jewish Christian context, the Pastor's instruction to pray for all people should be seen as a specification of the love command. In the Sermon on the Mount, the Matthean Jesus authoritatively interprets the love command (Lev.

19:18) for a Jewish Christian audience by saying, "Love your enemies and pray for those who persecute you" (*proseuchesthe hyper tōn diōkontōn hymas*, Matt. 5:44). Expanding on his exhortation to genuine love, Paul writes, "Bless those who persecute you; bless and do not curse them" (Rom. 12:14). The Pastor's directive that believers should pray for everyone would seem to intimate that not even those who were causing difficulties within the community should be excluded from its prayer.

Among those for whom Christians are to pray, particular mention is made of kings and those in authority (see the exhortation to obey legitimate authorities in Titus 3:1). The practice of prayer for civil rulers is one that the Pastor's readers had received from their Jewish forebears. The book of Baruch, of date unknown, claims that the practice dates to the time of the Babylonian exile (Bar. 1:11–12). Before the Temple was destroyed in 70 C.E., prayers and sacrifices for the well-being of the empire had been offered in the temple on a daily basis (1 Macc. 7:33; see 1 Esdr. 6:31). Epigraphic evidence from Jewish synagogues in the Diaspora confirms the loyalty of Jews to the empire. Philo boasts that the Jews are not to be outdone by any other nation in Europe or in Asia in their prayers for the emperor:

> In all matters, in which piety is enjoined and permitted under the laws, it [Judaism] stood not a whit behind any other either in Asia or in Europe, in its prayers, its erection of votive offerings, its number of sacrifices not only of those offered at general national feasts but in the perpetual and daily rites through which is declared their piety, not so much with mouth and tongue as in intentions formed in the secrecy of the soul by those who do not tell you that they love their Caesar but love him in very truth. (*Gaius* 280; see 68, 232, 317–18, 356–57)

Rabbinic Judaism urged that prayers be offered for the authorities. Rabbi Hanina, the "Prefect of the Priests," is reported to have taught, "Pray for the peace of the ruling power, since but for fear of it men would have swallowed up each other alive" (*m.'Abot* 3:2; see *t. Sukk.* 4). This Mishnaic teaching is similar to that of 2:2 insofar as it gives a reason why prayers should be offered for the ruling authority.

The pious practice that the Pastor urges upon the community is similar to Jewish practice and radically different from Gentile practice. The community was to pray *for* the emperor and not *to* the emperor, as was then the case in the cult of divinized emperors. The community's practice was also different from various pagan forms of prayer in which offerings were made to the emperor through the medium of statues or images, similar to the idols used in the worship of civic deities. The Pastor's list of four kinds of prayer to be offered (2:1) excludes the kind of idol worship that pagans might employ in the cult of the emperor.

The Pastor's concern for social order is reflected when he, along with Rabbi Hanina, mentions the commonweal as the reason why prayers should be offered for those in authority. These prayers are important. Their purpose is that the people itself can lead a serene life without being swallowed up in chaos. A long prayer in Clement's letter to the Corinthians asks that the Lord direct the counsel of sovereigns so that they might "administer in peace and gentleness with godliness the power which You have given them" (*1 Clem.* 61:2). The Pastor's motivational clause contains some measure of self-interest. He desires that all people, but particularly the faithful ("we"), be able to live with godliness and dignity in all respects. In the Hellenistic world, "godliness" sums up the virtue of religiosity, while "dignity" can be taken as the epitome of social virtue. In 1 Thessalonians the apostle himself had written about the importance of the serene life (1 Thess. 4:11–12).

Excursus 2: Christians in the World

In his classic commentary on the Pastoral Epistles, Henrich Julius Holtzmann wrote, "The civic life is the sphere in which the inner Christian life is outwardly expressed as Christianity in the world" (Holtzmann 307). Since then commentators have often used Holtzmann's language, that of the bourgeois ethic (*bürgerliche Ethik*), in their discussions of ethics in the Pastoral Epistles. Dibelius and Conzelmann describe this kind of morality as "the ideal of good christian citizenship" (Dibelius and Conzelmann 39–41).

Clearly the formulation of the Pastor's moral exhortation, his *paraenesis,* is Hellenistic in its formulation. Prayer must be offered for those in authority so that believers might live "a peaceful and quiet life in all godliness and dignity" (1 Tim. 2:2; see Titus 3:1; 1 Thess. 4:11). The qualities that those who aspire to be overseers or to serve the community must have (1 Tim. 3:2–10, 12; see 2 Tim. 2:22–24) are those that people everywhere hope to find in a husband or father, a civil or religious authority, a relative or neighbor. Women in the community are expected to have "modesty" (1 Tim. 2:15). In Hellenistic society modesty is the epitome of feminine virtue. "Modesty" (*Sōphrosynē*) sums up all the qualities that one would expect to find in a responsible woman in the Greco-Roman world. The qualities of dignity and fidelity that women ministers in the community are to have (1 Tim. 3:11) are desirable in any woman.

The Pastorals promote the ideal of a good and functional household and urge family values, parental and filial piety. The epistles encourage men to be faithful to their wives (1 Tim. 3:2, 12; Titus 1:6) and wives to be faithful to their husbands (1 Tim. 5:9; Titus 2:4). Men are to manage their households properly (1 Tim. 3:4, 12). Women are expected to raise a family, take care of the household, and be good homemakers (1 Tim. 2:15; 5:14; Titus 2:4). Fathers are to raise their children properly (1 Tim. 3:4, 12); women should be devoted mothers (Titus 2:4). Older women are to train younger women (Titus 2:3–5). People are to remember their teachers (2 Tim. 3:14) and take care of the elderly unable to provide for themselves (1 Tim. 5:4). Older people are to be treated with respect

(1 Tim. 5:1, 2, 16). Leaders of the community are expected to be hospitable (1 Tim. 3:2; Titus 1:8). Such social values are an essential part of the fabric of the moral exhortation found in the Pastorals.

A grateful and prudent use of the necessities of life is urged. First Timothy 4:3 rejects an asceticism that denigrates marriage and urges abstinence from foods created by God. Marriage and food are gifts of God to be received with prayer and thanksgiving (4:4–5). God gives them to use for enjoyment and happiness (6:17). Men and women are expected to marry and have children. A person should be attentive to his or her health (5:23). A moderate amount of wine is good (5:23); some physical exercise useful (4:8). Men (3:3, 8; Titus 1:7) and women (Titus 2:3) are reminded not to be overindulgent in regard to drink. With exhortations like these, the Pastorals attend to the well-being of the members of the community, but with a theological perspective. All that contributes to human well-being is the gift of God.

The love of money is a source of many kinds of evil (1 Tim. 6:10), but people should have enough of this world's goods to ensure their own sustenance (1 Tim. 6:8). The farmer deserves the first fruits of his crops (2 Tim. 2:6). Men should not be sordidly greedy for money (1 Tim. 3:3, 8; Titus 1:7); women should not try to adorn themselves with gold, pearls, and lavish clothes (1 Tim. 2:9). Properly raised children are not profligate (Titus 1:6). Lazy gluttons are looked upon with disdain (Titus 1:12–13). The Pastor has strong words for those who pervert religion by making it a means for profit (1 Tim. 6:5) or who teach for the sake of sordid gain (Titus 1:11). First Timothy 6:17 reminds the well-to-do to place their hope in God, not in their riches.

The Pastorals' use of Hellenistic catalogs of virtues (1 Tim. 2:15; 3:2–5, 8–12; 6:11; 2 Tim. 1:7; 2:22; Titus 1:6–8; 2:12; 3:1–2) and vices (1 Tim. 1:9–10; 2 Tim. 3:2–5; Titus 1:16; 3:3) and the Pastor's use of elements of the household code (1 Tim. 5:1–2; 6:1–2; Titus 2:2–10) promote the common ethical vision of the day. Titus 2:1–10 offers a good example. This pericope begins with an exhortation, "Say what is appropriate to sound teaching." It then presents a household code delineating the respective responsibilities of older men and women, younger women and men, and slaves. Slaves were included as part of the normal household structure and economic system of the times.[16] In urban centers, slaves would constitute a sizeable part of the population. One of the vice lists excoriates those who unjustly traffic in slaves (1 Tim. 1:10).

Hellenistic authors tended to adapt their use of the literary form of the virtue/vice catalog to their audience, as would have been required by the rhetorical canons of the day. This is true of the catalogs that appear in the Pastorals. Lists of virtues are given as "qualifications" for overseers and servers, particularly those that pertain to the good family man and to household management. The catalogs of vices focus on various kinds of antisocial behavior, be it unruly behavior or endless argument (see 2 Tim. 2:23–24; 3:2–4; Titus 3:3, 9).

16. The institution of slavery in the Greco-Roman world was quite different from slavery as it existed in nineteenth-century America. The slaves of whom the Pastor writes were not of a different race from their masters. With the notable exception of prisoners of war taken as booty and reduced to slavery, slaves were not a group of displaced persons. Some slaves wielded considerable power. Others were teachers and poets. Finally, slaves of the Greco-Roman world had the possibility of buying their freedom.

Encouraging the readers to say what is appropriate to sound teaching in this way and urging that those who have a leadership role within the community should be noted for their impeccable social demeanor, the Pastor has not only stated that proper social behavior follows upon sound teaching but he has also implied that nonbelievers should be able to regard believers as people who accept their social and civic responsibilities. Proper social behavior on the part of a believer, even of the slave who is a believer, brings honor to the teaching of God the Savior (Titus 2:10). Believers are to live according to the common social norm so that no opponent can say bad things about them and so that the word of God is not blasphemed (Titus 2:5; see 1 Tim. 3:7).

A desire for good social order is also manifest by particular directives and exhortations that are scattered throughout the epistles. Men who come to prayer are expected to be without anger and to have no quarrels (1 Tim. 2:8); quarreling is to be avoided by the person who belongs to God (2 Tim. 2:24). People who deal with sinners should not show any partiality (1 Tim. 5:21). Slaves are not to take advantage of Christian masters (1 Tim. 6:2). Women who are servants in the community must avoid slander. Young women, without husband or children, are not to gad about, interfering in other peoples' households, being gossips and busybodies.

Some of the buzzwords that pervade the documents confirm that the ethical model proposed by the Pastoral Epistles is basically a conventional ethic. "Godliness" (*eusebeia*), piety accompanied by appropriate moral behavior, is held in high esteem throughout the texts (see Excursus 7). A number of related words carrying the nuance of prudence, discretion, or moderation (*sōphrōn, sōphronizō, sōphroneō, sōphronōs, sōphrosynē*) are to be found throughout the Pastorals. These words help to limn the Pastor's vision of the demeanor appropriate to the life of a believer.

Titus is to show himself a model of "good works" (*kalōn ergōn*) in every respect (Titus 2:7). He is to insist that people of faith choose good works (Titus 3:8). People chosen by our Savior, Jesus Christ, should be eager for good works (Titus 2:14), rich in good works (1 Tim. 6:18). Good works demonstrate the quality of a widow's life (1 Tim. 5:10). The "good conscience" (*syneidēseōs agathēs*) is yet another buzzword found in the Pastorals. The good conscience accompanies a pure heart and genuine faith (1 Tim. 1:5, 19). Paul is described as having been thankful that he served God with a clear conscience (2 Tim. 1:3).

The Pastorals characterize the behavior of their opponents as self-serving, corrupt, and motivated by money. These accusations are stock charges that Hellenistic moralists make against their competitors or opponents (see p. 30). The Pastor's extensive remarks on material wealth (1 Tim 6:5–10, see also vv. 17–19) probably derive from conventional wisdom rather than indicating a major problem within the Pastor's community.

The paraenesis of the Pastoral Epistles generally proposes a conventional moral wisdom similar to that of the Stoics and other philosophic moralists. For example, the list of qualities that an overseer should possess apparently includes the qualities that the philosophers describe as the four cardinal virtues: prudence, justice, temperance, and fortitude (Titus 1:8). As a rule, the Pastorals do not deal with specific behavioral issues that affect the community. In contrast, the apostle Paul dealt very concretely with specific moral behavior. He did so especially in his First Letter to the Corinthians and his

Letter to Philemon. The Pastorals fail to offer encouraging advice with respect to the ethical tradition as did Paul in the first of his letters (1 Thess. 4:1–12). In addition, the ethic of the Pastorals lacks the urgency that characterizes much of Paul's moral exhortation. That urgency derives from the apostle's expectation of an imminent Parousia. Paul does not advocate what some scholars have called "an interim ethic," but there is no doubt that the expectation of the Parousia provided urgency, focus, motivation, and sharpness for Paul's paraenesis when he wrote to the Corinthians and to the Thessalonians. There is nothing of this kind of urgency in the Pastorals, and the coming of the Lord does not provide the community with the kind of motivation expressed by Paul in Phil. 4:4–7.

What is proposed in the Pastoral Epistles is that Christians accommodate themselves to the world in which they live. The reader of the epistles does not experience any tension between the Christian life and the world like that found in the Johannine corpus (John, 1–3 John, Revelation). The Pastorals are directed to Christians living in an urban setting in the Hellenistic culture of the late first century C.E. Their ethic is that believers, no matter their gender or social status, should be good citizens of the world in which they live. That world is here to stay; believers must find an appropriate place within it. The Pastorals present an ideal of the Christian life from which an expression of the transitoriness of the world and the expectation of an imminent Parousia are virtually absent. They offer an ethic for believers who must come to grips with life in the secular world.

In some respects, the ethic of the Pastorals is an individual ethic. Emphasis on the good conscience is an expression of what would today be called personal moral responsibility. The Pastorals urge mutual responsibility within the household structure, fathers' responsibility for their children, the responsibility of older women to teach younger women, the care of widows by members of the family, and so forth. The Pastorals do not, however, give evidence of the social outreach, particularly to other Christian communities, found in Paul's writings (e.g., Phil. 2:4). The collection for the poor Christians of Jerusalem is a remarkable example of this kind of outreach (see Rom. 15:25–27; 1 Cor. 16:1–4; 2 Cor. 8–9; Gal. 2:10).

Notwithstanding the differences between the Pastor's ideal of the good Christian life and the ideal of the Christian life proposed by Paul's paraenesis and by the Johannine corpus, a decidedly Christian dimension is present in the Pastoral Epistles' moral exhortation. The Pastorals affirm that good moral behavior stems from the sound teaching of the community. Good theology leads to good morality. The Pastor affirms that sound words about the Lord Jesus Christ, the sound teaching of the community, issue forth in godliness (1 Tim. 6:3). The purpose of Jesus' self-oblation is that his people be eager for good works (Titus 2:14). Titus 1:1 affirms that the purpose of Paul's apostolate was the faith of the community, the kind of knowledge that leads to godliness. Those who assent to faith are expected to choose to do good works, things that are good and beneficial to human beings (Titus 3:8).

A sense of eschatological urgency is generally absent from the Pastoral Epistles. Thoughts of the impending Parousia would not immediately come to the minds of the Pastor's audience as they listen to his paraenesis. The Pastor's moral exhortation is not, however, utterly devoid of any suggestion of an eschatological sanction. First Timothy 5:24–25 speaks of condemnation and of sins that cannot be hidden. The Pastor speaks of the misuse of wealth as leading to utter destruction (1 Tim. 6:9). On the other hand, he encourages the members of his community to act so as to obtain real life (1 Tim. 6:19) and urges them to keep the commandment spotless and irreproachable until the appearance of the Lord Jesus Christ (1 Tim. 6:14). The apostle Paul is, for the Pastor, the preeminent example of conversion and of life lived with faith (see Collins, "Image of Paul," 165–72). He is one who in his dying moments awaits the appearance of the Lord, the just judge (2 Tim. 4:8). Christ Jesus is to judge the living and the dead (2 Tim. 4:1).

An important feature of Hellenistic paraenesis was the moral authority of whoever was making the exhortation. The strength of the exhortation lay not in its intrinsic value; rather, it lay in the authority from which the exhortation came. The ethic of the Pastorals is not rationalistic. For the most part, it is innocent of the argument from advantage. Essentially, the ethic of the Pastorals derives its persuasive force from the authority of Paul and the authority of his delegates, Timothy and Titus. Their ethos is a model for the community. Only secondarily does the warrant of eschatological sanction enter into the Pastorals' moral exhortation.

The Scriptures are said to be useful for training in righteousness so that those who belong to God are thoroughly prepared for every good work (2 Tim. 3:16–17). In spite of this programmatic statement on the importance of the Scriptures, focused reflection on the ethical teaching of the Scriptures does not significantly enter into the ethic proposed in the Pastorals. With the exception of Deut. 25:4 in 1 Tim. 5:18, no scriptural text is cited as a warrant for appropriate behavior.[17] First Timothy 1:8–11 seems almost to disparage the use of the Scriptures in the development of a Christian ethic.

Second Timothy 3:16–17 speaks of righteousness, but neither righteousness nor holiness receives any particular emphasis in the Pastorals. Nonetheless, the Pastor's "godliness" is akin to the "righteousness" of Judaism, and the "good conscience" is rather similar to the "pure heart" of the Jewish Scriptures. Apart from these two ideas, as rooted in the Jewish ethos as they are in Hellenistic morals, the paraenetic language used in the Pastorals and the values that are urged are those of the philosophic moralists of the era. First Timothy 1:9–10's list of vices follows the order of the Ten Commandments, but the Decalogue does not receive the kind of explicit emphasis that it does in Rom. 7:7, 13:8–10, or Jas. 2:10–11. In addition, the Pastorals do not use the kingdom of God as an all-embracing cipher in moral exhortation.

The Pastorals' emphasis on godliness reflects, nonetheless, the Jewish and Christian covenantal notion in which responsibility toward God is inherently linked to responsibility toward others within the community. Within the perspective of a covenantal relationship with God, piety and social responsibility go hand in hand. Among the biblical texts that reflect this vision are Exod. 20:1–17 (the Decalogue) and Matt. 22:34–40 (Jesus' twofold love command). Philo says that some may be justly called "lovers of men" (*philanthrōpous*) and others "lovers of God" (*philotheous*). "Both come," he writes, "but halfway in virtue; they only have it whole who win honor in both departments" (*Decalogue* 110).

17. The only other explicit citation of the Jewish Scriptures in the Pastoral Epistles is to be found in 2 Tim. 2:19, which describes an "inscription" that is an amalgam of scriptural texts (Num. 16:5; Sir. 17:26; Isa. 26:13). These passages are not identified as having come from Scripture.

The use of examples or models (*paradeigmata*) is very important in Hellenistic ethics (see Fiore). The Pastorals do not, however, cite Abraham as a model of righteousness (cf. Rom. 4:3), nor do they offer Rahab as a model of hospitality (cf. Jas. 2:25). For the Pastor, *the* model of behavior that is in accordance with sound teaching is Paul, whose own behavior is to be modeled in turn by Timothy and Titus. Thus, the Pastor's moral exhortation is rather different from the paraenesis of the authentic Pauline letters. There are some similarities, for instance, the use of appropriate lists of virtues and vices in both sets of writings. On the other hand, the Pastorals lack the focus on love, the epitome of the Christian life in Paul's letters (e.g., Rom. 12:9–10; 13:8–10; 1 Cor. 13; 1 Thess. 1:3; 3:12; 4:9–10).

Despite the appearance of the formula "to live in godly fashion in Christ Jesus" in 2 Tim. 3:12, the ethic of the Pastorals does not in any great measure derive from christological insights. This formula links the Hellenistic notion of godliness with Paul's notion of being "in Christ Jesus." Paul's phrase does not, however, punctuate the Pastorals' paraenesis as it does Paul's exhortation. Second Timothy 4:1, 8 present Christ Jesus as the ultimate judge of one's life, but the Pastorals fail to mention the motif of the imitation of Christ found in Phil. 2:5 (see 1 Cor. 11:1; 1 Thess. 1:6).

Rather than being christological in emphasis, the religious aspect of behavior appropriate to the Christian is related to God and to faith as shared belief within the community (see 1 Tim. 4:3–5). Thus, immoral behavior is presented as being clearly out of step with sound teaching (1 Tim. 1:10). As a leader of the community, Timothy is to deal seriously with the presence of sin in the community (1 Tim. 5:20–25). Abominable and disreputable behavior is a practical denial of God (Titus 1:16). In contrast, those who are useful to the master of the house are ready for every good work (2 Tim. 2:21).

Christians are to accept the ordinary things of this life as God's gifts to them (1 Tim. 4:4; 6:17) and are to share these gifts with others. In order to motivate Christians to share, the Pastor reminds them that such sharing provides a good foundation for what is to come, namely, eternal life (1 Tim. 6:19). First Timothy urges its readers to keep "the commandment" spotless and blameless until the appearance of the Lord (1 Tim. 6:14). The Pastorals do not highlight the love command despite its relevance as the hallmark of the moral exhortation of both Jesus and Paul. The Pastorals limn their own profile as they offer moral exhortation to their readers.

[3–4] The Pastor's plea for prayers on behalf of kings and those in authority is hardly as detailed in its outline of believers' responsibilities toward public authority (*hyperochē ontōn* in 2:2; *hyperechousais* in Rom. 13:1) as is Paul's exhortation in Rom. 13:1–7. Paul essentially expresses a Jewish point of view toward authority. The Pastor, however, must argue his case. He offers a reason why believers are to pray for authorities. Prayer for public authorities is good in itself; it is pleasing in the sight of God (see 5:4). Emperor worship was to be avoided, however, as idol worship was to be avoided. Nonetheless, it was good and proper to pray for public authorities. The Pastor speaks with apologetic overtones when he calls God "our Savior." The reigning emperor is not *Sōtēr*. That designation belongs to God and to God alone.

The Pastor then explains why it is that God is Savior (see 4:10). God is Savior almost by definition. The Pastor's apologetic intent continues to be expressed in his affirmation that God wills that all humans be saved. This echoes the universalism of verse 1 in which believers are urged to pray for "all human beings," a motif reprised and specified in verse 2 where mention is made of all (*pantōn*) in authority. The Pastor's emphasis on the salvation of all humans serves to counter any suggestion that salvation is reserved to Jews and/or to Gentile Christians who faithfully observe the Jewish law. To the extent that an incipient Gnosticism was a problem for the Pastor's community, his affirmation rejects out of hand the notion that only an elite privy to "knowledge" (*gnōsis*) were capable of being saved. The Pastor's subsequent emphasis on the "full knowledge" (*epignōsin*) serves to reinforce the subtle apologetic of his rhetoric against any divisive elitism.

The aorist passive form of the Pastor's verb implies punctiliar action and suggests that God's universal will of salvation is accomplished at a definite moment in time. In addition to willing that all people be saved, God also wills that they come to "the full knowledge of truth" (*epignōsin alētheias*; see 2 Tim. 2:25; 3:7; Titus 1:1). This expression is a household word within the Pastor's community. It designates the full message of the Christian gospel issuing forth into a life characterized by godliness (see p. 97 and Excursus 7). This "profound knowledge" accrues only to those to whom God has given the gift of conversion.

[5–6] With implicit deference to the canons of rhetoric, the Pastor divides the question. He first explains God's universal salvific will, telling the audience why God alone is Savior and how it is that God effects salvation (vv. 5–6). Then he talks about access to the profound knowledge of the truth (v. 7).

Echoing the Jewish Shema (Deut. 6:4) and Paul's hymnic confession (1 Cor. 8:6; see Gal. 3:20), the Pastor affirms the uniqueness of God. The confession of "one God" (*heis theos*)—the Shema proclaims "one Lord" (*heis kyrios*)—is a familiar topos in the apologetic literature of Hellenistic Judaism. There are not many gods and many lords; there is only one God, one Lord (see Eph. 4:4–6). Since there is only one God (see 1:17; 6:16), this one God alone is capable of designating the one(s) through whom salvation comes. No human sovereign, not even an emperor, can designate the one through whom salvation comes.

Adopting a rhythmic tone, the Pastor then affirms that there is only one mediator between God and human beings (*heis . . . mesitēs theou kai anthrōpōn*). The Pastor uses the noun *anthrōpos*, "human," "a person," to designate human beings. His usage follows the practice of other New Testament authors who regularly use this generic term to designate human beings as distinct from God. Throughout the New Testament, "human" (*anthrōpos*) stands always in explicit or implicit contrast with "God" (*theos*).

The Pastor then affirms that the sole mediator is human (*anthrōpos*). By affirming the humanity of the mediator before he identifies the mediator, the Pastor demonstrates his apologetic intent. The mediator is not a divinized emperor; the mediator is a human being. Then, and only then, does the Pastor identify the mediator as Christ Jesus. Apart from the letter to the Hebrews, which speaks of Jesus as the mediator of a new covenant (Heb. 8:6; 9:15; 12:24), 1 Tim. 2:5 is the only New Testament passage to speak of Jesus as the mediator. He is mediator, writes the Pastor, not insofar as he is Lord but insofar as he is human. The humanity of Christ Jesus is a very important factor in the Pastor's theological scheme. This is due to his subtle polemicizing against the divinization of emperors and his radically Jewish view of God—unique, dynamic, and transcendent.

The effect of the aorist participle in the expression "who gave himself as a ransom for all" (*ho dous heauton antilytron hyper pantōn*; see Titus 2:14) is to identify Christ Jesus not only as the ransom for all people but also as one who has taken the initiative in this regard. The idea of a human life being offered as a ransom is rooted in Hellenistic Judaism. Texts from the Maccabean literature speak of people who offer themselves on behalf of the nation (4 Macc. 6:29; 17:21–22; see 2 Macc. 7:37–38; 4 Macc. 6:27–29). Fourth Maccabees 6:29 and 17:21–22 (with *antipsychon*) and the Pastor (with *antilytron*) use a word for "ransom" whose Greek prefix *anti* underscores the substitutionary function of the ransom that is offered.

The Maccabean texts lack the universal reference of the Pastor's affirmation. The Pastor's universal reference is consistent with the general all-inclusiveness found in his words about prayer (see 2:1, 2, 4). It also underscores Christ Jesus' solidarity with all humanity insofar as he is a human, an *anthrōpos*, one among and in relationship with other human beings. Jesus' own saying, "to give his life a ransom for many" (*dounai tēn psychēn autou lytron anti pollōn*, Mark 10:45; see Matt. 20:28) also has a universal referent. The Jesuanic logion employs the Semitizing "for many" (*anti pollōn*) to speak of a ransom made for all. The expression is an example of culturally imbedded synecdoche, in which mention of a part evokes the reality of the whole.

Paul speaks of "redemption" (*apolytrōsis*) in Rom. 3:24; 8:23; and 1 Cor. 1:30. Otherwise Paul does not use language derived from the root *lytr-*.[18] On the other hand, he uses the image of the ransom of slaves, of their being bought and fully paid for, as a theologoumenon, an evocative image for the theological reality of "redemption" (1 Cor. 6:20; 7:23; see 1 Pet. 1:18; 2 Pet. 2:1).

18. The word "redemption" (*apolytrōsis*) is used ten times in the New Testament. Related words—three nouns, *antilytron*, *lytron*, and *lytrōsis*, and a verb, *lytroomai*—are found in nine other passages (1 Tim. 2:6; Titus 2:14; Matt. 20:28; Mark 10:45; Luke 1:68; 2:38; 24:21; Heb. 9:12; 1 Pet. 1:18).

The Pastor's "testimony at the appropriate time" represents a kind of inter-pretive punctuation. In this regard it is similar to the *pistos ho logos* formula of 1:15; 3:1; and 4:9 (see 2 Tim. 2:11; Titus 3:8). The Pastor's words affirm the public nature of Christ Jesus' ransoming act as witness to God's universal will of salvation. Similar use of the language of "testimony" and the "appropriate time" recurs in 6:13–15, where there is also emphasis on universality and the witness of Jesus. "At the appropriate time" (*kairois idiois*) is idiomatic. The expression is used in Titus 1:3 to state that according to God's plan, Paul's min-istry took place at the appropriate time. The idiom appears twice in 1 Timothy, highlighting the crucial moments chosen by God for the manifestation of sal-vation: Jesus' ransom of all people publicly attested by his death and the final appearance of Jesus, his eschatological manifestation (6:15).

[7] Having affirmed the uniqueness of God the Savior, the Pastor makes an affirmation that points to the means chosen by God that enable all people, specifically non-Jews, to come to full knowledge of truth (2:4). The role of the apostle Paul in this regard is underscored by means of an apostolic oath, "I am telling the truth, I am not lying" (*alētheian legō ou pseudomai*) and the presen-tation of Paul as the teacher of the Gentiles in regard to faith and truth (*en pis-tei kai alētheia*).

Paul occasionally uses asides to confirm the truth of his message. He calls on the experience of the community ("as you know" in 1 Thess. 2:2, 5) and the witness of God ("God is my witness" in 1 Thess. 2:5; see Rom. 1:9). Paul's oath in Rom. 9:1 appears to be echoed in 2:7. The Pastor's oath has a judicial tone, which focuses on "the truth." Emphasis is placed on "the truth" by its mention as the first word of the oath, the explicit contrast between telling the truth and lying—an example of rhetorical *contradictio* (see Rom. 9:1)—and the mention of "truth" as the last word in the sentence. The judicial tone of the oath recalls the testimonial nature of Christ Jesus' ransom of all people (2:6b).

Readers are to understand, by the Pastor's use of an epexegetical *kai*, an explanatory "and," that faith, the objective content of the Christian message, is the truth (see Excursus 4). People with whom the Pastor has to deal have turned from the truth and shipwrecked the faith (1:19; 6:5; see 2 Tim. 2:18; 3:7–8; 4:4; Titus 1:14). Paul, on the other hand, kept the faith (2 Tim. 4:7). He has pre-served the faith that he has taught.

The formal language of "appointment" and of the triple description of the Pauline office in verse 7 (see 2 Tim. 1:11) continues the solemn style with which the Pastor emphasizes the testimonial nature of Christ Jesus' self-donation. Paul's appointment is related to the testimony offered by Christ Jesus, the act by which God's universal salvific will has been accomplished. The office to which Paul has been appointed—obviously by God, for "have been appointed," *etethēn*, is a so-called divine passive—is that of apostle. The opening words of

2 Timothy express a similar thought. Apart from the announcement of God's universal will of salvation in 2:4, 2 Tim. 1:1 contains the only mention of God's will in the Pastoral Epistles.

Paul's office is explained by means of an interpretive triad. Paul is not only an apostle; he is also a herald and teacher. "Herald" (*kēryx*) and "teacher" (*didaskalos*) embrace and interpret "apostle." The roles of herald and teacher were well known in the Hellenistic world. The former evokes images of messengers who bring news of recent events, generally good news (*eu-angelion*, with the prefix *eu* suggesting "good" or "well"), to a hastily assembled crowd before they move on to the next town or village. The latter evokes images of the philosophic teachers anxious to impart sound teaching to those who would listen. "Herald" and "teacher" translate the Semitic institution of *shaliach*, "apostolate," into Hellenistic idiom. Heralds and teachers have related but somewhat different functions.

The idea that Paul was a "herald" recalls the apostle's missionary activity. He moved from place to place in the Greco-Roman word to announce the good news of salvation. Thus, the word "herald" is a kind of cipher that captures the memory of Paul's missionary activity. The image of Paul as "teacher" conveys the idea of the revered figure whose teaching deserves to be passed on from generation to generation. First Timothy itself is an example of how the teaching of the apostle would continue to be revered and have an influence in the years after the apostle's death.

The use of interpretive triads is a characteristic feature of the Pastoral Epistles (see p. 37). In 2 Tim. 1:11 Paul is similarly described as "herald, apostle, and teacher." Thus, the Pastor's use of an interpretive triad in 2:7 is not particularly surprising. What is striking is the Pastor's expansion of his three-term rhetoric. He qualifies Paul's role as teacher by adding "of the Gentiles in faith and truth." Later generations of Christians would call Paul the "apostle to the Gentiles"; the Pastor describes him as "teacher of the Gentiles" (see Gal. 2:2). The designation of Paul as the teacher of the Gentiles (*didaskalos ethnōn*) is an important element in the Pastor's rhetoric. The word "Gentiles," meaning "the nations," is vocabulary that properly belongs to Jewish discourse; it represents the language of others, the voice of those who are different.

The basic sociological vision of the Jews was that humanity was divided into two distinct groups: "the [chosen] people" who knew God and "the nations" who did not. From this point of view, "the Gentiles" are all people who are not Jewish. Paul himself shared this perspective (e.g., 2 Cor. 11:26; Gal. 2:9, 14; 1 Thess. 4:5). Unlike Peter, who was an apostle to the circumcised, Paul considered himself as having been sent to the Gentiles (Gal. 2:8; see 2 Cor. 10:13–16). In the conduct of his mission, Paul found supportive inspiration in Deutero-Isaiah's prophetic vision (Isa. 49:6). Nonetheless, the scandal of God's election of the Gentiles became a hurdle that met Paul at virtually step of his way.

The universal scope of Paul's apostolate is reiterated in 2 Tim. 4:17. In that passage a dying Paul reflects on his life and affirms that "the Lord stood by me and strengthened me so that my work of proclaiming the gospel continued to be carried out and all the Gentiles [*panta ta ethnē*] heard it." The universal scope of Paul's apostolate to which the Pastor makes reference in designating Paul as "the teacher of the Gentiles" is an important element in the Pastor's understanding of God's universal will of salvation. God wills all people to be saved and to come to the full knowledge of truth (2:4). Salvation is accomplished through Jesus' self-donation on behalf of all (see 1:15). People's coming to the full knowledge of truth is accomplished through the apostolate of Paul, whose work as herald of the gospel is continued in the teaching that is handed on.

What the Pastor writes about God's universal will of salvation and about Paul's role as one appointed to announce and explain this truth represents an important rhetorical digression from the "liturgical directives" with which he began the pericope. It supports those directives insofar as it provides a significant theological reason, in addition to the self-interested reason cited in verse 2, why the members of the community should pray for everyone. In the following section, the Pastor returns to the task at hand, namely, directives on communal prayer.

Men and Women at Prayer
1 Timothy 2:8–3:1a

In this pericope the Pastor focuses more on the comportment of believers engaged in prayer than he does on prayer forms, the object of prayer, and the suitability of Christian prayer. Those aspects of the community at prayer were treated during the first section of his instruction, specifically in 2:1–3. Now his attention is turned to the community that gathers for prayer. The praying community consists of both men and women. There is, says the Pastor, appropriate demeanor for believers of either sex. The Pastor's initial comments in regard to both men and women focus largely on externals, on the posture of men at prayer and on the attire of women at prayer. For each group, however, the Pastor has a word to say about the kind of lives that should be led by those who gather for prayer. Men are urged to come to prayer with no anger in their hearts or quarreling on their record. Women are urged to come to prayer with lives characterized by good works.

The Pastor's division of remarks with regard to the externals and quality of life aspects of Christian prayer might strike a contemporary reader as patriarchal or sexist. The exhortation on women that is inserted into the instruction on prayer intensifies this impression. The Pastor urges women to be submissive and reflects that they are saved by childbearing. The Pastor's remarks must be understood within the context within which they were written. Christians were coming under attack as being disturbers of the social order (2:2). Moreover, some who deviated from the truth of the faith were making inroads into the community and were denying the importance of marriage (4:3). In this troubled context, the Pastor's response consists of an exhortation to respect social order and to recognize the importance of the value of marriage and childbearing within the social order and God's plan of salvation.

2:8 Therefore I wish all men everywhere to pray lifting up pure hands without wrath and quarreling. 9 And similarly the women should adorn themselves with proper decorum with self-respect and modesty, not with braided hair, gold, pearls, or lavish garments; 10 rather, it is fitting for women to show devotion to God through good works.

11 Let a woman learn quietly and in all submission, 12 and I do not allow a woman to teach or to have power over a man but to live quietly. 13 For Adam was first formed, then Eve. 14 And Adam was not deceived but the woman, thoroughly deceived,[a] was in a state of transgression; 15 and she will be saved through childbearing if they remain in faith, love, and holiness with modesty. 3:1 This is a trustworthy[b] saying.

a. The Byzantine manuscripts read a simple *apatētheisa,* "deceived," rather than the emphatic *exapatētheisa,* "thoroughly deceived." The intensive form is used by Paul in 2 Cor. 11:3.

b. As was the case in 1:15, some witnesses to the Western text type read *anthrōpinos,* "human," rather than "trustworthy." One manuscript (256) lacks the formula of affirmation.

[2:8] The Pastor's initial "therefore," an inferential *oun,* indicates that having exhorted the readers to pray, the Pastor is about to give further instructions on prayer. He first addresses all adult males. Not only should the prayer of believers make petitions on behalf of everyone; everyone within the community should pray. The Pastor's "everywhere" (*en panti topō*) should not be construed as if the epistle were a circular letter to be read in several different communities; rather, the geographical references promote the traditional practice of daily prayer no matter where one might be at the time of prayer. Prayer was not to be restricted to a "place of prayer."

Later rabbinic tradition attests to a similar concern. The rabbis prescribed that prayers should be recited three times a day (see Ps. 55:17; Dan. 6:10): morning, afternoon, and evening (*m. Ber.* 4:1). Morning prayer corresponded to the hour of the morning oblation (Ps. 5:3), afternoon prayer to the late afternoon sacrifice (1 Kgs. 18:36; Ezra 9:5). The Eighteen Benedictions, the additional *Teffilah*, could be pronounced at any time (*m. Ber.* 4:1, 7), but it was customary to recite this additional *Teffilah* on Sabbaths and feast days when an additional offering was to be made in the temple. The Mishnaic tractate *Berakoth*, "Blessings," gives specific instructions on how a man in a dangerous place, riding on an ass or journeying by sea, is to pray at the appointed hours (*m. Ber.* 4:4–6). Craftsmen could recite the Shema but not the *Teffilah* while seated in a tree or on top of a course of stones.

The Bible attests to various postures for prayer. The normal posture was standing (1 Sam. 1:26; 1 Kgs. 8:22; see *m. Ber.* 5:1) with arms outstretched (1 Kgs. 8:22; Ps. 28:2; 63:4; 68:31; 77:2; 88:9; 134:2; 141:2; 143:6; see Ps. 44:20; *m. Ber.* 5:4). According to the Talmud, Rabbi Joshua ben Levi taught that a priest who does not lift his hands in prayer is not to raise his hands in blessing (*b. Sotah* 39a). When the Pastor states that a man at prayer should lift up "pure" hands, he is simply stating that a man's hands are to be washed,[19] "purified," before prayer (see Mark 7:2; cf. *1 Clem.* 29:1).

In addition to having washed his hands, the man at prayer is expected to have no anger in his heart and to be involved in no feuding. A similar hortatory remark derived from Matthew's proper material, a Jewish source, was included in the Sermon on the Mount and embedded in a pericope that speaks about anger (Matt. 5:23–24; see Mark 11:25; Luke 12:57–59). Pious Jews waited an hour before reciting the Eighteen Benedictions so that their hearts might be totally directed to God (*m. Ber.* 5:1). The rabbis required that a man have a peaceful heart when he prays, a disposition that Rashi, the great eleventh-century Jewish scholar, related to Sir. 7:10 (Str-B 3:645). The extended and open hands of a man express a state of neediness in the presence of God. Hands open in God's presence are, moreover, unable to conceal or grasp a weapon that might be used in anger.

[9–10] Having addressed the demeanor of Christian men at prayer, the Pastor turns his attention to women. His instructions for women are similar to those of 1 Pet. 3:1–6. Women, the Pastor writes in his tightly knit phrase, are to "adorn themselves with proper decorum." When used of women, the verb "adorn" (*kosmein*) generally means "to dress, to attire oneself" (so Homer, Hesiod, and other classical authors). The noun "decorum" (*katastolē*; see *Jewish War* 2.8.4 §126) refers to demeanor in both its inward and outward aspects. The Pastor urges female believers to be clothed with "self-respect and modesty."

---

19. Aeschylus, the ancient Greek dramatist, also used the phrase *hosiai cheires* to mean "clean hands."

Among the Stoics, self-respect (*aidōs*) was an important virtue. Musonius considered it to be the greatest good (frag. 3.42.24). Hellenistic Jewish authors, Philo included (*Moses* 2.234; *Contemplative Life* 33; *Flaccus* 89), considered "self-respect" to be a typically feminine virtue. It consisted of "a self-respect and a sense of honor that is often identified with modesty" (*TLNT* 1.42). Among Hellenists, modesty or self-control (*sōphrosynē*) was considered the most important of a woman's virtues. Men were expected to possess this virtue as well, but among men the quality was configured differently from the way that it was to appear among women. In women the virtue of modestly implied that she was well ordered in the conduct of her life, chaste in her marriage, and above reproach. In his "Advice to the Bride and Groom," the Stoic moralist Plutarch disagreed that women lost their modesty when having sexual relations with their husbands:

> Herodotus was not right in saying that a woman lays aside her modesty [*aidō*] along with her undergarment. On the contrary, a virtuous woman puts on modesty [*aidō*] in its stead, and the husband and wife bring into their mutual relations the greatest modesty [*malista aideisthai*] as a token of greatest love. ("Advice to the Bride and Groom" 10; *Moralia* 139C)

A woman's self-respect and modesty were reflected in her outward demeanor, the way that she appeared in public. The Pastor's words about a woman's outward appearance are similar to Philo's allegory on a man's two wives (based on Deut. 21:15–17). Philo sees the two wives as respectively representing pleasure (*hēdonē*) and virtue (*aretē*). Personifying virtue, Philo indicates that modesty is the mother of a whole host of virtues, many of which appear in the Pastor's lexicon:

> She [Virtue] appeared with all the marks of a free-born citizen, a firm tread, a serene countenance, her person and her modesty [*to aidous*] alike without false coloring, her moral nature free from guile, her conduct from stain, her will from craft, her speech from falsehood, reflecting faithfully the honesty of her thoughts [*dianoias hygious*]. Her carriage was unaffected, her movements quiet, her clothing plain [*metrian esthēta*], her adornment that of good sense and virtue, which is more precious than gold [*chrysou*]. And in her company came piety [*eusebeia*], holiness [*hosiotēs*], truth [*alētheia*], justice, religion, fidelity to oaths and bonds, righteousness [*dikaiosynē*], equity, fellow-feeling, self-control, temperance [*sōphrosynē*], orderliness [*kosmiotēs*], continence, meekness, frugality, contentment, modesty [*aidōs*], a quiet temper, courage, nobility of spirit, good judgment, foresight, good sense, attentiveness, desire for amendment, cheerfulness, kindness, gentleness, mildness, humanity, high-mindedness, blessedness, goodness [*agathotēs*]. (*Abel and Cain* 26–27)

Similarly, the Pastor notes that a woman's true qualities are reflected not in ostentatious trappings and luxurious clothing; rather, they are to be seen in her behavior, her "good works" (*ergōn agathōn*; see 5:10; 2 Tim. 2:21; 3:17; Titus 1:16; 3:1). The Stoics and other philosophic moralists also placed a high value on the simple lifestyle. Thus, Epictetus asks, "Can it be that the human is the only creature without a special virtue but must resort to his hair, clothes, and ancestors?" (frag. 18). Within Hellenistic Judaism, *The Testament of Reuben* offers a biting critique of women's elaborate adornment:

> By reason of their lacking authority or power over man, they [women] scheme treacherously how they might entice him to themselves by means of their looks. . . . Accordingly, order your wives and your daughters not to adorn their heads and their appearances so as to deceive men's sound minds. (*T. Reub.* 5:1, 5)

Braided hair was probably included on the list of things to be avoided by the virtuous woman because elaborately braided hairstyles were, along with gold and pearls, an expression of wealth. Only a woman who had slaves had the time and the possibility to have an elaborate coiffure. The Pastor had strong views on the use of wealth (6:6–10). These views may well have motivated his critique of women who wear their finery when they appear in an assembly of people at prayer. In the Hellenistic world, philosophers such as Musonius Rufus (frag. 21) and Epictetus (e.g., *Discourses* 2.21.15–16) wrote about the way that men and women were to wear their hair in public. Ancient cults often had specific regulations on the grooming, hairstyle, jewelry, and clothing of those who participated in worship. Paul, who wrote about men and women's hairstyles in 1 Cor. 11:2–16, shared the concerns of these philosophers and liturgists. The Pastor continues this tradition as he writes about women showing devotion to God (*epangellomenais theosebeian*) by their good works rather than by showing off their physical beauty and their wealth.

[11–12] Hellenists placed great value on the virtue of quiet or tranquility (*hēsychia*), which the Pastor expects women to have (see *P. Mert.* 98.6; *P. Adl.* 1.2.2; Philo, *Abraham* 216). His exhortation hearkens back to his prayer that believers might be able to live a peaceful and quiet life (*hēsychion bion*, 2:2). To live quietly was to live without agitation, disputes, idle curiosity, or meddling in other people's business. Philo describes the worthless person as one who has "not been trained in that tranquility which in season is most excellent." That person is one who

> haunts market-places, theaters, law-courts, council halls, assemblies [*ekklēsias*], and every group and gathering of people; his tongue he lets loose for unmeasured, endless, indiscriminate talk, bringing chaos and confusion into everything, mixing true with false, fit with unfit, public with private, holy with profane, sensible

with absurd. . . . His ears he keeps alert in meddlesome curiosity, ever eager to learn his neighbor's affairs, whether good or bad, and ready with envy for the former and joy at the latter. (*Abraham* 20–21; see 1 Tim. 5:13)

As does Philo, the Pastor believes that virtuous quiet is a practice that must be learned. The Pastor highlights submission (*pasē hypotagē*; see *1 Clem.* 1:3) as a particular aspect of this social virtue. The Hellenistic idea of submission was not so much a matter of obedience (see Eph. 5:21–22 and 6:1, 5; and Col. 3:18, 20, 22) as it was a matter of keeping one's place (Eph. 5:21) so as to assure the stability and order of the whole, be that the world (*kosmos*), the city (*polis*), or the household (*oikia*). Plutarch wrote at length about the importance of submission within a Hellenistic household ("Advice to the Bride and Groom" 11, 31–33 [*Moralia* 42 C.E.]; see Titus 2:5, 9). The Pastor's language implies that he holds that the social order (of the church? of the household?) would be disturbed were a woman to teach or rule over a man, presumably her husband. She is to learn, not teach; she is to be submissive, not exercise authority over her husband (see Philo, *Hypothetica* 7.14).

In the Greco-Roman household, the paterfamilias exercised virtually absolute authority not only over his children but also over his wife. The Pastorals often cite examples, most commonly the example of Paul himself (e.g., 1 Tim. 1:13–16; 2 Tim. 3:10–11), to make a point. Plutarch also uses examples as a rhetorical device:

Theano,[20] in putting her cloak about her, exposed her arm. Somebody exclaimed, "a lovely arm." "But not for the public," said she. Not only the arm of the virtuous woman but her speech as well, ought to be not for the public, and she ought to be modest and guarded [*sōphronōs . . . aideisthai kai phylattesthai*] about saying anything in the hearing of outsiders, since it is an exposure of herself; for in her talk can be seen her feelings, character, and disposition.

Pheidias[21] made the Aphrodite of the Eleans with one foot on a tortoise, to typify for womankind keeping at home and keeping silence. For a woman ought to do her talking either to her husband or through her husband, and she should not feel aggrieved if, like the flute-player, she makes a more impressive sound through a tongue not her own.

. . . So it is with women also; if they subordinate themselves [*hypotatousai . . . heautas*] to their husbands, they are commended but if they want to have control, they cut a sorrier figure than the subjects of their control. And control ought to be exercised by the man over the woman, not as the owner has control of a

20. Theano was the wife of the philosopher Pythagoras; see Clement of Alexander, *Stromata* 4.121.2–3 (PG 8.1332).

21. Pheidias was a fifth-century B.C.E. Athenian sculptor. The example given by Plutarch is his interpretation of Pheidias's statue of the goddess Aphrodite.

piece of property but, as the soul controls the body, by entering into her feelings and being knit to her through goodwill. ("Advice to the Bride and Groom" 31–33, *Moralia* 142C–E; the example of Pheidias' statue is also cited in "Isis and Osiris" 75 *Moralia* 381E to teach the same lesson)

In "Advice to the Bride and Groom," Plutarch also has something to say about a married woman's feelings and about her friends:

> The wife ought to have no feeling of her own but she should join with her husband in seriousness and sportiveness and in soberness and laughter. ("Advice" 14, *Moralia* 140 A)

> A wife ought not to make friends of her own but to enjoy her husband's friends in common with him. ("Advice" 19, *Moralia* 140 D)

Christians for whom the Pastor wrote his epistle lived in the Greco-Roman world. What Plutarch wrote about a married woman and her husband, her public demeanor, her feelings, and her friends is illustrative of the mores of the society to which the Pastor and his readers belonged. In the Pastor's world it was generally considered unseemly for a woman to have power over her husband, but this does not mean that it never happened. The Pastor's view that the members of the community should adopt the acceptable social standards of the day dominates his paraenesis. Thus, his reference to women neither teaching nor having power over their husbands does not necessarily indicate that the Pastor's community was troubled by false teaching coming from a group of liberated and charismatic women (as claimed by Perriman and Low).

[13–14] Following social custom and urging a woman to live quietly and submissively, the Pastor offers an explanation of and a warrant for his exhortation that stems from his Jewish background. His explanation consists of a midrash, a written explanation and contemporary application of a text of Scripture, on the Yahwist's stories of creation (Gen. 2:7, 21–23) and the fall (Gen. 3:6, 12).

The Pastor follows early Christian tradition in seeing the creation narratives of Genesis 1–2 as providing the basic paradigm for the relationship between man and woman (Matt. 19:5; Mark 10:7; 1 Cor. 6:16; Eph. 5:31). Early Christian tradition regarded Adam and Eve as the prototypical human beings. In 1 Cor. 11:2–16 Paul uses the creation narratives as a theological warrant for his own exhortation on the type of hairstyle appropriate to men and women at prayer. The apostle inserts the text, "the two shall become one flesh" (Gen. 2:24), in his reflection on men's use of prostitutes (1 Cor. 6:12–20). In later correspondence with the Corinthians, Paul writes about Eve's deception (2 Cor. 11:3). The Pastor picks up the same theme in verse 14.

The Pastor takes over the verbs "formed" (*eplasthē*) and "deceived" (*ēpatēthē*) from the Greek Bible. Adam possesses relative superiority over Eve because he was created before her (*prōtos*). In the rabbinic tradition, that which was first narrated enjoys priority. Paul uses this hermeneutical principle to good advantage when he writes about righteousness and faith in Rom. 4:9–12 and about the promise and the law in Rom. 4:13–15. Similarly, in early rabbinic thought what God first created was more important (see *Sipra Deut.* 11:10; Str-B 3:256–58; 645–46). In his explanation of the Genesis story of the creation of woman, Philo asks, "Why was not woman, like other animals and man, also formed from earth, instead of the side of man?" He gives a four-part response to his own question:

> First, because woman is not equal in honor with man. . . . Fourth, he counsels man figuratively to take care of woman as of a daughter, and woman to honor man as a father. And this is proper. (*Questions and Answers* 1.27)

The Pastor considers Eve's being deceived before Adam a sign of her weakness. He uses an intensive form of the verb "deceive" to speak of Eve's deception but a simple form of the verb to speak of Adam's deception.[22] She was *really* deceived. The Pastor emphasizes the extent of Eve's deception by adding that she existed in a state of transgression (*en parabasei gegonen*).

Inferences that the Pastor draws from the biblical story are comparable with rabbinic midrash on the same Genesis narrative. Thus, *Gen. Rab.* 18:2 explains that the woman was formed from man's rib so that she should be modest. Had she been formed from the ear, mouth, heart, hand, or foot, she would have been an eavesdropper, overly talkative, very jealous, overly acquisitive, or a gad-about, respectively. These are the same defects that Philo attributes to a person who has not been taught tranquility.

Jewish women were generally unlearned. Philo held that women were easily deceived (*Genesis* 1.23, 46). Women were not obliged to study the Torah; rather, they were to encourage their sons and husbands to study (*b. Ber.* 17a). They themselves were to learn about the Torah from their husbands (see Philo, *Hypothetica* 7.14). Not having studied the Scriptures herself, a woman was unqualified to teach.

Yahweh decreed that the husband should rule over the wife (*autos sou kyrieusei*, Gen. 3:16 [LXX]) as a punishment for her having allowed herself to be deceived (Gen. 3:13). The Hebrew word for "husband" is *baal*, "lord."[23] The Greek Bible has Sarah calling Abraham her "lord" (*kyrios mou*, Gen. 18:12). As late as the Middle Ages, the Jewish philosopher Maimonides would write

---

22. The intensive form used of Eve is *exapatētheisa* (see 2 Cor. 11:3 and above, p. 65n*a*). The form used for Adam is a simple *ēpatēthē*.

23. See Gen. 20:3; Exod. 21:3, 22; Deut. 22:22; 24:4; 2 Sam. 11:26; Prov. 12:4; 31:11, 23, 28; Hos. 2:18; Joel 1:8; Esth. 1:17, 20.

that the sages "laid down that a wife shall honor her husband exceedingly and shall accept his authority and abide by his wishes in all her activities" (*Mishneh Torah, Ishut* 15:20).

One of the Pastor's overarching concerns is domestic tranquility and social stability. The Pastor's exhortation promotes these values with specific regard to the role of women in his community (vv. 11–12). As did other authors writing from within Hellenistic Judaism, the Pastor uses the Jewish Scriptures to endorse cultural values. Thus, Philo extends the ambit of the Decalogue's commandment to honor one's parents (Exod. 20:12; Deut. 5:16) to children's willingness to hearken to the commands of their parents and obeying them in everything that is just and profitable (*Special Laws* 2.236). The author of Ephesians inserts this same precept of the Decalogue into a household code in order to provide a scriptural warrant for a principle of social order, namely, the obedience of children to their parents (Eph. 6:2). The Pastor does something similar when he uses a midrash on Scripture as a warrant for women's quiet submission (vv. 13–14).

Excursus 3: The Pastor's Perspective on Women

Père Lagrange, the founder of the world renowned *École biblique et archéologique* in Jerusalem and its leading light for more than four decades, was fond of saying that the Bible must be interpreted in light of its "text and context." The pun remains as insightful now, after the passing of a full century, as it did when he first uttered it.

Jewish and Christian Scriptures must be understood in the two-beamed light of their text *and* their context. Archaeological finds help to shed light on the context insofar as these discoveries attest to the life and culture of the people by and for whom biblical texts were written. Literature contemporary with biblical texts sheds further light on the context within which these texts were written. To some extent the texts themselves bear witness to the context. The interdependence of language and culture is inevitable. Culture produces language; language shapes culture.

The Pastor's words about women must be situated within the context of his desire to actualize the teaching of Paul for his own congregation. That is the burden of the choice of the literary form of a letter (1 Tim. 1:1–2) and of the development of a Pauline ethos as the warrant for his own paraenesis. Paul's own letters are remarkable in what they have to say about women. His basic principle is that "there is no longer male and female; for all of you are one in Christ Jesus" (Gal. 3:28). In the enunciation of this principle, Paul seems to have quoted an early baptismal formula. In Christ, men and woman are equal. Theirs is a basic equality, "for just as woman came from man, so man comes through woman" (1 Cor. 11:12). With regard to marriage and the sexual relationship, men and women have complementary, mutual, and equal roles and responsibilities (1 Cor. 7:1–16).

The most striking aspect of Paul's attitude toward women is the way in which he writes about various women. Romans, 1 Corinthians, Philippians, and Philemon mention the names of women associated with Paul's ministry of evangelization (see Gill-man). Romans mentions not only Phoebe, a deacon of the church at Cenchreae and Paul's benefactress to whom he had given some task to fulfill in Rome (Rom. 16:1-2), but also Prisca, who with her husband Apollos shared their shop with Paul, provided him with hospitality, evangelized with him, and once saved his life (Rom. 16:3–4). The final greetings of Paul's letter to the Romans continue with mention of Mary, who had worked hard among the Romans; Junia, prominent among the apostles; Tryphaena and Tryphosa, workers in the Lord; the mother of Rufus, who proved to be a mother to Paul; Julia; and the sister of Nereus (Rom. 16:6–16). First Corinthians mentions Prisca and Aquila (1 Cor. 16:19), hosts to a household church, and Chloe, the woman who may not have been a Christian but whose people apprised Paul about the situation in Corinth (1 Cor. 1:11). Philippians cites the names of Euodia and Syntyche, who struggled beside Paul in the work of the gospel (Phil. 4:2–3). Finally, Paul's shortest letter is addressed, among others, to Apphia, whom Paul esteems as his sister (Phlm. 2).

First Corinthians shows that Paul's attitude on the role of women in the church was not accepted by all with readiness and prudence. In 1 Cor. 14:32a–36 Paul counters the view of conservatives who held that women should be silent in church, submissively seeking to learn from their husbands (on the interpretation of this difficult passage, see Collins,[24] 513–17, 520–22). In 1 Cor. 11:2–16 Paul writes about men and women pray-ing and prophesying side by side, but he is obliged to say something in response to those whose views on the radical equality between men and women would lead them to vio-late the canons of social propriety (Collins, 393–416).

While they have more to say about women than do other New Testament texts, the Pastoral Epistles, when compared with the letters of Paul, are relatively restrained in what they say about women. With exception made for the name of Eve in 1 Tim. 2:13, neither 1 Timothy nor Titus mention the name of any woman. Second Timothy mentions Lois and Eunice as, respectively, the grandmother and mother of Timothy (2 Tim. 1:5). The final greetings of this farewell letter cite the names of Prisca and Claudia, but the relationship between these women and Paul is not specified.

Rather than affirming the radical equality of men and women in Christ, 2 Timothy speaks demeaningly of women who are unable to attain to the full knowledge of the truth (2 Tim. 3:6–7; see 1 Tim. 5:13). First Timothy and Titus speak of women in more pos-itive terms, but they emphasize the domestic role of women (see Philo, *Special Laws* 3.169; *Virtues* 19; *Genesis* 1.26). Young women are to marry, raise their children, and take care of the household (1 Tim. 5:14). Older women should be holy and venerable, teaching younger women how to be good wives, mothers, and homemakers (Titus 2:3–5). Women are to take care of the widows in their family (1 Tim. 5:16), but the Pas-tor warns that women who become widows at an early age are liable to abandon their social responsibilities (1 Tim. 5:11–14).

Alone among the Pastorals, 1 Timothy has something to say about the role of women in the house of God, the church. It implies that women participate in the assembly at prayer without actually saying that they pray, still less saying that they prophesy (1 Tim. 2:9). First Timothy considers in only brief review the qualities appropriate for a female

24. Raymond F. Collins, *First Corinithians* (SP 7; Collegeville: Liturgical Press, 1999).

server in the house of God (1 Tim. 3:11).[25] Its most extensive reflection on women comes when the Pastor writes about widowed women in 1 Tim. 5:3–16. He distinguishes three categories of widows: senior citizens who have no one to care for them, older women whose children and grandchildren should look after them, and young widows who are encouraged to become married again. The church itself should care for the first group of women; in turn, they should continue in prayer and in their petitions to God.

A twenty-first-century reader of the Pastoral Epistles finds what the Pastor writes about women in 1 Tim. 2:11–15 particularly difficult to understand if not truly problematic. This text must be understood within the specific context of the socioreligious circumstances in which the Pastor was writing. His circumstances were decidedly complex. Would-be teachers of the law who really did not know what they were talking about had apparently disturbed his community (1 Tim. 1:7). In 1 Timothy the Pastor affirms the goodness of the law and identifies the purpose of its legal prescriptions (1 Tim. 1:8–11). He urges Timothy to pay attention to the reading of the Scriptures (1 Tim. 4:13). Second Timothy 3:15–17 affirms that the Scriptures are inspired by God and talks about the different ways in which leaders of the community can use the Scriptures. Nonetheless, the Scriptures can be misunderstood (1 Tim. 1:7) and misused (Titus 1:13–14).

The Pastor's midrash on the creation narrative (1 Tim. 2:13–15) is to be understood within the context of this search for an appropriate use of the Jewish Scriptures by the community. As does Paul (1 Cor. 6:16) and the Synoptics (Matt. 19:4–6; Mark 10:6–8), the Pastor uses the Genesis creation narratives as the basis on which the male-female relationship is to be understood. In the Judaism of his day, only men were considered capable of teaching. Women were to be silent and learn from men (see 1 Cor. 14:33a–34). The Pastor's halakah on women (1 Tim. 2:13–15) is an appropriation of the Jewish tradition to his own community.

That appropriation occurred within the Hellenistic culture of the Greco-Roman world in which the Pastor and his community lived. Jewish Christian communities living closer to the time of Jesus than did the Hellenistic Christian communities of the late first century C.E. were able to profit from the tolerance accorded to Jews because of the *religio licita* principle of Roman jurisprudence. A generation or two later, when the expectation of an imminent Parousia had waned, Hellenistic Christian communities had to find their own place in the Greco-Roman world (see Ascough).

Mid-first-century C.E. Christian gatherings in Corinth were characterized by some analogies with the gatherings of people belonging to religious and fraternal associations and the various trade guilds. The Greco-Roman world of the late first century was familiar with such associations, but if it were to abide any of these associations it was imperative that they fit into a society characterized by the household unit at the microlevel and the structures of the Roman Empire at the macrolevel. The concern evidenced throughout the Pastorals for social stability, the integrity of the customary household structure, respect for kings and those in authority, the impression made on nonbelievers (see 1 Tim. 2:1–2; 5:14; 6:1–2; Titus 2:1–10), and the Hellenistic ethos is a sign of the desire of early

---

25. One can note that both 1 Tim. 2:9 and 3:11 use the word "similarly" (*hōsautōs*) in comparing the roles of men and women in the church.

Christian leaders to form the community of faith so that it had its place not only in the history of salvation but also in the world where believers lived and experienced salvation. What the Pastor writes about women in 1 Tim. 2:13–15 is part of that effort. What the authors of Col. 3:18–4:1 and Eph. 5:22–6:9 said about the household and of a wife's subordinate role within the household unit—as well as what the author of 1 Pet. 2:18–3:7 writes about slaves, wives, and husbands—is part of this same picture.

When the Pastor's efforts are interpreted hermeneutically by twenty-first-century readers, due attention must be paid to the literary context in which his teaching and paraenesis were expressed. His chosen literary form is that of the apostolic letter. The genre allows the Pastor to invoke the authority of the apostle Paul as a warrant for the didactic, hortatory, and organizational content of the epistle. Of its very nature, the content of a letter is shaped by the circumstances in which it is written. Of all literary genres it is the epistolary genre that is most conditioned by the coordinates of time and space, historical and relational circumstances. Thus, scholars speak of the *occasional* nature of letters. They are ad hoc compositions whose essential import relates immediately and directly only to the situation that dictated their composition.[26]

Undoubtedly the Pastor continues his midrash of Genesis 3 with a reference to child-bearing (1 Tim. 2:15) because some people in his circles, most probably the anonymous "some" of the previous chapter, forbade marriage (4:3; see Kimberley; Kroeger; Kroeger and Kroeger 174–76). His words about child-bearing are a partial response to that kind of false asceticism. He continues the fray in 5:14–15, encouraging young widows of child-bearing age to marry, bear children, and take care of their households.

The anonymous folks who disparaged marriage and child-bearing shared the kind of enthusiastic asceticism, born of an anthropological dualism that dissociated spirit and body, that Paul himself rebutted in 1 Corinthians 7. This perverted view of human sexuality would later become a tenet of Gnosticism, a second-century Christian heresy. A classic critique of this heresy was written by Irenaeus, who described Gnostics as people who held "that marrying and generating come from Satan" (*Against Heresies* 1.24.2; cf. 1.28.1; see also Tertullian, *Prescription against Heretics* 33).

[2:15–3:1a] The authors of Ephesians, Colossians, and 1 Peter used the literary structure of the household code in a pastoral attempt to urge their readers to adapt their Christian life to the social structures in which they were living their lives. Each of these authors incorporated into his use of the household code the language of Christian theology. In doing so, he implied that living within accepted social structures was not only obligatory but also the Christian thing to do. In similar fashion, the Pastor adds to his exhortation on women and his midrashic explanation a theological perspective. His motif is salvation, arguably the dominant theological motif of his epistle (see, e.g., 1:1; 2:3–7).

---

26. Epistolary context-specific paraenesis cannot be treated as some sort of timeless truth. The modern reader of a text such as 1 Timothy must be attentive to the ways in which a contemporary context differs from the context envisioned by the Pastor.

In verse 15 the Pastor relates God's gift of salvation for women with their giving birth (*tēs teknogonias*). Aristotle held that the ideal time for a woman to give birth was after she had reached twenty-one years of age. "After thrice seven years," he wrote, "the women have reached a favorable state for childbearing (*pros tas teknogonias ēdē eukairōs, History of Animals* 9.1.29). More than a half century earlier Hippocrates, the father of Greek medicine, responded to people who lacked discretion and discernment, deriding both the bad and the good by stating that childbearing was "wholly good" (*holōs agathon, Epistles* 17.21).

The Pastor reaffirms the traditional maternal role of women. What he writes about childbearing continues his midrashic exposition of the biblical story of Eve's deception by the serpent. "To the woman," Yahweh said, "I will greatly increase your pangs in childbearing; in pain you shall bring forth children [*texē tekna*], yet your desire shall be for your husband, and he shall rule over you" (Gen. 3:16). Apropos of this verse Philo wrote, "This experience comes to every woman who lives together with a man. It is meant not as a curse but as a necessity" (*Genesis* 1.49). Jewish tradition held that the burden of Gen. 3:16 was somewhat mitigated when a woman gives birth (Philo, *Allegorical Interpretation* 2.217–19; see John 16:21).

The Pastor states that "she will be saved" (*sōthēsetai*) through childbearing (*dia tēs teknogonias*). The verb is in the singular, employing a divine passive that indicates God as the source of her salvation. Some authors interpret the singular number of the verb as a reference to one particular woman. They take the noun to refer to a particular birth, the birth of *the* child, that is, the birth of the Messiah (see, e.g., Knight 144–48). "She" is the mother of the Messiah of whom Eve is the type. Such typological reading of biblical texts is characteristic of patristic exegesis. Limited second-century patristic witness exists in support of a messianic reading of 2:15 (Justin, *Dialogue* 100; see Ign. *Eph.* 19).

Were the messianic reading the correct interpretation of 2:15,[27] the Pastor's midrash would consist of a messianic reading of Genesis 3:15. It seems more likely, however, that the Pastor's use of a verb in the singular number is dependent on the singular form of the noun *gynē* (meaning "women" in general), used by the Pastor when he began his exhortation in verse 11. Insofar as Eve was more fully deceived than was Adam, she was the prototypical female, Adam the

27. This interpretation has been soundly rebutted by Stanley E. Porter, "What Does It Mean to be 'Saved by Childbirth'? [1 Tim 2:15]," *JSNT* 49 (1993): 87–102, 98–102, and Thomas R. Schreiner, "An Interpretation of Timothy 2:9–15: A Dialogue with Scholarship," in *Women in the Church: A Fresh Analysis of 1 Timothy 2:9–15*, ed. Andreas J. Köstenberger, Thomas R. Schreiner, and H. Scott Baldwin (Grand Rapids: Baker, 1995), 105–54, 146–53.

prototypical male. Support for taking "she will be saved" as a reference to women in general is confirmed by the Pastor's shift to a verb in the plural: "*she will be saved* [*sōthēsetai*] through childbearing if *they* remain [*meinōsin*] in faith, love, and holiness with modesty."[28]

Woman finds her place in God's salvific economy not in teaching and public ministry but in her domestic role, rearing godly children. The Pastor's codicil indicates that, in itself, the physical bearing of children is not necessarily in conformity with God's salvific activity; childbearing fits in with the plan of salvation when it is accompanied by faith, love, holiness, and modesty. These four virtues are typical of the "good works" mentioned in 2:10. The mother who is a believer should possess these virtues if she is to participate in the worship of the community. The Pastor's mention of the first three virtues is particularly apropos in a context that speaks about worship (2:8–13a). The dyad of faith and love is the hallmark of Christian existence (*en pistei kai agapē*; see, e.g., Gal. 5:6; 1 Thess. 5:8). Holiness (*hagiasmō*) expresses a condition of belonging to the Lord. Polycarp of Smyrna uses essentially the same triad when he says that women should conduct themselves in faith, love, and purity (*pistei kai agapē kai hagneia*, Pol. *Phil.* 4:2).

The Pastor concludes his description of the female worshiper and believing mother with the notation that in addition to possessing the "theological" virtues, she must have modesty (*meta sōphrosynēs*). She must possess that quality that Hellenistic society considered to be the epitome of feminine virtue. The worshiping woman should be well regarded by the society in which she lives. At about the same time that the Pastor was writing, Clement of Rome used the phrase "with all modesty" (*pany sōphronousas*) to conclude his description of the responsibilities of Christian women (*1 Clem.* 1:3).

The Pastor brings the pericope to a close with an affirmation that he has faithfully passed along the tradition. He affirms that what he has written is a "trustworthy saying" (*pistos ho logos*). This use of the phrase of affirmation is rather different from other uses of the phrase (1:15; 2 Tim. 2:11; Titus 3:8). In 3:1 the Pastor's endorsement is immediately attached to a midrash, an explanation of

28. Some commentators take "they" as a reference to a mother's children. Her childbearing is complete if her children (see 3:4; *b. Ber.* 17a) abide in faith, love, holiness, and modesty. See, e.g., Jarl H. Ulrichsen, "Noén bemerkninger til 1. Tim 2,15," *NTT* 84 (1983): 19–25; "Heil durch Kindergebären: Zu I Tim 2,15 und seiner syrischen Version," *SEÅ* 58 (1993): 99–104; Johnson, *Letters to Paul's Delegates,* 134; *EDNT* 3.340. Holmes, *Text in a Whirlwind,* argues that the conditional clause belongs to the finale of the pericope and refers to both the men and the women in the community. In fact, the four virtues cited in the Pastor's short catalog are qualities that both men and women should have. The presence of "modesty" in the final, climactic position, grammatically set off from the other three virtues, and the fact that Hellenists consider the particularly feminine form of modesty to sum up their positive qualities suggest that this particular catalog relates specifically to women.

Jewish Scripture. The formula ratifies the Pastor's exposition of his views on Christian women. More broadly, it confirms the teaching on salvation that began in 2:3–4 with the affirmation that God wills all people to be saved and to come to the full knowledge of the truth. The Pastor's hope is that they do so within the context of a peaceful and quiet life.[29]

Overseers
1 Timothy 3:1b–7

The Pastor's instruction about the conduct of men and women in the assembly provided him an opportunity to write about the broader topic of the role of women in the community (2:11–15). He urged that cultural expectations regarding the relationship between men and women be respected and that women not forget that childbearing is part of God's plan of salvation. Then the Pastor turns his attention to some individuals who have specific functions within the community. These functions are those of overseer (*episkopos*) and server (*diakonos*).

"Overseers" and "servers" appear together in Phil. 1:1, but apart from the etymological implications of the terms, Paul gives no specific indication of the role of the overseers and servers within the community. The Pastor, however, develops a profile of the qualities that one should expect to find in someone who is to serve the community as an overseer. To do so, the Pastor makes use of the classic literary form of a catalogue of virtues. Apart from not being a neophyte, the qualities are those that one would expect to find in anyone who is an upright, responsible, and respectable husband and father. For the Pastor, this profile is very important. His rhetorical aside (v. 5) makes it clear that if a person cannot even run his own household very well, he is incapable of taking care of the community. Moreover, unless the community's leadership enjoys a good reputation among the outsiders who can observe it, not only will its leadership fall into disrepute, so too will the community itself. Such a situation would be an eschatological disaster!

> 3:1b If someone aspires to be an overseer, he desires a good thing. 2 In all events the overseer should be blameless, the husband of one woman, sober, temperate, well-mannered, hospitable, able to teach, 3 neither addicted to wine nor ready for a fight,[a] but balanced, not contentious, not a money lover, 4 having managed his own household well, having chil-

---

29. Leland E. Wilshire has suggested that the Pastor's words about women were specifically intended to counter violence within the community ("1 Timothy 2:12 Revisited: A Reply to Paul W. Barnett and Timothy J. Harris, *EvQ* 65 [1993]: 43–55).

dren who are submissive, with all dignity—5 If someone does not know how to manage his own household, how can he take care of the church of God?—6 not a neophyte so that he be not puffed up and fall into the devil's judgment. 7 He should have good testimony from outsiders so that he not fall into censure and the devil's trap.

a. A relatively few minuscules add *mē aischrokerdē*, "not sordidly greedy for gain," perhaps under the influence of Titus 1:7.

[3:1b] This pericope, closely joined to and paralleled by the following passage (3:8–13), begins with a conditional clause. The Pastor wants to say something about someone who desires to exercise the function of oversight in the community. The term "oversight" (*episkopē*) designates a function within the community, not a permanent position or office.[30] An "overseer" (*episkopos*) is someone who watches over another or over others in order to see that things are going smoothly. On the basis of Phil. 1:1, in which mention is made of overseers and servers (*episkopois kai diakonois*), it would appear that the functions of overseers and servers were features of Paul's foundations (see Acts 20:28). Elsewhere in the Pastoral Epistles, the "overseer" is mentioned in Titus 1:7, the end of a passage that gives a list of qualifications for "overseers" similar to that found in 1 Tim. 3:2–7.

The Pastor prefaces his list of qualities with a remark to the effect that it is a good thing to aspire to be an overseer. Despite the fact that some Hellenists, especially the philosophical moralists, used the verbs "aspire" and "desire" in a negative sense—the former to refer to greed, the latter to sexual desire—the verbs were often used in an ordinary sense. "Aspire" would connote striving after something good, even the kingship (see, e.g., Plutarch, *Solon* 29.3; *Phocion* 17.1; Josephus, *Life* 13 §70, a passage that uses both "aspire" and "desire"). Philo puts such ambition into a religious perspective. "How could anything," he asks, "fail to be great and worthy of our efforts [*oregei*] which God offers and gives?" (*Abraham* 39).

[2–6] This list of sixteen qualities is a classic catalog of virtues. The Pastor affirms that the would-be overseer must be an exemplary person. He adds that the person should be well regarded within the community at large (v. 7). Except for the Pastor's rhetorical question (v. 5) and the remark about why it is not appropriate for a neophyte Christian to be an overseer (v. 6), the Pastor's list of

30. The term *episkopē* appears elsewhere in the New Testament only in Luke 19:44; Acts 1:20; and 1 Pet. 2:12. In Luke and in 1 Peter the term designates God's exercise of the function of oversight on the day of judgment; hence, it is translated as "visitation" in the NRSV. Acts 1:20 quotes Psalm 109's oracular judgment against the wicked man. Luke uses the Scripture, "Let another seize his position" (Ps. 109:8), in his scriptural apologetic on Judas' betrayal of Jesus. In the flow of his argument, it prepares for the selection of Matthias as one of the Twelve.

desirable qualities is hardly distinguishable from lists of virtues found in the writings of philosophical moralists. Epictetus, for example, asks about the qualities that we should honor in a human being. He responds to his own rhetorical question by saying, "the duties of citizenship, marriage, begetting children, reverence to God, care of parents, in a word, desire, avoidance, choice, refusal, the proper performance of each of these acts" (*Discourses* 3.26). The emphasis of such a long list lies in its cumulative effect (see also 1:9–10). If an author wants to praise someone, he cites a long list of virtues. If he wishes to condemn someone, he rehearses a similarly long list of vices.

Scholars have debated whether the specific virtues or vices on these list are chosen at random or whether they pertain particularly to the object of the author's praise or blame. Analysis of the vices that appear in the New Testament lists reveals that there is a measure of both generic use and ad hoc application in most lists. Some of the virtues or vices appear because they pertain to the situation at hand. Others are cited either because the rhetor presumes that the audience will expect to hear them or because the author must fill out the list in order to achieve the desired rhetorical effect.

This list of virtues is similar to a list of qualifications cited by Onasander, a Platonic philosopher. He writes about the choice of a military officer. We must choose a general, writes Onasander, "because he is temperate, self-restrained, vigilant, frugal, hardened to labor, alert, free from avarice, neither too young nor too old, indeed a father of children if possible, a ready speaker, and a man with a good reputation" (*The General* 1.1). Still closer to the Pastor's list is the profile of the elder-overseer in Titus 1:6–9 and the description of the server's qualities in 3:8–10 and 12–13. The Pastor uses shorter lists of virtues to describe "women" (3:11; see commentary) and women of marriageable age (2:15). Three short lists appear in Titus 2:2–5, respectively for older men, older women, and younger women (see also 1 Tim. 5:14). Another catalog is found in the exhortation of Titus 3:1–2.

With regard to younger men, Titus gives not a list but only a single virtue, discretion (*sōphrosynē*, Titus 2:6). This virtue appears on six of the nine lists of virtues in the Pastoral Epistles (2:15; 3:2; Titus 1:8; 2:2, 4, 5). It appears to be a sine qua non for those who live in the Pastor's Christian community. The Pastor does not specifically mention this virtue among the qualities to be desired in servers and "women" (3:8–13). The omission hardly implies that servers were not expected to possess the virtue of discretion as befitting their gender and age. The Pastorals affirm that discretion is expected of all older men and older women, all younger men and younger women. Those chosen by the community as its servers could hardly have lacked this virtue.

The term *sōphrosynē* refers to the cardinal virtue of prudence. The ancients were well aware that this virtue plays out differently in the lives of men and women[31] (see Aristotle, *Politics* 1.13.9). They considered the virtue to be one of the most important qualities for any adult, male or female, to have. Onasander cites it as the first quality to be sought in a would-be general: "The general must be temperate [*sōphrona*] in order that he may not be so distracted by the pleasures of the body as to neglect the consideration of matters of the highest importance" (*General* 1.2).

The virtue of discretion (*sōphrona*) is the fourth virtue cited on the Pastor's list of qualities expected of the overseer. His list begins with "blameless" (*anepilēmpton*), a comprehensive virtue that provides a good start for this kind of list.[32] This quality is a stock item on a list of virtues. Euripides and Thucydides write about people against whom nobody can bring any accusation. An ancient letter sent by the church of Smyrna to the church of Philomelium describes the former martyred bishop, Polycarp, as someone "who had a blameless life from the beginning" (*tēn aparchēs anepilēpton politeian, Mart. Pol.* 17:1). In the New Testament, the word is used only by 1 Timothy, in reference to the overseer (3:2), the real widow (5:7), and God's person, the "man of God" (6:14).

That the overseer should have but one wife (*mias gynaikos andra*, literally "a man of one woman," a one-woman man) implies marital fidelity and the avoidance of sexual immorality. The same expression is found in the list of qualities expected of the server (3:12). The phrase is used to describe the elder in Titus 1:6. Similarly, the mature woman who is to be enrolled as a "widow" must likewise have been "married only once" (1 Tim. 5:9). The phrase indicates that those recognized as capable of exercising these functions within the church have been married, but it does not so much set forth a requirement that they be married—it presupposes that they are married!—as articulate the expectation that they be faithful to a single spouse. After twenty centuries it is difficult for a commentator to ascertain exactly what kind of marital fidelity is meant by "one-woman man" and "one-man woman."

The Pastor's circles knew what the similar phrases meant. The words occur four times in the Pastorals but are never once explained. They clearly exclude polygamy and polyandry, but a prohibition of bigamy is not likely to have been the reason why office-holders were expected to have but one wife and enrolled widows to have had but a single husband. Nothing in the New Testament suggests that either polygamy or polyandry was a matter of concern for first-century Christians. Nor is it likely that the phrases simply meant that the over-

---

31. The translation of *sōphrōsynē* in this commentary attends to the difference by rendering the term "discretion" when it is used of men and by "modesty" when it is used of women. On "modesty," see the commentary on 2:15.

32. The two lists in Titus begin with the virtually synonymous *anenklētos*, "beyond reproach" (Titus 1:6, 7).

seer or enrolled widow should not be guilty of adultery. All Christians were expected to shun adultery and avoid sexual immorality.

Why then does the Pastor specify that the overseer be a man of one wife? Philo's allegory on the marriages of Abraham, Isaac, and Jacob may provide some clue. In contrast with his father and his son, Isaac had only one wife. So Philo praises him because "his lawful wife is the one who shares his home throughout" (*monē d'hē kouridios achri pantos synoikei, Preliminary Studies* 34). Another clue comes from 1 Tim. 5:9–10 in which "the wife of one husband" seems to imply that a woman who is to be recognized as a "real widow" is a woman who had not taken a second husband after the death of her spouse. On the basis of these clues, the phrase "the husband of a single woman" may mean that the would-be overseer (3:2) or server (3:12) should not have remarried after divorce or the death of his spouse. The thrust of the Pastor's phrase is, nonetheless, positive. He is urging that the would-be overseer be faithful to his wife.

The third quality on the Pastor's list is "sober" (*nēphalion*), a word that qualifies the "women" of 3:11 and is used to describe old men in Titus 2:2. Josephus uses the adjective to designate abstinence from wine (*Ant.* 3.12.2 §279). Philo (*Sobriety* 2; *Moses* 1.187) contrasts sobriety with drunkenness. Thus, in itself, the word "sober" here is basically synonymous with another quality on the list, "not addicted to wine" (3:3). Hence, "sober" is probably to be taken in a metaphorical sense. Classical authors sometimes used the term to mean clearheaded or self-controlled, and some New Testament authors, including Paul, occasionally used the related verb, *nēphō*, "to be sober," in a figurative sense (1 Thess. 5:6, 8; 1 Pet. 1:13; 4:7; 5:8; 2 Tim. 4:5).

Next on the Pastor's list is the virtue of temperance, moderation, discretion—the ubiquitous *sōphrona* of these lists in the Pastoral Epistles and a sine qua non for all members of the Pastor's community. The fifth expectation the Pastor has of the overseer is that he be "well mannered" (*kosmion*). The adjective means "orderly." Used of persons, it means orderly, regular, quiet, and discreet. Aristotle, Plato, and a bevy of later philosophers used the adjective to describe people who are well behaved and well mannered. Among New Testament authors, the Pastor alone uses the adjective (see 2:9). A sensitivity to good order is an important requisite for one who is to manage the household of God.

Another quality of the good householder is that he be "hospitable" (*philoxenon*). Christian hospitality was of crucial importance in the life of the early church. Hospitable Christians provided lodging for traveling missionaries (e.g., Phlm. 22; 3 John 5–8) and letter-carrying traders whose services provided an important means of communication among Christian communities. The Pastor's emphasis on the hospitality of an overseer is to be seen within this context.

In the seventh item on the list the Pastor expresses the desire that the overseer be willing to learn and able to teach (*didaktikon*, see 2 Tim. 2:24). These qualities are indispensable for someone with a teaching function in the community (Titus 1:9). Philo relates the ability to teach with leadership and the acquisition of virtue. Writing about Abraham, he says, "The leader in adopting the godly creed came to the fullness of what he could be by virtue gained through instruction" (*didaktikē chrēsamenos aretē pros alētheian, Rewards and Punishments* 27). Again, "the virtue that comes through teaching, which Abraham pursues, needs the fruits of several studies" (*Preliminary Studies* 35). Possession of this quality enables the overseer to correct with sound teaching and to confute opponents of that teaching (see 1:19–20).

The Pastor then lists a pair of qualities that are negative in their formulation, "neither addicted to wine nor ready for a fight" (*mē paroinon mē plēktēn*). Each of these vices was well known in antiquity. The Athenian orator Lysias (*Discourses* 4.8) and the Attic poet Aristophanes (*Wasps* 1300) spoke about those given to wine (*paroinon, paroinikos*). Plutarch knew of people ready for a fight (*plēktēn; Dion* 30.8).

The Pastor contrasts the pair of negative qualities with three virtues. The overseer must be "balanced" (*epieikē*), "not contentious" (*a-machon*), "not a money lover" (*a-philargyron*). The first two are virtually a given. All members of the community are expected to be balanced and peaceful (see Titus 3:2, which mentions these very qualities). "Balance" is a quality that one expects to find in judges, magistrates, and rulers. When found in persons exercising such functions, "balance" evokes a sense of equity in the application of law and the exercise of civil leadership. The term was not, however, confined to the judicial sphere and the leadership function. "Balance" was a quality that all good folks should aspire to. Thus, the Pseudo-Plato defined balance as "condescendence in giving in one's rights and interests; moderation in business relations; right measure of the reasonable soul in matters related to good and evil" (*Definitions* 412b).

The overseer who is not contentious is an overseer who is not prone to quarreling with others. He is one who knows how to get along with people and does not get involved in petty disputes. The twelfth quality on the Pastor's list, "not a money lover," begins a short series of virtues that are requisite for householders. Philosophical moralists praised those who were not tainted by avarice. In their judgment the absence of avarice was particularly important for a leader who was expected to be incorruptible in his leadership (see Pol. *Phil.* 6:1). Onasander explains:

> this quality of freedom from avarice [*aphilagryron*] will be valued most highly, since it is largely responsible for the incorruptible and large-minded management of affairs. For men who can face the shields and spears of a host with courage are blinded by gold; but gold is a strong weapon against the enemy and effective for victory. (*General* 1.8)

This quality of the overseer (see Titus 1:7) is similar to one of the server's qualities. Servers should be "not sordidly greedy for gain" (*mē aischrokerdē*, 3:8).

With the thirteenth and fourteenth qualities on his list, the Pastor expresses his expectation that the overseer should be a good paterfamilias. In the Pastor's Greco-Roman world, the paterfamilias was clearly the head of the household, with absolute control over his wife, children, and servants/slaves. Autocratic rule did not necessarily imply oppression. Thus, the Pastor could compare the leader of the community with the paterfamilias who managed his household well. The overseer should be someone who has managed his household well (*tou idiou oikou kalōs proistamenon*) and has raised children who are submissive (*tekna echonta en hypotagē*). Their submissiveness is a sign of their having been reared well. Children's submission to their father is analogous to the submission of believing women to their husbands (see 2:11, where the phrase *en hypotagē* likewise occurs). The household codes of Eph. 5:22–6:9 and Col. 3:18–4:1 attest to the submission of wives, children, and slaves to the head of the household in the Greco-Roman world. The Pastor adds to the list of household virtues within the larger list of virtues the idea that the overseer should be characterized by his "dignified bearing" (*semnotētos*), the *gravitas* of Latin philosophers. The Pastor expects that men (3:8) and women (3:11) also have dignified bearing (see Titus 2:2, apropos older men).

Having listed fifteen qualities that he expects an overseer to have, the Pastor interrupts the accumulation of virtues with a pointed rhetorical aside. The aside emphasizes the importance that he attaches to the overseer's domestic virtues. Managing the household of God is the basic function of the overseer (see 3:15). The Pastor asks, "If anyone does not know how to manage his own household, how can he take care of the church of God?" The expected answer is negative. Anyone who is incapable of managing his own household is incapable of managing the church of God.

The Pastor's rhetorical question evokes the image of the church as the household of God. The image of the household is the dominant ecclesiological metaphor in the Pastoral Epistles (see 3:15). Second Timothy 2:19 describes God's firm foundation of the house. Titus 1:7 identifies the overseer as God's steward, that is, God's household manager. The church, the assembly of the people of God, is where God dwells. The imagery of the church as the house of God recalls imagery used by Paul in 1 Cor. 3:9b–17. There the apostle identified "God's building" (*theou oikodomē*) as the temple of God in which the Spirit of God dwells (*oikei en hymin*, "dwells in you [plural]").

As a final notation, the Pastor adds a sixteenth quality to his list: The overseer should not be a neophyte (*mē neophyton*); he must not be a seedling, "newly planted" in the Christian community. This is the only specifically Christian virtue on the Pastor's list; the fifteen other qualities are found in many different lists of virtues in Hellenistic literature. This virtue is identified as "not a neophyte." The word "neophyte" would later become a technical term in the jargon of the church, describing people who had recently adopted the Christian faith and entered the Christian community. Many generations later the use of the metaphor was extended so that it could be used of any person who is new to a discipline or way of life. Originally, however, "neophyte" was an agricultural term; the Pastor was the first to use it as a metaphor. The Pastor's juxtaposition of architectural (house) and agricultural (new planting) imagery was not unusual in ancient literature, whether Greek[33] or Jewish.[34] The ploy was successfully used by the apostle in 1 Cor. 3:5–17.

The reason why it is not desirable for the overseer to be a neophyte is that he should not be puffed up (*typhōtheis*; see 6:4; 2 Tim. 3:4). Having the responsibility of managing God's household could lead to a kind of pride that would make the manager fall victim to the judgment of the devil. The "devil" (*diabolos*, a substantivized adjective meaning "slanderer"; see 2 Tim. 3:3) is an eschatological figure often equated with Satan[35] (Rev. 12:9) or the tempter (see Matt. 4:1, 3, 5, 8, 10, 11; cf. Luke 4:2, 3, 6, 13). In early Christian usage "the devil" is the equivalent of the Jewish eschatological figure named Belial or Beliar (see commentary on 2 Tim. 2:26). The Pastor's mention of the devil (3:6, 7; see 2 Tim. 2:26) is a sign of the times. His language shows that he considers the times in which he was living as the final times, times in which the agelong opposition between God and the devil was coming to a decisive head. The "devil's judgment" is to be interpreted in the light of the more common phrase, "the devil's trap" (v. 7). The devil does as he wills with those who fall victim to his trap.

[7] Verse 7 serves as a kind of peroration for the Pastor's review of qualities that the overseer should possess. It adds the idea that the overseer should—note the repetition of *dei*, "should" in verses 2 and 7—enjoy a good reputation. The Pastor's "have good testimony" (*martyrian kalēn echein*) is analogous to the contemporary expression, "receive a good recommendation." The Pastor should be well regarded by people who do not belong to the Christian community. Rather than revile and censure the overseer, outsiders should be able to say good things about him. They will be able to do so if the overseer has the profile that the Pastor has drawn up for him.

From the outset, Pauline foundations were concerned with the impact that they had on outsiders (1 Thess. 4:12; 1 Cor. 14:23–25; see 1 Tim. 5:14). The

---

33. See Plato, *Laws* 1.643b; Dio Chrysostom, *Discourses* 71.5; Philo, *Allegorical Interpretation* 3.48; *Cherubim* 100–102. See also Luke 17:28.

34. See Deut. 20:5–6; Jer. 1:10; 18:7–10; 24:6; 31:28; 42:10; Sir. 49:7; 1QS 8:5; 11:5.

35. The Septuagint often translates the Hebrew *haśśāṭān* as *diabolos* (e.g., Job 2:1; Zech. 3:1–2).

Pastor's own community continued to share that concern. Hence, he required that the would-be overseer be someone to whom good witness could be borne, someone whom people could recommend for a leadership position. Were an overseer not to have a good public reputation, he would likely fall into derision. Along with him the community itself could possibly be derided.

If the overseer's life were such as to be a source of shame, then indeed he would have fallen into the devil's trap (*pagida tou diabolou*, see 2 Tim. 2:26). The biblical sounding phrase echoes the language of the Dead Sea Scrolls that mention the snares of Belial (CD 4:15; see 1QH 3:26; 4:12). These snares are fornication, wealth, and the profanation of the temple. By concluding his list of the overseer's qualities with a reference to the devil's trap, the Pastor has brought the overseer into the horizon of Jewish eschatology. The overseer who lacks the qualities required for his role will not only bring censure upon himself, he will also fall into the devil's trap. The Qumran parallels would suggest that an overseer's failure to have the requisite qualities is tantamount to his being the cause of the profanation of the house of God, the church (3:15).

Servers
1 Timothy 3:8–13

Having listed the qualities of the overseer, the Pastor turns his attention to another group of people who have a specific role in the community (see Phil. 1:1). They function as servers (*diakonous*). Were the noun *diakonous* to be transliterated as "deacons" rather than translated as "servers," there would be considerable risk of anachronism in the interpretation of the Pastor's text. Used as a technical term in much later periods of church history, the word "deacon" connotes a fixed role with specific duties, but the Pastor does not specify the nature of the service rendered by those whom he designates as *diakonous*. The one function that would seem to be excluded from their role in the Pastor's church is that of household management (see commentary on v. 12).

As he had done with regard to the overseer, the Pastor uses the literary form of a catalog of virtues to list qualities expected in someone who aspires to serve the church (vv. 8–9). The final item on the Pastor's list pertains to the faith of the would-be server. Verse 10 suggests that the community is to exercise due discernment before allowing anyone to serve. In the following verse (3:11) the Pastor writes about the qualities of "women" within the community. These women are female servers. The qualities listed in their regard are similar to the qualities that a male server should have (3:8). In verse 12 the Pastor adds a short list of domestic qualities that should be found in the male server. The three virtues are qualities that a well-regarded male should possess. The final verse (3:13) functions as a kind of peroration to the Pastor's exposition. This is similar to the function of 3:7 at the end of the list of the overseer's qualifications.

> 3:8 Similarly, servers must be dignified, not having a forked tongue, not given to much wine, not sordidly greedy for gain, 9 holding the mystery of faith with a clean conscience. 10 Let them first be judged, then let those serve who are beyond reproach. 11 Similarly, women must be dignified, not slanderous, sober, and faithful in all things. 12 Let servers be the husbands of a single wife, supervising their children well, and managing well their own households. 13 For those who serve well procure for themselves a good position and sufficient confidence with regard to faith in Christ Jesus.

[3:8–10] The list of qualities expected in "servers" (*diakonous*) is similar to (*hōsautōs*) but shorter than the list for the overseer. There are, in fact, two lists, verses 8–9 and verse 12, with a total of just eight virtues. The first list consists of five items. Three of these—"not given to much wine," "not sordidly greedy for gain" (see Titus 1:7), and "beyond reproach" (see Titus 1:6, 7)—substantially appear on the list for the overseers albeit with somewhat different wording. A newcomer on the list is "not having a forked tongue" (*mē dilogous*). This quality is not otherwise mentioned in the New Testament, yet it appears as an expectation for servers in Polycarp of Smyrna's list of expectations (Pol. *Phil.* 5:2). Among classical authors such as Xenophon, the word *dilogos* meant "repetitious." The adjective retained this meaning well into the second century C.E. (BAGD). The Pastor and Polycarp seem to have used the term in a different connotation, to suggest a lack of sincerity in speech. As such, "not having a forked tongue" is synonymous with *diglōssos*, "double-tongued," which appears on Philo's long list of vices (*Abel and Cain* 32).

The fifth item on the Pastor's list of qualifications for servers breaks the staccato rhythm of the first four qualities. The participial phrase "holding the mystery of faith with a clean conscience" is of major importance. The expectation expresses one of the Pastor's major concerns. From the outset of his missive he has been concerned with genuine faith (1:2). The expression of this concern in 3:9 provides an early example of the way in which Hellenistic writers, including some Christians, adapted the classic list of vices to a specific context and their own personal agenda. The Pastor had done something similar in adding "not a neophyte" to his list of the overseer's qualifications (3:6). The overseer should not be a neophyte; the server should hold on to "the mystery of faith with a clean conscience."

In contemporary Hellenistic culture the "mystery" was typically some sort of occult knowledge or a rite associated with initiation into an occult faith but Paul writes about the "mystery of God" (1 Cor. 2:1). Paul and Apollos were the custodians of that mystery (1 Cor. 4:1). The "mystery" designates the content of Paul's preaching of the gospel. Later in 1 Corinthians, Paul uses the term "mystery" to speak of apocalyptic revelation (1 Cor 13:2; 14:2; 15:51). The Synoptic Gospels use the term "mystery" in this apocalyptic sense (Mark 4:11; Matt. 13:11; Luke 8:10). The ultimate reality of the mystery is hidden until God reveals himself in his fullness. Deuteropauline texts speak about the "mystery of God" (Col. 2:2; see Rev. 10:7), the "mystery of Christ" (Eph. 3:4; Col. 4:3), and the "mystery of the gospel" (Eph. 6:19), but none of them speaks about the "mystery of faith," as the Pastor does.

For the Pastor the "mystery of faith" is the content of faith, the "sound teaching" whose content is well known within the Pastor's circles (see Excursus 4). The core of Christian faith is the paschal kerygma, a faith that is expressed in the terse language of a hymnic structure (3:16b). The Pastor then goes on to say that "Timothy," to whom his epistle is directed, has closely followed and been nourished by the message of faith and good teaching (4:6). Servers who hold on to the mystery of faith are like Timothy, who is a "good servant"[36] (*kalos diakonos*) of Christ Jesus.

The faith of the Christian, especially the faith of a would-be server, must be accompanied by an appropriate lifestyle. Faith should give rise to appropriate mores. Accordingly, Helmut Krämer writes that "mystery" is to be understood as the "'ineffable ultimate ground (root, basis)' of a particular mode of conduct" (*EDNT* 2.448). The Pastor had previously linked faith with a good conscience (1:5, 19). Now he specifically directs that someone who is to serve the community hold on to the faith "with a clean conscience" (*en kathara syneidēsei*). "Conscience" (*syn-eidēsei*, literally, "shared knowledge") has an ethical connotation as it does elsewhere in the epistle (1:5, 19; 4:2). One example of a person with a clean conscience is Paul (2 Tim. 1:3). In 4:2 the Pastor writes about people who have cauterized their consciences by rejecting marriage and imposing a regimen of inordinate dietary abstinence. These people fail to recognize the goodness of God's many gifts to his people (4:2). Unlike them, the server must maintain the basics of the faith and live accordingly. He must, says the Pastor, hold "the mystery of faith with a clean conscience."

Verse 10 indicates that before a person assumes the role of server in the community his demeanor must be scrutinized by the community: such persons must be "judged first" (*dokimazesthōsan prōton*). "To be judged" means "to be scru-

---

36. The Greek *diakonos* is rendered "servant" in 4:6 to highlight the subordinate role of Timothy vis-à-vis Jesus; it is rendered "server" in 3:8, 12 to highlight the functional role of servers within the house of God.

tinized." This was a technical term used in the Athenian court to refer to the screening of a candidate for public office. The process is comparable to the contemporary hearings in which some public agency or legislative committee vets candidates for appointive office. Only after the nominees have been scrutinized are they appointed to office. This is the situation that obtains in the community. The Pastor does not specify who it is that conducts the scrutiny. Most likely the scrutinizers are the members of the community to whom the epistle is sent (see the plural pronoun in the epistle's final greeting, 6:21).

The Pastor's text indicates that a process is to be followed. The proper sequence is important. The Pastor juxtaposes "first" and "then" so that his readers understand that the candidates must first be scrutinized; only then may they serve. If the scrutiny concludes that the candidates for service are "beyond reproach" (*anenklētoi*), then they are allowed to serve. "Beyond reproach" is a summary assessment. It would suggest minimally that the would-be server have the five qualities that the Pastor had rehearsed in verses 8 and 9 (see Titus 1:6–8). The Pastor's use of technical language in verse 10 clearly implies that the verb "serve" (*diakoneitōsan*) designates some specific function within the community. Not all members of the community are called to service in this technical sense.

The process that must be followed before candidates are allowed to serve (v. 10) indicates that even as the Pastor was writing, "service" was on its way to becoming a particular function within the church and that this function would be fulfilled by designated "servers" (*diakonoi*). In the early second century, Polycarp wrote about "servers" in much the same way as the Pastor had some few decades previously:

> In like manner, deacons [*diakonoi*] should be blameless in the presence of His righteousness, as deacons of God and Christ and not of men; not calumniators, not double-tongued, not lovers of money, temperate in all things, compassionate, diligent, walking according to the truth of the Lord who became a server of all [*diakonos pantōn*]. (Pol. *Phil*. 5:2)

The Pastor gives a list of five qualities that a server should possess; Polycarp provides a list of seven (see Pol. *Phil*. 4:3). One of these qualities, "not having a forked tongue," appears on the Pastor's list as well as on Polycarp's. The rest of them, with the exception of the final quality, are stock items in Hellenistic catalogs of virtues. Two of these appear on other lists of virtues in the Pastorals, namely, "not lovers of money" (3:3) and "temperate" (Titus 1:8).

Polycarp seems to have been influenced by the Pastor, since he concludes his list of qualities on a religious note as did the Pastor. Polycarp says that the server must "walk according to the truth of the Lord who became a server of all." The Pastor says that the server must "hold the mystery of faith with a clean conscience." As did the Pastor, Polycarp mandates that the faith of the server be expressed in appropriate conduct. "The mystery of faith" and "the truth of the Lord" respectively sum up the content of Christian faith for the Pastor and Polycarp. A "clean conscience" and "walking according to the truth" are their respective ways of speaking about the Christian life. Both the Pastor and Polycarp make a rhetorical appeal to servers, urging them to believe and to act as they should. The Pastor attempts to motivate servers by mentioning the advantages that will accrue to them (3:13, an example of the *pathos* appeal in Hellenistic rhetoric). Polycarp offers the example of the Lord himself, who became the server of all, to motivate servers (an example of the *ethos* appeal in Hellenistic rhetoric).

[11] Before continuing his list of qualifications expected of the server, the Pastor turns his attention to women (*gynaikas*). These are neither all Christian women (see Titus 2:3–5) nor the wives of the servers. Rather, they are women who have a role analogous to that of servers within the community, as is indicated by "similarly" (*hōsautōs*). The Pastor lists a triad of functions within the community—overseers, servers, women—each with its respective list of requisite qualities. Verses 8–10 give the qualifications of servers, indicating that men are to be scrutinized before being given a role of service within the community. Verse 11 indicates that the group of women to be scrutinized must possess the appropriate personal qualities. Were verse 11 to refer to the wives of the servers, one would have expected that verse 11 appear after verse 12, which identifies the server as a family man. Moreover, had "women" referred to the wives of the servers, it should have been qualified by an appropriate pronoun (see Pol. *Phil.* 4:2, *epeita tas gynaikas hymōn*, "then your wives"). Finally, it would have been very strange for the Pastor to list the qualities expected to be found in the wives of servers when he has not listed any specific expectations for the wives of overseers.

Paul had used the word "server" (*diakonos*, a masculine form) to describe Phoebe, one of his female associates (Rom. 16:1). Phoebe was a benefactor of the church at Cenchreae, one of the port towns that served the city of Corinth. Paul asked the Romans to assist Phoebe in carrying out the task that Paul had entrusted to her. Paul's use of the noun "server" to describe a woman marks the very first time that the word was used of a female. Writing shortly after Paul, Josephus used the word to describe Rachel (*Ant.* 1.19.7 §298). Early in the second century, Pliny the Younger wrote about two Christian slave women "whom they [Christians] call deaconesses" (*quae ministrae dicebantur*). Pliny had these women tortured in order to gain information about the growing Christian movement (*Epistle* 10.96).

The Pastor does not specifically identify the women of 3:11 as "servers." He had no need to do so. The pericope is about servers. Were people to regard the community's servers as upright individuals, they had to possess the qualities that society deemed important. Hellenistic society believed that some household responsibilities were the charge of men while others fell to women. From the time of Aristotle, Hellenistic moralists had taught that some virtues were appropriate for men, others for women. They also believed that men manifest various virtues in ways that are different from the ways in which these same virtues appear in the lives of women. Thus, the Pastor writes about the qualities of male servers, then he writes about the qualities of female servers.

Dignity, sobriety, fidelity, and the absence of slander are among the qualities that a female server should possess. Dignity was the first quality cited for a male server and dignity (*semnas*) appears first on the list for female servers. These servers are also expected not to be slanderous (*mē diabolous*). Polycarp also mentions that this vice of the tongue should not be found in "servers" (Pol. *Phil.* 5:2). The Pastor's circles expected mature women to possess this quality (Titus 2:3). They also expected that male servers avoid vice in their speech (3:8). The concern that the members of the church and especially its leaders avoid various kinds of malicious speech is also found in other late New Testament texts (Eph. 4:29; 5:4; Jas. 1:26; 3:1–12, 14; 4:11; see 1 Tim. 4:7, 12). Polycarp says that the church's widows are to abstain from all slander, evil reports, and false witness (Pol. *Phil.* 4:3).

The Pastor next states that female servers should be sober (*nēphalious*). This quality may refer to the woman's sobriety in bearing, but it might also be a matter of moderation in the use of alcoholic beverages. Overseers and servers are expected to be not addicted to wine (3:3; Titus 1:7); servers and mature women should not be given too much wine (3:8; Titus 2:3). One would expect that a similar quality should be found in the female server and that this is what the Pastor intends when he writes about the sobriety of female servers.

The final quality on the Pastor's list is that female servers be "faithful in all things" (*pistas en pasin*). The appearance of fidelity in an ancient list of virtues usually evoked the general idea of trustworthiness or loyalty. This is probably not what the Pastor intends when he writes about a female server being faithful. The Pastor's previous lists of qualities concluded with the mention of a specifically Christian virtue (3:6, 9; see 3:13). This practice, along with the fact that his circles used words belonging to the *pist-* word group to speak about Christian faith, suggests that the expression "faithful in all things" refers to the woman server's faith (see Titus 1:6).

[12] The Pastor's first series on male servers presented the expectation that servers be upright in their demeanor (3:8–10). After the list of qualities of female servers, the Pastor gives a second series of qualities that male servers are to possess. The server should be the husband of a single wife, he should supervise his children well, and he should manage his own household in an acceptable fashion (3:12).[37]

---

37. The translation of 3:12 renders the phrase *kalōs proïstamenoi,* which appears only once, as both "manage well" (for households, see 4:4) and "supervise well" (for children).

The expectation that the server be a good family man is similar to the expectations set out for the overseer. The overseer should be the husband of a single wife (3:2), should manage his own household well, and should have raised children who are obedient (3:4).

[13] The architectural imagery used in the Pastor's listing of an overseer's qualifications returns in verse 13 as the Pastor describes a double benefit accruing to a server who does the job well. Persons who serve well earn for themselves a good position (*bathmon heautois kalon*). The language comes from the construction industry. The Pastor employs the word "step" (*bathmos*), a word that normally denoted the base of a statue, the first step, the threshold, or one of the steps on a stairway. Figuratively, the term was used in reference to military rank.

It is difficult to determine what exactly the Pastor means when he writes about servers attaining a good step. Could it be that he is speaking of a step in the server's spiritual journey (see 3:13b)?[38] An argument in favor of this understanding is that later Christian literature uses the word "step" in this way. Does "step" mean that one who serves well has found his or her niche within the community?[39] Or does the word suggest that good servers have attained a position in which they can demonstrate their competence and thus be deemed qualified to move on to another position of responsibility within the community?[40] The fact that the Pastor is speaking about serving well within the community—not about the server's moving on to some other function in the community!—argues against this possibility.

Paul's own views on ministry in the church appear in his writings about spiritual gifts, especially in 1 Corinthians 12–14. With regard to these gifts manifest in the ministries of the church, Paul's byword was essentially "to each his own or her own." Thus, many recent commentators think that the ambiguity of the Pastor's expression should be left as it is.[41] The Pastor affirms that one who serves well is in good standing and is well regarded by the community and by God. The Pastor's thought is similar to that of Clement, who writes "he that shall have done this [strive for peace] shall win for himself great renown in Christ, and every place will receive him" (*1 Clem.* 54:3).

Another result of good service is "sufficient confidence" (*pollēn parrhēsian*). The noun literally means to "say all things" (*pas-rhēsis*). Originally, as the writings of Demosthenes show, the term was used in regard to orators in the political arena. "Speaking everything" was a matter of openness and frankness of speech.

---

38. See Holtz 86.
39. See Dornier 65.
40. See *TLNT* 1.250–51.
41. See commentaries by Dibelius and Conzelmann, Brox, Kelly, and Marshall.

This was the kind of freedom of speech that was—or should have been—characteristic of the democratic city-state. Sometimes the expression was used metaphorically to describe a person's openness. Aristotle, for example, wrote that the magnanimous person "must be open both in love and in hate, since concealment shows timidity; and care for the truth rather than for what people will think; and speak and act openly" (*parrhēsiastēs*; *Nicomachean Ethics* 4.3.35).

Eventually the expression "sufficient confidence" (*pollēn parrhēsian*) was used as a cipher for courage and confidence in the presence of important people. In Jewish and Christian literature it sometimes indicated courage and confidence in the presence of God. This kind of courage was an attribute of the prophets. Paul could speak about himself as being "bold enough in Christ" (*pollēn en Christō parrhēsian*, Phlm. 8). He relates this openness and confidence to his faith. Servers who serve well can expect to gain similar confidence in their faith. "With regard to faith in Christ Jesus" (*en pistei tē en Christō Iēsou*) is the way that the Pastor qualifies this confidence. Such language is the language of his circles; the reader would hear familiar echoes in both the reference to faith and the mention of Christ Jesus.

In the Pastor's circles "faith" usually refers to what people believe. In the phrase "Christ Jesus," "Christ" functions more as part of a two-part name than as a title. Thus, given the way that the Pastoral Epistles speak about faith, the words "in Christ Jesus" may be but little more than formulaic and used adjectivally. If so, the Pastor's phrase simply means "with regard to Christian faith."

Excursus 4: Faith

Faith (*pistis*) is one of the most important themes in Paul's letters. In his letter to the Thessalonians he describes how he remembers the faith, love, and hope of that Christian community (1 Thess. 1:3). Sent to visit the community at Thessalonica in Paul's stead, Timothy returned with good news about the community's faith and love (1 Thess. 3:6). Paul urges the Thessalonians to put on the breastplate of faith and love, fitting armor for eschatological times (1 Thess. 5:8). During a decade of writing letters, Paul continued to talk about faith. The controversy with infectious Judaizers who maintained that the members of the church had to follow various Jewish practices, including circumcision, led the apostle to refine his thoughts on faith and to share those thoughts at length with Christian communities located in Rome and various places in the Galatian region.

As do the apostle's letters, 1 Timothy speaks at length about faith. The discerning reader of this epistle quickly comes to realize the Pastor has an understanding of faith that is somewhat different from what Paul means by the term. The epistolary salutation describes Timothy as Paul's "true son in faith" (*gnēsiō teknō en pistei*; see also Titus 1:4). The designation affirms that Timothy is a real son, a genuine son of Paul, but not in the physical sense. Timothy is a son of Paul "in faith." A Jewish rabbi was considered to be the father of his pupils. Those students who appropriated the tradition passed on by the master were considered his sons (see *b. Qidd.* 22a; *b. Sanh.* 19b; 1 Cor. 4:17; Phlm. 10). Similarly, Timothy is Paul's true son in faith because he has appropriated Paul's teaching. "Faith" designates the content of what Timothy had learned from Paul.

This approach to faith continues throughout the epistle. The Pastor writes about a "genuine faith" as something that one is able to possess, along with a pure heart and a good conscience (1:5, 19). He writes about a lack of faith (1:13) and about those who are without faith (5:8). He speaks about deviating from the faith (6:10), missing the mark with regard to faith (6:21), and giving up the faith (4:1). The Pastor describes Paul as a teacher "in faith and truth" (2:7). He talks about "the mystery of faith" (3:9), an expression apparently interchangeable with "the mystery of godliness" summarized in a traditional hymn (3:15–16). The Pastor knows "the message of faith," which he calls "good teaching" (4:6), and speaks about the "good fight of faith" (6:12).

The Pastor juxtaposes "faith" and "love" in 1:14; 2:15; 4:12; and 6:11. In 2:15; 4:12; and 6:11, the juxtaposed pair is part of a larger unit, a short catalog of virtues. The "faith and love" dyad does not stand alone as a summary description of the Christian life as it does in Paul's letters. "Hope" is occasionally added to the traditional pairing (1 Cor. 13:13; 1 Thess. 1:3; 5:8). Nonetheless, "faith and love" are together a constant factor in Paul's description of the Christian life (see, e.g., Gal. 5:6; 1 Thess. 3:6)

First Timothy 3:13 speaks of "faith in Christ Jesus," but that mention of faith seems to be rather similar to what the Pastor calls the mystery of faith, the mystery of godliness. The idea that the Pastor's circles looked upon faith objectively, as that which is to be believed, rather than subjectively is confirmed by a reading of the two other Pastoral Epistles. Second Timothy and Titus mention faith in short lists of virtues that always mention love but not necessarily adjacent to faith (see 2 Tim. 2:22; 3:10; Titus 2:2). Second Timothy 1:5 speaks about a "genuine faith," and 2 Tim. 2:18 mentions those who subvert the faith.

Second Timothy 4:7 speaks of fighting the fight of faith, as does 1 Tim. 6:12. The epistolary greeting of Titus uses "faith" in much the same way as does the greeting in 1 Timothy. Titus 1:4 speaks of Titus as Paul's "true son according to the common faith." This expression is roughly equivalent to 1 Timothy's "true son in faith" (1:2), yet adds the idea that what Paul has passed on to Titus is shared by others as well. In this sense it is a common faith.

Other passages in 2 Timothy and Titus confirm that the Pastor's circles use the word "faith" to designate the content of faith, what they believed.[42] Thus, Titus is encouraged to correct Cretans so that they might be "sound in faith," not like those who have turned away from the truth (Titus 1:13). People who oppose the truth can be described as "unqualified with regard to the faith" (2 Tim. 3:8).

The phrase "in faith" was used in the epistolary salutations to describe Timothy and Titus as Paul's sons in faith. Coupled with "love" the phrase is also found in the farewell greeting of Titus: "Greet those who love us in faith" (Titus 3:15). In 2 Tim. 1:13 the Pastor speaks of "faith and love that is in [*en*] Christ Jesus," a phrase with a distinctively Pauline ring. The Pastor's words describe how Timothy is to receive the message, identified as "the model of sound words that you heard from me" (2 Tim. 1:13) and as "the

---

42. The content of faith is what scholastic theologians would later call the *fides quae*, "faith which" is believed, as distinct from *fides qua*, "faith by which" we believe.

precious treasure entrusted to you through the Holy Spirit" (2 Tim. 1:14). "Faith in Christ Jesus" appears in 1 Tim. 3:13. Here, as in 2 Tim. 1:13 and 3:15, the Pauline expression "in Christ Jesus" appears to be merely formulaic. It was the virtual equivalent of the adjective "Christian," not yet in current use (see Acts 11:26; cf. Acts 26:28; 1 Pet. 4:16).

The expression "faith in Christ Jesus" recurs when the Pastor writes about the usefulness of the Scriptures in 2 Tim. 3:14–17. He states that the Scriptures, the sacred writings of the Jews, are "capable of instructing you with regard to salvation through [*dia*] faith in Christ Jesus" (2 Tim. 3:15; cf. 1 Tim. 1:4). Today readers might think that the Pastor is referring to Paul's teaching on justification by faith. Paul, however, does not use the phrase "salvation through faith," nor do the Pastorals speak about justification by faith. In 2 Tim. 3:15 the Pastor states that the Jewish Scriptures are useful for teaching about salvation as that is understood in the tradition of Paul and the Pastorals.

Teaching

Second Timothy 3:16 identifies "teaching" (*didaskalia*) as one of Timothy's mandated activities. Timothy had observed Paul's teaching (2 Tim. 3:10) and was to teach in similar fashion. By citing "teaching" as the first of various aspects of Paul's life observed by Timothy, the Pastor implies that Paul is a teacher above all else. Other passages in the Pastorals confirm that this is so.

The Pastorals know that there are many teachers who captivate the occasional attention of the wayward (2 Tim. 4:3) but that there is only one teacher whom the community is to revere. That is Paul, who alone merits the title "teacher" (*didaskalos*). Paul is described as a herald, apostle, and teacher in 1 Tim. 2:7 and 2 Tim. 1:11. The interpretive triad used in these two passages is designed so that the recipients might understand that, as an apostle, Paul is a teacher. As the apostle, he is the teacher par excellence. This is especially clear in 1 Tim. 2:7, where a mild oath emphasizes the notion that Paul is "teacher of the Gentiles in faith and truth." The Pastoral's understanding of Paul as the teacher sheds light on the way that Paul's apostolate is presented in Titus's epistolary greeting: "Paul, God's slave and apostle of Jesus Christ for the sake of the faith of God's chosen ones, the full knowledge of truth that is for the sake of godliness" (Titus 1:1).

Paul is portrayed as the "herald, apostle, and teacher" in 2 Tim. 1:11. Immediately thereafter Timothy is exhorted to "preserve the model of sound words that you heard from me" (2 Tim. 1:13). What Timothy has heard from Paul is a paradigm (*hypo-typosin*; see 1 Tim 1:16) of sound teaching. "Sound" or "healthy" (*hygiainontōn*, a word that does not occur in Paul's letters) is part of the characteristic vocabulary of the Pastorals. "Teaching" (1 Tim. 1:10; 2 Tim. 4:3; Titus 1:9; 2:1), "faith" (Titus 1:13; 2:2), "message" (*logon hygiē*, Titus 2:8), and "words" (1 Tim. 6:3; 2 Tim. 1:13) are described as "sound." One can hope that older men are "sound in faith" (Titus 2:2); one wishes that the correction of opponents is so effective that they become "sound in faith" (Titus 1:13).

Homer (*Iliad* 8.524) characterized some speech as "sound" (*hygiēs*) long
before the Pastor did. "Sound" appeared in the writings of many philosophers,
beginning with Plato (*Republic* 9.584e) and including some philosophers,
more or less contemporary with Paul and the Pastorals. Herodotus, the fifth-
century historian, spoke of soundness in matters political or religious
(Herodotus 7.157). Epictetus considered that what philosophers teach is sound
(*Discourses* 1.11.28) and that the essential quality of any judgment is that it
be sound (*Discourses* 2.15.2; see 3.9.2–5). What was true or valid was by definition also sound and salutary. Thus, Philo concludes his praise of Abraham
by saying that the patriarch followed a sound impulse even without the benefit of the written Scriptures (*Abraham* 275). In the same treatise, Philo uses
the very expression "sound words," also used by the Pastor in 2 Tim. 1:13
(*Abraham* 223).

This contemporary philosophical discourse suggests that when Paul's teaching (1:13) is proposed as a paradigm of sound discourse, its content is reasonable and its message beneficial to those who listen to it. Sound teaching is
implicitly set over and against teaching that is not healthy. Undoubtedly there
was some teaching in the air that could not be considered sound. So each of the
three Pastorals contrast sound teaching that leads to godliness with teaching that
leads to moral perversity (1 Tim. 1:9–10; 6:3; 2 Tim. 4:3; Titus 1:9, 13). First
Timothy 6:3–5 is particularly graphic in this regard. The Pastor employs medical metaphors to contrast those whose "faith" is healthy with those whose
minds are diseased: "If anyone teaches otherwise and does not agree with the
sound words about our Lord Jesus Christ, the teaching that leads to godliness,
that person is puffed up, . . . having a diseased appetite for arguments and verbal warfare from which come . . . the constant disputations of people who have
lost their minds."

Paul had been concerned that the kerygma be faithfully passed down (1 Cor.
12:23; 15:1–3). The Pastor's "model of sound words" is essentially the kerygma
proclaimed by Paul then passed on by his disciples. It is said to have been heard
from Paul (2 Tim. 1:13) and is described as a precious treasure (2 Tim. 1:14).
"Sound teaching" is a cipher for the Pauline kerygma. Accordingly, the Pastor
writes about "sound teaching according to the glorious gospel of the blessed
God, which has been entrusted to me" (1 Tim. 1:10–11). The message concerns
Christ Jesus (1 Tim. 6:13), as does the mystery of godliness (1 Tim. 3:16). As
Paul's true son in faith, Titus is to hold on to this treasure (Titus 1:9; cf. 2 Tim.
1:13–14) and to speak out the healthy message (Titus 2:1, 8). In doing so he can
encourage the community (Titus 1:9) and correct opponents (Titus 1:9, 13; 2:8).

Occasionally the Pastorals employ a banal "these things" (*tauta*) to designate what it is that Timothy and Titus have heard from Paul, the things that they
are expected to convey to believers in Ephesus and on Crete (see 1 Tim. 4:6,

11; 5:7; 6:2; 2 Tim. 2:2, 14; Titus 2:15; 3:8). "These things" are all that Paul has taught (see 1 Tim. 3:14; 5:21).

The Full Knowledge of Truth

Using philosophical language to describe the preservation and passing along of the Pauline kerygma, the Pastor's circles anticipated the efforts of later apologists who sought to explain Christianity in philosophical terms. Their efforts were akin to those of Philo, who sought to explain the Torah to his Hellenistic contemporaries by means of allegory and other philosophical categories. The expression, "the full knowledge of truth" (*epignōsis alētheias*, 1 Tim. 2:4; 2 Tim. 2:25; 3:7; Titus 1:1; see Heb. 10:26), with its philosophical ring appears to be part of an attempt to explain the Christian message to Hellenists. The fixed expression clearly designates the norm of Christian faith.

The epistolary salutation of Titus uses the expression to explain what is meant by "faith." The Pastor writes about "Paul, God's slave and apostle of Jesus Christ for the sake of the faith of God's chosen ones, the full knowledge of truth that is for the sake of godliness" (Titus 1:1). In 1 Tim. 4:3 the faithful are described as "those who have full knowledge of the truth" (*epegnōkosi tēn alētheian*; see 2 John 1). "The full knowledge of truth" seems to be a technical term used in the Pastor's circles to designate the norm of Christian truth, the "faith." Paul was the teacher of the Gentiles in faith and truth (1 Tim. 2:7). The church, God's house, is the pillar and foundation of truth (1 Tim. 3:15). Timothy was expected to teach the message of truth (*ton logon tēs alētheias*, 2 Tim. 2:15).

The formulaic expression "the full knowledge of truth" does not seem to have been in general use in philosophical writings. It does not even appear in the writings of Plato. An exception to the general nonuse of the expression is Epictetus, who writes that "man has received from nature measures and standards for discovering the truth" (*eis epignōsin tēs alētheias*, *Discourses* 2.20.21). Epictetus then goes on to talk about godliness (*Discourses* 2.20.22), as does the author of Titus 1:1.

The relationship between the full knowledge of truth and godliness (see Excursus 7) indicates that Christian belief is related to a type of conduct that is appropriate to one's piety. People who are captivated by sin and beholden to their passions cannot reach the full knowledge of truth (2 Tim. 3:7). God might give a gift of repentance so that those who have opposed the Christian message might come to the full knowledge of truth (2 Tim. 2:25). God's will is that all people be saved and come to the full knowledge of truth. The faithful who have full knowledge of truth accept God's good gifts. Those who are not faithful turn from the message of truth (see 2 Tim. 4:4). They miss the mark of truth. Thus,

Hymenaeus and Philetus say that the resurrection has already occurred (2 Tim. 2:17–18). By teaching in this way, they subvert some people's belief. They oppose the truth, as did the legendary Jannes and Jambres (2 Tim. 3:8). In sum, heterodox teachers are simply deprived of the truth (1 Tim. 6:5).

Creedal Formulas

"Faith" is what the faithful are to believe. It is the truth, the full knowledge of the truth. With the aid of the teaching of the church, the pillar of truth, the faithful are able to arrive at full knowledge, while their opponents are deprived of this knowledge. Despite this emphasis on the content of faith, the Pastoral Epistles do not employ any creedal formulae in the narrow sense of the term.

Traditional creedal formulae are generally introduced by some form of the verb "to believe" (*pisteuō*), followed by "that" (*hoti*), with an affirmation of the death and resurrection of Christ, or at least one of these claims. The classic case is 1 Cor. 15:3–5. Not all of the characteristic elements of the creedal formula are present in every creedal formula cited by Paul. In every instance, however, sufficient indicators are present for the reader to fully understand that Paul is passing along a terse formulation of the traditional faith of the church.

Notwithstanding the relative absence of traditional creedal formulae from the Pastoral Epistles, these writings contain a number of isolable passages that express some of the core beliefs of the early church. Their traditional nature is indicated by their stylized formulation and one or another explicit indication that the author is sharing traditional faith formulations with his readers. One such indication is the formula "This is a trustworthy saying" (*pistos ho logos*, see Excursus 1), which appears in both a shorter version (1 Tim. 3:1; 2 Tim. 2:11; Titus 3:8) and an expanded version (1 Tim. 1:15; 4:9). The formula is the Pastor's guarantee of the reliability of the tradition that he is passing along to his readers.

First Timothy also uses another formula to identify a traditional formulation of faith. This is "the mystery of godliness" (1 Tim. 3:16), otherwise described as the "mystery of faith" (1 Tim. 1:9). Both of these formulae highlight the idea that the hymn found in 1 Tim. 3:16 reflects the faith of the church.

In 2 Tim. 2:8, the verb "remember" (*mnēmoneue*) is used to introduce words that hearken back to the creedal formulae of Paul's authentic letters. The Pastor writes, "Remember Jesus Christ, raised from the dead, of the seed of David, in accordance with my proclamation" (2 Tim. 2:8). The traditional nature of this formulation is indicated not only by the fact that this is the only place in 2 Timothy in which the name "Jesus" precedes the "Christ" title but also by the fact that the words "raised from the dead" (*egēgermenon ek nekrōn*) are not found elsewhere in the Pastoral Epistles. They are, however, a pointed expression of the faith that Paul so often shared with the recipients of his letters. As the Pastor was writing 2 Timothy he remembered the traditional creed of the church; he would have his readers remember it as well.

The Church's Great Confession
1 Timothy 3:14–16

First Timothy 3:14–16 is one of the most important passages in the letter. It gives the reason why the epistle was written. The patronymic author expresses a desire to visit the recipients of his missive but expresses some concern that he might be delayed. In the meantime (see 4:13), they will have his epistle.

Hellenistic letters frequently spoke of the writer's desire to visit those to whom he was writing, as do modern letters, but the expression of a possible delay in the fulfillment of those desires is an unusual trait in both Hellenistic and modern letters. Mention of the desire to visit provides additional verisimilitude to the epistle. The Pastor's writing about a delay is an indication that the visit is not likely to occur. This reflects the pseudepigraphic nature of the Pastor's missive. Paul will not be able to visit Timothy and those who were with him because he is long since dead. The motif of the prisoner in the deuteropauline "captivity epistles" serves a similar function (Eph. 3:1; 4:1; Col. 4:18).

Another important feature of this pericope is its rich ecclesiology. The church is described as the house of the living God who has assembled people together to serve as his householders. The metaphor of the house continues as the author describes the role of God's people. They are the pillar and foundation of the truth.

The magnificent christological hymn of verse 16 expresses the great mystery of the Christian faith. Hanna Stettler has described the hymn as a Christ-psalm that offers a christological summa (Stettler 86, 299). Bart Ehrman comments that this is "one of the finest specimens of a preliterary creed in all of the New Testament: its lapidary character . . . , the striking syntactical parallelism of its six clauses . . . , and the dependence of each clause on the introductory relative pronoun" (Ehrman, 77).[43] The Pastor has strategically placed his christological hymn between his reflections on those who are to serve the

---

43. Bart D. Ehrman, *The Orthodox Corruption of Scripture: The Effect of Early Christological Controversies on the Text of the New Testament* (New York: Oxford University Press, 1993).

community in responsible positions and the apocalyptic warning of 4:1–5. The hymn portrays Christ as the risen and enthroned one. This motif provides an authoritative warrant for the paraenesis of the encompassing pericopes.

3:14 I am writing these things to you,[a] hoping to come to you soon, 15 so that, if I am delayed, you know how you ought to conduct yourself in the house of God, which is the assembly of the living God, the pillar and foundation of the truth. 16 Everyone agrees: Great is the mystery of godliness:

(He) who[b] was manifest in the flesh,
    was vindicated in the spirit,
appeared to angels,
    was proclaimed among the nations,
believed in in the world,
    lifted up in glory.

a. "To you" (*pros se*) is omitted by F, G, and a few other manuscripts.

b. The masculine singular relative pronoun, *hos*, is generally attested in the oldest manuscripts (e.g., ℵ, A, C, F, G, 33) and is found in other New Testament hymn fragments (see Phil. 2:6; Col. 1:15). Some late manuscripts read *theos*, a reading that could reflect a deliberate alteration or a misreading of *hos* (ΟΣ) as an abbreviation of the word "God" (ΘΣ).

[3:14–15a] It is not unusual for a letter writer, ancient or modern, to state the purpose of the letter and to express a desire to visit those to whom he or she is writing. Most of Paul's letters state the reason why he wrote (Rom. 15:15; 1 Cor. 4:14; 5:11; 9:15; 2 Cor. 9:1; 13:10; Phil. 3:1; Phlm. 19, 21; see also 2 Cor. 2:3, 4, 9, 7:12; Gal. 1:20; 1 Thess. 4:9; 5:1). The apostle often expressed a desire to visit those to whom he was writing (Rom. 1:11; 15:22; 1 Cor. 16:3, 5–7; 2 Cor. 12:14; 13:1–2; 1 Thess. 2:17–3:5; Phlm. 22; see Phil. 1:27). Occasionally he even wrote about the length of his stay or the intended purpose of his visit.

What the Pastor says about the purpose of this missive and of Paul's desire to visit (vv. 14–15) is unique within the New Testament's Pauline corpus. The author makes provision for Paul's "delay" and states what the recipients of the epistle are to do during the period of the apostle's absence. The Pastor's explicit mention of the desire to visit enhances the epistolary nature of his text. Telling its recipients what they are to do during the time of Paul's absence contributes to its verisimilitude.

Paul was dead when the epistle was written. It was impossible for the apostle to visit with this community. Paul's "delay" is thus an excuse for Paul's protracted absence, his permanent absence from the community. The Pastor's explicit reflection on his revered mentor's indefinite absence provides cover for the timely advice that he now offers in Paul's name. His writing about what the recipients of the epistle are to do during the time of Paul's absence in this way is an indication of the pseudepigraphic nature of his missive.

[15b–d] The purpose of the epistle is that "Timothy" should know how he is to conduct himself. He should know how to behave in the place where God dwells. The verb *anastrephesthai* (used by Paul only in 2 Cor. 1:12; see Eph. 2:3) does not so much refer to Timothy's private behavior as it does to his activity as leader of the community. Timothy leads the community by exhorting its leadership and its membership. Thus, the real purpose of the epistle is that the members of the community know how it is that they should act as members of the household of God.

"The household of God is described as the assembly of the living God." description that serves the Pastor's apologetic interests. From the outset of his missive the Pastor has been concerned with would-be teachers of the law (1:7–8). His use of the Adam and Eve tradition (2:13–15) demonstrates his own familiarity with the Torah as well as his ability to derive appropriate teaching therefrom. With a haggadic use of a biblical motif, the Pastor now describes his community as "the assembly of the living God." The biblical tradition of the assembly is realized anew in the assembly of the Pastor's community.

Polemical intent is also evident in the Pastor's description of God as the "living God." The participle describes God in his original trait, that by which God is distinguished from all else. Swearing by the living God was the form of the biblical oath (e.g., 2 Sam. 12:5). God is alive and dynamic. God has created the universe; God continues to maintain the existence of the universe. God has created humanity and God has chosen the people among whom he dwells. The apostle Paul was heir to this tradition. He uses the phrase "the living God" in Rom. 9:26; 2 Cor. 3:3; 6:16; 1 Thess. 1:9 (see Heb. 3:12; 9:14; 10:31; 12:22). In 1 Thess. 1:9, the apostle uses traditional language to contrast the living God with the inert idols of the Gentiles (see Ps. 115). Some polemical intent may be discerned in the Pastor's reference to "the assembly of the living God." The God to whom the community belongs is not merely the God of the past, to whom the Torah might testify, nor is their God a dead emperor who has been "divinized."

Verse 15d continues with architectural imagery. The Pastor describes the house-assembly as "the pillar and foundation of the truth." The pieces of construction cited by the Pastor convey the idea of solidness. The Greek term for "pillar," *stylos*, generally denoted a column used as a support or bearing. In the New Testament, the term is used in a metaphorical sense to refer to people: Cephas, James, and John in Gal. 2:9, the one who conquers in

Rev. 3:12,[44] and the community in this verse. The Greek term *hedraiōma*, "foundation," is related to an adjective used by Paul (1 Cor. 7:37; 15:58; see Col. 1:23). The word is synonymous with *themelios*, which Paul uses in the construction metaphor of 1 Cor. 3:10–12 to describe his own function in the construction.

In the post-Pauline construction of the house of God, the community is comparable with Paul in its foundational role. The pairing of "pillar" and "foundation" may be a hendiadys used to convey the idea of a firm foundation. The assembly is the firm foundation of "the truth." The truth (*tēs alētheias*) is "the faith," the full knowledge of which (*epignōsis alētheias*, 2:4; 2 Tim. 2:25; 3:7; Titus 1:1; see 1 Tim. 4:3; cf. Heb. 10:26) is a hallmark of the community's existence. The Pastor's description of the church is analogous to the way the Qumran community viewed itself: "They shall lay a foundation of truth for Israel, for the community of an eternal covenant" (1QS 5:5). Qumran's imagery was apparently derived from Isa. 28:16 (see 1QS 8:7–10).

Excursus 5: "The House of God": Theology and Sociology

The "house" or the "household" (*oikos* or *oikia*)[45] is the dominant ecclesiological metaphor in the Pastoral Epistles. No other passage in the corpus in which this metaphor is used is as rich in its theological import as is 1 Tim. 3:15. This verse contains one of the most succinct ecclesiological formulations in the entire New Testament. Its tripartite formula affirms that the community is(1) the house of God (see 2 Tim. 2:19), (2) the assembly of the living God, and (3) the pillar and foundation of the truth. The profound theological understanding of the Christian community expressed in the triad is unmatched by any other early Christian text.

With the "house of God" metaphor (see 1 Pet. 4:17), the Pastor brings a profound reflection to bear on the assembly-in-a-house that is the church. This house belongs to God. The living God is not, however, an absentee landlord. The house of God is God's dwelling place. Within the biblical tradition, the house of God (Dan. 1:2; see 1 Kgs. 3:1) was the temple in which God dwelt (2 Sam. 7:1–6, 12–13; 1 Kgs. 5:5; 6:11–14). The idea that there should be a dwelling place for God among his people goes back to the tradition of the ark of the covenant (see Exod. 25–31, 36–40). A biblical tradition states that David built a tent to enshrine the ark (2 Sam. 6:17; 1 Chr. 15:3). Carried about inside the tent (2 Sam. 7:6), both the ark and the tent were brought into the temple during the reign of Solomon (1 Kgs. 8:4; 2 Chr. 5:5). Josephus reports that "this was a sign of God's being present and dwelling . . . in the place which had been newly built *Ant.* 8.4.1 §102. The temple to which the people came was the place where God dwelt. Thus, the motifs of assembly and dwelling place come together in the biblical notion of the "house of God." There God dwells; there God's people come together to meet God.

44. The term "pillar" is also found in Rev. 10:1, in a simile derived from Exod. 13:21–22.
45. The two words are virtually synonymous. They designate a building or a group of people who share a common habitation.

These two ideas are also present in the Synoptic passages that refer to the temple as "the house of God" (Mark 2:26; 11:17 and par.; Matt. 12:4; 21:13; Luke 6:4; 19:46; see John 2:16–17). The Epistle to the Hebrews describes the heavenly temple as "the house of God" (Heb. 10:21). The apostle Paul did not write about "the house of God." Nonetheless, Paul called the Christians of Corinth "God's building" (*theou oikodomē este*, 1 Cor. 3:9b). The terms that he used to describe the construction of this building and its quality control were commonly found in contracts for construction work. Paul's exposition ends with a rhetorical question: "Do you not know that you are God's temple and that God's Spirit dwells in you [*oikei en hymin*] (1 Cor. 3:16). This architectural metaphor may have inspired the Pastor's use of architectural imagery in 3:15b–d.

The Pastor writes about the "house of God" some time after the destruction of the Jerusalem temple (see 1 Pet. 4:17;[46] cf. 1 Pet. 2:5). Lest there be any misunderstanding, the Pastor explains what he means by "the house of God." It is not a building made of stone or adobe; it is "the assembly of the living God" (v. 15c). The phrase *ekklēsia theou zōntos* is generally translated "the church of the living God." It is, however, preferable to retain the root meaning of *ekklēsia* and translate the phrase as "the assembly of the living God." The house of God is where God's people come together.

As does the "house of God" tradition, "assembly" likewise hearkens back to the Exodus tradition. The Bible frequently describes Israel during the time of its salvific journey from Egypt to the promised land as a "gathering," an "assembly" (*qāhāl*), or more specifically as the "assembly of Yahweh" (*qĕhal YHWH*). The Greek Bible renders the Hebrew word as *synagōgē* or *ekklēsia*; Deuteronomy frequently uses the phrase *ekklēsia Kyriou*, "assembly of the Lord," to render the Hebrew *qĕhal YHWH* (see, e.g., Deut. 23:2–4 [LXX]). The Israelites assembled to hear the word of the Lord spoken through Moses (Deut. 4:10; 9:10; 18:16; 31:30). The Pastor actualizes that tradition by using the phrase "assembly of the living God" to refer to the church. For the benefit of his audience, he "remembers" Israel's primary experience of salvation, implying that the Christian community is in the midst of a primal experience of salvation.

The qualification of the church as "the house of God" and "the assembly of the living God" brings the Pastor's understanding of the church into a specifically theological perspective. The Pastor's ecclesiology is a function of his theology, his understanding of God. At the beginning of the epistle, the Pastor states that the recipient of the missive is to avoid any kind of speculation that would deter from "God's plan of salvation [*oikonomian theou*] in faith" (1:4). The Greek word *oikonomia*, derived from *oikos*, "house," and *nomos*, "law" or "custom," is literally "the law of the household." The term basically meant household management, the task of a "steward" (*oikonomos*), the chief of the householder's staff and generally a slave. The term was sometimes used to connote principles of administration or management. Used of God, the term designates God's management plan, which later generations of theologians would describe as God's plan of salvation.

The Pastor uses household imagery to speak of God again toward the end of his epistle. Its final doxology proclaims God as one "who inhabits [*oikōn*] unapproachable light"

---

46. This is the only other New Testament passage that explicitly calls the church "the house of God." The literary form of 1 Peter and the circumstances of its composition are similar to those of 1 Timothy.

(6:16). The notion that God inhabits unapproachable light is novel within Jewish and Christian literature, but the underlying ideas are deeply rooted in biblical tradition. Judaism often spoke of God's glory. To speak of God's glory the Greek Bible uses the term *doxa* as a translation of the Hebrew *kābôd*. This Hebrew term conveys an image of weightiness. Gradually the image of tremendous luminosity became associated with the idea of God's glory. "Glory" is essentially a metaphor that bespeaks the transcendence of God. The Pastor's doxology evokes this imagery when it describes God as inhabiting, that is, dwelling or making a home, in unapproachable light. The unapproachability implies that God cannot be seen. The God to whom the Pastor offers praise is radiant in glory and active where he dwells.

With a mention of God's plan of household management at the beginning of the epistle (1:4) and a mention of God's dwelling place at the end of the epistle (6:16), the Pastor has encompassed the entire missive within the theological perspective of God's house. The significance of this theological perspective is unfolded in 3:15 when the Pastor writes about "the house of God, which is the assembly of the living God." Rich in its theological significance, the image of the house to describe the church is similarly rich in its sociological and ecclesiological significance.

Household language is used to describe the Christian church throughout the New Testament. The use of domestic idioms reflects the social situation of early Christianity. The first generations of believers gathered in one another's homes. This situation is patent when Paul writes about "the church in their/your house" (*tēn kat'oikon autōn ekklēsian*, Rom. 16:5; 1 Cor. 16:19; Phlm. 2; see Col. 4:15). The Christian household is the *Sitz im Leben* of New Testament epistolary literature. These letters were written to groups of believers who gathered in people's homes. The gathering together of Christians in household units is suggested almost as often as the New Testament uses household language.

The early church existed "at home." The house was where the church happened, where it came together as an assembly. There the members of the assembly listened to passing missionaries whose lodging had been provided by a hospitable Christian householder. Those who gathered in a household church could provide assistance to those who could not be present. Thus, the household of Onesiphorus attended to the needs of the imprisoned Paul (2 Tim. 1:16). At home, in the house, Christians discussed traditional stories about Jesus and listened to the reading of letters from Paul. Sometimes Paul asked that his greetings be extended to another household (Rom. 16:11; see 2 Tim. 4:19). In the house, the reader could explain the apostle's words; there, too, the assembly discussed the meaning of the kerygmatic message. There, finally, the assembly could break bread and celebrate its traditional meal, the "Lord's Supper" (1 Cor. 11:18–34).

The household was the cell of Hellenistic society, its basic constitutive unit. The empire was largely composed of cities. Cities were composed of households (Titus 1:5). These households were organized according to traditional social patterns, with the paterfamilias as the head. He had power over his wife, his children, his slaves, and assorted clients. Within the household each one had his or her place and function. Several New Testament texts implicitly reflect the structure and organization of a Hellenistic household. Second Timothy gives a good description of the well-ordered house: "In a large house there are not only golden and silver vessels but also wooden and crockery vessels, some for noble use, others for ignoble use. If anyone cleanses himself or herself from these things, he or she will be a noble vessel, sanctified, useful for the master of the house, and ready for every good work" (2 Tim. 2:20–21).

"Household codes," whose origins date to the time of Plato and Aristotle, summarized the way that members of the household were to relate to one another. Via Hellenistic Judaism and the dominant Stoic ethic of the era, household codes entered into Christian paraenesis. These codes fostered social order, social responsibility, and respect for one another's role in society. Several passages in the Pastoral Epistles provide examples of the Christian use of this literary form (see 1 Tim. 2:8–15; 5:1–2; 6:1–2; Titus 2:1–10; 3:1). Household codes are also found in other late New Testament texts (see Col. 3:18–4:1; Eph. 5:21–6:9; 1 Pet. 2:11–3:12) and some early patristic texts (*1 Clem.* 1:3; 21:6–8).

The household codes that appear in 1 Timothy 2, 5, and 6 show not only that the Pastor was firmly rooted in the culture of the Greco-Roman world but also that he was concerned that the members of the community respect the social conventions of the times. If people lived in well-ordered households where order and responsibility reigned, it was important that Christians live in well-ordered households, with its structures and mutual responsibility. Were they not to do so, they would not gain that respect and admiration from those outside the community for which the Pastor strove (see 2:2; 3:7). The respectability and acceptance of the Christian household was one of his pastoral concerns.

Linked closely with the household code as a conveyer of social expectations and requirements was the Hellenistic catalog of virtues. Two such catalogs appear in 1 Timothy 3, just a few verses before the Pastor's pregnant sayings on the church and the mystery of godliness in 3:15–16. The first is a list of qualities for one who would serve the church as an overseer (3:2–6).

Among other things, the Pastor expects the would-be overseer to have managed his own household well and to have raised children who are submissive. Of the fifteen qualities cited in the Pastor's profile, effective household management is particularly emphasized. The Pastor makes his point with an effective rhetorical question: "If someone does not know how to manage his own household, how can he take care of the church of God?" (3:5).[47] If the overseer is to be a manager of the church, he must have proven himself as a successful manager of his own household. That experience serves as a test of his fitness for the awesome task of overseeing God's household.

Similar thoughts on the importance of household management are found in the Epistle to Titus: "The overseer should be without reproach as God's steward" (Titus 1:7; see 1 Cor. 4:1). In the Greco-Roman world, the steward (*oikonomos*), generally a slave, had responsibility for overseeing the other slaves in the household. He assigned their tasks and coordinated their work so that the entire household functioned smoothly and effectively. When Christians came together in the homes of those who served as patrons of the "house church," a good manager, the steward, had responsibility for assuring the good order of the assembly.

The Epistle to Titus describes the qualities expected of someone who is to function within the church as an overseer. First Timothy adds to the list of qualities expected in

47. Since the church is an assembly (*ekklēsia*) of God's people, the rhetorical question may imply that the assembly gathers together in the home of the overseer.

the overseer a list of qualities expected of a server (*diakonos*) in the community (1 Tim. 3:8–13). It is expected that servers in God's household, as the overseer (3:4), should have managed their own households well (3:12). The way that the Pastor describes the domestic responsibilities of the overseer and servers within their own households provides an analogy for their activity within God's household (*oikō theou*, 3:15).

The Pastor's concern for a well-ordered and socially responsible community continues to be evident in the way that he speaks about widows (5:3–16). Twice the Pastor talks about the responsibility of younger adults to take care of the widowed members of their household. "They should first of all learn how to act in godly fashion toward their own households [*ton idion oikon*] and pay back their forebears," he writes (5:4) and again, "If anyone does not provide for his or her kin, especially if they are members of the household, that person has denied the faith and is worse than someone who is without faith" (5:8). When his attention turns from the care of elderly widows to younger widows, the Pastor continues to focus on the importance of the household. He encourages young widows to marry, raise a family, and take care of their households (*oikodespotein*, 5:14), rather than being busybodies, gadding about, and visiting other people's houses (*tas oikias*). Young Christian widows should not trouble other households.

Second Timothy and Titus express great apprehension lest evil people disturb the Christian household. In its description of evildoers who will arise in apocalyptic times, 2 Tim. 3:6 says that some will enter homes (*tas oikias*) and captivate silly little women. Speaking of some stubborn and malicious Cretans, especially those from among the Jewish population, the Epistle to Titus urges its recipient to rein in those who "subvert whole households [*holous oikous*], teaching what ought not to be taught for the sake of sordid gain" (Titus 1:11).

The household was the basic unit of society in the Greco-Roman world, an essential principle of its stability. First Timothy and Titus exploit this social reality and the fact that the church functioned within household units to present various ideas on church order. Church order was to be achieved by following contemporary patterns of social organization. In addition to providing a vehicle for a reflection on church order, the idea of the household provided the Pastor an opportunity to offer profound theological reflection on the church, the house of God.

[16a] Verse 16 offers a tightly structured christological hymn.[48] The Pastor provides a formal introduction for this hymn: "Everyone agrees: Great is the mystery of godliness." Formed from the present passive participle of the verb *homologeō*, which Paul uses in regard to the confession of faith (Rom. 10:9–10), the rarely used adverb *homologoumenōs* (4 Macc. 6:31; 7:16; 16:1) means "admittedly," "undoubtedly," "obviously." Jurists and Stoic philosophers used the term to speak of something that was beyond dispute, something that everyone could agree to. The nuance of the term in its literary usage was not so absolute. It simply meant "by common consent." Thus, the Pastor's use

---

48. See E. Testa, "L'inno sul 'Sacramentum pietatis' (1 Tim 3,16)," *SBFLA* 46 (1996): 87–100.

of the expression suggests that what is to follow is almost a confession of covenanted faith. Spicq suggests the translation, "Yes, as we all agree, great is the mystery of godliness" (*TLNT* 2.584).

What the Pastor's community confesses is "the mystery of godliness." The adjective "great" reflects the moderate polemic of the pericope. Hellenists may have the mysteries, which they celebrate in their various cults, but the core of the Christian faith is the *great* mystery. Servers are specifically exhorted to hold on to this mystery (3:9). Only those who do so are qualified to become servers within the community.

The motif of godliness appears in each of the Pastorals, although it is particularly important in this epistle (see Excursus 7). "Godliness" sums up the entirety of the Christian life (2:2; 4:7, 8; 6:3, 5, 6, 11). The introduction to the hymn speaks of the mystery of godliness (*to tēs eusebeias mystērion*, the Vulgate's *pietatis sacramentum*). The confessional hymn expresses the content of this mystery, namely, the paschal reality. The paschal reality is the mystery of godliness insofar as it leads to the Christian life. What believers confess leads them to act as they do. They are different from others because of their specific profession of faith and the way of life that they lead in consequence of that belief.

[16b–c] The christological hymn opens with a relative pronoun, as do the christological hymns in Phil. 2:6–11 and Col. 1:15–20. It is characterized by its tight structure and its economy of words. Apart from the introductory "who" (*hos*), there are but seventeen words in the hymn. Each of its six stichs begins with a verb in the aorist passive followed by a nominal construction in the dative. With the exception of "angels" each noun in the dative is the object of the preposition "in" (*en*). The formal unity of the hymn is constituted not only by the parallelism of its six stichs but also by the literary devices of homoioteleuton and paronomasia.[49] Each of the aorist verbs ends in *thē*, thus providing a tone that echoes throughout the hymn.

The Pastor presents the hymn as if it is well known in the community, not as one that he himself had composed for this epistle. He states that the hymn is their common confession, a traditional expression of their faith. One stich (*a*) in each of the three pairs speaks of an earthly reality, the other (*b*) speaks of a heavenly reality. The pairs are arranged in a chiastic *a-b, b-a, a-b* order.

Key terms in the first pair of stichs identify two spheres of reality, the flesh (*en sarki*) and the spirit (*en pneumati*). These terms reflect the Pauline and biblical antithesis between the created order and that of the Creator, the material and the divine. This kind of contrast between "flesh" and "spirit" appears in the creedal fragment found in the greeting of Paul's letter to the Romans (Rom. 1:3–4; see Gal. 5:19, 22). The creed in Romans 1 focuses on the Pauline

---

49. These literary devices are, respectively, the use of similar endings and the repetition of similar sounds.

kerygma, whose core is the resurrection of Christ (see 2 Tim. 2:8). It distinguishes the Son "according to the flesh" from the Son "according to the Spirit." First Peter 3:18 similarly confesses that Christ "was put to death in the flesh, but made alive in the spirit."

In the hymn, as in these creedal fragments, the word "flesh" must be taken in its most basic biblical sense.[50] The Hebrew *bāśār*—sometimes translated "flesh" (*sarx*), sometimes "body" (*sōma*)—when used of humans, identifies them as living creatures united with one another in a common, embodied existence. This is the sense that the term *sarx*/flesh has in Rom. 1:3 and John 1:14 and the sense in which "in flesh" is to be understood in 1 Tim. 3:16b. Using an antithesis similar to that found in 3:16b–c, Ignatius describes Jesus Christ as "both fleshy and spiritual" (Ign. *Eph.* 7:2).

How then is the entire phrase "was manifest in the flesh" (*ephanerōthē en sarki*) to be understood? The Fathers generally understood the phrase as referring to the incarnation of Christ Jesus. Thus, the *Epistle of Barnabas*, one of the earliest of Christian texts, uses the phrase four times, each time in reference to the incarnation (*Barn.* 5:6; 6:7, 9; 12:10; see 14:5). Second Timothy also uses the expression "was manifest," but without the qualification "in the flesh," to refer to the incarnation (2 Tim. 1:10). When the phrase "manifest" or "manifest in the flesh" is understood in this way, it clearly implies the preexistence of Christ Jesus.

On the other hand, "was manifest in the flesh" can be understood as a phrase that makes generic reference to the appearances of the risen Jesus. Belief in the "fleshy" reality of the risen Jesus is underscored by such narratives as Luke 24:36–43 and John 20:24–29 (see John 20:5, 17, 20, 27; 21:13–14). A similar expression is used in reference to the risen Jesus in Acts 10:40: "God raised him on the third day and allowed him to appear [*auton emphanē genesthai*]." Epilogues to the Markan and Johannine gospels use the word "manifest" to speak of the risen Jesus (Mark 16:12, 14; John 21:1, 14). So too does the *Epistle of Barnabas*: "Jesus rose from the dead and having been made manifest [*phanerōtheis*] ascended into the heavens" (*Barn.* 15:9). In the *Epistle of Barnabas* two passages that use "manifest" to speak of the incarnate Jesus do so in order to undergird Christian hope in the resurrection of the dead (see *Barn.* 5:6; 6:14). Thus, "manifest in the flesh" might well be a proclamation of the bodily resurrection of Jesus.

The arguments advanced in favor of taking "manifest in the flesh" as a reference to the incarnation are weighty. So too are those in favor of taking the phrase as a reference to resurrection appearances. It is difficult to opt for one over the other. On structural grounds some preference must be given to the sec-

---

50. In 1 Tim. 3:16, "flesh" does not have the specific nuance with which it occasionally used by Paul, that is, to signify humanity, which, in the weakness of its created condition, is prone to sin.

ond option, which takes the phrase in reference to the resurrection (Stettler 94). The structural parallelism of the hymn makes it likely that the entire hymn speaks of the risen One. Moreover, the Pastor's circles had to deal with people who were off target with regard to the resurrection (2 Tim. 2:8). Among the three Pastorals, 1 Timothy stresses the human reality of Jesus' trial and death (2:5–6; 6:13). An interpretation of 3:16b–c that understands verse 16b as a reference to the resurrection appearances of Jesus in the flesh affirms the bodily resurrection of Jesus and counters any incipient docetic, perhaps gnosticizing, tendencies to deny the reality of bodily resurrection (see 1 Cor. 15:35, 44). Early Christian belief in the bodily resurrection of Jesus is dramatically expressed in the Johannine narrative of the appearance of Jesus to a doubting Thomas (John 20:24–29).

Verse 16c, "was vindicated in the spirit" (*edikaiōthē en pneumati*), recalls the language used in the opening confession of the epistle to the Romans to speak about the resurrection of Jesus: The Son "was declared to be Son of God with power according to the Spirit [*kata pneuma*] of holiness" (Rom. 1:4). The *Odes of Solomon* (ca. 100 C.E.) use the language of vindication, being pronounced righteous, to speak of the bodily form of Jesus: "His face was justified because thus his Holy Father had given to him" (*Odes Sol.* 31:5).

There is a strong possibility that the Pastor's use of vindication language derives from Isa. 53:11. The conclusion of Deutero-Isaiah's fourth Servant Canticle (Isa. 53:11–12) celebrates the victory of the Servant and speaks of the Servant, the righteous one, who will make many righteous. According to the Septuagint, the Servant is made righteous (*dikaiōsai dikaion*, Isa. 53:11). This phrase seems to lie behind verse 16c. The canticle played an important role in the New Testament's scriptural apologetic; it was used to reflect on the passion, death, and resurrection of Jesus.[51] In Isaiah's reference to the vindication of the Servant of Yahweh, the church found a key by which it could come to some theological understanding of the resurrection. Many scholars hold that Isaiah 53 is the principal source of the christological hymn in Phil. 2:6–11. Some opine that the Isaian text is the principal referent of the traditional formula "in accordance with the scriptures" (*kata tas graphas*, 1 Cor. 15:3, 4). The Servant theme is evoked in Rom. 4:25 and then exploited in the argument of Romans 5. The hymnic and creedal character of the Pastor's phrase "was vindicated in the spirit," coupled with these Pauline passages, makes it likely that the Isaian Servant Canticles lie behind the Pastor's formulation of resurrection faith.

[16d–e] Paul's demonstration of the reality of Christ's resurrection in 1 Cor. 15:3–11 speaks of appearances to Cephas, then to the Twelve, to five hundred brothers and sisters, to James, and finally to Paul himself. The apostle uses the verb "appeared" (*ōphthē*) to describe these postresurrectional christophanies (1

---

51. See also Matt. 8:17.

Cor. 15:5, 6, 7, 8; see Luke 24:34; Acts 13:31). This same verb, characteristically used of a theophany (see Matt. 17:3; Mark 9:4; Luke 1:11; 22:43; Acts 7:30), is used in the phrase "appeared to angels" (*ōphthē angelois*, v. 16d).

Who are the messengers before whom the risen Christ Jesus made himself visible? Jerome Murphy-O'Connor "Redactional Angels"[52] and Raimund Lülsdorff think that "angels" are the human messengers (*angeloi*) to whom the risen Christ appeared. Lülsdorff finds some support for this view in 1 Tim. 5:21 (see Rev. 1:20). The canonical Gospels contain several accounts that describe the risen Jesus telling those to whom he appeared that they had a message to convey (Matt. 28:18–20; [Mark 16:15–16]; Luke 24:44–49; John 20:17, 21; Acts 1:8). According to the Pauline tradition, Cephas, the Twelve, the five hundred, James, all the apostles, and Paul (1 Cor. 15:5–8) can be considered "angels" in this sense.

The traditional view that "angels" refers to heavenly angels appears to be a preferable interpretation (see 1 Tim. 5:21). Taking "angels" as a reference to heavenly beings preserves the heavenly and earthly foci of the second pair of stichs. These angels stand in contrast with (all) the nations. Taking "angels" as a reference to heavenly angels is likewise consistent with traditional resurrection imagery that presents the resurrection as the enthronement of Jesus at the right hand of the Father. Angels are the attendant courtiers. A scriptural apologetic using Psalms 2 and 110 is a strong feature of this enthronement Christology (see Dan. 7:10). Other New Testament passages that evoke an angelic presence before the risen Christ are Phil. 2:9–11; Eph. 1:20–21; Heb. 1:3–4, 1 Pet. 3:22; and Rev. 5:8–14. Not to be overlooked in the panorama are the Gospel narratives about angels who proclaim the resurrection of Jesus at the empty tomb (Matt. 28:2–7; Mark 16:5–8; Luke 24:4–9; John 20:11–13).

The Pastor's hymn states that the risen Jesus was "proclaimed among the nations" (*ekērychthē en ethnesin*). His circles considered Paul to be the primary herald of the risen Jesus among the nations (2:7). Paul himself had spoken about proclaiming the gospel among the Gentiles (*kēryssō en tois ethnesin*, Gal. 2:2) and often used the verb "to proclaim" when writing about his mission (see Rom. 10:8; 1 Cor. 1:23; 9:27; 15:11; 2 Cor. 1:19; 11:4 [with "Jesus"]; Gal. 2:2; 1 Thess. 2:9). The object of Paul's proclamation was "Christ" (1 Cor. 1:23; 2 Cor. 4:5; 11:4; Phil. 1:15; see 1 Cor. 15:12; 2 Cor. 1:19). For the Pastor and his community, Paul was the one par excellence who proclaimed the risen Christ among the nations. Paul's mission was to be continued by the Pastor himself, by Timothy, and by others.

The Pastor's circles undoubtedly thought of Paul and his successors in ministry when they heard the phrase "proclaimed among the nations." Luke brought the first part of the two-part opus, Luke-Acts, to its close with this reflection:

---

52. Murphy-O'Connor holds that the stich is an interpolation into an original five-line hymn.

"Thus it is written, that the Messiah is to suffer and to rise from the dead on the third day, and that repentance and forgiveness of sins is to be proclaimed in his name to all nations [*kērychthēnai . . . eis panta ta ethnē*, see Matt. 28:19], beginning from Jerusalem" (Luke 24:46–47). The evangelist continued his story in part two, presenting Paul as the chief evangelist and Christian spokesperson among the nations, the Gentiles.

[16f–g] The final pair of stichs in the christological hymn provide a summary to the whole composition. With regard to the earthly sphere, the hymn proclaims that Jesus was "believed in in the world" (*episteuthē en kosmō*). The New Testament rarely uses the verb "to believe" (*pisteuō*) in the passive voice,[53] but the hymn does so. The juxtaposition of "proclaimed" (v. 16e) and "believed in (v. 16f) provides yet another key to the dynamic of the hymn. The first, third, and fourth stichs speak of manifestation or proclamation; the second, fifth, and sixth stichs speak of acceptance, that is, by God, humans, and angels (see Lau 91).

The risen Christ Jesus is to be believed in. The hymn enthusiastically proclaims that the risen Christ Jesus is believed in throughout the world (*en kosmō*). This enthusiasm stems from the universalism of the Isaian vision and the hope of Israel that all the nations will gather around Zion when the kingdom of God is ultimately realized (Isa. 2:2–4; 11:10; 60:1–16; see, e.g., Ps. 86:9; Mic. 4:1–3; Zech. 9:9–10). The hymn contemplates the resurrection of Christ Jesus in terms of its eschatological completion (see 1 Cor. 15:27–28).

Were the first stich of the hymn to be taken in an incarnational sense, the final stich, "lifted up in glory" (*anelēmphthē en doxē*), might be taken as its antithesis. The hymn does not, however, contrast an abasement in flesh with an exaltation in glory (see Phil. 2:5–11). Rather, the hymn concludes on a note that recalls the Lukan motif of the ascension of Jesus (Acts 1:2, 11, 22; see Mark 16:19; cf. Luke 9:51). The emphasis of the hymn's finale lies not so much on the lifting up as it does on the notion of Jesus' exaltation in glory. The hymn concludes with a note that speaks of the glory of the risen One. The risen Jesus shares in that glory that properly belongs to the only God (1:11, 17; 2 Tim. 4:18; see 2 Tim. 2:10; Titus 2:13).

The Pastor's citation of this hymn offers a fitting conclusion to his vision of the church as a well-organized household. In the house of God various functions are assumed by those who are qualified to do so and in which everyone knows how to behave. This vision of the church is a peaceful vision. As the Pastor develops his thought, his optimistic vision gives way to a pessimistic view of the times in which the church lives. Those times, about which the Spirit has said some ominous things, present a challenge that the church and its leaders must face (see 4:1–7).

53. A passive form with the meaning "be entrusted with" appears in 1:11; Titus 1:3; 1 Thess. 2:4.

Latter Times
1 Timothy 4:1–5

Chapter 3 concluded with a christological hymn that presents the resurrection of Christ Jesus from earthly and heavenly vantage points. Its final lines put forth a vision of the gospel preached throughout the world and of Christ Jesus in glory. This eschatological vision contrasts with the reality of the world in which the Pastor and his community lived. Traditional apocalyptic schemes typically present a scene of evil run amok prior to the realization of God's ultimate victory. The Pastor's description of penultimate evil is sparing in its use of apocalyptic imagery, but it is nonetheless a description of eschatological times. The Spirit of the end times, the divine power that raised Christ Jesus from the dead (3:16c), is the source of the Pastor's description.

The final times are times of eschatological error and deceit. People abuse food and procreation, God's vital gifts. In typically apocalyptic style, yet still without its dramatic imagery, the Pastor contrasts the evil of those who have gone astray with the hopeful steadfastness of those who have the full knowledge of the truth and receive the gifts of God's creation with prayer and thanksgiving.

4:1 The Spirit clearly says that in latter times some will give up the faith, following deceiving spirits and the teachings of demons, 2 with the hypocrisy of liars cauterized in their own conscience. 3 They[a] hinder marriage and urge[b] abstinence from food that God has created to be received with thanksgiving and enjoyed by the faithful and those who have full knowledge of the truth. 4 For everything that God has created is good and nothing received with thanksgiving is to be rejected, **5** for it is sanctified by the word of God and invocation.

a. The Greek text of verse 3 is a relative clause modifying "liars."
b. The language is elliptical; BDF 479.2 suggests that the verb to be supplied is *keleuontōn*, generally similar in sound with the previous *kōluontōn*, "hinder."

[4:1–3a] The Spirit, that is, the Spirit of God, is rarely mentioned in the Pastorals. Second Timothy and Titus mention the Spirit just once each. These passages, 2 Tim. 1:14 and Titus 3:5 (see 2 Tim. 3:16), identify the Spirit as the Holy Spirit. The Spirit is the Spirit of sanctification, which dwells in human beings and sanctifies them. In 1 Timothy, the Spirit is mentioned in two successive verses, 3:16 and 4:1. In this brace of verses the Spirit, the power by which "He" had been vindicated, appears as the prophetic Spirit who speaks about the final times. The Pastor affirms that the Spirit speaks clearly and distinctly (*rhētōs*) but fails to mention how the voice of the Spirit is heard. The message of the

Spirit is clear: In the final times "some" (*tines*) will give up the faith. Instead of following the warnings of the Spirit who speaks about the end times, they will follow deceiving spirits and the teaching of demons.

The Pastor's brief description (see 2 Tim. 3:1–5) of the latter times (*en hysterois kairois*), the final times (*en eschatais hēmerais*) of 2 Tim. 3:1, is characterized by the contrast between those who depart from the faith (see *T. Levi* 16:1) to follow various deceptive spirits, and the faithful with their full knowledge of the truth. The contrast between truth and deception is natural, but the Pastor has raised the stakes in his description of the final times. The truth of which he writes is not simple truth (*alētheia*) but the full knowledge of the truth, here expressed in a verbal form that recalls the formulaic *epignōsin alētheias* of 2:4; 2 Tim. 2:25; 3:7; and Titus 1:1 (see pp. 97–98). The deceit about which the Pastor speaks is not simple error but a going astray that results from the activity of deceiving spirits (*pneumasin planois*) and demons.

Hellenistic Judaism was familiar with the idea that deceit is characteristic of the end times (see *T. Levi* 10:2; 16:1). This notion is found in the Markan apocalypse (Mark 13:5–6, 22) whence it was taken over by Matthew and Luke (Matt. 24:4–5, 11, 24; Luke 21:8; see Matt. 18:12–13). Mark and Matthew attribute this end-time deception to false Christs and false prophets (Mark 13:22; Matt. 24:24; see Matt. 24:11).

The Pastor's brief but dualistic description of the final times derives from postbiblical Judaism, where deceit, or seduction to sin, is attributed to various demonic powers. The idea that God's people are led astray by demonic powers is found both in the Dead Sea Scrolls (1QS 3:22; CD 2:17; 1QpHab 10:9) and in the *Testaments of the Twelve Patriarchs* (*T. Dan* 5:5; *T. Benj.* 3:3). Mysterious "spirits of deceit" figure mightily in the eschatology of the *Testaments of the Twelve Patriarchs* (e.g., *T. Reub.* 2:1–2; *T. Sim.* 6:6; in the singular, e.g., *T. Sim.* 3:1). Mention of these spirits of deceit appears most prominently in *The Testament of Judah* (e.g., *T. Jud.* 14:8; 20:1). In this testament a spirit of deceit is contrasted with the spirit of truth. These spirits are locked together in a contest for the minds and hearts of human beings (*T. Jud.* 20).

Because of this end-time activity of deceitful spirits and demons, those who are led astray embrace demonic teachings (*didaskaliais daimoniōn*). The plural form of "teaching," used only here in the Pastorals, suggests a morass of teachings, similar to the confusion caused by false prophets of which the Markan apocalypse speaks (see Mark 13). These teachings sharply contrast with the sound teaching that is extolled throughout the Pastorals. The results of this demonically inspired confusion is that those who go astray are liars and impostors who do not speak the truth. The Pastor characterizes them as *pseudologōn*, "speakers of falsehood," a rarely used term appearing only occasionally in cultivated Greek literature (see Aristophanes, *Frogs* 1521; Strabo, *Geography* 2.1.9). Their lack of truth is the result of hypocrisy (*hypokrisei*), a quality that the evangelist Matthew untiringly attributes to Jewish teachers who do not accept his Christian interpretation of the law (Matt. 6:2, 5, 16; 7:5; 15:7; 22:18; 23:13, [14], 15, 23, 25, 27, 28, 29; [24:51]; see also Gal. 2:13). This hypocritical untruth stands in sharp contrast with the full knowledge of the truth (v. 3; see 2:4) to which the members of the Pastor's community are committed (see 4:6).

In contrast with the pure and clean conscience (1:5, 19; 3:9) the members of the community ought to have is the scarred conscience (*kekaustēriasmenōn*) of those who have gone astray. The image is strong; it recalls the branding of a slave by his master. Those who have gone astray have done this to themselves. The searing of their consciences has destroyed living tissue, with a consequent loss of feeling, a loss of sensitivity to the Spirit and the truth. These unfortunate "some" have branded their own consciences with the result that they forbid marriage and enjoin abstinence from food.

The false asceticism that results from demonic teachings is part of the confusion of the end times. The Pastor's mention of this undue asceticism indicates the kind of deviance with which he and his circles had to deal. While in 2 Timothy the Pastor decries the rampant lust of the final times (2 Tim. 3:3–4, 6; see 1 Tim. 5:6), in 1 Tim. 4:1–3 the Pastor writes about those same times and states that some people reject marriage and certain foods.

In the Pastorals' vision of things, the good and clean conscience rejects both extremes, rampant lust and undue asceticism. The Christian life is one of moderation (1 Tim. 2:9, 15; 3:2–3, 8, 11, 12; 5:11, 14–15, 23). The Pastor attempts to set things right in his exhortation to women to realize the importance of childbearing in God's plan of salvation (2:15). He urges young widows to marry and have children (5:14) and suggests that the moderate use of alcohol is a good thing (5:23).

In 4:3–5 the Pastor confronts the problem head on. This is the only time in the Pastoral Epistles that the author identifies a specific issue that he finds troubling and then proceeds to refute it with an explicit, logical argument. Using an enthymeme, a rhetorical syllogism in which one of the premises is assumed rather than stated, he affirms the goodness of what the false teachers reject: Everything created by God is good; the things that "some" are rejecting were created by God; hence, these things are good and are to be received with prayer and gratitude.

Excursus 6: The Debate on Marriage and Food

The two extremes, rigid asceticism and licentious antinomianism with regard to food and sex, were later associated with Gnosticism. Irenaeus, in particular, wrote about the gnostics' opposition to marriage in his classic work, *Against Heresies*:

They declare also, that marriage and generation are from Satan. Many of those, too, who belong to his school [the school of Saturninus], abstain from animal food, and draw away multitudes by a feigned temperance of this kind. They hold, moreover, that some of the prophecies were uttered by those angels who made the world, and some by Satan. (*Against Heresies* 1.24.2; *ANF* translation)

Springing from Saturninus and Marcion, those who are called Encratites (self-controlled) preached against marriage, thus setting aside the original creation of God, and indirectly blaming Him who made the male and female for the propagation of the human race. Some of those reckoned among them have also introduced abstinence from animal food, thus proving themselves ungrateful to God, who formed all things. (*Against Heresies* 1.28.1; *ANF* translation)

A hundred or so years after Irenaeus, the great church historian Eusebius of Caesarea attributed an ambiguous slogan "everyone ought to abuse his own flesh" to Nicolaus, a proselyte from Antioch (see Acts 6:5). This Nicolaus may be the one from whom the Nicolaitans of Revelation 2 took their name. According to Eusebius, Nicolaus himself understood this saying to mean the suppression of passion. Hence, he was faithful to his wife, and his son and daughters lived as virgins (Eusebius, *Ecclesiastical History* 3.29). Clement of Alexandria similarly described Nicolaus as an ascetic (*Stromata*. 3.25.5–3.26.2).

On the other hand, Eusebius reports that some people took the saying literally and rushed into fornication. Earlier, Hippolytus had claimed that Nicolaus himself departed from true doctrine (*Refutation of All Heresies* 7.24). Tertullian writes about a gnostic and satanic sect whose members were known for their lustful conduct (see *Against Marcion* 1.29; *Heretics* 33; *Modesty* 19). He compares the group with the Nicolaitans of Rev. 2:14–15. A fourth-century text describes the Nicolaitans, who invoked the name of Nicolaus as their founder, as "shameless in uncleanness" (*Apostolic Constitutions* 6.8).

Clement of Alexandria twice mentions the adage "everyone ought to abuse his own flesh" (see *Stromata* 2.118.3 and 3.25.7). He explains how one and the same saying could lead both to sexual asceticism and to sexual license:

When we mentioned Nicolaus' remark we omitted one point. They say that he had a pretty wife. After the Savior's resurrection he was accused of jealousy by the apostles. He brought his wife out into their midst and offered her to anyone who wanted her in marriage. They say that his action was consistent with the saying "The flesh is to be treated with contempt." Those who are members of his sect follow his word and act simply and uncritically, and indulge in unrestrained license.

However, I learn that Nicolaus had relations with no woman other than his wedded wife, and of his children the girls grew to old age as virgins, and the son remained innocent. In these circumstances it was a rejection of the passions to wheel out the wife, over whom he was charged with jealousy, into the middle of the apostles; and his control of the generally acknowledged pleasures was a lesson in "treating the flesh with contempt." (*Stromata* 3.25.5–3.26.2).

Clement also notes that some people attribute abstinence from sex and the prohibition of eating beans to "Pythagoreans" (see *Stromata* 3.24.1–2).[54] Patristic texts like this have led many commentators on the Pastoral Epistles to opine that the false asceticism to which 4:3 refers derives from a gnostic or gnosticizing view characterized by a strong anthropological and ethical dualism. The church's second-century antignostic polemic has consequently been cited as an argument in favor of the view that the Pastorals were composed as late as the second century C.E. Tales told in the second-century *Acts of Paul* show that some Christians of that era believed that abstinence from marriage was a matter of faithfully following Paul's teaching. These stories tell about a woman named Thecla who went to extreme lengths in order to safeguard her virginity.

An asceticism that derives from a gnosticizing dualism may well be an important piece of the problem confronted in the Pastoral Epistles. The patristic texts and the *Acts of Paul* show that issues of sex and marriage were a matter of heated debate among second-century Christians. The church of the first century was, however, not innocent of debates about food and sex. The epistolary warnings of the book of Revelation suggest that some Christians were lax in regard to restraint of the appetites for food and sex (Rev. 2:14–15, 20–25). Revelation associates this excess with the teaching (*didachē*) of Balaam and of the Nicolaitans (2:14–15).

Four of Paul's own letters attest to some of the earliest Christian discussions about food and sex (see Rom. 14:13–21; 1 Cor. 7:12–16; 8:1–13; 10:25–31; Gal. 2:11–14; 1 Thess. 4:3–6). Paul writes at length (1 Cor. 7:1–40) about a number of matters that arose from a Corinthian fascination with the ill-conceived slogan "it is good for a man not to touch a woman" (1 Cor. 7:1). Systematically and very strongly he argues in favor of marriage and the use of sex within marriage (1 Cor. 7:2–6). As far as food is concerned, Paul spells out various possible scenarios with regard to food that had been offered to idols (1 Cor. 8, 10). He advises the Christians of Corinth to "eat whatever is sold in the meat market without raising any question on the ground of conscience, for 'the earth and its fullness are the Lord's'" (10:25–26). On the other hand, he addresses harsh words to those who eat and drink, even to the point of drunkenness, without any consideration of others within the community (11:17–22).

Paul adds a confrontational codicil to his reflection on all things belonging to the Lord: "If I partake with thankfulness, why should I be denounced because of that for which I give thanks?" (1 Cor. 10:30). This emphasis on God's creation and people's giving thanks is echoed in what the Pastor writes in 1 Tim. 4:4. The vision derives from the Bible's wisdom tradition:

> This is what I have seen to be good: it is fitting to eat and drink and find enjoyment in all the toil with which one toils under the sun the few days of the life God

---

54. To a large extent, the antiheretical argument of many of the early church fathers is based on anecdotal evidence. Clement admits that some of this evidence falls into a category that would now be described as hearsay. "It is said," he writes, "that the Pythagorians abstain from sex" (*Stromata* 3.24.1). The critical historian must carefully weigh the value of the various anecdotes cited by the Fathers. In many instances they are not confirmed by an independent source even if some of the Fathers repeated what early Fathers have said. Such caution must be exercised with regard to many of the traditions about Nicolaus and the Nicolaitans.

gives us; for this is our lot. Likewise all to whom God gives wealth and posses-sions and whom he enables to enjoy them, and to accept their lot and find enjoy-ment in their toil—this is the gift of God. (Eccl. 5:18–19)

Unlike Paul, the Synoptic tradition does not have much to say about marriage—apart, that is, from the issue of divorce (Matt. 5:31–32; 19:3–9; Mark 10:2–12; Luke 16:18). Two passages nonetheless identify marriage as a reality of the world in which people live. In response to the disciples' thoughtless outburst that "it is better not to marry," the Matthean Jesus utters an enigmatic saying about eunuchs (Matt. 19:10–12). Only some, he says, have been called by God to abstain from marriage. In response to an objection posed by the Sadducees, the Lukan Jesus responds with a rejoinder that includes the obser-vation that "those who belong to this age marry and are given in marriage" (Luke 20:34).

With regard to the eating of food, Mark 7:19 says that Jesus declared all foods clean. The evangelist Matthew revised the Markan gospel for a Jewish Christian readership. Apparently he found Mark's parenthetical remark on the cleanness of all foods so strong that he omitted it from his own version of the Gospel (see Matt 15:17). According to Acts 15, the "Council of Jerusalem," under the guidance of the Spirit, offered guidance to Gentile Christians with regard to food and marriage (Acts 15:20, 29). Peter's thrice-repeated vision at Joppa, with its solemn declaration that "what God has made clean, you must not call profane" (Acts 10:15), prepared the way for the conciliar decision.

The early Christian debate about sex and food was to a large extent a discussion about the relationship between Jewish and Gentile Christians and the acceptability of their respective mores within a single Christian fellowship. The Pastor's exhortation to a bal-anced and moderate view with regard to sex and diet may well be located within his own discussion with judaizing elements and false views of the law. On the other hand, he was concerned that his community find its place within the Greco-Roman world. Social sta-bility and societal acceptance were among his goals. Christian asceticism and gnostic libertinism were part of the scene as the first century drew to a close. The Pastor's plea for moderation and his urging that all that God had created was good, to be accepted with prayer and thanksgiving, are an attempt to find a Christian balance amid a conflu-ence of different trends.

[3b–5] Having cited immoderate asceticism with regard to sex and diet as a consequence of the end-time activity of the deceitful spirits and demons, the Pastor offers a reflection on how Christians should regard sex and food. A rel-ative clause states that God has created food to be received and enjoyed (*eis metalēmpsin*, a phrase that suggests both reception and fruitful use). The Pas-tor's words echo what the apostle had said in writing to the Romans: "Do not, for the sake of food, destroy the work of God. Everything is indeed clean" (Rom. 14:20; see Titus 1:15). Similar thoughts were expressed repeatedly by the voice that spoke to Peter: "What God has made clean, you must not call pro-fane" (Acts 10:15).

The Pastor does not make use of the ritual language of "cleanness" or "purity" to speak about food (see Rom. 14:20; Acts 10:15). Neither does he use the social language of good nor the medical language of health to speak of diet. Rather, the Pastor gets to the heart of the matter, as did Paul with regard to sex (1 Cor. 6:16). According to the Pastor, food and sex are good because they have been created by God. They are God's gifts to human beings. As such, they are to be received with thanksgiving (*meta eucharistias*) and used.

God's gifts are for all human beings. Those who are faithful and have full knowledge of the truth—that is, the Pastor's community—are to receive them with thanksgiving. Some people outside the community shun God's gifts rather than receive them with thankful acceptance. Led astray by the deceitful spirits, these outsiders do not enjoy the full knowledge of the truth about God. God's fidelity to those he has created requires that some means for sustenance and the continuation of their race be provided. Those outside the community do not understand this. Captivated by falsehood, they do not accept the ethical standards of those who fully know the truth and thus find themselves outside the community of faith (see 5:8).

The Pastor's solemn reflection on the goodness of creation (vv. 4–5) is introduced by the conjunction *hoti*, "for."[55] His affirmation reprises the vocabulary of verse 3b. "God," "creation," "received," and "thanksgiving" are the common themes. God is the Creator. God's people are to receive what God has created with thanksgiving. All that God has created is good (*kalon*)—"very good" (*kala lian*) according to Gen. 1:31—and therefore not to be rejected.

The Pastor adds a further explanation: What God has created and people have received with thanksgiving is sanctified. It is holy; it is not profane. This sanctification of God's gifts owes to God's word and human prayer. "God's word" (*logou theou*) in this context is God's creative word (Gen. 1:3, 6, 9, 11, 14, 20, 24, 26), endorsed by the divine reflection that what had been created was good (Gen. 1:4, 10, 12, 18, 21, 25), even very good (Gen. 1:31). The thanksgiving with which the gifts of creation are to be received takes the form of a prayer in which the name of God is invoked (*enteuxis*; see 2:1, where it is juxtaposed with "thanksgiving"). The primary meaning of the root *enteug-*, used by the Pastor, is "to meet someone." In both its nominal and verbal use it means to have a conversation with someone (Polybius, *Histories* 4.30.1; Plutarch, *Fabius Maximus* 20.2). In effect, to receive God's gifts with thanksgiving is to have an encounter with God. God has spoken through his creation; humans respond with a prayer of thanksgiving. Accordingly, the psalms praise the Lord for the works of his creation (Pss. 8, 104, 135).

---

55. The elliptical construction—there is no verb (see 2 Tim. 3:16)—makes it difficult to determine whether *hoti* introduces a supporting argument ("*because* everything created by God is good . . .") or simply makes explicit what the Pastor means by "the truth" ("*namely, that* everything created by God is good . . ."). The first argues for the goodness of created things, the second assumes it as self-evidently true.

The Pastor's words on the reception of God's gifts with a prayer of thanksgiving specifically pertain to the gift of food. They can readily be extended to the use of sex within marriage. The Pastor recalls the creation of Eve as he encourages women to bear children (2:13–15). For the Pastor, the bearing of children is salvific provided that it is accompanied with a Christian attitude and social responsibility. Moreover, the Pastor urges young widows to marry and bear children lest the adversary revile the community (5:14). The way in which the Pastor writes about their getting married and raising a family suggests that he sees the failure to do so not only as an occasion for the community to be disparaged but also as the work of Satan himself (5:15).

A Charge to Timothy
1 Timothy 4:6–16

This charge to Timothy is the longest of the pastoral charges in the Pastoral Epistles. Various asides contribute to the Pastor's argument but lengthen its exposition. The charge focuses on how Timothy is to teach and how he should live. The creative tension between Timothy's ministerial responsibility and his personal life mutually enriches the two foci of the charge.

With regard to Timothy's teaching the Pastor presents a contrast between the kind of things that Timothy should avoid and those that he should present to the faithful. The charge concludes with a rhetorical peroration in three segments (vv. 14–16) that respectively underscore the idea that Timothy's ministry results from the spiritual gift that he has received, that it is a matter of his personal progress, and that it concerns the salvation of himself and of those who listen to him. The charge includes elements that commonly appear in the Pastorals and some that are novel or at least rarely expressed. Among the usual themes are teaching, godliness, the promise of life to come, a trustworthy saying, and God as Savior. On the other hand, some of the motifs expressed in this pericope distinguish this exhortation from other hortatory material in the Pastorals. One such element is the use of the metaphor of physical training. Still another is the Pastor's highlighting of "progress," a Stoic ideal. Most significant are the elements of church order that emerge from the pericope. Among these are the idea of the faithful as a community of brothers and sisters, the notion that Timothy is a servant (*diakonos*), that "reading" is integral to the community's life, the idea of a group of elders (the "presbyterate"), and the idea that Timothy's ministry is conferred on him through the laying on of hands.

4:6 If you set these things before the brothers and sisters you will be a good servant of Christ Jesus, nourished by the message of faith and the good teaching that you have closely followed. 7 Avoid[a] impious speech and old wives' tales.

Train yourself in godliness. 8 Physical training is of some benefit but godliness is beneficial for everything. It[b] bears the promise of life in the present and of life to come. 9 This is a trustworthy saying, worthy of full acceptance. 10 Because of this[a] we toil and struggle,[c] since we have hoped in the living God who is the Savior of all people, especially of the faithful.

11 Announce and teach these things. 12 Let no one look down on your youth but be an example for the faithful in your speech, way of life, love, faith, and holiness. 13 Until I come, be attentive to the reading, admonition, and teaching. 14 Do not neglect the spiritual gift that is in you, which has been given to you through prophecy with the imposition of the hands of the group of elders. 15 Take care of these things; deal with them so that your progress may be visible to everyone. 16 Pay attention to yourself and to the teaching. Keep on doing[b] so; if you do, you will save yourself and those who listen to you.

a. Arguably verses 6–7a constitute a single sentence in Greek (see *GNT*). The explanatory *gar* and the inferential *eis touto* make it possible to read verses 9 and 10 as a single Greek sentence, as does *GNT*.

b. Verses 8 and 16 are each a single sentence in Greek.

c. Most of the ancient majuscules read *agōnizometha*, "struggle." Most minuscules read *oneidizometha*, "suffer reproach" (so the AV, based on the reading of the Textus Receptus).

[4:6–7a] The tone of the Pastor's language changes when he turns his attention to Timothy's responsibilities. He had described Timothy as Paul's true son (1:2); now he describes Timothy as someone who can be a good servant of Christ Jesus, on the proviso that he lay "these things" (*tauta*) before the community. "These things" are the instructions that have been given thus far. If Timothy shares these instructions with the community, he will prove not only that he is a real disciple of Paul but also that he is a good servant (*diakonos*, see 3:8, 12) of Christ Jesus. Pursuit of his ministry will demonstrate Timothy's fidelity to Paul and his service to Christ Jesus.[56]

Another shift in language occurs in the description of the community as Timothy's "brothers and sisters" (*adelphois*).[57] Paul commonly uses kinship language, especially "brothers and sisters," when writing to communities with

56. 1 Cor. 12:5 describes the charisms as varieties of services (*diakoniōn*). In contrast there is but "one Lord" (*ho autos kyrios*).

57. Since at least the time of Euripides (fifth century B.C.E.), the plural masculine form, *adelphoi*, referred to both males and females when it was used of an assembly.

which he has a warm relationship. Kinship language evokes the bonds that link Paul and the members of the community together. It also suggests that those who have assembled are family members bound together by family ties. The Pastor uses this language (see 6:2; 2 Tim. 4:21) in a context that juxtaposes the community and the anonymous "some" of the previous pericope. "They" are anonymous; believers are a family. The Pastor's use of language so often used by Paul suggests that Timothy is to have a relationship with the community similar to Paul's relationship with his communities.

By placing before the community these things, the teaching of "Paul" that Timothy has closely followed (see 2 Tim. 3:10), Timothy will show that he has been well nourished by the "message of faith." The message of faith (note the plural *logois*, literally "words") includes the creed of 1:15, the midrash in 2:13–15, and what is to be said about godliness in 4:8. "These things" extend beyond these trustworthy sayings to include whatever is said pertaining to faith in Christ Jesus (see 3:13). Thus, Timothy is loyal to Christ Jesus and he is being loyal to Paul, his teacher.

The obverse side of Timothy's responsibility is avoidance of impious speech and old wives' tales. The epistle's peroration warns Timothy to avoid empty sounding and impious speech (*bebēlous*, 6:20; see 2 Tim. 2:16). The Pastor makes no other mention of "old wives' tales," which he describes as "myths" (*mythous*). Elsewhere in the Pastorals, "myths" are the stories embraced by those who have gone astray in latter times (2 Tim. 4:4). They appear to be judaizing stories (1:4; Titus 1:14) that have no place within the Pastor's community. By deriding them as the tales of "old hags" (*graōdeis*, a term used by Strabo in his *Geography*), the Pastor reflects a patriarchal, cultural bias in which women are considered to be silly little people led astray by their passions, whose ability to learn is such that they should not be allowed to teach "real men" (2:11–12; see 2 Tim. 3:6). The colloquial expression "old wives' tale" is a faint echo of that cultural prejudice.

[7b–8] Having set out Timothy's pastoral task, positively and negatively, the Pastor gives a brief exhortation on training. The exhortation is similar to some of the hortatory material in Stoic writings. These often employ the agon motif, the military or athletic image of a struggle used to speak of the quest of and defense of the truth. The Pastor speaks about preparations for the struggle, the necessary training. "To train" (*gymnaze*) and "physical training" (*sōmatikē gymnasia*) are expressions that are not generally found in the New Testament (see Heb. 5:14; 12:11; 2 Pet. 2:14). Paul does not use these terms, but he does evoke the image of the athletic regime and the pains of sparring as he speaks of runners and boxers in his use of the agon motif at 1 Cor. 9:24–27.

Timothy's "training," his preparation for ministry, consists of godliness, piety working itself out in a virtuous life. "Godliness" (*hē eusebeia*) is one of the most important motifs of the Pastoral Epistles, especially 1 Timothy (see

2:2; 3:16; 6:3, 5, 6, 11; 2 Tim. 3:5; Titus 1:1; see Excursus 7). The Pastor highlights the importance of godliness by contrasting it with physical training. Physical training, he says, is only partially beneficial. Godliness, on the other hand, is beneficial for everything. Speaking in this way, the Pastor uses a rhetorical appeal to advantage, a common ploy in deliberative rhetoric, to underscore the importance of godliness. As compared with physical training, which offers only limited advantages, godliness is advantageous in every respect (*pros panta ōphelimos*). It is useful for all forms of human activity.

The reason why godliness is so advantageous is that it carries with it the promise of life (*epangelian echousa zōēs*) in the present age (*tēs nyn*) and in the age to come (*kai tēs mellousēs*). The contrast between the present age and the age to come derives from Jewish apocalyptic thought. The present age is the age in which people are actually living; the age to come is the eschatological age. The Pastor's use of the apocalyptic scheme is most appropriate in a section of his epistle that speaks of latter times (4:1). In other sections of the missive the Pastor speaks about life in the age to come as "eternal life" (1:16; 6:12; see Titus 1:2; 3:7) and as "real life" (6:19). This is "life in Christ Jesus" (2 Tim. 1:1), the object of the promise of God (2 Tim. 1:1) and of the hope of Christians (Titus 1:2; 3:7).

According to the Pastor's anthropology, godliness brings with it not only reward in the life to come but also some benefit in the present age. His views on godliness are consistent with his views that those to whom he is writing are to live out their beliefs in the real world, that is, the Greco-Roman world with its Hellenistic culture. Godliness manifests itself in qualities that express a human being's relationship with God *and* in those virtues that enable life in social relationship with others, particularly within the Christian community. In the polemical context of chapter 4, godliness bears with it a healthy attitude toward marriage and food. Insofar as the believer's relationship with God is concerned, marriage and food are to be received as gifts of God for which thanksgiving is the appropriate response. Insofar as the believer's relationship with others is concerned, these gifts are to be enjoyed (4:3). They are necessary for life in the real world.

Excursus 7: Godliness

In the Hellenistic world, godliness (*eusebeia*) was a much esteemed virtue. The apostle's near contemporary, Epictetus, the Stoic philosopher, described godliness as the combination of piety and correct behavior, of an appreciation of the gods that leads to proper conduct. He wrote, "In piety towards the gods I would have you know the chief element[58] is this, to have right opinions about them—as existing and as administering the universe well and justly—and to have set yourself to obey them and to submit to everything that happens, and to follow it voluntarily, in the belief that it is being fulfilled by the highest intelligence" (*Encheiridion* 31). Philo wrote that "piety and religion

---

58. The Greek text uses *to kyriōtaton*, that is, the reigning or dominant element.

[*eusebeian de kai hosiotēta*] are the queens among the virtues" (*Decalogue* 119). Godliness encompassed respect for existing values and value structures. Thus, Hellenistic Jews considered godliness to be a matter of living according to the tradition of their ancestors, in fidelity to God and to one another.

Despite the widespread contemporary emphasis on godliness, the writings of the New Testament do not often speak about godliness. Apart from the Pastorals, the New Testament mentions godliness only five times.[59] First Timothy is a notable exception to the New Testament's relative silence about godliness. The epistle uses the noun "godliness" or "piety" eight times (2:2; 3:16; 4:7, 8; 6:3, 5, 6, 11) and the related verb "to act in godly fashion" once (*eusebein*, 5:4). Words belonging to this lexical cluster appear in the other Pastoral Epistles as well. Thus, in striking fashion the salutation of the epistle to Titus says that Paul's apostolate was "for the sake of godliness, in the hope of eternal life" (Titus 1:1–2). Second Timothy 3:5 expresses concern for the proper understanding of godliness. "Godly" (*eusebōs*) is found in 2 Tim. 3:12 and Titus 2:12.[60]

Godliness is an important element in the paraenesis of the Pastorals, especially in that of 1 Timothy. For the Pastor, godliness is essential for an acceptable quality of life in society. Accordingly, the Pastor urges "Timothy" and with him the whole community to pray especially for kings and those in authority so that Christians "might live a peaceful and quiet life in all godliness and dignity" (2:2). Encouraging this kind of prayer is one of his primary pastoral responsibilities; "I urge you, first of all," he writes in 2:1. The urgency of his plea derives from the ominous situation that is on the horizon. Pliny the Younger would soon write about the torture of Christian deaconesses (*Epistle* 10.96). Second Timothy reminds its readers that "all who desire to live in godly fashion in Christ Jesus will be persecuted" (2 Tim. 3:12).

Godliness was imperative for anyone who desired to live peacefully in the Greco-Roman world. Godliness was understood as reverence for the gods, a kind of piety that called forth respect for traditional values and practices and the structures that promote those values and practices. Godliness included "family values," the domestic virtues of taking care of one's own household, parents for their children and children for their parents. These values were highly regarded in the Pastor's circles and well esteemed in the world in which they lived. Thus, the Pastor urges that Christians act in godly fashion toward the members of their own households and offer some return to their living forebears, who need their support (see 1 Tim. 5:4).

Luke, a fine Hellenistic author in his own right, equated the Hellenistic "godliness" with the Semitic notion of "righteousness" or "justice" (see Acts 10:2, 22). The latter term (*dikaiosynē* in Greek, *ṣĕdāqâ* in Hebrew) designated the quality of a life lived in proper relationship with God and God's people. In the words of Philo, "justice and God's covenant are identical" (*Dreams* 2.224). Godliness/piety and righteousness/justice went hand in hand in Hellenistic Judaism. According to Philo,

---

59. See Acts 3:12; 2 Pet. 1:3, 6, 7; 3:11. A related verb appears in Acts 17:23; a related adjective in Acts 10:2, 7; 2 Pet 2:9. Of the twenty-two uses of the root *euseb-* in the New Testament, thirteen occur in the Pastorals, four in Acts, and five in 2 Peter. No instances of words with this root are to be found in the apostle's undisputed letters.

60. The adverb is not used in 1 Timothy.

Among the vast number of particular truths and principles there studied,[61] there
stand out practically high above the others two main heads: one of duty to God
as shown by piety and holiness, one of duty to men as shown by humanity and
justice, each of them splitting up into multiform branches, all highly laudable"

(*Special Laws* 2.63; see *Every Good Man Is Free* 83–84). Philo suggests not only that
godliness and righteousness go together but also that they are virtually inseparable: "The
nature which is pious," he writes, "is also kindly and the same person will exhibit both
qualities, holiness to God and justice to people" (*Abraham* 208).

The pairing of godliness with justice, a correct attitude and proper devotion toward
the gods with appropriate behavior toward others, is a Hellenistic idea. Plato writes,
"This then is my opinion, Socrates, that the part of the right [*to meros tou dikaiou*] which
has to do with attention to the gods constitutes piety and holiness, and that the remaining part of the right is that which has to do with the service of people" (*Euthyphro* 12e).
Hellenistic Judaism appropriated some of these ideas, along with their idiom, in order
to present in Hellenistic terms some of the basic ideas associated with the covenant.

Philo claims that godliness and justice belong together. He sees each of them as a
generic virtue, the root of other virtues. Speaking of students in the Sabbath school, Philo
affirms that they are taught according to the tradition of the past and that "they are trained
in piety, holiness, justice, domestic and civic conduct, knowledge of what is truly good,
or evil, or indifferent, and how to choose what they should and avoid the opposite, taking for their defining standards these three, love of God, love of virtue, love of people"
(*Every Good Man Is Free* 83).

The Pastor's circles were familiar with people who did not pursue the triad of virtues
extolled by Philo. Such people love pleasure rather than God, money rather than virtue,
and themselves rather than other people. They are "lovers of self, lovers of money,
impostors, arrogant, defamers, disobedient to parents, ingrates, unholy, heartless,
implacable, slanderers, lacking in self-control, uncivilized, haters of good, traitors, reckless, conceited, lovers of pleasure rather than lovers of God, having the appearance of
godliness while denying its power" (2 Tim. 3:2–5). Any appearance of godliness in people who do not really love God and others is but a sham.

The Pastor understands the relationship between godliness and righteousness in
much the same way as Philo. He urges Timothy to flee "these things," including a false
understanding of godliness, and to "pursue righteousness, godliness, faith, love, steadfastness, gentleness" (6:11). He exhorts Timothy to avoid the sophistry and denial of
truth of those who hold that "godliness is a means for profit" (6:5; see *2 Clem.* 20:1–4).
In the Pastor's view, true godliness is not related to the acquisition of material wealth.
Money, he writes, is a root of evil (6:10). True godliness does not lead to amassing profit
for the sake of profit.

This does not mean that godliness is unprofitable. "There is," says the Pastor, "great
gain in godliness with self-sufficiency; we have brought nothing into the world so that
we can take nothing out of the world; and having food and covering we will be satisfied
with these" (6:6–8). This is the first time in extant literature that self-sufficiency
(*autarkeia*) is coupled with the virtue of godliness. The Pastor's reflections are particu-

---

61. Studied, that is, in thousands of Jewish Sabbath schools.

larly apropos in the light of a philosophic tradition that apparently goes back to the time of Socrates. Socrates is reputed to have been asked, "Who is the wealthiest human?" to which he replied, "The one self-sufficient with least; for self-sufficiency is the wealth nature gave us" (*Gn. Vat.* 476). Diogenes, the early Cynic (fourth century B.C.E.), also championed self-sufficiency. To a question similar to the one Socrates was asked, Diogenes is said to have responded, "The self-sufficient person" (*Gn. Vat.* 180). In later times, Cynics extolled the virtue of self-sufficiency in opposition to those philosophers who received in recompense for their teaching what Cynics considered to be excessive amounts of money. For them, the simple life was sufficient.

In the light of the philosophic tradition, it appears that the Pastor aims to put the man of God, the one who is to teach the community (6:2, 11), on guard against any desire to profit excessively from his role as a teacher. Teaching or preaching for profit's sake is a hallmark of sophists and false teachers, far removed from the ideal of the apostle Paul, who worked with his hands to provide for his physical needs (1 Thess. 2:9) and could contrast himself favorably with those teachers whose words were a pretext for greed (1 Thess. 2:5).

The Pastor considers "godliness" for the sake of profit to be characteristic of false teachers who do not "agree with the sound words about our Lord Jesus Christ, the teaching that leads to godliness" (6:3). His description of these teachers closely links together sound Christian teaching and godliness, just as the greeting of the Epistle to Titus joins "the full knowledge of truth" with godliness. "Sound teaching" and "the full knowledge of truth" are ciphers for what the Pastor's circles considered to be authentic and healthy Christian teaching (see Excursus 4). Both Titus 1:1 and 1 Tim. 6:3 unabashedly affirm that good Christian teaching is to be accompanied by a good Christian life.

Epictetus wrote about correct opinions about the gods. For the Pastor, the core teaching on which the Christian life is to be based is the paschal mystery. Thus, he writes about the community's confession of the great mystery of godliness, which is summed up in a traditional hymn about the risen One (3:16). More generally, the Pastor's circles linked godliness with a belief that the appearance of Christ Jesus is a manifestation of God's saving beneficence. Thus, Titus 2:11–12 states that "the saving beneficence of God has appeared to all people, teaching us to deny impiety and worldly passions and to live modestly, justly, and in godly fashion in the present age."

Titus 2:11–12 connects righteousness/justice with godliness/piety as did Hellenistic Judaism. Because they associated godliness specifically with teaching about Christ Jesus, the Pastor's circles could sum up the Christian life as "to live in godly fashion in Christ Jesus" (2 Tim. 3:12). The words echo Pauline mysticism, whose motif is life "in Christ Jesus," with the generic Hellenistic virtue of godliness. Living in Christ Jesus is to live in godly fashion.

It is imperative that "Timothy" strive for godliness (6:11). Echoes of the Stoic agon motif are present in the way that the Pastor urges Timothy to train himself in godliness (4:7). The recipients of his letter, who have been nourished by the message of faith and the good teaching that has been followed, are to train themselves in godliness (4:7). Hellenistic moralists generally do not give reasons why people should follow their moral advice, although they sometimes offer specific examples of good behavior.[62] Apart from

---

62. These are the *paradeigmata* of Hellenistic rhetoric. See Fiore.

the use of examples, the paraenetic genre relies on the authority of the speaker, his rhetorical *ethos*, and the inherent value of what is being exhorted to provide sufficient motivation for the audience.

The Pastor's discourse on godliness deviates somewhat from that of other Hellenistic moralists. In cultivating the example of Timothy, he provides a model for the community to follow. In addition, and this is unusual, he argues against a wrong notion of godliness. He explains that people who think that godliness is a means for profit have lost their minds (6:5). Second Timothy 3:2–5 excoriates those who claim to be godly, yet do not manifest godliness in their lives. Theirs is an appearance of godliness, a godliness that is but a farce since it is deprived of its power. The Pastor employs the rhetorical argument of advantage in urging those to whom he is writing to pursue godliness. First Timothy 4:7–8 argues that godliness is advantageous in every respect. Godliness bears within itself promise for this life as well as promise for the life to come. In 1 Tim. 6:6 the Pastor again proclaims that there is great gain to be had from godliness, provided that it is accompanied by self-sufficiency.

Godliness, as the Pastor understand it, is a comprehensive quality that is difficult to achieve. Hence, he employs the agon motif in 1 Tim. 4:7–8 in urging Timothy to train in godliness. The virtue of godliness requires practice. The Pastor appropriates the philosophic ideal of godliness, rooted, however, in the great mystery of faith rather than in an understanding of pagan gods. Godliness is something for which the members of his community and its leaders ought to strive. Godliness affects their relationships with other members of the Christian household. In the Pastor's view, godliness is an all-important virtue, bearing within itself the promise of eternal life. The Pastor underscores the importance of godliness by adding to the exhortation in 1 Tim. 4:7–8 the endorsement, "This is a trustworthy saying, worthy of full acceptance."

[9–10] This is the second time that 1 Timothy uses the expanded formula of approval, "This is a trustworthy saying, worthy of full acceptance" (see 1:15; 3:1, see Excursus 1). Use of the formula brings the polemic argument of 4:1–8 to a new level. In latter times, those who give up the faith are engaged in hypocrisy and lies. Presumably they are engaged in impious speech and old wives' tales. Contrasted with their perversion of the truth is a saying upon which the faithful who have the full knowledge of the truth can rely: Godliness is beneficial for everything. It bears the promise of life in the present and of life to come (4:8–9).

First Timothy 4:9 stands alone among the "trustworthy sayings" of the Pastoral Epistles inasmuch as the Pastor spells out some of the implications of the teaching that the formulaic saying has endorsed. His "explanation" is complex; it involves three distinct but related elements: human struggle, hope in the living God, and God's gift of salvation.

Because godliness is the kind of virtue that it is, those who accept the saying on godliness in faith must toil and struggle. Timothy was to train in godliness; people of faith must toil and struggle for godliness. God has promised the life to come, but this does not mean that life in the present is easy (see 2 Tim.

3:12). Writing to his beloved Thessalonians, Paul reminds them that the Christian life is difficult. The Christian life is characterized by faith, love, and hope, but this demands hard work, effort, and endurance (see 1 Thess. 1:3). The long beatitude preserved by Matthew and Luke affirms the ultimate happiness of those who persist despite manifold difficulties encountered on account of the Son of Man (Matt. 5:11; Luke 6:22; see 2 Tim. 3:12).

The Pastor uses a verbal hendiadys, "toil and struggle," to reflect the difficulty of the Christian life. "Toil" (*kopiōmen*)[63] is not merely "work." Toil is sometimes tedious; it always demands energy and sometimes wears people out, even to the point of exhaustion. "Struggle" (*agōnizometha*) implies difficulty from without, some form of opposition. The pairing of the two verbs suggests the idea of inherent difficulties and of difficulties from outside. Both words are derived from roots (*kop-* and *agōn-*) that early Christians used to describe the work of evangelization. In 4:10 the terms primarily relate to the struggle of the Christian life, but they are not without an evangelical component. Life and word alike proclaim the gospel message.

The second element of the Pastor's explanation of the saying on godliness speaks about Christian hope. His community, and he with them, toil and struggle, "since we have hoped in the living God." Christians hope for the life to come (4:8; Titus 1:2; 3:7; see 1 Tim. 1:16; 6:12, 19); they hope in the living God (*epi theō zōnti*). David and the Israelites of old swore by the living God. As a divine attribute, "living" is the root trait of God (see, e.g., 1 Thess. 1:9). God is "alive"; God gives life to his people through the Spirit. Although the Pastorals often use the abstract language of Hellenistic philosophy to speak about God, the Pastor describes God by means of God's primary biblical trait in a context that recalls the God of creation (4:4). Christians have hope because God lives; God is "the God of the living" (Luke 20:38). Only the living God can impart life to come (see 4:8). Hence, the ultimate object and ground of Christian hope is the living God.

The third element of the Pastor's explanation focuses on God's gift of salvation. This element is crucial. Each and every time that the "trustworthy saying" formula appears in the Pastorals it refers to some aspect of salvation (1:15; 2:15; 2 Tim. 2:10; Titus 3:6). Christians not only can, they also must rely on these formulae of faith—these formulae pertain to their salvation.

In 4:10 the Pastor speaks about God as the Savior of all human beings (*Sōtēr pantōn anthrōpōn*), not Savior of the faithful alone. Earlier he had used hymnic material to explain God's will of universal salvation and its realization through Christ Jesus (2:4–6). Then the Pastor recalled that God, the Savior, is the "one" God of the biblical tradition. Now, as he again speaks about God's

---

63. The related noun is used by Paul in 1 Thess. 1:3 when he writes about "the labor of love."

will to save all people, the Pastor uses the epithet "living" to evoke the biblical God for his audience.

God is the Savior of all, but he is especially the Savior of the faithful (*malista pistōn*) The God who wills that all people be saved also wills that they come to the full knowledge of the truth (2:4). Those who do so are the "faithful" (*pistōn*) whom God particularly wills to save. The Pastor's words about God as the Savior of all and about God who especially saves the faithful specifically relate to his teaching on godliness. Godliness is a virtue for which upright Hellenists strove; the Pastor's community is to strive for godliness, but the virtue as they are to understand it has a specifically Christian nuance.

[11–12] After the interlude on godliness, the Pastor's charge to Timothy (4:6–16) returns to "these things," what Timothy is to set before the members of the community. He is to announce and teach these things (*parangelle tauta kai didaske*). Evangelization and teaching is his ministry. In addition, notwithstanding his youth, Timothy is to serve as an example for the faithful. Paul himself not only preached, he also provided an example for those to whom he preached (1 Thess. 1:5–10; 2:9–12). Timothy is to do likewise.

Paul expected that his example would motivate people and that a chain of Christian evangelization and witness would be established. The Pastoral Epistles suppose that Timothy had learned from the teaching of Paul (see 2 Tim. 3:14) and had observed Paul's way of life (see 2 Tim. 3:10–11). He now is presented as a vital link in the chain of Christian exemplars. He is to serve the community in word and in life (see Titus 2:7–8). He is to announce and teach the things that Paul has passed on to him. He is also to serve as an example (*typos*, see Titus 2:7) for the faithful (*pistōn*), those whom God especially wants to save (4:10).

The wish that no one look down on Timothy's youth recalls a recommendation that Paul had made with regard to Timothy: "see that he has nothing to fear among you . . .; let no one despise him" (1 Cor. 16:10–11). The reference to Timothy's youth suggests that the Timothy whom the Pastor has in mind is a young man in his twenties (see 2 Tim. 2:22). The detail is consistent with the Pastor's presentation of Timothy as Paul's true son (1:2). Timothy is portrayed as a younger man to whom the ministry of Paul, the old man, has been entrusted. The five-item list of qualities that Timothy is to model for the sake of the community is comparable to the list of seven qualities that Timothy observed in Paul (2 Tim. 3:10). "Love" and "faith" appear on both lists. In the early church, the pair presented a cameo picture of the Christian life (1 Thess. 3:6; 5:8; Gal. 5:6).

The first two items on the list of exemplary demeanors that Timothy is to demonstrate are his "speech" and his "way of life." "Speech" (*en logō*) is a reference to the content, tone, and manner of Timothy's speech rather than a specific reference to the gospel message. His "way of life" (*en anastrophē*) recalls that Paul provided Timothy with the model of his own way of life (*tē agōgē*, 2 Tim. 3:10). The final quality that Timothy is to demonstrate is "holiness" (*hag-*

neia, see 4:12; 5:2). He should be undefiled, free from anything that would contaminate himself or his ministry. In 5:22 the Pastor again exhorts Timothy to be holy (*seauton hagnon tērei*). Holiness is a quality that should impact on a person's relationships with others. Thus, it should be evident in Timothy's relationship with young women (5:2). The list of qualities is evidence that the community expects the legates to the churches, and other church leaders as well, to be exemplary in regard to conduct (see Titus 2:6–7). They provide an example to the young men in the community (see the references to young men/youth in Titus 2:6; 1 Tim. 4:12a).

[13] "Absence" and "presence" (*apousia* and *parousia*) are common themes in Hellenistic letters, especially "friendly letters" that Pseudo-Demetrius described as belonging to the friendly type [typos philikos] of letter. The theme of presence, using the very word *parousia*, frequently appears in the letter writer's expressed wish to come to those to whom he is writing. Paul's own letters (Rom. 15:22, 29, 32; 1 Cor. 16:5; 2 Cor. 13:1; 1 Thess. 2:18; 3:10; Phlm. 22) often speak in this way. The idea is absent from Paul's censorious letter (*typos epitimētikos*) to the Galatians, as it is from the letter to the Philippians (but cf. Phil. 4:1), written while Paul was in prison.

The Pastor's use of the absence-presence motif in 4:13 represents one of the few truly epistolary traits of his composition. Along with the epistle's opening and closing, the phrase "until I come" imparts epistolary verisimilitude to the text. The Pastor's earlier use of the motif of Paul's coming had spoken of a delay in Paul's arrival (3:14–15a). The phrase "until I come" reinforces the idea that there is to be a delay. In the meantime, Timothy is to get on with his ministry.

Timothy is to be attentive to reading, admonition, and teaching. "Reading" (*anagnōsei*) is a technical term for the reading of the Scriptures in the assembly (see Acts 13:15; 2 Cor. 3:14; Philo, *Hypothetica* 7.14). The Pastor's plea that attention be paid to the reading of the Scriptures is consistent with the Pastorals' emphasis on the utility of the Scriptures (2 Tim. 3:16–17). Proper attention to the reading of the Scriptures will prove helpful to Timothy and the community in dealing with would-be teachers of the law, the misunderstanding of the law, and (Jewish) myths (1:7–11; 4:7).

By citing the reading of the Scriptures before making mention of Timothy's responsibility to admonish and teach, the Pastor implies that the Scriptures are the foundation for Timothy's paraenetic and didactic activity. Second Timothy 3:16 explicitly states what the Pastor implies in 4:13: The Scriptures are useful for teaching, convicting, correcting, and training for righteousness. The Scriptures are the basis for Timothy's admonition and teaching.

"Admonition" (*paraklēsei*) means giving someone motivation to change their behavior. It can imply either reprimand or encouragement. Given the admonitory character of so much of 1 Timothy and the understanding of the use of the Scriptures in 2 Tim. 3:16, the meaning of "admonition" in 4:13 is probably similar to the "conviction and correction" of 2 Tim. 3:16. Comparison and contrast highlight what Timothy is to do in addition to providing for the reading of the Scriptures. The positive side of his work is teaching. In this short summary of Timothy's responsibilities "teaching" (*didaskalia*) is to be understood as Timothy's activity as a teacher rather than as a cipher for the content of his teaching. Timothy is to teach "these things" (4:11; 6:2; see 4:6, 15), ultimately the "sound teaching" of the epistle.

[14–16] Verses 14–16 are the peroration of the Pastor's lengthy charge. The verses explain what is at stake in Timothy's faithful fulfillment of his ministry. First of all, Timothy must not neglect the spiritual gift (*charismatos*) that is in him. Paul coined this term in order to meet head-on some Corinthians' fascination with ecstatic phenomena (see 1 Cor. 12:1–11). The term "spiritual gift" or "charism" underscores the idea that, with regard to the Spirit, the extraordinary is not what matters; what really matters is the *gift* given by the Spirit. The gift is not a static gift; it is an active gift, a dynamo. God acts among his people through spiritual gifts. Through the exercise of spiritual gifts the Lord and his community are served.

Timothy's fulfillment of the charge addressed to him is thus understood to be a matter of acknowledging the gift that he has received and of being so responsive to the gift that he enables it to be active in his life (see 4:13–15). Were he not to fulfill the charge given to him, he would be unfaithful not only to Paul but also to the Spirit in him. Paul does not associate the reception of the spiritual gifts with any specific kind of ritual activity. His position is that all who have been baptized receive appropriate spiritual gifts. The Pastor, however, writes about the spiritual gift "which has been given to you through prophecy with the imposition of the hands of the group of elders." The language is similar to that of 2 Tim. 1:6, where Timothy is exhorted to rekindle "the gift of God which is in you through the laying on of my hands." These passages associate Timothy's "spiritual gift" with a "laying on of hands" (*epitheseōs tōn cheirōn*). This is a ritualized gesture signifying a transfer of power, communicating to the one upon whom hands are laid something that resides in those who impose their hands (see Acts 8:17–18 for the imparting of the gift of the Spirit).[64]

A striking difference between the two passages, 1 Tim. 4:14 and 2 Tim. 1:6, is that the former identifies a "group of elders" (see Luke 22:66; Acts 22:5) as those who impose hands, while 2 Tim. 1:6 mentions only Paul.[65] By its silence

---

64. The gesture later became a rite of entrance into an order of ministry (see Acts 6:6; 14:23), the rabbinic *semikhah* (see Str-B 2:646–61; *semikâ* means "laying," literally, "leaning," of hands), and Christian ordination.

65. The two passages employ different prepositions in reference to the laying on of hands: "with" (*meta*) in 1 Timothy, "through" (*dia*) in 2 Timothy. The causal connotations of "through" should not be exaggerated. At most, "through" suggests God's chosen instrument; minimally, it might only suggest that the gift was given during the ritual gesture.

with regard to others, 2 Tim. 1:6 implies that Paul alone imposed hands on Timothy and communicated the spiritual gift to him. It has occasionally been proposed that "of the group of elders" (*tou presbyteriou*) represents a qualifying genitive, which suggests that Timothy was coopted into a group of presbyters. The parallelism between 4:14 and 2 Tim. 1:6 suggests, however, that the wording of 4:14 means that a group of elders laid hands on Timothy.[66] According to Acts 6:6 the group of twelve apostles imposed hands on the seven disciples, who were then recognized as servants in the community.

The Pastor's circles apparently knew of a tradition that elders had imposed hands on Timothy as well as a tradition that Paul had laid hands upon Timothy. There is no real contradiction between these traditions. The Jewish horizon of 1 Timothy means that the Pastor had every interest in stating that a group of elders, a revered group among Jews, coopted Timothy into ministry. The literary form of 2 Timothy suggests that the emphasis should be placed on the specific role of the departing Paul in the cooptation of Timothy.

Another difference between 4:14 and 2 Tim. 1:6 is that 4:14 has the qualification "through prophecy" (*dia prophēteias*, see 1:18), while 2 Tim. 1:6 does not. Some interpreters have suggested the prepositional phrase means that some form of prophetic oracle designated Timothy as one upon whom hands should be laid. It is preferable to take the preposition as indicating circumstances: The laying on of hands took place in the context of the community at prayer (see Acts 6:6). According to Paul, prophecy is the sine qua non of the Christian community (see 1 Cor. 12–14). When Christians come together for prayer, the gift of prophecy is present and active.

Having instructed Timothy not to neglect the spiritual gift that he has received, the Pastor concludes the charge with a series of staccato imperatives: "Take care of these things; deal with them[67] so that your progress may be visible to everyone. Pay attention to yourself and to the teaching. Keep on doing so." Taken together, the directives emphasize the importance of the charge to Timothy.

The idea of "progress" (*hē prokopē*) appears elsewhere in the New Testament only in Phil. 1:12, 25, where it means "advancement." The Pastor's choice of this expression seems to reflect the technical sense of the term as employed by the Stoics and other philosophers to speak of a person's moral and spiritual evolution. Epictetus devoted an entire treatise to "Progress" (*peri prokopēs*, *Discourses* 1.4). Plutarch considered progress to lie somewhere in the middle between natural dispositions and perfection (see "Table Talk," 2.3.2, *Moralia* 636B). Chrysippus (third century B.C.E.) and his disciples held that the truly wise person is someone who has progressed from folly to wisdom and from vice

66. The genitive is to be taken as a subjective genitive rather than as a qualifying genitive.
67. "Deal with them" translates the Greek *en toutois isthi*, literally "be about them" (see Luke 2:49).

to virtue (frag. 217, 425, 530, 532; see *SVF* 3.51.37; 104.18; 142.17). Posido-
nius cited Socrates, Diogenes, and Antisthenes as individuals whose progress
is proof of the reality of their virtue (*SVF* 3.7.91). Philo also wrote about
progress (e.g., *Allegorical Interpretation* 3.249). Writing from his Jewish perspective, Philo noted that "all progress is due to God" (*Allegorical Interpretation* 2.93; see *Dreams* 2.237).

The Pastor is well aware of the categories used by the philosophers. Stating
that Timothy's "progress" should be visible to everyone, he emphasizes that
Timothy's moral and religious development should be able to serve as an example for the faithful (see 4:12). The Pastor's final plea is that Timothy pay attention to himself and to the teaching and that he "keep on doing so" (v. 16). In the
fashion of perorations, the first clause sums up what the Pastor has thus far said
to Timothy. Timothy must pay attention to himself and to the teaching so that
he might provide an example to the community and that his teaching be sound
(see 4:6). The reiterative "keep on doing so" (*epimene autois*)[68] stresses that
Timothy must be constantly concerned with the example that he gives and the
teaching that he offers. Both are necessary in order to confound those who have
gone astray while continuing to instruct the community.

What is at stake in all of this is salvation itself (see v. 10). If Timothy fulfills
his charge, he will save not only himself but also those who listen to his words
(see *2 Clem.* 19:1). God is the Savior of all people, but he has coopted Timothy
into his plan of salvation by means of the spiritual gift given to this good servant of Christ Jesus (4:16).

The long charge addressed to Timothy in 4:6–16 follows immediately after
the Pastor's brief reflection on the times in which the church lives (4:1–5).
Together these two pericopes interrupt the Pastor's grand reflection on the
church as the house of God. Having concluded the exposition of the charge with
the series of rapid-fire exhortations (vv. 15–16), the Pastor is able to return to
the household motifs that he had developed so insightfully in chapter 3.

Responsibilities to Men and Women
1 Timothy 5:1–2

The Pastor's exposition of duties toward younger and older people includes
elements of a household code (vv. 1–2). The directives are expressed as imperatives in the second person singular, as if they were intended for Timothy alone.
In fact, they have a wider purpose, namely, church order itself. They are not so

---

68. On the figurative sense of the verb *epimene*, see BAGD 292.2.

much personal exhortations to Timothy as they are an overall plan for church order (see Titus 1:5). The Pastor's intention is that they be heard by the "you," in the plural, to whom the epistle is ultimately addressed (6:21). The use of the singular number in the exposition of these directives suggests that, although the directives are intended for the community, each member of the community ought to follow them. Corporate order implies individual responsibility.

The fragmentary household code describes in general terms the way that believers should treat older and younger men, and older and younger women. Children are the responsibility of their parents (3:4, 12; 5:14). Sensitivity to people of different ages is one of the features of the Pastoral Epistles. What is presented here is the reverse side of what is found in Titus 2:2–5. There the duties of people in different age groups are described. Here the responsibilities of adult believers to people of different age groups are described. The Pastor's use of a household code to describe these responsibilities is quite apropos in a document that describes the Christian community as the household of God (3:15).

The Pastor's remarks with regard to older and younger men and women are succinct. These remarks lead him to consider two particular groups within the community—namely, widows, especially older widows (5:3–16), and older men, particularly those engaged in service to the community in word and teaching (5:17–19). This in turn leads to remarks about the way that the leader of the community should deal with sinners (5:20–24). Only after these particular considerations—the remarks on widows and elders are so extensive that they virtually constitute a digression in the Pastor's use of the literary form—does the Pastor return to the simplicity of the format of a household code. He does that in 6:1–2 when he takes up the matter of the responsibility of slaves toward their masters.[69]

5:1 Do not rebuke an older man but encourage him like a father, younger men like brothers, 2 older women like mothers, younger women like sisters in all holiness.

[5:1–2] The Pastor begins his exposition of the household code with a brief exhortation on how Timothy is to treat people of different age groups. The terse exhortation is classic in its brevity. It is also classic with regard to its grouping of people according to their ages. Philo divides the human community into six groups according their ages: "old men, young men, boys, and then, old women, grown women, maidens" (*Gaius* 227). The late first-century letter of *1 Clement* mentions four groups of people toward whom Christians have particular

---

69. Unfortunately, Stephen Langton's thirteenth-century division of the New Testament into chapters did not take into account the literary form of the texts. Thus, the household code of 1 Timothy is now read in two chapters (5:1–6:2), as are the household codes of Ephesians (5:21–6:9) and Colossians (3:18–4:1). Langton's ignorance of the literary form leads many contemporary readers of the New Testament to separate from one another the elements of a single literary unit.

responsibilities: "old men, young men, women, and children" (*1 Clem.* 21:6–8). The Pastor's grouping includes older and younger men, and older and younger women. Older people would be men and women in their early fifties; younger people would be in their twenties (see p. 343).

The Pastor pays more attention to older men than to the other groups, highlighting his paraenesis with a contrast between what is not to be done and what is to be done. The double exhortation provides evidence of the author's pastoral sensitivity. It is preferable to commend rather than condemn.

The book of Sirach expresses similar concern for men in their old age: "Help your father in his old age, and do not grieve him as long as he lives; even if his mind fails, be patient with him; because you have all your faculties do not despise him. For kindness to a father will not be forgotten" (Sir. 3:12–14; see Exod. 20:12; Deut. 5:16). The Pastor's hortatory words come from the same font of human wisdom as the sage's exhortation. Older men are to be encouraged, like the fathers that they presumably are.

What the Pastor says about Timothy's consideration of an older man serves as a paradigm for how one should treat other members of the community. Within the household of God, Christians are to consider people of various ages as members of the family. Younger men are to be treated like brothers, older women like mothers, and younger women like sisters. Within the household of God (see Excursus 5), obligations toward one's kin are to be extended to all members of the community. Similarly, Philo taught that "one who pays respect to an aged man or woman who is not of his kin may be regarded as having remembrance of his father and mother" (*Special Laws* 2.237).

Since the Pastor more than once expresses his awareness that the community lives in the presence of those who are not members of the community, it is possible that he is urging that all people, not merely Christians, be treated as members of one's family. His final words are a reminder that all members of the community should be encouraged "in all holiness" (*en pasē hagneia*; see 4:12). The Pastor had previously used this phrase as a complement to the classic pair, "faith and love," and as the final element in his profile of the exemplary life that Timothy is to lead. Members of the community should treat people of every age group with that same kind of holiness and dedication to God for which Timothy was noted.

"Real Widows" and Other Widows
1 Timothy 5:3–16

The Pastor pays greater attention to widows than to the members of different age groups. He sets out his expectations of widows and describes the way in which widows are to be cared for. He distinguishes three categories of widows. The first group consists of "real widows," women over sixty whom the community is to register and care for on the proviso that these widows have lived an acceptable Christian life and continue in a life of prayer (vv. 3, 5–7, 9–10). The second group consists of widows who are not "real" widows because they are not really alone. The members of a widow's household should take care of her (vv. 4, 8, 16). Finally, there are young widows, widows who are still of marriageable age. Like Paul, his mentor, the Pastor has realistic attitudes with regard to the sexual drive (see 1 Cor. 7:2–9; 1 Thess. 4:3–6). He recognizes that young widows will someday want to marry. Accordingly, he urges younger widows to remarry rather than lead dissolute and idle lives (vv. 11–15).

In showing concern for widows of various sorts, the Pastor reflects his biblical tradition. Yahweh, "God of gods and Lord of lords" (see 1 Tim. 6:15), is described as the protector of widows, orphans, and aliens (Deut. 10:17–18; see Ps. 68:5; 146:9; Mal. 3:5). Deuteronomic laws sought to protect the rights of economically vulnerable widows and orphans (Deut. 14:29; 16:11, 14; 24:17–21; 26:12, 13; see Job 31:16–23). During the renewal of the covenant, a curse is laid upon those who deprive any of these disadvantaged people of their due (Deut. 27:19; see Exod. 22:22–24). Prophetic oracles called for people to do right by orphans and widows. They railed against those who did not do so. With encouragement and threats the prophets urged the people of Israel to remember the needs of the alien, the orphan, and the widow:

> Thus says the LORD of hosts, the God of Israel: Amend your ways and your doings, and let me dwell with you in this place. . . . For if you truly amend your ways and your doings, if you truly act justly one with another, if you do not oppress the alien, the orphan, and the widow, . . . then I will dwell with you in this place." (Jer 7:3–7; see Isa. 1:17; Jer. 22:3; Zech. 7:9–10)

The Pastor capitalizes on this biblical concern as he develops a kind of casuistry that shows what kind of provision needs to be made for various kinds of widows. Young widows are encouraged to remarry. Their support will come from their new husbands. Widows who have kin are to be supported by these people. Older widows without apparent means of support, "real widows" in the Pastor's jargon, are confided to the care of the community. The Pastor digresses at some length about the responsibilities of "real widows" who are registered by the community. The Pastor's expression of concern for these older widows stems from a pastoral care for these older women, who are to be treated like mothers (5:2). Mothers deserve support in declining years (see Exod. 20:12; Deut. 5:16).

5:3 Honor widows who are real widows. 4 If any widow has children or descendants, they should first of all learn how to act in godly fashion toward their own households and pay back their forebears. This is acceptable before God. 5 The real widow, left all alone, has placed her hope in God[a] and continues in petitions and prayers night and day. 6 But the widow who runs wild, even if she is alive, has died. 7 Announce these things so that they may be blameless. 8 If anyone does not provide for his or her kin, especially if they are members of the household, that person has denied the faith and is worse than someone who is without faith. 9 Let a widow be enrolled if she is not less than sixty years of age, the wife of one husband, 10 well regarded because of her good works, if she has raised her children, has entertained strangers, if she has washed the feet of the holy ones, if she has assisted those in need, and if she has pursued every good work.

11 Decline young widows, because when they behave wantonly against Christ they want to marry, 12 having to face condemnation because they have put aside their first troth. 13 At the same time they learn to be idle, going about visiting houses, being not only idle but also gossiping and being busybodies, saying what ought not to be said. 14 I want young widows to marry, raise a family, take care of the household, giving no occasion to the Adversary because of their abuse. 15 For some have already turned aside after Satan. 16 If any woman of faith[b] has widows, she must assist them; let not the assembly be burdened, so that it can assist true widows.

a. Some manuscripts read "the Lord" (*ton kyrion*) instead of "God" (*theon*). Two important majuscules, ℵ and D, originally read "the Lord," but later copyists changed the reading to "God."

b. "Woman of faith" (*pistē*) is well attested in the majuscules, but it has been changed by some scribes who have adapted the text to their cultural situations. Some Western witnesses read "man of faith" (*pistos*); others read "men or women of faith" (*pistos ē pistē*). Some manuscripts of the Vetus Latina and of the Vulgate read *pistas*, thus, "if anyone has faithful widows."

[5:3] As the Pastor turns his attention to widowed women, he begins with the exhortation, "Honor widows who are real widows." The exhortation recalls the fifth precept of the Decalogue, "Honor your father and mother" (Exod. 20:12; Deut. 5:16), a provision of the law requiring that care be taken of one's elderly forebears. The biblical "honor," as the Pastor's *tima*, "honor," connotes physical and financial support. The commandment was specifically addressed to individual Jewish males. Now the Pastor directs Timothy, the leader of the community, to ensure that care be taken of "real widows" (*ontōs chērais*; see 6:19). These are, as the Pastor will quickly point out, elderly widows, previ-

ously married women more than sixty years of age, who have no family to care
for them (vv. 5, 9).

The Hebrew Bible's "widows" (*'almānôt*) were once-married women who
no longer had any means of financial support and therefore required special care
and legal protection. Women such as Ruth, Orpah, Naomi, Abigail, and
Bathsheba were not considered to be widows in this technical sense because,
on the death of their husbands, they were not without financial support. Israel's
understanding of "widows" was similar to that reflected in other strata of Near
Eastern culture. A Middle Assyrian law, dating from sometime around 1076
B.C.E., for example, stipulated:

> If a woman is residing in her own father's house, her husband is dead, and she
> has sons [. . .],[70] or [if he so pleases], he shall give her into the protection of the
> household of her father-in-law. If her husband and father-in-law are both dead,
> and she has no son, she is indeed a widow [*almattu*]; she shall go wherever she
> pleases. (MAL A.33; see MAL A.28, A.33–34, A.40, A.45–46, the Laws of Ur-
> Namma 10–11, and the Laws of Hammurabi 171–73, 176a–77)

[4] Having spoken of the community's need to provide for "real widows,"
the Pastor writes about widows who cannot be categorized as "real widows."
This second category consists of widows who have children or grandchildren.
Since the Pastor speaks about descendants[71] as well as about children, he is
really considering the case of an older woman whose husband has died and
whose sons might also have died. In such a case, responsibility for the widow's
care devolves upon her descendants, that is, her sons and her grandsons. Under
Jewish and Near Eastern law, male offspring bore the responsibility to care for
women whose husbands had died (see 5:16).

Exhorting male offspring to provide for their widowed forebears, the Pastor
reminds them that this fulfillment of household responsibility is a matter of acting in godly fashion (*eusebein*). Taking care of the widows in one's own family
is an expression of filial piety. Sons and grandsons are to pay them back (*amoibas
apodidonai*) for the sustenance and care provided over the course of years.

The care of elderly widows to whom a man is related might not come easily to a son or grandson. It is something that he must learn to do, behavior to
which he must become accustomed. Public piety and concerns for social welfare (see MAL A.46) should motivate men to care for their widowed relatives,
but the Pastor adds that caring for widows is also a matter of doing something

70. MAL A.46 provides a clue as to how the ellipsis can be interpreted, namely, of the woman's
right to move into the home of whichever son she chooses.

71. This fragment of a legal code is the only New Testament text to make use of this broad kinship language, "descendants" (*ekgona*) and "forebears" (*progonois*). The only exception is the use
of "forebears" in 2 Tim. 1:3.

that is acceptable to God. The support of widows is, like prayer for authorities, not only a civic duty but is also something that is pleasing to God (see 2:3). The Pastor's addition of the element of religious motivation to his exposition of a household code recalls the way that similar formulae are used in the household codes of Eph. 5:22–6:9 and Col. 3:18–4:1.

[5–7] As if tradition had not been enough to explain what the Pastor meant by "real widow," the Pastor offers an explanation of what he means by this terminology. The real widow is one who has been left all alone (*kai memonōmenē*). The real widow has no one to take care of her; she relies on God alone. In this respect she is one of those poor, the *ʿănāwîm* to whom reference is so often made in the Psalms. These poor are God's clients; they cry out to him in their need. The plight of the solitary widow who relies on God alone is exemplified in the description of her as one who continues in petitions and prayers night and day (see Luke 2:37; 1 Tim. 2:1). "Night and day" underlines the constancy of her prayer; it reflects the Jewish way of considering each day as "evening and morning" (see, e.g., Gen. 1:5, 8, 13, 19, 23, 31). The widow's prayer is not only a prayer of praise and gratitude; it is necessarily also a prayer of supplication (*tais deēsesin kai tais proseuchais*).

In any society there are always people who do not live up to expectations. Widows who have been left with no descendants are no exception. Some Near Eastern legislation placed restrictions on what a widow could do and how she should appear in public (Laws of Hammurabi 171; MAL A.40). The Pastor mentions widows who have run amok (*spatalōsa*). These seem to be widowed women who have spent the time of their widowhood not in prayer and petition but in the pursuit of pleasure (see Jas. 5:5). In the Pastor's judgment such women, although physically alive, are really dead (*zōsa tethnēken*). For the Pastor, real life is eternal life (6:19). Pleasure-seeking widows do not share eternal life.

The Pastor's comment in regard to people who, though physically alive, are really dead echoes a notion found in Hellenistic moralists: The virtuous person is truly alive; an evil person is really dead. Philo reflects this philosophic tradition. In commenting on Deut. 30:15, he writes, "Goodness and virtue is life, evil and wickedness is death" (*Flight and Finding* 58). Earlier he had written:

> I attended the lectures of a wise woman, whose name is Consideration. . . . [S]he taught me that some people are dead while living, and some alive while dead. She told me that bad people, prolonging their days to extreme old age, are dead, deprived of the life in association with virtue, while good people, even if cut off from their partnership with the body, live for ever, and are granted immortality. (*Flight and Finding* 55)

The Pastor concludes this part of his legislative text with an exhortation addressed directly to the recipient of his letter. The language that it uses—

"announce," "these things," and "blameless"—is characteristic of 1 Timothy.[72] Timothy is to give the word (see 1:3; 4:11) to widows; he should tell them these things. The reason why Timothy is to exhort widows in this fashion is so that they be blameless. The thought echoes that of Paul, who prayed that those whom he had evangelized should be blameless (*amemptōs*) at the coming of the Lord Jesus Christ (1 Thess. 3:13; 5:23).

[8] Kin must especially take care of widows who are members of the household. It is possible to construe the "especially" clause to mean that within the context of a general obligation to take care of their widowed relatives, Christians are particularly expected to take care of widows who live within their own households. It is, however, more likely that the words "members of the household" (*oikeiōn*) make reference to fellow Christians. The noun has this meaning in its other New Testament uses (Gal. 6:10 and Eph. 2:19). The sentence mentions "faith" twice, suggesting that one should take the term to mean "the household [of faith]." Finally, taking the expression as a reference to believers coheres with the ecclesial reference of the *oik-* root in the Pastorals. The assembly, the church itself, is the household of God (*oikō theou*, 3:15; see Excursus 5).

Verse 8 urges that special attention be given to widowed women within the community of believers. Should those who are related (in faith) to these widows neglect them, this neglect is tantamount to a denial of the faith. As regards the faith, they are no better off than someone who has no faith, the unbeliever (*a-pistou*). In fact, such people are worse than unbelievers. By speaking about faith as he does in verse 8b, the Pastor has clearly expressed that the faith, fully understood and accepted, bears with it moral responsibilities, in this instance, moral responsibilities toward the disadvantaged members of the community.

[9–10] The Pastor's use of the technical term "enrolled" suggests that there was a well-defined group of real widows in the community.[73] In common parlance, "enrolled" (*katalegesthō*) was used of those who were enlisted or conscripted into an army. A number of conditions were stipulated in order that a woman be recognized as a true widow and enrolled in this group. In all, eight conditions were set forth.

The first was that she should be no less than sixty years of age. The second was that she should be the wife of one husband (*henos andros gynē*). The quality of marital fidelity is similar to one that is stipulated for those who serve the community as overseer or server (3:2, 12; Titus 1:6). Theodore of Mopsuestia held that "wife of one husband" means that the widow had been chaste and was faithful to her husband: "If she has lived in chastity with her husband, no matter

---

72. See 1:3; 4:11; 5:7; 6:13, 17 for "announce" (*parangellō*); 3:14; 4:6, 11, 15; 5:7; 6:2 for "these things" (*tauta*); 3:2; 5:7; 6:14 for "blameless" (*anepilēmptoi*).

73. The technical sense of this verb has led many commentators on this passage to speak of an "order of widows" within the Pastor's community.

whether she has had only one, or whether she was married a second time . . ." (Commentary or Timothy 2.161 [66.944]; see Theodoret, *Interpretation of Timothy* 2.64 [PG 82.817]). On the other hand, the previously cited Near Eastern texts (see p. 137) seem to indicate that a real widow is a woman who had been married just once. Roman society—not so, however, Greek society—held that it was ideal for a widow not to remarry after her husband's death. Livy, the historian, tells us that only widows who had been married not more than once could serve at the altar of Pudicitia (see *Roman History* 10.23.9). Nevertheless, both the *lex Julia* of 18 B.C.E. and the *lex Papia Poppaea* of 9 C.E. strongly encouraged widows and unmarried men to get married.

The first two characteristics of a real widow listed by the Pastor concern her status in society at large. The remaining six indicate that a widow who is to be enrolled in the "real widows" group must be a woman noted for her virtue and Christian character (see Pol. *Phil.* 4:3). The idea of "good works" and "every good work" in verse 10 provides a literary inclusion that delineates her Christian profile (see 2:10). Both "good works" and "every good work" describe the virtuous and Christian life in its entirety.[74] A real widow should pursue the Christian life in every respect. If she does so, her conduct will provide evidence of her uprightness to those outside the community.

The enrolled widow should have raised her family well and provided hospitality. These conditions are similar to those set out for a man desiring to be the overseer (3:2, 4; see Titus 1:6, 8), but different terminology is employed. A widow is to have "raised her children" (*eteknotrophēsen*) and "entertained strangers" (*exenodochēsen*); the overseer is to be hospitable and to have children who are well behaved (3:2, 4). In using different terms to describe the different but complementary responsibilities of husband and wife, the Pastor reflects conventional notions of the household responsibilities proper to men and women (see Titus 2:2–6).

The hospitality expected of a woman who one day would be enrolled as a real widow was probably the sort of hospitality that was offered to fellow Christians, perhaps especially to traveling Christians and evangelists. Washing a guest's feet was a common gesture of hospitality in ancient times, particularly in the Near East (see Luke 7:44). "The holy ones" (*hagiōn*) are fellow Christians. The expression describes believers as belonging to God, as being God's "own" people. Use of this terminology to describe believers is common in the New Testament, especially in Paul (Rom. 1:7; 12:13; 15:25, 26, 31; 16:15; 1 Cor. 1:2; 6:2; 14:33; 16:1, 15; 2 Cor. 1:1; 8:4; 9:1, 12; 13:12; Phil. 1:1; 4:22; 1 Thess. 3:13; Phlm. 5, 7), but this is the only time that the epithet is used in the Pastorals.

The final condition that a sixty-year-old widow must meet if she is to be

---

74. For "good works" (*ergois kalois*) see 5:25; 6:18; Titus 2:7, 14; 3:8, and 14. For "every good work" (*pan ergon agathon*) see 2 Tim. 2:21; 3:17; Titus 1:16; and 3:1.

enrolled in the group of widows is that she should "have assisted those in need." This striking terminology is used only within this pericope in the New Testament. The verb (*epērkesen*) connotes both financial and personal support. "The needy" (*thlibomenois*) is a participial form derived from a root that Paul often uses in reference to the distress of the end times. The Pastor seems not to be using the participle with that nuance; he uses it to speak of the needy, the object of Christian love and concern.

[11–15] Verse 11 orders Timothy not to enroll young widows. The reason alleged is that these young widows will want to marry. The verb "to marry" (*gamein*) is in the active voice, as it is in verse 14. In the culture of the times, men married (active voice) and women were married (passive voice, see Luke 20:34–35). The use of the active voice in 5:11 (see 5:14; Mark 10:12; 1 Cor. 7:28) may suggest that the Pastor was thinking about young widows taking the initiative with regard to a second marriage, thereby contravening social convention and perhaps indicating that they did not want to enter the household of their in-laws.

Wanting to marry, young widows are likely to behave wantonly (*katastrēniasōsin*) toward Christ.[75] "When they feel sensuous impulses that alienate them from Christ" is the way that BDF renders the Pastor's terse phrase. This would be consistent with the negative attitude toward desire, especially sexual desire (*epithymia*), seen in the writings of the philosophic moralists. Early Christians took the sexual drive seriously (see 1 Cor. 7:2–9; 1 Thess. 4:3–4). The Pastor does as well. He urges young widows to marry (v. 14). They were certainly free to marry (see 1 Cor. 7:39).

The situation envisioned by the Pastor in verses 11–12 may have been that a young widow, having amorous desires at Christ's expense, would marry someone who was a non-Christian. Such a marriage would not have been in accord with Paul's teaching that widows should marry "in the Lord" (1 Cor. 7:40). Were a young widow to marry a non-Christian, she would be under considerable social pressure to abandon the Christian faith, her first troth. Social customs of the time dictated that a wife follow the religion of her husband (see Plutarch, "Advice to the Bride and Groom" 19, *Moralia* 140D). Were a Christian widow to marry a non-Christian and succumb to the social pressure to follow the gods of her husband, she would have abandoned her faith in Christ. Thus, she would deserve condemnation (*krima*, see 3:6).

Were young widows not to marry, it is possible that they might become gadabouts. Having nothing to do, and without responsibilities for household or children, they might while away the time visiting one household after another. What then? Not only would they have nothing to do, they would compound the

75. 1 Tim. 5:11 is the only passage in the Pastorals in which "Christ" is used without being conjoined with the name "Jesus."

problem of their idleness by gadding about, gossiping, and being busybodies (*phlyaroi kai periergoi*). The Pastor uses a three-item list of vices to describe the wanton state of these young widows. The final element in the Pastor's negative description of these young widows is that they say things that ought not to be said. His cultural conditioning is such that he can conceive of these young widows only as being up to no good.

Rather than allowing young widows to fall into the trap of idleness or of marriage to a non-Christian, the Pastor urges young widows to remarry, just as other young women are expected to marry (2:15; Titus 2:4–5). The mere condition of having been widowed at a young age should not deter these women from assuming the social role that young women are expected to have. Women of a marriageable age were expected to marry, raise a family, and take care of their household (*gamein, teknogonein* [see 2:15], *oikodespotein*).[76] The trio of verbs that describes what is expected of a young widow stands in contrast with the three items that appear in the Pastor's negative description of the state into which an idle young widow might fall (v. 13).

If young widows act as they should and do not engage in abusive activity (*loidorias*), they will not give the adversary (*tōantikeimenō*) any occasion to cause difficulties for the community. The "Adversary" appears elsewhere in the New Testament in reference to the ultimate apocalyptic foe (see 2 Thess. 2:4; cf. Luke 13:17; 21:15; 1 Cor. 16:9; Phil. 1:28). Here it has reference to Satan (see 1:20), the legendary antagonist of the people of God in Jewish apocalyptic thought (see Rom. 16:20; 1 Cor. 7:5; 2 Cor. 2:11; 11:14; 12:7; 1 Thess. 2:18; 2 Thess. 2:9). The Pastor's chosen description for the Adversary implies that he has been influenced by the apocalyptic tradition (see 4:1). Already "some" have succumbed to the wiles of Satan. The reference to the anonymous "some" (1:6, 19; 4:1; 6:10, 21) shows that the Pastor was well aware that the danger of apostasy was real not only for men within his community but was also a danger to which women, especially young widows, were prone.

[16] The final element in the Pastor's exhortation on widows is specifically addressed to women of faith (*pistē*). Should there be members of their households who are widows, the Pastor enjoins the women to provide for these widows. The Pastor's exhortation indicates that women had a role in the community that would have been considered unusual at the time. Women were exhorted to take care of widows. In the culture of the times that responsibility normally devolved upon men, the heads of households. In contrast, the Pastor urges women to take care of widows. Their Christian faith should prompt them to do so. Moreover, the Pastor urges women of faith to be attentive to the needs and abilities of the Christian

76. "Marry" is again in the active voice (see 5:11). The other two verbs do not appear elsewhere in the New Testament. The rarity of this linguistic usage is an indication that the Pastor is, as it were, using "borrowed material," that is, the traditional language of household codes, in the epistle.

community. Previously he had indicated that women believers had some responsibility toward the church when he urged young widows not to give any occasion to the Adversary (v. 14). Now women of faith are encouraged to take responsibility for some widows within the community. They are not to wait for their husbands to take on this responsibility, nor are they to expect that the church should do so. Any woman of faith has a responsibility to take care of widows among her kin. The burden of providing for these widows should not be relegated to the members of the assembly. The members of the assembly are to take care of widows who are really widows, without kin and deprived of financial support. Let an additional burden not be placed on the community, says the Pastor as he brings his lengthy expansion of the household code to its conclusion. Women have important responsibilities within the house of God.

The Rights of Elders
1 Timothy 5:17–19

The Pastor began chapter 5 with some elements of what might be considered a household code in reverse; his initial words identified those to whom obligations were owed rather than those who had various duties within the household. Household codes customarily describe the respective responsibilities of the members of a household (see Titus 2:2–5); the Pastor's household code exhorts the members of the community to treat various groups of people in the household in appropriate and familial fashion (5:1–2). His exhortation on the treatment of widows in the community was so extensive as to virtually constitute a rhetorical digression (5:3–16) within the exposition of his household code.

In 5:17 the Pastor turns his attention to elders, especially those who labor in word and teaching. Elders who are engaged in the ministry of prophecy and teaching must be taken care of by the community. The Pastor cites a passage from Scripture and an appropriate adage to remind the community of this responsibility. Elders engaged in prophecy and teaching have a right to be supported; they also have a right to their good name. The Pastor evokes biblical jurisprudence to remind Timothy that a charge should not be brought against an elder except if there are at least two witnesses ready to testify against him. With its halakhic or regulatory use of Scripture, this pericope (5:17–19) is unlike any other passage in 1 Timothy. Concerned with elders' rights to a just wage and "judicial" equity, the pericope contains a kind of elder's bill of rights.

17 Let elders who manage well be considered worthy of a double honor, especially those who labor in word and teaching. 18 For the scripture says, "Do not muzzle the ox that is threshing" and "The worker is worthy of

his wages."ᵃ 19 Do not accept any charge against an elder except on the
testimony of two or three witnesses.

a. With the exception of ℵ, the textual witnesses almost unanimously read "wages"
(*tou misthou*). The Codex Sinaiticus reads "food" (*tēs trophēs*), undoubtedly under the
influence of Matt. 10:10.

[5:17–18] Philo says that Moses applied "the name of elder not to one who
is bowed down with old age but to one who is worthy of precedence and honor
[*ton gerōs kai timēs axion*]" (*Sobriety* 16). The Pastor writes in the same vein.
The elders of whom he writes are not the "older men" of 5:1; rather, they are
the overseers whose qualifications he had surveyed in 3:1–7. The Pastor treats
elders in much the same way that he treats widows. Not all widows are to be
supported by the community; only those older and destitute widows who pray
for the community are to be supported by the community. So it is with elders.
The community has a responsibility to provide for elders who have a particular function in the community. Titus 1:5–9 apparently uses "elders" and "overseers" almost interchangeably. The elders of whom the Pastor writes in 5:17–19
would thus seem to be elders who have leadership responsibilities within the
community.

Those who fulfill their task[77] well are worthy of a double honor. "Honor"
(*timēs*) is something rendered to someone or something on the basis of the
recipient's worth or value. The word itself can mean "esteem" or "dignity"; it
can also mean "payment" or "wages." Some commentators read the Pastor's
"double honor" as if he were suggesting that the elder who manages well
deserves double pay. The Pastor clearly states that the community must provide an elder with his sustenance. He cites Scripture in support of this position. Rather than suggesting double wages, it is likely that "double honor"
means that the elder ought to be held in esteem by the community as well as
be sustained by it. The implied reference to the regard in which the elder is to
be held by the community anticipates verse 19. Verse 18 expands on the elder's
right to sustenance; verse 19 expands on the elder's right to esteem. In providing both sustenance and high regard, the community renders double honor
to an elder.

Elders who labor in word and teaching (*hoi kopiōntes en logō kai didaskalia*)
are especially worthy of honor and appropriate compensation. Paul uses the
verb "labor" to describe the work of those who have positions of leadership in
the community: "respect those who labor [*tous kopiōntas*] among you and have
charge [*proïstamenous*] of you in the Lord" (1 Thess. 5:12). The Pastor echoes
and gives substance to Paul's words in 1 Tim. 5:17. Those who have charge of

---

77. The Pastor uses the verb *proïstēmi*, "manage." See 3:4–5; cf. 1 Thess. 5:12.

the community have a twofold task: to profess the prophetic word, that is, to be God's spokespersons, and to teach. Teaching is the ministry of catechesis, teaching a community that has already been evangelized. The work of teaching, passing along the tradition of sound teaching, is one of Timothy's principal tasks. The elders of the community carry on that teaching. To a large extent teaching consists of the faithful transmission of the trustworthy sayings and the explanation of the Scriptures (see 2 Tim. 3:16). The Pastor's use of Scripture immediately after (5:18) he speaks of the work of teaching is just one indication that teaching involves the use of Scripture.

The ministry of word and of teaching does not imply that all who have this leadership ministry exercise it well (note the use of "well" [*kalōs*] in 5:17), nor does it imply that all who have the ministry of leadership have the gifts of prophecy and teaching. Prophecy and teaching are, after the apostolate itself, the second and third spiritual gifts given to the community for its welfare (see 1 Cor. 12–14, esp. 12:28–29). Prophecy is, in fact, a sine qua non of the Christian community. Prophecy and teaching are not, however, the only spiritual gifts given to people who serve the community and may even do so well (note the use of "especially" [*malista*] in 5:17). Paul specifically mentions the gift of "leadership" itself (*kybernēseis*) in 1 Cor. 12:28.

"Labor" (*kopiaō*) describes the ministry of those engaged in the ministry of prophecy and teaching. The use of this verb suggests that the ministry of prophecy and teaching demands effort. It is time-consuming and fatiguing. Had the Pastor used the verb "to work" (*energeō*), as Paul often did, he would have been implying that ultimately the ministry of prophecy and teaching is the work of God (1 Cor. 12:6; see 1 Thess. 2:13). In his pragmatic presentation of the ministry of elders, the Pastor has not only made mention of their due compensation but also reminds them that their ministry is a matter of human effort. No wonder that all do not do it well!

To provide a warrant for his assertion that elders deserve to be supported, the Pastor follows his mentor, Paul, in citing Deut. 25:4 (see 1 Cor. 9:9). This verse is taken from the Torah's agricultural law. In keeping with a rabbinic principle of biblical interpretation, the principle of *qal-wa-homer*, an argument from the lesser to the greater, the Pastor applies the scriptural quotation in *a fortiori* fashion to the situation with which he is concerned: If animals are to be fed when they work, even more so should working preachers and teachers. The Pastor then reinforces his claim that elders should receive compensation with an early church adage: "The worker is worthy of his [*autou*] wages." The adage is similar to a logion from Q that Matthew and Luke have incorporated into their respective versions of Jesus' missionary charge (Luke 10:7; Matt. 10:10). In Matthew the saying appears in an instruction to the twelve apostles (see Matt. 10:1–4). In Luke the same saying appears in the instruction directed to seventy disciples (see Luke 10:1).

The Pastor seems to identify both the passage from Deuteronomy and the logion as "scripture" (*hē graphē*), but Christian writings were not yet regarded as Scripture at this point in the history of the early church. It is, moreover, quite unlikely that the Pastor had available a written version of Q,[78] Matthew, or Luke. Matthew's use of the saying with a small difference of wording (see note a, above) suggests that the adage circulated in the early Christian community. It may even have been a proverb, expressing the common wisdom of the times. Familiarity with the saying may have led the Pastor to have inadvertently identified it as "scripture."[79] Since Deut. 25:4 is certainly a "scripture," the adage might have been taken as a paraphrase of Moses' charge to the Israelites with regard to the material welfare of Levites (Num. 18:31; see 2 Chr. 15:7).

[19] Having argued that the elder is worthy of honor and compensation, the Pastor turns his attention to a corollary of the assertion that elders who fulfill their task well are worthy of twofold honor. Deserving of honor as elders are, Timothy is not to accept any charges against them except when two witness come forward to accuse them of wrongdoing. The exhortation is a biblical injunction (see Deut. 19:15; cf. Matt. 18:16). The Pastor's allusion to traditional Jewish legal practice may imply that the community may have faced a troubling situation in which false teachers were unjustly accusing the community's elders.[80]

Pastoral Care of Sinners
1 Timothy 5:20–25

Mention of the judicial equity due to elders leads the Pastor to express his thought on the pastoral care of sinners (5:20–25). In doing so, he deviates from the scheme of the household code that he had begun in 5:1 and that he will take up again in 6:1. The Pastor may have considered that after he had had something to say about old men, young men, old women, young women, widows, and elders it was important for him to say something about another group within the community, namely, sinners. How should a church leader deal with the sinners in the community? Paul (1 Cor. 5) and Matthew (18:15–20) had written about the responsibility of a community and its leaders toward inveterate sinners. Now the Pastor sets forth his views on the topic. First of all, he directs that sinners be

---

78. The Pastoral Epistles provide no evidence that the Q collection was available to the Pastor's circles.

79. A similar phenomenon is to be found in Pol. *Phil* 12:1. There Eph. 4:26, cited immediately after Ps. 4:4, is apparently identified as "scripture."

80. At about the same time that 1 Timothy was written, Clement of Rome wrote his letter to the church of Corinth. The letter was written because insubordination was rife and some duly appointed elders had been unlawfully deposed.

examined in the presence of the entire community. Such scrutiny should be beneficial for the community. Knowledge of the sins of others (see 5:14) should lead the rest of the community to the fear of God and the fear of sin.

Timothy's responsibility with regard to people who persist in their sin is weighty. He must not act capriciously in their regard. The Pastor warns Timothy to exercise this responsibility without prejudice and partiality. Another caution reminds Timothy that sinners are not to be reconciled too quickly to the community. Sin has an ugly habit of clinging to people (5:24). Using the metaphor of yeast and a batch of dough, Paul reminds the Corinthians that sin has the power to corrupt a community (see 1 Cor. 5:6b–7). Accordingly, the Pastor urges Timothy to think twice before imposing hands on the sinner and restoring him or her to participation in the life of the community.

The Pastor interrupts his discourse on the discipline of sinners with an expression of concern for Timothy's well-being, advice for Timothy to be attentive to his own spiritual and physical condition (5:23). After this aside the Pastor returns to the topic at hand, namely, sinners and their sin. He contrasts the sins of the troublesome "some" with the good works of the members of the community. Sin, always visible, seems to cling to "some." In similar fashion good works are visible, even when members of the community try to do their good deeds in secret.

5:20 Cross-examine sinners in the presence of all so that everyone else might be afraid. 21 I solemnly charge you in the presence of God, Christ Jesus, and the chosen angels that you maintain this practice without prejudice, doing nothing as the result of partiality. 22 Do not impose hands hastily on anyone lest you share in the sins of others. Keep yourself holy. 23 No longer drink only water; use a little wine for the stomach's sake and because of your frequent illnesses. 24 Some people's sins are blatant, leading to condemnation; for some, they follow close behind as well. 25 Just as[a] good works are manifest, works of the other kind cannot be hidden.

a. Verses 24 and 25 constitute a single sentence in Greek.

[5:20–21] The Pastor's recalling of the biblical tradition on the necessity of two witnesses in corroborating a charge of wrongdoing indicates that the Pastor has begun to consider the jurisprudence that ought to operate in the fledgling community. Words taken from the juridical register—"cross-examine," "in the presence of," "solemnly charge," "prejudice," and "partiality"—confirm that the Pastor is evoking a judicial setting in these verses.

"Solemnly charge" (*diamartyromai*; see 2 Tim. 2:14; 4:1) is a term taken from Attic law. "In the presence of" (*enōpion*, vv. 20 and 21) suggests a face-to-face encounter, not unlike that of the common-law right of the accused to face his or her accusers. The Pastor's words indicate that one who continues in sin (*hamartanontas*) is to be brought before the entire assembly (see Matt. 18:17; 1 Cor. 5:4–5) and questioned. This is done so that everyone else who is present (*hoi loipoi*, "the rest") have the fear of God put into them, thereby motivating them to avoid similarly sinful behavior. The Pastor concludes his exhortation on pastoral jurisprudence with a solemn reminder that justice is to be administered with neither "prejudice" (*prokrimatos*) nor "partiality" (*prosklisin*). His use of a pair of assonant terms—in Greek they begin with the same sound—emphasizes the importance of the Pastor's plea. An impartial administration of justice must always be maintained (*tauta phylaxēs*).

To further underscore the importance of this charge, the Pastor solemnly calls on God and the entire heavenly host as his witnesses. The cohort includes Christ Jesus, witness par excellence, and the chosen angels. "Chosen" (*eklektōn*) is a word that is often used in the New Testament to describe Christians, generally calling attention to their eschatological status (see Mark 13:20–27). Only here is it used of angels (*angelōn*). The idea that some angels are God's chosen ones while others are not evokes a judicial motif of postexilic Judaism. Satan and the fallen angels are not members of the divine court.

[22a] Earlier the Pastor had made mention of hands being imposed upon Timothy (4:14; see 2 Tim. 1:6). The gesture, symbolizing the transfer of power, functioned as part of an ordination ritual. Elsewhere in the New Testament, the gesture symbolizes healing (Mark 6:5; 8:23; Luke 4:40; 13:13; Acts 9:12, 17), blessing (Matt. 19:13, 15), "confirmation" with the gift of the Spirit (Acts 8:17; 19:6), or commissioning for a function within the church (Acts 6:6; 13:3). Scholars disagree over the symbolism of the ritual gesture mentioned in 5:22. Some think it is a commissioning ritual (see 4:14; 2 Tim. 1:6; Acts 13:1–2); others think it is a sign of reconciliation.

Arguments in favor of the view that laying on of hands is a commissioning ritual are the proximity of this pericope to the Pastor's words on the rights of elders, the fact that 1 Timothy has as one of its main concerns the quality of people admitted to leadership, and the weighty interpretation of some church fathers. After asking a rhetorical question about the meaning of the Pastor's "hastily," Chrysostom replied "Not upon a first, nor a second, nor a third trial but after frequent and strict examination and circumspection. For it is an affair of no common peril. For you will be responsible for the sins committed by him, as well his past as his future sins, because you have delegated to him this power" (*Homily* 16 on 1 Timothy [PG 62.587]; see "Priesthood" 4.2 [PG 48:663]). Servers are to undergo scrutiny before being admitted to service (3:10). If the imposition of hands in verse 22 is a reference to a commissioning ritual, Timothy is being exhorted to ensure that the process of scrutinizing church leaders not be conducted with undue haste. Only after the proper process has been followed should Timothy impose hands, just as hands had been imposed on him when he assumed a leadership position within the church (4:14).

The immediate context of verse 22 is, however, a discussion of sinners and sin; verses 20–25 deal with the pastoral care of sinners. Verse 22 makes specific mention of sin. Thus, contextual and linguistic considerations make it likely that verse 22, with its mention of the ritual of the imposition of hands, has to do with the church's pastoral practice toward sinners. Paul had been concerned about this. He severely criticized the church at Corinth for its tolerance of the sin of incest (1 Cor. 5:1–8). Matthew 18:10–18 speaks about the responsibility of church leaders with regard to sinners and those liable to sin.

As leader of the community, Timothy has a responsibility vis-à-vis sinners (5:20). He is to have no complicity in the sins of others. Thus, he is exhorted not to impose hands hastily lest he "share in the sins of others" (*mēde koinōnei hamartiais allotriais*). Timothy is not to restore them to communion with the church without due consideration and probably not without appropriate conversion and penance on their part. The symbolism of the laying on of hands as a gesture of forgiveness and reconciliation is similar to the laying on of hands for healing or baptism. In the Jewish world, sickness was generally viewed as God's punishment for sin. The imposition of hands would confer healing and symbolize forgiveness (see Matt. 9:5; Mark 2:9; Luke 5:23). Christian baptism with the imposition of hands was baptism for the remission of sins. In context, the laying on of hands in 5:22 is a gesture of forgiveness and reconciliation (see Heb. 6:2). With managerial responsibility for the household of God, Timothy is exhorted to reconcile to the community only those who have properly repented of their sins.

[22b–23] The Pastor emphasizes this injunction with a reminder to Timothy that he keep himself holy (*hagnon*; see 1 Tim. 4:12; 5:2). To this he adds a rejoinder that Timothy keep himself fit and healthy: "No longer drink only water; use a little wine for the stomach's sake and because of your frequent illnesses." This rejoinder apparently interrupts the flow of the Pastor's thought, but given the less-than-systematic order of 1 Timothy, this aside is not quite the interruption that it may seem to be at first sight. "Timothy" bears a heavy responsibility for the church of Ephesus (1:3). In 5:22b–23 the Pastor expresses his concern that Timothy be spiritually and physically fit for the task at hand. Negatively and positively the Pastor urges Timothy to attend to his spiritual state. He is not to share in the sins of others; he is to keep himself holy. In verse 23 the Pastor turns his attention to Timothy's physical well-being. He must attend to his health.

People of ancient times were well aware of gastric difficulties. Epictetus, for example, wrote that those "with a weak stomach throw up their food" (*Discourses* 3.21.1). As a remedy, Greco-Roman doctors prescribed a bit of wine. The Talmud states that Jewish elders believed wine to be the primary medicine: "First among the medicines am I, Wine. Where there is no wine, people seek drug potions" (*b. B. Bat.* 58b).[81] In Jewish teaching the moderate use of wine was thought to relate to a person's general well-being. "Wine has two virtues," says the Talmud, "it nourishes and brings joy" (*b. Ber.* 35b). Rabbi Hanan is reputed to have taught, "Wine was not created except to console mourners and to give the wicked their just reward, as it is said, 'Give drink to those who are lost and wine to those of heavy heart'" (*b. Sanh.* 70b).

In urging Timothy to drink a little wine (see 3:3, 8) and not restrict himself to water, the Pastor is urging him to avoid undue ascetic practices. Abstinence from wine was enjoined upon the Nazirites (Num. 6:1–4) and practiced by the Rechabites (Jer. 35:5–6), but Rabbi Joshua stated that most of the congregation were unable to practice this kind of abstinence (*b. B. Bat.* 60b). The Mishnah suggests that eating bread with salt and drinking water by measure, apparently a quart (one sixth of a hin) at set times (see Ezek. 4:11), was a regimen to be followed by those seeking knowledge of the law (*m. 'Abot* 6:4). Timothy is to avoid this kind of asceticism and take care of his health. Earlier in his missive the Pastor had argued against demonic teachings that promote undue abstinence, thereby denigrating what God had created (4:3–5). The Pastor does not want Timothy himself to fall victim to the conduct that the false teachers were advocating.

Commenting on 5:23, Clement of Alexandria stressed not only the medicinal value of wine but also the fact that wine is a "creature of God": "Both[82] are creatures of God [*tou theou poiēmata*], and for this reason a combination of both, water and wine, contributes to health, since life combines the necessary and the useful" (see *Paedagogus* 2.2; PG 8:416). Many other church fathers argued along the same lines. Thus, Chrysostom posed the question, "Don't you know that bodily infirmity no less than infirmity of soul injures both us and the Church?" (*Homily* 1 *on Titus* [PG 62.670]).

[24–25] After his digression on Timothy's well-being, the Pastor returns to the topic at hand in this pericope, namely, sinners and their sin. He contrasts "sins" and "good works." Both are easy to see. Sins (*hai hamartiai*) lead to judgment and condemnation. The thought continues the judicial motif of the earlier part of the pericope. Sinful deeds are manifest (*prodēloi*); they merit the scrutiny and condemnation that comes with the sinner's cross-examination in the presence of the assembly (v. 20). Conversion from sin is not easy to achieve. Sin tends to follow people around, particularly the enigmatic "some" (*tisin*) about whom the Pastor has written so often in this epistle. Sin, as it were, almost sticks to these people (*tisin de kai epakolouthousin*). Our contemporaries might have said that it follows them like the plague.

---

81. The translation of these passages from the Talmud is that of Betty Sigler Rozen, who translated Shulamit Valler, *Women and Womanhood in the Talmud,* BJS 321 (Providence: Brown Judaic Studies, 1999), 77, 78.

82. That is, wine and water.

Good works are also manifest (*prodēla*). "Good works" is a cipher for proper conduct as the Pastor and his community understood it. Good works[83] are the hallmark of the Pastor's community, a sign that they have heard the message and live accordingly. To emphasize his point that good works are as visible as sinful deeds, the Pastor adds a pithy phrase with an unusual construction: "works of the other kind [*ta allōs echonta*] cannot be hidden." Such works are not immediately obvious.[84] Good works done in secret—even if the person doing good deeds intends that they not be seen—"cannot be hidden" (*krybēnai ou dynantai*). They too will be made manifest (see 1 Cor. 4:5).[85]

Slaves and Masters
1 Timothy 6:1–2

With this pericope the Pastor completes his version of the household code (5:1–6:2). Slavery was the common condition of a major segment of the populace in the Greco-Roman world. Thus, Hellenistic codes typically included a section on the responsibility of slaves. In this respect, the Pastor's words about slaves are no different from those of other household codes, including those household codes in the New Testament that conclude with an exposition of the duties of slaves (see Titus 2:9–10; Eph. 6:5–8; Col. 3:22–25; 1 Pet. 2:18–25). Writing about slaves, the Pastor follows the traditional pattern of the household code rather than the reverse pattern that he has been using thus far. Rather than writing about the duties of older men, younger men, older women, younger women, widows, and elders, the Pastor has talked about the way that the members of the community were to treat these various categories of people. In 6:1–2 the Pastor reverts to the traditional pattern and writes about the responsibilities of slaves. The reversion suggests that the community at Ephesus (1:3) was largely comprised of slaves. Although reverting to traditional form in speaking about the duties of slaves, the Pastor's exposition differs from other household codes, including the other New Testament household codes, insofar as the Pastor distinguishes behavior toward masters who are believers from behavior toward masters who do not believe.

---

83. For "good works" in the plural (*ergois Kalois*), see 5:10; 6:18; Titus 2:7, 14; 3:8, 14. A singular form appears in 1 Tim. 3:1. For "every good work" with a synonymous adjective (*pan ergon agathon*), see 5:10; 2 Tim. 2:21; 3:17; Titus 1:16; 3:1; the plural form (*erga agatha*) is used in 1 Tim. 2:10.

84. The unusual construction, with an adverb that does not appear elsewhere in the New Testament, could possibly be taken as a reference to sinful deeds.

85. Similar ideas are expressed in the Sermon on the Mount (see Matt. 5:14; 6:3–4, 6, 17–18).

6:1 Let all slaves who are under the yoke regard their masters as worthy of complete honor so that the name of God and the teaching are not blasphemed. **2** Let those who have masters who believe not treat them with disdain because they are brothers or sisters, but let them serve as slaves still more because those who benefit from their service are people who believe and are loved. Teach and urge these things.

[**6:1**] Slavery was an integral component of the social and economic fabric of first-century Greco-Roman society. In the urban environments of the Greco-Roman world, slaves constituted a large part of society, perhaps even the vast majority.[86] Some slaves rose to high positions within the household. At the top was the position of *oikonomos*, the household manager or chief of staff. Other slaves were military officers, philosophers, poets, and pedagogues. Some had substantial wealth, enough to purchase freedom for themselves and their families at the appropriate time. The one thing that slaves lacked was freedom.

For the Pastor and Paul before him, slavery was a factor of social life. Paul's own attitude toward slavery was complex. He urged slaves to remain in their condition (1 Cor. 7:21–24), but theologically he recognized that the relationship between Christian slaves and their masters was ironic. Christian slaves are freed persons who belong to the Lord. Conversely, even the freedman is a slave of Christ (1 Cor. 7:22). Paul's short letter to Philemon and those gathered in his house was sent to urge Philemon to welcome the slave Onesimus no longer simply as a slave but as a beloved brother (Phlm. 16). Although he was still a slave, Onesimus was to be regarded as kin, just as Timothy and Apphia were considered as kin (Phlm. 1–2).

As Paul before him, the Pastor accepted slavery as a social institution. Slaves were members of the household. Slaves, the Pastor says, are to regard their masters (*tous idious despotas*; see Titus 2:9) with complete honor (*pasēs timēs axious*; see 5:17). Elders in the community who serve well are to be tendered double honor (5:17); slaves are to honor their masters in every respect. The Pastor's exhortation is very pointed. He defines his terms: Slaves are those actually under the yoke of slavery (*hypo zygon*; see Gal. 5:1); masters are those who benefit from the service of a slave (*tēs euergesias*, 1 Tim. 6:2; see Acts 4:9). The Pastor does not speak of the slave's attitude toward the general class of slaveholders, nor does he address the issue of a master's responsibilities toward slaves (see Eph. 6:9; Col. 4:1). Neither does he speak about manumission (see 1 Cor. 7:21b) nor about freedmen who were formerly slaves. He speaks only of

---

86. See the discussion in S. Scott Bartchy, *First Century Slavery and 1 Corinthians 7:21*, SBLDS 11 (Atlanta: Scholars Press, 1973), 58nn183–84.

those actually under the yoke of slavery and of their responsibilities toward their own masters.

The New Testament household codes typically offer some form of theological reflection as to why slaves should respect their masters (see Eph. 6:5–8; Col. 3:22–25; 1 Pet. 2:18–25). In the Pastorals such theological reflection is of a more practical sort. Thus, Titus 2:9–10 cites the testimonial value of slaves' proper behavior: "Slaves should be subject to their masters in all things: well-pleasing, neither speaking against their masters nor stealing from them but showing complete loyalty to them so that they bring honor in every way to the teaching of our Savior, God." Similarly, 1 Tim. 6:1 speaks of the witness value of the behavior of Christian slaves, albeit in a negative fashion:[87] Christian slaves are to conduct themselves properly so that neither the name of God (Exod. 20:7; Deut. 5:11) nor the teaching are blasphemed.

[2] The Pastor has special words to say apropos those slaves whose masters are believers (*pistoi*). The Christian slave is not to forget that even though the slave owner may be a believer and therefore a brother or sister in the Lord, the slave owner remains nonetheless a master (*despotas*). The fact that a slave-holder is a believer provides no excuse for the slave to disregard the master's wishes or otherwise try to take advantage of the latter's Christian faith. Quite to the contrary! The fact that the owner of a slave is also a believer should provide the slave with additional reason for being a devoted servant, as the Pastor explains in his a fortiori argument. Masters who are believers especially deserve to be well served by their slaves who are believers. Not only is the believing master to be honored and obeyed as a master, the master is also a sibling who deserves to be treated as a member of the family, loved like a sister or brother[88] (see 1 Thess. 4:9–12).

The Pastor concludes this exhortation in the format of a household code with a kind of peroration: "Teach and urge these things" (*tauta didaske kai parakalei*). Were these words to be only a conclusion to the exhortation on slaves, they would be unduly formal. In fact, the summary exhortation is a peroration to the entire household code (5:1–6:2), with all its seeming digressions. It is appended for the sake of emphasis. The Pastor had told "Timothy" that the instructions that he was writing had as their purpose that people know how to conduct themselves in the house of God (3:14–15). First Timothy 5:1–6:2 provides a few directives.

---

87. This is an example of the Pastor's use of litotes, the use of understatement to make an assertion by the negation of its contrary.

88. The meaning of the Pastor's elliptical phrase is ambiguous (see the discussion in Marshall 631–33). The interpretation given here seems to be the best rendering of the Pastor's difficult words: *pistoi eisin kai agapētoi hoi tēs euergesias antilambanomenoi*, literally, "those who benefit from good service are believers and loved."

False Teaching
1 Timothy 6:3–10

In this pericope the Pastor returns one more time to the subject of false teachers, one of his major concerns since the outset of the epistle. His words are in the form of an ad hominem argument against "someone," the representative of the anonymous and pervasive "some" of his missive (1:3, 6, 19; 4:1; 6:10, 21; see 5:15). Having rejected sound teaching that leads to godliness, this someone is presented as totally diseased and depraved. Such people are always in a state of conflict, prone to jealousy and suspicious of others. Their minds are in a state of constant confusion. Proof of their miserable condition is that they consider godliness to be a means for material gain.

The Pastor's rejoinder to these people who have lost their minds consists of a reflection on wealth that at once echoes the sapiential tradition of right and wrong attitudes toward wealth (see Eccl. 5:10–20; Job 1:8–10, 21; 41:10–15) as well as Stoic ideas on self-sufficiency and root vices. The Pastor's reflection on wealth looks back to 4:1–5, where the Pastor had spoken about the deception of the final times and had urged his community to acknowledge, use, and be thankful for the goodness of God's creation. The reflection also looks ahead to 6:17–19, with some words on wealth directed to the wealthier members of the community.

6:3 If anyone teaches otherwise and does not agree[a] with the sound words about our Lord Jesus Christ, the teaching that leads to godliness, 4 that person is puffed up, understanding nothing but having a diseased appetite for arguments and verbal warfare from which come jealousy, strife, slander, malicious suspicions, 5 the constant disputations of people who have lost their minds and are deprived of the truth, holding that godliness is a means for profit.[b] 6 There is, on the other hand, great gain in godliness with self-sufficiency; 7 we have brought nothing into the world so that we can take nothing out of the world; 8 and having food and covering we will be satisfied with these. 9 Those who want to amass riches fall into temptation, a trap,[c] and many unimaginable and harmful desires that sink people into utter destruction, 10 for the love of money is a root of all kinds of evil. Some[d] who have been eager for it have deviated from the faith and have stabbed themselves with much pain.

a. The verb *proserchetai*, literally, "approach" or "come to," figuratively, "agree with," is widely attested but is a difficult reading. A clarifying *prosechetai*, "hold" (see 1:4; 3:8; 4:1, 13; *Titus* 1:4) is found in ℵ and some Latin witnesses.

b. Several majuscules, most minuscules, several ancient versions, and many patristic witnesses (e.g., Irenaeus, Basil, Chrysostom) add "stay away from such persons" (*aphistaso apo tōn toioutōn*). Incorporated into the Textus Receptus, this phrase appears in the AV as "from such withdraw thyself." The shorter reading is preferable. The short reading is found in the better Alexandrian and Western manuscripts, several Fathers, and a wide variety of ancient versions. Moreover, it is difficult to think of a plausible reason why a scribe would have omitted the phrase had it appeared in his prototype.

c. The manuscript tradition, especially Western manuscripts and some of the Latin Fathers, offers some evidence for the expanded reading, "the devil's trap" (*pagida tou diabolou*), undoubtedly under the influence of 1 Tim. 3:7 (see 2 Tim. 2:26).

d. Verse 10 is a single sentence in Greek.

[6:3–5] This long sentence presents a movement in three parts: a condition (v. 3), an immediate result (v. 4a), and a consequent result (vv. 4b–5). Each part is complex.

The conditional clause (v. 3) identifies the situation: someone who "teaches otherwise" (*heterodidaskalei*, see 1:3). The Pastor writes of the one involved in heterodox teaching as actively doing so. He speaks of the heterodox person as teaching something different, emphasizing that he does not agree with sound doctrine. The content of the heterodox teaching is not identified; it is simply contrasted with sound teaching. These sound words (see Excursus 4) relate to Jesus Christ, further identified as "our Lord" (*tou Kyriou hēmōn*). The full christological formula, so common in Paul's own letters, is rarely used in the Pastoral Epistles (see 1:2, 12; 6:3, 14; 2 Tim. 1:2). The presence of the full christological designation in 6:3 and in 6:14 helps to delineate 6:3–16 as a discrete literary unit. Although the Pastor often identifies Jesus as "Lord" (see 1:2, 12, 14), the three uses of "Lord" in this literary unit (6:3, 14, 15) add additional rhetorical force to what the Pastor is saying.

For the Pastor and his community, sound teaching does not stand alone. It leads to a way of life, identifiable patterns of appropriate behavior. That behavior can be summed up as "godliness" (*eusebeia*), the kind of religious devotion that leads to a corresponding way of life. The motif of godliness runs throughout the missive (2:2; 3:16; 4:7, 8; see Excursus 7), but it comes especially to the fore in this unit, which contrasts the Christian pursuit of godliness with godliness that has gone astray (see 6:5, 6, 11).

The immediate result (v. 4a) of not giving sound teaching its due is a totally unhealthy situation. The Pastor describes the heterodox teacher as puffy and diseased (*tetyphōtai . . . nosōn*). The vocabulary is striking. Within the New Testament, these words appear only in the Pastorals, "to be puffy" here and in 3:6 and 2 Tim. 3:4, "diseased" only here. The image is that of a person in terrible physical condition, almost repugnant to look at. These puffed-up people understand nothing at all. The Pastor then makes it abundantly clear that understanding nothing is indeed a woeful condition. It manifests itself in a diseased appetite for arguments and verbal conflicts (*logomachias*), "making war" (*machomai*) with "words" (*logos*). Second Timothy 2:23 echoes the idea that foolish and stupid arguments lead to conflict. These conflicts appear to be over the law (see Titus 3:9; 1 Tim. 1:6–7). They are debilitating and lead to destruction (see 2 Tim. 2:23). The Pastor's reference to verbal warfare is consistent with his use of the agon motif. The terminology appears to have been coined within the Pastor's own circles. A related adjective (*logomachos*) appears in Hellenistic literature, but the first known uses of "verbal warfare" (*logomachias*) and the related verb (*logomacheō*, 2 Tim. 2:14) are to be found in the Pastoral Epistles.

The Pastor uses a catalog of vices to describe what happens as a result of verbal warfare (vv. 4b–5). There are jealousy, strife, slander, malicious suspicions, and constant disputations.[89] The community is in total disarray, with one member pitted against another. This image of community disaster results from the cumulative effect of the Pastor's catalog of vices. As for the heterodox teachers themselves, they who understand nothing, they have "lost their minds" (*diephtharmenōn ton noun*; see BDF 159.3). They are consequently "deprived of the truth" (*apesterēmenōn tēs alētheias*). The pair of participles—lost their minds, deprived of the truth—contributes to the vituperative tone of the passage.

The Pastor's vitriolic diatribe concludes by observing that heterodox teachers simply do not understand what godliness is all about.[90] For them it is a matter of gaining riches (*porismon*, 6:5, 6). This is an obvious misunderstanding of the virtue of godliness. Aristotle said, "The life of money-making [*chrēmatistēs biaios*] is a constrained kind of life, and clearly wealth [*ploutos*] is not the good we are in search of, for it is only good as being useful, a means to something else" (*Nicomachean Ethics* 1.5.8). Those who were listening to the Pastor's diatribe may have heard in his words an echo of his earlier, harsh remarks about the law. The Pastor speaks of these heterodox teachers as "holding" (*nomizontōn*) that godliness is a means for profit. The verb was commonly used in Hellenistic Greek to refer to holding an opinion, thinking, or believing. Its etymology suggests something else. The verb is *nomizō*, literally, creating a custom or making a law.

[6–8] Before arriving at the end of his diatribe, the Pastor offers a few thoughts on the relationship between godliness and wealth. Godliness, he says, accompanied by self-sufficiency, is advantageous. Unlike other New Testament authors, including Paul (2 Cor. 9:8; see Phil. 4:11), the Pastor talks about the virtue of self-sufficiency (*autarkeias*) in much the same way that Stoics did.

---

89. "Constant disputations" (*diaparatribai*) is an intensive form of the noun and may suggest the possibility of some violence.

90. Jas. 1:26–27 similarly attempts to set straight some people who had an erroneous idea about religion and the kind of behavior that ensues from religion.

For these philosophers, self-sufficiency is found in a person who is satisfied with himself or herself. That person is independent and has no need to rely on others. In this way, Marcus Aurelius wrote about the ideal of self-sufficiency (*Meditations* 4.25; 10.1.1; 11.15.4–6), as did Epictetus. Epictetus described Socrates as a person who spurned Archelaus's intention to make him rich. He preferred self-sufficiency to riches. Socrates is reputed to have replied to the king's messenger, "Look you, if what I have is not sufficient for me, still, I am sufficient for it, and so it too is sufficient for me" (Curt Wachsmuth and Otto Hense, *Joannis Stobaei; Anthologiam* [reprint: Berlin: Weidman, 1974] 1912, 4.33.28). Earlier, too, than the Stoics was Plato, who asked, "Will not the good [person], insofar as he is good, be in that measure sufficient for himself?" Plato answered his question in this way: "Yes. And the sufficient [person] has no need of anything, by virtue of his sufficiency" (*Lysis* 215A).

For the Pastor, the virtue of self-sufficiency is the antithesis of the love of money (*philargyria*, 6:10; see 2 Tim. 3:2; Heb. 13:5). He writes, "We have brought nothing into the world so that we can take nothing out of the world" (v. 7). The contrast between "bringing nothing into" (*ouden eis-ēnenkamen*) and "taking nothing out of" (*oude ex-enenkein*) delineates an entire human life. The Pastor's reflection recalls the moral of the book of Job. Confronted with untold deprivation, Job falls to the ground, worships, and says, "Naked I came from my mother's womb, and naked shall I return there; the LORD gave, and the LORD has taken away; blessed be the name of the LORD" (Job 1:21; see Ps. 49:10, 16; Eccl. 5:15; Philo, *Special Laws* 1.295). A modern would surely quip, "You can't take it with you."

As did the philosophic moralists, the Pastor uses the verb *arkeō*, "to satisfy," in his discourse on the virtue of self-sufficiency. Self-sufficiency is a matter of being satisfied. From birth to death, self-sufficiency is attained when one is satisfied with food and clothing, literally, sustenance and covering or shelter (*diatrophas kai skepasmata*; see Philo, *Rewards* 99). The Pastor's words recall those that Diogenes Laertius used to describe Cynic philosophers. Writing about their sense of self-sufficiency, Diogenes said that they eat only sufficient food (*autarkesi chrōmenois sitios*), wear a single garment, and are content with any kind of covering (*Lives of Eminent Philosophers, Menedemus* 6.104).

Earlier in this epistle (4:6–8) the Pastor expressed a few pregnant ideas about the nature of godliness (see Excursus 7). His understanding of godliness is an important component of his anthropology. He expressed the view that godliness is beneficial for life in the present. In 6:6–8 he expands on his ideas on the virtue of godliness as it relates to life in the present. For the Pastor, godliness is to be accompanied by the virtue of self-sufficiency. This virtue eschews the accumulation of riches (6:9). Within the Pastor's theological perspective it includes the thought that what is necessary for human sustenance is a gift from God that believers are to use but for which they are also to give thanks (4:4–5).

[9–10a] Having expressed an opinion on the nature of the virtue of self-sufficiency, the Pastor turns his attention to people who want to amass riches (*hoi boulomenoi ploutein*). These are money-lovers (*philargyroi*, see 3:3). People who want to accumulate wealth fall into a trap. The Pastor explains the image by means of an interpretive triad.[91]

The trap into which money-lovers fall is temptation (*eis peirasmon*). Temptation is something about which Paul had written in the Corinthian correspondence (1 Cor. 7:5; 10:9) and in his letter to the Galatians (6:1). The Synoptics speak about the temptation of Jesus (Matt. 4:1–11 and par.). Early Christian catechesis included the petition "Do not bring us to the time of trial" (*eis peirasmon*, "into temptation") in its paradigm of the disciples' prayer (Matt. 6:13). When the Pastor speaks about temptation, he reflects the early Christian understanding of temptation. "Temptation" is ultimate temptation, the ultimate test of one's loyalties. It is the danger of being totally at odds with God's salvific plan. Temptation is not a matter of being tempted to one or another incidental failing; it is temptation with eschatological consequences. Temptation is the work of the "tempter" (*ho peirazōn*), Satan, the devil, the evil one.

The devil's trap (see 3:6–7; 2 Tim. 2:26) is manifest in the many disordered and inordinate desires that lead to utter destruction. The Pastorals share with the Stoics a very negative idea of "desire" (*epithymia*, 2 Tim. 2:22; 3:6; 4:3; Titus 2:12; 3:3). The moralists used the word "desire" generally but not exclusively to connote inordinate sexual desire. The Pastor's adjectives indicate that he is thinking of more than merely sexual desire. The immoderate desires into which the love of riches leads are "many," "unimaginable," and "harmful." These "unimaginable" desires are literally "mindless" (*a-noētous*; see 5:8); they are silly and foolish, the condition of people who have not yet come to believe, who have not yet attained the fullness of truth (see Titus 3:3). When the Pastor describes these desires as "harmful" (*blaberas*), he suggests that they lead to disastrous deterioration (see also Aristotle, *Politics* 3.15.13; 1286b).

The Pastor explains what he means by noting that these inordinate desires cause people to sink into ruin and destruction. The imagery of sinking is consistent with that of the pit into which the money-lovers fall, that is, the pit of ruin and destruction. The hendiadys suggests utter and final ruin. "Ruin" (*olethron*) is eschatological ruin (1 Thess. 5:3; 2 Thess. 1:9), the work of Satan (1 Cor. 5:5). "Destruction" (*apōleian*) is ultimate ruin, the work of the Destroyer, a familiar figure in Jewish apocalyptic thought.

The Pastor's rhetoric evokes special comparison with the Dead Sea Scrolls. The opponents of the sect are described as "children of perdition" (*bĕnê haššaḥat*, literally, "children of the pit" [1QS 9:16, 22; CD 6:15]). In biblical Hebrew, "pit" (*šaḥat*) has a figurative meaning of "perdition" (Ezek. 28:8); the

91. In Greek the three elements of the triad are connected by *kai*, "and."

Greek Bible renders the Hebrew term as "destruction" (*apōleia*, see Ezek. 28:8 LXX). Qumran's *Manual of Discipline* describes "destruction" as an expression of God's vengeful wrath: "The visitation of all those who walk in it[92] will be many afflictions by all the angels of Punishment, eternal perdition by the fury of God's vengeful wrath, everlasting terror and endless shame, together with disgrace of annihilation in the fire of murky Hell" (1QS 4:12–13). The *Damascus Document* associates this kind of perdition with the inordinate desire for wealth. Having exhorted the sectarians to keep apart from the children of destruction, the document urges that they "refrain from the unclean wealth of wickedness acquired by vowing and devoting and appropriating the wealth of the sanction, and not rob the poor of His people, that widows might be their spoil and that they might murder orphans" (CD 6:15–17).

In verse 10 the Pastor explains why the desire to amass wealth leads to such dire consequences: "The love of money is a root of all kinds of evil." The philosophic moralists considered that there are root vices just as there are root virtues. Philo taught that desire (*epithymia*, *Decalogue* 173; *Special Laws* 4.84, 87–88; *Virtues* 100), inequality (*anisotētos*, *Special Laws* 1.121; *Contemplative Life* 70; *Gaius* 85), pride (*typhos*, *Decalogue* 5, and falsehood (*Contemplative Life* 39) are vices that spawn other vices. The Pastor considers the amassing of wealth to be a root vice.

Polycarp observes that "the love of money is the beginning of all troubles. Knowing therefore that we brought nothing into the world neither can we carry anything out, let us arm ourselves with the armor of righteousness and let us teach ourselves first to walk in the commandment of the Lord" (Pol. *Phil.* 4:1). Polycarp comments on 6:10, using 6:7 as a horizon. He interprets the Pastor's phrase "a root of all kinds of evil" as the beginning of all kinds of trouble (*archē pantōn chalepōn*). To ward off these troubles, Polycarp exhorts those of the church at Philippi to arm themselves with righteousness (*dikaiosynēs*) and follow the Lord's commandment (*tē entolē tou Kyriou*). Biblical righteousness is a matter of right relationships. Yahweh's righteousness, expressed in concern for the poor, widow, orphan, and alien was to serve as a model for the rulers in Israel. The Lord's commandment (see 6:14) is a reference to the new commandment of love (John 13:34; 15:12; see 2 John 5). Thus, Polycarp sees "Christian charity" as the antidote to the vicious pursuit of wealth (see 6:17–19).

[10b] As he often does in this epistle, the Pastor concludes the pericope with a kind of peroration. He opines that "some" who are eager for money have deviated from the faith and cause themselves untold difficulty. These "some" are the Pastor's anonymous antagonists, those who are causing trouble for the community. "The faith" from which they turn consists of "sound words about our Lord Jesus Christ, the teaching that leads to godliness" (6:3). In rejecting that

92. That is, "in inextinguishable desire."

faith, they have a skewed concept of godliness, thinking it to be a means of personal profit. Such deviant thinking, with its moral and personal consequences, is described as stabbing themselves with many a pang. The metaphor "stabbing themselves" (*heautous periepeiran,* literally, "piercing with a spit") is an old one. Philo wrote that Flaccus Avillius "stabbed many people with deadly evil" (*Flaccus* 1) in describing his oppression of the Jews. In their pursuit of inordinate wealth, the anonymous some have inflicted much pain (*odynais pollais*) upon themselves, both physical and mental. As Polycarp said, they have brought all sorts of trouble upon themselves.

Final Exhortation to Timothy
1 Timothy 6:11–16

This final exhortation, addressed to Timothy, who receives the distinctive epithet "man of God," parallels the missive's epistolary thanksgiving (1:12–17). Taken together, the two pericopes form a literary *inclusio* for the body of the letter. An important feature of their similarity is the two doxologies (1:17; 6:15–16). Their respective positions within the epistle mark an intriguing feature of their similarity. They are not immediately adjacent to the epistolary opening and closing. The epistolary thanksgiving is separated from the opening salutation by another pericope, the "excursus" on the law (1:3–11). The final exhortation is separated from the epistolary closing by an exhortation to the rich (6:17–19).

The exhortation itself uses classic paraenetic techniques, namely, the catalog of virtues and the agon motif (vv. 11–12). The plea is enhanced by the Pastor's calling on the mighty and life-giving God as his witness, a rare reference to Jesus' trial before Pilate, and the minatory reference to the coming appearance of the Lord Jesus Christ. The end-time appearance of the Lord promises eternal life to those who remain faithful but bodes ill for those who do not. The extensive list of divine attributes (6:15–16) that precedes the final doxology gives this passage a theological density that is rarely found within the Pastoral Epistles.

Polemic and apologetic concerns may have influenced the wording of the doxology. Its formulation clearly relates to the situation of the Pastor's community in the Greco-Roman world. Popular legend had it that the gods dwelt on Mount Olympus, not very far from the city of Thessalonica where Paul had founded one of the earliest Christian communities in what is now called Europe. In the Greco-Roman world, "Sovereign" was a epithet used for Zeus. Zeus, considered to be "the most powerful, the mightiest of the gods, the far-seeing master who fulfills everything" (Homeric *Ode to Zeus* 1–2), revealed himself from the heights of Olympus. He was thought to be the protector of wealth (see 6:10, 17), lord of justice, and guarantor of social and moral order. Five centuries prior to the Pastor, Sophocles used the epithet "Sovereign" (*dynastēs*) to describe Zeus. The Pastor's doxology proclaims that the only Sovereign dwells in unapproachable light.

For a century or so prior to the writing of the Pastorals, the Roman emperors were considered to be gods or the manifestation of God. The title "Lord" was readily applied to the gods and to the emperor. Having been declared savior and father of the country, the Roman general Lucius Cornelius Sulla acquired the title (or name) *Felix*, the blessed one, equivalent of the Greek *makarios*. Thereafter, blessedness/happiness (*phelichitas*) and eternity (*aeternitas*) were cited among the emperor's attributes. Pompey and other generals of the empire were considered to be blessed with *phelichitas* and heaven-sent fortune (*divinitus adiunct fortuna*; see Cicero, *Manilian Law* 16.47; cf. 16.28, 48).

The Pastor's theological reflection (6:14–16) affirms that there is only one blessed Sovereign, the one who dwells in unapproachable light. That only and blessed Sovereign is "King of those who reign and Lord of those who exercise power" (see 2:2). He alone possesses immortality. The only and blessed Sovereign cannot be seen; it is Jesus Christ who is to appear as our Lord. Idol worship was the counterpoint of Paul's affirmation of the uniqueness of God (see 1 Cor. 8:6). The divinized emperors of the Greco-Roman world are the counterpoint of the Pastor's affirmation that there is only one God. To God alone belong the attributes of beatitude and immortality, for he alone is the blessed Sovereign to whom is due all honor and might.

> 6:11 You then, O man of God, flee these things. Pursue righteousness, godliness, faith, love, steadfastness, gentleness. 12 Fight the good fight of faith, obtain eternal life, to which you have been called and for which[a] you have made a good confession in the presence of many witnesses. 13 In the presence of God who quickens all things and of Christ Jesus who made a good confession before Pontius Pilate, I charge you: 14 Keep the commandment spotless and irreproachable until the appearance of our Lord Jesus Christ, 15 which the blessed and only Sovereign will manifest at the appropriate time, the King of those who reign and Lord of those who exercise power, 16 who alone has immortality, who inhabits unapproachable light, whom no single person has seen or can see; to him[b] be honor and everlasting might. Amen.

a. One prepositional phrase, *eis hēn*, is translated "to which" and "for which" in this verse.

b. The Greek text has a relative pronoun.

[6:11] The use of an emphatic pronoun, the rhetorically emphatic "Ō," and the antithetical "flee-pursue" enhance the force of this appeal. "Timothy" is addressed as a "man of God" (*ōanthrōpe theou*, see 2 Tim. 3:17), language that is used in the Hebrew Bible for a person with a prophetic function (see, e.g., 1 Sam. 2:27; 1 Kgs. 13:1). The recipient of the letter belongs to God and has a responsibility to fulfill the function that God has entrusted to him. Addressed in this fashion, "Timothy" is obligated to avoid zealously the false teaching and deviation from the faith with the baneful consequences that the Pastor has just described. On the other hand, Timothy must strive for righteousness, godliness, faith, love, steadfastness, and gentleness.

The antithetical pairing of "flee" and "pursue" (*pheuge diōke*) is classic paraenesis; the Greek terms follow immediately after one another so that the contrast between them is clearly articulated (see 2 Tim. 2:22; 1 Cor. 6:18; 10:14). Timothy is to seek after virtue as eagerly as he is to flee from false teaching. To explain what Timothy is to do, the Pastor gives a list consisting of three pairs of virtues: righteousness and godliness, faith and love, patience and gentleness. On the relationship between righteousness and godliness, see pp. 123–124. The Pastor's reflections on godliness and the desire for money (6:5–10) suggest that by "righteousness" or "justice" (*dikaiosynēn*) he is specifically thinking in terms of a proper use of wealth (see 6:17–19; Pol. *Phil.* 4:1). Timothy is to be a model for the members of a community (4:12) whose leaders are not to be eager for sordid gain (3:3, 8).

The second pair of virtues that Timothy must pursue is faith and love (see 4:12), the epitome of the Christian life (1:14; 2:15; 2 Tim. 1:13; 2:22; Titus 2:2) in Pauline communities. The third pair of virtues is steadfastness (*hypomonēn*) and gentleness (*praupathian*). Steadfastness, joined with faith and love in 1 Thess. 1:3 and Titus 2:2 (see 2 Tim. 3:10), is patience and constancy in the face of adversity. The Pastor's mention of this particular virtue, as his use of the agon motif (4:7–8; 6:12), evokes the difficulties that Timothy will encounter in fulfilling his God-given task.

Plato and Aristotle expected that all good people would possess the virtue of gentleness (see Plato, *Laws* 5.731d). The gentle person is one who maintains his or her serenity and is ready to forgive. Plutarch wrote extensively on gentleness (see various references in *TLNT* 3.165). For Plutarch, the gentle person has a smiling countenance and tranquil demeanor, is charming and gracious, easygoing and conciliatory. The mild person does not like quarrels and remains patient, as was Socrates with his shrewish wife and stupid children. Hellenists particularly expected that good rulers and good leaders, kings, and generals would possess gentleness. In leaders, gentleness implies calmness toward one's subordinates and a moderation that facilitates reconciliation. It is the opposite of rage and brutality (see Pindar, *Pythian Odes* 3.71; 4.136; Thucydides, *His-*

tory of the Peloponnesian War 4.108.3; Plato, *Critias* 120e; Josephus, Ant. 19.7.4 §334). Philo says that Abraham possessed the virtue of gentleness (*Abraham* 213). The patriarch was so mild-mannered that his servants and shepherds became quarrelsome and out of control.

[12] In verse 12 the agon motif[93] is used to reinforce the antithetical appeal of verses 10–11. "Timothy" is instructed to fight the good fight[94] (see 2 Tim 4:7) and to obtain eternal life. Timothy is involved in the struggle for the faith; the reward is eternal life. Paul described the reward as the victor's crown, an imperishable wreath (1 Cor. 9:25). The Pastor's circles revered Paul as having received a crown of righteousness because he had fought the good fight and had maintained the faith. Those who follow Paul's example (1:16), who have fought the good fight and long for the appearance of the Lord, can likewise obtain the crown of righteousness (2 Tim. 4:7–8). The Pastor describes Timothy as having been called to obtain eternal life (see 1:16; Titus 3:7; cf. 6:19, "real life"). God has called us, says 2 Tim. 1:9, with a holy call.[95]

The Pastor's observation that Timothy has already "made a good confession" is literally "confessed a good confession" (*hōmologēsas tēn kalēn homologian*, see 6:12). The construction, a verb with its cognate noun as object, is common in Hellenistic uses of the agon motif. "Confession" implies common consent or agreement; the etymology implies the "same speech" (*homo-logos*). The Stoics employed the terminology for something that ought to be agreed to and professed. In the juridical sphere, terms with the root were used to describe matters of common agreement, which then could be used as an argument in a court of law. In Philo's writings the terminology has theological connotations. Confession, he writes, "is the act of a sober and well-ordered reason to acknowledge [*homologein*] God as the Maker and Father of the universe" (*Posterity* 175; see *Cherubim* 107; *Drunkenness* 117; *Migration of Abraham* 85; cf. *Allegorical Interpretation* 1.80–82; 2.95; 3.26; *Abraham* 203). As Philo, Christians used confessional language with theological implications. Confessional language was used in regard to the gospel message (2 Cor. 9:13; see Heb. 3:1; 4:14; 10:23; 11:13; 13:15), the baptismal creed (Rom. 10:9–10), the Pastor's christological hymn (3:16), and judgmentally of those who profess to know God but deny him by their deeds (Titus 1:16). To make a good confession is to profess a common faith (see Titus 1:4) with other Christians and to do so in the presence of many witnesses (*enōpion pol-*

---

93. See 1:18; 4:7–8; 2 Tim. 2:3–5; 4:7–8.

94. The same metaphor, "fight the good fight" (*agōnizou ton kalon agōna*), appears in 2 Tim. 4:7. A similar metaphor, with the root *strat-*, "to fight like a soldier," appears in 1 Tim. 1:18.

95. 1 Tim. 6:12 and 2 Tim. 1:9 are the only passages in the Pastorals that use vocational language, the language of "calling." Paul often used the motif, especially in 1 Thessalonians, 1 Corinthians, and Romans.

lōn martyrōn). Timothy's own confession is, as it were, a matter of public record (see 4:12).

[13] The judicial register evoked by the reference to "many witnesses" in verse 12 continues in verse 13 with its allusions to the heavenly court and to Pilate's hearing chambers. The Pastor's discourse moves from the level of human witnesses (v. 12), to the witness of God and Christ Jesus, and then to Pilate, who witnessed Jesus' confession. This verse serves as a solemn introduction to the resumptive exhortation of verse 14. Its basic meaning is almost equivalent to the apostle's "I swear by the living God and by Christ Jesus, keep the commandment" (see 5:21).

The Pastor qualifies both God and Christ Jesus.In the biblical tradition "living" is the root attribute of God (see 1 Thess. 1:9). Swearing by the living God is the traditional formulation of the Jewish oath (see, e.g., 1 Sam. 19:6). God lives in the sense that God both creates life and continues to be active in the world that has been created. Anything that lives has the life that God gives. For the Pastor, God quickens all things (*tou zōogonountos ta panta*; see Luke 17:33; Acts 7:19); God makes them alive and maintains them in life.

The Pastor's virtual oath recalls "the good confession" that Christ Jesus made before Pontius Pilate. The reference to Christ Jesus anticipates the reference to his appearance (v. 14) and places the exhortation directed to Timothy between Christ Jesus' appearance before Pilate and his eschatological appearance. Memory of Christ Jesus' good confession provides a model for Timothy's good confession (v. 12). The Pastor does not, however, say that Christ Jesus "confessed" (*homologeō*) a good confession. He says that Jesus "testified" (*tou martyrēsantos*) a good confession. This language goes beyond the judicial allusions of the Pastor's earlier description to the formal language of the judicial register, the language of the courtroom.

The Pastor's reference to Pontius Pilate is striking because it is so rare. Pilate was the fifth Roman prefect (*eparchos*) of Judea (see Josephus, *Ant.* 18.3.1–3 §§55–64, etc., and Philo, *Gaius* 299–305), but apart from 6:13 and Luke 3:1; 13:1,[96] the only New Testament references to Pilate are in passages about Jesus' passion and death. The letters of Paul have little to say about the life and death of Jesus other than that he was born (Gal. 4:4) and that he died, which Paul sometimes specifies as death on a cross (see, e.g., Phil. 2:8). The only memory of Jesus recounted by Paul is in his account of the Lord's Supper (1 Cor. 11:23–25). On the other hand, Ignatius of Antioch, for whom Paul was "the Apostle," argued against certain heretics by emphasizing historical realities. Thus, three of his letters mention that Jesus had suffered under Pontius Pilate (see Ign. *Magn.* 11; *Smyrn.* 1:2; *Trall.* 9:1).

[14] This is the only reference to "the commandment" (*tēn entolēn*) in the

96. Witnesses in the New Testament use the full name, Pontius Pilate.

entire corpus of the Pastoral Epistles. The definite article suggests that the Pastor has some specificity in mind, but he does not give any precise indication of what that is. This final exhortation is in the form of a solemn charge directed to Timothy. In this context it is likely[97] that the commandment refers to the commission, the ministerial task entrusted at the laying on of hands (4:14). As such the commandment would encompass Timothy's didactic responsibilities and his obligation to provide moral leadership in the form of his own good example. The pair of synonymous adjectives that qualify the commandment, "spotless and irreproachable" (*a-spilon an-epilēmpton*),[98] evoke Timothy's moral responsibility to carry out the mandate.

Timothy is to keep the commandment in this fashion until "the appearance of our Lord Jesus Christ" (*tēs epiphaneias tou kyriou hēmōn Iēsou Christou*). This is 1 Timothy's only use of the appearance motif, which was familiar to his readers as an important and distinctive element of Christology. The Pastor's reference to the appearance differs from the other uses of the theme in the Pastorals (see 2 Tim. 1:10; 4:1, 8; Titus 2:11, 13; 3:4) insofar as he describes the appearance as that "of our Lord Jesus Christ," using the full christological designation of the Pauline tradition (see 1:2, 12; 6:3). "The appearance of our Lord Jesus Christ" is a reference to the eschatological Parousia of the risen Lord expressed in the theological jargon of the Pastor's circles (see Excursus 8). The Pastor's use of the motif expresses convictions similar to those expressed by Paul in 1 Thess. 3:13 and 5:23 without, however, suggesting that the appearance will occur in Timothy's lifetime (see 2 Tim. 4:6–8). Paul's early letters reflected the expectation of an imminent Parousia (see especially 1 Thess. 4:15–17). The mitigated eschatology of the Pastorals (see 1:16; 4:1, 8; 6:19) does not include the expectation of an imminent appearance.

[15–16] The doxology of 6:16 is similar to the doxology of 1:17 in many respects, including their long lists of divine attributes. Each of the doxologies proclaims that God is king (*basileus*), that God is the only (*monos*) God, and

---

97. Knight offers a range of eight different possibilities (266); Marshall offers seven possibilities (664). Among them are the possibilities that "commandment" refers to the whole Christian life, the instructions given in the letter, and the "treasure" to which 6:20 makes references. Ernst Käsemann's seminal 1954 essay, "Formular eine neutestamentliche Ordinationsparänese," provided the impetus for a range of modern commentators (Brox, Roloff, Marshall, and Quinn-Wacker; see also Limbeck [*EDNT* 1.460]) to adopt the "ordination mandate" interpretation. Käsemann argues that 6:11–16 was a preexistent liturgical piece, part of an "ordination ritual," that the Pastor had incorporated into his missive.

98. Both adjectives are used only rarely and in late strata of New Testament texts, "spotless" in Jas. 1:27; 1 Pet. 1:19; 2 Pet. 3:14; and some manuscripts of Jude 24; "irreproachable" in 1 Tim. 3:2; 5:7; 6:14. Such early second-century Christian texts as *Herm. Sim.* 5.6.7; *Herm. Vis.* 4.3.5; and 2 *Clem.* 8:6 also employ the term "spotless."

that God cannot be seen. This doxology is different from the earlier one insofar as the series of attributes in 6:16 precedes the doxology itself (6:16b), whereas the attributes are given in the doxological formula itself in 1:17. Each of the doxologies concludes a personal vignette, respectively on Paul and on Timothy, that repeatedly mentions Christ Jesus. The multiplication of epithets creates a degree of difference between Christ Jesus and God. Christ Jesus belonged to the world (1:15; 6:13); God does not. Jesus testified in the presence of Pontius Pilate; the One proclaimed in the doxology dwells in unapproachable light, has never been seen and will never be seen. God will manifest the appearance of our Lord Jesus Christ; God is responsible for the eschatological appearance of our Lord. A subtle contrast is established between the unseen and unseeable One and Jesus Christ, who will make an appearance, who will be seen.

Using images of visibility—epiphany, showing, light, being seen—the Pastor affirms that the appearance of Jesus Christ is a future reality that God directs. The blessed and only Sovereign will manifest Jesus Christ at the appropriate time, in his own time (*kairois idiois*). In 1 Thessalonians, Paul uses the imagery of sound to say that the time of the Parousia is controlled by God: "The Lord himself, with a cry of command, with the archangel's call and with the sound of God's trumpet, will descend from heaven" (1 Thess. 4:16). In 1 Corinthians, Paul exploits an apocalyptic time scheme to say that the Parousia of Jesus belongs to the eschatological sequence defined by God: "Christ has been raised from the dead, the first fruits of those who have died. . . . Each in his own order: Christ the first fruits, then at his coming those who belong to Christ. Then comes the end, when he hands over the kingdom to God the Father, after he has destroyed every ruler and every authority and power" (1 Cor. 15:20–24). The Pastor's visual imagery is different from the aural and temporal imagery of Paul, but the insight is the same: the appearance/Parousia of Jesus Christ is under God's control.

The Pastor's first description of God—even though "God" (*ho theos*) is not used in these verses (see 1:17)!—is that God is the blessed and only Sovereign. In the Greek Bible the designation was used of God (Sir. 46:5, 7; 2 Macc. 12:15; 15:4, 23). The Lord God is the great Sovereign of the world, dwelling in heaven to whom his embattled people can cry out in times of difficulty. Luke uses the epithet to describe human potentates (Luke 1:52; Acts 8:27); the Pastor is the only New Testament author to speak of God in this way. Clement of Rome described God as the "great Creator and Sovereign of everything [*despotēs tōn hapantōn*]," concluding his description with a doxology, as does the Pastor (*1 Clem.* 20:11–12; see 20:8). The Pastor praises God as "the blessed and only Sovereign." The Pastor is alone among New Testament authors in calling God "blessed" (*makarios*), an adjective typically used to describe human happiness and good fortune (see 1:11 and commentary). His other adjective, "only" (*monos*), is used in reference to God in New Testament prayers of praise (1:17; 6:16; Rom. 16:27; Jude 25; Rev. 15:4).[99]

The Pastor's prayer of praise describes the blessed and only Sovereign as "the King of those who reign and Lord of those who exercise power" (*ho basileus tōn basileuontōn kai kyrios ton kyrieuontōn*; see 1:17, *tō basilei tōn aiōnōn*). The Pastor's laudation is often translated "King of kings and Lord of lords" (see Deut. 10:17). That terse translation is well struck but fails to pay due attention to the rhetorical force of the participles (see Rev. 17:14 and 19:16, whose language is closer to that of Dan. 2:47 than it is to 1 Tim. 6:15). The two verbs clearly proclaim the sovereignty of God over all reigning monarchs and potentates, the kings and those in authority for whom the community should pray (2:1–2). First Timothy is the only one of the three Pastoral Epistles to speak of kings and of God as king. Immediately after exhorting the community to pray for kings, the Pastor has reminded his readers that God is our Savior (*tou ōstēros hēmōn theou*, 2:3) and has affirmed that there is but one God and one intermediary (*heis gar theos heis kai mesitēs*) between God and humans (2:5). That emphasis on the uniqueness of God, to whom alone mortals owe obedience and adoration, is best explained as having an apologetic intent, as does the royal language of the doxologies.

Verse 16 continues to focus on the one God. The only and blessed Sovereign alone (*monos*) possesses immortality. This Sovereign alone inhabits unapproachable light. It is he alone whom no one has seen nor can see. For the most part this trilogy of ideas is expressed in Hellenistic language. It speaks of God in negative abstractions, as *im*mortal, *un*approachable, and *in*visible. Even the adjective "alone" (*monos*, vv. 15, 16) reflects the philosophic idiom of Hellenism. Jewish tradition speaks of God as the "one" (*heis*) God rather than as the only God. In speaking of the one God, the confessional hymn of 1 Cor. 8:6 reflects this biblical tradition, as does the Pastor in 2:5.

The Pastor's early doxology praised God as "incorruptible and invisible" (1:17). Similar ideas are expressed in 6:16: "who alone has immortality, . . . whom no single person has seen or can see." The "immortality" (*a-thanasian*) attributed to the blessed and only Sovereign in 6:16 corresponds to the "incorruptible" (*a-phthartō*) of 1:17. Both terms are abstract and begin with a privative alpha. The biblical tradition speaks of the living God rather than of the immortal God. Hellenistic literature, on the other hand, often speaks of immortality as one of the attributes of the deity (e.g., "you have made the great Osiris immortal" [*sy ton megan Osirin athanaton epoiēsas*, *P.Oxy.* 1380.242–43]).

---

99. Jude 4 also uses the adjective of Jesus Christ, identified as "our only Master and Lord" (*ton monon despotēn kai kyrion hēmōn*). "Master" translates the Greek word that Clement employs as a divine attribute.

The words "whom no single person has seen or can see" (*hon eiden oudeis anthrōpōn oude idein dynatai*) correspond to the "invisible" (*a-[h]oratos*) of 1:17. This description of the blessed and only Sovereign evokes a biblical notion (see Exod. 33:20; John 1:18; 1 John 4:12[100]), but it lacks the concreteness of the passage about Moses at the burning bush, whose narrative terms tell about God's invisibility and unapproachability (Exod. 3:2–6).

The idea that God inhabits unapproachable light (*phōs oikōn aprositon*) is novel, but it is deeply rooted in Jewish tradition. The description underscores the traditional Jewish notion of the transcendence of God, the total otherness of which contemporary theologians write. Classic biblical tales of Moses graphically demonstrate that the God of Israel is unapproachable and cannot be seen (Exod. 3:2–6; 19:20–23). Within the New Testament, the Johannine corpus uses ideas of light and dwelling to speak about God. As the manifestation of God, Jesus is the light of the world (John 8:12; 9:5; see John 1:7–10). The Johannine Jesus speaks about his Father's house (*oikia tou patros mou*, John 14:2). Where Jesus and where the Father dwell is a major theme in the Fourth Gospel (e.g., John 1:38–39; 14:10). The Pastor's description of the dwelling of the Sovereign does not use the Johannine "dwell" (*menein*, "to abide") but rather "inhabit" (*oikōn*, "to live in a house"), calling to mind the household imagery that runs throughout the Pastorals (see Excursus 5).

The doxology that follows the exposition of divine epithets is relatively short: "to him be honor and everlasting might. Amen." The word "doxology" derives its name from *doxa*, "glory," a term found in all thirteen New Testament doxologies with the single exception of 6:16. A pair of nouns, "honor and might," takes the place of "glory" in the Pastor's doxology. These terms appear alongside "glory" in the doxology of Rev. 5:13 (see 1 Tim. 1:17; Rev. 7:12). Thus, the binomial attribute used by the Pastor fits well within the New Testament's doxological tradition. The terms "honor" and "might" appear in the doxologies of Clement's letter to the Corinthians (*1 Clem.* 64; 65:2), written during the persecution of Domitian, and in a doxology of the *Martyrdom of Polycarp* composed shortly after Polycarp's death (*Mart. Pol.* 20:2).

The doxology's proclamation that honor (*timē*) is due to God calls to mind the fact that honor is due to one's master in the Pastor's social world (6:1). The doxology's proclamation of the might of God (*kratos*) must be understood in the light of the immediately preceding description of the blessed and only Sovereign as one who reigns over earthly kings and is Lord over earthly lords. The presence of "might" in the doxologies of 1 Pet. 4:11; Jude 25; Rev. 1:6, 5:13 bespeaks the beleaguered situation of the church, expressing the conviction that God's might will win out over the hostile forces that were confronting the Christian community. The Pastor's community may not have been oppressed by the

---

100. These Johannine passages likewise specify that "no one" (*oudeis*) sees God.

empire, but it had every interest in proclaiming that might belonged to the King of those who reign, the Lord over those who exercise power.

Doxologies typically proclaim that the praise of God is everlasting (see 1:17). The Pastor's doxology stands alone among New Testament doxologies in proclaiming that God's might is everlasting (*aiōnion*). The emphasis does not so much suggest that the Pastor's community was experiencing pressure or persecution as it indicates that the Pastor was concerned to affirm that the quality of God's might was unique indeed, distinct from the might and power of any king or potentate. To this the congregation could only reply "Amen" (see 1:17).

Exhortation for the Wealthy
1 Timothy 6:17–19

Verses 17–19 seem to constitute an interlude in the exhortation addressed to Timothy. Alternatively, the preceding exhortation (6:11–16) can be seen as an interruption[101] in the Pastor's discourse on wealth (6:3–10, 17–19). In either case, this pericope returns to the topic of wealth, the theme of 6:3–10. The sound of riches is heard throughout the short pericope. The literary and rhetorical device of paronomasia, repetition of the same sound, contributes to the unity of the pericope and enhances its rhetorical force of the Pastor's charge. Four times the sound *plous-* or *plout-* was heard by those who listened to the reading of the epistle: *plousiois . . . ploutou . . . plousiōs . . . ploutein*, "the rich . . . riches . . . generously [richly] . . . to be rich," respectively a personal noun, an objective noun, an adverb, and a verb.

Paul wrote about financial matters in each of his undisputed letters. His principal concerns were apostolic support (1 Cor. 9:4–15; Gal. 6:6; Phil. 2:25; 4:14–18; 1 Thess. 2:5, 9) and the collection on behalf of the saints in Jerusalem (Rom. 15:25–28; 1 Cor. 16:1–4; Gal. 2:10; see Phlm. 18–19). Second Corinthians 8–9 offers a profound theological and christological reflection on Christian generosity. First Timothy 6:17–19 lacks the length and depth of Paul's administrative letter. This is a short pericope that uses Hellenistic language and the rhetorical argument from advantage. The Pastor speaks of this advantage in terms appropriate to his theological anthropology. His thoughts are similar to ideas expressed by the evangelist Luke (see Luke 12:20–21, 32–34; 16:9).

6:17 Tell the rich in this age not to be haughty or to hope in uncertain riches but in God who generously grants everything to us for enjoyment, **18** to

---

101. R. A. Falconer, *The Pastoral Epistles* (Oxford: Clarendon, 1937) (158) considers the preceding pericope, 6:11–16, to be an interpolation into the text.

do good, to be rich in good works, to be generous and sharing, 19 storing up for themselves a good foundation for what is to come so that they may obtain real[a] life.

a. Along with the majority of the Byzantine manuscripts, 075, and some manuscripts of the Coptic and Vulgate versions, the Textus Receptus reads *aiōniou* (see 1:16; 6:12; Titus 3:7). The AV consequently renders the phrase "that they may lay hold on eternal life." This reading is a scribal clarification for *ontōs*, rarely used in the literature of the times but similarly used by the Pastor in 5:3.

[6:17–19] For the fifth time in this epistle the Pastor addresses a charge to Timothy using the verb *parangellō*, "I charge you" (see 1:3; 4:11; 5:7; 6:13). This time Timothy is commanded to give the word to those who are rich. The notation that these people are rich in this age (*en tō nyn aiōni*, see Titus 2:12) serves the Pastor's argument in several different ways. It shifts the readers' attention from the future appearance of the Lord Jesus Christ (6:14) to the present. It recalls the Pastor's earlier reflection that wealth cannot be taken with us (6:7), and it prepares for the contrast with what is to come. As such, it strengthens the antithesis between hope in uncertain riches and hope in God.

The rich must not build castles in the sky or set their hopes on ephemeral wealth; rather, they are to hope in God. The vocabulary used by the Pastor in the negative portion of the antithesis is unusual.[102] The rich are "not to be haughty or to hope in uncertain riches." Both of the expressions suggest something unreal, beyond one's control, with the result that the Pastor's words mean something like "tell the rich not to get ideas." Instead, they should place their hope in God (see 4:10; 5:5), the Savior (1:1) and Benefactor who generously distributes his benefaction. God generously gives everything (*panta*) to human beings.

The Pastor notes, as he did earlier (4:3–4), that God's gifts are given for a reason. The Pastor identifies four uses for riches. The first is enjoyment. The phrase, *eis apolausin*, "for enjoyment," recalls what he had previously said about God's gifts of marriage and food given to be enjoyed with thanksgiving (4:3–5). Hellenistic Jews such as Philo (*Moses* 2.70; *Rewards* 135) and Josephus (*Ant.* 1.1.4 §46; 8.6.1 §153) used this phrase of the basic necessities of life, those with which Christians should be satisfied (see 6:8; cf. Heb. 11:25). Clement wrote about the everflowing springs that sustain human life and have been created by God for the enjoyment and health of humans (*pros apolausin kai hygian, 1 Clem.* 20:10). Unlike the false teachers who deny the value of such

102. The phrase "in uncertain riches" (*epi ploutou adēlotēti*, literally, "the uncertainty of riches") employs a reverse genitive of quality (see BDF 165). The noun "uncertainty" (*adēlotēti*) and the verb "to be haughty" (*hypsēlophronein*) do not appear elsewhere in the New Testament. The expression *ta hypsēla*, "lofty or sublime things," sometimes referred to the heavens (see Heb. 1:3).

gifts, the Pastor urges that people make ·the most of God's gifts (see Eccl. 5:18–20).

Having affirmed that such possessions as people have are God's gifts, the Pastor elaborates in a series of three infinitive phrases on the use to which wealth is to be put. Grammatically, the three infinitives are part of what Timothy is to tell the rich (see v. 17); in fact, they tell the reader how wealth is to be used. It is to be used for doing good (*agatho-ergein*; see Acts 14:17). The term is essentially synonymous with *agatho-poiein*, also "to do good," which in the Greek Bible and the New Testament means to do a good deed for another person.[103] It appears in Luke's Sermon on the Plain in reference to the material support of others (Luke 6:33, 35). *The Testament of Benjamin* highly esteems doing good, especially for the impression that it makes on others (see *T. Benj.* 5:1–2).

The Pastor emphasizes what he has just said by affirming that those who have material possessions should use them in such a way that they become rich with good deeds (*ploutein en ergois kalois*). They are to be as lavish in sharing their possessions as God is in giving the gifts of his creation. Those who are rich because of God's generosity have a responsibility to be generous toward others. The Pastor reinforces this idea by instructing Timothy to tell the rich "to be generous and sharing," a kind of hendiadys in which one element reinforces the other. The basic meaning of "generous" (*eu-metadotous*) is giving what one has to someone else. The prefix (*eu*) implies liberality and/or joy in doing so. The idea of generosity is accentuated by the Pastor's suggestion that members of the Christian community share things in common (*koinōnikous*). This vision of a believer in a community of believers approaches that of Luke, who describes the "ideal" Christian community in Jerusalem as one in which "no one claimed private ownership of any possessions, but everything they owned was held in common [*hapanta koina*]" (Acts 4:32).

On the other hand, what the Pastor says with regard to ephemeral wealth is similar to what Menander had said some four centuries earlier. The dramatist presented this dialogue between Kallippides and his son Sostratos (*Dyskolos* 797–817):

> *Sostratos:* You speak of money, an unstable substance. If you know
>   that it will stay with you for ever, guard it and don't share
>   with anyone. But where your title is not absolute and all is
>   on lease from Fortune [*Tychē*], not your own, why grudge
>   someone a share in it? . . . So long as you control it, use it
>   generously, aid everyone, and by your acts enrich all whom
>   you can. Such conduct never dies . . .

---

103. See Num. 10:32; Judg. 17:13 (mss. A); Tob. 12:13; Zeph. 1:12; 1 Macc. 11:33 (mss. A); 2 Macc. 1:2; Luke 6:9.

Kallippides: . . . No need for sermons. You may dispose, and give, and
               share [*porizeō, didou, metadidou*].

Having directed Timothy to urge Ephesian Christians to be generous with
their material wealth, the Pastor moves his financial discourse to a new level.
Once again his final words are a kind of peroration to the exhortation. The verbs
"store up" (*apothēsaurizontas*) and "obtain" (*epilabōntai*; see 6:12) belong to
the same semantic domain as the "riches" (*plous-*) about which the Pastor has
been writing. In verse 19 the Pastor employs these financial terms to speak of
real gain.

If the members of the community are as generous with their material wealth
as he urges them through Timothy to be, they would be amassing a real fortune
for what is to come (*eis to mellon*). What they would do is to store up for themselves a solid foundation (*themelion kalon*) for their future. In modern terms,
they would be investing in their future. What is the yield on this investment?
The Pastor says that it is "real life." "Real life" is eternal life (see pp. 169–70,
na), the kind of life that Timothy is urged to pursue (6:12; see 1:16; Titus 3:7).
The Pastor's use of the qualifier "real" (*ontōs*; see 5:3) underscores the difference between life based on fleeting wealth and the kind of life that only God
can give. The purpose of God's gifts is not that they be stored up (see Jas. 5:1–6;
Luke 6:24), but that they be used as a foundation, used, that is, in such a way
that God will reward their users with the gift of true life. Ultimately, this is what
the blessedness of God really means (see comments on 1:11; 6:15).

Epistolary Closing
1 Timothy 6:20–21

In addition to saying farewell, the epistolary closings of Hellenistic letters generally had a resumptive function. These closings often recapitulated and emphasized the main themes of the letter. In this respect they are similar to a rhetorical
peroration. With a direct appeal to Timothy, the epistolary closing of 1 Timothy hearkens back to the direct appeals of 1:18 and 6:11 and creates a ring construction with 1:2, which identifies the epistle as a literary unit. The "impious
nonsense" that Timothy is to avoid recalls the exhortation of 4:7. The anonymous "some" who missed the mark were first mentioned in 1:6. These provide
the negative horizon for the task that Timothy is to pursue.

Timothy is urged to preserve zealously the treasure that has been entrusted
to him, avoiding irreverent and vacuous speech and devoting his energies to the
defense of the faith. Thus recalling Timothy's apologetic task, the Pastor reverts
to the epistolary style he had abandoned from the beginning of his "epistle,"

bringing his composition to a close with the customary Christian greeting "Grace be with you."

> **6:20** O Timothy, preserve the treasure, turning away from impious nonsense and the objections of falsely called knowledge. **21** Professing this,[a] some people have missed the mark concerning the faith. Grace be with you.[b]

a. Verses 20–21a constitute a single sentence in Greek.
b. The Byzantine manuscripts and a few older witnesses read "with you" in the singular (*meta sou*). This is a scribal "correction" to make the epistolary closing correspond with an epistolary opening that designates Timothy alone as the recipient of the missive (1:1). "Amen" appears at the end of the text in several different manuscripts. This is a result of the use of the text in liturgy.

[6:20–21a] The Pastor's direct appeal to Timothy is short and forceful: "O Timothy, preserve the treasure." These striking words of direct address use the emphatic and attention-getting "O" of koine Greek (see 6:11) and call upon Timothy by name (see 1:18). Hellenistic letters customarily began with the names of the sender and the recipient. Typically, neither of these names appeared again in the letter except when the author added his handwritten signature or personal postscript. The terse exhortation "preserve the treasure" capitalizes on the financial language of the previous pericope. The word *parathēkēn*, "treasure," often has the connotation of a deposit. The treasure that Timothy is to preserve is the gospel message, the full knowledge of the truth. Second Timothy 1:14 describes this as the precious treasure entrusted by the Holy Spirit.

If Timothy is to preserve this treasure, he must also turn away from inane chatter and falsehood. The Pastor's description of this other side of Timothy's task repeats vocabulary that he had previously used in the epistle: "turning away from" (1:6) and "impious" (1:9; 4:7; see 2 Tim. 2:16). "Falsely called" (*pseudō-nymou*) echoes the "liars" (*pseustais*) of 1:10 and, by contrast, the "authentic" (*anypokritou*) of 1:5. Timothy must not fall victim to objections[104] that arise from the teaching that goes by the misnomer of "knowledge." "Some" people have done just that. These anonymous "some" are a leitmotif of the entire epistle, populating its negative horizon. They engage in empty-sounding impious nonsense and have missed the point, the target, of the faith (see 1:6; 2 Tim. 2:18).[105] Perverting the law (1:5–7), God's gifts of marriage, food, and wealth

104. Tertullian identified these "objections"—the word *antitheseis* is used only here in the entire New Testament—with Marcion's 140 "Antitheses" (*Against Marcion* 1.19; PL 1:267, 361). Tertullian's views were sometimes used by critics who assigned a late date to the composition of 1 Timothy.
105. See Philo, *Cherubim*, 42: "The sacred revelation is not for those others who, under the spell of the deadly curse of vanity, have no other standards for measuring what is pure and holy but their barren words and phrases and their silly usages and ritual."

(4:3; 6:10), godliness (6:5), knowledge (6:20), and the truth (6:5), these anonymous "some" provide a negative example for Timothy and his community.

[21b] The Pastor's final greeting, "Grace be with you" (*hē charis methō 'hymōn*) is the shortest of the New Testament epistolary literature's final farewells (see Col. 4:18). Hellenistic letters typically ended with "farewell" or "good-bye" (*errōso* or *errōsthe*). In place of this customary epistolary Paul wrote "Grace be with you" in some expanded form. The short greeting, similar to the Semitic "Peace be with you," seems to have replaced the Semitic greeting among Hellenistic Christians and was used by them in their liturgical gatherings.

Paul customarily included second-person ("Greet so-and-so") or third-person ("So-and-so greets you") greetings at the end of his letters. First Thessalonians contains second-person greetings and Philemon third-person greetings, while Romans, 1–2 Corinthians, and Philippians have both second- and third-person greetings. Among Paul's letters only Galatians lacks any form of final greeting. This omission is surely due to the strained relationship between Paul and those communities. Both 2 Timothy and Titus have both second- and third-person greetings. Thus, 1 Timothy is alone among the Pastorals in omitting any greetings apart from the mandatory farewell. A similar omission occurs in the deuteropauline Ephesians and 2 Thessalonians.

2 TIMOTHY

INTRODUCTION

The Second Epistle to Timothy comes from the same cloth as 1 Timothy. The two texts have similar epistolary frameworks. "Paul, apostle of Christ Jesus . . . to Timothy, beloved son, grace, mercy, and peace from God the Father and Christ Jesus our Lord" is the epistolary greeting of 2 Timothy. This is the same as the greeting in 1 Timothy except for its designation of Timothy as "beloved" rather than as "true." As an epistolary farewell, both 2 Timothy and 1 Timothy read, "Grace be with you."

Similarities and Differences

Some of the distinctive phraseology that characterizes the Pastoral Epistles as a whole is found in 2 Timothy. The use of the cachet "This is a trustworthy saying" (2:11; see 1 Tim. 1:15; 3:1; 4:9; Titus 3:8) is a case in point. So too would be the use of "to be sound" (1:13; 4:3; 1 Tim. 1:10; 6:3; Titus 1:9, [13]; 2:1, [2]) and "the full knowledge of truth" (2:25; 3:7; 1 Tim. 2:4; Titus 1:1) to describe the doctrine of the community. With the other Pastorals, 2 Timothy uses the expression "every good work" to designate a pattern of fully acceptable behavior (2:21; 3:17; 1 Tim. 5:10; Titus 1:16; 3:1). With regard to theology, 2 Timothy shares with 1 Timothy, but not with Titus, a manifest preference for "Christ Jesus" (the title preceding the name) as a way of speaking about Jesus. Other features of the theology of 2 Timothy that resemble those of the other Pastorals are its use of the distinctive "appearance" scheme (1:10; 4:1, 8; 1 Tim. 6:14; Titus 2:13; cf. Titus 2:11; 3:4) and of the title "Savior" (1:10; 1 Tim. 1:1; 2:3; 4:10; Titus 1:3, 4; 2:10, 13; 3:4, 6).

These striking similarities nonetheless cloak some significant differences. One might note, for example, that 2 Timothy employs the expression "in Christ Jesus" seven times (1:1, 9, 13; 2:1, 10; 3:12, 15). In contrast, this distinctive phrase appears only twice in 1 Timothy (1 Tim. 1:14; 3:13) and not at all in the epistle to Titus. The Pastorals make distinctive use of the "Savior" title, but the title appears just once in 2 Timothy whereas it appears three times in 1 Timothy (1 Tim. 1:1; 2:3; 4:10) and six times in Titus (1:3, 4; 2:10, 13; 3:4, 6). Second Timothy uses the "Savior" title of Christ, whereas 1 Timothy uses it for

God; Titus uses it for both God and Jesus Christ. With 1 Timothy and Titus, 2 Timothy speaks about "every good work" (*pan ergon agathon*), but it does not share with them the virtually synonymous expression "good works" (*erga kala*; see 1 Tim. 5:10, 25; 6:18; Titus 2:7, 14; 3:8, 14).

Persons and Places

The most striking difference between 2 Timothy and the other Pastorals is the sheer number of references to persons and to places. First Timothy is the longest of the Pastorals, but apart from the mention of Timothy as the fictive addressee in 1 Tim. 1:2 and two direct appeals embedded in the body of the epistle (1 Tim. 1:18; 6:20), the only persons mentioned by name in 1 Timothy are Hymenaeus and Alexander, whom Paul is presumed to have handed over to Satan so that they might learn not to blaspheme (1 Tim. 1:20). The only geographical references in 1 Timothy are to Macedonia and Ephesus. Timothy is said to have been left behind in Ephesus while the apostle was making his way to Macedonia (1 Tim. 1:3).

The relatively modest use of personal and geographical names in 1 Timothy contrasts sharply with the appearance of names in 2 Timothy. Apart from the name of the fictive addressee, the names of Lois, Eunice (1:5), Phygelus, Hermogenes (1:15), Onesiphorus (1:16; 4:19), Hymenaeus, Philetus (2:17), Demas, Crescens, Titus (4:10), Luke, Mark (4:11), Tychicus (4:12), Carpus (4:13), Alexander (4:14), Prisca, Aquila (4:19), Erastus, Trophimus (4:20), Eubulus, Pudens, Linus, and Claudia (4:21) appear in 2 Timothy. This cumulative list is much longer than any other in the New Testament, with the exception of the series of greetings appended to the letter to the Romans (Rom. 16). It far exceeds the list of eleven names in Col. 4:7–17.

Second Timothy does not contain as many geographical references as it does personal names; nonetheless, the epistle cites several different locations: Asia (1:15), Rome (1:17), Ephesus (1:18; 4:12), Antioch, Iconium, Lystra (3:11), Thessalonica, Galatia, Dalmatia (4:10), Troas (4:13), Corinth, and Miletus (4:20). Apart from the travelogue that appears at the end of the epistle (Titus 3:12–14), Titus is as sparing in its use of personal and place names as is 1 Timothy. It mentions only that Titus, to whom the epistle is addressed (Titus 1:4), has been left behind in Crete (Titus 1:5). Thus, the abundance of personal and geographic names in 2 Timothy distinguish it not only from 1 Timothy but from Titus as well.

Three of the personal names mentioned in 2 Timothy, Titus (4:10), Prisca, and Aquila (4:19), appear in Paul's own letters.[1] Some of the persons named in 2 Timothy appear in the deuteropauline epistles or in the Acts of the Apostles. Other names do not appear elsewhere in the New Testament; among these are

1. For Titus, see Gal. 2:1–3; 2 Cor. 2:12–13; 7:6–7, 13–15; 8:5–6, 16–19, 23–24; 12:18. For Prisca and Aquila, see Rom. 16:3; 1 Cor. 16:19; cf. Acts 18:2, 18, 26.

Lois, Eunice, Phygelus, Hermogenes, Onesiphorus, Philetus, Crescens, Carpus, Eubulus, Pudens, Linus, and Claudia. These individuals constitute fully half of the group of persons named in 2 Timothy. Hymenaeus appears in 1 Tim. 1:20. A man named Tychicus, perhaps the "Fortunatus" of 1 Cor. 16:17, appears in Titus 3:12; Acts 20:4; Eph. 6:21; and Col. 4:7. In Acts 20:4 Tychicus appears in the company of Trophimus, mentioned again in Acts 21:29. The Epistle to the Colossians cites not only the name of Tychicus but also the names of Demas, Luke, and Mark (see Col. 4:10, 14). These three names appear in the greetings of Paul's short note to Philemon (Phlm. 24). A city official by the name of Erastus appears in Rom. 16:23 (see Acts 19:22). This name has been found on an epigraph discovered by archaeologists in the area around the agora of Corinth.

The identification of the Luke and Mark who appear in 4:11 is somewhat problematic. Are they to be identified with the persons to whom the canonical Gospels according to Luke and Mark are attributed? In turn, is "Luke" to be identified with Lucius, the coworker of Paul (Rom. 16:21), or with Lucius of Cyrene (Acts 13:1)? Is "Mark" to be identified with John Mark, sometime companion of Paul (see Acts 12:12, 25; 15:37, 39) or with the Mark identified as Peter's son in 1 Pet. 5:13?

A further complication is the identity of Alexander. He is called a coppersmith in 4:14. The only other person to be identified by trade or profession in the Pastorals is a lawyer named Zenas (Titus 3:13). The unusual mention of Alexander's trade prompts one to ask whether he is to be identified with the son of Simon of Cyrene (Mark 15:21), the priestly Alexander of Acts 4:6, or the otherwise unidentified Alexander of 1 Tim. 1:20. On the other hand, one might suggest that the naming of Alexander as a metalworker is for the purpose of identifying him with or distinguishing him from the Alexander present with Paul during the riot of the Ephesian silversmiths (Acts 19:33).

The late second-century *Acts of Paul* also mentions a man by the name of Alexander (*Acts of Paul* 3.26–36). He is described as coming from Antioch in Syria, a confidant of the governor, and a leader of the games, the highest honor conferred upon a local official in imperial times. The apocryphal *Acts* portrays Alexander in opposition to Paul because of Alexander's love for a woman named Thecla who rejects him because she is a disciple of Paul who, in turn, is said to have urged celibacy for the sake of sharing in a future resurrection.

A man named Zeno is mentioned in passing in *Acts of Paul* 3.2, but he is not identified as a lawyer. On the other hand, the apocryphal *Acts* describes a coppersmith who took a stand against Paul, but his name is Hermogenes (*Acts of Paul* 3.1–17). Together with Demas, Hermogenes portrayed Paul as denying marriage and proclaiming a future resurrection whereas, said they, the resurrection takes place in one's progeny and the knowledge of God. A person named Hermogenes who abandoned Paul appears in 2 Tim. 1:15. He is contrasted with Onesiphorus, who ministered to the imprisoned Paul (1:16; see 4:19). *Acts of*

Paul 3.1–17 presents opposing pictures of Hermogenes and Onesiphorus, who happens to count Zeno among his children.

Acts of Paul 11.1 narrates that Luke from Gaul and Titus from Galatia were waiting for Paul just before his imprisonment. These same names appear in 2 Tim. 4:10–11, which says that Titus had gone to Dalmatia but that Luke remained with Paul. Second Timothy 4:21 sends greetings on behalf of Eubulus. *Acts of Paul* 8.1.1 speaks of a Corinthian presbyter named Eubulus who joined with Stephanus and three other presbyters in writing a letter to Paul. It describes Demas as a coconspirator with Hermogenes; a person named Demas is described as having left Paul in the lurch in 2 Tim. 4:10.

In sum, many of the people cited in 2 Timothy whose roles in Paul's ministry are difficult to identify on the basis of his letters and the Acts of the Apostles have names that occur in the apocryphal *Acts of Paul*. The names are similar, but the roles and relationship to Paul are not always the same. These data suggest that a number of individual names were bandied about as legends about the apostle developed in the centuries after his death. They were stock figures in a divided church's battle for theological loyalty, providing a cast of characters for a graphic description of the battle. To a large extent the battle raged around the image of Paul. The Pastor portrays a hagiographic image of Paul, his hero. *Acts of Paul* offers another portrait, that of a teacher who urged his followers to adopt an ascetic lifestyle and even forgo marriage. At the center of the battle was faith in the resurrection.

In contrast with the personal names cited in 2 Timothy, Paul wrote about most of the places named in 2 Timothy. Paul wrote letters to Christians living in Rome, Corinth, Galatia, and Thessalonica. He wrote about his visits to Antioch (Gal. 2:11), Ephesus (1 Cor. 15:32; 16:8), Troas (2 Cor. 2:12), and Asia (2 Cor. 1:8; see Rom. 16:5; 1 Cor. 16:19). In addition, Acts mentions Paul's visits to Iconium (Acts 13:51; 14:1, 19, 21; 16:2), Lystra (Acts 14:6, 8, 21; 16:1, 2), and Miletus (Acts 20:15, 17), as well as his activity in Asia, Ephesus, Antioch, Thessalonica, Galatia, Troas, Corinth, and Rome in the accounts of the various Pauline journeys. Of all the places named in 2 Timothy, the coastal region of Dalmatia stands alone as not being otherwise mentioned in the New Testament as a site for Paul's ministry of evangelization.

A concentration of personal and geographic names occurs in the epistle's final two pericopes, its postscript (4:9–18) and its epistolary closing (4:19–22). Demas, Crescens, Titus, Luke, Mark, Tychicus, Carpus, and Alexander are mentioned in the postscript, which also cites Thessalonica, Galatia, Dalmatia, Ephesus, and Troas as being among the locations that were important in Paul's ministry. The epistolary closing's farewell greetings mention Prisca, Aquila, the household of Onesiphorus, Eubulus, Pudens, Linus, and Claudia. Finally, an odd aside in the epistolary greetings cites the personal names of Erastus and Trophimus, respectively situated in Corinth and Miletus.

Literary Genre

The amount of "personalia" scattered throughout 2 Timothy indicates that it is a different sort of epistle from the other two Pastorals. As written, the epistle appears to be a very personal communication from Paul to Timothy, his beloved son. These two provide foci for the entire epistle. The epistle mentions Paul's ministry in different places and offers a portrait of Paul who is about to depart this life and is grateful for the memories that he has and that he now shares with Timothy. The apostle is said to have remembered[2] his own ancestors (1:3), as well as the mother and grandmother of Timothy (1:5). He remembers the tears of Timothy (1:4) and the kindness of Onesiphorus (1:16–18). The Paul who is presumed to have written this epistle is one who has completed his ministry and is now facing death, the time of his departure (4:6–7). Paul is able to face his death with confidence because he has previously experienced deliverance (4:17–18) and has longed for the appearance of the Lord (4:8).

In the Pastor's portrait of Paul who remembers the past and is about to move into the future reserved for him by the Lord, attention is also drawn to the present. The present is characterized by the apostle's suffering (1:8, 12; 2:9, 10); he suffered persecution in Antioch, Iconium, and Lystra (3:11), and evil things from Alexander the coppersmith (4:14). He writes from a prison where he has been shackled for the sake of the gospel (1:8; 2:9). At his trial (4:16) and in his final moments, Paul experiences loneliness and abandonment (1:15; 4:10–12). Left in the lurch and abandoned by all but Luke (4:11), Paul desires the presence of Timothy (1:4; 4:9) and remembers the prayer of the just person who has been abandoned and oppressed (4:17, a reminiscence of Ps. 22:21).

The portrait of Timothy that emerges from the epistle is that of a man who has been well reared in the faith (1:4–5; 3:14) and trained in the Scriptures from his youth (3:15). He is Paul's beloved son (1:2), a man of God (3:17), and a qualified person (2:15; see 3:17). He has received a charism, the gift of God through the laying on of Paul's hands. This ritual gesture, accompanied by the filial epithet (1:2; 2:1), suggests that Timothy is to succeed Paul in his ministry. With Paul he shares a calling and apostolic suffering (1:8–9). He is to preserve the basic outline of Paul's teaching, a treasure imparted by the Spirit who dwells in Paul and Timothy alike. He is to continue in what he has learned, recognizing those who have been his teachers (3:14). Paul expresses confidence that the Lord will provide Timothy with the type of understanding that is required for this ministry (2:7).

Timothy is to explain to others what he has heard from Paul (2:2) and to remind them of the kerygma that Jesus Christ has been raised from the dead and of the trustworthy saying that speaks of their future participation in the reign of

---

2. Note the recurrence of the memory motif in 2:8, 14.

God (2:8–14). He is to be zealous in his work (2:15) and fulfill his ministry (4:5). He is to proclaim the word and preach the gospel in circumstances that are favorable and in circumstances that are difficult (4:2, 5). He is to teach the message of truth correctly and avoid godless nonsense (2:14–16; 3:5). With a truly pastoral attitude, with patience and sound teaching, Timothy must be ready to convince, warn, and encourage people (4:2). In this effort he is to use the sacred Scriptures, for these are not only useful for teaching about salvation through faith in Christ Jesus but are also helpful for convicting, correcting, and training people in righteousness.

In effect, Paul, the presumed author of 2 Timothy, rehearses his legacy for the benefit of his disciple and entrusts to him responsibility for continuing his ministry. Paul had been appointed herald, apostle, and teacher (1:11). Paul's apostolate was a foundational charism expressed in the work of proclamation and of teaching. This twofold ministry is entrusted to Timothy in the laying on of Paul's hands (1:6). These ideas—succession in ministry, the conferral of the Spirit, and the laying on of hands—often appear together in the Jewish Scriptures and New Testament literature. All this leads one to characterize 2 Timothy as a piece of literature that deals with succession in ministry, perhaps even in office.

On the other hand, the extensive reminiscences about Paul contained in the personalia and the thoughts expressed about his death link 2 Timothy with such portions of the Bible as Deuteronomy 29–32; Gen. 47:29–49:33; 1 Kgs. 2:1–9; and 1 Macc. 2:49–70. These texts present farewell speeches by Moses, Jacob, David, and Mattathias as they are about to depart this life. All of them are literary compositions for which the author of the book in which they appear is responsible rather than the presumed speaker. These texts are generally described as "farewell discourses" or "testaments."

This literary genre was refined and reached its high point during the Second Temple period. *The Testaments of the Twelve Patriarchs*, the *Testament of Job*, the *Testaments of the Three Patriarchs* [Abraham, Isaac, Jacob], the *Testament of Moses*, the *Testament of Solomon*, and the *Testament of Adam* are among the best-known examples of the genre, but the list could also include the *Testament of Hezekiah*, the *Testament of Zosimus*, and the *Testament of Orpheus*. Perhaps the list should also include the second-century B.C.E. book of *Jubilees*, sometimes known as the *Testament of Moses*.[3] New Testament examples would include the farewell discourses of the Fourth Gospel (John 13–17), Luke 22:21–38, and Paul's farewell discourse in Acts 20:18–35.

The genre is not well defined. It often incorporates other types of material, such as paraenetic, apocalyptic, and midrashic. In general, works that belong to the testamentary type of literature present a hero from the past who gathers family and close friends around him as he faces his own death. He frequently rem-

---

3. This second-century text must not be confused with the first-century C.E. *Testament of Moses*.

inisces about his past, pointing to an occasional failing that he urges his family and friends to avoid after his departure. He urges those left behind to carry on the tradition or the work that he has begun, sometimes giving instructions for how this is to be done and even naming those who are to succeed him in his work (e.g., 1 Macc. 2:65–66; *T. Reub.* 6:8–12; *T. Sim.* 7:1–3; *T. Jud.* 21:1–5; *T. Naph.* 8:2). Those about to be left behind are frequently exhorted to lead an ethical life. Often the person who is about to die speaks about the future in apocalyptic terms. Often, but not always, the discourse closes with curses and blessings.

Most of the features of the testamentary genre are found in 2 Timothy. Were it in the form of a speech rather than the form of a letter, one could almost characterize 2 Timothy as a model of the farewell discourse. Before dismissing this possibility out of hand, the reader of 2 Timothy must take into account the fact that Hellenistic writers considered letters to be a form of speech. These speeches were composed in epistolary form so that they could be delivered at another time and in another place. This consideration allows one to identify 2 Timothy as a testamentary epistle, albeit not the classic testamentary letter, which is really a last will and testament. The epistolary genre was suggested by the importance of the apostolic letter in the early church and that community's association of letter-writing with the apostle Paul.

The recognition that 2 Timothy is an epistolary testament points to its unique situation among the Pastorals. The genre explains to a large degree why the epistle is composed as it is. The epistle's last words—"The Lord be with your spirit. Grace be with you"—have a dual function. They function as an epistolary farewell and as a testamentary blessing. The dual foci of the epistle, Paul and Timothy, highlight the succession of the latter in the ministry of the former, who is about to depart the present life.

Testamentary literature frequently includes ethical material. This is the case in 2 Timothy, where an abundance of paraenetic material is scattered throughout the epistle: 1:6–9, 13–14; 2:3–6, 15–17, 22–25; 4:5. Second Timothy 2:22 exhorts Timothy to pursue a life of righteousness, illustrated by means of a short catalogue of virtues. The exemplarity of Paul, particularly with respect to his ministry and his suffering, ultimately has a paraenetic function. The epistle's second exhortation, 2:1–7, employs typically Hellenistic illustrations: the farmer, the athlete, and the soldier. The latter are often exploited by Hellenistic rhetors in their use of the agon motif, the metaphorical description of human struggle for truth or virtue.

Jewish testamentary literature often speaks of the future in apocalyptic terms in the guise of a dream or visions, granted to the work's protagonist. Second Timothy speaks of neither dreams nor visions, but it does employ a variety of apocalyptic motifs. Among these are the author's early reference to "the appearance of our Savior Christ Jesus, who destroyed death and brought life and imperishability to light through the good news" (1:10). This describes the Christ event in apocalyptic terms as it relates that salvific event to the gospel. The trustworthy saying of 2:11–13 speaks of future life and the future kingdom and employs a Paul-like sentence of holy law. The kingdom is rarely mentioned in Paul's own letters, but it is implied by 2:12 and is specifically mentioned in 4:1, 18.

"That day," the mysterious day of the Lord of the prophetic tradition, is mentioned in 1:12, 18; and 4:8. "That day" will be a time of judgment for the living and the dead (4:1, 8). Those who long for the appearance of the just judge can hope for life, a future reign (2:12), and a crown of righteousness (4:8). These people are the elect, who shall gain salvation with eternal glory in Christ Jesus (2:10). The appearance of our Savior Christ Jesus is the definitive event that issues forth in life and imperishability.

Dualism is a common feature of apocalyptic literature. Salvation is for the elect. Opposite the elect are people who are up to no good. Their evil will increase and multiply in the final times. The author briefly mentions the devil's trap (2:26). Immediately thereafter he uses a long catalog of vices to categorize those who oppose the truth and pursue their own folly (3:1–6). Thoroughly corrupt and with rotten minds (3:8), they are no good at all. In typical apocalyptic fashion, the author speaks of the final times as those in which evil will get still worse; leading astray and being led astray will be the order of the day (3:13). In 4:3–4 the author gives a colorful description of those who will be led astray. They scratch their ears as they run from teacher to teacher and turn from the truth. In 3:8–9 Jannes and Jambres are cited as examples of people who previously had opposed the truth and whose folly was subsequently laid bare for all to see. The legend to which the author refers[4] may well have been a pre-Christian midrashic tradition elsewhere known from the Palestinian Targum on Exod. 7:11–12. This would be the only indication of the author's familiarity with the Jewish midrashic tradition despite his evident appreciation for the sacred Scriptures (3:15–17; 4:13).

The distinctive literary genre of 2 Timothy sets it apart from 1 Timothy and Titus within the small corpus of the Pastoral Epistles. In many ways, 2 Timothy is essentially a reflection on the ministry of Paul and how that ministry is to be continued after Paul's death. It presents Timothy as one who has been with Paul in many of the locations of his apostolic ministry and has learned from him. Properly qualified, he has been coopted into succession of the Pauline ministry by the ritual gesture of the laying on of hands. Thus conceived, 2 Timothy lays a foundation for 1 Timothy and Titus. These are concerned with the organization of the church in the post-Pauline era.

Second Timothy is concerned with the issue of who should organize the church and why that person is qualified to do so. Motivated by this concern and

---

4. A common feature of apocalyptic literature is its rehearsal of material contained in earlier texts.

framing the argument within an epistolary farewell discourse, the author has no need to set out detailed parameters for the organization of the household church or to give instructions for a worshiping community (1 Tim. 2:8–12). For the purposes of 2 Timothy, it suffices that exhortation be addressed to Timothy, for whom Paul is the model of excellence in faith and ministry.

The testamentary genre also explains why the Scriptures are presented differently in 2 Timothy from the way they appear in 1 Timothy and Titus. In those texts, the author's concern is with those who misuse the Scriptures, the would-be teachers of the law who do not understand the Scriptures and their true halakic and haggadic use (see 1 Tim. 1:6). In 2 Timothy, Paul's successor is said to have been well formed in the Scriptures since his youth (3:14–15), as Paul himself undoubtedly was. Paul's undisputed letters illustrate the apostle's familiarity with the Jewish Scriptures and give evidence of his adroit ability, undoubtedly learned from his own rabbinic masters, to use the Scriptures in different ways. Paul was someone who used the Scriptures in teaching, conviction, correction, and training in righteousness (see 3:16). It is no wonder that when the author of 2 Timothy uses the image of a building to describe the church, he presents it as having an epigraph from Scripture inscribed on the foundation (2:19–21).

Second Timothy's testamentary genre explains the appearance of another unique feature within the epistle, the anamnesis motif in 2:8–14. The pericope is framed by the idea of remembering and reminding others about what has been remembered (2:8, 14). What is to be remembered is the core of the Pauline kerygma, the proclamation that Jesus Christ was raised from the dead. The author's recalling the early Christian creed in this pericope stands alone within the three-letter corpus. The proclamation of this creed motivated Paul's preaching and led to his suffering. The Pastor's memory of Paul's proclamation prompts him to rehearse some elements of the introduction of Paul in Rom. 1:1–7 and to adopt and modify the baptismal hymn of Rom. 6:8.

Authenticity

The testamentary genre of 2 Timothy gives it a Pauline character that does not as markedly typify the other two Pastoral Epistles. The Pauline features of 2 Timothy have prompted a number of theories as to the composition of the text, namely, that 2 Timothy incorporates authentic Pauline fragments (see pp. 4–6), that it was written by an amanuensis who worked at Paul's behest, or even that it was written by Paul himself.

It is, however, not necessary to adopt any of these positions. In fact, two of the characteristic traits of 2 Timothy militate against its possible Pauline authorship. The first is its literary genre. A characteristic of the genre is that farewell discourses are composed by authors writing about their heroes; they are in no way verbatim reports of those who are about to depart this life. The second is the apocalyptic elements incorporated into the epistle and scattered here and there throughout the text. The apocalyptic elements of 2 Timothy are not so extensive or so characteristic of the epistle as a whole as to warrant the designation of epistolary apocalypse, a description that might aptly be applied to the deuteropauline 2 Thessalonians. Nonetheless, the apocalyptic elements present in 2 Timothy suggest that the epistle was not written by the apostle. It is characteristic of the apocalyptic genre that these works are not composed by the seers to whom the texts' "prophetic" elements are attributed.

An Outline of 2 Timothy

1:1–2	The Salutation
3–5	The Thanksgiving
6–14	First Exhortation
15–18	A Personal Note
2:1–7	Second Exhortation
8–13	The Kerygma Reinterpreted
14–21	A Pastoral Charge
22–26	Third Exhortation
3:1–9	The Final Times
10–17	Final Exhortation
4:1–8	Farewell
9–18	Postscript
19–22	Epistolary Closing

The Salutation
2 Timothy 1:1–2

Hellenistic letters typically begin with a three-part salutation that includes the name of the author, the name of the recipient, and a formula of greeting. New Testament letters follow this pattern, expanding it and giving a specifically Christian cast to each of its three parts. The salutation of 2 Timothy anticipates the content of the epistle. Paul's apostolate is presented within a perspective that looks forward to life in Christ Jesus. Timothy is characterized as a beloved son. This double characterization is in keeping with the farewell character of the epistle.

> 1:1 Paul, apostle of Christ Jesus through the will of God, in accordance with the promise of life that is in Christ Jesus, 2 to Timothy, beloved son, grace, mercy, and peace from God the Father and Christ Jesus our Lord.

[1:1] The epistle begins with the name of Paul, the Greek form of the Latin name of an Aemilian clan. With the exception of those passages in Acts[5] where Paul is identified by his given name, Saul,[6] this is the name by which Paul is known throughout the New Testament. Appended to the name is a title, the *intitulatio*, corresponding to the signature block of a modern letter. The title identifies the author in such a way as to specify the quality of the author's claim for the attention of his correspondents. The *intitulatio* of 2 Timothy is longer than the titles typically found in Hellenistic letters and in Paul's own letters.[7] It identifies Paul as an apostle of Christ Jesus and emphasizes Paul's apostolic authority by identifying its source, the will of God, and its purpose, life in Christ Jesus.

The expression "apostle of Christ Jesus through the will of God" has been taken over from 2 Cor. 1:1 (see 1 Cor. 1:1; Col. 1:1; Eph. 1:1). Among the Pastoral Epistles only 2 Timothy speaks of God's will. Paul had appropriated the idea of "God's will" from Jewish piety. In using the idea, the Pastor shows his dependence on Paul and echoes Paul's conviction that his apostolate was

---

5. Acts 7:58; 8:1, 3; 9:1, 8, 11, 22, 24; 11:25, 30; 12:25; 13:1, 2, 7, 9 (*Saulos*); 9:4, 17; 22:7, 13; 26:15 (*Saoul*).

6. Saul is the name of the great king of the tribe of Benjamin to which Paul belonged (Rom. 11:1; Phil. 3:5).

7. Paul did not use a title in the first of his extant letters, 1 Thessalonians. Later he did so, identifying himself as apostle (Romans, 1–2 Corinthians, Galatians), servant (Romans, Philippians), and prisoner (Philemon).

intended by God and originated from God. The will of God determined the shape of Paul's life and work as an apostle of Christ Jesus. When Paul placed the title "Christ" before the name "Jesus" in the salutation of 2 Corinthians, he emphasized the death and resurrection of Jesus. He may even have intended to evoke (Jewish) messianic expectations among his audience. Neither the resurrection of Jesus nor messianic expectation is emphasized in 2 Timothy. The Pastor has simply borrowed a convenient title from one of Paul's own letters.

Paul's apostolate and this epistle are to be seen within the context of the promise of life that is in Christ Jesus. "Promise of life" is an expression proper to the Pastoral Epistles (1 Tim. 4:8). The object of God's promise is eternal life (1 Tim. 1:16; 4:8; 6:12, 19; Titus 1:2; 3:7). God has promised and guarantees the gift of eternal life (see 2:13; Titus 1:2), a gift mediated through Christ Jesus (see 1:10). Promised by God, eternal life is the object of Christian hope. Eternal life is not only future salvation (1 Tim. 4:8), it also helps to shape the present. The hope of eternal life motivated the apostolate of Paul; similarly, hope of eternal life should motivate the readers of the epistle.

[2] Describing Timothy as Paul's "beloved son" (see 2:1[8]), the Pastor defines the relationship between the putative Paul and the putative Timothy. Paul had described Timothy as his beloved son, the exemplary big brother who was to be imitated by the Corinthians (1 Cor. 4:17). As a son, Timothy worked with Paul in the proclamation of the gospel (Phil. 2:22). The idea that Timothy had been faithful to Paul and could serve as an example for believers is implicit in the Pastor's choice of "beloved son" as a descriptive epithet. It is particularly appropriate in a letter that has a testamentary character. The genre is one in which a dying father (see 4:5–6) is often portrayed as conveying his last will and testament to the beloved children whom he will leave behind.

The typical Hellenistic greeting is "rejoice" (*chairein*); the typical Semitic greeting is "peace" (*eirēnē*). Paul typically combines both of these greetings, adding a Christian twist. His salutation (see also 1 Tim. 1:2; 2 John 3; Jude 2) was generally "grace [*charis*] and peace from God the Father and Christ Jesus our Lord." Paul hoped and prayed that God the Father and Christ Jesus would not only look favorably upon his correspondents but would also share with them that peace which is both the fullness of covenantal blessings and the fullness of well-being that humans desire.

Second Timothy adds a third element to the traditional greeting, namely, mercy. In the biblical tradition mercy is a divine attribute. Mercy is an expression of Yahweh's benevolence to his people (Jer. 3:12; 9:24 [9:23 LXX]). In the

---

8. Here as in 1:2, the Pastor uses the generic *teknon*, "child," rather than the gender-specific *huios* to identify Timothy as Paul's son. This is the consistent usage of the Pastoral Epistles (see 1 Tim. 1:2, 18; Titus 1:4), which do not use the word *huios* at all. The other Pastoral Epistles use the plural form, *tekna*, to speak of the children of overseers, servers, and widows (1 Tim. 3:4, 12; 5:4; Titus 1:6).

Greek Bible, "mercy" (*eleos*) frequently renders the Hebrew *ḥesed*,[9] a virtually untranslatable term often rendered as "covenantal love" or "steadfast love." The term *ḥesed* evokes the idea of God's favorable disposition toward his people. One of its qualities is that it lasts forever, down to the thousandth generation in the concrete imagery of the Hebrew idiom (see, e.g., Exod. 20:6). Thus the Chronicler proclaims, "Give thanks to the LORD, for he is good; for his steadfast love [*ḥesed*] endures forever" (1 Chr. 16:34).

Paul never uses "mercy" in his epistolary greetings and rarely writes it. Nonetheless, a prayer in Gal. 6:16 wishes mercy upon those who follow Paul's rule, his "canon," and upon the house of Israel. Paul's prayer was innovative insofar as it prayed that mercy be extended even to those Gentiles who belong to the Israel of God (Rom. 9:24; 11:31; 15:9). Adding "mercy" to the traditional Pauline epistolary greeting in 1:2, the Pastor endorses Paul's idea of the extension of God's covenant blessings to the Gentiles (see Luke 1:72; cf. Luke 1:54, 58, 78). In the Pastor's community Paul is remembered as a prime example of someone to whom God had shown mercy (1 Tim. 1:16).

In greeting "Timothy" as he does, the Pastor expresses the hope that those to whom the letter is addressed (see the plural "you" in the final greeting, 4:22) will be the beneficiaries of the grace, mercy, and peace that comes from God the Father and Christ Jesus our Lord. The choice of "Timothy" as Paul's protégé is a fictive device that enables the Pastor to address all who would be faithful to Paul's apostolic legacy as the Pastor understands it.

In using the epithets of "Father" for God and "our Lord" for Christ Jesus, the Pastor appropriates Paul's favorite theological and christological titles, those titles that were commonly used in the salutations of his letters (Rom. 1:7; 1 Cor. 1:3; 2 Cor. 1:2; Gal. 1:3; Phil. 1:2; 1 Thess. 1:1; Phlm. 3). God and Christ stand together as being the source of the triple blessing. Christ is the mediator of the beneficence that comes from the Father (see 1:1).

The Thanksgiving
2 Timothy 1:3–5

Following Hellenistic epistolary form, in which words of thanks to one or another god for a specific benefit received often replace or are added to the traditional wish for good health (see 3 John 2), Paul's letters typically begin with words of thanksgiving addressed to God. Among his extant letters there are only two exceptions: 2 Corinthians, where the thanksgiving has been replaced by a benediction that recalls the Jewish *berakah*, and Galatians, where Paul's irate

---

9. The Greek noun *eleos* was also used to translate six other Hebrew terms.

mood has apparently led him to omit the customary words of thanksgiving. Second Timothy is the only one of the Pastoral Epistles to begin with a thanksgiving. The thanksgiving period is generally similar to the thanksgivings of the authentic Pauline letters, but its vocabulary, style, and themes are different from those found in Paul's own correspondence.

The thanksgiving periods of the Pauline letters have both an epistolary and a rhetorical function. Their expression of affection for the addressees helps the letter to fulfill the purpose of *philophronesis*, an expression of warm positive regard, in Hellenistic letters. They serve as a kind of *captatio benevolentiae*, an implicit appeal to the reader's favorable disposition. Paul's epistolary thanksgivings introduce the main themes of his letters. Thus, they fulfill the rhetorical function of the *diēgēsis* (*narratio*). Coming between the rhetorical introduction (*proemium*) and the speaker's announced purpose (*propositio*), the *diēgēsis* sets out some of the facts on which both the writer and his audience agree as he begins to address them. This corresponds to the forensic rhetor's rehearsal of facts. In the thanksgiving period of 1:3–5, the recipient of the letter is almost overwhelmed by the author's expression of concern and confidence. Verse 5 establishes Timothy as someone who has been formed in the faith since his youth (see 3:14–15). Verse 4, on the other hand, initiates the reader to the idea that the "writer" is about to depart.

> 1:3 I am thankful to God—whom I serve, as my ancestors did, with a clear conscience—as I remember you constantly in my prayers night and day. 4 Remembering your tears, I yearn to see you so that I might be filled with joy. 5 I have a memory[a] of your genuine faith that first dwelt in your grandmother, Lois, and your mother, Eunice. I am convinced that it is also in you.

a. Verses 4–5 have been translated as three independent sentences. In Greek these verses are a single complex sentence.

[1:3] Hellenistic letters typically include some sort of health wish or expression of thanks to the deity after the opening salutation. An early second-century C.E. letter begins, "Antonius Maximus to his sister, Sabina, very many greetings. Before all else I pray that you are well, for I myself am well. Making mention of you before the gods here . . ." (BGU 2.632).[10]

The Pastor's expression "remember you" (*echōtēnperi sou mneian*) is similar to Antonius's "making mention of you." Paul's thanksgivings begin with the verb "to give thanks" (*eucharisteō*) and make use of the word "always" (*pantote*), to qualify either the word "thanksgiving" (1 Cor. 1:4; 1 Thess. 1:2; see 2 Thess. 1:3) or Paul's prayer of gratitude (Rom. 1:10; Phil. 1:4; Phlm. 4;

---

10. See John L. White, *Light from Ancient Letters* (Philadelphia: Fortress, 1986), 160.

see Col. 1:3). The Pastor's thanksgiving employs other words: "I am thankful" (*charin echō*, corresponding to the Latin *gratias ago*; see 1 Tim. 1:12) in place of "I give thanks," and "constantly . . . night and day" (*adialeiptōs*; see Rom. 1:9; 9:2; 1 Thess. 1:2) instead of "always." Striking features of this thanksgiving are its description of the one who gives thanks (see Rom. 1:10–15), the expression of a desire to see the recipient, and the use of personal names.

In this thanksgiving Paul's profile, already outlined in the *intitulatio* of 1:1, is further developed. Mention is made of Paul's having served or worshiped as his ancestors did (see Phil. 3:5). He followed the example of his forebears and did so "with a clear conscience" (see Acts 23:1; 24:16). This phrase can be taken in a moral sense (see "good conscience" in 1 Tim. 1:5, 19; "clean conscience" in 1 Tim. 3:9), but it might well mean "with undivided attention" so as to affirm that Paul was single-minded in his service to the God of his ancestors. This proclaims the Pastor's conviction about Paul's Jewishness. He never abandoned the God of his ancestors. Such a description of Paul should motivate Timothy, whose own ancestors, Lois and Eunice, had such a genuine faith (1:5).

Timothy is said to be remembered in prayers of petition or intercession (*en tais deēsesin*). The terminology suggests that these prayers request that God confer some specific blessings on Timothy. The expected blessings are not specified, but the context suggests that fidelity to the faith of his ancestors, including Paul, his father in faith (1:2), is one gift that God might grant to Timothy. Constancy in prayer is a trait of Christian piety (see 1 Tim. 5:5; Luke 2:37; 5:33; Acts 10:2; Phil. 4:6; 1 Thess. 5:17). The merism "night and day" reflects the Jewish division of "a day" and suggests that the Pastor prays for Timothy all the time. Paul prayed constantly; so too does the Pastor.

[4] Paul's desire to see Timothy frames and colors the entire letter. Before the letter is brought to its close, Paul is described as urging Timothy to come quickly to Paul and to bring Mark along (4:9, 11, 21). This literary inclusion sets the entire letter in the context of Paul's absence and Timothy's presence. Absence and presence are among the typical motifs of Hellenistic letters. So too is joy, especially joy that results from the writer having had a visit or received a letter from the one to whom he is writing (see, e.g., 1 Cor. 16:17–18).

Paul's desire—"yearning," the *pathos* motif (see Phil. 4:1)—to see Timothy is self-interested. He wants to see his beloved son so that he himself might be filled with joy. Although joy is a typical epistolary motif, early Christian texts spoke of joy with a particular nuance. In these texts joy accompanies the reception of a divine gift; joy is experienced in the presence of the Lord. Thus, Paul experienced joy in the presence of one or another missionary who shared with him news about the well-being of a community that he had evangelized (1 Thess. 3:9; 1 Cor. 16:17–18; 2 Cor. 2:3; Phil. 4:1). He begged the community at Philippi to "make his joy complete" by being a community that is one in faith and love.

Ostensibly motivating the apostle's desire to visit with Timothy is his memory of the latter's weeping. Timothy's tears are enigmatic. The New Testament gives no indication as to when, where, or why Paul would have experienced a weeping Timothy, nor does the New Testament provide any information about Paul's having been told of Timothy's sadness. One can only conjecture that the reason for the disciple's sadness is that the apostle has been imprisoned (1:8) and abandoned by his coworkers (1:15; see 4:10, 16). There is some indication in the New Testament, but no conclusive evidence, that Timothy was somewhat fearful in the exercise of the task that Paul entrusted to him (see 1 Cor. 16:10–11). The mention of Timothy's tears may perhaps result from the fact that in his desire to eulogize Paul the Pastor did not want to present his hero as someone who was concerned only with his own personal well-being.

[5] In addition to remembering Timothy's tears, the apostle is said also to have remembered (*hypomnēsin labōn*) Timothy's genuine faith. Paul remembered the dynamic faith of the Thessalonians (1 Thess. 1:3, 7) and Philemon's faith in the Lord Jesus (Phlm. 4–6). Here he is said to have remembered Timothy's "genuine faith" (*anypokritou pisteōs*; see 1 Tim. 1:5). This genuine faith includes "intellectual orthodoxy, pious conduct, faithfulness, and loyalty in keeping obligations" (*TLNT* 1.134–38, 135). It is at once a faith that is whole and a faith that is not perverted. Suggesting that Timothy's genuine faith had previously resided in his mother and grandmother adds yet another nuance to the idea of genuine faith. Genuine faith transcends the generations; it is passed on from generation to generation.[11] Without employing the "tradition" word group, the author has set the groundwork for an understanding of tradition. Paul received a religious tradition from his ancestors. Timothy is Paul's "beloved son" in the faith (see 1 Tim. 1:2). Before Timothy had genuine faith, his grandmother and mother did. That same genuine faith is presumed to remain with Timothy. He had received it from his mother (see Acts 16:1) and his grandmother; he is to pass it on to the people of Ephesus so that their faith might be genuine (see 1 Tim. 1:5; Rom. 1:5). There is a chain of tradition in passing genuine faith along from generation to generation. Men and women are involved in the passing along of this tradition. Paul and Timothy are vital links in the chain of tradition.

The names of Eunice and Lois do not appear elsewhere in the New Testament. Timothy's mother is mentioned in Acts 16:1, but her name is not given; she is identified only as a Jewish woman who was a believer. Luke says that

11. In addition to the difficulty of trying to harmonize 2 Timothy's bibliographic "data" about Paul with information provided in Paul's own letters and the Acts of the Apostles, there is some tension between the Pastor's description of Timothy's pious upbringing (1:5; 3:14–15) and what Luke says about Timothy in Acts 16:1–3.

Timothy's father was a Greek (*hellēnos*), but does not give his name. Second Timothy does not mention Timothy's biological father; Paul is Timothy's father insofar as he had passed the faith along to him. The epistle does not specifically mention who it was that evangelized Eunice and Lois, but the implication is that Paul has done so. On the one hand, he is said to have remembered their faith, implying that he had experienced their faith. On the other hand, in the absence of any mention of Timothy's biological father, Paul and Eunice are Timothy's parents in faith. They shared not only their Jewish ancestry (1:2; Acts 16:1) but also a common Christian faith (see Titus 1:4).

According to the Pastor, Timothy had been instructed in the Scriptures from infancy (3:15). Luke's notion that Timothy was an adult who not yet been circumcised (Acts 16:3) could suggest that Eunice was a lax Jew. Her marriage to a Gentile (Acts 16:1, 3) would, in any case, have been frowned upon by pious Jews. Timothy was well regarded in his hometown of Lystra as well as in the neighboring town of Iconium (Konya in contemporary Anatolia). Despite the Pastor's assertion that Timothy had been instructed in the Scriptures from infancy, there remains some doubt about whether he would have been considered a Jew. Within Judaism, children born to Jewish mothers were normally considered to be Jews but, observes Shaye J. D. Cohen, "when the Israelite woman moved abroad to join her Gentile husband, her children were considered Gentile."[12] In the Greco-Roman world, women were expected to defer to their husbands in matters religious (see Plutarch, "Advice to the Bride and Groom," 19; *Moralia* 140D).

In ancient Israel the family was the principal instrument for passing traditional lore and customs from one generation to the next. To this day the Passover seder attests to the importance of the family in this regard (see Exod. 13:8; *m. Pesah.* 10:4–6; see Exod. 20:12; Deut. 5:16; see also *b. Qidd.* 143 for a discussion about the role of the grandfather in teaching the Torah to his grandsons). Locating the faith of both Paul and Timothy within the Jewish tradition, Paul's ancestors, and Timothy's formative scriptures is the Pastor's descriptive way of affirming that genuine faith is firmly rooted within the Jewish tradition.

The thanksgiving, a virtual exercise of Paul's memory ("remember . . . remembering . . . memory"), concludes with an expression of the apostle's convictions (see 1:12). He is convinced that genuine faith is to be found in Timothy. This short, independent sentence whose real subject is genuine faith is an apostolic seal of approval that confirms Timothy's authority. The Pastor's words are similar to the description of Timothy as Paul's "true son" in the salutation of 1 Timothy (1 Tim. 1:2; see Titus 1:4). Timothy is one who has been endorsed by the apostle Paul.

---

12. Shaye J. D. Cohen, "Was Timothy Jewish (Acts 16:1–3)? Patristic Exegesis, Rabbinic Law, and Matrilineal Descent," *JBL* 105 (1986): 266.

First Exhortation
2 Timothy 1:6–14

One of the main purposes of testamentary literature is to encourage those who have been left behind to carry on the legacy of the departed person. The encouragement often takes the form of an exhortation. The first exhortation in 2 Timothy is structured chiastically as an *a-b-c-b'-a'* pattern in which the two *a* and *b* elements correspond with one another. At the center of the scheme is the hymn-like 1:9–10. This is the focal point around which the other elements of the pericope are organized. Suffering is the dominant motif of the *b* elements (1:8; 1:11–12). The *a* elements (1:6–7; 1:13–14) speak about the spirit and delimit the pericope as a literary unit. The ring construction, a literary *inclusio*, is marked by two lexical elements, "spirit" (*pneuma*) and "in" (*en*). These terms appear in both *a* and *a'*.

In this exhortation Timothy is challenged to follow the example of Paul, who has designated him as his successor by means of the ritual gesture of the laying on of hands. Timothy is specifically encouraged to hold on to the model of the sound words that he has received from Paul (v. 13), but the idea that Timothy is to follow Paul's example is implicit throughout the exhortation. Timothy is not to be ashamed (v. 8), as Paul was not ashamed (v. 12). Timothy is to join in suffering (v. 8), as Paul suffered (v. 12). Timothy is to preserve what has been entrusted to him (v. 14). The Pastor portrays Paul as entrusting his legacy to Timothy (vv. 13–14) even as Paul commends the results of his own ministry to God's safekeeping (v. 12).

1:6 For this reason I remind you to fan into flame the gift of God which is in you through the laying on of my hands. 7 For God did not give us a spirit of cowardice but of strength, love, and moderation. 8 Do not be ashamed of the testimony about our Lord or of me, his prisoner. Join[a] with me in suffering for the good news with the help of the power of God, 9 who saved us and called us with a holy calling, not according to our works but according to his own purpose and the beneficence shown to us in Christ Jesus before the eternal ages. 10 This beneficence is now made manifest through the appearance of our Savior Christ Jesus,[b] who destroyed death and brought life and imperishability to light through the good news. 11 For this proclamation I have been appointed herald, apostle, and teacher.[c] 12 For this reason I too suffer these things, but I am not ashamed, for I know the one in whom I have trusted, and I am convinced that he is able to preserve what has been entrusted to me until that day.
13 Preserve the model of sound words that you heard from me in faith and love that is in Christ Jesus. 14 Hold fast the precious treasure entrusted to you through the Holy Spirit dwelling in us.

a. Verses 8–11 are a single sentence in Greek.

b. Christian scribes had a tendency to affirm the divinity of Jesus. Thus, a fifth-century manuscript (I) reads "the appearance of our Savior, God." A similar phenomenon occurs in the manuscript tradition of 1 Tim. 1:1 and Titus 3:6.

c. Almost all of the ancient manuscripts have a qualifying phrase, "of the nations" (*ethnōn*), after "teacher." The oldest manuscripts, א and A, do not have this qualification. The modifier was introduced into the manuscript tradition under the influence of 1 Tim. 2:7.

[1:6] The first exhortation begins with a continuation of the remembrance theme that served as the leitmotif of the thanksgiving period (vv. 3–5). Not only does the author begin the pericope with "For this reason," he also "reminds"[13] Timothy to fan into flame the gift of God that he has received through the laying on of Paul's hands. This is a remarkable opening gambit for an exhortation. Most often Hellenistic hortatory passages begin with *parakalō*, "I exhort you." Instead of using the familiar language of Hellenistic paraenesis, whose rhetorical force derives from the authority of the one who says "I exhort you," the Pastor's exhortation begins with a "think back" motif and goes on from there.

Timothy is exhorted to rekindle the gift of God (*charisma tou theou*). During the late first century C.E, the verb "rekindle" (*anazōpyrein*, literally, "fan into flame") was commonly used in a figurative sense, as various papyri texts and the writings of Josephus, Plutarch, and others indicate. The metaphor was a good one for the Pastor to use. The image of fire was used in early Christian literature to describe gifts of God's Spirit, beginning with Paul's first literary reference to a charism, in which he exhorts the Thessalonians not to extinguish the Spirit, and including Luke's description of the first Christian Pentecost (1 Thess. 5:19; Acts 2:3–4, 19).

In 1 Tim. 4:14, Timothy was told, "Do not neglect the spiritual gift that is in you, which has been given to you through prophecy with the imposition of the hands of the group of elders." The thought is reiterated here in 2 Tim. 1:6. The use of the term *charisma*, "gift," to indicate what it was that Timothy received as a result of the laying on of hands is an indication of the dependence of the Pastorals on Paul. Ancient literature does not provide any evidence of the use of the term "gift" (*charisma*) prior to Paul. Thus, it appears that the term was coined by Paul. He chose the term to contrast the real gifts of the Spirit with ecstatic phenomena that are too readily characterized as spiritual phenomena (*pneumatika*; see 1 Cor. 12:1–4). Thereafter, the term is used in the New Testament only in the writings of Paul and in the literature dependent on him (1 Tim. 4:14; 1 Pet. 4:10). The term highlights the gratuitous nature of the gifts of God and points to their ecclesial function. The charisms are gifts given by

---

13. The construction, with the verb *anamimnēskō* followed by an accusative and an infinitive, has the sense of reminding someone to do something.

the Spirit for the upbuilding of the church as the body of Christ. The section of 1 Corinthians (chaps. 12–14) that Paul devotes to the charisms are the most extensive explanation of the "gifts" of God in the New Testament.[14] For Paul, charisms are not only gifts; they are also a service to the community and a means by which God acts, through the Spirit, in the world.

The specific nature of the charism entrusted to Timothy is not identified in 1:6, but one might suggest that the charism of which the author is thinking is the gift of prophecy. The gift of prophecy, the only charism found on all four of the apostle's lists of charisms (Rom. 12:6; 1 Cor. 12:10, 28, 29; see also Eph. 4:11; 1 Pet. 4:11), is the single charism without which a Christian community cannot exist. A Christian community needs to have someone in its midst who speaks on behalf of God and on behalf of God's people. This is the function of the biblical prophet and the gift of prophecy (*pro-phēteia*). The exhortation to fan the gift into flames is an exhortation to Timothy to use the gift, the charism, that is his (see 1 Cor. 12:11). Paul did not link the gift of charisms to any ritual whatsoever. In the face of an elitism that threatened the unity of the church at Corinth, he taught that all believers have charisms.

In contrast, both 1 and 2 Timothy use the language of charism only in regard to Timothy. Moreover, these texts associate Timothy's charism with the ritual gesture of the imposition of hands. The church's use of the imposition of hands to symbolize the transference of power, appointment to office (see Acts 14:23),[15] and conferral of the gift of the Spirit (see Acts 8:16–19; 9:17; 19:5–6) as a kind of "ordination ritual"[16] was parallel with a similar development in late first-century and early second-century Judaism. The Talmud relates that Rabbi Johannan ben Zakkai (d. ca. 80 C.E.), the Tannaitic sage who was Judaism's leading rabbi in the years following the destruction of the temple, ordained his disciples with a ritual imposition of hands (see *b. Sanh.* 13b–14a). The same passage observes that in earlier times each rabbi ordained his own pupils.

The ritual gesture is well attested in the biblical tradition. The Lord directed

14. Paul uses the metaphor "the body," an important feature of his theology, to explain the interrelationship among the charisms (1 Cor. 12:12–27). Unfortunately, this hermeneutical key is absent from the Pastorals. For John A. T. Robinson the omission of any "body" theology from the Pastorals is almost compelling evidence that the Pastorals were not written by Paul (see John A. T. Robinson, *The Body: A Study in Pauline Theology.* SBT 5 (Chicago: Regnery, 1952), 10).

15. Luke's account of Paul's dealings with Timothy does not give any indication that Paul or another Christian prophet laid hands on Timothy (see Acts 16:1–3).

16. It is anachronistic to speak of the "ordination" of Timothy. Some commentators (e.g., Roloff 255–59, 263–82; and Oberlinner 1.208–11) nonetheless use this language to speak about the charism given to Timothy with the imposition of hands. Other authors (e.g., Von Lips 247–48, 281–82, 286–87; and Wolter 187–88) write about the institutionalization of the charism. Ordination and the institutionalism of charisms place 1–2 Timothy in a context of a developing catholicism (*Frühkatholizismus*).

Moses to lay his hand upon Joshua as an indication that Joshua was to succeed Moses in the leadership of Israel. Thereupon in the presence of the priests and the whole congregation Moses laid his hands on Joshua in a ceremonial commissioning (see Num. 27:18–23). The Deuteronomist comments that Joshua was full of the spirit of wisdom because Moses had laid hands on him (Deut. 34:9).

Rabbinic tradition saw in the imposition of hands a symbol of the transfer of the divine spirit. The seventy elders chosen to assist Moses (Num. 11:16–17, 24–25) were considered to have received a share of Moses' spirit by a similar ritual gesture (*semikhah*, the laying on of hands). These in turn imposed hands on their successors so that there was an unbroken chain in the transmission of the divine spirit from Moses down to the time of the Second Temple. Reception of the *semikhah* was required for participation in the Great Sanhedrin and lesser sanhedrins. As a ritual of ordination, the practice of the *semikhah* continued into the fourth century C.E., but some Jewish authorities claim that it continued until the eleventh or twelfth century.

First Timothy 4:14 says a group of elders laid hands on Timothy but makes no specific mention of Paul's participation in the ritual. It can be argued that there is no real contradiction between 1 Tim. 4:14 and 2 Tim. 1:6. Conceivably, Paul and the elders laid hands on Timothy either simultaneously or successively. Arguments that seek to harmonize the two traditions easily overlook the fact that the texts are intended to make different points. Having spoken about the relationship between Paul and Timothy (1:3–5), 2 Timothy highlights the idea that Timothy is the designated successor (see the "us" in v. 7) of Paul and one who has received the gift of the Spirit (1:5–6) through the laying on of hands. First Timothy presents an overview of Timothy's ministry.

[7] The Pastor explains the gift given to Timothy with a contrast, the classic rhetorical device often employed by the apostle himself. On the one hand, Timothy was not given a spirit of cowardice. Cowardice (*deilias*) renders a person unfit for battle (Sir. 37:11; see Philo, *Moses* 1.233, 236; Dio Chrysostom, *Discourses* 11.101; 71.7; Epictetus, *Discourses* 1.24.3). The Lord told Joshua not to be cowardly (Deut. 31:8; Josh. 1:9; 8:1); the Lord would be with him and the people (Josh. 10:25; see Deut. 1:21). "Have neither fear nor cowardice" appears to have been an ancient military charge. Paul had been a good soldier (4:7). Timothy was expected to be a good soldier (2:3). Cowardice was something to be avoided, especially by a soldier. "Don't be a coward," an appeal to a person's sense of shame, was a familiar motif in Hellenistic rhetoric. Thus, a letter addressed by the church of Smyrna to the church of Philomelium describes Polycarp as hearing a voice from heaven, "Be strong, Polycarp, and play the man," just before his martyrdom (*Mart. Pol.* 9:1). Such exhortations served to prod those to whom they were addressed to do what had to be done, despite the effort to be made and the danger to be faced.

Rather than being a coward, Timothy was to have a triad of qualities as a result of God's gift: the spirit of strength, love, and moderation. Within the Pauline tradition "love" is the most important and the most basic gift of the Spirit. All other charisms are but expressions of this fundamental charism (Rom. 5:5; 1 Cor. 12:31b–14:1). Here, in verse 7, God's gift includes strength, love, and moderation. The Pastor will again speak of love in 1:13; 2:22; and 3:10. In this exhortation, it is likely that "love" is to be considered as the fundamental gift of God à la Paul, and that strength and moderation are specific articulations of the virtue of love in Timothy's ministry. Taken together, the three terms appear in the form of an interpretive triad in which the central term, often a familiar term of the Pauline tradition, is encompassed by two terms that would be readily understood in the Pastor's Hellenistic world. The literary device is often used in the Pastorals (see, e.g., 1:11; 1 Tim. 1:13; 2:7).

Immediately contrasted with cowardice, "strength" evokes military courage, the strength to lead soldiers in battle. In a leader, "moderation" (*sōphronismou*) implies good judgment and prudence. Words derived from the root *sōphron-* were used in imperial documents in the sense of good judgment or discretion in administration (MM 4996). That would seem to be its sense here. Hellenistic moralists frequently extolled virtuous "good judgment." Words derived from the root are used throughout the Pastorals, in various verbal (Titus 2:4, 6), adverbial (Titus 2:12), adjectival (1 Tim. 3:2; Titus 1:8; 2:2, 5), and nominal forms (1 Tim. 2:9, 15), to suggest a kind of self-discipline that is expressed in modest, chaste, and restrained forms of behavior. Moulton-Milligan suggest that in 1:7, "moderation" clearly suggests the meaning "self-control," "self-discipline" (MM 4995).

Timothy has received the God-given gifts of strength to fight the good fight and good judgment to lead the community. These are qualities that Paul possessed. They are qualities that should be found in those who would succeed him in the leadership of the church.

[8] The second specific exhortation addressed to Timothy is that he should be ashamed neither of testimony about the Lord nor of testimony about Paul (see Rom. 1:16). "Testimony about our Lord" is not synonymous with "the gospel," the message of the good news. Rather, it should be taken as a reference to the trial and eventual death of Jesus (see 1 Tim. 2:6; 6:13). Jesus died by crucifixion, a form of punishment meted out to slaves and criminals. Testimony about Paul would be similar. Paul is a prisoner,[17] chained and treated like

---

17. The motif of Paul the prisoner (see 1:16; 2:9) provides a reason for the epistle. Paul is not able to come to Timothy, nor does he express any desire to do so. Rather, Timothy is urged to come to Paul (1:4; 4:9). That Paul is unavoidably absent from the community functions as a pseudepigraphic device for the Pastor. Paul is absent from the community because, in fact, he has already died. A similar use of the prisoner motif is found in Eph. 3:1 and 4:1.

a malefactor because of the message that he proclaimed (1:16; 2:9; see Phil. 1:7). Since the Roman judicial system did not use imprisonment as a form of punishment, the apostle is either awaiting trial (note the use of "first defense" in 4:16) or the death penalty (4:6–8).

Shame and honor were strong social and motivational forces in late first-century Mediterranean culture. Timothy and other Christians might well experience some shame with regard to both the fate of Jesus and the situation of Paul. Timothy's association with them would be something for which he would lose face. Rather than being ashamed, Timothy is exhorted to join with Paul in suffering for the sake of the gospel. Paul's own letters speak of his suffering not only in circumstantial catalogs (2 Cor. 6:4–5; 11:23–27) but also here and there throughout his correspondence (see Rom. 16:6, 12; 1 Cor. 15:10; 16:16; 2 Cor. 1:6; Gal. 4:11; Phil. 2:16; 1 Thess. 2:14; 5:12).

A stylistic feature of the Pastorals is the use of compound nouns and verbs. "To join in suffering" (*synkakopatheō*, combining *syn*, "with," *kakon*, "evil," and *patheō*, "suffer") is one such term. In 1:8 the connotation of the compound verb (see 2:3; note also the use of *kakourgos* in 2:9) is suffering as a good soldier might suffer. This is not suffering for the sake of suffering. It is suffering for a cause. In 1:8 the cause is the proclamation of the gospel. Paul suffered for the sake of that message (2:8–10). Timothy, his beloved son, is to do likewise.

The Pastor's evocation of a military charge in the twofold exhortation (1:6–8), especially in his references to courage, moderation, and suffering, must be understood in terms of the agon motif of Stoic philosophy and Hellenistic rhetoric. The truth of the gospel is something for which one must struggle and be ready to die. The ability to suffer for the sake of the gospel is a gift from God. The Pastor says that both Paul and Timothy have an ability to sustain suffering "with the help of the power of God." This translation of the Pastor's words employs the language of piety to express some of the theology of the Pastor's phrase, *kata dynamin theou*, "with the help of the power of God." The Greek phrase indicates that God, who empowers the soldier with the gift of courage (note the use of the same word, *dynamis*, in 1:7 and 1:8), is the source and norm of Paul and Timothy's power to maintain courage in the midst of their suffering for the sake of the gospel.

[9–10] The mention of the name of God in verse 8 issues forth in a paean of praise. The Pastor's theological hymn begins with a pair of participial clauses that describe "God." God is the God of the biblical tradition, who has saved and called his people, including the Pastor's community. The unspoken idea of divine election binds together the two ideas of salvation and vocation. The God who calls his people is the God of our salvation.

Not only has God saved us, God has also called us with a holy calling. One of Paul's favorite ideas is that of God's call (Rom. 8:30; 9:6–26; 1 Cor. 1:9;

7:15, 17–24; 15:9; Gal. 1:6, 15; 5:8, 13; 1 Thess. 2:12; 4:7; 5:24). Paul emphasizes three aspects of God's call but does not specifically describe God's call as
a "holy" call. First of all, God's call is divine election, a call to participate in
the history of salvation. Secondly, the call is a gratuitous gift effected in the new
era of salvation through Jesus Christ (Rom. 9:11–12; Gal. 1:6, 15). Thirdly, the
call is a vocation. It is a call to mission and an appropriate style of behavior (1
Cor. 1:9; 7:15; 15:9; 1 Thess. 2:12; 4:7). These three ideas are summed up in
the Pastor's reference to God's "holy call." The call is holy not only because it
proceeds from God; it is also holy insofar as it is a call to live a holy life, a call
to participate in the life of God's holy people.

The Pastor emphasizes the gratuity of God's call by the contrast between
one's accomplishments on the one hand, and the divine purpose and grace given
in Christ Jesus on the other. The contrast recalls Paul's discussions of justification without works in Rom. 3:24, 28; and 4:1–6, and the election of Jacob in
Rom. 9:11–12, "even before they had been born or had done anything good or
bad (so that God's purpose of election might continue, not by works but by his
call)." As did Paul, the Pastor speaks of God (*theos*), the call (*kalesantos*), the
divine purpose (*prothesin*), and human works (*erga*), formulating an antithesis
between human works and the gratuity of God's purpose. Although the idea of
divine purpose is biblical (see, e.g., Isa. 5:19; 14:26; 25:1),[18] the Pastor's language echoes that of the apostle. Like Paul, the Pastor uses the word *prothesis*
to speak of God's salvific purpose, God's salvific will.

The notion that God's salvific will is accomplished independently of human
acts is biblical and Jewish. Philo speaks of Noah and Abraham finding favor
before God prior to any good works on their part (*Allegorical Interpretation*
3.77, 83). The Pastor adds the idea of "beneficence" (*charin*; see Titus 2:11) to
the notion of God's purpose. God's purpose is characterized by its gratuitous
nature. The Pastor attributes three qualities to God's salvific purpose: (1) It is
gratuitous, a gift that has been given (*dotheisan*; see Rom. 12:3, 6; 1 Cor. 1:4;
3:10; Gal. 2:9); (2) it is accomplished in Christ Jesus; and (3) the initiative
derives from all eternity (*pro chronōn aiōnōn*, "before eternal ages"; see 1QS
2:23). The idea that God's plan of salvation is realized in Christ Jesus adds a
Christian twist to the Jewish notion of divine favor.

The christological dimension of the divine plan of salvation is further
explained in verse 10. God's gratuitous plan of salvation has been made manifest in the appearance of our Savior Christ Jesus. This descriptive language is
striking. Key to the exegetical crux is how to interpret the epithet "savior"
(*sōtēr*), sometimes applied to Christ Jesus, sometimes applied to God within the

18. The Greek Bible generally uses words derived from the root *boul-* ("will" or "plan") to speak
of God's purpose (see also 1QS 1:8, 10; 2:23).

circles from which the Pastoral Epistles have come (see Excursus 9). By his "appearance," Christ Jesus is said to be the manifestation of the divine purpose and favor. Insofar as Christ Jesus appears as the bringer of good gifts, he appears as our savior. Instead of death, Christ Jesus has brought life and immortality, gifts that only God can give.

The antithesis between the two participial constructions emphasizes the nature of the divine beneficence manifest in Christ Jesus. Christ Jesus is the one who has destroyed death. He is the one who has brought to light life and imperishability. Through the good news, life and imperishability are known. The contrast between death and life is classic; the contrast between destruction and revealing is not as readily apparent. Key to the understanding of this antithesis is the fact that words belonging to the *epiphan-* word group often mean "shine on." An "appearance" takes place either because whoever has appeared has entered into one's field of vision or because there is a new form or intensity of light that enables the one who appears to become visible.

By his appearance, Christ Jesus has made manifest God's gifts of life and imperishability. According to the biblical tradition, life is the core attribute of God. God is the living God who imparts life to his people. The Pastor adds a qualification[19] to his identification of life as a gift of God: The life that God gives is "imperishable." The Pastor is not talking about ordinary human viability and vitality. He is writing about the same kind of imperishability that Paul discussed in 1 Cor. 15:42–55. Imperishability comes with the resurrection of the dead. The Pastor does not fall back on the apocalyptic image of resurrection from the dead; for him it is sufficient to write that Christ destroyed death (see also 1 Cor. 15:26).

The unusual vocabulary used in 1:9–10 suggests that the Pastor's theological hymn is an alien piece that the Pastor has borrowed from somewhere else and incorporated into his epistle. Four of the key terms used by the Pastor in verse 10b ("destroy," "death," "bring to light," and "imperishability") do not occur elsewhere in the Pastorals, let alone in 2 Timothy. In the Pastorals the word "gospel" appears only in 1 Tim. 1:11; 2 Tim. 1:8, 10; and 2:8, where it is associated with the proclamation of the resurrection of Jesus from the dead. The Pastor's hymn proclaims that the revelation of life and imperishability occurs through the proclamation of the good news, that is, through the announcement of the kerygma summarized as "Jesus Christ raised from the dead" (2:8). It probably originated in Pauline circles in dependence on 1 Cor. 15:42–45.

---

19. He does so by using the common literary practice of the epexegetical *kai.* What follows the conjunction "and" (*kai*) explains what preceded the conjunction. The conjunction is more or less equivalent to "which is" or "i.e."

Excursus 8: The Appearance of Our Savior Jesus Christ

Second Timothy 1:10 proclaims the beneficence of God that "is now made manifest through the appearance of our Savior Christ Jesus *phanerōtheisan de nyn dia tēs epiphaneias tou sōtēros hēmōn Christou Iēsou* who destroyed death and brought life and imperishability to light through the good news." Later in the epistle the Pastor describes Paul as living in anticipation of his impending death. He solemnly entrusts his ministry to Timothy, his beloved son, saying, "Before God and Christ Jesus who is about to judge the living and the dead, I charge you by his appearance *tēn epiphaneian autou* and his kingdom: Proclaim the word, be ready in good times and in bad, convince, warn, and encourage with all patience and teaching" (2 Tim. 4:1–2). A few verses later, having entrusted the ministry to Timothy and reflecting that he himself had already run the race, "Paul" concludes his goodbye to Timothy with, "For the rest, there is reserved for me a crown of righteousness, which the Lord, the just judge, will give to me on that day, not only to me but also to all who long for his appearance" (*kai pasi tois ēgapēkosi tēn epiphaneian autou*, 2 Tim. 4:8).

These three passages speak of the "appearance" (*epiphaneia*) of our Savior Jesus Christ, the "epiphany" of the Savior (see 1 Tim. 6:14; Titus 2:13). In the New Testament only the Pastorals use this kind of language. The single exception is 2 Thess. 2:8, which speaks of the annihilation of the lawless one "by the manifestation of his [the Lord Jesus'] coming" (*tē epiphaneia tēs parousias autou*). Second Thessalonians speaks of this "epiphany" in conjunction with the Parousia of the lawless one. "Parousia" is a technical term that Paul used to denote the future "coming" of the Lord, his eschatological presence (1 Cor. 15:23; 1 Thess. 2:19; 3:13; 4:15; 5:23). The Pastor uses the term "appearance" in 2 Tim. 4:1, 8 in much the same way that Paul used "Parousia." The eschatological connotation of both terms is readily apparent.

In 2 Tim. 1:10, however, the Pastor used the word "appearance" in reference to a past appearance of the Savior. According to the Pastor, Paul lived between a past appearance of the Savior Christ Jesus who destroyed death and brought life, and a future appearance of Christ Jesus who is to judge the living and the dead at some indeterminate moment. Christian life lies between these two appearances of Christ Jesus. Christ Jesus first appeared as savior; later he will appear as judge.

The term "appearance" or "epiphany" belongs to a group of Greek words that are derived from the root *phan-*, "manifest." Several of these words are used in the Pastorals. A related verb (*phaneroō*) appears in 1 Tim. 3:16; 2 Tim. 1:10; Titus 1:3; a different verb (*epiphainō*) in Titus 2:11; 3:4; and an adjective (*phaneros*) in 1 Tim. 4:15. Words from this semantic group are thus used three times in 1 Timothy, four times in 2 Timothy, and four times in Titus; only 2 Timothy uses the noun more than once. These related words speak about an appearance that is central to the understanding of salvation and judgment in the Pastoral Epistles.

The idea of a magnificent appearance of a powerful presence was deeply rooted within Hellenistic culture. Hellenistic texts frequently speak about the "appearance" (*epiphaneia*) of some one or other. Two series of texts are particularly significant for the interpretation of 1:10 and the other passages in the Pastoral Epistles that employ "epiphany" language. One group of texts speak about the appearance of a god or goddess.

The cult of Asclepius, the god of healing, was spread throughout the Mediterranean basin. Dozens of temples were built in his honor. The god is said to have brought about many cures through his appearances in the temple at Epidaurus (*SIG*, 1169, 34) and elsewhere.

"Epiphany" language was, however, not reserved to the cult of Asclepius. A number of deities were known for their "appearances" (*epiphaneiai*). There exists, for example, a report of "the appearance of the goddess" (i.e., Artemis) to the Epirotes (*SIG*, 867, 35). The Septuagint, the Bible of Hellenistic Jews, also employs "epiphany" language. The Septuagint uses the word group to translate a variety of Hebrew words derived from the root *wr*. The book of 2 Maccabees, a Hellenistic text from the first century B.C.E., describes God's manifestations on behalf of Israel as "epiphanies" (2 Macc. 2:21; 3:24; 5:4; 12:12; 14:15; see 3:20).

Another group of Hellenistic texts, about one hundred altogether, employs "epiphany" language to speak about such deified emperors as Claudius, Caligula, Diocletian, and Valerian. "Epiphany" language was used to describe their births, their coming into power, their enthronement, their imperial visits, their victories, and their victorious return home from foreign lands. Thus, Julius Caesar is said to have been "god made manifest, [born] of Ares and Aphrodite, the common savior of human life" (*SIG* 347, 760,6). The fact that an inscription with this particular wording was found in Ephesus, the city to which 2 Timothy was presumably sent, renders the epigraph particularly apropos to the interpretation of 2 Tim. 1:10.

2 Timothy 1:10

Caesar was said to be god made manifest because he was savior (*sōtēr*). "Savior" was an epithet attributed to kings and emperors, and sometimes to lesser personalities as well, known for their generous benefaction to a city or region. Caesar was god made manifest because of his generosity to all humanity. Emperors were considered to be visible manifestations of the deity insofar as they made visible the help that one or another god rendered to human beings. The emperor's generosity manifested the beneficent presence of the deity. The Pastor's identification of Jesus as "Savior" (2 Tim. 1:10) is analogous to the Ephesian epigraph's description of Caesar as "savior." Christ Jesus appears as Savior insofar as he is the bringer of good gifts. As such he is our gracious benefactor, our Savior.

Apologetic and polemic interests move the Pastor to write about Christ Jesus as he does in 1:10. It is not Caesar or some other emperor who is Savior; Christ Jesus is Savior. Not Caesar, but Christ Jesus is the manifestation of divine benevolence. There is ultimately a very basic difference between the way that the Pastor speaks about the appearance of Christ Jesus and the way that many Greco-Roman contemporaries spoke about the appearance of some emperor or other. The Pastor's understanding of the epiphany of Christ Jesus is rooted in his theological monotheism (see 1 Tim. 2:5): The appearance of Christ Jesus is the manifestation of the beneficence of the one God of the biblical tradition.

The gifts brought by Christ Jesus are life and imperishability, not death. Only God can give such gifts as these. God gives these gifts through Christ Jesus, our Savior. With the affirmation that life and imperishability are given through the appearance of our Savior Christ, the Pastor has echoed the words of Paul, who proclaimed that "the last enemy to be destroyed is death" (1 Cor. 15:26). Paul speaks about the victory over death that God has wrought through our Lord Jesus Christ and of the imperishability with which the dead will be raised (see 1 Cor. 15:52–57). The theology of 2 Tim. 1:10 is thoroughly Pauline; it reflects what Paul wrote to the Corinthians.

The language of 1:10, however, just as clearly reflects Hellenistic religious idiom. The Pastor uses the Hellenistic concepts of "appearance," "Savior," and "reveal" to express the apostle's thought to his audience. He has taken the core of Paul's gospel (see 1 Cor. 15:1–2) and expressed it in language that virtually everyone in the Hellenistic world could understand. Giving the gifts of God, Christ Jesus is the manifestation of the divine purpose and favor. The appearance of Christ Jesus is what Hellenists could call a *theia epiphaneia*, a "divine appearance," "an appearance of God."

2 Timothy 4:1–8

In 2 Tim. 4:1–8 the Pastor reflects on what is in store for Paul after his departure from this life. The pericope is a tightly knit literary unit, encompassed by mentions of judgment and of the appearance. The judgment and the appearance are to take place on "that day," the eschatological day of the Lord proclaimed by the prophets of old and more recently by the apostle himself. In the Pastor's vision of things, the appearance and the judgment are correlative notions: On "that day," Christ Jesus is to appear as judge.

The Pastor speaks of a coming appearance and of a comprehensive judgment. The living and the dead are to be judged: "Before God and Christ Jesus, who is about to judge the living and the dead, I charge you by his appearance and his kingdom" (2 Tim. 4:1). The Pastor places the appearance of Christ Jesus as judge within the context of the kingdom of God. The appearance of Christ Jesus as eschatological judge marks the beginning of the ultimate manifestation of the kingdom. In the words of Andrew Lau, "God's eternal kingdom will be finally established on the day of judgment and His sovereignty will be revealed in the *epiphaneia*-event" (Lau 238). The appearance of Christ Jesus is the definitive sign of the kingdom in which Christ Jesus acts as God's eschatological agent. Paul himself had taught that with the Parousia comes the end, when Christ "hands over the kingdom to God the Father, after he has destroyed every ruler and every authority and power" (1 Cor. 15:24).

What the Pastor writes about the judgment, the appearance, and the kingdom in 2 Tim. 4:1 provides a horizon for the solemn charge to Timothy, who is about to assume the responsibilities of the dying Paul. At the end of the pericope the Pastor returns to the ideas of the appearance and of judgment. He writes about what Paul can expect after his "departure" (2 Tim. 4:6). Speaking in Paul's name, the Pastor writes, "For the rest, there is reserved for me a crown of righteousness, which the Lord, the just judge, will give to me on that day, not only to me but also to all who long for his appearance" (2 Tim. 4:8). The scenario is apocalyptic, as was the scene evoked at the beginning of the pericope (2 Tim. 4:1). The appearance of the Lord, the just judge, is the hallmark of the day of Yahweh. On that day a crown of righteousness is to be given to Paul and, with him, to all who have longed for the appearance of the Lord.

Two elements in the Pastor's apocalyptic scenario must not be overlooked. First, as the Pastor writes about the conferral of the crown of righteousness, he does not use the verb *didōmi*, "to give" (see 2 Tim. 1:16, 18). Rather, he uses the verb *apodidōmi*, "to give [back]." The prefix *apo* provides a nuance of paying back what is due, in this case, the honor that is associated with a crown of righteousness. Second, the Pastor writes about "all those" (*pasi tois*) who have longed for the appearance of the Lord. This phrase, coupled with the mention of the judgment of the "living and the dead" in verse 1, provides an element of universality (see "the common savior" of the Ephesian inscription in honor of Caesar) and finality in the Pastor's eschatological scenario. The eschatological appearance of Christ Jesus is of ultimate significance.

In 1 Thessalonians (1 Thess. 2:19; 3:13; 4:15; 5:23) and again in 1 Corinthians (1 Cor. 15:23) Paul used the language of coming (*parousia*, "presence" or "coming") to speak of the appearance of Jesus as Lord of the day of Yahweh (1 Thess. 5:2). He used the title "Lord" (*Kyrios*) to designate Jesus as the risen One whose coming on that day means salvation for those who belong to him. Paul's "coming" (*parousia*) and the Pastor's "appearance" (*epiphaneia*) are virtually synonymous (see Dupont 74; *TLNT* 2.66–67n5). In common Greek parlance, these two terms were used almost interchangeably to speak about the appearance of a king or victorious general on the occasion of his solemn and joyful entry into a city. The terms conjure up the notion of a magnificent victory parade.

1 Timothy 6:14

The semantic similarity between "appearance" and "coming," and the fact that they were virtually interchangeable as Hellenists spoke of the coming of an emperor or his victorious general for a victory celebration, suggest that the

Pastor's apocalyptic use of "epiphany" language in 2 Tim. 4:1–8 represents something of a "rereading" of Paul's words about the Parousia. That the Pastor's circles understood Paul's words about the Parousia in language that speaks about the appearance of Christ Jesus is confirmed by 1 Tim. 6:14: "Keep the commandment spotless and irreproachable until the appearance of our Lord Jesus Christ."

The Pastor's admonition echoes passages such as the wish prayers of 1 Thess. 3:13; 5:23. Paul prayed, "May [the Lord] so strengthen your hearts in holiness that you may be blameless before our God and Father at the coming of our Lord Jesus with all his saints" (1 Thess. 3:13); again, "May your spirit and soul and body be kept sound and blameless at the coming of our Lord Jesus Christ" (1 Thess. 5:23). A striking similarity between 1 Tim. 6:14 and these wish prayers is that the full designation of the one who is to appear, "our Lord Jesus Christ"[20] is found in both. The Pastor's legal language, "keeping the commandment," is more appropriate in the peroration of his text than the Jewish anthropological language of 1 Thessalonians would be. The Pastor's peroration is hortatory; Paul's language is that of prayer. What the Pastor shares with Paul is that "blamelessness" is to be hoped for by those who are awaiting the appearance/Parousia.

In the verses that follow 1 Tim. 6:14, the epiphany motif is placed within a monotheistic theological context. The Pastor writes about the appearance of our Lord Jesus Christ "which the blessed and only Sovereign will manifest at the appropriate time, the King of those who reign and Lord of those who exercise power, who alone has immortality, who inhabits unapproachable light, whom no single person has seen or can see; to him be honor and everlasting might. Amen." (1 Tim. 6:15–16). This proclamation is crafted in Hellenistic language; it proclaims the one transcendent God of Jewish tradition.

The affirmation that at the appropriate time the one and only God will make the appearance of our Lord Jesus Christ manifest declares that the eschatological scenario is controlled by the sovereign God. Paul uses apocalyptic imagery to affirm this same idea; he presents the apocalyptic events as being introduced by extraordinary fanfare, the archangel's call and the sound of God's trumpet (see 1 Thess. 4:16). In 1 Cor. 15:51–57 Paul uses the apocalyptic term "mystery" to speak about the Parousia. In this passage, Paul writes about "immortality" (1 Cor. 15:53, 54), the divine attribute that is recalled in the Pastor's doxology in 1 Tim. 6:16. Paul's language is apocalyptic; the Pastor's idiom is that of imperial celebration.

---

20. Within the Pastorals, this full christological designation is found only in 1 Tim. 1:12; 6:3, 14; and the epistolary greetings of 1 and 2 Timothy (1 Tim. 1:2; 2 Tim. 1:2).

Titus 2:11–14

The eschatological aspect of the future "appearance" of Jesus Christ is clearly evident in Titus 2:13. In this verse the Pastor uses an appearance clause to explain believers' blessed hope. He writes about "awaiting the blessed hope, that is, the appearance of the glory of the great God, our Savior, Jesus Christ,[21] who gave himself for us, to redeem us from all lawlessness and purify for himself a chosen people, eager for good works" (Titus 2:13–14). The Pastor's use of the verb "await" (*prosdechomai*) and his reference to "glory" (*tēs doxēs*) evoke the expectation of some sort of future glory; these characteristic terms bespeak the expectation of the eschaton.

It is noteworthy that the Pastor identifies the awaited one as one who had already given himself as a ransom. The purpose of this self-donation is the purification of a chosen people. The Pastor's ecclesiological focus is evident in the way that the Pastor writes about what Jesus had done. "Jesus [is] Lord" (*kyrios Iēsous*) was a familiar acclamation in Pauline churches (see 1 Cor. 12:3; Phil. 2:11). The acclamation identifies the Lord, the risen and expected One, with Jesus, whose death these communities remembered, professed in the creedal formulae, and commemorated in the eucharistic meal. In Titus 2:13–14 the Pastor similarly identifies the awaited one with a historical figure of human experience—the man named Jesus. He uses Hellenistic "epiphany" language to speak of the future, the cultic and economic language (redemption) as well as the election language (chosen people) to speak of the past.

The Pastor's circles occasionally used "epiphany" language to speak of Jesus (see 2 Tim. 1:10), but Titus 2:14 does not use this terminology to speak of the "historical" Jesus. Nonetheless, the epistle to Titus sometimes uses "epiphany" language in oblique references to the historical Jesus. For example, before speaking of the end-time appearance of Jesus Christ, the Pastor writes, "For the saving beneficence of God has appeared [*epephanē*] to all people, teaching us to deny impiety and worldly passions and to live modestly, justly, and in godly fashion in the age" (Titus 2:11–12). Later in his missive he writes, "When appeared *epephanē* the goodness and benevolence of our Savior, God, not from works of righteousness that we ourselves have done, but according to his mercy, he saved us through the washing of rebirth and renewal by the Holy Spirit, which he poured out on us profusely through Jesus Christ, our Savior" (Titus 3:4–6).

Titus 2:11 and 3:4 make use of the verb *epiphainō*, "manifest," a verb belonging to the "epiphany" word group but not otherwise used in the Pastorals

---

21. The meaning of "the great God, our Savior, Jesus Christ" is one of the great cruces in the interpretation of the Pastoral Epistles. See the exegesis of Titus 2:13 and Excursus 9.

(see Luke 1:79; Acts 27:20). The two passages speak of a manifestation of God's salvific goodness. They bring together three related ideas—God's goodness, its manifestation, and our salvation—which are key elements in the Pastor's theological vision. For the Pastor, our salvation is the manifestation of God's goodness (see 2 Tim. 1:10).

These passages relate the manifestation of God's salvific goodness to a teaching for the present age (*en tō nyn aiōni*; Titus 2:11–12) and a baptismal ritual (Titus 3:4–6). This washing of rebirth is linked to Jesus Christ our Savior, to God's grace, and to the hope of eternal life. The teaching for the present age is apparently linked with Paul. The epistle's lengthy opening salutation speaks about God who "manifested *ephanerōsen* his word at the appropriate time in the proclamation with which I have been entrusted by the order of our Savior, God" (Titus 1:3; see 2 Tim. 1:10–11). As always in the Pastorals, it is God who makes something manifest—the appearance of Christ Jesus or the word given to Paul. The manifestation of God's word to Paul is pertinent to our salvation and hope for eternal life. That salvific word has been given to Titus for him to proclaim with exhortation and correction in the present age (Titus 2:12, 15).

1 Timothy 3:16 and 2 Timothy 1:10

Of the four words belonging to the "epiphany" word group that is so characteristic of the Pastorals' soteriology and Christology, only two appear in each of the three epistles: the noun *epiphaneia* (1 Tim. 6:14; 2 Tim. 1:10; 4:1, 8; Titus 2:13) and the verb *phaneroō* (1 Tim. 3:16; 2 Tim. 1:10; Titus 1:3). Second Timothy 1:10 mentions the beneficence of God "now made manifest [*phanerōtheisan*] through the appearance of our Savior Christ Jesus." In 1 Tim. 3:16 the verb "to manifest" (*phaneroō*) is found in a terse phrase, "was manifest in the flesh" (*ephanerōthē en sarki*), which is used in the first stich of a christological hymn. The Fathers generally understood the phrase as one that referred to the incarnation of Christ Jesus, but it is preferable to take the phrase as a reference to the appearances of the risen Jesus (see the discussion on p. 108). The verse brings the resurrection of Jesus, the focal point of the traditional Christian kerygma, under the umbrella of "the appearance" of Christ Jesus.

Summary

The Pastorals' use of "epiphany" language is a hallmark of their theology, Christology, and soteriology. "Epiphany" language highlights specific events related to the manifestation and realization of God's universal salvific will. God's universal salvific will exists from before all ages (Titus 1:2). It was manifest in time through the appearance of Christ Jesus, our Savior, who purified a chosen people. In the manifestation of God's word to the apostle Paul, God's salvation was further manifested and again concretized. His proclamation of the gospel made the death-destroying and life-bringing appearance of Christ Jesus manifest (Titus 1:3; 2 Tim. 1:10). God's saving goodness is made manifest to the chosen people through the waters of rebirth and renewal. This chosen people exists in the present age (2 Tim. 1:10; Titus 2:12) while it awaits the appearance of Christ Jesus as savior and judge. Thus, God's chosen people lead lives motivated by the manifestation of God's word to Paul between appearances of Christ Jesus, our Savior. They are an "epiphany" people, people of the appearance of Christ Jesus, the manifestation of God's saving benevolence.

[11–12] The center of the chiasm that serves as the organizational structure of 2 Tim. 1:6–14 focuses on God's beneficence manifested in the appearance of Christ Jesus (1:9–10). In verses 11–12, the Pastor returns to the theme of suffering that he had begun to develop in verse 8, the *b* element of the chiastic structure. In verse 8, Timothy was invited to join in Paul's suffering for the sake of the good news. He was exhorted not to be ashamed of Paul, who had suffered for the sake of the gospel. Verses 11–12 complement verse 8 by stating more fully why it was that Paul had suffered and providing the example of Paul's personal conviction as a model for Timothy's perseverance in suffering.

The good news is instrumental in making life and immortality known. Paul had been appointed herald, apostle, and teacher for the sake of this good news (see 1 Tim. 2:7). The description has an official ring about it. There is little doubt that Paul considered himself to be an apostle. Four of his most important letters began with a reminder to his congregations that he was an apostle (Rom. 1:1; 1 Cor. 1:1; 2 Cor. 1:1; Gal. 1:1). In his first letter to the Corinthians, Paul wrote about the theological foundations of his being named an apostle (1 Cor. 15:3–11) and the practical consequences of his being an apostle for the sake of the gospel (1 Cor. 9:1–23). In 1 Thess. 2:4 he evokes the political process of official scrutiny and conferral of a mission as he speaks about the responsibility that he shares with Silvanus and, fellow apostles of Christ (1 Thess. 2:7) to proclaim the good news.

The Pastor adopted Paul's customary self-designation as apostle in the opening salutation of the epistle (1:1). There is, therefore, nothing surprising about the Pastor's description of Paul as one who has been appointed apostle. The use of official sounding language—"I was appointed" (*etethēn*, a divine passive)—in conjunction with Paul's apostolate seems appropriate. Paul himself said that he had been called or named apostle (*klētos apostolos*, Rom. 1:1; 1 Cor. 1:1). The apostle is someone who has been sent on a mission, the legate of Christ Jesus. He had been scrutinized for this mission, approved by God, and entrusted with the gospel (1 Thess. 2:4).

The Pastor does not only call Paul an apostle; he also describes him as a herald (*kēryx*) and teacher (*didaskalos*). Paul does not use these terms to describe his own ministry. Except for Noah, (2 Pet. 2:5), no one else is called a herald in the New Testament. The role was, however, familiar to Hellenists. It was the role of the herald to announce good news (*euangelion*), typically an army's victory in battle or events of imperial importance, such as a birth in the imperial household, an emperor's accession to the throne, even an imperial edict. For his work the herald was given a reward originally designated as an *euangelion* (see Homer, *Odyssey* 14.152–53).

In the Hellenistic world of the late first century, the figure of the herald also appeared in religious literature. In this literature the herald had the role of a prophet and a teacher. From this perspective it may be that the use of the term "herald" to describe Paul may be the Pastor's attempt to interpret his apostolate for the benefit of those living in the Hellenistic world. Spicq (TLNT 1.370) suggests that the term may have been chosen in order to contrast the apostle with the heralds who functioned in the Ephesian temple of Artemis.

Similar reflections can be made apropos the description of the apostle as a teacher. The figure of the teacher was well known in the Hellenistic world and in early Christianity. The teacher was one who expounded his ideas in systematic fashion. The term suggests intelligence, authority, and organization. Luke was fond of using the epithet as a form of address to Jesus (e.g., Luke 7:40). Paul identifies teaching as one of the charisms given to individual Christians, listing it immediately after the charisms of the apostolate and prophecy in the enumerated list of 1 Cor. 12:28 (see 1 Cor. 12:29). Teaching is one charism that Paul never claimed for himself. When the Pastor uses the title of teacher to describe Paul, he is presenting Paul in a role that would make him readily comprehensible in the Hellenistic world. The Pastor may have chosen this term in order to project the figure of Paul as the master teacher (1:13), in contrast to the many teachers who tickle people's fancy (4:3).

What the Pastor has done is to explain Paul's charism as an apostle for the benefit of a Hellenistic readership. Paul's apostolate is likened to the well-known functions of the herald and the teacher. In somewhat similar fashion, he explains the fundamental charism that had been given to Timothy as one of strength and administrative discretion. The Pastor's use of the triad—one of Paul's favorite rhetorical constructions—is similar to but quite different from the apostle's own use of a three-term series. Paul used triads for the sake of emphasis (see, e.g., 1 Thess. 2:10). The Pastor used triads in order to interpret traditional but unfamiliar ideas, in this case (1:11) the apostolate by means of the familiar images of the herald and teacher.

Because of his apostolate, the Pastor says in verse 13 that Paul suffered as he did. Were the epistle to be an ordinary letter, the reader might ask what it was that the apostle was enduring. Was Timothy to have remembered the hardships cited in 2 Cor. 6:4–5 and 11:23–28 in a letter written at a time when Timothy was with Paul (see 2 Cor. 1:10)? Thus far the only suggestion of Paul's suffering in 2 Timothy is the hint contained in verse 8, where mention was made of

Paul's imprisonment and his suffering. Perhaps that was enough. The lot of prisoners in the Greco-Roman world was well known. Prisoners were subject to forced labor, malnutrition, and disease.[22]

Yet to come are the Pastor's references to Paul's persecutions and sufferings in Antioch, Iconium, and Lystra (3:11) and the several references to Paul's sense of having been abandoned (1:15; 4:10, 16). The recipient of the epistle is presumed to know about the former; the epistle itself imparts information about the latter. Offering himself as an example to Timothy, Paul notes that he was not ashamed of his sufferings (1:12). Timothy had been encouraged not to be ashamed because of Paul (1:8); now the Pastor's Paul presents himself as someone who has not been shamed by his sufferings. Rather than shame, he has experienced trust and confidence. Paul is convinced that the one in whom he trusted[23] will be able to maintain the treasure that has been entrusted to him. With this conviction Paul can offer himself as an example for Timothy to follow.

What is the treasure that had been entrusted to Paul, the treasure to be maintained (see 1:14; 1 Tim. 6:20)? In common parlance a treasure or deposit (*parathēkē*) was something—money or a harvest of grain, for example—that was entrusted to another for safekeeping. Since the relationship of trust was so important, the gods were frequently invoked when something was handed over as a deposit. Thus, preservation of the deposit became a sacred duty:

> The most sacred of all the dealings between human beings is the deposit on trust. . . . He who repudiates a deposit . . . acts most wrongfully. . . . He has set at nought both the human and the divine and repudiated two trusts, one that of him who consigned the property, the other that of the most veracious of witnesses who sees and hears all whether they intend or do not wish to do what they say. (Philo, *Special Laws* 4.30, 32; see also Josephus, *Ant.* 4.8.38 §285)

The word "treasure" did not always, however, describe some material thing. Philo, for example, describes the sacred story and the knowledge of divine rites as a treasure to be preserved (*Abel and Cain* 60). The Pastor's use of the word "treasure" is similar to that of Philo. For the Pastor, the treasure entrusted to Paul would appear to be the good news (1:8), the sound words that Timothy has heard from Paul (1:12). The idea that the deposit of the good news would be preserved until "that day" adds another dimension. "That day" is the day of the Lord, the final day of the present world order. That day was well known in Pauline circles.

The apostle wrote about that day in five of his letters. In his first letter he refers to the "day of the Lord" (1 Thess. 5:2; see 5:4), using an expression taken

---

22. See Werner Eisenhut, "Die römische Gefängnistrafe," *ANRW* 1, no. 2 (1972): 268–82.

23. In 2 Timothy the verb *pisteuō* is used only in this passage, where it has its ordinary connotation, "I trust." In his letters Paul himself characteristically used the verb with the meaning "I believe" (see, e.g., Phil. 1:29; 1 Thess. 1:7; 4:14).

from the prophetic tradition (Amos 5:18, 20; Joel 2:1, 11, 31 [=3:4 LXX/MT]; Zeph. 1:7, 14 [2x]; see Zech. 14:1). Later Paul identifies that day as the "day of the Lord Jesus Christ," sometimes using the full christological formula (1 Cor 1:8), sometimes using a shorter formula, "the Lord" (1 Cor 5:5), "the Lord Jesus" (2 Cor. 1:14), "Christ" (Phil. 1:10; 2:16), or "Jesus Christ" (Phil. 1:6). In his letter to the Romans, Paul speaks of it as "the day of wrath" (Rom. 2:5), describing it more fully as "the day when, according to my gospel, God, through Jesus Christ, will judge the secret thoughts of all" (Rom. 2:16). That day is the day when Jesus Christ will be fully revealed as Lord, the day when Christ will be revealed as God's vicegerent and agent in the realization of eschatological judgment.

The Pastor has more to say about "that day" (*ekeinē tē hēmera*) later in this letter (see 1:12, 18; 4:8; see also 2 Thess. 1:10). That day will follow penultimate difficult days (3:1). That day is the day on which the Lord will appear as "our Savior" (1:10). Toward the end of the epistle, the Pastor describes "that day" as the day of the appearance of Christ Jesus (4:1–8). On that day, Christ, the just judge, will give a crown of righteousness not only to Paul but to all who long for his appearance (4:8).

The Pastor's use of the demonstrative adjective "that" suggests that he is indeed making reference to the "day" that was so well known in the Pauline circles to which he belonged. Coincidentally, he has employed an expression that many of the prophets of old had used to speak of the eschatological day of the Lord (Hos. 1:5; 2:16 [=2:18 LXX/MT]; 21 [=2:23 LXX/MT]; Joel 3:18 [=4:18 LXX/MT; see Joel 2:29; 3:1]; Amos 2:16; 8:3, 9, 13; 9:11; Obad. 8; Mic. 2:4, 4:6; 5:10 [=5:9 LXX/MT]; 7:11, 12; Zeph. 1:9, 10, 12, 15; 3:11; Hag. 2:23; Zech. 2:11 [=2:15 LXX/MT; see Zech. 8:6]; 3:10; 9:16; 11:11; 12:3, 4, 6, 8, 9, 11; 13:1, 2, 4; 14:4, 6, 8, 9, 13, 20, 21).

By adding a qualifying eschatological note to the treasure entrusted to Paul, the Pastor has put the gospel proclaimed by Paul, the sound words that he had passed along to Timothy, within an eschatological perspective. In his view, the gospel shall continue to be proclaimed until the coming of the day of the Lord. This conviction is presented as the source of Paul's confidence at a time of suffering and imprisonment. Given the hortatory purpose of the epistle, Paul's confidence is cited not only for the sake of Timothy. It is mentioned for the sake of the Pastor's community, who may themselves have been experiencing suffering of various kinds.

[13–14] Verses 13–14 round off the chiastic pattern of 1:6–13. Its references to the Spirit, to Paul ["my," "me"], and what has been given to Timothy create a neat literary inclusio and delineate the pericope as a unit. In the parallel verses (1:6–7), Timothy was asked to rekindle the gift that had been given to him; now he is asked to preserve the sound words that he has heard.

Paul was described as a herald, apostle, and teacher. The words that Timothy has heard from him are now described as a paradigm, a model (the compound *hypotyposin*; see 1:16) of sound teaching. The *hygia-* word group, suggesting "sound" or "healthy," is not used by the apostle himself but is often used in the Pastoral Epistles, where it qualifies "words" (1 Tim. 6:3; Titus 2:8), "teaching" (4:3; 1 Tim. 1:10; Titus 1:9; 2:1), and "faith" (Titus 1:13; 2:2). Contemporary philosophic discourse suggests that when Paul's teaching (1:11) is proposed as a paradigm of sound discourse the message is beneficial to those who hear it and its content is reasonable (see pp. 95–97). That teaching is implicitly set over against teaching that is not sound but is presumed to be in the air.

The treasure that Paul has received is apparently the "model of sound words" that has been passed along to Timothy. The phrase is a cameo description of the gospel message, the essence of the creed, a norm for catechesis. Paul had reminded the Christians of Thessalonica and of Rome that the good news is a message that is "heard" (1 Thess. 2:13; Rom. 10:14; see Gal. 3:2; cf. Heb. 4:2). According to 1:13 the message was heard "in faith and love that is in Christ Jesus." The formulaic phrase is also found 1 Tim. 1:14. Given its formulaic nature and the fact that the word "faith" as used in the Pastoral Epistles tends to designate the contents of one's belief rather than the relationship of faith, the phrase "in faith and love that is in Christ Jesus" is to be understood as a succinct description of the Christian way of life.

The binomial expression "faith and love" is Paul's summary of the Christian life (Gal. 5:6; [1 Cor. 13:13]; 1 Thess. 1:3; 3:6; 5:8; Phlm. 5; see 2 Tim. 2:22; [3:10]; 1 Tim. 1:14; 2:15; 4:12; 6:11; Eph. 6:23). For Paul, faith is the acceptance of the gospel message and the relationship with the Lord that this acceptance entails. "Love," which is a Spirit-inspired task (Rom. 5:5; 1 Thess. 1:3), describes the kind of relationship with others, especially one's fellow Christians, that results from one's relationship with the Lord (Gal. 5:6).

The "model of sound words" is the precious treasure that had been entrusted to Timothy. That treasure, whose import is emphasized by the adjective "precious," appropriate to the metaphor "treasure," is the treasure that had been entrusted to Paul (v. 12). Acting to ensure the proper transmission of the treasure for safekeeping from one generation to the next is the Holy Spirit.

Only rarely do the Pastorals mention the Spirit of God (see 1 Tim. 3:16; 4:1; Titus 3:5). The designation of the Spirit as "Holy Spirit" appears only here and in Titus 3:5. The only pericope that reflects any more than a merely formulaic pneumatology is 1:6–14, a passage delineated by its spirit language. Describing the Holy Spirit as dwelling in Timothy, the Pastor appropriates Paul's idiom (Rom. 8:11; 1 Cor. 3:16; see also 1 Cor. 6:19). For Paul, the indwelling Spirit is the sanctifying Spirit, the Spirit of holiness. Paul highlights this function of the Spirit by his frequent use of the descriptive adjective "holy" (Rom. 5:5; 9:1; 14:17; 15:13, 16; 1 Cor. 6:19; 12:3; 2 Cor. 6:6; 13:13; 1 Thess. 1:5, 6; 4:8) and the powerful image of the temple in which the Spirit dwells (1 Cor. 3:16; 6:19). For Paul, the Spirit is the Holy Spirit because the Spirit is God's Spirit, but the

Spirit is also the Spirit of holiness, the potent force that enables believers to be God's own people. For Paul, the Holy Spirit is also the vivifying Spirit (Rom. 8:11). In 1:14 the Holy Spirit is the power of God that faithfully preserves the model of sound words, the gospel message, from one generation to the next.

A Personal Note
2 Timothy 1:15–18

This "personal note" is quite distinct from the hortatory sections that precede and follow it. The first of four autobiographical passages in the epistle (see also 3:11; 4:6–8; 4:16–18), it provides a certain measure of verisimilitude for the entire epistle. The passage helps to capture an image of Paul about to die and reminiscing about his life. The frequency of such passages in 2 Timothy and the fact that they contain a number of proper names, often of people who are not otherwise known to have been in Paul's company, however, gives the passage a distinctively non-Pauline character.

In 1921 Harrison argued that this first autobiographical passage (without v. 15) comprised one of four Pauline fragments that an editor incorporated into the epistle. Thirty-four years later he revised his earlier opinion and suggested that 1:16–18—along with 3:10–11; 4:1, 2a, 5b, 6–15, 16–19, 21b, and 22a—constituted one of two fragments assimilated into the extant epistle. In 1997 Miller suggested that the pericope may perhaps have been a collection of two formerly independent notes that were later incorporated into a more comprehensive text.

The pericope, like the preceding one (1:6–14), is chiastically structured on an *a-b-c-b'-a'* pattern. Verses 15 (*a*) and 18b (*a'*) speak about some of the things that Timothy knows about the church in Asia, especially the church in the provincial capital of Ephesus. Specifically, Timothy is said to know about Paul's abandonment by Phygelus and Hermogenes and the service rendered by Onesiphorus. Verses 16a (*b*) and 18a (*b'*) are a repeated prayer that the Lord have mercy on Onesiphorus and his household. The center of the chiasm (the *c* element, vv. 16b–17) offers an image of Paul in prison.

This biographical note is the Pastor's first expression of the theme of Paul's being without ordinary human contact. The motif recurs toward the end of the epistle (4:9–16). Together the two passages, 1:15–18 and 4:9–16, help to define and focus the literary unity of the epistle. Lying just inside two passages that identify the text as an epistle—1:1–5, the salutation and thanksgiving, and 4:19–22, the greetings and final salutation—the biographical passages focus on the loneliness of Paul. They identify him as a lonely prisoner about to die. His epistle thus becomes a kind of testamentary farewell.

1:15 You know this, that all those in Asia, including Phygelus and Hermogenes, have abandoned me. 16 May the Lord have mercy on the household of Onesiphorus because he often refreshed me and was not ashamed of my chains. 17 Once in Rome he quickly sought me out and found me. 18 May the Lord grant him to find mercy with the Lord on that day. You know full well how much he served[a] in Ephesus.

a. A few manuscripts (104, 365, among others) specify the text by adding a clarifying *moi*, "to me." By doing so, Onesiphorus is identified as one who assisted the apostle, rather than as having served the Ephesian church in general.

[1:15] Timothy is presumed to know that all the Asian Christians had abandoned Paul. This could mean that at the time of an arrest in Asia no one came to help him (thus Marshall) or that Asian Christians abandoned Paul while he was languishing during an imprisonment in Rome. Spicq and Dornier suggest that "all in Asia" is a Semitism meaning "all from Asia." The expression is in any case hyperbolic. Not everyone had abandoned Paul, certainly not Timothy, Paul's son, to whom the pastoral charge of the church in Ephesus, the provincial capital, had been confided (1 Tim. 1:3), nor Onesiphorus, who is praised because he offered his assistance to Paul. It is difficult to determine which of the two scenarios the Pastor intended to evoke, an abandonment in Asia or an abandonment in Rome. His purpose was not so much to provide accurate biographical data as to create the literary image of Paul's solitary existence.

He specifically identifies Phygelus and Hermogenes as two Asians who had abandoned Paul. The negative example of Phygelus and Hermogenes serves to accentuate the positive role attributed to Onesiphorus and the members of his household. The name of Phygelus does not appear in any other early Christian text. The name of Hermogenes does not appear elsewhere in the New Testament, but a coppersmith named Hermogenes is mentioned in the *Acts of Paul* (3.1–17) along with a person named Demas (see 2 Tim. 4:10). These two are portrayed as opposing Paul's teaching on celibacy and resurrection from the dead. Since the apocryphal *Acts of Paul* may have relied on traditions independent of those reflected in 2 Timothy, it is possible that Hermogenes was a historical figure who had veered from the gospel preached by Paul.

[16a] The household of Onesiphorus is mentioned in the New Testament only in 1:16 and 4:19. The two references, coming shortly after the epistolary opening and just before the epistolary closing, narrowly construed (1:1–2; 4:22), contribute to the ring construction that constitutes the epistle as a single literary unit. The apocryphal *Acts of Paul* (3.2–7, 15, 23–26, 42) portrays Onesiphorus as a significant and heroic figure in Paul's ministry. Onesiphorus is said to be a resident of Iconium (see Acts 13:51; 14:1, 19, 21; 16:2) who, together with his wife Lectra and his sons Simmias and Zeno, welcomed the

apostle to Iconium and hosted him during the time of his stay. Paul's appreciation of Onesiphorus's hospitality provoked Demas and Hermogenes to jealousy and contributed to their opposition to Paul. According to these apocryphal *Acts* (3.7–8), the legendary Thecla sat transfixed by a window and listened to Paul for three days and three nights as he was preaching in Onesiphorus's house. This prompted her to break her engagement to Thamyris and become a disciple of the apostle. Subsequently imprisoned and then released from prison, she followed Paul to Myra, whence she was sent back to Iconium to preach the gospel. There she entered the house of Onesiphorus and pronounced an impassioned doxology (*Acts of Paul* 3.41–42).

The legendary tales of these apocryphal *Acts* underscore the importance of the household (*oikos, oikia*) in early Christianity (see Excursus 5). The household was the nucleus of Greco-Roman society, but it was also the nucleus of the early Christian movement. The household served the missionary efforts of early Christians by providing hospitality to traveling missionaries as well as a locale in which these missionaries could preach the gospel. The household served as the venue for early Christian gatherings. It was there that they gathered to discuss the meaning of the Christian message, listen to the reading of Paul's letters, and celebrate the ritual of their Eucharist. Baptisms of entire households are mentioned in Acts (Acts 16:15, 31–33; 18:8; see 10:2; 11:14) as well as by Paul himself (1 Cor. 1:16).

Paul's prayer, "May the Lord have mercy on the household of Onesiphorus," recalls the intercessory prayers Paul offered in the thanksgiving periods of some of his letters (Rom. 1:9–10; Phil. 1:3–4; 1 Thess. 1:2–3; Phlm. 4–6). The prayer echoes the language of the traditional prayer of the just (e.g., 25:6–7 [24:6–7 LXX]; Tob. 8:4) and the central phrase of the Aaronic blessing (Num. 6:25). The prayer's traditional nature suggests that "the Lord" is the Lord God rather than the Lord Jesus. The Greek Bible describes God as "rich in mercy" (*polyeleos,* rendering the MT's *rab-ḥesed*; Num. 14:18; Joel 2:13; Ps. 86:5, 15 [85:5, 15 LXX]). Paul's prayer asks God to show his love and mercy for Onesiphorus with an abundance of gifts and favors.

[16b–17] Writing about his own prayer, especially in the thanksgiving periods of his letter, Paul typically spoke about the reasons why he prayed as he did, the circumstances that moved him to prayer. The Pastor does something similar by mentioning that Onesiphorus invigorated (*anepsyxen*) Paul by visiting him. The verb suggests some easing of anxiety as well as the satisfaction of physical needs. Onesiphorus is said to have assuaged Paul's anxiety by seeking him out just as soon as it was possible for him to do so. The text suggests that Onesiphorus had come to Paul almost immediately after his arrival in Rome, thus evoking the scenario of a Roman imprisonment for Paul and a Roman origin for this epistle.

Onesiphorus's efforts to be with Paul contrast with the defection of Phygelus and Hermogenes (1:15; see 4:10). Unlike them, Onesiphorus was not ashamed of Paul's imprisonment.[24] The mention of Onesiphorus's lack of shame is significant. In the Greco-Roman world, honor and shame were strong motivational forces. Onesiphorus's lack of shame in going to visit Paul was clearly countercultural. The fact that he was not ashamed to visit the imprisoned Paul and take care of his emotional and physical needs should serve as an example for Timothy, who is exhorted not to be ashamed of what is being said about the prisoner Paul (1:8). Does Timothy want to be like Onesiphorus, or like Phygelus and Hermogenes?

The reference to Rome in 1:17 is one of the "biographical" traits of 2 Timothy that are difficult to reconcile with what is known about Paul's life and ministry from his own letters and the account of the apostle given by Luke in the Acts of the Apostles. Scholars who wish to reconcile this datum with these other witnesses to the life and ministry of Paul resort to various stratagems to explain the phrase "once in Rome" (*genomenos en Rōmē*). Mullins, for example, suggests that Onesiphorus was in Rome when he heard about Paul's difficulties and proceeded immediately to Corinth in order to be able to help Paul. Gineste holds that the phrase "in Rome" describes Onesiphorus's spiritual and moral strength as someone who really was able to help Paul. As a common noun, the word *rōmē* means "force" or "impetus."

[18a] Paul's prayer for the household of Onesiphorus was motivated by the relief that Paul had found in Onesiphorus's visit. The repetition (the *b'* element in the chiasm) of the prayer for mercy in verse 18a suggests that Onesiphorus came to Rome to help Paul unaccompanied by the members of his household, who presumably remained behind in Ephesus (4:19). Paul's first prayer for mercy (v. 16a) was on behalf of the household of Onesiphorus. His second prayer (v. 18a) is on behalf of Onesiphorus himself.

With its reference to "that day" (see 1:12) and the incorporation of a traditional salvific formula, "with the Lord" (see 1 Thess. 4:14), Paul's prayer for Onesiphorus acquires an eschatological tone. The author prays that the Lord might grant to Onesiphorus the gift of finding mercy, implicitly a reference to mercy in the future contrasting with mercy in the present, the focus of the first prayer (v. 16a). The difference between the two prayers and the eschatological coloration of the second conceivably suggest that Onesiphorus was dead when the epistle was written. If that is the case, not only is the prayer of verse 18 one of the earliest examples of Christian prayer for the dead (see 2 Macc. 12:42–45), but it also adds the name of Onesiphorus to that of Paul as someone whose death is hinted at in the epistle.

The two prayers for mercy may be dependent on one of Paul's own letters written while he was in prison. In the letter to the Philippians Paul talks about the mercy that God had shown to Epaphroditus (see Phil. 2:25–27). He suggests

---

24. It is possible to discern the beginnings of the Christian cult of the martyrs in vv. 16b–17.

that Epaphroditus, who was sent to Paul by the Philippians, received mercy because he had ministered to Paul. The prayers for mercy differ from the intercessory prayers that Paul offers in various letters. The apostle offered those prayers to God on behalf of those to whom he was writing, thus enhancing his rhetorical *ethos* and implicitly creating a spirit of receptivity among his correspondents.

[18b] An emphatic *kai* introduces the final element of the chiastic structure. As Timothy is presumed to have known about the shameful conduct of Phygelus and Hermogenes (1:15), so he is presumed to know about the exemplary conduct of Onesiphorus. The geographical references contrast Onesiphorus's behavior in Rome (*genomenos en Rōmē*) with his behavior in Ephesus (*hosa en Ephesō*). Ephesus, the locale of much of Paul's apostolate, was the capital of the Roman province of Asia. The mention of the two cities recalls the idea of Paul going to Rome as a prisoner, his desire to go there on the way to Spain frustrated forever, and his successful ministry in Ephesus, the home of a vibrant Christian church for years to come.

"Full well," a comparative form (*beltion*, "better [than I]"), suggests that the Pastor is evoking Onesiphorus's ministerial service to the community of Ephesian Christians rather than his service to Paul (see p. 215, note a). The author provides no specific information on the nature of Onesiphorus's service to the community. Notwithstanding the lack of evidence, the hospitality of Onesiphorus became legendary in the early church (see *Acts of Paul* 3).

Second Exhortation
2 Timothy 2:1–7

The Pastor now returns to the hortatory mode that he had temporarily abandoned in order to insert a prayerful biographical note (1:15–18). This second exhortation reprises the theme of the gift that had been given to Timothy in Christ Jesus (1:6, 9). This exhortation is like the first in that both are identified as literary units by means of the literary device of ring construction (*inclusio*). What the Lord has given to Timothy delineates each of the two pericopes (1:6, 14; 2:1, 7).

The second exhortation moves beyond the first. The first exhortation focused on the charism, the gift of God given through the Holy Spirit. The second exhortation highlights the task that has been entrusted to Timothy. Timothy is to act as Paul's beloved son, following Paul's example and teaching what Paul had taught. To make his point, the Pastor cites the examples of the soldier, the athlete, and the farmer. These are classic examples, appearing in a number of Hellenistic texts and in Paul's own letters. The soldier and the athlete are examples of the agon motif, the Stoic trope that made use of the image of an athletic contest or armed conflict to portray the struggle on behalf of the truth.

2:1 You, therefore, my son, be strengthened by the grace that is in Christ Jesus. 2 Explain[a] the things that you have heard from me with many witnesses to people of faith such as are qualified to teach others in turn. 3 As a good soldier of Christ Jesus, share in suffering. 4 No one who is soldiering[b] gets entangled in the affairs of life, so as to please the one who enlisted him. 5 If anyone competes in an athletic contest, he is not crowned unless he competes according to the rules. 6 A hardworking farmer should receive the first of the produce. 7 Consider what I say, for the Lord shall provide you with understanding in all things.

a. Verses 1 and 2 are a single sentence in Greek. Verse 2 begins with "and" (*kai*).

b. Lest the military metaphor be misunderstood, some manuscripts of the Western family (F, G, the Vetus Latina, some manuscripts of the Vulgate, Cyprian, and the Ambrosiaster) have inserted an explanatory "for God," thus, "who is fighting on behalf of God."

[2:1–2] With a resumptive "therefore," the Pastor returns to the direct mode of exhortation temporarily interrupted by the personal note (1:15–18) that precedes this pericope. The charge is addressed to Timothy as "my son" (literally, "my child"; see 1:2), the form of direct address used in 1 Tim. 1:18. Paul himself used similar forms of direct address in many of his paraenetic appeals (see, e.g., 1 Cor. 10:14; 15:58).

Before defining the charge, the Pastor affirms that the grace of Christ Jesus (see 1:9) will strengthen Timothy for his task. The word "grace" (*chariti*) is to be understood in its usual sense, "gift" or "benefit," rather than in the specific connotation of God's merciful disposition that the term acquired in Paul's letters to the Romans and the Galatians. Plutarch used the term to speak of a wide variety of gifts (*Parallel Lives*, "Solon" 2.1; "Cato the Elder" 5.2; "Alexander" 30.6; etc.). Philo and Epictetus used the expression *hai charitai* to speak of God's gifts to humankind. Philo says that God gives these gifts in accordance with the capacities of the recipients, not in proportion to the greatest of his own bounties (Philo, *Creation* 23; see *Allegorical Interpretation* 3.78; *Special Laws* 1.285; Epictetus, *Discourses* 1.16.15). The gift given to Timothy is an empowering force (see 4:17; Phil. 4:13)[25] that will enable him to fulfill his mandate and complete the mission entrusted to him.

Verse 2 defines the commission. Empowered by the gift of Christ Jesus, Timothy is to explain to believers what he has heard from Paul (see Rom. 10:14; 1 Thess. 2:13). The Pastor's language is different from what Paul himself would

25. The verb *endynamoō*, "to strengthen," "to confer power on," continued to be used in this sense in other early Christian literature (*1 Clem.* 55:3; *Herm. Man.* 12.6.4; *Herm. Sim.* 6.1.2; 9.1.2).

have written. The Pastor says that Timothy is to "explain" (*parathou*) the things (*tauta*, see pp. 96–97) that he had heard. The primary sense of the Greek verb used by the Pastor is "pass along" or "distribute." Derivatively, the verb means "explain" but not without the idea of an explanation of something that is being passed along. In Rom. 8:32; 1 Cor. 11:2, 23; and 15:3, Paul used the verb "transmit" (*paradidōmi*) to speak of the process of faithfully passing along a tradition that has been received. Paul's language is derived from rabbinic usage; the word used by the Pastor is cognate with the "treasure" word group that he had used in 1:14 of the "model of sound words" that Timothy is presumed to have heard from Paul.

Although the vocabulary is different from Paul's, the text nonetheless speaks about a chain of tradition. In 1 Tim. 1:18 Paul is said to have explained (*paratithēmi*) the message to Timothy. In 2 Tim. 2:2 Timothy is urged to explain what he had heard from Paul to people of faith. Timothy is portrayed as being engaged in a kind of catechetical activity, a point emphasized by his reference to people of faith (*pistois anthrōpois*,[26] literally, "faithful people"). Timothy is not alone in passing along what he has heard from Paul; there are many witnesses to what Paul has said. The emphasis is on "many" (*pollōn*). Paul's message has been heard and been rehearsed by others in the community. It was this corporate catechesis, not a particular brand of Paulinism à la Timothy, that Timothy, Paul's son, was expected to impart to the faithful.

On the other hand, the Pastor's reference to these many witnesses is part of his overarching agenda, the faithful handing on of the tradition that comes from Paul. This calls for some discretion on the part of the community and its leaders. Among the many witnesses, Titus and Timothy are faithful witnesses, but others are not—for example, Alexander, who heard what Paul said but took a stand against his words and did many evil things (4:14–15).

[3–4] In verses 3–4 the Pastor uses the example of a soldier to illustrate that fulfilling the charge that has been given to him will involve some suffering by Timothy and that his responsibility should be fulfilled with singleminded devotedness. Aristotle said that metaphor "gives perspicuity, pleasure, and a foreign air, and it cannot be learnt from anyone else" (*Rhetoric* 3.2.8). In the Corinthian correspondence, Paul shows that he was well versed in the effective use of metaphor. Paul uses the very metaphors employed by the Pastor: the soldier (1 Cor. 9:7; 2 Cor. 10:3–4; see Rom. 13:12; Phil. 2:25; 1 Thess. 5:8; Phlm. 2), the farmer (1 Cor. 3:6–9; 9:7), and the athlete (1 Cor. 9:24–27; see Phil. 3:14).

The Pastor draws two inferences from his use of the military metaphor. The first is that Timothy be ready to suffer for the sake of Christ Jesus (see 1:8, 12).

---

26. Paul typically used a participial form of the verb *pisteuō*, "to believe" (Rom. 1:16; 1 Cor. 1:21; Gal. 3:22; 1 Thess. 1:7) to describe those who accepted his message: "those who believe" rather than "people of faith."

The other is that he be singleminded in his dedication to Christ. Both inferences were warranted by the real situation of soldiers in the imperial army. The sufferings of soldiers were legendary (see, e.g., Josephus *Jewish War* 3.7.28–29, §271–82; 3.10.9, §§525–29). They had to be ready to suffer together for the common good (see Tacitus, *Annals* 14.44). The soldier who cowered in the face of danger and left his place in the line of battle was subject to his fellow soldiers' beating him with clubs and throwing stones at him. This was the dreaded *fustuarium*, which usually led to the coward's death. Military life involved a total commitment. Until the end of the second century C.E., soldiers in the imperial army were neither allowed to marry (Dio Cassius, *Roman History* 60.24) nor to conduct any business on the side. The soldier knew that he had to be totally committed to the emperor. Likewise, Timothy must be utterly dedicated to Christ Jesus.

[5] The Pastor draws other inferences from his second example, the athlete. The image of a person taking part in an athletic contest is used to highlight the importance of competing according to the rules if victory is to be won. The rules also included mandatory months of training and a final period of exercising in the gymnasium. Paul seems to have been familiar with the Isthmian games celebrated just outside of Corinth; he was also aware that athletes could be disqualified (1 Cor. 9:27). For example, if a runner in a race of more than a single lap failed to circle a post at the turn, he was struck by an umpire who held a stick in his hand for this very purpose (see *2 Clem.* 7). The winner was crowned with a wreath, a pine wreath at the Isthmian games and a laurel or celery wreath in other games. The image of the athlete (see 4:7–8) suggests that Timothy must be properly prepared—in 1 Tim. 4:7–8 Timothy is exhorted to train himself in godliness—and faithfully fulfill his charge if he is to receive the crown of (eschatological) salvation.

[6] Paul uses the image of the farmer in 1 Cor. 3:6–9. He describes the church at Corinth as "God's field," in which he served as a planter and Apollos served as one who watered. Those who worked the field in this way would receive appropriate wages for their work. The Pastor borrows the image from Paul and draws the same lesson: The laborer deserves due reward (see 1 Tim. 5:17–18; 1 Cor. 3:8; 9:7–10; Luke 10:7). He has added to the image details that are not found in Paul. The Pastor's farmer is a "hardworking farmer" (*kopionta geōrgon*). Both the verb and the noun are used elsewhere in the New Testament as metaphors for evangelization. The farmer's pay is not Paul's generic "wages" but the work-specific "first of the produce" (*prōton tōn karpōn*).[27]

[7] Verse 7 is a kind of peroration. It summarizes the entire exhortation (2:1–7), bringing it to a close with a reference back to verses 1–2. The Pastor

27. The idiom is well chosen. "Firstfruits" (*aparchē*) were traditionally offered to God (see 1 Cor. 15:20, 23).

assures Timothy that the Lord will give him the gift of understanding so that he can carry out his catechetical task. "Understanding" (*synesis*) is the gift of intelligence and discernment, distinct from the gift of "wisdom" (*sophia*) of which there is no mention in the Pastoral Epistles.

The Kerygma Reinterpreted
2 Timothy 2:8–13

Having exhorted Timothy to listen carefully to what the apostle has to say, the Pastor cites a creedal fragment, "Jesus Christ, raised from the dead," which he describes as Paul's gospel and as the word of the Lord. He emphasizes the traditional nature of this material by adding a few biographical details about Paul. These details demonstrate that the preaching of the gospel continues despite difficulties and suffering. God's word cannot be fettered.

The Pastor concludes the pericope by characterizing Paul's gospel as a "trustworthy saying." The "trustworthy saying" formula was well known in the Pastor's community (see 1 Tim. 1:15; 3:1; 4:9; Titus 3:8; see Titus 1:9), but this is the only time that it is used in 2 Timothy. What the Pastor identifies as a trustworthy saying is basically a paraphrase of Paul's baptismal catechesis.

> 2:8 Remember Jesus Christ, raised from the dead, of the seed of David, in accordance with my proclamation, 9 for which I suffer even to the point of being shackled like a malefactor. But the word of the Lord is not bound. 10 For this reason, I endure all things for the sake of the elect, so that they too might gain salvation that is in Christ Jesus with eternal glory. 11 This is a trustworthy saying.
>
> For if we die together, we shall also live together. 12 If we endure, we shall also reign together. If we deny [him], he shall deny us. 13 If we are unfaithful, he remains faithful, for he cannot deny himself.

[2:8–9a] Each of the key expressions in verse 8 does not appear again in 2 Timothy. The presence of so many significant terms otherwise unemployed in a document is prima facie evidence that an author is making use of borrowed material. These important terms, "remember," "Jesus Christ" (with "Jesus" preceding), "raised from the dead," "of the seed of David," and "according to my proclamation," indicate that in verse 8 the Pastor is recalling the traditional faith of the church, summed up in the words of an early creedal formula. In New Testament usage, the verb "remember" (*mnēmoneue*) means to remember something significant with regard to the faith. The Pastor's use of this language underscores the traditional nature of what he is about to say: "Jesus Christ, raised from the dead."

The early church's creedal formula was not cast in stone, even if it had already become traditional by the time that Paul wrote 1 Corinthians (see 1 Cor. 15:1–2). The creedal formula admitted of several different formulations (see, e.g., 1 Cor. 15:3–4; 1 Thess. 4:14). "Raised from the dead" (*egēgermenon ek nekrōn*) was common creedal language; it is the language that Paul normally used to talk about the resurrection of Jesus. He sometimes used the verb in the active voice, saying that God raised Jesus from the dead (Rom. 4:24; 8:11 [2x]; 10:9; 2 Cor. 4:14; Gal. 1:1; 1 Thess. 1:10). At other times he used the verb in the passive voice, saying that Jesus was raised from the dead (Rom. 6:4, 9; 7:4; [8:34]; 1 Cor. 15:12 [15, 16, 17], 20). Whether he used "God" as the subject of the verb "raise" or employed a divine passive "be raised," Paul always affirmed that God was the one who acted in the resurrection.

"From the dead" (*ek nekrōn*, in the plural) implies that Jesus Christ has been raised from among the dead. This reflects the traditional Jewish belief that even the righteous dead have entered Sheol, the abode of the dead, where they await the resurrection of the dead. In raising Jesus from the dead, God effected the firstfruits of resurrection. Jesus' resurrection is a harbinger of the resurrection of those who belong to him and thus the ground of the believer's hope. The sequence of "Jesus Christ," with the name preceding the title, points to the humanity of Jesus (see 1 Tim. 2:5). It was Jesus called the Anointed One[28] who was raised from the dead.

The expression "of the seed of David" (*ek spermatos Dauid*) is another bit of Paul's own language. The expression, derived from Rom. 1:3, identifies Jesus as the Messiah, the expected ideal king of Israel. The fact that the Pastor does not otherwise exploit the messianic character of Jesus and the fact that the "seed of David" formula appears in Rom. 1:3 in a confession of faith confirm that the Pastor is echoing the traditional faith of the church when he writes about the seed of David. The formula highlights the Davidic origins of Jesus, an idea that appears principally in the Synoptics and the book of Revelation (Matt. 1:1, 6, 17; Mark 12:35–37; Luke 1:32; 3:31; Rev. 5:5; 22:16; see John 7:42; Acts 2:30) and receives hardly an emphasis in Paul and the epistolary literature of the New Testament.

In Romans, Paul uses the "seed of David" formula to explain his proclamation (*euangelion*, Rom. 1:1, 9) and to introduce himself as an apostle set aside for that proclamation to a community that he had not personally evangelized or yet visited. In similar fashion, the Pastor uses traditional creedal language to sum up the essence of Paul's preaching, the proclamation for the sake of which Paul suffered as he did (1:8; 2:8–9).

Paul writes about the preaching of the good news (*euangelion*) in each of his undisputed letters. Occasionally he uses the expression that the Pastor employs

---

28. "Christ" and "Messiah" are respectively transliterations of Greek and Hebrew verbal adjectives that mean "anointed" or, substantivized, "the anointed one."

in 2:8, namely, "my proclamation" (*to euangelion mou*; Rom. 2:16; [Rom. 16:25]; see 1 Cor. 15:1; 2 Cor. 11:7; Gal. 1:11; 2:2). Elsewhere Paul writes about "our proclamation" (*to euangelion hēmōn*; 2 Cor. 4:3; 1 Thess. 1:5), expressing his conviction that he is not alone in proclaiming the gospel. The Pastor's use of a pronoun in the singular is in keeping with the Pauline reductionism of the Pastoral Epistles, their singular focus on Paul and Paul alone as the apostle par excellence and the norm of Christian preaching. The words "in accordance with my proclamation" (*kata to euangelion mou*) have a formulaic ring. They indicate that Timothy is to recall the traditional Christian creed such as it had been proclaimed by Paul. For the Pastor, who would have Timothy know this, Paul's preaching is the norm of the believer's faith.

The Pastor adds a degree of poignancy and realism to the norm by adding that Paul was suffering for the sake of the gospel that he preached. The Pastor has already noted that Paul had suffered and had been imprisoned on account of the gospel (1:8). In 2:9 the Pastor reprises this motif and dramatizes it by comparing Paul to a common criminal in chains because of his evil deeds (*kakourgos*; see Luke 23:32, 33, 39). The Pastor's mention of Paul's suffering the fate of the common criminal—and experiencing no shame because of his lot (1:12; see Rom. 1:16)—was to provide an example to the community, which may well have been experiencing its own difficulties.

[9b] Notwithstanding Paul's own situation, the gospel cannot be contained. The gospel is powerful (Rom. 1:16; 1 Cor. 1:17–18, 24). The word of the Lord cannot be bound. By describing Paul's proclamation as the word of the Lord, the Pastor not only employs a traditional expression with good effect; he also prepares for the characterization of Paul's gospel as a trustworthy message (2:11).

The Pastor's use of the verb "bound," not otherwise found in the Pastorals, is striking. It creates a sharp contrast between Paul who is shackled (*desmōn*) and the word of the Lord that is not fettered (*ou dedetai*). Both Greek terms derive from the same root. Unlike its human instruments, even one as important as Paul, the word of the Lord cannot be contained. This graphic contrast is rooted in the traditional Pauline vision, which commonly contrasts the human (*anthrōpos*) with the divine (*theos*). In 1 Thess. 2:13 the apostle contrasts the word of God with the words the Thessalonians actually heard. God's word, he writes, is powerful. It energizes the Thessalonian believers (see Phil. 1:14). The apostle uses the expression "the word of the Lord" in 1 Thess. 1:8 and 4:15 (see 2 Thess. 3:1). The expression is classic in the Greek Bible (e.g., Isa. 1:10; 2:1), where it identifies the word of God as a force that, once spoken, will move to its fulfillment despite human indifference or opposition.

[10] After the aside on the power of the word of the Lord, the Pastor returns to the idea of Paul's suffering. Paul endures suffering for the sake of the gospel and for the sake of God's chosen people. From the time of Aristotle and Plato, endurance (*hypomonē*) was considered to be one of the most noble of virtues (see also Plato's use of *karteria*, "perseverance," in *Laches* 192b–d). The philosophic moralists extolled the virtue of endurance, especially the Stoics, for whom resistance to passion was an ideal of the ethical life. Philo considered endurance a manly virtue (*Change of Names* 153, 197; *Moses* 2.184; see also 4 Macc. 1:11; 5:23; 17:4, 23), a characteristic of athletes (*Abel and Cain* 46; *Every Good Man Is Free* 26), and one of the mightiest of virtues (*Cherubim* 78). Rebekah is the symbol of endurance; popular Hebrew etymology interpreted her name to mean "strong confidence" (*Cherubim* 47; *Preliminary Studies* 36). Within the Pastorals endurance is a virtue for which all mature men and Timothy in particular were to strive (1 Tim. 6:11; Titus 2:2).

Philo speaks of endurance as an ability to bear with all sorts of pain and adverse circumstances, including imprisonment (*Unchangeableness of God* 115). Within the community from which the Pastoral Epistles derive, Paul's endurance was legendary (see 3:10–11). The characterization of Paul as a man who endured all things (see 1 Cor. 13:7) eulogizes Paul in the categories of Hellenism. The Pastor is quick to note, however, that Paul does not endure suffering for suffering's sake. Paul suffers for the sake of the elect (see Titus 1:1) in order that they might be saved. Within the Pauline tradition salvation results from the proclamation of the gospel (see Rom. 10:13–14; 1 Cor. 1:17–18). Lest readers misconstrue the author's intention by thinking that the salvation about which he was writing was deliverance from physical danger, the Pastor clearly indicates what he means. Salvation comes through Christ Jesus (note the reprise of the author's more familiar usage with "Christ" preceding "Jesus," see 2:8). It is eschatological salvation, salvation with eternal glory (*meta doxēs aiōniou*).[29]

In Hellenistic literature, including the writings of Hellenistic Jews such as Philo and Josephus, the word *doxa* means opinion, fame, or reputation, occasionally even a bad reputation. In the Septuagint and the New Testament, the term generally had a different connotation because of the LXX's use of *doxa* to translate the Hebrew *kābôd*, "glory." In the biblical tradition "glory" was essentially a divine attribute, one to which Paul made reference in many of his letters. The Pastorals employ the term in its traditional biblical sense in two doxologies (4:8; 1 Tim. 1:17) and three other passages (1 Tim. 1:11; 3:16; Titus 2:13). Titus 2:13 specifically associates the glory of Christ with his "appearance." The only exception to this general usage is 2:10, where the expression "with eternal glory" clearly means "in the presence of God for all eternity."

[11a] "This is a trustworthy saying" (*pistos ho logos*) is a formula commonly used in the Pastoral Epistles to identify and endorse traditional material that has been handed down (see Excursus 3). The vocabulary, form, and content of the

---

29. Note that 4:7–8 also links others' eternal salvation with the ministry of Paul.

material are evidence of its traditional nature. Sometimes the formula follows the material to which it is appended and serves as a kind of endorsement (1 Tim. 3:1a; 4:9; Titus 3:8). At other times, the formula precedes the traditional material and serves as a kind of call for attention and faithful acceptance (1 Tim. 1:15a).

It is difficult to specify the precise referent of the formula used in 2:11a. Given the dense content and the complex yet tightly knit structure of the pericope, it may be best not to be overly specific. Much of the preceding material is traditional, especially verse 8. On the other hand, verses 11b–13 are well crafted. The verses contain a pair of distichs. The formulation allows creedlike material to be easily remembered and handed down. The first distich (vv. 11b–12a) echoes Paul's baptismal catechesis. The second distich (vv. 12b–13a) contains a sentence of holy law. The material they contain is written as an explanation of the creedal material in 2:8b–c and the salvation of the elect expressed in 2:10b. The Pastor's explanation opens with an explanatory "for" (an epexegetial *gar*). The particle introduces the traditional material in 1 Tim. 2:13–15, which is followed by the *pistos ho logos* formula (1 Tim. 3:1a). In sum, it is likely that the words "This is a trustworthy saying" (2:11a) introduce the pair of distichs to follow, but these are offered as an explanation of the traditional material in 2:8b–c (see 2:10b). Hence, "This is a trustworthy saying" confirms the preceding traditional material and introduces the following. In 2:11a the Pastor's formula of approval does double duty.

[11b–12a] The pair of distichs are virtually a hymn whose simple literary structure is characterized by parallelism and antithesis. The synonymous parallelism of the first distich highlights the present condition of the members of the community and the eschatological state that awaits them. Its language is Paul's language. "To die," "to live," and "to reign" are words that belong to his epistolary and theological vocabulary.[30] "To die" and "to live" appear in all of Paul's letters but Philemon. He uses the verb "to reign" in Romans and 1 Corinthians. He uses the compound forms "die together" (2 Cor. 7:3; see Mark 14:31), "live together" (Rom. 6:8; 2 Cor. 7:3), and "reign together" (1 Cor. 4:8).[31] Specifically, verses 11b–12a appear to be a succinct formulation of Rom. 6:8: "If we have died with Christ, we believe that we will also live with him" (*ei de apethanomen syn Christō, pisteuomen hoti kai syzēsomen autō*).

Paul introduced these words with a creedal lemma: "we believe that" (*pisteuomen hoti*). He had previously used the same lemma in 1 Thess. 4:14, which

---

30. Paul uses the verb "die" forty times, "live" fifty-one times, "reign" nine times.

31. Apart from 2:11b–12a and Mark 14:31, Paul is the only New Testament writer who uses these three compound verbs. The oddity is even more striking insofar as the Pastor has a predilection for compound verbs, particularly those with *syn*, but does not elsewhere use these three particular verbs.

likewise articulates a belief that Christ has died and that Christians will ultimately be with him. Similar ideas are expressed in 2 Tim. 2:11b, confirming that the *pistos ho logos* formula is jargon used in the Pastoral Epistles to identify creedal formulations. Paul incorporated the creedal formula of Rom. 6:8 into his baptismal catechesis. The formula expresses the ultimate meaning of baptism. Through baptism, Christians enter into solidarity with the humanity and death of Christ, as a result of which they believe that they will have ultimate life with Christ.

Paul's double use of "with" (*syn, sy-zēsomen*) is reflected in the compound used in the Pastor's hymn. The prepositions suggest that the primary object of the Pastor's reference is Christ Jesus: We are united with Christ Jesus in death and in life. Only secondarily is the Pastor writing about the community's solidarity with one another in death and in future life. An element of Christian solidarity is never absent from the Christian idea of salvation. Christians are together in having died together with Christ in baptism and in awaiting the future life that will be given at the appearance of the Lord and that is rooted in the resurrection of Jesus from the dead (2:8; see Rom. 6:5–11; 2 Cor. 4:14; 1 Thess. 4:14–17).

The Pastor does not speak of the resurrection; rather, he draws an encouraging inference for a beleaguered community: "If we endure, we shall also reign together." Paul, from the traditional belief of solidarity with Christ in death and in life, who is about to die, is a model of endurance for the community to imitate (see 2:10; 4:7–8). If they endure,[32] they will reign together,[33] that is, with Christ, and presumably with Paul and those who along with him wear a crown of righteousness (4:8). "To reign with" Christ Jesus is to share in the "kingdom of God" (*basileia tou theou*), the traditional symbol of God's eschatological reign (see 4:1, 18), the focus of Jesus' own preaching of the good news (see Mark 1:15).

[12b–13] The second distich is as well crafted and as tightly knit as the first. As the first, the second distich draws from earlier tradition. Its traditional nature is suggested by a rare use of the verb "deny" (*arneomai*)[34] and the fact that it is subsumed under the rubric of a trustworthy saying. The earlier tradition is cited in the form of the sentence of holy law. A sentence of holy law is a kind of eschatological law

32. "We endure" (*hypomenomen*) is the only verb that does not use the prepositional prefix *syn* in the first stich. The implication may be that endurance is something that each member of the community must do.

33. The rarely used verb "reign together" (*symbasileuō*) first appeared in Polybius, *Histories* 30.2.4, where it referred to a royal military union. Paul himself used the verb only in a well-turned trope (1 Cor. 4:8) that he used to counter the claims of some haughty individuals who were acting as if they were kings.

34. The verb is used in 2 Timothy only in 2:12b.

of retribution characterized by the use of the same verb in the protasis and the apo-dosis, that is, in the description of both the crime and the punishment.[35]

This sentence of holy law hearkens back to a Q logion (Matt. 10:33 = Luke 12:9). Those who deny that one[36] in the present life will be denied by that same one in the life to come. "He," "that one"[37] is mysterious; his identity is not revealed. He is an enigmatic eschatological figure. The Pastor uses the related adjective *ekeinos* in reference to the eschaton (see 1:12, 18; 4:8; see 2:26; 3:9), the day of the Lord. The Lord is expected to grant mercy (1:18) and confer a crown of righteousness on that day (4:8). It may be that 2:12 speaks enigmati-cally of "that one" rather than of the "Lord" because the Lord is Savior (*Sōtēr*), a beneficent figure, whereas "that one" is a vindicator.

Verse 13a is ironic. The symmetry of the distich's four stichs and the sen-tence of holy law in verse 12b would lead the reader to expect that the final stich of the composition would be, "If we are unfaithful, he will be unfaithful to us." Instead of affirming that "that one" will cast aside his fidelity and sever his rela-tionship with those who have not been loyal, the hymn concludes with a virtual confession of faith: "He [*ekeinos*] remains faithful." Fidelity (*'ěmet*) is one of the essential characteristics of the God of the Hebrew biblical tradition (see 2:19). Use of the word speaks of God's covenantal loyalty to his chosen peo-ple. Paul proclaims that God is faithful (*pistos*; see 1 Cor. 1:9; 10:13; 2 Cor. 1:18; 1 Thess. 5:24). Verse 13 speaks of "that one's" fidelity; "that one" is Christ Jesus. The Pastor's circles were accustomed to attributing divine attributes to Christ Jesus (thus, *sōtēr*, *kyrios*). Fidelity is among those divine attributes that can be attributed to Christ Jesus (see 2 Thess. 3:3). Doing so, the Pastor echoes an apocalyptic notion: The agent of eschatological judgment shall remain faith-ful despite the unfaithfulness of human beings (see 2 Thess. 3:3).

To clarify and emphasize the point, the Pastor adds a catechetical explana-tion: "for [*gar*] he cannot deny himself." This explanation reprises the key verb of the Q logion. The principle of noncontradiction derives from Hellenistic reflection on the God of the biblical tradition. The use of Hellenistic thoughts and phrases to develop discourse about God ("theology," "words about God") is characteristic of the Pastoral Epistles. The use of "appearance" (*epiphaneia*) and "savior" language as well as the use of abstract adjectives in the descrip-tion of God (1 Tim. 1:17; 6:15–16; Titus 1:2) are striking examples of the phenomenon.

35. See Ernst Käsemann, "Sentences of Holy Law in the New Testament," in *New Testament Questions of Today*, NTL (Philadelphia: Fortress, 1969), 66–81.

36. Technically, the Pastor's omission of a direct object for the verb "deny" is an example of zeugma. The omission may have been intended to ensure the symmetry of the four stichs of the composition.

37. The Attic form *kakeinos* means "that one." This word, created by the elision of *kai* and *ekeinos,* is an example of crasis, a figure of speech that allows an orator or writer to avoid the hia-tus of a harsh transition.

A Pastoral Charge
2 Timothy 2:14–21

The pastoral charge addressed to Timothy urges him to be well qualified with no cause for shame. His task will be to remind his charges of the kerygma but to do so in such a way as to present the message of truth, not falling into the error of those who misrepresent the resurrection from the dead by saying that it has already occurred. This kind of false teaching creates a state of confusion.

The house of God, on the other hand, is orderly. It stands on a firm foundation. The use of household images allows the Pastor to talk about some of the various kinds of materials from which household items were made. Some items are used for noble purposes; others serve a less noble purpose. Effectively, the Pastor charges Timothy to make a decision about what kind of building material he would like himself to be in the building up of God's house (see 1 Tim. 3:15).

2:14 Remind them of these things, charging them before God[a] not to engage in verbal warfare, which redounds to no useful advantage but leads only to the destruction of those who listen. 15 Be zealous to present yourself to God as someone who is qualified, a worker who has no cause for shame, teaching the message of truth correctly. 16 Shun impious nonsense, for it will further advance impiety 17 and their word will spread like gangrene. Among them are Hymenaeus and Philetus, 18 who miss the mark of truth, saying that the resurrection has already occurred. They subvert some peoples' faith. 19 The firm foundation of God, however, stands fast. It bears this inscription: "The Lord knows those who belong to him," and "Let whoever calls on the name of the Lord turn from wrongdoing." 20 In a large house there are not only golden and silver vessels but also wooden and crockery vessels, some for noble use, others for ignoble use. 21 If anyone cleanses himself or herself from these things, he or she will be a noble vessel, sanctified, useful for the master of the house, and ready for every good work.

a. The preponderance of textual evidence, including the ancient versions, read "God." Some manuscripts, among them A and the Byzantine manuscripts, read "Lord" (see AV).

[2:14] Timothy is initially charged to remind "them" of "these things." "These things" (*tauta*) is throughout the Pastorals a cipher for the Pauline tradition that Timothy and Titus are to pass along. In 2:14 these things are especially the formulae of faith endorsed in the previous pericope by "This is a trustworthy saying." The memory motif that introduced that pericope recurs in the introduction to this pericope's pastoral charge. Timothy is to remember (2:8) and remind (2:14). The Pastor does not identify those to whom the reminder should be addressed. "Remind" lacks the expected indirect object. Presumably, Timothy is to remind the members of the community, the people of faith, the elect of the previous pericopes (see 2:2, 10).

With the appended clause, "charging them before God," the Pastor adds solemnity to the charge (see 4:1; 1 Tim. 5:21; 6:13) and places Timothy's activity in an arena that has the aura of God's courtroom. Using phrases such as "engage in verbal warfare" (*logomacheō*)[38] and "redounds to no useful advantage" (*chrēsimon*) that are not otherwise found in the New Testament, the Pastor urges Timothy to avoid the kind of sophistry that can only lead to the destruction of the witnesses. The Pastor's phraseology skillfully explains the relevance of the rhetorical argument of advantage. Verbal warfare results in no advantage at all; rather, it results in great disadvantage, that is, utter destruction (*katastrophē*). The eschatological horizon reflects the tone of the sentence of holy law in the immediately preceding verse. In verse 14 the Pastor sets before Timothy the ultimate consequences of the way in which he conducts himself as a teacher. He teaches in the presence of God. His failure to teach as he ought will have catastrophic consequences, namely, the ultimate destruction of those who listen to him (see 1 Tim. 4:16).

[15] The initial charge to Timothy is reinforced with an encouragement to Timothy to get immediately involved in the task at hand. *Spoudason* literally means "hurry up"; figuratively it means "be zealous." Urgency and commitment are involved. Timothy is to present himself to God as a qualified worker (*dokimon . . . ergatēn*) who has no reason for shame. The work is immediately identified as teaching. The metaphors of verses 19–21 suggest that the work is to be construed as a kind of construction work (see 1 Cor. 3:10–17). The task at hand is building the house of God (see 1 Tim. 3:15). Paul often used words derived from the root *erg-*, meaning "work," to describe the activity of people who announced and proclaimed the word of God. The "work" was evangelization.

Timothy is expected to be qualified and competent (*dokimos*), ready for his task and able to avoid self-defeating procedures. Describing his own role in a similar construction project, Paul identified himself as a "skilled master builder" (*sophos architektōn*, 1 Cor. 3:10).[39] Hellenists used the adjective "qualified" (*dokimos*) to characterize a person who had a demonstrated competence. Philo writes about competent craftsmen (*Heir* 158), mathematicians and astronomers (*Creation* 128), physicians (*Unchangeableness of God* 65; *Special Laws* 3.117), and priests (*Special Laws* 1.166). He knows of those who are competent in one specific area of endeavor (*Planting* 81) as well as those who are virtually omnicompetent (*Joseph* 114).

---

38. The compound verb (*logo-macheō*) is a neologism first used in 2:14; the cognate noun logomachia occurs in 1 Tim 6:14.

39. It is likely that 1 Cor. 3:10–17 provided the Pastor with inspiration for the imagery of 2:14–21.

The task for which Timothy is qualified is teaching the message of truth correctly. Timothy has assumed the Pauline mantle of teacher (1:11; 1 Tim. 2:7). He was urged to remain in Ephesus for this purpose (1 Tim. 1:3). There can be no doubt that Timothy is a teacher. The participial clause, "teaching the message of truth correctly" (*orthotomounta ton logon tēs alētheias*), identifies what it is that Timothy is to teach and how he is to teach it. Specifying that he is to teach correctly, the Pastor echoes the concern of Hellenistic rhetoricians that speech be characterized by *orthoepeia*, the quality of "exactness and precision, without error or flaw, respecting the linguistic proprieties" (*TLNT* 2.595). Timothy is to teach correctly "the message of truth" (*hon logon tēs alētheias*). This well-turned phrase recalls Paul's description of his proclamation as a message (*logos*; 1 Cor. 14:36; 2 Cor. 5:19; Phil. 2:16; 1 Thess. 1:8; 2:13) and his conviction that he spoke the truth (Gal. 2:5, 14; 5:7; 2 Cor. 4:2; 6:7).

The expression was first used by Paul himself to describe his own ministry (2 Cor. 6:7; see 2 Cor. 7:14); thereafter, it became a technical term that post-Pauline communities used to designate the Pauline gospel. The epistle to the Colossians thus refers to "the word of the truth, the gospel that has come to you" (Col. 1:5–6).[40] The expression has a biblical ring (see Ps. 119:43; *T. Gad* 3:1; *Odes. Sol.* 8:8), but the truth to which it makes reference is not God's fidelity (*ʾemet*). Rather, it a reference to a Hellenistic notion of truth, truth contrasted with falsehood. In Colossians, the message of the truth is contrasted with the philosophy and empty deceit summarized in Colossians 2. The Epistle to the Ephesians develops the same idea (see Eph. 1:13), probably in dependence on Colossians, but pays greater attention to the idea of divine fidelity (see Jas. 1:18) than Colossians does.

Timothy is expected to teach carefully the message of truth, avoiding impious nonsense (2:16) and foolish and ignorant disputes (2:23) that stray far from the truth. If he does so, Timothy will have nothing of which to be ashamed (*anepaischynton*). The contrast between the impious nonsense (*tas bebēlous kenophōnias*) that Timothy is to avoid rigorously and the message of the truth that he is to teach correctly focuses his "job description." The sequence (in Greek) of the Pastor's words, "correctly teaching the message of truth; shun impious nonsense," forms a chiasm in which "the message of truth" and "impious nonsense" are antithetically juxtaposed with one another. The sharp contrast is difficult to capture in English translation.

[16–18] The rhetorical contrast emphasizes the importance of the charge to Timothy. Not only is he to teach zealously and correctly the message of truth;

---

40. Commenting on Col. 1:5, Jean-Noël Aletti has noted that this is the first designation of the gospel message as "the word of truth." See *Saint Paul: Épitre aux Colossiens*, EBib 20 (Paris: Gabalda, 1993), 61.

232 2 Timothy 2:14–21

he is also to avoid impious nonsense. These two elements are connected by the particle *de*, which often has the meaning "but" and introduces contrary ideas. There is, moreover, a verbal contrast between the "message [*ton logon*] of truth" and the "word [*ho logos*]" that "will spread like gangrene."

Timothy must shun "impious nonsense" (*tas bebēlous kenophōnias*; see 1 Tim. 6:20). A combination of "empty" or "vain" (*kenos*) and "sound" (*phōn-*), yields the neologism *tas kenophōnias*, "empty sounds," hence, nonsense. The adjective "impious" (*bebēlous*) was widely used in the metaphorical sense of "profane," especially in the Septuagint and Hellenistic Jewish writings (see 1 Tim. 1:9; 4:7; 6:20; Heb. 12:16). The term had ritual, social, and moral overtones. The Epistle to the Hebrews describes Esau as an "immoral and godless person [*tis pornos kai bebēlos*], who sold his birthright for a single meal" (Heb 12:16). The term "profane" appears in a catalog of vices in 1 Tim. 1:9–10 and in Philo (*Abel and Cain* 32). According to Philo, "the shameful is profane, and the profane is surely unholy" (*Abel and Cain* 138). A prostitute is "profane in body and soul," unfit for marriage to a priest even after she has abandoned her profession (*Special Laws* 1.102).

The word "profane" implies a contrast with "holy," which describes something or someone dedicated to God. Profane speech is the antithesis to godliness (*eusebeia*). First Timothy 4:7 contrasts profane myths and old wives' tales with the words of faith and sound teaching, strongly implying that this kind of profanity is opposed to godliness (*eusebeia*). First Timothy 6:20 describes "impious nonsense" as failing the faith and being opposed to true knowledge. "Impious nonsense" is a well-found cipher to describe the teaching of those whose opposition to the Pauline gospel must be eradicated from the community.

The Pastor reminds Timothy that impious nonsense enables people to advance further in impiety—*epi pleion . . . prokopsousin asebeias*, an ironic phrase, since the verb connotes progress (see the similar construction in 3:13). Initially the Pastor does not identify the subject of the verb. He will give the example of Hymenaeus and Philetus. Before he does so he warns that the noxious word will spread like gangrene. Moderns might say that the word would spread like wildfire, but the Pastor's medical metaphor is more appropriate in a community that commonly speaks about sound or healthy teaching (1:13; 4:3; 1 Tim. 1:10; 6:3; Titus 1:9, 13; 2:1, 2, 8).

The use of examples (*paradeigmata*) is a characteristic ploy of Hellenistic rhetoric. Hymenaeus and Philetus are cited as examples of those whose impious nonsense spreads like gangrene. The Pastor assumes that Hymenaeus and Philetus were known to the community. Philetus, however, is otherwise unknown to us. Hymenaeus is most likely one of the persons mentioned in 1 Tim 1:20—Alexander is the other—who scuttled the faith and were consequently handed over to Satan.

Hymenaeus and Philetus are said to have "missed the mark"[41] (*ēstochēsan*; see 1 Tim. 1:6; 6:21), a metaphorical description of serious error used by Polybius, Plutarch, and other Hellenistic writers (see, e.g., Plutarch, "On Listening to Lectures" 151, *Moralia* 46A; "Obsolescence of Oracles" 10, *Moralia* 414F; "Table-Talk" 7.5 *Moralia* 705C; cf. Josephus, *Jewish War* 4.2.5 §116). Hymenaeus and Philetus have missed the mark of "truth." In contrast, the "full knowledge of truth" is the hallmark of the Pastor's community (2:25; 3:7). The peroration of 1 Timothy speaks of "some" who have missed the mark with regard to the faith (1 Tim. 6:20–21). Implicitly these people are described as speaking impious nonsense and raising objections on the basis of ideas that are wrongly called knowledge.

The deviation of Hymenaeus and Philetus from the truth is expressed in a claim that the resurrection (*tēn anastasin*) has already occurred. This departure from the truth is different from the denial of the resurrection with which the apostle dealt in 1 Cor. 15:12–13. The Corinthian deviation concerned the possibility of resurrection. Some members of that Hellenistic and cosmopolitan Christian community had difficult understanding the Jewish apocalyptic notion of the resurrection of the dead (see Acts 17:18, 32). Paul rebutted their position by affirming that the core of the Christian kerygma is the reality of Jesus' resurrection from the dead.

The deviation from the truth in 2:18 may have involved a spiritualizing reinterpretation of the notion of resurrection, perhaps as no more than a metaphor for one's conversion. In practical terms, such a spiritualization would be tantamount to denying the reality of a future, bodily resurrection (see 2:8, 10).[42] Paul himself may have contributed to the difficulty that Hellenists had in understanding the concept of resurrection by speaking of the new life that is consequent upon moral conversion and Christian baptism (see Rom. 6:4, 11).

Paul's discourse about the new life employs language similar to that of Philo and Hellenistic moralists who speak about "being dead" in reference to an evil life and about "being alive" in reference to a morally good life (see Philo, *Flight* 55, 58). On the other hand, the denial of a future resurrection may stem from the Jewish notion that future life is realized in one's progeny, or from a Hellenistic notion that authentic existence is to be found in a kind of immediate experience of the deity. The apocryphal second-century *Acts of Paul* offers an

41. The verb *hamartanō* is the word most commonly used in the LXX and the New Testament with the meaning "to sin" (1 Tim. 5:20; Titus 3:11). Synonymous with *astocheō*, its primary meaning is "to miss the mark."

42. "Resurrection" (*anastasis*) is a Pauline term, although the apostle with but one exception (Rom. 6:5) always writes of the "resurrection of the dead" (with *nekrōn*; 1 Cor. 15:12, 13, 21, 42) or of the resurrection of Christ (Rom. 1:4; 6:5; Phil. 3:10). The lack of either qualifier in 2:18 suggests that the error of Hymenaeus and Philetus is a denial of resurrection after death.

interpretation of the Pastor's words. This book describes individuals named Demas and Hermogenes who oppose Paul's teaching.[43] On the one hand, they claim that Paul teaches a future only for those who are "chaste," that is, only for those who have not married (*Acts of Paul* 7.12). On the other hand, they endeavor to "correct" what Paul has said to Thecla "concerning the resurrection which he [Paul] says is to come, that it has already taken place in the children whom we have and that we are risen again in that we have come to know the true God" (*Acts of Paul* 7.14).

It is impossible to determine accurately the source of Hymenaeus and Philetus's deviation from the truth. The Pastor offers no rebuttal of their error; rather, he focuses on some of its consequences. Having missed the mark and engaged in godless chatter, they subvert (*anatrepousin*; see Titus 1:11) the faith of some members of the Pastor's community. John 2:15 uses this verb in the portrayal of Jesus overturning the tables of the money changers in the temple. Titus 1:11 suggests that the verb in 2:18 should be taken in the figurative sense of "subvert" or "undermine," a usage found in Diodorus Siculus, who writes about a pledge that is subverted (*Library of History* 1.77.2).

Titus 1:10–11 describes teachers who subvert whole households for the sake of money. These many teachers are especially from a "Jewish" group (see the exegesis of Titus 1:11). Like those to whom the Pastor refers in 2:18, the many teachers of Titus 1 are characterized by vices of the tongue. One significant difference between Titus 1 and what the Pastor writes in 2:18 is that Titus speaks of the subversions of entire households whereas 2:18 speaks about the subversion of "the faith." "Faith" in the Pastoral Epistles refers to the content of Christian belief rather than to a personal relationship with God (see Excursus 7). Second Timothy 2:8–21 virtually equates Paul's gospel (2:8), the word of God (2:9), the trustworthy saying (2:11), and the message of truth (2:15) with "the faith" (*tēn pistin*, v. 18). It is the content of faith that is being upset by such characters as Hymenaeus and Philetus; the focus of Christian belief has been confused and distorted by the likes of Hymenaeus and Philetus. By their false teaching with regard to the resurrection, they have skewed the basic message of the Christian faith.

The way in which the Pastor deals with the error of Hymenaeus and Philetus, as serious as it is, is quite different from the way in which Paul dealt with the denial of the resurrection in 1 Corinthians 15. Skilled rhetorician that he was, Paul developed a *pathos* and *logos* appeal; that is, he appealed to the interests of the audience (*pathos*) and attempted to argue a logical rebuttal (*logos*).[44]

---

43. The names have apparently been borrowed from 4:10 and 1:15 respectively.

44. The "artificial"—that is, the product of human intelligence—arguments of classical rhetoric were the appeals from *pathos, logos,* and *ethos*, appeals based on the moral stature of the speaker. See Aristotle, *Rhetoric* 1.2.3.

The Pastor alluded to the tradition about the resurrection (2:8, 11–13) but dismisses Hymenaeus and Philetus out of hand by speaking about them in a blatantly negative fashion.

[19] In contrast with the situation of Hymenaeus and Philetus going awry and the faith of some people being turned upside down as a result is the stable solidity of God's firm foundation. The Pastor emphasizes the idea of the foundation's solid nature by using the verb "stand fast" (*histēmi*) and the adjective "firm" (*stereos*). The imagery is that of a building that is constructed on a solid foundation. The image comes from Paul, who uses it as a metaphor for the local church (Rom. 15:20; 1 Cor. 3:10–12). The Pastor uses the imagery for his own purpose (see Eph. 2:20). He looks at the building in the way that a construction engineer would. He first inspects the foundation, then the rest of the building. This is the way in which Paul looks at the Corinthian church in 1 Cor. 3:9b–17.

The Pastor, as does Paul, makes one point while looking at the foundation and another while looking at the building. He draws the readers' attention to the epigraph on the foundation. The inscription is presented as a pair of tersely formulated texts with a gnomic ring. It contains three allusions to the Greek Bible: "the LORD will make known who is his" (Num. 16), "return to the Most High and turn away from iniquity" (Sir. 17:26), and "we acknowledge your name" (Isa. 26:13). These texts are the only biblical texts cited in the Pastor's missive. None of them appears elsewhere in the New Testament. For the most part, the wording of the inscription is according to the LXX, but none of the three texts is cited exactly as it appears in the Greek Bible.

The citation of Num. 16:5 is particularly appropriate to the Pastor's situation. He is concerned with a community, some of whose members are turning from the faith because of the influence of Hymenaeus, Philetus, and people like them. The biblical citation is taken from a passage that describes the revolt of Korah, Dathan, and Abiram against the leadership of Moses (Num. 16:1–35). Responding to Korah and his ilk, Moses says, "In the morning the LORD will make known who is his, and who is holy, and who will be allowed to approach him; the one whom he will choose he will allow to approach him" (Num. 16:5). This is the language of a royal court where only the king's own men were allowed into the royal presence. Applied to priests, the language suggests that at least at some stage of the tradition there were divisions among priests. In his citation of Num. 16:5 the Pastor uses "Lord" (*kyrios*) rather than the LXX's "God" (*ho theos*); the MT has the Tetragrammaton (YHWH). The emendation may reflect the influence of the classic expression "the name of the Lord" (e.g., Joel 2:32; see also 1 Cor. 1:2, 10; 5:4), which appears in the Pastor's citation of Isaiah.[45]

---

45. In the manuscript tradition the homogeneity was further developed in א, which adds a qualifying "all" to the citation of Num. 16:5.

The second epigraph appears to be a combination of allusions to Sir. 17:26 and Isa. 26:13. The words "turn from wrongdoing" allude to the call to repentance (Sir. 17:25–26) with which the sage begins a hymn on repentance and God's great mercy (Sir. 17:25–32). The verb in Sir. 17:26 (*apostrephe*) has been replaced by a verb in the aorist imperative (*apostētō*), implying a conversion experience. The reference to Isaiah, "whoever calls on the name of the Lord," comes from a prayer for deliverance (Isa. 26:1–27:1). The invocation of Isa. 26:13–14 is one in which the people proclaim their loyalty to the one God after having acknowledged other lords. Though found within another literary form, its conversion motif is similar to that of Sirach's prophetic call. The Pastor constructed a participial form (*onomazōn*) from the first person plural (*onomazomen*) found in Isa. 26:13. In addition, he has replaced Isaiah's "your" by "of the Lord," with the result that the epigraph contains the classic phrase, "the name of the Lord."

The cumulative effect of the three citations, articulated as but two, is that the edifice—ultimately the church (see 1 Tim. 3:15; 1 Cor. 3:10–17)—has been established on the basis of the divine call and the conversion of humans. Each of these two elements is discriminating. God chooses whom he will. Humans change their lives or they do not. The inscriptions are minatory. They warn the community not to follow the path taken by Hymenaeus and Philetus. If anyone calls upon the name of the Lord but does not live accordingly, that person should know that God is not fooled (see Matt. 7:21–22; Luke 6:46; 13:25–27). God knows those who truly belong to him and show that they belong to him (their holiness) by the way in which they live.

[20–21] In verses 20–21 the Pastor turns his attention from the foundation to the building itself. The building is a large building, a kind of mansion. The image of a relatively large edifice allows the Pastor to mention a wide variety of material from which the utensils used in lighting, cooking, and eating were made. Had the Pastor been thinking of the homes of the poor, he would have been able to mention only vessels made of wood and crockery. The reference to the large house also says something about the social status of the community for which the epistle is intended. It does not, however, imply that some members of the community were affluent. The vast majority of the population in Hellenistic cities were slaves. Chief among them would have been the *oikonomos*, the household manager. Household slaves would be quite familiar with the variety of utensils used by their masters. Slaves were responsible for using and taking care of these vessels.

The Pastor's description of the utensils makes a twofold distinction. His extended metaphor distinguishes among the material from which the vessels are made and the uses to which they are put. With regard to the material, a distinction is made between vessels made of precious metal, gold and silver, and those made of ordinary material, wood and clay. With regard to the use of the vessels, some are used for a more noble purpose (*eis timēn*), others for an ignoble purpose (*eis atimian*). The contrast between the two phrases is clear; the expressions are antonyms. Vessels used for less seemly purposes, such as a chamber pot or garbage container, would have been made of material less valuable than gold or silver. If the contrast is not taken at face value but as one simply between more honorable and less honorable uses, the Pastor may have been alluding to the fact that gold and silver plates and utensils would have been used on more festive occasions, while those made of wood or crockery would have been used in more mundane circumstances.

The exhortation of verse 21 is an inference abruptly drawn from the image of the vessels. The Pastor writes about cleaning the vessels. Anyone following the Pastor's image would immediately think of washing (*ekkatharē*) the dishes and other vessels so that they can be used again, perhaps for another purpose. The Pastor, however, draws the reader's attention to a person who is washing him or herself. A person is like a dish insofar as both have to be clean in order to be put to another use. A person must be clean of "these things" (*apo toutōn*), whose only clear referent is the "wrongdoing" mentioned in verse 19 (= Sir. 17:26). The image suggests conversion, a new start.

The image of washing may be an allusion to baptism, the symbolic celebration of conversion by means of a water ritual. There is no clear New Testament evidence of the use of the verb "to clean" (*ekkathairō*) for Christian baptism, but various purification and expiation rituals (*katharismoi*) were celebrated in the Greco-Roman world. The use of water for cleansing was part of the initiation rite at Qumran (1QS 3:6–9). Frequently the thought world of the Pastorals can be clarified by means of parallels from the Dead Sea Scrolls. The Pastor's use of washing may well be a case in point. He describes the person who has been washed as noble, sanctified, useful for the master of the house, and ready for every good work.

The idea that a person who is washed is a noble vessel (*skeuos eis timēn*) reprises the imagery of verse 20. The other descriptions of the person who has been newly washed pertain to the Christian state. A person who has been washed has been "sanctified" (*hēgiasmenon*; see 1:9). Such a person has been consecrated and set apart for use by God. This cultic language is clarified by the apposite "useful for the master of the house." The metaphor suggests that once a dish has been washed it can be used in any way that the householder (*despotē*; see 1 Tim. 6:1, 2; Titus 2:9) wants it to be used.

In the early church, household language was as often as not ecclesial language (see Excursus 5). The church is "the house of God" (1 Tim. 3:15). The Pastor evoked this motif in the reference to God's foundation (2:19). From the standpoint of the implied referent of the metaphor, the idea that the person who has been washed is useful for the householder implies that the person is now ready for use by God, the householder, much in the fashion in which Mark was

"useful" for Paul's ministry (4:11). More broadly, says the Pastor, such a person has been prepared for any and every good work. Minimally this implies the
ethic of good citizenship to which so much of the paraenesis of the Pastorals is
directed (see Excursus 8).

Not only is the person who is washed ready to be used by God; that person
also is answerable to God, the Master. In the Greek Bible "master" (*despotēs*)
was a common designation for God (see, e.g., Gen. 15:2, 8; Jonah 4:3; Jer. 1:6;
4:10; Job 5:8; Dan. 9:15; Tob. 8:17). This usage was continued by Hellenistic
Jewish writers (see e.g., Philo, *Heir* 22; Josephus, *Ant.* 8.4.3; *Jewish War* 7.8.6
§323) and early Christian writers (see, e.g., *1 Clem.* 7:5; *Barn.* 1:7; *Diogn.* 8:7;
Herm. Sim 1.9; *Herm. Vis.* 2.2.5). A striking example is the compound term
"master of the household" (*oiko-despotēs*), used in the parables of Jesus (Matt.
13:27; 20:1, 11; 21:33; 24:43; Luke 12:39; 13:25; 14:21; see Matt. 10:25). The
literary character portrayed as the "master of the household" is ultimately a
metaphor for God.

The epigraph on the building's foundation (2:19) indicates that the building
belongs to God and warns those who would enter to turn from wrongdoing. The
description of the utensils has a hortatory function but contains a veiled threat.
It warns those who are not ready and able to serve God's purpose that God is
the *oikodespotēs*, the master of the house. In effect, the image of the vessels
suggests ideas similar to those evoked by the double inscription on the foundation. Both the image and the epigraph speak of belonging to God and the
importance of conversion.

Third Exhortation
2 Timothy 2:22–26

The pastoral charge addressed to Timothy in 2:14–21 was hortatory; in 2:22–26
the Pastor adopts a decidedly paraenetic tone. He first exhorts Timothy to abandon the ways of youth and pursue a path of righteousness. The Pastor's real concern is the welfare of the community, its peace. So that peace can be achieved,
Timothy must avoid the kind of foolish discourse that provokes disagreement.
He is to deal gently with his opponents in the hope that God will give them the
gift of conversion.

The pericope offers two descriptions of conversion. Each of them mentions
the negative and the positive aspects of conversion, the turning from and the
turning to. Timothy's conversion is described in classic Hellenistic language:
flee from and pursue (2:22). He is to pursue righteousness, to which the Pastor
adds "faith and love," the traditional summary of the Christian life. The conversion of the opponents, on the other hand, is described in almost sectarian

terms (2:25b–26). The linguistic modes used to describe their conversion echo the language of the Dead Sea Scrolls.

2:22 Flee youthful passions; pursue righteousness, faith, love, and peace together with those who invoke the Lord with a pure heart. 23 Avoid foolish and stupid arguments, knowing that they produce quarrels. 24 The servant of the Lord must not quarrel; rather, he must be gentle with all, able to teach, and forbearing, 25 correcting opponents with gentleness. Perhaps[a] God might give them the gift of repentance to the full knowledge of truth 26 so that they come to their right senses and escape from the devil's trap after they had previously been held captive by him in order to do his will.

a. In the Greek text, 2:24b–26 is a single sentence.

[2:22] In the Greek text, the contrast between the two parts of the Pastor's hortatory remark is accentuated by the juxtaposition of the verbs "flee" (*pheuge*) and "pursue" (*diōke*). Since the Pastor uses two antonymic verbs, the contrast could hardly have been sharper. The same construction, with the juxtaposition of the same two contrasting verbs, appears in 1 Tim. 6:11. There the man of God is urged to flee "these things" and pursue righteousness, godliness, faith, love, steadfastness, and gentleness. In 2:22 Timothy is urged to flee youthful passions (*neōterikas epithymias*).

The Pastorals share an aversion to the passions (3:6; 4:3; 1 Tim. 6:9; Titus 2:12; 3:3) that was characteristic of the Stoic ethic, the dominant ethic of the times. For the Stoics, submission to one's passions was the antithesis to the ideal of *apatheia*, freedom from one's passions. "Passions" generally connotes sexual urges and desires. See Paul's similar exhortation in 1 Cor. 6:18: "Shun fornication!" (*pheugete tēn porneian*). For the Stoics, not only must sexual misconduct be shunned, passion itself must be avoided. The Pastor describes the passions that Timothy is urged to avoid as "youthful" (*neōterikas*). This qualification has a pejorative sense. Youths are presumed to be unable to control their passions (see Titus 2:6). Leaders, like Timothy, are presumed to be mature individuals (*presbyteroi*, a term that does not appear in 2 Timothy but is to be found in 1 Tim. 5:1, 2, 17, 19; Titus 1:5) who can keep their passions under control.

Fleeing passion, Timothy is urged to pursue (*diōke*; see 1 Tim. 6:11; 1 Cor. 14:1) righteousness, faith, love, and peace. Lists of virtues such as this were a well-known literary form in the Hellenistic world (see p. 55). Twenty such lists are found in the New Testament, including three in Paul's own writings (2 Cor. 6:6–7a; Gal. 5:22–23; Phil. 4:8). Such lists were frequently used to spell out the qualifications and characteristics of people in positions of

leadership. This is the case in 2:22. The Pastor's short list of four virtues contains three of the six virtues on the list in 1 Tim. 6:11, namely, righteousness,
faith, and love. The dyad "faith and love" is a classic Pauline description of
the Christian life (see, e.g., 1 Thess. 3:6; Gal. 5:6). "Faith" expresses one's
relationship with God; "love" expresses one's relationship with other human
beings.

Faith and love are frequently found in the New Testament's catalogs of
virtues (e.g., Titus 2:2). "Righteousness" (*dikaiosynēn*), on the other hand, is
not commonly found in these lists. Among Paul's three lists of virtues, "righteousness" appears only in Phil. 4:8; among the fifteen lists of virtues in literature dependent on Paul, "righteousness" occurs only in 2:22; 1 Tim. 6:11; Titus
1:8; and Eph. 5:9 (see Eph. 6:14). In these passages righteousness is one of several desirable ethical qualities. Righteousness is one of the cardinal virtues (see
Philo, *Allegorical Interpretation* 2.18; *Sobriety* 38; *Migration of Abraham* 219),
a quality of a person who is in correct relationship with other humans and, consequently, is in right relationship with God. Neither here nor elsewhere in the
Pastorals does the term "righteousness" have the theological nuances that it did
in Paul's correspondence with the Romans and with the Galatians.

The fourth item on the Pastor's list is "peace." The appearance of "peace"
on the list is somewhat exceptional. This is the only place in the body of any of
the Pastoral Epistles that speaks of peace (see 1:2; 1 Tim. 1:2; Titus 1:4). Among
the New Testament's catalogs of virtues, peace is cited only in Gal. 5:22 and
here. Philosophic moralists conceived of peace in negative terms, as the
absence of armed conflict on the macroplane and as the absence of pain on the
microplane. The New Testament, however, uses the term "peace" (*eirēnē*) to
designate the fullness of God's covenantal blessings to his people. In the New
Testament, "peace" is the biblical shalom.

Paul encouraged the Romans to pursue what makes for peace (*ta tēs eirēnēs
diōkōmen*) and mutual upbuilding (Rom. 14:19; see also Luke 19:42). His
exhortation follows the affirmation that "the kingdom of God is not food and
drink but righteousness and peace and joy in the Holy Spirit" (Rom 14:17). The
Pastor's exhortation that Timothy pursue peace echoes what Paul wrote to the
Romans. Like Paul, the Pastor writes about pursuit, righteousness, and peace.
An exhortation to pursue peace is particularly appropriate in a document such
as 2 Timothy. Continuing good relationships among those left behind is a common motif in farewell discourses (see John 14:27).

Peace is not a value to be pursued by Timothy alone; it is to be pursued by
all who invoke the Lord, who call upon the Lord's name with a pure heart. The
invocation of the name of the Lord is a traditional biblical idea (see, e.g., Gen.
12:8; 13:4; 21:33; 26:25). Paul used this kind of language in Rom. 10:12–14
and 1 Cor. 1:2; for him, the name of the Lord is Jesus Christ (Phil. 2:9–11). The
Pastor does not focus on the name of the Lord; rather, he uses the traditional

formula to indicate that Timothy is not alone in being urged to conversion and the pursuit of peace. Timothy is united with all those who similarly call on the name of the Lord (see 1 Cor. 1:2). To "invoke the Lord" has a cultic ring; it evokes a prayer formulation addressed to the Lord. The Pastor's words recall what Christians do when they come together as a worshiping assembly (see 1 Tim. 2:8–10). Timothy's conversion is not merely a personal experience; it is expressed in his participation in the liturgical life of the believing community.

His participation must be authentic (1 Tim. 2:8–10). He and all Christians must invoke the Lord with a pure heart (*ek katharas kardias*). In so doing, they are like Paul who, as his ancestors, served God with a clear conscience (*en kathara syneidēsei*, 1:3). The Pastor states that the worship of God that follows upon conversion must proceed from the depths of one's being; it must rise from the heart. In biblical anthropology the heart (*kardia*; in Hebrew, *lēb*) is the very core of the human being. The Pastor's idea that Timothy must be purified through an external ritual cleansing with water (2:21) and in the depths of his being (2:22) is similar to the Qumranite notion that initiation into the community involves both an external cleansing and an internal cleansing (1QS 3:4–9). The ideas that the Pastor expresses in 2:22 are traditional; at no other place in this missive does he use either "heart" or "invoke."

[23] Having exhorted Timothy to radical conversion and participation in the worshiping community, the Pastor formulates an exhortation that directly bears upon Timothy's leadership function. Just as he is to encourage the community not to engage in verbal warfare (*logomacheō*, 2:14), so he himself is to avoid foolish and stupid arguments (*mōras kai apaideutous zētēseis*). First Timothy 6:4 associates "arguments" with verbal warfare; Titus 3:9 associates "arguments" with genealogies. These kinds of arguments lead only to dissension within the community (see Titus 3:9–11). Such a state of affairs would be the antithesis of the peace that Timothy is to pursue (2:22).

[24–25a] If he is not to engage in quarrels (*machas*, a term used of military conflicts but also of athletic contests), how is the servant of the Lord to correct the errant members of a congregation? "Servant" (*doulos*, literally, "slave") is an appropriate epithet in this context. Timothy has been described as being in the company of those who call on the name of the lord (*kyrios*, 2:22). "Slave" and "lord" are correlative terms. A lord has slaves; slaves have their lord. If Timothy has a real Lord, then he is truly a slave. The expression "servant of the Lord" does not otherwise occur in the New Testament (see Jonah 1:9, LXX; Luke 1:38 and "man of God" in 1 Tim. 6:11). Paul did, however, identify himself as a servant of Christ (see, e.g., Rom. 1:1; Gal. 1:10). The salutation of the epistle to Titus describes Paul as a servant of God (Titus 1:1).

The servant of the Lord who endeavors to deal pastorally with those in error must be a person who is gentle, able to teach, and forbearing. Gentleness is not so much a personal quality as it is a pastoral quality, one that characterized

Paul's apostolic activity. It is a "style of teaching and of apostolic authority, without sharpness or bitterness arising from overzealousness" (*TLNT* 2.174). When the Pastor states that gentleness is be to extended to all, he intimates the difficulty experienced by a leader who must deal with people in error. Even with those in error, the good pastor, the servant of the Lord, must be gentle. He must also be able to teach. This ability is one that overseers should also possess (1 Tim. 3:2). If the servant of the Lord is to teach others, he must be well taught himself, particularly with regard to the Scriptures (3:14–17). Finally, the servant of God must be patient. The Pastor has come up with a new word to describe the kind of patience that he expects Timothy to have. Rather than use the common terminology, "patience" (*makrothymia*; see 3:10; 4:2), he has coined a new word, *anexikakon*, literally, "bearing evil" (*anechomai* + *kakon*). The task at hand is the correction of opponents in a kind and mild manner (*en prautēti*). The Pastor uses a double compound participle (*antidiatithemenous*; see *TLNT* 1.128–30, 128) to describe the complex task of correcting opponents.

[25b–26] The gentleness of the servant of the Lord may provide God with a window of opportunity, as it were, to lead the opponents to repentance. It may be (*mēpote*, "perhaps") that God will give them the gift of repentance (*dōē autois . . . metanoian*, literally, "give them repentance"; see Acts 5:31; 11:18). Repentance is a gift of God. It is God who hardens the heart and God who has mercy; it is God who withholds or gives the gift of repentance. "Repentance" (*metanoia*) is literally a "change of mind." Speaking about repentance as a change of mind is to speak of repentance from a Hellenistic point of view. The Greek Bible and the New Testament use the term "repentance" and its cognates to translate biblical ideas expressed by the Hebrew *šûb* and its cognates. That verb means to "turn around," "change directions," "reorient oneself." Used in a religious sense, the Hebrew term means a total reorientation of one's life, classically a turning to the one true God from idol worship (see 1 Thess. 1:9).

The gift of repentance that God might give to the opponents is like the conversion to which Timothy has been urged (2:22). Repentance and conversion have a positive and a negative facet. The terms represent a turning from and a turning to (see 1 Thess. 1:9). The Pastor describes the potential repentance of the opponents in positive terms as a turning to the "full knowledge of truth" (*epignōsin alētheias*), the technical term used in the Pastorals to designate the community's understanding of the truth (see 3:7; 1 Tim. 2:4; Titus 1:1; see pp. 97–98).

Repentance also entails a turning from. As the Pastor describes this, he says that the opponents might come to their right senses and escape from the devil's trap. "Come to their right senses" (*ananēpsōsin*) is literally "to become sober again" [*ana-nēphō*]. Used figuratively in Hellenistic literature, it indicates the process of repentance. Commenting on the story of Noah, temporarily without virtue because of his drunkenness (Gen. 9:21), Philo writes, "he becomes sober again [*ananēphei*], that is to say, he repents [*metanoei*] and recovers as from an illness" (*Allegorical Interpretation* 2.60). Philo's comment is virtually a definition of the figurative sense of the verb "to come to one's right senses." Philo's comment is also a good example of the way contemporary moralists often used the metaphor of physical health to describe a person's moral well-being. The Pastor frequently makes use of comparable language (see 1:13; 4:3; 1 Tim. 1:10; 6:3; Titus 1:9, 13; 2:1, 2, 8). Second Timothy 3:8 speaks of those who undermine the faith as people with rotting minds; 1 Tim. 6:5 describes heterodox teachers as people who are out of their minds.

The register of the Pastor's discourse changes as he writes about the devil's trap. Hygienic language is the language of Hellenistic moral discourse; "the devil's trap" is the language of Jewish apocalyptic circles. The Pastor portrays the opponents prior to their possible conversion as having been trapped (*ek tēs tou diabolou pagidos*) and captured by the devil (*ezōgrēmenoi hyp'autou*). His language is similar to that of the Dead Sea Scrolls that speak of the snares of Belial (CD 4:15) or the snares of the pit (1QH 3:26; see 1QH 4:12). For the Qumranites, the snares are fornication, wealth, and the profanation of the sanctuary. The word used as Qumran, *měṣûdâ*, "snare," can be translated into Greek as *pagis*, "trap" (see Ps. 66:11[65:11 LXX]), the word used by the Pastor in 2:26. Qumran's use of sexual and purification language in the enumeration of the traps of Belial is similar to that used by the Pastor to describe the repentance of Timothy in 2:21–22.

The Pastor enhances his imagery by describing the opponents as having been captured by the devil. They were trapped and captured (*ezōgrēmenoi*). This verb, generally used in reference to war or hunting, literally means "to be taken alive" (*zōon-agreō*; see *TLNT* 2.161–63). It includes the idea of not being killed. In war some of the enemy are killed; others are taken prisoner, degraded, and enslaved. Trapped by the devil, the opponents have become his slaves, forced to do his will. It may be interesting to note that the term "will" (*thelēma*) is used only twice in the Pastoral Epistles, here to designate the will of the devil and in 1:1 to designate the will of God. The will of the devil is in sharp contrast with the will of God.

God's gift of repentance is in fact a kind of redemption; it is liberation from enslavement to the devil. The convert is no longer a slave of the devil (*doulos tou diabolou*); he or she is a slave of the Lord (*doulos tou kyriou*; see 2:24). In the process of repentance, one's allegiance is transferred from the devil to the Lord. The Dead Sea Scrolls use similar ideas to describe the initiation of a neophyte into the community: "All those who enter into the order of the community, shall enter into the covenant before God to act according to everything which he has commanded; they must not turn back from following after Him because of any terror or dread, affliction or agony during the reign of Belial" (1QS 1:16–18).

First Timothy 3:6–7 also suggests that a new convert is free from the snare of the devil. Explaining why an overseer should not be a new convert, the Pastor writes that he must not be "a neophyte so that he be not puffed up and fall into the devil's judgment. He should have good testimony from outsiders so that he not fall into censure and the devil's trap [*pagida tou diabolou*]" (1 Tim. 3:6–7). The Dead Sea Scrolls speaks about the snares of Belial; 1 Tim. 3:7 and 2 Tim. 2:26 speak about the devil's trap. Although the terminology is different, the ideas are similar.

The Final Times
2 Timothy 3:1–9

In the classic apocalyptic worldview, whether Jewish or Christian, the times just prior to the appearance of God as king will be characterized by the onslaught of terrible evils. The "little apocalypse" of Mark's Gospel speaks of a cosmic cataclysm and of suffering such as has not been seen since the time of creation (Mark 13:19–25). The book of Revelation speaks of war, famine, and pestilence (6:3–8) and of cosmic upheaval (8:6–13). The Pastor's vision of history has been partially formed by this apocalyptic tradition. He portrays the penultimate times not, however, as times of cosmic upheaval or of a disturbance of "nature" but as a time of moral upheaval, where there will be all sorts of evil characters who will cause difficulties for God's people.

To describe the evil of the end times, the Pastor has employed a well-known Hellenistic literary form, a list of vices (see p. 55). His long list identifies all sorts of misdeeds. The cumulative effect of the list is a description of the end times as times when moral evil will abound in virtually all its forms. The list has been compiled with some literary artistry. Nine of the eighteen vices are designated by a Greek word that begins with a privative alpha. People will appear who are impostors, disobedient, ingrates, unholy, heartless, implacable, lacking in self-control, uncivilized, and haters of good (*a-lazones, a-peitheis, a-charistoi, an-[h]osioi, a-storgoi, a-spoudoi, a-krateis, an-[h]ēmeroi, a-philagathoi*). The use of the privative alpha indicates that these end-time malefactors will lack the qualities to which each of these vices is opposed. The end-time evildoers are no good and will be up to no good.

Another striking stylistic feature of the Pastor's list is his use of the root *phil*, "love." His list begins and ends with a pair of words that employ this root: "People will be lovers of self, lovers of money, . . . lovers of pleasure rather than lovers of God" (*philautoi, philargyroi, philēdonoi . . . philotheoi*). Another word with the prefix *phil-* appears in the middle of the list, "haters of good" (*a-phil-agathoi*), that is, people who do not love the good. The term may have been coined by the Pastor or by someone in his circle to sum up the attitude of the evildoers. They simply do not love what is good.

The Pastor's use of these *phil-* words creates important contrasts. By placing "lovers of self" at the beginning of his list and "lovers of God" at the end, the Pastor creates a strong antithesis between a selfish egotist and a person whose life is dictated by the love of God (see Philo, *Abel and Cain* 3; *Worse Attacks the Better* 32; *Flight* 81; *Genesis* 1.60). Juxtaposing "lovers of money" with "lovers of self," the Pastor reflects an idea that is prevalent in his circles— namely, that the love of money is a root of all kinds of evil (see 1 Tim. 6:10). Egotism manifests itself in greed. The Pastor brings his list to its conclusion with the contrast between "lovers of pleasure" and "lovers of God." At this point the Pastor seems to be reflecting the dominant Stoic ethic of his day— see, for example, Dio Chrysostom, *Discourses* 4.115, which mentions "lovers of pleasure" (*philēdonoi*) as people enslaved to delusion—but puts this ethical concern into a religious context. Ultimately, all vice is a matter of not loving God.

Lest his readers think that these various vices describe what "others" will do, the Pastor reminds those readers that his list of vices also has a hortatory purpose. Avoid these vices, he says to his readers before developing his thought any further. The Pastor's description of the end times continues with a graphic description of the false teachers who will arise in the final times. He describes them as stealthily creeping into people's houses and leading astray those who are weak. In this regard they are like Jannes and Jambres, the legendary court magicians of Pharaoh who opposed Moses. The Pastor tells his readers that such false teachers are out of their minds. In the coming eschaton they will be revealed for who they are.

3:1 Know[a] this, that in the final days difficult times will occur. 2 For people will be lovers of self, lovers of money, impostors, arrogant, defamers, disobedient to parents, ingrates, unholy, 3 heartless, implacable, slanderers, lacking in self-control, uncivilized, haters of good, 4 traitors, reckless, conceited, lovers of pleasure rather than lovers of God, 5 having the appearance of godliness while denying its power. Avoid them! 6 For among them are those who enter houses and captivate silly little women, overwhelmed by sins and led by passions[b] of various sorts, 7 always learning, and yet never able to arrive at the full knowledge of truth. 8 Just as Jannes and Jambres[c] opposed Moses, so also these people oppose the truth. They are people whose minds are rotted, unqualified with regard to the faith. 9 They will progress no further for, as happened to them, their folly will be quite visible to all.

a. A few ancient manuscripts read the exhortation in the plural rather than the singular.

b. A few manuscripts, along with the Syriac Harklean version, add "and pleasures" (*kai hedonais*), presumably under the influence of Titus 3:3.

c. Some Western witnesses have "Mambres" (e.g., F, G, vg, it, Cyprian, Ambrosiaster, Augustine). In rabbinic writings, "Mambres" (see *b. Menah.* 85a; *Exod. Rab.* 7:11) is one of four attested forms of the name "Jambres" (*TDNT* 3.192–93).

[3:1] The Pastor continues his exhortation to Timothy with an instruction on the final times. It opens with a disclosure formula, "know this" (*touto de ginōske*), not otherwise used in the epistle. The formula is similar to other hortatory formulae with verbs in the imperative second person singular, which were used to introduce the earlier exhortations (2:1, 8, 14, 22). Timothy is to know that the conditions in which he, Paul's designated successor (1:2, 6; 2:1), will be exercising his ministry are those of the approaching final times (see 1 Tim. 4:1–3).

The phrase "in the final times" (*en eschatais hēmerais*, "in the last days") appears in the well-known oracle of Joel cited in Acts 2:17 (see Joel 3:1–5 [LXX]). The LXX reads, "after these things" (*meta tauta*), but Luke has replaced this phrase with "in the last days" when he cites the biblical passage to describe the Christian Pentecost. The biblical oracle speaks of signs and portents that will occur in a remote, almost mythic future.[46] The oracle describes the gift of the Spirit, God's vital force, to those who prophesy and the cosmic portents that will herald the coming great and terrible day of the Lord.

The Pastor, like Joel, distinguishes between "the last days" (*en eschatais hēmerais*) and "that day" (*en ekeinē tē hēmera*, 1:18; 4:8), the day of the Lord, the day when the Lord will appear as the just judge. This is a kind of two-stage eschatology. The final times culminate on that day. Prior to "that day" are "those days," the penultimate period of the eschatological era. In those days dangerous circumstances will arise (see *TLNT* 3.494–95). Those will be perilous times for the household of God, the church. It will be beset by people who will harm the faithful (see 2:18b) with their cruelty, violence, and aggressiveness.

[2–5] The Pastor describes what people will be like in those days by using a list of vices (see *T. Levi* 17:11). Paul's letters contain six such lists (Rom. 1:29–31; 13:13; 1 Cor. 5:10–11; 6:9–10; 2 Cor. 12:20–21; Gal. 5:19–21). The Pastor's list of eighteen vices is the second-longest list in the New Testament, exceeded in length only by the twenty-one vices in Romans 1. Long enough to characterize the evildoers of the final times, the Pastor's list is far shorter than Philo's list of 146 vices (*Abel and Cain* 32).

No single person is presumed to have each and every one of the eighteen vices. The literary genre is such that it conveys its point by an accumulation of terms rather than by using terms whose definitions are clearly distinct from one another. The global impression is what is important. The Pastor wants to con-

46. See James L. Crenshaw, *Joel,* AB 24C (New York: Doubleday, 1995), 164, 167.

vey the idea that the final times will be difficult times for the church. Accordingly, his list employs terms that indicate various forms of asocial and antisocial behavior.

The Pastor begins by saying that the people of those days will be lovers of self (*philautoi*), crass egocentrists. This vice is one that contemporary ethicists may describe as the root of all evil, but the Pastor and his contemporaries lacked such ethical sophistication. The second vice on the list is the love of money (*philargyria*; see Luke 16:14; Pol. *Phil.* 4:3), the vice that was thought to be a source of many evils (see 1 Tim. 6:10).

Among the people of those days, some will be impostors (*alazones*, a term that appears on Philo's long list of vices; see also Rom. 1:30). They will be wolves in sheep's clothing, ready to lead God's people astray. Some will be arrogant (*hyperēphanoi*), the kind of persons to whom God himself is opposed (see Prov. 3:34; Jas. 4:6; 1 Pet. 5:5). Others will defame, disparage, and ridicule (*blasphēmoi*). "Blasphemy" is a term that appears in many Hellenistic lists of vices as a general description of antisocial behavior. Its root (*blasphēm-*) is often used in the New Testament to describe those who ridicule the name of God.

In the final days will also appear people who are disobedient to their parents (*goneusin apeitheis*). This is not the failure of the child who says no to his or her parents; it is the rebellion of the adult who refuses to obey the head of the household. The description of the end-time evildoers as disobedient begins a series of five vices characterized by alliteration. Each begins with a privative alpha. The evildoers are disobedient, ingrates, unholy, heartless, and implacable (*a-peitheis, a-charistoi, an-[h]osioi, a-storgoi,* and *a-spondoi*). They lack docility, graciousness, holiness, affection, and a willingness to make peace (*pithanos,*[47] *charis, hosiotēs, storgē, spondē*). Such words, both the vices and their antonyms,[48] are rarely used in the New Testament. The infrequency of the use of these words in the New Testament suggests that the Pastor has appropriated the common coin of Hellenistic moralists to compose his list.

The lack of graciousness (*acharistoi*) that characterizes end-time evildoers contrasts them with God, whose overwhelmingly generous beneficence is celebrated throughout the biblical tradition. When the Pastor describes these persons

47. The word *peithos* is a late koine form of *pithanos*.
48. Among these words the adjective "disobedient" appears the most frequently in the New Testament, six times in all, including four times in a list of vices (3:2; Titus 1:16; 3:3; Rom. 1:30). "Unholy" and "heartless" are each found on another vice list (see 1 Tim. 1:9; Rom. 1:31). "Ingrates" is contrasted with "gracious" (*chrēstos*) in Luke 6:35. "Implacable" does not occur elsewhere in the New Testament. "Graciousness" or "grace" (*charis*) is often used in Paul's writing, but the other words that describe the qualities these evildoers lack are also similarly of infrequent occurrence in the New Testament. "Affection," "willingness to make peace," and probably "docility"—the word appears as a disputed reading in 1 Cor. 2:4—are used just one time; "holiness" only twice (Luke 1:75; Eph. 4:24).

as unholy (*anosioi*), he is indicating that they are not in a right relationship with God. "Holiness" is a quality that is often cited in the writings of Hellenistic Jewish authors who frequently pair it with the term "justice" (*dikaiosynē*). Philo, for example, writes that "the nature which is pious is also kindly, and the same person will exhibit both qualities, holiness to God and justice to men" (*hosiotēs men pros theon, diakaiosynē de pros anthrōpous, Abraham* 208; see also Wis. 9:3; Josephus, *Ant.* 19.6.3 §300; 1 Thess. 2:10; *1 Clem.* 48:4).

The evildoers are lacking in affection, the kind of affection that normally binds parents and children. Since the Pastor has already spoken about disobedience, he may have specifically wanted to suggest that some of the evildoers even lacked affection for their children.[49] Moreover, some of the evildoers are implacable (*a-spondoi*). A *spondē* was a libation, an offering of wine poured out to the gods. Such offerings were frequently made prior to the banquets celebrating a truce. Hence, the term came to be used of the truce itself. Those who are implacable are basically unwilling to make peace with others.

The list of evildoers whose presence will be a sign of the impending end time continues as the Pastor speaks of slanderers, the intemperate, the uncivilized, and haters of good. "Slanderers," the substantivized adjective *diabolos*, is a term that frequently appears on lists of vices, as it does in Philo's classic list of 146 vices. In the New Testament it appears on three such lists, all in the Pastoral Epistles (1 Tim. 3:11; 2 Tim. 3:3; Titus 2:3). The term is more commonly used in the New Testament to designate the slanderer beyond all others, the devil.

After mentioning slanderers, the Pastor resumes his list with an additional three vices with a privative alpha: *a-krateis, an-[h]ēmeroi,* and *a-philagathoi,* "lacking in self-control," "uncivilized," and "haters of good." As was the case with the previous series of alpha privatives, the reader meets unfamiliar words. None of these three terms are used elsewhere in the New Testament. Nor do they appear on Philo's list of 146 vices. The terms describe persons who lack power, gentleness, and a love for the good, respectively, *kratos, hēmerotēs,* and *philagathon.* To lack power is not so much to be weak as to lack self-control. Classic authors used the adjective to describe those who could not contain their anger (Thucydides), their tongue (Aeschylus), or their love for wine (Xenophon, Aristotle). "Uncivilized" (*anēmeroi*) is a term that is used of wild and savage animals or of uncultivated plants that grow wildly. Used derogatorily of humans, it describes people who lack common politeness and gentleness, people who act as if they are not civilized. Those who lack any love for the good would be those whom contemporary authors might describe as having no orientation whatsoever toward the moral good.

---

49. Since "heartless" (*astorgoi*) appears in the New Testament only in lists of vices (3:3; Rom 1:31), the modern reader cannot be sure of the precise nuance intended by the author.

The next pair of vices on the Pastor's list are also joined by alliteration. They are *pro-dotai* and *pro-peteis*, "traitors" and "the reckless." Neither of these terms appears on another New Testament vice list, nor do they appear on Philo's list in *Abel and Cain*. They do, however, appear in Luke-Acts. The former describes Judas (Luke 6:16) and those Jewish leaders who were responsible for Jesus' death (Acts 7:52). "Reckless" (see Acts 19:36) appears frequently in philosophical and biographical literature to describe those who act impulsively and take wild chances, whose frenzy results in unjust actions (see *TLNT* 3.189–90).

The next group on the Pastor's list are the "conceited" (*tetyphōmenoi*, literally, "those surrounded by smoke"). The idea underlying the metaphor, if not the imagery, is similar to ideas expressed by Paul in 1 Corinthians. He used the verb *physioō*, "to puff up [with pride]," to describe those whose attitude was disruptive of good order in the community (1 Cor. 4:6, 18, 19; 5:2; 8:1; 13:4). The Pastor similarly uses the verb *typhoomai*, "to be surrounded by smoke," metaphorically to describe people whose ambition and vainglory leads them to be deluded (see 1 Tim. 3:6; 6:4). Philo also used the term with this metaphorical meaning, especially in describing an orator who is so caught up in the art of his rhetoric that he is unable to perceive the truth. For Philo, "pride" (*typhos*)[50] is a source of many kinds of evil, even contempt for divine realities (see *Decalogue* 4–6).

The name of the Egyptian god Typhon is derived from the verb *typhoomai*. Greek mythology speaks of Typhon, a many-headed (often a hundred snake heads) fiery monster who threatened the supremacy of Zeus. He was slain by a bolt of thunder and buried under Mount Etna. Typhon appears as a wicked god, the son of Gaia and Tartarus, in some Greek myths. This evil god is often considered to be the Greek equivalent of the Egyptian god Seth.

Finally, the Pastor notes, there will appear in those awful end times people who are "lovers of pleasure rather than lovers of God" (*philēdonoi mallon hē philotheoi*), contrasting terms that are used only here in the New Testament. Philosophic moralists of the Pastor's times considered "pleasure" (*hēdonē*; see Titus 3:3; and p. 246 note b), especially in the sense of sensory pleasures or lust, to be a vice, the most shameful passion (see Philo *Special Laws* 2.135). It was the source of many other vices (see Philo, *Allegorical Interpretation* 2.106–8; 3.113). It is likely that the Pastor used the term "pleasure-lovers" to describe people who were prone to various forms of sexual misdeeds. The vice that appears most often on lists of vices in the New Testament is *porneia*,[51]

50. Philo considered the golden calf (see Exod. 32:1–20; 1 Kgs. 12:28–33) to be a symbol of the Egyptian god Typhon. For him, the calf symbolized Egyptian folly (see *Drunkenness* 95; *Flight* 90; *Special Laws* 1.79; 3.125).

51. The term is not used in any of the Pastoral Epistles.

sexual immorality. Neither this vice nor any specific sexual vice, adultery for example, appears on the Pastor's list. This absence and the moralists' understanding of "pleasure" suggest that the term "lovers of pleasure" really means those who pursue illicit sexual pleasure.

The Pastor's vice list concludes with a contrastive reference to those who love God, the God-lovers (*philotheoi*). The term goes back to the time of Aristotle, who used it to describe the religious or the pious (*Rhetoric* 2.17.6). Reserving this term until the end of his list, the Pastor suggests that all forms of vice are inconsistent with the love of God, that is, an *authentic* love of God as he explains in verse 5. He uses a phrase with contrasting participles, "having" (*echontes*) and "denying" (*ērnēmenoi*), to distinguish a sham religiosity from the kind of love of God that imparts a directive force to one's life.

The Pastor brings his list of vices to a conclusion with a summary exhortation: "Avoid them!" His readers live in the difficult final times. They must nonetheless "turn away from" (*apo-trepou*) all the vices that the Pastor has just listed. God-lovers are to be engaged in a kind of ongoing conversion; they must constantly turn from a love of themselves and the various vices to which they had been prone prior to their acceptance of the full knowledge of truth with its concomitant demand for all good works (see 3:7, 17; 2:21).

[6–7] It is bad enough that there are people living in the final times who can be described by any of the terms that the Pastor has just rehearsed for his readers. It is even worse that some of those people prey on the weakness of some members of the community and undermine their faith. They are as bad as Jannes and Jambres of old who undermined the work of Moses. They "enter houses and captivate silly little women." This is a dramatic image of the false teachers of the end times. The idea that false teachers and false prophets will appear in the final times is characteristic of early Christian apocalyptic thought (see Matt. 24:23–26; Mark 13:21–22). Given the ecclesial use of household language in the Pastoral Epistles (e.g., 2:20–21), the description is virtually a parable about the church.

The Pastor's choice of a verb, *hoi endynontes*[52] instead of the common *hoi eiserchomenoi*, "enter," probably suggests a stealthy entrance (perhaps, as in BDF 100, "creeping in"). Having entered the houses of these silly little women, the evildoers easily capture them (*aichmalōtizontes*; see Luke 21:24; Rom. 7:23). The Pastor's imagery is not of women being kidnapped from their homes; it is of their becoming seduced by teaching that deviates from "the full knowledge of truth," the norm of Christian faith. Morally, emotionally, and intellectually weak, the silly little women of the Pastor's caricature are easily led astray by the malefactors of the final times.

---

52. An alternative form of the verb, *endyō*, is sometimes used with the meaning "to put on," as one would put on clothes.

The language used by the Pastor to describe the harm that the evildoers will wreak on the house of God is a byproduct of the cultural prejudices of the time. Wanting to show that evildoers prey on the weak and unsuspecting, he says that they will lead astray "silly little women" (*gynaikaria*, a diminutive of *gynē*, "woman"; see BAGD 168). This derogatory term appears only here in the New Testament. It is, however, one of several words derived from the root *gyn-* that were used in derogatory fashion by Epictetus, the first-century moralist, and other writers of the day.

The Pastor lists three stereotypical characteristics to spell out what he means by "silly little women." Silly little women, he says, are burdened by sin,[53] prone to passion, and never really intelligent (see *T. Reub.* 5:1–7; Philo, *Genesis* 1.33, 46). He says that the silly little women on whom evildoers prey and about whom he writes are overwhelmed by sin. Unlike those who really love God, they are dominated by their passions. Their several passions—*poikilais* has connotations of both plurality and variety—lead them astray. True, they can learn (see 1 Tim. 2:11–12) and they can be taught, but, says the Pastor, they are never able (*mēdepote . . . dynamena*) to arrive at the "full knowledge of truth" (*epignōsin alētheias*; see 2:25), the gospel message as it was understood by the members of the Pastor's community. People who are afflicted with sin and passion are unable to reach this level of insight into the gospel message.

The cultural prejudice reflected in the Pastor's words about silly little women is a classic topos in the writings of Hellenistic moralists. The prejudice was shared by Philo, for whom courage and intellect are masculine and susceptibility to passions and the senses are feminine. In his allegorical interpretation of the biblical story of creation, Adam is a symbol of the mind, Eve of the body and the senses (see *Allegorical Interpretation* 3.49–50). A radical expression of this prejudice is found in the final logion of the Coptic *Gospel of Thomas* (*Gos. Thom.* 114). In response to Simon Peter's objection that Mary Magdalene is not worthy of life, Jesus is said to respond, "Lo, I shall lead her, so that I may make her a male, that she too may become a living spirit, resembling you males. For every woman who makes herself a male will enter the kingdom of heaven."

[8–9] One of the features of the apocalyptic genre is its reference to the past as somehow providing a key to the future. The Markan apocalypse, for example, makes reference to the "desolating sacrilege" (Mark 13:14). The expression comes from Dan. 9:27; 11:31; 12:11, where it alludes to the pagan altar that Antiochus Epiphanes built over the altar of burnt offerings in 168 B.C.E.

To illustrate the malevolence of those final-time agents who undermine the faith, the Pastor cites Jannes and Jambres. According to a pre-Christian rabbinic tradition, Jannes and Jambres (see p. 246, note c) were Egyptian magicians who

---

53. This is the only time that the word "sin" (*hamartiais*, a plural form), is used in 2 Timothy. On the related verb, see note 41.

vied with Moses and Aaron in the contest of the plagues before the exodus (see Exod. 7:11–8:19). They continued to oppose Moses and Aaron even after the wizards' defeat (Exod. 8:18). They are said to have used their magical arts in an effort to hinder the work of Moses and Aaron at the time of Israel's passage through the Red (Reed) Sea. It is they who are said to have instigated the apostasy of Israel in the incident of the golden calf (Exod. 32:1–20).

Mention of Jannes and Jambres appears in non-Jewish as well as Jewish sources. The church fathers often mention these wizards. At some point in time the tradition about them was written down in what Origen calls the *Book of Jannes and Jambres* ([Mambres]; see *Celsus* 41.51, PG 11:1111–12; *Commentary on Matthew* §117, PG 13:1769). The Gelasian Decree describes this as a confession (*poenitentia*, see *Decretum*, PL 59:163). Its extant fragments (Greek and Latin) show the influence of both the Septuagint and of Christianity. Since the "confession" is a Christian genre, decidedly not a Jewish one, it is generally considered that the *Book of Jannes and Jambres* is a Christian text, although some scholars consider that its origins are pre-Christian.

The false prophets of the end times oppose the truth just as Jannes and Jambres had opposed God's messengers at the decisive moment in the history of Israel's salvation. Later the Pastor will remind his readers that Alexander, the wicked coppersmith, had similarly opposed Paul (4:14). The difficulties caused by false teachers that the Pastor's readers are encountering are nothing new. In every moment of history, in the pre-Pauline era, at the time of Paul, and in the post-Pauline era, there are those who oppose the word of God. The Pastor's readers are to find strength and consolation in this history. Citing examples as he does, the Pastor encourages his community according to the canons of classical rhetoric. Examples, particularly examples drawn from history, were considered to be a powerful buttress for an argument based on reason.

The Pastor says that the opponents who were troubling the weaker members of his community were like Jannes and Jambres in opposing the truth (*anthistantai tē alētheia*), that is, the truth of which the members have the full knowledge (*epignōsis alētheias*, 2:25; 3:7). The false teachers are described as people whose minds are thoroughly corrupt (*anthrōpoi katephtharmenoi*[54] *ton noun*) and who are therefore incapable of attaining the truth, let alone teaching it (3:7). With minds that are thoroughly ravaged, they are simply incapable of knowing and instructing the truth. Spicq notes that today we would speak of them as people who had lost their minds (see *TLNT* 2.279).

These people cannot teach the truth. They are "unqualified" (*a-dokimos*) with regard to the faith, that is, the faith that is to be believed. In its proper and technical sense, the adjective suggests that someone or something is not up to

---

54. This is an intensive form of the verb *phtheirō*, "to corrupt," used eight times in the New Testament.

par; he or she does not meet acceptable standards (see the use of *dokimos* in 2:15). Etymologically, the term generally implies a judgment (*doki-*) on the part of appropriate authority. Some runners are not qualified to run the final heat; only some citizens are judged qualified to hold public office, and so forth. The term was also used in a metaphorical sense to describe a person who was deemed to be disreputable and reprobate (see Titus 1:16). Thus, the Pastor's words in 3:8 could be taken to mean that the false teachers are disreputable with regard to the faith (*adokimoi peri tēn pistin*). Given the Pastor's graphic description of the corruption of the minds of the false prophets, it is probable that he intends to portray these subverters of the faith of the weak as people who are simply unqualified with regard to the content of faith.

They have gone as far as they can go. Epictetus says that "it is absurd that someone will make progress [*prokopsei*] in anything about which he has not learned" (*Discourses* 2.17.4). Like other Stoics, Epictetus used the verb "to progress" to describe moral and intellectual growth. From this perspective, the Pastor is suggesting that the false teachers' growth will be stunted with regard to the intellectual and ethical aspects of the faith. The eschatological aspect of the pericope provides for another understanding of the Pastor's words: The stealthy evildoers are about to go as far as they can go; they will be stopped.

In the eschaton, these false teachers will be revealed for who and what they are (see, e.g., 1 Cor 4:5); their folly will be plain enough for everyone to see. The word *anoia*, "folly," usually means ignorance, but in the light of what the Pastor has just said about the condition of the false teachers' minds, it must be taken in the sense of mindlessness (*a-noia*, "without a mind"), thus, "folly." With "as happened to them" the Pastor expresses his conviction that the fate that awaits the false teachers is no less certain than the legendary fate of Jannes and Jambres. Later he will tell his readers that Paul himself expected that the eschatological Lord would pay back the infamous Alexander for his misdeeds, especially for his opposition to Paul's preaching (4:14).

Final Exhortation
2 Timothy 3:10–17

In the immediately preceding pericope, the Pastor used the literary form of a catalog of vices to illustrate the evil that would infect his community in the final times (3:1–9, esp. vv. 2–4). As he begins his final exhortation, the Pastor uses another catalog to paint a picture of the apostle that can serve as a model for Timothy to imitate. The list given in verses 10–11 is a kind of *Mischform*. It can be read both as the juxtaposition of a seven-item catalog of virtues and as a circumstantial catalog with three items. Mention of the apostle's steadfastness

(v. 10) provides a transition between the Pastor's topical eulogy and his recalling some historical circumstances that beset the apostle during the course of his ministry.

The way in which the Pastor speaks of the apostle's suffering continues to evoke the apocalyptic idea that evil will abound in the final times (3:1). Those are times when there will be evil and more evil. Paul had been persecuted. So too will those who live in the final times be persecuted, that is, if they desire to live piously in Christ Jesus. The tradition that those who live their lives in accordance with the gospel message will be persecuted derives from the teaching of Jesus himself (see Luke 6:22; Matt. 5:11; cf. Matt. 5:10; 1 Pet. 4:14), but the motif that the "good guys" will suffer at the end time is a stock motif in apocalyptic literature.

Apocalyptic literature, both Jewish and Christian, is replete with allusions to and quotations of the Scriptures. The Pastor's epistle is not an expression of the apocalyptic genre per se. Nonetheless, the Pastor has made fruitful use of apocalyptic motifs (2:9–12; 3:1–9). Thus, it is not surprising that when the Pastor exhorts Timothy to stand fast in what he has learned, he speaks especially about the Scriptures. The Pastor writes that the Scriptures, which Timothy learned in his early childhood, are inspired and useful in every respect for the man or woman who truly belongs to God. Equipped with these Scriptures, Timothy is qualified for his work (2:15).

3:10 You have closely followed my teaching, my way of life, my purpose, my faith, my patience, my love, my steadfastness, 11 my persecutions,[a] and my suffering the things that happened to me in Antioch, Iconium, and Lystra. Such persecutions I endured! But the Lord delivered me from all of them. 12 Indeed, all who desire to live in godly fashion in Christ Jesus will be persecuted. 13 Evil people and swindlers will get worse, leading astray and being led astray.

14 As for you, continue in what you have learned, what you have acquired in faith, conscious of those from whom you have learned,[b] 15 and that from your infancy you have known the sacred writings, which are capable of instructing you with regard to salvation through faith in Christ Jesus. 16 All Scripture is inspired by God and[c] suitable for teaching, for conviction, for correction, and for training in righteousness, 17 so that the person who belongs to God is ready and thoroughly prepared for every good work.

a. Verses 10–11 are a single sentence in Greek.

b. The plural "by whom" (*para tinōn*) is well attested, but a singular form, *para tinos*, appears in many ancient versions as well as in the Byzantine and lectionary manuscript traditions. A scribal tendency to enhance the portrait of Paul as the instructor par excellence of Timothy is a probable cause of the switch to the singular.

c. Several ancient translations and various Fathers omit the "and" (*kai*). The sentence is elliptical; the verb "to be" is implied. If "and" was present in the text, two attributes are made of Scripture—inspiration and utility. If "and" was not present in the text, it would be possible to read the verse as if it meant that inspired Scripture is useful. Instead of being affirmed, inspiration would be presumed.

[3:10–11] Timothy stands in contrast to the malicious people of the final days; he is said to have closely followed various aspects of the apostle's "career." The verb (*parekolouthēsas*; see MM 3877) evokes Timothy's familiarity with the qualities and circumstances indicated by the Pastor. It has, nonetheless, a studied nuance and suggests close attention and careful study (see 1 Tim. 4:6; Luke 1:3). Epictetus uses the term to describe one who closely follows an argument or philosophic demonstration (*parakolouthein logō de apodeixei, Discourses* 1.7.33; 2.24.29).

What is it in Paul's life that Timothy is presumed to have paid such careful attention to? The list that follows provides the answer. First and foremost, Timothy is presumed to have closely followed the apostle's teaching. More than two-thirds of the New Testament's uses of the term "teaching" (*didaskalia*) are found in the Pastoral Epistles. Singular "teaching" is virtually a technical term for "apostolic or Christian teaching as a whole" (*EDNT* 1.316–17). The Pastoral Epistles are consistent in distinguishing between "teaching" (*didaskalia*) in the singular, that is, authentic teaching, and "teachings" (*didaskaliai*) in the plural, that is, false teachings. "Teaching" is authentic teaching mediated by the apostle Paul himself. Throughout the epistle, the Pastor has shown just how much and how faithfully Timothy has learned from Paul (see 1:13–14; 2:2, 8–9, 11–13). Thus, he can write in 3:10 that it is Paul's teaching, "my teaching," that Timothy has followed.

Closely related to the idea of Timothy's following Paul's teaching is the notion that he has closely followed Paul's way of life. The term *agōgē*, "way of life" (see *1 Clem.* 47:6; 48:1), sometimes used in reference to a person's training or reputation, suggests that a characteristic lifestyle has been adopted because someone has imitated a teacher or master. Hellenists used the word "purpose" (*prothesis*) as a designation for a statement of purpose, the thesis to be demonstrated. Its basic sense is, however, simply "purpose." Paul's purpose would have been one with God's purpose in choosing him for the work of the apostolate (1:9).

The triad "my teaching, my way of life, my purpose" means that Timothy was quite familiar with what Paul had taught, how he taught it, and why he taught as he did. In effect, Timothy was familiar with Paul's faith (*pistei*). Since the connotation of "faith" is objective (*fides quae*),[55] the Pastor is affirming that

55. The sequence of faith, patience, love, and steadfastness seems to be derived from the Pauline triad of faith, love, and steadfastness (or hope). To the extent that the legacy of this triad impinges on the Pastor's words, the relational dimension of faith cannot be excluded from the Pastor's understanding of Paul's faith.

Timothy was familiar with the content of Paul's faith, of which the Pastoral Epistles' "trustworthy sayings" are so many summaries (2:11; 1 Tim. 1:15; 3:1; 4:9; Titus 3:8). The Pastorals repeatedly affirm that belief is accompanied by action, "good works" being a phrase often used to describe the activity that follows upon belief. Paul's "godliness" (see Excursus 4) is expressed in his faith as well as in his patience, love, and steadfastness.

The threesome identifies the virtues of the apostle engaged in the work of teaching. All three qualities appear in the various catalogs of virtues of Hellenistic authors. "Patience" (*makrothymia*) is found in the New Testament on such lists in 3:10, in Paul (2 Cor. 6:6; Gal. 5:22; 1 Thess. 5:14), and in the other deuteropauline literature (Eph. 4:2; Col. 1:11; 3:12). Essentially the term designates forbearance, an ability to control one's anger. Second Timothy 3:10 suggests that it is a quality to be had by those who would teach, and Eph. 4:2 suggests that such patience is a result of love.

"Love" (*agapē*) is the epitome of Christian virtue (1 Corinthians 13), the empowering gift of the Spirit (Rom. 5:5). Paul frequently expressed his love for those to whom he preached the gospel. Only one of his extant letters has a postscript after the final greeting. It is "my love be with all of you in Christ Jesus" (1 Cor. 16:24). He addressed the Corinthians as his beloved siblings (1 Cor. 4:14; 10:14; 15:58; 2 Cor. 7:1; 12:19; see Phil. 2:12; 4:1; 1 Thess. 2:8; Phlm. 1, 16). With the exception of his scolding letter to the churches of Galatia, all of Paul's letters speak of his love for those to whom he had preached the word of God. As one familiar with the life and ministry of Paul, Timothy could not have been unaware of Paul's love for those to whom he preached.

"Steadfastness" (*hypomonē*) is more or less synonymous with "patience," to which it is sometimes joined in the various catalogs and descriptive phrases (e.g., Col. 1:11). If there is a nuance of difference between the two terms, it is to be found in the idea that "patience" has an internal referent, "steadfastness" an external referent. Patience is a matter of controlling one's anger. Steadfastness is a matter of coping with difficulties. It is a quality of the athlete who puts up with pain and opposition (so Philo, *Every Good Man Is Free* 26). Because of its use in regard to athletes, the term *hypomonē*, steadfastness or endurance, entered into the vocabulary of the philosophers' agon motif (see 4 Macc. 5:23). It is characteristic of someone who faces difficulties, even death, with courage. The evangelist Luke uses it to describe the spread of the word of God in spite of the many difficulties that it encounters (Luke 8:15).

Mention of the apostle's endurance allows the Pastor to expatiate on that theme. The paraenetic intent of his writing is served by filling in the picture of his hero, Paul, as one who had willingly experienced various kinds of suffering and opposition for the sake of the gospel. To illustrate the extent of the bad things that happened to Paul, the Pastor uses a classic literary form, the circumstantial or peristatic catalog. Its form and function are related to the catalogs of virtues and vices that appear throughout the Pastorals. Paul used similar lists of circumstances, particularly in his correspondence with the Corinthians (1 Cor. 4:10–14; 2 Cor. 6:4–10; 11:23–27; 12:10), to describe the difficulties that he encountered when preaching the word of God. In his own words, he suffered much as a servant of God (2 Cor. 6:4) or of Christ (2 Cor. 11:23; see 2 Cor. 12:10). His language makes it appear as if hardship and difficulty were the accepted lot of someone who was a servant.

The Pastor's use of a catalog of circumstances in a comprehensive reflection on the work of the apostle has a twofold purpose. On the one hand, it underscores the steadfastness of the apostle. No matter the difficulty, he continues his ministry. No matter the obstacle, he continues to preach the gospel. The circumstantial catalog enhances the image of Paul, the personal example that is such an important feature of the Pastor's epistolary exhortation (see Fiore).

On the other hand, the use of a circumstantial catalog by the Pastor and by Paul underscores the very power (*dynamis*) of the gospel message. No matter the obstacles that humans place in the way of the spread of the gospel, God's word will be spread by the messengers whom God empowers and enables to fulfill their prophetic mission. The word of God achieves its effect despite the difficulties that it encounters (see Matt. 13:18–23; Mark 4:13–20; Luke 8:11–15[56]), as the very existence of the Pastor's community implicitly attests.

"Persecutions" (*tois diōgmois*) are among the difficulties that Paul encountered. "Persecution" is a hardship to be endured; the term essentially connotes untoward treatment, generally of a physical nature and generally at the hands of an unruly group. Paul admits to having persecuted the church of God (1 Cor. 15:9; Gal. 1:13, 23; Phil. 3:6); rarely does he speak of himself as having been "persecuted" (see Gal. 5:11). Nonetheless, he twice cites "persecutions" among the hardships that he lists as an illustration of his dedication to the preaching of the gospel (1 Cor. 4:12; 2 Cor. 12:10; see Rom. 8:35, another catalog of adverse circumstances). The literary scheme adopted by Luke to describe the missionary activity of Paul is constant in portraying the apostle as one who preached in the synagogue, was harassed by mobs of Jews, was brought before Roman authorities for disturbing the peace, and was eventually forced to leave town. The several scenarios in Acts that develop this theme reflect the memory of the persecutions suffered by Paul and his coevangelists (see Acts 13:50).

The persecutions suffered by Paul are the stuff from which the Pauline legend developed. The Pastor underscores the extent and variety of Paul's persecutions with an exclamation: "Such persecutions I endured!" (*hoious diōgmous hypēnenka*). Nestled between his two mentions of Paul's persecutions is the memory of Paul's suffering in the cities of Antioch (in Pisidia), Iconium, and

---

56. Luke notes that those who hear the word of God and hold it fast in their heart bear fruit "with patient endurance" (*en hypomonē*).

Lystra. The Pastor has used a familiar triadic construction (see 1:11) to cast Paul's sufferings (*tois pathēmasin*) as persecution. The lesson would not have been lost on his readers.

Paul's suffering was part of his struggle, his *agōn* on behalf of the gospel. In his first letter he told his beloved Thessalonian correspondents about his suffering in nearby Philippi (1 Thess. 2:2; Phil. 1:29–30). He was even imprisoned for the sake of the gospel (Phlm. 13; see Phil. 1:7, 14; Phlm. 1, 10). In this catalog, the Pastor does not mention Paul's imprisonment (see 1:8, 16; 2:9), nor does he mention his suffering in the Macedonian city of Philippi. What he does mention is the suffering endured by Paul in three cities of the Roman province of Galatia (3:11). Luke notes that Timothy came from Lystra (Acts 16:1–2), one of the three cities.

Luke gives an account of Paul's visit to the three cities in Acts 13:1–14:23. A summary verse, Acts 14:21, makes mention of a return visit when Paul spoke about his persecutions: "It is through many persecutions that we must enter the kingdom of God" (Acts 14:22). In his stylized, longer account of Paul's visit to the cities, Luke describes Paul's persecution (*diōgmon*) by Jews in Antioch (Acts 13:50). Paul and Barnabas then went to Iconium, about ninety miles away. The same thing (*egeneto . . . kata to auto*, Acts 14:1) happened to the apostles in Iconium as had occurred in Antioch. When these apostles learned that a group of Jews and Gentiles were going to mistreat and stone them, they moved on to Lystra, some twenty-four miles to the south. Some Jews from Antioch and Iconium followed Paul to Lystra. They stoned him and dragged him outside the city, thinking that he was dead (Acts 14:19). Luke's picture is that of a courageous apostle, determined to preach the gospel, beset by Jews who sought to kill him. The Pastor's mention of Paul's persecution in the three cities recalls the events described in Luke's dramatic narrative.

The Pastor may have been familiar with the Lukan account, but it is more likely that he was aware of the stories on which Luke's dramatic narrative is based. By the end of the first century C.E., various stories about Paul were circulating in the early church. Some of them would eventually give rise to the body of apocryphal literature about Paul, of which the second-century *Acts of Paul* and various pseudepigraphic letters are the most important examples. The *Acts of Paul and Thecla* describe Paul as having been bound and imprisoned, scourged and expelled from the city of Iconium, the most important of the three cities in 3:11, because of a woman named Thecla, whom he had converted to the faith (see *Acts of Paul* 3.17, 21).[57] Demas (see 2 Tim. 4:10) and a coppersmith named Hermogenes (see 2 Tim. 1:15; cf 4:14), Paul's traveling companions dur-

---

57. Reference to the legend of Paul's having been persecuted in Iconium because of Thecla appears as a marginal gloss in two late Greek manuscripts of 2 Timothy, a ninth-century majuscule (K) and a tenth-century minuscule (181), as well as on the Syriac Harklean manuscript.

ing the escape from Antioch to Iconium, were the instigators of these troubles (*Acts of Paul* 3.4, 12, 14, 16). The turncoats are described as being "full of hypocrisy" and as having "flattered Paul as if they loved him" (*Acts of Paul* 3.1).

The Pastor brings his list of circumstances to closure with two relative clauses that are best rendered in English an independent sentences since they are virtually a pair of parenthetical remarks. The first is a commentary on the extent of Paul's persecutions. It underscores the magnitude of Paul's suffering. "How much I suffered!" says "Paul" to his readers. Then he expresses a note that has the force of a thanksgiving, without using the language of gratitude. The epistle's putative author notes that the Lord had saved him from all the oppressive circumstances that he had faced.

These comments are to be read in the light of the apocalyptic scheme of the preceding pericope and the paraenetic purpose of the letter. The apocalyptic scheme speaks of the penultimate times as those of terrible evil and the final day as the day of redemption for those who have remained steadfast. In the Pastor's almost parenthetical comment on the list of hardships, Paul is presented as having suffered a great deal (*hoious diōgmous hypēnenka*). But the Lord has delivered him from all of them (*ek pantōn me errysato ho kyrios*). Paul's example is offered to encourage the readers of the epistle. They are facing great difficulties. The final times in which they will live, the penultimate period, will be difficult (3:1). As the Lord has delivered Paul, so he will deliver those who stand fast in spite of the difficulties that they encounter (see 4:18).

[12–13] The Pastor's eschatological perspective and hortatory intent become more explicit in this pair of verses. He reminds his readers that persecution (*diōchthēsontai*) is the lot of all those who desire to live in godly fashion in Christ Jesus. The idea that the final (penultimate) times will be characterized by an inevitable onslaught of tremendous evil (see, e.g., Dan. 12:1; *As. Mos.* 8:1; *Jub.* 23:13–21) is a constant feature of apocalyptic thought. Passages such as 1 Thess. 3:3–4 and 1 Cor. 11:19 reflect the apostle's conviction that some form of eschatological tribulation will beset Christian communities. The Pastor capitalizes on this Pauline tradition to say that those who remain steadfast in living their Christian faith will be persecuted, as Paul himself had been persecuted (3:11).

The Pastor uses a formulaic expression, "to live in godly fashion in Christ Jesus" (*eusebōs zēn en Christō Iēsou*), to sum up the Christian life. He speaks of those who have made a decision (*thelontes*) to live such a life. His description of the Christian life uses one of the apostle's favorite expressions, "in Christ Jesus." It is found in all of Paul's letters (e.g., Rom. 3:24; 1 Cor. 1:2; Gal. 2:4; Phil. 1:1; 1 Thess. 2:14; Phlm. 23) with the exception of 2 Corinthians. Second Corinthians has the shorter formula "in Christ" (e.g., 2 Cor. 2:14), which Paul uses in some of his other letters as well. Here (see 1:1, 9, 13; 2:1, 10; 3:15) as in 1 Timothy (1 Tim. 1:14; 3:13) the "in Christ Jesus" expression is merely formulaic; it lacks the depth inherent in Paul's almost mystical use of the formula. For the Pastor, living in Christ Jesus is living a Christian life, that is, living as a Christian or in a Christian fashion.

"In godly fashion" (*eusebōs*; see Titus 2:12) belongs to a word group (a noun, verb, adjective, and adverb with the root *euseb-*) whose appearance in the Pastoral Epistles is a striking feature of their *lexis*, their choice of vocabulary (see Excursus 4). Hellenistic Jews used this language to describe a life lived in keeping with the religious traditions of their ancestors (see, e.g., 4 Macc. 9:29–30). The language describes what the biblical tradition calls the "fear of the Lord" (see Towner, *Goal of Our Instruction,* 147–54).

The Pastor provides Christian characterization for this common language when he qualifies it with a reference to life in Christ Jesus. He will explain concretely what that means in verses 14–17. Before doing so, he enlarges on the apocalyptic scenario by describing the penultimate times as times in which evil folks (*ponēroi*), the kind of people illustrated in verses 2–5, and swindlers (*goētes*) will appear. "Swindlers," a term that literally means "magicians" or "jugglers," must be taken in its more general and figurative sense. It describes those who dupe people. In his address to the people of Alexandria, Dio Chrysostom spoke of the good fortune of a lucky city. It is one in which people speak out of goodwill and concern for their fellow human beings; but, notes Dio, "to find such a man as that is not easy . . . so great is the dearth of noble, independent souls and such the abundances of toadies, mountebanks, and sophists [*kolakōn kai goētōn kai sophistōn*]" (*Discourses* 32.11).

In the final times things are going to get still worse (*prokopsousin epi to cheiron*).[58] Evildoers (*ponēroi anthrōpoi*) and false teachers (*goētes*) will fall into still greater error and lead others astray (see 3:1–9). Going astray (*planē*) was a classic topos, even the subject of novels, in antiquity; it implied some sort of seduction: moral, intellectual, or both. Dio Chrysostom said that false teachers, having been led astray themselves, lead others into error and confusion (see *Discourses* 4.33; 4.37).

The New Testament uses the language of "going astray" to describe the moral, intellectual, and religious confusion that is characteristic of the final times. In scenes reminiscent of Jewish apocalyptic writings (see *Sib. Or.* 3.68–69), the book of Revelation describes Satan as the great deceiver (*ho planōn*, Rev. 12:9) and the beast as deceiving (*plana*, 13:14) the inhabitants of the earth. "Deceit" is virtually a code term for final, eschatological error. The Pastor speaks about the moral and religious confusion of the (penultimate) final times by saying that evildoers and false teachers will arise, leading astray and being led astray.

[14–15] In the midst of this eschatological confusion (vv. 1–9, 12–13) and with Paul's example before him (vv. 10–11), Timothy is exhorted to carry on.

---

58. See the similar construction in 2:16.

Timothy is presumed to be among those who desire to live in godly fashion in Christ Jesus (3:12). Since godliness encompasses respect for the traditions of one's ancestors, Timothy is exhorted to continue in what he has learned and what has been entrusted to him (see 1:5). The exhortation is phrased in the imperative with an emphatic subject (*sy de mene*, "as for you"; see 3:10). Timothy is urged to continue in what he has been taught, what he has acquired in faith (*kai epistōthēs*).[59]

A participial clause, "conscious of those from whom you have learned" (*eidōs para tinōn emathes*) provides motivation for Timothy to continue in what he has been taught. The motivation is an element of godliness, namely, respect for one's teachers. Primary among Timothy's teachers is Paul.[60] Timothy is Paul's beloved disciple (1:2). He has closely examined the content of the apostle's teaching. He was familiar with how and why the apostle taught as he did. He knew the faithful formulations that he had learned (3:10a).

The plural "from whom" (*para tinōn*) suggests that in addition to Paul, Timothy had other teachers. The idea that Timothy knew (*oidas*) the sacred writings from the time he was an infant (*apo brephous*) also suggests that he had had other teachers. Among them were certainly Timothy's mother and grandmother, whose faith he shared (1:5). The Scriptures, with which Timothy had been familiar since infancy, continued to have an influence on his life.[61] These are the "sacred writings" (*ta hiera grammata*).

That expression is a technical term used in secular Hellenistic literature, as well as in the writings of Hellenistic Jews. In secular writing, "sacred writings" are official imperial letters. Among Hellenistic Jews, "sacred writings" (*ta hiera grammata*, a Greek translation of the synagogal formula *kitbê haqqōdeš*) were the Jewish Scriptures.[62] Philo and Josephus sometimes used the expression in specific reference to the Torah (*Moses* 2.292; see *Confusion of Tongues* 50 and Josephus, *Ant.* 3.15.3 §322, which use *grammata* without *hiera* in reference to the Torah). Philo describes the banquet that takes place on

59. The verb *pistoō* occurs only here in the New Testament. In the active it means "to make trustworthy"; "to feel confidence" is the usual connotation when it is employed in the passive. The editors of the *EDNT*, capitalizing on the root *pist-*, render the verb as "acquire in faith" (3.98). This understanding implies that the *kai* should be construed as an epexegetical *kai*, an explanatory "and."
60. See p. 254, note b.
61. In the New Testament the perfect form of the verb *eidō*, "to see," generally has a present-tense value, "to know." Here, however, the context makes clear that the formative influence of the Jewish Scriptures on Timothy began long before (3:14a–15b). Hence, this translation reads the verb as a true perfect, that is, as designating a past action with present effect.
62. See Josephus, *Ant.* 10.10.4 §210; 13.5.8 §167; 16.6.4 §164; 20.11.2 §261; *Against Apion* 1.10 §54, 1.18 §127; Philo, *Rewards* 79; *Special Laws* 2.159, 238; *Moses* 2.290, 292; *Gaius* 195; *Contemplative Life* 28, 75, 78. Josephus also used the expression "sacred writings" to refer to Egyptian sacred writings (see *Against Apion* 1.26 §228).

the Feast of Pentecost and mentions the presider's exposition of the sacred writings (see *Contemplative Life* 78).

In *Gaius* 195, Philo writes, "Either you have not the genuine feelings of the nobly born or you were not reared or trained in the sacred writings." His comment reflects the assumption of pious Jews that young men would have been trained in the Scriptures from their youth (see Ps. 71:17; Matt. 19:20). A rabbinic adage says that "at five years old [one is fit] for the scripture, at ten years for the Mishnah, at thirteen for [the fulfilling of] the commandments, at fifteen for the Talmud" (*m. 'Abot* 5:21). This expectation of pious Jews with regard to the Scriptures is reflected in the Pastor's comment about Timothy's having been trained in the sacred writings from his earliest years.

The clause, "which are capable of instructing you with regard to salvation through faith in Christ Jesus," affirms the importance of the (Jewish) Scriptures for the members of the Pastor's community (see 1 Tim. 4:16). His thoughts on the importance of the Scriptures are a byproduct of his understanding that believers are to live in godly fashion in Christ Jesus (3:12), that they are to respect the traditions of their forebears but in a way that is decidedly Christian. The Pastor emphasizes that the Jewish Scriptures are capable of instructing Timothy (*sophisai*, literally, "making him wise"; see 2 Pet. 1:16) with regard to salvation through faith in Christ Jesus. This is the point that the Pastor wants to emphasize in verses 14–17. The outside elements of the Pastor's chiastic structure speak of learning and formation (vv. 14 and 17, *a*, *a'*). The inside elements speak of the Scriptures (vv. 15a, 16). The center of the chiasm is the achievement of wisdom through faith in Jesus Christ.

The expression, "through faith in Christ Jesus" (*dia pisteōs tēs en Christō Iēsou*), reflects the Pauline tradition of salvific faith. The apostle used the very same expression as he argued about the salvific value of the works of the law (Gal. 3:26; see Rom. 3:22; Phil. 3:9 [with "through" (*dia*); cf. Rom. 3:26; Gal. 2:16; 3:22 [with "from" (*ek*)]). That is not the Pastor's argument. His argument is directed against evil people, swindlers with rotten minds who lead people astray, completely out of the picture with regard to the faith (3:8) and turning from the truth to follow myths (4:4), presumably "Jewish myths" (Titus 1:14; see 1 Tim. 1:4; 4:7).

Thus, the Pastor speaks not about "justification through faith in Christ Jesus" (see 2:22; 3:15; 4:7) but about "salvation through faith in Christ Jesus." Salvation (see Excursus 9) is related to Jesus Christ and is fulfilled in eternal glory (2:10). The qualifying phrase, "through faith in Christ Jesus," is formulaic. The Pastor uses the phrase to affirm that the sacred writings in which Timothy had been instructed since his youth explain salvation in the light of the message about Christ Jesus.

The Pastor's professed acknowledgment that the Jewish Scriptures have a significant purpose in his community's understanding of salvation is an indication of Hellenistic Jewish influence on the Pastor and the community. His epistle formally uses the Jewish Scriptures just once (2:19), but it is important to the Pastor that Timothy be aware of the importance of the Jewish Scriptures for an understanding of salvation. His epistle was written at a time when Christian "teaching" (*didachē*, see 3:16) had begun regularly to make use of the Scriptures to interpret and explain the mission of Jesus. Paul, the Pastor's hero, frequently quoted the Scriptures. Writing for a Hellenistic readership, the author of Luke-Acts had portrayed Jesus as the expositor of the Scriptures (Luke 4:16–30; 24:13–35; these pericopes embrace the Lukan story about Jesus). Writing for a Jewish Christian audience, Matthew spoke about the fulfillment of the Scriptures (e.g., Matt. 1:22).

[16–17] The importance of an understanding of the Jewish Scriptures in the life of the early church was a lesson that the Pastor did not want Timothy to forget. Hence, he writes about the different uses to which these Scriptures may be put. Before he does so, he states the basic reason why they are so important: The (Jewish) Scriptures are "inspired by God" (*pasa graphē theopneustos*). Throughout the years this phrase has been the subject of much discussion. What is meant by "all Scripture" (*pasa graphē*)? What did the author mean when he used the new expression "inspired by God" (*theopneustos*)?

The first crux deals with the meaning of "all" (*pasa*). Is the word to be taken distributively, that is, as meaning each and every part of Scripture? Or is it to be taken globally, that is, the Scripture in its entirety? Arguments can be advanced for either position. Commentators disagree over which of the interpretations is more adequate. Ancient rabbinic traditions of biblical interpretation suggest that every part of Scripture is important, no matter how small.[63] In the light of these principles, it would seem that the word *pasa* should be taken distributively: Each and every part of Scripture is inspired.

The second crux concerns the meaning of the rare verbal adjective *theopneustos*, "inspired." Found only here in the New Testament, the term is formed from *theos*, "God," and *pneō*, "to breathe," in a way similar to that in which Paul had coined the expression "God-taught" (*theo-didaktoi*, 1 Thess. 4:9). The adjective "God-breathed" appears in only four pre-Christian texts and the *Sibylline Oracles*. Should this term be taken in an active sense, that is, that all Scripture is inspiring? Or should it be taken in a passive sense: to mean that all Scripture comes from God? Hellenistic religious literature sometimes describes the mantic experience of an "inspired" prophet. Thus, it seems preferable to take

63. The *gezerah shavah* principle, the principle of the comparison of like expressions and the second of the famous thirteen rules of interpretation of Rabbi Ishmael, states that if one and the same word is found in two passages of the Torah, either passage could be used to interpret the other. The rule of *ribbui* and *mi'ut*, the rule of inclusion and exclusion, a principle especially used in the school of Rabbi Akiva, implied that even particles are important since they suggest either an inclusion (e.g., *'et*) or an exclusion (e.g., *'ak*).

the term in its passive sense.[64] Moreover, the church fathers generally take the term in this latter sense.[65]

A final crux derives from the fact that the sentence (vv. 16–17) is elliptical. There is no principal verb; the verb "to be" must be supplied, but where? Does the Pastor mean that all inspired Scripture is useful (thus, NEB and REB; see *EDNT* 2.140), or does he mean that all Scripture is inspired and useful for many different purposes (thus, AV, RSV, NIV, NRSV, and revised NAB)? The first alternative would imply that only the inspired parts of Scripture are useful. It supposes an unprecedented distinction between inspired Scripture and Scripture that is not inspired. The aforementioned rules of rabbinic hermeneutics militate against such a restrictive interpretation. The Pastor affirms the divine origin of the Scriptures that instruct Timothy regarding salvation through faith in Christ Jesus and acknowledges the various uses to which these Scriptures can be put. The many citations of 2 Tim. 3:16 in the patristic era—more than one hundred in all!—emphasize the usefulness of the Scriptures far more than they do their inspiration. According to the Pastor, the Scriptures are useful for teaching, for conviction, for correction, and for training in righteousness.

Timothy has observed Paul the teacher at work (3:10). He is to be a teacher (2:15) and to train future teachers (2:2). As the Scriptures served Paul in his work of teaching (1:11), so they can be usefully employed in the teaching of Timothy. The Scriptures are also suitable for conviction (*pros elegmon*) and for correction (*pros epanorthōsin*). The first term is a variant of *elenchos*, correction or reproof; the second is found in epigraphic inscriptions with the meaning of restoring, repairing, or rebuilding.[66] In the papyri, this term is used to describe the correction of a text. Used of persons, the term suggests change for the sake of improvement (*TLNT* 2.30–31). In 3:16 the terms are virtually synonymous. Nestled between "teaching" and "training in righteousness," the pair of terms points to Timothy's role in correcting people who have fallen into error (2:24–26). The Scriptures will prove to be useful for that aspect of Timothy's ministry. They will help him to deal with the doctrinal and moral errors that he must confront.

The Scriptures are also deemed to be useful for training in righteousness (*pros paideian tēn en dikaiosynē*). This is the high point of the Pastor's reflections on the usefulness of the Scriptures. Using the rhetorical technique of climax (*climax* or *gradatio*), he has placed "training in righteousness" at the end of his list and provides emphasis by adding a purpose clause (v. 17). "Training" (*paideia*) was often stressed by philosophic moralists. "Training" embraced

---

64. See A. Piñero, "Sobre el sentido de *theopneustos*: 2 Tim 3,16," *FNT* 1 (1988): 143–53.

65. Such a reading of 3:16 does not, however, mean that the Scriptures are not inspiring. See Raymond F. Collins, "Inspiration," *NJBC* 65:9–24, 62.

66. Neither term appears elsewhere in the New Testament.

everything that enters into the proper rearing of an individual so that he or she may assume the role of a mature person in society. The Pastor, however, gives a religious twist to this Hellenistic concept by saying that the training, for which the use of the Scriptures is appropriate, is training in righteousness (*tēn en dikaiosynē*; see 2:22).

"Righteousness" does not connote Paul's thoughts on justification. Rather, the Pastor's use of the term reflects the Hellenistic Jewish idea of right relationship, with God and with others. The Mishnaic adage quoted above indicates just how the use of the Scriptures fits into a program of training in righteousness. One begins with the Scriptures, proceeds to the Mishnah, then becomes a son of the commandment (*bar mitzvah*), and finally moves on to the Talmud (*m. 'Abot* 5:21). The rabbinic rules for the interpretation of Scripture were, for the most part, employed for the development of halakah that would enable God's people to live as they ought. The Pastor's words about the suitability of the Scriptures for training in righteousness echo the use that Judaism made of those same Scriptures.

The Pastor waxes eloquent on this idea, identifying the real purpose for which they are to be used. Timothy and other teachers are to use the Scriptures for training so that the person who belongs to God is ready (*artios*) and thoroughly prepared (*exērtismenos*) for every good work. Timothy is such a person; he is a person who belongs to God (*ho tou theou anthrōpos*; see 1 Tim. 6:11). He is to present himself to God as being ready for the task at hand (see 2:15).

Writing as he does, the Pastor stresses the life-purpose of training in righteousness. Such training is about getting ready and being prepared. The Pastor joins together the ideas of belonging to God and of accomplishing every form of good work (*pros pan ergon agathon exērtismenos*). The person who truly belongs to God gives evidence of a theocentric relationship in the life that he or she lives. To that end, the inspired Scriptures are eminently useful.

Farewell
2 Timothy 4:1–8

The announcement of Paul's departure, that is, his impending death, provides the occasion for a five-point charge that is given to Timothy. The image of a solemn ceremony, recalling that of a court, whether judicial or regal, is evoked as the Pastor outlines this charge. Timothy is to succeed Paul in his ministry of evangelization and teaching. In doing so, he is to follow Paul's own example. He is to preach as Paul preached. He is to expect suffering as Paul had suffered. By framing the commissioning "ceremony" within an eschatological perspective, the Pastor has provided Timothy with an authority, importance, and urgency that he might not otherwise have had.

The motifs of judgment and of the appearance (vv. 1, 8) encompass the pericope and define it as a discrete literary unit. These motifs provide an eschatological framework for what the Pastor writes, similar in many respects to what is found in 1 Tim. 6:11–17. He continues to maintain the two-stage eschatology with its distinction between the final times and "that day" (see 3:1). Paul's departure and the time that is to come precede "that day," the day of the appearance of Christ Jesus. In the penultimate eschatological times, people will prove to be dilettantes and skeptics, amassing for themselves a plethora of teachers. On that day, the crown of righteousness will be given to those who stand fast in their longing for the appearance, as did Paul.

> 4:1 Before God and Christ Jesus, who is about to judge the living and the dead, I charge you by his appearance and his kingdom: 2 Proclaim the word, be ready in good times and in bad, convince, warn, and encourage with all patience and teaching.
>
> 3 For there will be a time when they will not accept sound teaching but, following their own desires, they will accumulate teachers for themselves, as they scratch their ears. 4 They will turn their ears from the truth and turn aside to myths. 5 As for you, be sober in all things, endure hardship patiently,ᵃ do the work of preaching the gospel, fulfill your ministry. 6 For I, on my part, am already being poured out as a libation, and the time of my departure is at hand. 7 I have fought the good fight. I have finished the race. I have kept the faith. 8 For the rest, there is reserved for me a crown of righteousness, which the Lord, the just judge, will give to me on that day, not only to me but also to all who long for his appearance.

a. The Codex Alexandrinus has added a simile, "like a good soldier of Christ Jesus," apparently under the influence of 2:3.

[4:1–2] The farewell charge begins with a formula that recalls that of a solemn oath (see 2:14; 1 Tim. 5:20, 21; 6:12, 13). "Before God" (*enōpion tou theou*) recalls the biblical expression "before the LORD" (*lipnê Yĕhwāh*; 1 Sam. 7:6; See Ps. 56:13; 61:7; 68:3 [=55:14; 60:8; 67:4 LXX]:8; 68:4; etc.), a formula frequently used with respect to judgment or rites of atonement. In the Hellenistic world, similar formulas were used in regard to legal acts of succession (see Spicq, *Saint Paul,* 798). The Pastor's formula associates the name of Christ Jesus with that of God (see 1 Tim. 5:21), describing Jesus as one "who is about to judge the living and the dead." "Judgment," whether by the gods or by a human judiciary, was a familiar topos in Hellenistic rhetoric (see [Aristotle] *Rhetoric to Alexander 1,* 1422a.25–28). Indicating that Christ Jesus is the judge, the Pastor counters any claim that one of the gods or the emperor is the ultimate judge.

The Pastor's words are similar to the description of Jesus as judge found in Peter's précis of the ministry, life, death, and resurrection of Jesus in the house of Cornelius:

> They put him to death . . .; but God raised him on the third day and allowed him to appear, not to all the people but to us who were chosen by God as witnesses. . . . He commanded us to preach to the people and to testify that he is the one ordained by God as judge of the living and the dead. All the prophets testify about him. (Acts 10:39–43; see also *2 Clem.* 1:1)

In comparison with the speech attributed to Peter, the Pastor's affirmation is quite terse, almost formulaic.[67] The Pastor makes no explicit reference to the death and resurrection of Jesus. His formula lacks the "subordination" that is to be found in the Lukan account, where God is identified as the agent principally responsible for judgment: God, who had raised Jesus from the dead, appointed him as judge of the living and the dead. This nuance of the relationship between God and Jesus is absent from the Pastor's juxtaposition of God and Christ Jesus. The Pastor attributes the judiciary function to Christ Jesus alone.

Notably lacking from the Pastor's summary reference to Christ's judicial function is his qualification as "Lord" (*kyrios*; see 4:18). "Lord" is, moreover, Paul's favorite christological title. The apostle typically uses this title to designate Jesus who has been raised and who will come again as the eschatological Lord (see, e.g., 1 Thess. 1:3; 2:19). The title is also present in the beginning of Peter's speech. In a rhetorical aside, Peter says that "he is Lord of all" (Acts 10:36).

Paul expected that the Parousia of Jesus as the eschatological Lord was imminent. Initially he seems to have thought that it would take place during his own lifetime (see 1 Thess. 4:15, 17). The urgency of that expectation seems to have waned during the course of the years; Paul's later letters do not suggest that the Parousia is on the immediate horizon. The Pastor's use of the participial expression "about to" (*tou mellontos*) remains as a sign of the lingering influence of the notion that judgment is almost at hand. The Pastor writes about "the living and the dead." This is an example of merism, the use of antithetical expressions to indicate "all" (see v. 2). All people will be judged by Christ, although, as the apostle himself was fond of saying, not all will be dead at the moment of the Parousia (1 Cor. 15:51; 1 Thess. 4:15–17).

The Pastor's reference to "his appearance and his kingdom" (*kai tēn epiphaneian autou kai tēn basileian autou*) was bound to provoke curiosity. Traditional "kingdom" language, going back to the apocalyptic preaching of Jesus (see, e.g., Mark 1:15), is rare in Paul (eight occurrences) and just as rare in the deuteropaulines (six occurrences). In the Pastorals, kingdom language

---

67. The formula was reprised by the Christian church and eventually incorporated into the Nicean-Constantinopolian creed.

appears only in the final chapter of this epistle (vv. 1, 18). In 4:1 the Pastor adds "kingdom" language to the familiar language of "appearance" (*epiphaneia*; see Excursus 8). His binomial expression could be taken as a hendiadys with the meaning "the manifestation of his kingdom" (BDF 442.16) were it not for the initial *kai,* which suggests a "both . . . and" understanding of the text. Lau notes that "God's eternal kingdom will be finally established on the day of judgment and His sovereignty will be revealed in the *epiphaneia*-event" (Lau 238).

The Pastor has made an abrupt transition from the genitives used for "God" and "Christ Jesus" to a pair of accusatives, namely, "appearance" and "kingdom." The shift appears to stem from the Pastor's use of "charge" (*dia-martyromai*). The word belongs to the register of judicial vocabulary; its technical meaning is to "call as witness."[68] Jewish tradition demands a pair of witnesses in a judicial procedure (Deut. 17:6; 19:15). In the biblical tradition, inanimate creatures, especially "heaven and earth," were called upon as witnesses to divine action.

The Pastor's complex construction[69] highlights the by now traditional faith of the church that Christ will be the eschatological judge. The appearance of Christ as the eschatological judge marks the beginning of the final manifestation of the kingdom of God. A kind of chiasm exists between the prepositional phrase "before God and Jesus Christ" and the phrase "his appearance and his kingdom." To "God" corresponds the Judeo-Christian notion of "kingdom."

The solemn charge followed by a fivefold enumeration of duties evokes the scenario of a transition in office (see Spicq, *Saint Paul,* 798). Timothy is solemnly charged to proclaim the word, be ready at all times, convince, warn, and encourage people (see 3:16). "Preaching the word" (*kēryxon ton logon*) sums up the mission of evangelization. As a cipher for that mission, the phrase does not occur elsewhere. Mark characterized the ministry of Jesus as one of preaching (Mark 1:14). Thereafter, Mark (nine times), followed by Matthew and Luke (nine times each), continued to describe Jesus as engaged in the task of preaching. What Jesus preached was the "good news," "the gospel" (*to euangelion*; Matt. 4:23; 9:35; 24:14; 26:13; Mark 1:14; 13:10; 14:9; see Mark 16:15; Luke 8:1; Gal. 2:2; 1 Thess. 2:9).

In Acts, Luke spoke of the church's task of preaching in Jerusalem (Acts 10:42), Samaria (Acts 8:5) and all the ends[70] of the earth, where Paul preaches (9:20; 19:13; 20:25; 28:31). He summarized Paul's ministry as "preaching the kingdom" (Acts 20:25; 28:31). In each of his letters, with the exception of

---

68. See Deut. 4:26; 8:19; 30:19; 31:28; and Jdt. 7:28, which uses a simple *martyromai.*

69. In Greek the phrase "his appearance and his kingdom" is separated from the verb by twelve words. The verb "charge" is the first word of the verse in Greek.

70. The program was announced by the Lukan Jesus in Acts 1:8. In this passage, "ends" (*eschatou*) is in the singular ("end"), pointing to Rome, the capital of the empire, Paul's ultimate destination.

Philemon, Paul wrote about his preaching. In Romans, the most systematic of his writings, he explains the importance of his preaching: "But how are they to call on one in whom they have not believed? And how are they to believe in one of whom they have never heard? And how are they to hear without some-one to proclaim him? And how are they to proclaim him unless they are sent? As it is written, 'How beautiful are the feet of those who bring good news!'" (Rom. 10:14–15; see Isa. 52:7). It is little wonder that the Pastor's circles remembered Paul as a preacher and herald (1:11; see 1 Tim. 2:7).

In commissioning Timothy, Paul charges him to preach the word. One might have expected that the Pastor's Paul would have charged Timothy to "preach the gospel" (see v. 5) or that he would have used Luke's phrase "preach the king-dom," but he has not done so. In the Pastor's circles, "the word" (*ho logos*) was used as a cipher for the Christian message. "The word" is the word of God (2:9; 1 Tim. 4:5; Titus 1:3; 2:5), the message of truth (2:15), the words of faith (1 Tim. 4:6). This word is summarized in trustworthy sayings (*pistos ho logos*). Charged with preaching the word, Timothy is to proclaim Paul's gospel mes-sage. The ministry of the word of God is the one ministry without which a Chris-tian community cannot exist (see commentary on 1 Tim. 4:14).

Timothy must be ready to do this (*epistēthi*) in good times and bad. He must be on the qui vive all of the time, ready to preach no matter the circumstances, in good times and in bad (*eukairōs akairōs*). The merism, similar to the Latin *per fas et nefas* or the English "in fair weather and foul," is all the more intense because it lacks a connecting particle. The Pastor uses a juxtaposition of two antithetical terms to speak about all times. His language reflects Greco-Roman concerns with the opportune time for speaking. Timothy is supposed to be well aware that bad times lie ahead (3:1–9, 12). The "bad times" are times of encounter with those whose teaching is causing problems in the Pastor's com-munity. Lest Timothy miss his point, the Pastor will digress upon the time (*kairos*) that lies ahead immediately after he has completed the charge (4:3–5).

That charge continues as Timothy is told to convince, warn, and encourage people. None of these three words are used elsewhere, but each of them was reg-ularly used by philosophic moralists to describe related but somewhat different activities of the wise teacher. Good and wise teachers must convince people by dissuading them from moral or intellectual error (see 3:16). They must warn them, even blame them, so as to lessen their evil or prevent it altogether (see Demos-thenes, *Olynthiac I* 1.16). Finally, they must encourage people, urging them to conduct themselves in a way that is appropriate to their calling (1 Thess. 2:12). As for warning and blaming those who are in error, Philo (*Joseph* 74) taught that this is the responsibility of parents, guardians, and teachers (*didaskaloi*).

In doing this, Timothy is to emulate Paul's patience and to carry on his teach-ing. Timothy had carefully observed Paul's patience and this teaching (3:10); now he is charged to carry on in Paul's stead. Earlier he had been warned about how he was to deal with his opponents; he is to treat them with gentleness and forbearance.

[3–4] Earlier in his epistle the Pastor had spoken about the difficult times that would face the Christian community, drawing particular attention to false teachers who would easily lead the gullible astray (3:1–9). Now that Timothy has been charged to be ready at all times, even in the bad times, the Pastor again writes about those times that lie ahead. Speaking of some indeterminate future, he says that "there will be a time." Then he describes how the anonymous "they" (see 3:6–9) will respond to Timothy's teaching. A pair of metaphors is used to describe how some people will react: They will scratch their ears and turn them in another direction.

He uses the metaphor of people scratching their ears (*knēthomenoi tēn akoēn*)[71] to conjure up a group of dilettantes. The metaphor suggests a kind of curiosity that is looking for interesting and spicy bits of information (BAGD 31, 437). These are people who follow their own whims and cater to their self-interests and their passions (*kata tas idias epithymias*) rather than accept the sound doctrine that is to serve as a standard in the Pastor's community (1:13; see Titus 1:13; 2:1, 2). First Timothy 1:9–10 (see also 1 Tim. 6:3; Titus 1:9) speaks of the kinds of deviance that accompany the rejection of sound teaching.

These people accumulate teachers, picking and choosing from among those teachings that suit their fancy. The number of their teachers—the Pastor says that there is an accumulation of teachers—contrasts with the Pastor's view of Paul as *the* teacher (1:11). Their various teachings contrast with the *single* message, the word (*ho logos*) to which the Pastor makes reference throughout his epistle. These people move from teacher to teacher until they find one who says what they want to hear.

Eventually these folks will undergo a negative conversion. Instead of listening to the truth, they will listen to myths. They will undergo a real conversion: They will turn their ears from (*apo . . . apostrepsousin*) one thing and turn them to another (*epi . . . ektrapēsontai*). They will turn from the truth (*alētheias*) to fables (*mythous*). Apart from 2 Pet. 1:16, "myth" is a term that appears in the New Testament only in the Pastoral Epistles (see 1 Tim. 1:4; 4:7; Titus 1:14). Since the age of Pindar, some six centuries before the Pastor, the Greeks were aware of the difference between myths and truth. Pindar wrote, "Sometimes the sayings of mortals leave truth behind; fables [*mythoi*] ornamented with clever fictions deceive us" (*Olympian Odes* 1.28–29; see *Nemean Odes* 7.22–23). Epictetus expressed skepticism about the myths of even Homer himself. "And do you take Homer and his tales [*tois mythois autou*] as authority for everything?" was his rhetorical question (*Discourses* 3.24.18). Philo urged that

71. Conversely, Philo writes about good philosophers and chroniclers who refuse to enervate peoples' ears (see *Planting* 159).

myths be avoided totally: "Flee . . . what is worst. . . . [That which is] worst is the fabulous fiction [*mythikon plasma*]" (*Flight* 42). Philo also emphasized the contrast between truth and myth (e.g., *Abel and Cain* 13; *Migration of Abraham* 76; *Special Laws* 4.178).

In many respects, what the Pastor has to say about the desires, conversion, and the rejection of sound teaching recalls what Philo said in his description of the seductions of personified Pleasure. "I see yonder," Philo wrote, "Pleasure (*hēdonē*; see 2 Tim. 3:4; 4:3), that lewd dealer in magic and inventor of fables [*mythologon*], tricked out as for the stage. . . . I feared lest being off your guard you should be deceived and consent to the worst of ills as though they were the highest good. Therefore, that you may not . . . purchase for yourself unwelcome misfortune, I judged it well to proclaim to you, before it was too late, the full truth [*pasēs alētheias*] of all that attaches to this woman" (*Abel and Cain* 28).

The Pastor's description of the final times as a period when the pursuit of pleasure will lead people from sound teaching and divert them to myths fitted in well with what Philo and other Hellenistic philosophers had to say about myth. In the Pastor's circles, myths were associated with the rejection of truth (Titus 1:14), endless genealogies (1 Tim. 1:4), and old wives' tales (1 Tim. 4:7), all of which were opposed to the divine economy.

[5] This series of short instructions exhorts Timothy to follow Paul's example. The series begins with an emphatic "as for you" (*sy de*; see 2:1; 3:10, 14), creating a contrast with an emphatic "I" (*egō*) in verse 6. In effect, Timothy is encouraged to compare himself with the apostle Paul. He is to be "sober in all things." The qualification "in all things" (*en pasin*) suggests that the exhortation is to be taken in a metaphorical sense. In fact, the figurative use of the term "be sober" (*nēphe*) is common in Jewish and Christian paraenesis (1 Thess. 5:6, 8; 1 Pet. 1:13; 4:7; 5:8).

Plato taught that sobriety is the quality of those who are fit for public service. Public servants need to exercise sober judgment within a context of moderation and restraint of personal desire (*Laws* 11 [918D]). Philo regarded sobriety as a quality of those who are subservient: slaves, children, and subjects. They must rise above their needs, including a desire for food or drink, so that they avoid transgression by word or deed (*Drunkenness* 131). Philo describes sober people as those who have set "training" (*paideia*) as their head (*Drunkenness* 153). Thus, Otto Bauernfeind describes sobriety as a readiness to bear the burdens of service in obedience (*TDNT* 4.937) and the NRSV sees the use of the verb in 1 Pet. 1:13; 4:7; 5:8 as an exhortation to "be disciplined." Sobriety clearly has an eschatological nuance here and in 1 Thess. 5:6–8. Lövestam holds that the eschatological nuance is characteristic of the New Testament's use of the term.[72]

---

72. Evald Lövestam, "Über die neutestamentliche Aufforderung zur Nüchternheit," *ST* 12 (1958): 80–102.

Timothy is next exhorted to bear hardship with patience, as a good soldier of Christ Jesus should. This is not masochism—"endure hardship patiently," *kakopathēson*, is literally "suffer evil"—but a matter of being willing, and even expecting, to endure suffering for the sake of the Christian message and being ready to bear it patiently. Timothy is presumed to have observed Paul's sufferings (3:10–11), among which was imprisonment (2:9). Following the example of his mentor, Timothy is likewise urged to endure suffering for the sake of the word. He had previously been exhorted to share suffering as a good soldier of Christ Jesus (2:3). The military metaphor may be implicit[73] in the exhortation to "endure hardship patiently." Josephus and Appian used the verb "suffer" in reference to the military life (see Josephus, *Ant.* 10.11.1 §220; Appian, *Civil Wars* 5.8; cf. Aristotle, *Nicomachean Ethics* 10.6.6).

Timothy is urged to do the work of preaching the gospel, the evangelist's work (*ergon euangelistou*; see Acts 21:8; Eph. 4:11). This is the task of preaching the good news, Paul's work (1:8; 2:15; see 1 Cor. 1:17), a task with regard to which he should bear no shame (1:8). Now that Paul is about to bid farewell, Timothy is urged to assume the task previously fulfilled by the apostle. Paul had been appointed for service, for ministry (1 Tim. 1:12). Now, as the period of Paul's service is about to come to an end (4:7), Timothy is told to fulfill the ministry faithfully. In this context, both the immediate context of 4:1–8 and the larger context of the entire farewell epistle, the exhortation to "fulfill the ministry" connotes the idea of succession in ministry. Timothy is expected to be a man of sober judgment and to bear suffering with patience, as he assumes the ministry of preaching the gospel now that the apostle is about to depart the human scene.

[6–8] Having intimated Timothy's succession in the ministry of preaching and teaching, the Pastor turns his attention to Paul, whose imminent departure is the reason for Timothy's succession to ministry. The Pastor opens his imaginative portrayal of the impending death of Paul with a solemn "for I, on my part" (*egō gar*). The emphatic *egō* brings the figure of Paul into the limelight. "I, on my part" contrasts Paul's "I" with Timothy's "you" (v. 5) and introduces the idea that Paul's imminent departure is the reason (*gar*) for Timothy's succession to ministry.

The imagery with which the Pastor writes about Paul's death is dominated by the use of the agon motif. Such imagery is used to describe Paul's completion of his own work and to speak of the reward that awaits him in the future. Apart from the use of this classical topos, the Pastor's thought on Paul's death appears to have been inspired by what the apostle wrote in Phil. 2:16–17: "It is by your holding fast to the word [*logon*] of life that I can boast on the day [*eis hēmeran*] of Christ that I did not run [*edramon*] in vain or labor in vain. But

---

73. The Codex Alexandrinus makes it explicit. See p. 266, note a.

even if I am being poured out as a libation [*spendomai*] over the sacrifice and the offering of your faith, I am glad and rejoice with all of you." The cultic imagery, "being poured out as a libation" (*spendomai*), situates Paul's ministry and death within a religious context.

Such imagery spoke to the Hellenistic world, where a libation of wine was often added to a sacrifice or a libation was poured out to the gods before drinking or after a meal. In the solemn meals of religious associations and trade guilds, a libation was usually offered to the divine patron between the meal itself and the discourse, the *symposion*, that followed. The biblical tradition also knew of a libation of wine being poured on or at the foot of the altar at the time of sacrifice (Num. 15:5; 28:7; 2 Kgs. 16:13; Jer. 7:18; Hos. 9:4; Sir. 50:15). Paul frequently used cultic imagery to speak of Christ (Rom. 3:25; 1 Cor. 5:7), his own ministry (Rom. 15:16), or the service of others (Rom. 12:1; 15:27; 2 Cor. 9:12; Phil. 2:25; 4:18), but it was only in Phil. 2:17 that he used the imagery of a libation being poured out, a reference to his death.[74] Having set the scene with cultic language, the Pastor's Paul makes his announcement: "The time of my departure is at hand." Since the mention of the final times in 3:1 (see also 4:3), a perspective on time has been on the Pastor's horizon. Now his focus turns to the time of Paul's departure (*ho kairos tēs analyseōs mou*), his death.

Clement of Rome, the Pastor's contemporary, composed his own reflections on succession in the apostolic ministry: "Afterwards they provided a continuance, that if these should fall asleep, other approved men should succeed to their ministration" (*1 Clem.* 44:2). He continued, "Blessed are those presbyters who have gone before, seeing that their departure was fruitful and ripe [*teleian*]; for they have no fear lest anyone should remove them from their place" (*1 Clem* 44:5). In his reflection, Clement spoke about apostles (*apostoloi*), overseers (*episkopoi*), and presbyters (*presbyteroi*), and of death as "departure" (*tēn analysin*[75]) and "falling asleep" (*ean koimōthēsin*). The latter is the metaphor for dying that Paul himself often used (1 Cor. 7:39; 11:30; 15:6, 18, 20, 51; 1 Thess. 4:13, 14, 15). He likewise used cultic terms, especially "ministration" (*leitourgia*), and spoke about completion (*teleian*). Clement's concern, language, and imagery are similar to those used by the Pastor in 4:6–7.

Paul has fought the good fight (*ton kalon agōna ēgōnismai*). This image comes from the military. An inscription from 267 B.C.E. uses similar language of a military battle against the Athenians and their allies, the Lacedaemonians: "They fought many and good fights with others" (*pollous kai kalous agōnas ēgōnisanto met'allēlōn*; see SIG 214). The Pastor has paired this military image with an athletic image, that of the runner (see 2:3–5): Paul has completed the

74. See Peter T. O'Brien, *The Epistle to the Philippians,* NIGTC (Grand Rapids: Eerdmans, 1991), 305–6.
75. This very term is used in 4:6 but does not otherwise occur in the New Testament.

race (*ton dromon teteleka*). Paul had used military and athletic imagery to speak of his ministry and of the Christian life (1 Cor. 9:7, 24–27; 1 Thess. 2:2; 5:8; see 2 Tim. 2:3–5). A similar pairing of military and athletic images appears in Epictetus's *Discourses* (1.24.1–10). The image of the race was, in fact, often employed by the philosophic moralists (see, e.g., Seneca, *Letters* 34.2; 109.6). Seneca even speaks of the importance of people cheering the runner on. The moralists used the images to speak of the struggle for the truth and the struggle of the moral life (see Philo, *Allegorical Interpretation* 3.14). The Pastor uses these same images to portray Paul's ministry in graphic and traditional language.

The verbs that the Pastor uses in his reference to the fight and the race are in the perfect, implying that the end has come but that the influence of Paul's ministry continues on. The Pastor employs the same tense with similar implications when he writes that Paul "had kept the faith" (*tēn pistin tetērēka*). The phrase is similar to one found on a second-century C.E. Ephesian inscription by (or to) Marcus Aurelius Agathopous,[76] but the meaning is quite different. The words in this epigraph, "kept the faith" (*hoti tēn pistin etērēsa*), refer to loyalty to an assembly, the Gerousia or the Senate. The Pastor's observation has to do with Paul having maintained the orthodoxy of the Christian message. His faith continues to have an effect. It has been passed on to Timothy, who is charged with maintaining it (1:13–14; 2:1–2).

The imagery of the games is resumed in verse 8 as the Pastor looks ahead to the reward that Paul can expect. The expression "for the rest" (*loipon*)—a closing formula in some Pauline letters (2 Cor. 13:11; 1 Thess. 4:1; see Phil. 3:1; Eph. 6:10; 2 Thess. 3:1)—introduces a description of what is to happen to Paul after he has successfully completed his assigned task. To the victor belongs the spoils. Paul is to receive the crown of righteousness. This is as it should be. Epigraphic evidence testifies to the conferral of the victor's crown after the fight. A second-century inscription honoring an athlete says that he fought three battles and was crowned twice (*ēgōnisato agōnas treis estephē duō*).[77] Paul's successful completion of the fight and the race will earn him a crown (see Philo, *Migration of Abraham* 27, 133).

Paul's crown will not be a floral wreath, the perishable crown of 1 Cor. 9:25, nor will it be a crown of precious metal. Rather, the apostle can expect to receive "a crown of righteousness."[78] The just judge will award the crown of righteousness. The link between the quality of the crown and the quality of the judge

76. See C. E. Newton, ed., *The Collection of Ancient Greek Inscriptions in the British Museum*, vol. 3, *Priene, Iasos and Ephesos* (Oxford: Clarendon, 1890), 587b.

77. See *Collection of Ancient Greek Inscriptions*, 3:604. Similar phraseology also appears on a mid-third-century inscription. See J. H. Moulton, "Deissmann's Light from the East," *ExpT* 12 (1908–1909): 33.

78. The Semitic genitive in the phrase *ho tēs dikaiosynēs stephanos*, "crown of righteousness," yields a meaning similar to "medal of honor."

is apparent: The just (*dikaios*) judge will reward Paul with a (metaphorical) crown that symbolizes the reward for a life lived in proper relationship with the Lord and his people (*dikaiosynēs*).

The crown will be awarded "on that day" (*en ekeinē tē hēmera*). The Pastor does not identify the judge, but he has just written about Christ Jesus, who will come to judge the living and the dead (4:1). He has also written about "the appearance of our Savior Christ Jesus" (1:10), our ultimate benefactor. The reader of the Pastor's missive is thus able to identify the just judge, the one for whose appearance people long, as Christ Jesus, God's eschatological agent. Hellenistic Judaism affirmed that God alone was just to the highest degree. God alone is just, says Philo (*Dreams* 2.194). He is the absolutely righteous judge (*Moses* 2.279; see *Flight* 82; cf. Josephus *Jewish War* 7.8.6 §323; *Ant.* 2.6.4 §108; 11.3.6 §55).

The Pastor's imaginative scenario of the judge presiding over life's "games" is an eschatological one. The crown of righteousness will be awarded "on that day" (*en ekeinē tē hēmera*, 1:18; 4:8), the mysterious day of the Lord (see commentary on 3:1). The apostle frequently mentioned the day of the Lord, Christ, or Jesus, beginning with his earliest letter (1 Thess. 5:2; see 1 Cor. 5:5; 2 Cor. 1:14; Phil. 1:6, 10; 2:16; cf. 2 Thess. 2:2 and 1:10, where the day of the Lord is "that day").

Writing of Paul's expectation of an eschatological reward, the crown of righteousness, the Pastor is careful to note that it is not Paul alone who will receive the victor's crown. Unlike the athletic games, where there is only one winner (1 Cor. 9:24), all who long for "his appearance" (*tēn epiphaneian autou*; see Excursus 8) will receive a similar crown. Paul often affirmed that there is solidarity in salvation. The Pastor carefully recalls this notion when he writes that all who long for (*ēgapēkosi*)[79] Christ's appearance will receive the reward. No less than this was implied when he referred to Christ Jesus as *our* Savior (1:10). In the imagery of 4:8, the Lord, our Savior, presides over the ultimate games and gives a reward to all who have longed for his appearance. His appearance is the fulfillment of Christian hope and the realization of salvation, the manifestation of God's ultimate beneficence.

The Pastor's characterization of "that day" as the day of the "appearance" (*epiphaneian*) may have been facilitated by the use of the Greek Bible in the early church. Zephaniah 1:14 speaks of the "great day of the LORD." As the description of that day unfolds, the prophet says that "the LORD will be terrible against them [malefactors]" (Zeph. 2:11). The Greek translators misunderstood the Hebrew *nôrā'*, "be fearsome" (from the root *yr'*) as "become visible" (from the root *r'h*) and rendered the text as "the Lord will appear [*epiphanēsetai*] against them." A similar phenomenon occurred in Mal. 4:5

79. For this sense of the verb *agapaō*, "to love," see BAGD 5.2.

(3:23),[80] where the Hebrew text speaks of "the great and terrible day of the
LORD" but the Greek text has "the great and glorious [*epiphanē*] day of the
Lord." It occurs yet again in Joel 2:11 and 2:31(3:4). The awe-inspiring day of
judgment (in Hebrew) has become the day of the Lord's appearance (in Greek).

None of these texts appears in 2 Timothy, but Joel 2:31(3:4) was an important text in the scriptural apologetic of the early church. Luke cited the Greek
version of Joel 2:28–32 (3:1–5) to describe the Christian Pentecost (Acts
2:17–21). Mark 1:2–3 uses Mal. 3:1, inadvertently attributed to Isaiah, to provide an eschatological setting for the preaching of John the Baptist and the story
of Jesus. The Greek text of Mal. 4:5 (3:23) identifies the awaited prophet with
Elijah: "I will send to you Elijah before the great and glorious day of the Lord
comes" (according to the LXX).

Postscript
2 Timothy 4:9–18

With Paul's departure at hand and the charge entrusted to Timothy (4:1–8), the
Pastor can wrap things up. The Pastor's enhanced portrayal of the abandonment
of Paul bespeaks the isolation and loneliness of one who is about to die (see
4:6). The wrap-up mentions several people and various places associated with
the "history" of Paul's ministry.

"Name-dropping" is a feature of deuteropauline literature (see Eph.
6:21–22; Col. 4:7–9). The Pastor has already mentioned Lois and Eunice (1:5),
Phygelus, Hermonegenes, and Onesiphorus (1:15–16), Hymenaeus and Philetus (2:17). Now he mentions Demas, Crescens, Titus, Luke, Mark, Tychicus,
Carpus, and Alexander. Demas, Luke, and Mark appear in Paul's note to Philemon (Phlm. 24; see also Col. 4:10, 14). Tychicus was a name that was familiar
in some of the Pauline circles in Asia (Col. 4:7). Otherwise the characters are
unknown. Nonetheless, these "informative" details provide some verisimilitude for the epistle, but comparable biographical notes are not found in the
authentic Pauline correspondence.

The places cited in this postscript provide a highlighted map of the sphere
of Paul's activity: Thessalonica, Galatia, Dalmatia, Ephesus, Troas, Corinth,
and Miletus. The Pastor's mention of Paul's leaving coworkers behind in these
various places is a sign of the posthumous influence of Paul in the areas that he
had evangelized, namely, the Roman provinces of Macedonia, Galatia,

80. The references to the books of Joel and Malachi in these paragraphs follow the chapter and
verse enumeration of the NRSV. Many English translations follow the enumeration of the traditional
Hebrew text. This enumeration appears in parentheses.

Illyricum, Asia, and Achaia. Mention of them is another reflection of the Pastorals' overarching concern that Paul's legacy be continued (see, e.g., 1:6; 4:1–2; Titus 1:5).

These details enhance the epistolary profile of the apostle and serve a paraenetic function insofar as they illustrate the life of the apostle with traits that are worthy of imitation. The fact that Timothy is thrice urged to come to Paul (vv. 9, 11, 21) is a sign that within the Pauline tradition Paul is the center of unity and norm of the faith for the communities mentioned in the passage. In the exercise of his ministry, the apostle is described as eager to have a companion, Mark on this occasion, and wanting to use the books, unfortunately left behind in Troas. Paul carries on his ministry despite the difficulty of his circumstances. In God's providence the word will continue to be proclaimed. The word of God must be proclaimed to the Gentiles, no matter the opposition.

4:9 Make every effort to come to me as quickly as possible. 10 Demas, who loves this world, left me in the lurch and went to Thessalonica, Crescens to Galatia,ᵃ Titus to Dalmatia. 11 Luke is the only one with me. Get Mark and bring him with you, for he is useful for my ministry. 12 I have sent Tychicus to Ephesus. 13 When you come, bring the cloak that I left behind with Carpus in Troas and the books, especially the parchments. 14 Alexander, the coppersmith, did many evil things to me. The Lord will pay him back according to his deeds. 15 You too watch out for him! He took a stand against our words.

16 In my first defense no one came to my aid; everyone left me in the lurch. May it not count against them! 17 But the Lord stood by me and strengthened me so that my work of proclaiming the gospel continued to be carried out and all the Gentiles heard it; I was delivered from the lion's mouth. 18 The Lord will deliver me from every evil deed and he will save me for his heavenly kingdom. To him be glory for ever and ever. Amen.

a. The reading "Galatia" (*Galatian*) is found in a wide variety of ancient and more recent manuscripts in both the Eastern and Western textual traditions. Some ancient manuscripts, however, mostly of the Alexandrian family, read "Gaul" (*Gallian*). This alternate reading may have resulted from a visual error, but it is possible that it occurred because of the legend that Paul had traveled to the West (see Rom. 15:24), perhaps to Spain.

[4:9] Timothy is urged to go to Paul, to be in contact with Paul "as quickly as possible" (*tacheōs*). "As quickly as possible" is an epistolary cliché (P. Oxy. 2599.36; 2011.26; P. Sorb. 10.4; P. Med. 80.11; P. Michigan, 514.26; see BAGD 244.1). Were Timothy to do as he was urged, he would prove to be as faithful to Paul as was Onesiphorus, who is commended, greeted, and prayed for in the epistle (1:16–18; 4:19). The Pastor's wrap-up stresses the importance of Timothy's being in contact with Paul. Four times (vv. 9, 11, 13, 21) Timothy is urged to go to Paul.

The idea that Timothy should make every effort (*spoudason*, literally, "be eager to") to go to Paul, rather than vice versa, represents a reversal of the absence-presence feature of Hellenistic letters. Instead of Paul expressing a desire to go to see Timothy (see Phil. 2:24; Phlm. 22), the putative author of 2 Timothy expresses the desire that Timothy come to see him. While providing a certain measure of verisimilitude for the epistle, verse 9 ultimately affirms that the apostle is unable to visit Timothy, to whom the epistle is ostensibly addressed (1:2). His absence is due to circumstances beyond his control.

[10–11a] An ostensible reason for Paul's wanting to see Timothy (1:4) is given in a series of informational statements about various third parties. Six of the apostle's seven companions are no longer with him. Demas, Crescens, and Titus have abandoned Paul, leaving Luke alone with him. Their absence is the reason[81] why Paul asks Timothy to visit. Mention of their absence is sandwiched between two requests that Timothy come to visit.

In addition, Tychicus had been sent on a mission to Ephesus (4:12). Erastus remained behind in Corinth (4:20), and Trophimus, a sick man, was left behind in Miletus (4:20). The absence of these three is not presented as having contributed to Paul's solitude. Their absence is the result of the apostle's own initiative.

The Pastor describes Demas as someone who was in love with the present world. The Pastor's mention of "this world" (*ton nyn aiōna*) reflects an apocalyptic worldview in which the present age, deemed to be evil, is contrasted with the world to come (see 1 Cor. 1:20; 2:6, 8; 3:18; 2 Cor. 4:4; Gal. 1:4; Eph. 1:21). That Demas's love for this world led to his abandoning the imprisoned Paul makes that betrayal all the more poignant.

In his note to Philemon, Paul identifies Mark, Aristarchus, Demas, and Luke as his fellow workers in the task of evangelization (Phlm. 24). The presence of three of these names—Mark, Demas, and Luke—in 4:9–11 suggests that Phlm. 24 served as the source of the Pastor's inspiration. Colossians 4:10–14 was likewise influenced by Phlm. 24. This deuteropauline text mentions the names of Mark, Demas, and Luke along with Aristarchus and Epaphras (Phlm. 23). Both Colossians and 2 Timothy reflect a tradition of the church in Asia that Demas and Luke were companions of the imprisoned Paul.

In the early church, a legend developed around the figure of Demas. *Acts of Paul* 3.1–17 describes Demas as having accompanied Paul on the flight from Antioch to Iconium (Acts 13:49–51), a city where Timothy was well regarded (Acts 16:2). Demas is said to have been full of jealousy and to have flattered Paul as if he loved him. *Acts of Paul* says that Demas conspired with Hermogenes (see 1:15) in a plot against Paul in Iconium. Demas countered Paul's

---

81. The passage begins with an explanatory *gar* ("for").

teaching on the resurrection that is to come, saying "that it has already taken place [cf. 2 Tim. 2:18] in the children whom we have, and that we are risen again [cf. Col. 2:12; 3:1] in that we have come to know the true God" (*Acts of Paul* 3.14). The Pastor's description of Demas as having left Paul in the lurch is a reminder to the readers of 2 Timothy, particularly preachers and pastoral leaders, not to abandon the Paul of their tradition. They would do so were they to forsake Paul's futuristic (consequent) eschatology.

The anamnesis or remembrance of Paul in 4:9–18 provides an overview of the situation of the Pauline churches in the years after the apostle's death. The appearance in Thessalonica of Demas, to whom *Acts of Paul* 3.1–17 attributes an erroneous eschatology, may suggest that all was not well in the church of Thessalonica at the end of the first century. The author of the Pastorals may have known something about the eschatological misunderstanding that prompted the writing of 2 Thessalonians, a pseudepigraphic attempt to provide the Thessalonians with a correct eschatological perspective for their lives.

Crescens is a figure who, as so many others in 2 Timothy, is otherwise unknown in New Testament literature. Using the variant reading of 4:10 (see p. 277, note a), Eusebius mentions that Crescens was sent to Gaul (*Ecclesiastical History* 3.4.8 [PG 20:220]). *Acts of Paul* 11.1 says that "Luke [sic] from Gaul and Titus from Dalmatia" were waiting for Paul when the Neronian persecution was just beginning and Paul was about to be imprisoned. The Pastor's mention of Crescens's presence in Galatia attests to the continued existence of Pauline foundations in that Roman province (see Gal. 1:2; 1 Pet. 1:1). Luke describes the evangelization of three cities in the southern part[82] of the province: Antioch of Pisidia, Iconium, and Lystra (Acts 13:14–16:5; see 2 Tim. 3:11).

Dalmatia, to which Titus went, is a region of modern Yugoslavia located on the Adriatic coast. In the Pastor's day Dalmatia was the name of the southern part of the Roman province of Illyricum, an important tax base for the empire. Contemplating the extent of his work of evangelization, Paul reflects that he had preached the gospel from Jerusalem to Illyricum (Rom. 15:19).[83] Titus, who is said to have gone to Dalmatia, was a Gentile by birth (Gal. 2:3) who had accompanied Paul on a journey to Jerusalem. The occasion may have been the delivery of the collection for the saints in Jerusalem (see 2 Cor. 8:6). Later Paul would experience no little anxiety when Titus failed to make a rendezvous with the apostle in Troas (2 Cor. 2:13). Titus was Paul's trusted aide in dealing with

---

82. The ancient Galatians, a Celtic people, lived in the northern part of the province. There is considerable doubt over whether the apostle had visited the northern part of the province, in which the capital, Ancyra (present-day Ankara), was located.

83. Apart from 2 Tim. 4:10, Rom. 15:19 is the only mention of the province of Illyricum in the New Testament.

the church at Corinth, where he completed the collection. Paul commends him to the Corinthians as "my partner and co-worker in your service" (2 Cor. 8:23).

The idea that Titus had actually gone to Dalmatia is problematic. The New Testament makes no mention of a ministry of Paul in Dalmatia, and Titus 1:5 suggests that Titus had been left on Crete to continue Paul's work on that island. Notwithstanding the historical difficulty of the notion that Titus had been in Dalmatia, its mention in 4:10 confirms the existence of Pauline foundations in the region toward the end of the first century C.E.

The Pastor's mention of Crescens having gone to Galatia and Titus to Dalmatia contributes to his portrait of Paul's solitude and abandonment. It is not entirely sure that the Pastor wanted to present Crescens and Titus as having abandoned Paul, but several indications suggest that this was indeed his perception. These associates are cited together with Demas, who left Paul in the lurch. All three are contrasted with Luke, who alone remained with Paul. The names of all three are cited between two passages (vv. 9, 11b) in which Paul appeals for the presence of other people. Ultimately all three are contrasted with Tychicus, Erastus, and Trophimus. Tychicus was sent on a mission by Paul (v. 12); the other two remained behind as Paul continued on his travels (v. 20). Only Demas, Crescens, and Titus are portrayed as having gone away from Paul. On the other hand, while Demas is described as loving this world and leaving Paul in the lurch, no reason is given for why Crescens and Titus left Paul. Moreover, the very existence of the Epistle to Titus suggests that Titus was one of Paul's most reliable allies.

In verse 11a the Pastor highlights the loneliness of Paul by saying that Luke alone (*monos*) was with him. Luke's presence is contrasted with the absence of Demas, Crescens, and Titus. Most probably this Luke is to be identified with Luke the evangelist and with that Luke, Paul's coworker, who was with Paul (Phlm. 24) during the imprisonment to which the letter to Philemon makes reference. Origen suggests that this person is also to be identified with the Lucius of Rom. 16:21 (Commentary on Romans 10.39 [PL 14:1288]). The tradition of Luke's being with the imprisoned Paul is also reflected in Col. 4:14, which describes Luke as a beloved physician. Taken at face value, the "we sections" of Acts (Acts 16:10–17; 20:5–15; 21:1–18; 27:1–28:16) suggest that Luke was a companion of Paul during his missionary voyages. Commentators are, however, divided among themselves over whether these "we sections" reflect Luke's companionship of Paul or whether they are merely a literary device used by the evangelist.[84]

[11b] Timothy is told to go to Paul and to bring Mark with him. On his arrival, Paul will have in his company not only Timothy but also Luke and

84. See Joseph A. Fitzmyer, *The Acts of the Apostles,* AB 31 (New York: Doubleday, 1998), 98–103.

Mark. Mark, whose other name was John, was a companion of Paul during the latter's first missionary voyage (Acts 12:25; 15:37–39). Christian tradition reveres him as the author of one of the canonical Gospels. If this epistle was written at the very end of the first century C.E., as some authors contend, it cannot be excluded that the author of 2 Timothy intended to suggest by his reference to Luke and Mark that Paul had with him the authors, and perhaps the texts (see 4:13), of the gospels intended for Gentiles. Even these pillars of early Christianity find in Paul their center and norm.

The Pastor's reliance on Paul's note to Philemon continues to be evident in verse 11b. An almost offhand remark describes Mark as being "useful" to Paul (*moi euchrēstos*). Paul's note used a classic contrast between two antonyms as a pun in describing Onesimus as a useless slave (*achrēstos*) who became "useful to me" (*emoi euchrēston*; Phlm. 11). In Hellenistic Greek, *chrēstos* would have been pronounced the same way as *christos*, "Christ."[85]

[12] Tychicus is said to have been sent to Ephesus. Verse 12 is the only passage in the Pastoral Epistles in which missionary language is used of a person other than Paul (see 1:1, 11; 1 Tim. 1:1; 2:7; Titus 1:1), and it is the only place in which the verb "to send" (*apostellō*) is used. The description underscores the missionary character of early Christianity and the prominence of the church in Asia. It evokes the apostle's ongoing solicitude for the communities that he had evangelized, even after the departure of the first generation of evangelists.

Tychicus frequently appears in post-Pauline literature as an associate of Paul (Acts 20:4; Eph. 6:21; Col. 4:7; 2 Tim. 4:12; Titus 3:12). Acts portrays him as an Asian who was part of a group that accompanied Paul to Greece and then went to Troas (see 4:13) before Paul did when news of a plot led Paul to cancel his anticipated sea voyage to Syria (Acts 20:1–5). Colossians praises Tychicus as Paul's "beloved brother, a faithful minister, and a fellow servant in the Lord" (Col. 4:7).

Ephesus, to which Tychicus is said to have been sent, was the capital of the Roman province of Asia and a major locale for Paul's ministry (Acts 18:19–20:1; see 1 Cor. 16:7–8), as well as the home of Aquila and Prisca (4:19; see 1 Cor. 16:19). Luke records that Paul spent more than two years in Ephesus. From there the word of God could spread to "all the residents of Asia" (Acts 19:10; see 1 Cor. 16:19). Paul himself had something similar to say about the spread of the word from Thessalonica, the capital of the province of Macedonia (1 Thess. 1:7).

Tychicus's apostolate in Ephesus is as much a historical crux as is the ministry of Titus in Dalmatia (4:10). Titus 3:12 portrays Tychicus as a possible alternative to Artemas as the Pauline delegate in Crete. In that capacity, as in

85. See Eduard Lohse, *Colossians and Philemon,* Hermeneia (Philadelphia: Fortress, 1971), 200–201.

4:12, Tychicus would replace the principal pastor of that locale (see Titus 1:5; 1 Tim. 1:3; 2 Tim. 1:15, 18) as that pastor is recalled by Paul (Titus 3:12; see 2 Tim. 4:9, 11, 21). On the other hand, the tenor of the recommendation of Tychicus in Col. 4:7–9 suggests that Tychicus delivered the Epistle to the Colossians. The recommendation describes him as having been sent, along with Onesimus, to encourage the Colossians and as being capable of conveying news about Paul to the Colossians. A similar description, albeit dependent on Col. 4:7–9, appears in abbreviated form in Eph. 6:21–22. Notwithstanding these apparently competing traditions about the locale of Tychicus's ministry, the Pastor's mention of his apostolate in Ephesus attests to the importance of a Pauline church at the end of the first century C.E. (see also Rev. 2:1–7 and Ignatius's letter *To the Ephesians*).

[13] Some commentators suggest that the Pastor's reflection on Paul's having left his cloak (*phailonēn*) behind in Troas suggests a hasty departure, implying that Paul was arrested in Troas prior to a Roman imprisonment. No experienced traveler would readily move to another place without the cloak that served as a covering during the night. Alternatively, the Pastor may have been portraying Paul as having traveled during the summer, leaving his cloak behind prior to sailing for Assos (Acts 20:13). In any case he would have needed it before the winter began (4:21). The oldest extant Greek letter—a fourth-century B.C.E. leaden tablet found in Chaïdari, near Athens—requests covering for the winter: "Mnesiergus sends to those at this house greetings and health wishes and says that his situation is similar. If you are willing, send me some covering, either sheepskins or goatskins as plain as you have, and not broidered with fur, and shoe-soles. With luck [*tychon*] I will return them."

Paul is anxious to retrieve not only his cloak but also the books and especially the parchments. In New Testament usage, a "book" was generally a scroll. In the singular, the term was most often used with reference to one or another of the books of the Bible. The plural form (*ta biblia*) is used in 4:13, as well as in John 21:25 and Rev. 20:12 in reference to books that might conceivably be written about Jesus (John 21:25) and various heavenly books (Rev. 20:12). The "books" of 4:13 might simply be various "documents," but it is more likely that the Pastor had in mind some kind of biblical material.

The Jewish Scriptures were of considerable importance in the Pastor's circles. The Pastor's image of the house of God, the church, bears an inscription with three biblical citations (2:19). Second Timothy 3:14–17 reminded Timothy that he had been instructed in the Scriptures from his youth and explained why and how the Scriptures are to be used among God's people. First Timothy 1:4 and Titus 1:14; 3:9 also point to the value that members of the Pastor's community placed on the Scriptures. All of Paul's letters, with the exception of 1 Thessalonians, cite Jewish Scripture. The Pastorals' apparent allusions to some of the letters suggest some familiarity with these Scripture-quoting missives.

The Pastor's Paul especially wants to have the "parchments" (*membranas*).[86] Parchment is writing material distinct from the traditional papyrus. The plural form found in verse 13 may suggest that the Pastor is thinking of a small codex (see Martial, *Epigrams* 14.7, 184; also 14.186, 188, 190, 192). Paul, a leather worker (Acts 18:3), may have made such codices and occasionally may have used one as a kind of notebook in which were contained "quotable quotes" or information about various Christian communities. Such scraps of leather might also have served as writing material for some of his letters or for letters that he might have received.[87]

The Pastor's mention of the cloak and the books may be of more value than an expression of the Pastor's desire to impart verisimilitude to his portrayal of Paul. The entire epistle has been written from the perspective of Paul's impending departure (4:6–8); the apostle has run the race and is about to enter into the heavenly kingdom (4:18). The obvious successor to Paul in teaching and evangelizing is Timothy, his beloved child (1:2). Timothy has closely followed Paul's apostolic career (3:10–11). He has learned from Paul (3:10, 14). He has received the charismatic gift of ministry in the laying on of Paul's hands (1:6). Paul's desire to have available for use his cloak and his parchments may well symbolize a desire to have available for eventual transfer to Timothy the symbols of his ministry, namely, the mantle and the books.

The laying on of hands and the assumption of the mantle are important motifs in biblical accounts of the succession of prophetic ministry. In the Deuteronomistic History, Elisha serves as a model of the Mosaic prophet. The story of his accession to ministry as the successor of Elijah is modeled after the prototypical transfer of prophetic power from Moses to Joshua. That transfer took place with the laying on of hands (Num. 27:18–23; Deut. 34:9). As Moses laid hands on Joshua, so Paul laid hands on Timothy.

The assumption of the mantle symbolizes Elisha's succession to Elijah in the leadership of the company of prophets. Second Kings 2 tells the story of Elisha's assuming Elijah's prophetic office. A doublet of the story in 1 Kgs. 19:19–21, in which Elijah's mantle also appears, is an account of Elisha's initiation as the personal servant of Elijah. After Elijah has ascended into heaven in the fiery chariot (2 Kgs. 2:11)—a symbol of the eternal life that Elijah's successors deemed him to have (see 4:18)—Elisha picks up the mantle that had fallen from Elijah as he ascended into heaven.

A safe passage through water is a significant feature in the Moses-Joshua and Elijah-Elisha stories. The Torah's story features the rod of Moses. The

---

86. Along with *phailonēn*, the "cloak" of v. 13, *membranas*, "parchments," is a loan word from the Latin.

87. See Karl P. Donfried, "Paul as *Skēnopoios* and the Use of the Codex in Early Christianity," in *Christus bezeugen: Festschrift für Wolfgang Trilling zum. 65 Geburtstag*, ed. Karl Kertelge, Traugott Holtz, and Claus Peter März ETS 59 (Leipzig: St. Benno, 1989), 1:249–65.

Deuteronomist's story features the mantle of Elijah. Moses used the rod with which he had struck the river (Exod. 7:12–21) to strike the rock and obtain water (Exod. 17:5–7; Num. 20:1–13). He lifted up the rod as Israel passed on dry ground through the parted waters of the Reed Sea (Exod. 14:16–21). Joshua led the people of Israel across the Jordan on dry ground as they entered the promised land (Josh. 3:14–17). Elijah used the mantle to strike and divide the water so as to be able to cross over to the other side on dry ground (2 Kgs. 2:8). After he had retrieved Elijah's mantle, Elisha would perform a similar feat (2 Kgs. 2:13–14).

These biblical tales about water demonstrate the similar charismatic abilities of Moses and Joshua, Elijah and Elisha. With his mention of the cloak and the books, the Pastor may have remembered the classic stories about the transference of prophetic power and prepared the way for the later ordination ritual in which vestments and the Scriptures are given to the newly ordained. These are the symbols of office of those who assume the "mantle of leadership" within the community.

Paul is said to have left these symbols of office in Troas in the care of Carpus, an otherwise unknown individual. It may be that he was Paul's host when Paul visited Troas and that the church of Troas gathered in his house (see Acts 20:7–12). Troas, ancient Sigia, was an important port city in the northwestern part of Anatolia, the peninsula in Asia Minor. Strabo said that it was "one of the most famous cities of the world" (*Geography* 12.1.66). Paul seems never to have spent a great deal of time in Troas. The inspiration of the Spirit (Acts 16:6, 9), a desire to celebrate Pentecost in Jerusalem (Acts 20:16), an unexpected absence of Titus, and his desire to get to Macedonia were among the factors that prompted him to move on from Troas, where he nonetheless desired to preach the gospel (2 Cor. 2:12–13).

Paul's visits to Troas were brief, but the city played a significant role during his many travels. Luke recounts that Paul sailed from Troas to his European destinations during his second (Acts 16:8–11) and third (Acts 20:5–13) missionary voyages. It was in Troas that Paul, having been forbidden by the Holy Spirit to preach in Asia, had the vision of a Macedonian beckoning him to come and help (Acts 16:9–10). Later Paul stayed for a week in Troas, where he had met up with Tychicus and Trophimus (see vv. 12, 20), and participated in the breaking of the bread on the first day of the week (Acts 20:7). Paul himself realized that Troas, with its access to sea routes to Smyrna, Ephesus, Miletus, Neapolis, and Athens, was a natural place for preaching the gospel (2 Cor. 2:12–13). Its accessibility fit in well with his project of preaching the gospel in cities where the word could spread to outlying areas (1 Thess. 1:7; see 1 Cor. 16:19).

[14–15] On the presumption that the fictive recipient of this epistle was in Ephesus (1 Tim. 1:3), Alexander the coppersmith (*chalkeus*) may well be the Jew who was involved in the riot of the silversmiths in Ephesus (Acts

19:21–41). That he was involved in the metalworker's trade favors this identification. On the other hand, it may be that this figure is to be identified with another Alexander, the apostate and excommunicated Christian of 1 Tim. 1:20. The name was common in the Hellenistic world. It may be that the three post-Pauline traditions—4:14–15; 1 Tim. 1:20; and Acts 19:33–34—derive from the association of someone named Alexander who was involved in the opposition to Paul in Ephesus. He harmed Paul by speaking against him and the gospel that he proclaimed. The effects of Alexander's opposition lingered on; Timothy is warned about him.

Without identifying Alexander as a Jew or as a Christian, the Pastor names Alexander in order to be able to give an example for the community's sake. Alexander is someone who will be punished for his misdeeds. The idea of judgment and divine retribution is a Pauline notion, sometimes expressed in the form of a sentence of holy law (e.g., 1 Cor. 3:17). Paul associates judgment with the coming of the Lord (1 Cor. 4:5). According to Jewish tradition, God avenges wrongdoing. In 1 Thess. 4:6, Paul apparently alludes to a biblical citation about divine vengeance (Ps. 93:1 [LXX]) in reference to the Lord Jesus Christ. At the Parousia, the Lord Jesus ultimately will requite evil (see 2 Thess. 1:7–8; 2:8). The Pastor, who has already spoken about the appearance of Christ Jesus, a just judge who is about to judge the living and the dead (4:1, 8), now reminds his readers of the punishment that the Lord will mete out to evildoers, of whom Alexander is a good example.

Timothy is urged to be wary of Alexander, to be on his guard. The reason is simple. Alexander once took a stand against the gospel proclaimed by Paul and his companions, and Alexander's influence lingers on. The Pastor's unusual characterization of the gospel as "our words" appears to hearken back to 1:13, where Paul's message is summed up as "sound words . . . heard from me in faith and love." Timothy has responsibility for preserving and passing along this sacred treasure. He must be on guard lest he or any members of the community yield to the onslaughts of Alexander.

[16] Verse 16 continues the Pastor's focused description of Paul's isolation. At the time of Paul's first defense no one was available to help; he was all alone. The use of legal terminology (*apologia*, "defense") evokes an image of the judicial hearing that preceded the apostle's imprisonment and suggests a second hearing or trial that would lead to the apostle's anticipated death (4:6–8). At the time of that first trial no one stood by him; everyone left him in the lurch. The contrast between "no one" and "everyone" underscores Paul's isolation. The expressions are hyperbolic. Thus far in the Pastor's own narrative, only Demas is specifically identified as having abandoned Paul (4:10). Luke, on the other hand, is still with Paul (4:11).

As was the case in verses 14–15, the Pastor has created a literary scenario in verse 16 to provide a context for what is to follow. In what is virtually his final description of the apostle, the author portrays Paul as someone who prays for those who have abandoned him. He is a person of faith who relies on the help of the Lord. His prayer, "May it not count against them!" recalls prayers that Luke attributes to Jesus[88] (Luke 23:34 according to some manuscripts) and Stephen (Acts 7:60). The prayer contributes to the image of the apostle as a faith-filled martyr.

[17–18] Paul's reliance on the help of the Lord is another trait taken from traditional hagiography. The Lord stood by (*parestē*) Paul in contrast to all those who failed to appear at his side (*oudeis paregeneto*) in his hour of need. The use of a similar sound (paronomasia) accentuates the contrast. Human beings may have abandoned Paul, but the Lord strengthened the apostle (see 1 Tim. 1:12) so that Paul's task of proclaiming the gospel to the Gentiles was continued despite the difficulties that he encountered (see Phil. 1:12–14; 4:14; Ign. *Smyrn.* 4:2). Thus far he had been successful in defending himself before the authorities. As a result, Paul was able to carry on the work of proclaiming the gospel.

Paul's success in overcoming those difficulties is metaphorically described as his having been snatched from the jaws of a lion. This metaphorical description of deliverance from the hands of one's enemies derives from a Babylonian tradition. The lion's mouth was an image for serious conflict with one's enemies. From there the image entered into the biblical tradition (see Dan. 6:7, 16–24). Verse 17b uses this traditional, graphic metaphor to speak of Paul's difficulties. The Pastor had previously spoken of the manifold difficulties from which the Lord had rescued the apostle (3:11). In 4:9–11 the Pastor described Paul as being virtually all alone. A description of his loneliness in the face of impending death was described in the judicial metaphor of verse 16. The Pastor may have considered Paul's enemies as agents of the devil (see 2:26; see 1 Tim. 3:7; 5:15).

In the biblical tradition, deliverance from lions' mouths is the work of God. Within a context that makes reference to Paul's prayer (vv. 16b, 18b), mention of Paul's deliverance from the jaws of the lion may have been intended to evoke the words of the psalmist who prayed, "Save me from the mouth of the lion" (Ps. 22:21 [21:22 LXX]; see also Dan. 6:22). This psalm is a cry to God for help by one who is attacked and is all alone. The prayer was used in early Christian tradition to reflect on the isolation of Jesus, seemingly abandoned as he faced death on the cross (Matt. 27:46; Mark 15:34).

The Pastor continues to echo the prayer tradition of Judaism and Christianity in verse 18 as he portrays Paul's confidence that he will be delivered from every evil (see, e.g., Gen. 48:16; Ps. 17:12–13; Prov. 2:12; *b. Ber.* 16b; *b. Sanh.* 107a; *b. Qidd.* 81b; *b. Sukk.* 52b; the Seventh Benediction[89]; Matt. 6:13; *Did.*

---

88. See Eusebius, *Ecclesiastical History* 2.23.16.

89. That is, the seventh benediction among the Eighteen Benedictions, the weekday Amidah, which pious Jews recited three times a day during the Second Temple period. This seventh benediction was a prayer for the redemption of Israel.

8:2; 10:5). This language may reflect the liturgical tradition of the early church. The final petition in the versions of the Lord's Prayer cited by Matthew and the Didachist is "rescue us from the evil one" (*rhysai hēmas apo tou ponērou*), sometimes rendered as "deliver us from evil." The central petition of this prayer, that the kingdom come, is perhaps reflected in the Pastor's unusual use of "kingdom" language. Both Matthew and the *Didache* identify the one to whom the prayer is offered as the heavenly Father (see Matt. 6:9; *Did.* 8:2). Matthew does not specifically identify the kingdom whose coming is prayed for as the heavenly kingdom, but his Gospel leaves no doubt that this kingdom is the heavenly kingdom (see, e.g., Matt. 3:2; 4:17, 23; 5:3, 10, 19, 20).

The echo of the Lord's Prayer helps to interpret the metaphor in verse 17b. The verb "deliver" (*rhysetai*) appears in the metaphor and in the reminiscence of the prayer. The apostle's confidence that he will be delivered from all sorts of evil is based on his past experience (see 2 Cor. 1:10). According to the Pastor, Paul had been saved from all sorts of persecutions and suffering in the three cities of Galatia (3:11). The use of kingdom imagery and apocalyptic language bespeaks a conviction that Paul will attain eschatological salvation (see 3:8).

The Jewish-Christian prayer continues to be echoed in the doxology that follows mention of the Lord. Doxologies are not a typical feature in Hellenistic letters, but they were occasionally used by Paul (Rom. 11:36; [16:25–27]; Gal. 1:5; Phil. 4:20), whose own Judaism influenced this form of expression of praise to God. The doxology of 4:18 textually reproduces that of Gal. 1:5 (see also Heb. 13:21). Its presence at the end of the epistle derives from liturgical usage, suggesting that the epistle was intended to be read to a Christian assembly at worship (see 4:22b).

This suggestion is confirmed by the Order of the Prayer of Thanksgiving in *Did.* 10:1–7. The order of service concludes with "Maranatha! Amen!" (*Did.* 10:6). The final prayer of petition in the *Didache*'s eucharistic prayer is derived from the third petition of the *Birkat ha-Mazon*, the Jewish prayer after meals: "Be mindful, Lord [*Kyrie*], of your church to preserve it from all evil [*rhysasthai autēn apo pantos ponērou*] and to perfect it in your love. And once it is sanctified gather it from the four winds, in the kingdom [*eis tēn sēn basileian*] which you have prepared for it. For power and glory are yours forever [*hē doxa eis tous aiōnas*]."[90] The words of the petition, with its doxology, are remarkably similar to those found in 4:18. They appear to confirm that the Pastor has indeed incorporated into his missive the language of early Christian prayer.

---

90. The translation comes from Kurt Niederwimmer, *The Didache,* Hermeneia (Minneapolis: Fortress, 1998). Niederwimmer contends that the phrase "once it is sanctified" is a gloss (161). The prayer offers petition on behalf of the church; in Judaism's third benediction the prayer was offered on behalf of Israel, Jerusalem, and Mount Zion.

The Pastor's doxology contains the four elements of the classic New Testament doxology (see commentary on 1 Tim. 1:17). Its temporal element, "for ever and ever" (*eis tous aiōnas tōn aiōnōn*; Gal. 1:5; Phil. 4:20; 1 Tim. 1:17; Heb. 13:21; 1 Pet. 4:11; Rev. 1:6; 5:13; 7:12), with its plurals and doubling, reflects intensified Jewish formulas that speak of the eternity of God in this way 10:16 [9:37 LXX]; 41:13 [40:14 LXX]; see 89:29 [88:38 LXX]. The classic choral response, "Amen," confirms its liturgical use. It is difficult to determine to whom the Pastor addresses the doxology. The doxology praises the"Lord," but is the "Lord" to be understood as God or as Christ Jesus? Arguments can be advanced in favor of either interpretation. It is difficult to opt for one to the exclusion of the other, since divine salvation is realized in and through Christ. The Pastor shares with the apostle Paul the idea that Christ the Lord strengthens Paul (1 Tim. 1:12; 2 Tim. 2:1; cf. Phil. 4:13). Early church tradition held that Christ the Lord stood by Paul (see Acts 23:11). Accordingly, the Pastor is suggesting that Christ the Lord is the deliverer to whom the prayer of praise is addressed.[91]

Epistolary Closing
2 Timothy 4:19–22

Final greetings are a typical feature of Hellenistic letters. With the exception of the Epistle to the Galatians—an exception that confirms the strained nature of the relationship between Paul and those churches—all of the apostle's own letters conclude with a few words of final greeting. Some greetings are made by Paul himself (first person greetings; 1 Cor. 16:21; see Rom. 16:22). Sometimes the apostle indicates that those who are with him are also sending greetings (third person greetings). Sometimes Paul asks those to whom he is writing to convey greetings to others (second person greetings).

First Timothy omits the customary final greetings. Titus has second and third person greetings, but these are phrased in general terms. Second Timothy is alone among the Pastorals in citing individual names in its second and third person greetings. This corresponds to the name-dropping characteristic of this testamentary text. The absence of first person greetings from 2 Timothy may stem from its pseudepigraphal character. The Pastor has made no attempt to add a personal note from Paul, the kind of postscript that is found in 1 Cor. 16:21 and Gal. 6:11 (see Col. 4:18; 2 Thess. 3:17).

91. Similarly, Knight 47–73; Weima 136; Marshall 824–26. Oberlinner opines (*Pastoralbriefe*, 2:180–81), however, that vv. 17–18 primarily refer to God.

4:19 Greet Prisca and Aquila and the household of Onesiphorus. 20 Erastus remained in Corinth and I left the ailing Trophimus behind in Miletus. 21 Make every effort to come before winter. Eubulus greets you along with Pudens, Linus, and Claudia. All the brothers and sisters greet you. 22 The Lord be with your spirit. Grace be with you.[a]

a. The textual tradition shows considerable variation in the formulation of the epistle's farewell greeting; eight different forms appear in the various witnesses. One of them, a simple "Grace be with you," with "you" in the singular (*hē charis meth hymōn*), appears to be a scribal attempt to make the final greeting conform to the opening address (1:2).

[4:19] Second person greetings are to be conveyed to Prisca and Aquila and to Onesiphorus's household. Prisca and Aquila are among the most famous of early Christian couples (Acts 18:2, 18, 26; Rom. 16:3; 1 Cor. 16:19). Luke tells us that they were leather workers by trade who provided hospitality and a place for Paul to work during his long stay in Corinth. Prisca and Aquila accompanied Paul during his hasty departure from Corinth (Acts 18:18). Eventually they established themselves in Ephesus, where they appear to have again provided Paul with hospitality and a place for work. They worked with Paul in the proclamation of the gospel and risked their lives for him (Rom. 16:3–4). Finally they returned to Rome, from which they had been expelled as a result of the edict of Claudius in 49 C.E. The way that Paul greeted them at the end of his letter to the Romans suggests that the couple continued in the work of evangelization while they were in Rome. The association of Timothy, to whom this epistle is ostensibly addressed, with Ephesus (1 Tim. 1:3) creates a circumstance in which it was appropriate for the author to greet Prisca and Aquila. They were presumably residing in Ephesus at the time.

It is also appropriate that a household should be mentioned in the closing greetings (see Rom. 16:5; 1 Cor. 16:19) and that Onesiphorus's household[92] should be mentioned (see 1:16). Nonetheless the mention of Onesiphorus's household in a second person greeting is unusual. This is the only instance in the New Testament of the recipient being asked to convey greetings to an entire household (see Rom. 16:11).

[20–21a] In these verses the Pastor interrupts the epistolary greetings in order to highlight once again the loneliness of Paul and the need for Timothy to contact him immediately. This plea to Timothy and the accompanying personal and topical references echo the thoughts expressed in 4:9–13.

92. Manuscripts 181 (see note on 3:11) and 460 add the names of Onesiphorus's wife (Lectra) and sons (Simmias and Zeno) immediately after the name of Aquila in 4:19. In these manuscripts Aquila thus seems to have had two wives, Prisca and Lectra. This strange phenomenon may have resulted from a copyist's unwitting insertion into the text of a supralinear gloss containing the names of Onesiphorus's family in the manuscript from which he was copying.

Erastus is said to have remained in Corinth. The name of Erastus appears in the final greetings of Romans (Rom. 16:23), and the Corinthian origin of the letter to the Romans confirms the association between Erastus and Corinth. Paul identifies Erastus as the city treasurer. Paul's Erastus may well be the one whose name appears on a mid-first-century epigraph on a limestone paving block found not far from the municipal theater of Hellenistic Corinth: "Erastus in return for his aedileship [i.e., municipal leadership] laid [the pavement] at his own expense." There is no way of establishing with full certainty the identity of Paul's Erastus with the Erastus of the inscription, but there are sufficient indications to suggest that their identity is a likelihood. Both references are contemporaneous with each other, and both refer to public officials. Since the name Erastus was not altogether common, it is likely that the Erastus of the inscription, Paul's Erastus, and the Pastor's Erastus are one and the same person. Erastus is also linked with Timothy in Acts 19:22. They are described as two of Paul's helpers (*duo tōn diakonountōn autō*). They were with Paul in Ephesus and were then sent to Macedonia, where they were presumably to prepare the way for the apostle's visit. As is the case with other personal and topical names in 2 Timothy, it is difficult to reconcile Erastus's remaining in Corinth with other data in Paul's story. Nonetheless, 4:20a attests to the continued existence of a Pauline church in Corinth and the memory of a historical Erastus associated with Corinth.

As a locale for Paul's ministerial concern, Miletus, a city on the southwest coast of Asia Minor near the mouth of the Meander River, appears in the New Testament only in 4:20 and Acts 20:15–38. In Luke's story of the church, Paul asks the elders of the church of Ephesus to come to him at Miletus. There he delivers a farewell address (Acts 20:18–35). The Pastor says that Paul had left the ailing Trophimus behind in Miletus.[93] The idea that Trophimus had been left behind in Miletus because of illness (*asthenounta*) suggests that there were ailing persons among the leaders of Christian communities in the post-Pauline era.

The name Trophimus is actually a substantivized adjective meaning "nourishing." The substantivized form means "one who provides nourishment," that is, the master of the house, or "one who is nourished," that is, a nursling. Acts identifies Trophimus as one of a pair of Asians—the other being Tychicus (4:12)—who had been with Paul in Macedonia and Troas (Acts 20:4). Identified as an Ephesian, Trophimus is said to have been with Paul in Jerusalem (Acts 21:29). The presence of Paul and Trophimus in the holy city was the occasion of a near riot. Some Asian Jews, who presumed that Paul had brought the Gentile Trophimus into the temple with him, accused Paul of having profaned the temple. Some scholars believe that Trophimus and Tychicus participated in the

---

93. There is no evidence to support a conjecture advanced by Theodore of Beza and Dibelius/Conzelmann (125) that Trophimus was left behind in Malta rather than Miletus.

delivery of the collection to the saints in Jerusalem (1 Cor. 16:1–4), but there is no substantive evidence to support the conjecture.

Verse 21a expresses for the third time the apostle's desire to see Timothy (see 4:9, 13). For the third time, a sense of urgency is added to Paul's plea. He has begged Timothy to come as quickly as possible (4:9). He has told Timothy about the things that he needs (4:13) and has instructed him to bring Mark along (4:11). Now Paul pleads with Timothy to come before winter closes in. Once winter arrives, travel by sea would be out of the question (see 1 Cor. 16:6). Were Timothy not to arrive at Paul's side before winter, he would presumably not have been able to come until the following year.

[21b–c] With the third person greetings of 4:21b–c, the Pastor returns to the task of closing his epistle, which had been interrupted by yet another request that Timothy go to Paul. Third person greetings are conveyed by four individuals, including a woman, and a general greeting on behalf of all the brothers and sisters. Paul's ability to convey greetings on their behalf stands in tension with 4:11, where Luke alone is said to have been with the apostle. There is no easy way to resolve the tension except perhaps by suggesting that the four are presented as passersby who happened to be in Paul's company when the letter was being written. Luke, in contrast, is described as staying by Paul's side during his imprisonment.

The list of names resembles the series of names in the final greetings of various Pauline letters (Rom. 16:16, 21–23; 1 Cor. 16:19–20; Phlm. 23–24; see also Col. 4:10–14; 1 Pet. 5:13), but none of the four persons mentioned in 4:21—Eubulus, Pudens, Linus, and Claudia—appears elsewhere in the New Testament. Various hypotheses and legends developed with regard to each of the four figures identified by name. *Acts of Paul*, for example, identifies someone named Eubulus as a presbyter and companion of Stephanus (*Acts of Paul* 8.1.1). *Acts of Paul* appears to have exploited the personal notes in 2 Timothy (see commentary on 4:10, 19). On the other hand, it is possible the names may have come from an oral tradition on which both 2 Timothy and *Acts of Paul* are dependent.

Eubulus was, in any case, a common name in the Hellenistic world.[94] The name appears in many papyri and on several epigraphs. Of Pudens it has been said that he was the son of a Roman senator and a woman named Prisca.[95] Linus is occasionally identified with the Linus who appears in early ecclesiastical tradition as the first overseer of the church of Rome after the apostles.[96] Claudia, like Eubulus, was a rather common name. The name suggests that this woman

94. A freedwoman named Eubula appears in *Acts of Paul* 7.

95. See Jean Carnandet, ed., *Acta sanctorum quotquot toto orbe coluntur vel a Catholicis scriptoribus celebrantur. Maii*, vol. 4, new ed. (Paris: Palmé, 1863), 295–300.

96. See Irenaeus, *Against Heresies* 3.3.3 (PG 7:849); Eusebius, *Ecclesiastical History* 3.2, 13; 5.6 (PG 20:216, 248, 445); *Apostolic Constitutions* 7.46 (PG 1:1052–53).

was a member of the royal household, possibly as a slave or perhaps as a member of the *gens Claudia*.[97]

Traditions have developed about the relationship between Claudia and two of the men on the list. Some have suggested that Pudens was her husband. The name Pudens has been found on epigraphs in Chichester and Rome (see Martial, *Epigrams* 4.13; *Corpus inscriptionum latinarum* VI.15066; VIII.185). This Pudens was a friend of the poet Martial. He was married to a British woman named Claudia Rufina. The *Apostolic Constitutions* link Claudia with Linus. The Greek text *Linos ho Klaudias* could mean either that Linus was the son of Claudia or that he was Claudia's husband.

After these personal greetings, the epistle has a general third person greeting. Similar general greetings are found in 1 Cor. 16:20 and Phil. 4:22 (see also 2 Cor. 13:12; Titus 3:15; 3 John 15). Paul commonly referred to his fellow Christians as "brothers and sisters" (*adelphoi*). This term evokes the bonds of fictive kinship that bind Christians together and the memory of the households in which Christians gathered for their commemorative meals and the reading of Paul's letters. Paul frequently used the term in the vocative in writing to the churches that he had evangelized. It bespeaks the quality of the relationship that existed between Paul and those communities. The Pastor's use of the term, otherwise absent from 2 Timothy, is another example of his borrowing stock phrases from the Pauline tradition.

[22] The last verse of the epistle contains a kind of blessing. All of Paul's letters conclude with a final benediction. Its most common formulation is "the grace of the Lord Jesus Christ be with you," but there are variations. Romans 15:33 has "the God of peace be with all of you." Some manuscripts of Gal. 6:18; Phil. 4:23; and Phlm. 25 have "the grace of the Lord Jesus Christ be with your spirit," while others read "the grace of our Lord Jesus Christ be with your spirit." Paul's use of "spirit" (*pneuma*) is dependent on his Semitic anthropology; "your spirit" effectively means "you."

The liturgical character of the final benediction is underscored by the addition of a confirmatory "Amen." The appended "Amen" is found in Rom. 15:33 and Gal. 6:18. The manuscript tradition of the Pauline corpus includes an "Amen" after the final benediction of each of the letters, including 2 Timothy (see ℵ, C). This is surely a sign of liturgical usage, indicating not only that the formula of benediction was used in the liturgy but also that the epistles were read to a liturgical assembly.

---

97. The Emperor Claudius had the reputation of liberally freeing slaves (see Suetonius, *Claudius* 28), particularly those of the imperial household. In gratitude, many freedmen took the name of the emperor for themselves or members of their family. Thus was created the *gens*, a kind of extended family.

The final benediction of 2 Timothy is given in two parts, one in the singular, ostensibly for Timothy himself, the putative recipient of the epistle. The other is in the plural, corresponding to the real audience for which the document is intended (see 1 Tim. 6:21; Titus 3:15). The benediction in the singular resembles the liturgical finales (in the plural) of Galatians and Philemon, although it mentions only "the Lord." The benediction in the plural appropriates the grace motif from Paul's authentic letters, albeit in abbreviated form.[98]

This twofold benediction is not replicated in the New Testament. The other Pastoral Epistles have only a benediction in the plural. In its uniqueness, this double benediction provides a fitting conclusion to the epistle whose leitmotif is succession to the ministry of Paul (v. 22a) for the benefit of the church (v. 22b).

98. Harrison resolved the apparent tension between the two parts of the benediction by assigning each part to different letter fragments (see above, p. 5).

TITUS

INTRODUCTION

With but three chapters, the epistle to Titus is the shortest of the Pastoral Epistles. Its relationship with the other two epistles is evident. Among the many similarities between Titus and 1–2 Timothy are the important notions of Savior, the appearance, eternal life, sound teaching, the trustworthy saying, godliness, and good works. Its literary form is similar to that of 1 Timothy. Both share a concern for church and the household. Both contain a mixture of paraenesis and teaching. Both employ composite literary forms such as the household code and catalogs of virtues and vices. Both appear to be letters addressed to a close disciple of Paul, his "true son," who is thus enabled to convey the teaching of Paul on the authority of the apostle himself. Both conclude with a final benediction in the plural number. In each epistle, the community benefits from the authority and teaching of Paul without his personal presence and even without the hope that he would soon visit the community and further clarify his instructions.

There are, nonetheless, manifest differences between Titus and the two epistles to Timothy. Some of the more important differences appear in the first chapter, especially in the epistolary salutation (1:1–4). That the epistle is addressed to Titus rather than to Timothy is not as puzzling as it may appear to be at first sight. Both men were among Paul's disciples. Paul's own letters attest to his close association with each of them, but the sources, Paul's letters and the Acts of the Apostles, have more to say about Timothy than they do about Titus. Titus is not mentioned at all in Acts; we know nothing about him other than what Paul himself tells about his association with Titus. Paul occasionally employed both Titus and Timothy as emissaries sent on specific missions to particular churches.

First Timothy says that Timothy was sent by Paul with a mandate to reside in Ephesus (1 Tim. 1:3). Thus, it is imperative that an epistle with a similar function but concerned with the church in another locale be addressed to someone other than Timothy. No candidate appears more qualified for this role than Titus, who had accompanied Paul on one of his trips to Jerusalem (Gal. 2:1). After having not been found by Paul when the apostle was in Asia (2 Cor. 2:13), Titus rejoined Paul in Macedonia (2 Cor. 7:6). Titus was eager to go there (2 Cor. 8:16) and was sent there with a companion to continue the work of the collection on behalf of the saints (2 Cor. 8:6; 12:18). Titus was a particularly good candidate for a post on Crete. The island could easily be reached from the Corinthian port of Cenchreae (note also the implied reference to a voyage over the sea in 3:12).

Ancient sources indicate that there was a sizeable Jewish community on Crete. The Epistle to Titus is able to capitalize on motifs similar to those in Acts that describe Paul preaching in synagogues as it portrays Titus with a ministry on an island that had a substantial Jewish population. The Pastor begins his presentation on the qualifications and function of the overseer by evoking the image of the revered elder (1:5–6), a well-known figure in Jewish lore and biblical narrative. He speaks about a chosen people in 2:14. The Pastor exploits the Jewish factor when he contrasts the community's sound doctrine with Jewish haggadah and halakah (see the exegesis of 1:10, 14) and speaks of genealogies and quarrels about the law (3:9). The former is dispatched as "Jewish myth," the latter as "the commands of people who turn away the truth." In his paraenesis, the Pastor uses the Jewish notions of ritual purity and defilement (1:15). These elements suggest that believers on Crete were faced with some sort of "Jewish issue."

The Pastor attempts to delegitimize his opponents by saying that their minds and consciences are defiled (1:15). They are called abominable, disobedient, and unsuitable for any and every good work (1:16). A well-known proverb, "Cretans are always liars, evil beasts, lazy gluttons," made some residents of Crete easy prey for the Pastor's characterization of them as people who turned from sound teaching and were morally reprobate. The Pastor's dismissive treatment of his opponents' teaching and behavior is reprised toward the end of the epistle (3:9). There the Pastor says that arguments and quarrels about the law are useless and stupid. So much for his opponents!

The greeting of the Epistle to Titus offers a unique and very rich portrayal of Paul. Apart from Rom. 1:1–6, where Paul uses a summary of gospel faith to introduce himself, Titus's description of the sender of the letter (Titus 1:1–3) is the longest in the New Testament. It is all the more striking in that it contains a dense theological statement about the nature of Paul's apostolate. This is the most comprehensive explanation of the apostolate in the New Testament. The apostolate is presented in terms of God's eternal plan of salvation and the election of a chosen people.

The description of the sender of a Hellenistic letter, the *intitulatio*, functions in much the same way as does a signature block in the contemporary business letter. It identifies the role of the sender, thus providing authority for the letter's appeal. Had the Epistle to Titus been a real letter from Paul, to his close companion, coworker, delegate, and true son, there would have been no need for such a formal presentation of Paul's apostolate. Its presence at the beginning of the epistle makes it virtually impossible for the text to have been a letter from Paul to Titus. The epistle's final greeting, "Grace be with all of you" (3:15), confirms that the text is not a piece of personal correspondence between two men who had a long-standing friendship and a history of working together. The pronoun in the greeting, "you," is in a plural form enhanced by the addition of the word "all." "All of you" is the Pastor's designation of the community for which his exposition of Paul's apostolate in 1:1–3 is intended.[1]

The Pastor's theological reflection on the nature of Paul's apostolate mentions the manifestation of God's word (1:3). This language foreshadows one of the dominant theological motifs of the epistle, the appearance of Christ Jesus (see Excursus 8). The two passages in which the motif appears, 2:11–14 and 3:4–7, are tightly knit and theologically dense. They present a soteriology that includes traditional Christian ideas on redemption, baptism, and the Holy Spirit. These theological realities go virtually unmentioned in the epistles to Timothy.

A singular feature of these "epiphany" passages is that they speak of a salvific manifestation that has already occurred. With the exception of 2 Tim. 1:10, the epistles to Timothy reserve "epiphany" language for the future, eschatological appearance of Jesus. This idea is present in Titus 2:13, but the epistle stresses the salvific nature of the past appearance (2:11; 3:4) rather than the end-time appearance highlighted in 1–2 Timothy. The two epiphany passages in Titus reveal another unique feature of the epistle. Each of these passages uses the language of "salvation" or "Savior" in reference to both God (2:11; 3:4) and Jesus Christ (2:13; 3:6). First Timothy uses the epithet "Savior" only of God; 2 Timothy uses it only of Christ.

Coupled with Titus's wider use of specifically soteriological language is the fact that each of the epiphany passages refers to "Jesus Christ." In the Pastorals the title "Christ" generally precedes the name "Jesus." This is not the case in 2:13 and 3:6, nor is it the case in the theological presentation of Paul's apostolate (1:1). Thus, the name "Jesus" appears before the "Christ" title in three of its four occurrences in the epistle (see 1:4). In contrast, although both 1 Timothy and 2 Timothy mention Jesus more often than does Titus, these epistles rarely cite the name of Jesus before the title (1 Tim. 6:3, 14; 2 Tim. 2:8).

In sum, Titus enjoys a unique and distinguished position among the Pastorals in the fact that it contains three passages that are among the richest theological concentrations in the entire New Testament. These passages, the epistolary *intitulatio* and the two epiphany pericopes, constitute a real mini-summa of Christian theology. The epistle cites two hymnic fragments (2:14; 3:4–7) that are also very rich in theological content. These hymns use language that is not otherwise used in the Pastorals. To a large extent they represent cameo syntheses of Pauline theology.

While the literary genre of Titus is the same as that of 1 Timothy, the church structures suggested by Titus are fewer and simpler than is the church order

---

1. For further consideration of pseudepigraphy in ancient Christian literature, see "Introduction to the Pastoral Epistles," pp. 7–9.

described in 1 Timothy. Titus describes the qualifications of the overseer in 1:7–9, apparently suggesting that the overseer is to be chosen from among the community's elders. The epistle has, however, nothing to say about servers and female servers (see 1 Tim. 3:8–13). Nor does it have anything to say about properly qualified and enrolled widows for whom the community provides necessary sustenance (see 1 Tim. 5:3–10). Titus likewise has nothing to say about hands being imposed, as a kind of "ordination" ritual on Paul's delegate (see 1 Tim. 4:14; 2 Tim. 1:6), about order in the liturgical assembly (see 1 Tim. 2:1–2, 8–10), and the rights of elders (see 1 Tim. 5:17–19). What it has to say about discipline (3:10–11) is relatively simple when compared to the penitential discipline envisioned in 1 Tim. 5:20–25.

On the other hand, the household code used to expand on the notion of sound teaching in 2:2–10 is more fully developed than the elements of the household code found in 1 Timothy. Titus's household code has more to say about the formation of young people than any other household code in the New Testament. Older women are expected to train younger women in the domestic virtues. Titus is to act in such a way that he can serve as a role model for younger men. This concern for the younger members of the community so that they can become what today would be called "respectable members of society" is not otherwise replicated in the New Testament.

Titus's use of an expanded household code and its promotion of social virtues, including obedience to legitimate rulers, its affirmation of the multiform residential ministry of Paul's delegate, its concern with the formation of the next generation (2:3–4, 6–7) and succession in ministry (3:12)—no church should be left unattended! —and its restrained eschatology (1:2; 2:13; 3:7) are indications that the epistle was written for a Christian community that no longer lived with the imminent expectation of the Parousia. The Pastor's community was settling into the Hellenistic world for the foreseeable future.

Outline

1:1–4	The Salutation
5–9	Qualities of an Elder
10–16	Those Who Need Correction
2:1–10	The Christian Household
11–14	Salvation
15–3:3	Pastoral Exhortation
3:4–8a	A Baptismal Hymn
8b–11	Final Exhortation
12–15	Final Remarks and Farewell

The Salutation
Titus 1:1–4

The salutation of Paul's Epistle to the Romans (Rom. 1:1–7), the apostle's introduction of himself to a Roman congregation that he had not yet visited, is the longest of the epistolary greetings in the New Testament. It includes a kind of creed, a brief synopsis of the faith that the apostle shared with Roman Christians.

Apart from that lengthy salutation to the Romans, the salutation of the Epistle to Titus is the longest epistolary salutation in the New Testament. Its sixty-five words make it considerably longer than the salutation of the other Pastoral Epistles. These respectively contain thirty-two words (1 Timothy) and twenty-nine words (2 Timothy). The essential difference among the three salutations is that the salutation of the epistle to Titus contains a long reflection on salvation history that situates the apostle Paul at the crucial point within that history.

> 1:1 Paul, God's slave and apostle of Jesus Christ for the sake of the faith of God's chosen ones, the full knowledge of truth that is for the sake of godliness, 2 in the hope of eternal life, which God who does not lie promised before all ages 3 and manifested his word at the appropriate time in the proclamation with which I have been entrusted by the order of our Savior, God, 4 to Titus, a true son according to the common faith, grace[a] and peace from God the Father and Christ Jesus our Savior.

> a. Some important witnesses, including A, a few other majuscules, many minuscules, along with those in the Byzantine tradition, read "grace, mercy, and peace," undoubtedly under the influence of 1 Tim 1:2 and 2 Tim 1:2.

[1:1–3] As do other letters in the New Testament written by Paul or attributed to him, the epistle begins with the name of Paul. This is consistent with the Hellenistic style of letter writing in which the name of the sender appears at the beginning of the letter. The name of the sender is thus the first word to be read when the papyrus or leather scroll on which the letter is written is unrolled.

In more solemn and official letters, a title (*intitulatio*) was appended to the name of the author in much the same way that signature blocks are added to the signature in a contemporary business letter. The Epistle to Titus adds two titles to the name of Paul. These are "God's slave" and "apostle of Jesus Christ."

The first title, "God's[2] slave," is an unusual designation of Paul. The designation of Paul as a "slave" is familiar enough. Paul used this as a description of himself in many of his letters. He identified himself as a slave of Jesus Christ (Rom. 1:1; Phil. 1:1), and he used the image of the slave to describe his ministry (Rom. 1:1; 1 Cor. 4:1; 9:15–19; Phil. 1:1). In a world in which the vast majority of people were slaves—perhaps in excess of ninety percent in some of the urban centers of the empire—the image of the slave was a powerful one. The image did not so much suggest that the slave was demeaned as it meant that the slave was not free to follow his or her own will. The slave was subservient to one master, his or her "lord" (*kyrios*).

The apostle Paul did not use the title "slave of God" (1:1) to refer to himself; neither did the authors of the other deuteropauline letters. The expression "slave of God" was rarely used in the Hellenistic world (see, however, Acts 16:17). Plato did, however, call Socrates God's slave (*Phaedo* 85b), and the dramatist Sophocles presents Tiresias as describing himself as a slave (*doulos*) of Apollo (*Oedipus Tyrannus* 410). Hellenistic Jews would, on the other hand, be quite familiar with the title, which was frequently used in the Greek Bible. It was used of the elders (*tous presbyterous*). Thus, Tattenai's gubernatorial report to Darius, the king, stated that when the elders of the Israelites were asked to identify themselves by name, they replied, "We are the slaves of the God of heaven and earth" (Ezra 5:11). In various oracular utterances, Yahweh called the prophets "my slaves" (2 Kgs. 17:13, 23; see 21:10; 24:2; Ezek. 38:17; Zech. 1:6). Several individual prophets are described as the "slave" of God. The usage in the singular as an explicit personal title is comparatively rare. Among the individual prophets who are called God's slaves are Ahijah, Elijah, and Jonah.[3] Great leaders of Israel were also identified as God's slaves, especially Moses and David.[4] The language was also used of the patriarchs Abraham, Isaac, and Jacob,[5] as well as for Joshua, Solomon, and even Zerubbabel.[6] Isaiah speaks of "the slaves of God" (*hoi douloi tou theou*, Isa. 42:19) and of Israel as God's slave (Isa. 49:3).

2. The Epistle to Titus uses the name of God (*theos*, 1:1 [2x], 2, 3, 4, 7, 16; 2:5, 10, 11, 13; 3:4, 8) far more often than it does the name "Jesus Christ," used only four times, albeit once in inverted verbal sequence (see 1:4). Its emphasis on God rather than on Jesus distinguishes this epistle from the authentic letters of Paul as well as from 1–2 Timothy. On the theology of the epistle to Titus, see Collins, "Theology of the Epistle to Titus."

3. For Ahijah, see 1 Kgs. 15:29; for Elijah, 1 Kgs. 18:36; 21:28 [=20:28 LXX]; 2 Kgs. 10:10; for Jonah, 2 Kgs. 14:25; Jonah 1:9 [LXX only].

4. For Moses, see 1 Kgs. 8:53; 2 Kgs. 18:12 (*ho doulos Kyriou*); Neh. 9:14; 10:29 [=10:30 LXX]; Mal. 4:4 [=3:24 LXX]; cf. Rev. 15:3; for David, see 2 Sam. 3:18; 1 Kgs. 8:24–26; 1 Chr. 17:7 [cf. 1 Chr. 17:4]; 2 Chr. 6:42; Ps. 78:70 [=77:70 LXX]; Ezek. 34:23; 37:24–25; 1 Macc. 4:30; see the title of Ps. 36 [35:1 LXX].

5. See 2 Macc. 1:2. In addition, for Isaac specifically see Dan. 3:35 LXX = Prayer of Azariah 12; for Jacob see Ezek. 28:25; 37:25.

6. For Joshua (*doulos Kyriou*), see Joshua 24:29 [=24:30 LXX]; Judg. 2:8]; for Solomon, 1 Kgs. 3:7–8; 8:52; for Zerubbabel, Hag. 2:23.

"Slave" language is frequently found on the lips of individuals when they pray to God, especially in the Psalms.[7] Use of "slave" language in prayer speaks of the total submission of the one who prays to God from the depths of his or her being. The term "slave" is also found in oracular utterances to characterize those who do God's will (see Rev. 7:3). The usage confirms that these individuals were considered to be God's agents in the salvation of his people.

In the biblical tradition, David is the single individual most frequently so identified. Abner begrudgingly admitted that David was the slave of God (2 Sam. 3:18). His reported words elucidate some of the connotations of the term "slave" as it applied to David. "For the LORD has promised David," said Abner, "through my servant David I will save my people Israel from the hand of the Philistines, and from all their enemies."

The Pastor's use of the "slave of God" title as an attribute of Paul evokes this rich biblical tradition. Paul is situated within the history of God's people as an agent of Yahweh who faithfully executes his will. David was God's slave because he saved God's people. Paul was God's slave insofar as he was "the apostle of Jesus Christ." This second title appears as a formula in the salutation of the epistle. No other passage of the epistle uses this title. In no other place does the author call Paul an apostle. Neither does he exploit the rich connotations of "Christ," the anointed one (*Christos*, derived from *chriō*, "to rub or anoint with scented unguents"). He always uses the name "Jesus" in conjunction with the title "Christ" (1:1, 4; 2:13; 3:6) but never explores the meaning of either the name or the title. For him "Jesus Christ" (1:1; 2:13; 3:6) or "Christ Jesus" (1:4) was simply a name.

In the Hellenistic world, the slave was not usually a *factotum*, the proverbial jack of all trades and master of none. As a rule each slave, male or female, had a particular task. Among the most important tasks to which a slave might aspire was that of steward (*oikonomos*), the administrative head of the master's household. As slaves had a particular function to fulfill, so Paul had a task to fulfill. His task was to be an "apostle of Jesus Christ." This was his role in the history of salvation. "Apostle" is nonetheless used in a titular rather than a functional sense. The Pastor does not indicate that Paul was "sent" to anybody in particular (cf. 1 Cor. 9:2). Rather than describing Paul's mission, the Pastor states why the title is appropriate. Paul is apostle for the sake of the faith of God's chosen ones (*kata pistin eklektōn theou*).

Those who read the Pastor's missive from the perspective of Hellenistic Judaism would have recognized the reference to the "chosen people," God's chosen ones. The substantivized adjective *eklektoi* is frequently used in the New Testament to designate "the elect." The apostle Paul used such descriptive language (the root *ekleg-*), albeit sparingly (see 1 Cor. 1:26–27; 1 Thess. 1:4). The language appears especially in the letter to the Romans when Paul writes about

7. See, e.g., Ps. 19:11, 13 [Ps. 18:12, 14 LXX]; 36 [psalm title, =35:1 LXX]; 119:124–25 [118:124–25 LXX]; cf. Wis. 9:5.

Israel and God's chosen people and contemplates the role of that nation in the history of salvation (Rom. 9:11; 11:5, 7, 28; see 8:33; 16:13).

The Pastor presents Paul's servile role in the history of salvation as one whose purpose was the fidelity of God's holy people. He clarified this by adding that Paul was appointed the apostle of Jesus Christ for the sake of "the full knowledge of truth" (*epignōsin alētheias*), a catch phrase that was virtually a technical term to designate the norm of Christian truth (1 Tim. 2:4; 2 Tim. 2:25; 3:7; see pp. 97–98). The "full knowledge of truth" was not, however, merely a matter of correct intellectual understanding. It was also a matter of a life commitment. Thus, the Pastor adds that the full knowledge of the truth, the purpose of Paul's apostolate, is directed toward godliness (*eusebeian*). His readers knew what was meant by "godliness" (see Excursus 7). The Pastor's well-crafted words, "full knowledge of truth that is for the sake of godliness" (*epignōsin alētheias tēs kat'eusebeian*, 1:1), are virtually equivalent to a formula, *fides et mores*, used by Augustine and other patristic authors to describe the totality of the Christian life—correct belief accompanied by appropriate behavior.

In the following verse (1:2), the Pastor places the life of the Christian, the faith of the community, and the apostolate of Paul in the broadest possible historical framework ("transhistorical" if one prefers) by again making mention of God (1:1). Paul and his ministry are placed within God's eternal time frame. The Pastor's temporal perspective begins before all ages in the past and extends to the hope of eternal life in the future. From the standpoint of the Pastor's narrative, his time is all time. Rhetorically, this temporal perspective prepares for the Pastor's mention of the appropriate time in 1:3. The time is appropriate within the time frame of eternity.

The *terminus a quo* of the Pastor's temporal perspective is "before all ages" (*pro chronōn aiōniōn*). Commentators note that the Greek language contains two words for "time," *chronos* and *kairos*. The former, used only of time, evokes notions of chronological time (*tempus* in Latin). In the singular it designates a definite time. In the plural it indicates specific eras or periods of time. The latter term, *kairos*, used of place and of advantage, designates an opportune moment in time, the right time (*opportunas* in Latin). The Pastor uses both of these terms in 1:2–3, as did Paul in 1 Thess. 5:1 (see the doxology appended to Paul's letter to the Romans [Rom. 16:25]).

The Pastor's point of reference to the past is "before all ages" (*pro chronōn aiōniōn*, literally, "before the eternal ages"; see 2 Tim. 1:9). The Pastor is basically saying "before time began." In the New Testament and in Hellenistic Judaism, the Greek terms *aiōn* and *aiōnios*, the noun and its cognate adjective, reflect the Hebrew *'ôlām*, a term that connotes a remote time, either in the past or in the future. Semitic thought patterns were unable to conceive of "eternity" other than in temporal terms. For Semites, "everlasting ages" or "ages upon ages" comes close to what a Westerner might call "eternity." What the Pastor said when he wrote "before the eternal ages" might well be rendered by a Westerner as "from all eternity."

At the other end of the temporal spectrum is "eternal life" (*zōēs aiōniou*), for which God's chosen people hope. For Hellenistic Jews, "eternal life" was a contrasting expression. In the first-century B.C.E. *Psalms of Solomon*, eternal life is antithetically placed alongside "destruction" (see *Pss. Sol.* 3:12; 13:11; cf. 3:11 [*hē apōleia eis ton aiōna*]; 13:6 [*hē katastrophē*]). In the Greek Bible, eternal life is contrasted with shame and everlasting contempt (*eis oneidismon kai eis aischynēn aiōnion*, Dan. 12:2 LXX).

Some of the nuances of "eternal life" are expressed in the wisdom literature and the book of Daniel. That God lives eternally (*zēn eis ton aiōna*) is a given (see Sir. 18:1; 42:23). The *Psalms of Solomon* say that "those who fear the Lord shall rise up to eternal life, and their life shall be in the Lord's light, and it shall never end" (*Pss. Sol.* 3:12). When Michael, the great prince and protector of the people, shall arise, says the book of Daniel, "many of those who sleep in the dust of the earth shall awake, some to everlasting life, and some to shame and everlasting contempt" (Dan. 12:2). These texts suggest that eternal life is a gift that the Lord bestows upon the righteous (see Wis. 5:15; Sir. 37:26). Within the Hebrew Bible, Dan. 12:2 is the only text that is generally accepted as being a reference to the resurrection of individuals from the dead.

As is often the case, the Pastor uses the expression "eternal life" in a formulaic sense.[8] He does not exploit its traditionally antithetical character. He places his work within the perspective of the hope of eternal life. The phrase "hope of eternal life" serves as a kind of literary inclusion framing his epistle (1:2; 3:7).[9] In 1:2 the Pastor situates the relationship between God and the chosen people within this eternal time frame: God has promised (*epēngeilato*); the chosen people hope (*ep elpidi zōēs aiōniou*). Hope for eternal life drives the Pastor's rhetoric. He introduces the notion to qualify godliness. Doing so, he echoes the traditional understanding that links eternal life to the righteous life.

Hope for eternal life is based on God's promise, uttered before time began (*hēn epēngeilato ho apseudēs theos pro chronōn aiōniōn*). God's promise of salvation is a specifically Jewish idea that the Pastor and other New Testament authors have appropriated. *Second Baruch*, a second-century C.E. apocalyptic work closely linked to rabbinic tradition, links God's promise of life with the promise made to Abraham: "At that time [the time of Abraham], the belief in the coming judgment was brought about, and the hope of the world which will be renewed was built at that time, and the promise of the life that will come later

---

8. The expression occurs forty-three times in the New Testament, especially in the Johannine literature.

9. 1 Timothy, whose epistolary genre is similar to that of Titus, employs a similar technique (1 Tim. 1:16; 6:12).

was planted" (*2 Bar.* 57:2). The Pastor, on the other hand, situates God's promise not at the time of Abraham but before all ages.

If the promise was made before time began, how and to whom was it made known? In particular, when was the promise made for the sake of God's elect? The answer is given in verse 3. At the appropriate time, the opportune moment (*kairois idiois*), the God who does not lie manifested his word in the proclamation entrusted to Paul. God, who existed before time began and who will continue to exist after time, is the master of time. God determines the opportune moment. Because the promise of God, on which the chosen people's hope for eternal life is grounded, has been made known through Paul at the opportune moment determined by God, Paul becomes a central—indeed, the central—figure in the history of salvation. What the Pastor had implied in the "slave of God" epithet, attributed to Paul in verse 1, has now been unfolded: God has revealed the promise made from before time began through the proclamation of Paul.

The notions are deeply rooted within the Jewish mindset; the language used to describe them is Hellenistic. The Pastor writes about the God who does not lie (*ho apseudēs*) and the God who has manifested his word (*ephanerōsen ton logon autou*). The identification of God as "one who does not lie" employs an abstract term with a privative alpha (*a-pseudēs*). The adjective is part of that body of Hellenistic, almost philosophical terminology that the Pastor's circles used in their theological language (see 1 Tim. 6:15–16; cf. Rom. 16:27). The comparable Jewish notion is that the God of Abraham, Isaac, and Jacob is a faithful God, the God for whom "fidelity" (*'ĕmeth*) is one of the most defining attributes. Semites, including the biblical authors and the apostle Paul, would speak positively about God's truth and fidelity (e.g., 1 Thess. 5:24) rather than negatively and abstractly about the absence of lies with regard to God. In Jewish tradition, the notion of God's fidelity is closely linked with the covenant. God's "fidelity" (*'ĕmeth*) is God's loyalty to the oath that God has sworn and God's constancy in the magnanimous love (*ḥesed*) extended to the chosen people (see, e.g., Luke 1:72–73). Fidelity and magnanimous love are, along with God's righteousness (*ṣĕdāqâ*), the defining qualities of God's relationship with his people.

For Paul, the verb "to manifest" (*phaneroō*) is "a key term for the revelation of God's salvation in the gospel of Jesus Christ" (*EDNT* 3.413). As such, the verb is the practical equivalent of "to reveal" (*apokalyptō*; see Rom. 1:17 in comparison with 3:21). Paul-Gerd Müller notes that "the Pauline school continues this synonymous usage of *phaneroō* and *apokalyptō* within the framework of a revelatory scheme borrowed from the pre- Pauline tradition, and it does so in order to express God's revelation in Jesus Christ taking place in the proclamation of the gospel" (*EDNT* 3.413). This revelatory scheme dominates the use of the verb "to manifest" in its three occurrences in the Pastorals (1:3; 1 Tim. 3:16; 2 Tim.

1:10). The pre-Pauline revelatory scheme derives from Hellenistic usage in which the *phan-* word group is used of the manifestation of the deity.

According to the Pastor, God has manifested his word (*ton logon autou*) at the appropriate time in the proclamation that was entrusted to Paul. From 1 Thessalonians onward, "the word of God" (*logos tou theou*, see 1 Tim. 4:5; 2 Tim. 2:9; cf. 1 Thess. 2:13 [2x]) was virtually a technical term for the Christian message of salvation.[10]

The Pastor specifies that this Christian message was made manifest in the proclamation of Paul. The use of *phan-* language within a revelation scheme accentuated by temporal language (*chronos, kairos*) seems almost to suggest that it was only with the proclamation of Paul that the word of God was made manifest. Jürgen Roloff (*Apostolat-Verkündigung-Kirche*, 239) writes of Paul's exclusive relationship to the gospel. With reference to my own work (Collins, "Image of Paul"), Raymond Brown has stated that "apostolicity is personified in Paul—no other apostle is mentioned and no other is needed" (Brown 38). In any case, the author of the epistle to Titus intended to highlight the authority of Paul as one who was properly able and authorized to proclaim the word of God.

In common parlance, the "proclamation" (*kērygma*) of which the Pastor wrote denoted the public proclamation made by a herald. Use of the term connotes the public and official character of the content of the message. In 1:3, the "proclamation" designates the content of the Christian message (see 2 Tim. 4:17), for which Paul is the designated herald (see 1 Tim. 2:7; 2 Tim. 1:11). The authoritative character of his message is underscored by the phrases "with which I have been entrusted" and "by the order of our Savior, God." "With which I have been entrusted" recalls Paul's writing about how he had been "entrusted with the message of the gospel" (*pisteuthēnai to euangelion*, 1 Thess. 2:4; see 1 Tim. 1:11). Paul's words call to mind a process of official scrutiny of a designated candidate before a specific mission is entrusted to him, much in the way that designated candidates for the federal judiciary are scrutinized by members of the United States Congress before they are appointed to their positions.

The message was entrusted to Paul "by the order[11] of our Savior, God." BAGD 302 suggests that the nuance of the expression is that what has been given to Paul has been entrusted to him as a command. He has been described as a slave. It is appropriate for God to give orders to one of his slaves. Paul was commanded to execute the herald's task and to announce the gospel (see 1 Tim. 1:1; Rom. 16:26). The order was given by "our Savior, God." This links Paul's

---

10. See Matt. 15:6; Mark 7:13; Luke 5:1; John 10:35; Acts 11:1; Rom. 9:6; 1 Cor. 14:36; 2 Cor. 2:17; Phil. 1:14; Col. 1:25; Heb. 4:12; 1 Pet. 1:23; 1 John 1:10; Rev. 1:2; and so forth.

11. In the doxology appended to Paul's Epistle to the Romans, mention is made of "the command of the eternal God, to bring about the obedience of faith" (Rom. 16:26).

proclamation with our salvation; his kerygmatic ministry is to be seen from the perspective of our salvation. Thus, the command given to Paul is all the more urgent. It was not only a matter of Paul's subservience to the Savior; it was also of major importance for God's chosen people. It was not only Paul's fate that was at stake in the fulfillment of the command; also at stake was the salvation of God's chosen people.

Excursus 9: "Our Savior"

The importance of the cultural usage of the title "Savior" is underscored by the fact that the Pastor has not written about "God our Savior" (see 1 Tim. 1:1; cf. 1 Tim. 4:10; 2 Tim. 1:10; and the enigmatic Titus 2:13) but about "our Savior, God." He has first evoked the idea of our salvation. Then he identifies God as our Savior. "God" (*theou*) is placed in apposition to "our Savior" (*tou sōtēros hēmōn*). Within the Pauline circles to which the Pastor belonged, "God" was virtually the proper name of Yahweh, the God of Abraham, Isaac, and Jacob. By placing "God" in apposition to "our Savior," the Pastor has been able to create a neat *inclusio* for his presentation of Paul. He has written about "Paul, God's slave . . . by the order of our Savior, God."

Paul used the title "Savior" (*sōtēr*) only once in his extant writings. To the Philippians he wrote that "our citizenship is in heaven and it is from there that we are expecting a Savior, the Lord Jesus Christ" (Phil. 3:20). On the other hand, the use of the "Savior" title is one of the characteristic features of the Pastoral Epistles. The title appears three times in 1 Timothy (1 Tim. 1:1; 2:3; 4:10), once in 2 Timothy (2 Tim. 1:10), and six times in Titus (Titus 1:3, 4; 2:10, 13; 3:4, 6). In 1 Timothy the title is always used in a theological sense. In 2 Timothy it is used in a christological sense. In Titus the title is used in reference both to God (Titus 1:3; 2:10; 3:4) and to Christ Jesus (Titus 1:4; 2:13; 3:6). This repetitive but diverse usage suggests that the title is a key element of the soteriology, theology, and Christology of the Pastoral Epistles.

"Savior" in the Hellenistic World

In the Hellenistic culture from which the Pastoral Epistles arose, the title "Savior" was commonly used of both gods and human beings. Deities such as Zeus, Serapion (Asclepius), and Artemis were recognized as "Savior" in worship and in popular religious practice insofar as they had delivered human beings from various sorts of danger. Zeus, the most powerful of the gods, was Zeus *Sōtēr*, the "Savior" par excellence. Zeus is said to have rescued individuals from various situations of personal crisis as well as to have rescued communities from political turmoil, military attack, and natural catastrophes, including an earthquake. Accordingly, Zeus was the object of personal and communal prayer. His name appears on epigraphs that proclaim the gratitude of the rescued community. Zeus's daughter Artemis *Sōtēira* was celebrated for the protection that she afforded to the young approaching the crisis of puberty and adolescence and to women at the time of childbirth. As Savior, Artemis was invoked by cities threatened with destruction during a time of war. Serapion, the god of healing, merited the title "Savior" because he rescued individuals from various kinds of peril, from sickness to shipwreck.

From early times the title "Savior" was also applied to some human beings, namely, those who had performed some feat worthy of the divine (see Aeschylus, *Suppliant Women* 980–82; Thucydides, *History of the Peloponnesian War* 5.11.1). In Hellenistic times the epithet was used of emperors and kings, particularly deified emperors (see Cuss). Among the Emperor-Saviors, Ptolemy I (ca. 367–282 B.C.E.), successor to Alexander, was one of the first and one of the best known. Antigonos Doson (ca. 263–221 B.C.E.) was recognized as "Savior" some decades later but only after his death (see Polybius, *Histories* 5.9.10). During his lifetime Antigonos had been known as "Benefactor" (*Euergetēs*).

In the East, the "Savior" title was applied to a number of Roman emperors and occasionally to lesser imperial officials. These received the title because they had been generous benefactors of a city or region. Thus, despite his plunder of Asia and his disputes with Cicero Verres, the legate of the consul Cornelius Dolabela was recognized as "Savior." The "Savior" title was closely linked to the system of benefactors characteristic of Hellenistic society. Imperial officials who distributed benefits, including booty taken in warfare, could be recognized as "Savior."

The "Savior" title was, however, generally reserved for emperors. Emperors were sometimes deemed to be visible manifestations of the deity insofar as they gave visibility to the help that the divinity renders to human beings. In the era of divinized emperors, the recognition of an emperor as manifesting the beneficence of a deity was not far removed from the recognition of the ruler himself as a divine "Savior."[12] A first-century B.C.E. papyrus letter from Platon to the priests and other inhabitants of Pathyris says of Soter II, who twice came from Cyprus to rule Egypt, that "King Soter, the very great God [*ton megiston theon*], has arrived at Memphis and that Hierax has been appointed, with considerable forces, for quelling the Thebaid" (P. Bour. 12). Julius Caesar was recognized as the "common savior" as a result of his beneficence to all humanity. Manifesting the beneficent presence of the deity, Caesar was seen as god made manifest. Thus, an Ephesian inscription says of Caesar that he was "god made manifest, of Ares and Aphrodite, the common savior of human life" (SIG 347, 760.6).

12. An analogous phenomenon occurred in Hellenistic Judaism. 1 Macc. 4:11 proclaims Yahweh as "one who saves Israel" (*sōzōn ton Israel*). The same epithet was used of Judas Maccabee (1 Macc. 4:19).

Jesus As Our "Savior"

This epithet sheds light on the cultural situation in which the author of 2 Timothy wrote about the gospel, that is, "the good news with the help of the power of God, who saved us and called us with a holy calling, not according to our works but according to his own purpose and the beneficence [*charin*] shown to us in Christ Jesus before the eternal ages. This beneficence is now made manifest through the appearance of our Savior Christ Jesus, who destroyed death and brought life and imperishability to light through the good news" (2 Tim. 1:8–10).

These words were presumably written to a group of Christians in Ephesus (see 1 Tim. 1:3), the very location of the inscription in honor of Julius Caesar. In this regard it is interesting to note that apart from the Pastoral Epistles the only appearance of the "Savior" title in the deuteropauline New Testament corpus is in the household code of the epistle to the Ephesians (Eph. 5:22–6:9). There the author describes Christ as the Savior of the Church (Eph. 5:23). He exploits the title in a description of the purification effected by the Savior who is preparing his bride, the church, for marriage (Eph. 5:25–27).

In 2 Tim. 1:8–10 the Pastor says that "through the appearance" (*dia tēs epiphaneias*) of Christ Jesus, the divine purpose and favor has been made manifest (*phanerōtheisan*). Christ Jesus is "our Savior" insofar as he is the bringer of good gifts (see Titus 1:4). Life and immortality are gifts that only God can give. This manifestation of God's gifts are accordingly attributed to the power of God. Unlike the attribution of the "Savior" title to Caesar, said to have sprung from the divine couple Ares and Aphrodite, the Pastor's attribution of this title to Christ Jesus is rooted in his theological monotheism (see 1 Tim. 2:5–6; 6:15–16).

A similar relationship between God and Christ Jesus, to each of whom the epithet "our Savior" is applied, is to be found in the epiphany passage of Titus 3:4–7: "When appeared the goodness and benevolence [*hē chrēstotēs kai hē philanthōpia*] of our Savior, God, not from works of righteousness that we ourselves have done, but according to his mercy, he saved us through the washing of rebirth and renewal by the Holy Spirit, which he poured out on us profusely through Jesus Christ, our Savior, so that, justified by his grace, we may become heirs according to the hope of eternal life." This fragment of a baptismal hymn, which the Pastor calls a "trustworthy saying," applies the laudatory epithet "our Savior" to both God and Christ Jesus.

God As "Our Savior"

The Pastor's attribution of the title "Savior" to God in Titus 3:4 echoes his earlier usage in which "God" (*theos*) appears as an explanatory addition, an appositive, to "our Savior." Thus, in Titus 1:3 the Pastor writes about the order of "our Savior, God," and in Titus 2:10 he speaks of the honor even slaves are to bring to the teaching of "our Savior, God."

One might detect in these passages an apologetic and a soteriological interest as the Pastor writes about "our Savior, God." His rhetoric speaks of salvation before he identifies the Savior. Thus, the Pastor has appealed to the self-interest of his audience; they would be supremely interested in their salvation. The Pastor's apologetic concern then becomes manifest. He identifies the Savior, not as one or another emperor or civic benefactor but as "God," that is, the God of the Jewish tradition. His Bible often speaks of God as Savior. In the Psalms, God is addressed as "my Savior" (*sōtēr mou*, Ps. 25:5; 27:1, 9; 62:2, 6 [=LXX Ps. 24:5; 26:1, 9; 61:3, 7]; see also Luke 1:47) and as "our Savior" (*sōtēr hēmōn*, Ps. 65:5; 79:9; 95:1 [=LXX Ps. 64:6; 78:9; 94:1]). Hellenistic Judaism frequently used "Savior" as a divine epithet.[13] Using a baptismal hymn, the Pastor has explained how God saves us: "according to his mercy, he saved us [*esōsen hēmas*] through the washing of rebirth and renewal by the Holy Spirit, which he poured out on us profusely through Jesus Christ, our Savior" (Titus 3:5–6).

In the opening salutation of 1 Timothy, "our Savior" is used as a descriptive epithet for God as the author speaks of "the command of God our Savior" (1 Tim. 1:1; see Titus 1:3). Later in the missive, the Pastor affirms that God wills the salvation of all humankind. He writes of "our Savior, God, who wills that all people be saved and come to the full knowledge of truth" (1 Tim. 2:3–4) and again, of "the living God who is the Savior of all people, especially of the faithful" (1 Tim. 4:10). The emphasis on universal salvation serves to counter any suggestion that salvation is reserved to Jews and/or to Gentile Christians who faithfully observe the Jewish law. To the extent that an incipient Gnosticism was a problem for the Pastor's community, the affirmation that God wills the salvation of all people confronts the claim that only the elite, privy to some sort of esoteric "knowledge" (*gnōsis*), were capable of being saved. The Pastor's subsequent emphasis on the "full knowledge" (*epignōsin*) serves to reinforce the subtle apologetic of his rhetoric.

Each of these passages relates God's universal will of salvation to the Pastor's community. The community consists of "the faithful," those who have "the full knowledge of truth" (*epignōsin alētheias*). Because of the communal aspect of God's universal salvific will, the Pastor can affirm that God is "our Savior," that is, the Savior of the community in 1 Tim. 1:1. For the members of the community, there is no Savior other than "the living God" (see 1 Tim 3:15; 4:10; cf. 6:13).

"The Great God, Our Savior, Jesus Christ"

The Epistle to Titus uses the title "Savior" more often than do 1 and 2 Timothy combined. One of Titus's distinguishing features is that it uses the title to

---

13. See Philo, *Creation* 169; *Abel and Cain* 70, 71; *Confusion of Tongues* 93; *Migration of Abraham* 25, 124; *Abraham* 176; *Joseph* 195.

describe both God and Christ Jesus. With the exception of 1:1, the epistle always identifies Jesus Christ as "our Savior." It does so three times (1:4; 2:13; 3:6). In this missive, the Pastor also identifies God as "Savior" three times (1:3; 2:10; 3:4). Each time that the epithet is applied to God it appears in close proximity with a passage that applies the title to Jesus Christ. In effect, God is "our Savior," the source of our salvation; salvation is effected by Jesus Christ. Apart from 2:11–14, the epistle offers no specific reflection on why and how this is so.

Many of the salient ideas associated with the use of the "Savior" title in the Pastoral Epistles come together in Titus 2:11–14: "For the saving beneficence of God has appeared to all people, teaching us to deny impiety and worldly passions and to live modestly, justly, and in godly fashion in the present age, awaiting the blessed hope, that is, the appearance of the glory of the great God, our Savior, Jesus Christ, who gave himself for us, to redeem us from all lawlessness and purify for himself a chosen people, eager for good works." Present in this intricate statement are the notions of God as Savior, his universal will for salvation, the appearance of Jesus as Savior, and the salvation of the community.

The phrase "appearance of the glory of the great God, our Savior, Jesus Christ" is one of the great cruxes in New Testament interpretation. Some elements of the phrase are Hellenistic. Not only was the word *epiphaneia*, "appearance," commonly used to refer to the manifestation of a god, or of a monarch understood to be a representative or manifestation of a deity, but also the descriptive adjective *megas*, "great," was a common epithet for the deity in the Hellenistic world, just as it was in the Greek Bible (e.g., Deut. 10:17; Ps. 47:2). Sophocles, the fifth-century B.C.E. dramatist, called Demeter and Persephone, mother and daughter, respectively, the goddess of the grain and the goddess of spring, "great goddess" (*megala thea*). A third-century B.C.E. papyrus says of the goddess Isis that she made her husband, the great Osiris, immortal (*sy ton megan Osirin athanaton epoiēsas*, P. Oxy. 1380.242). Cybele, sometimes indistinguishable from Demeter and reputed to have raised Attis from the dead, was known as "the great mother" (see SIG 1014.83). Her Roman feast (April 4–10) was known as Megalesia, the celebration of greatness. Ephesians acclaimed the virgin goddess of the hunt with the words "Great is Artemis of the Ephesians" (*megalē hē Artemis Ephesiōn*; Acts 19:27, 28, 34).

In the Hellenistic world, the pair of words "god" (*theos*) and "savior" (*sōtēr*) was frequently used to describe emperors. The oldest such reference is in a third-century B.C.E. votive offering from Halicarnassus dedicated to "Ptolemy the savior and god" (*tou sōtēros kai theou*; see *The Collection of Ancient Greek Inscriptions in the British Museum* IV, 1, no. 906). An Ephesian inscription in honor of Julius Caesar (48 B.C.E.) used the pair of titles along with the idea of an appearance (*epiphanē*, see SIG 760). An Olympian inscription used the paired epithet, qualified by "great," for Augustus (*sōtēr Zeus aneteile megas*, Inschriften von Olympia 53).[14]

The Pastor's circles commonly used Hellenistic theological language to describe the God in whom they believed. This enabled them to interpret the monotheism of their ancestors in faith in the language of their Hellenistic culture. When the Pastor writes about "the appearance of the glory of the great God, our Savior" in Titus 2:13, he is clearly speaking about a manifestation of the divine. But what precisely do these words signify? Does the phrase, literally, "the great God and our Savior, Jesus Christ" (*tou megalou theou kai sōtēros hēmōn Iēsou Christou*; see 2 Pet. 1:1), mean that Jesus Christ is the great God and our Savior? Are "great God" and "our Savior" to be distinguished so that Christian hope is focused on the manifestation of both God and Jesus Christ? Or does the phrase "the great God and our Savior" refer to God alone and the name "Jesus Christ" appear within the complex expression in apposition to "glory," that is, the appearance of *the glory* (*tēs doxēs*) of the great God, namely, our Savior Jesus Christ?

For any number of reasons these questions are not easy to answer. One of the principal sources of difficulty is that in Titus, the "Savior" title is used of both God and Jesus. In 1 Tim. 4:10, God, to whom the epithet "Savior" is applied, is the object of Christian hope: "We toil and struggle, since we have hoped in the living God who is the Savior of all people, especially of the faithful." On the other hand, the opening words of that epistle speak of Christ Jesus as "our hope" (1 Tim. 1:1). First Timothy 1:1; 4:10; and Titus 2:13 are the only passages within the Pastorals that link Christian hope (*elpis*) with the "Savior" title.

Contributing further to the crux of Titus 2:13 is the fact that Jesus is but rarely, if at all, called "God" in the New Testament. Notwithstanding this difficulty, the phrase "the great God and our Savior" (*tou megalou theou kai sōtēros hēmōn*) ought to be taken as a titulary unit. The name "Jesus Christ" (*Iēsou Christou*) should be understood as an explanatory addition to the title. The two-part name identifies a human person, as it does throughout the Pastorals, in which neither "Jesus" nor "Christ" appears without the other. In these epistles "Christ" is nominal rather than titulary.

One of the principal reasons why "the great God and our Savior" should be understood as a single titular epithet is the widespread Hellenistic identification of a god, goddess, or divinized human as "god and savior." By calling Jesus Christ "God our Savior," the Pastor has appropriated a well-known Hellenistic expression (see 3 Macc. 6:29) to explain the significance of Jesus Christ to his readers. Support for this interpretation is found in the fact that a single definite article controls the two-part title. Were "God" and "Savior" to be distinguished from one another, common usage would have required that the article be

14. See Paul Wendland, *"Sōtēr," ZNW* 5 (1904): 343.

repeated before "Savior." Finally, "epiphany" language, one of the hallmarks of the Christian language of the Pastor's circles, is used exclusively of an appearance of Jesus Christ in the Pastoral Epistles (2:11; 3:4; 1 Tim. 6:14; 2 Tim. 1:10; 4:1, 8).[15]

Titus 2:13 is thus one of the first indications of the Christian use of "God language" in reference to Jesus. This usage is amply attested in the letters of Ignatius, who calls Jesus "our God" (Ign. *Eph.* prologue; 15:3; 18:2; *Rom.* prologue; 3:3; *Pol.* 8:3), "God" (Ign. *Eph.* 7:2; 19:3; *Trall.* 11:2; *Smyrn.* 1:1), and "my God" (Ign. *Rom.* 6:3) when referring to the passion of the historical Jesus.

"Our Savior" in Titus 2:11–14

When the crux of Titus 2:13 is thus resolved and the enigmatic phrase "the great God, our Savior" is understood as a reference to Jesus, it becomes clear that Titus 2:11–14 presents the Pastor's audience with a concise articulation of the common understanding of salvation by the Pastor's community. The pericope is presented as an explanation of the "teaching about our Savior, God" (Titus 2:10). The explanatory pericope is the only passage in the Pastorals to use the adjective "saving," in the phrase "the saving beneficence of God" (*hē charis tou theou sōtērios*, 2:11). This explanatory pericope uses the "Savior" title of Jesus Christ. Titus 1:1–4, 2:10–14, and 3:4–6 are the passages in the Pastorals in which the epithet is used of both God (1:3; 2:10; 3:4) and Christ (1:4; 2:13; 3:6). It is significant that in these instances the application of the title to God precedes its application to Christ.

Initially, some insight into 2:11–14 is to be gained from the Ephesian inscription in honor of Julius Caesar. The Pastor presents Jesus Christ as the manifestation of the saving beneficence of God. Jesus must be understood both as our Savior and as the great God, insofar as he is the expression of God's saving beneficence. Salvation ultimately comes from God (see 2:10). The Pastor is describing God's saving beneficence when he speaks of the appearance of Jesus Christ.

The Pastor's attribution of salvation to God is consistent both with his use of the adjective "saving" in reference to God in the pericope (2:11) and with his use of the "Savior" title in reference to God elsewhere in the epistle (1:3; 3:4; see 1 Tim. 1:1; 2:3; 4:10). In conveying the teaching about our Savior, God, to his audience, the Pastor echoes the conviction of God's will for universal salvation (2:11; see also 1 Tim. 2:4; 4:10). Writing about God's goodness and benevolence in 3:4–5, he tells us that God "saved us" ("God" being the implied subject of the verb "to save"; see 1 Tim. 2:4; 2:15 [a divine passive in Greek];

15. See further, Spicq, *Saint Paul*, 640–41, and Murray J. Harris, *Jesus as God: The New Testament Use of* Theos *in Reference to Jesus* (Grand Rapids: Baker, 1992), 173–75.

2 Tim. 1:9). We are saved not by our righteous works but according to God's mercy (3:5).

Salvation has past, present, and future dimensions. Because Jesus Christ gave himself for us, to redeem us from all lawlessness and to purify for himself a chosen people (2:14), he can be called "our Savior" (2:13; see 1:4; 3:6; 2 Tim. 2:10). In the Pastor's experience, God "saved us through the washing of rebirth and renewal by the Holy Spirit, which he poured out on us profusely through Jesus Christ" (3:5–6). Thus, we are justified by grace (3:7), and we have become heirs (3:7) and a chosen people (2:14). What God has effected through Christ Jesus, that is, through his redemptive self-donation and our baptisms, particularizes God's universal will of salvation. God's salvific will is made manifest in the salvation that God has accomplished in Christ Jesus. Hence, Christians can speak about "salvation in Christ Jesus" (2 Tim. 1:10; 3:15).

These purified and chosen people are to be eager for good works (2:14). That is, they are to shun impiety and worldly passions and live modestly, justly, and piously in the present age (2:12), notwithstanding the fact that they are not justified by their righteous works (3:5). These chosen people have been taught to live out their conversion experience. Inspired sacred writings, the Scriptures, are a key element in this teaching. They are apt for teaching, correcting, and training in righteousness. They are capable of instructing us with regard to salvation through faith in Christ Jesus (see 2 Tim. 3:15–16). Teaching about the Christian way of life—how his community should live—is an integral element of the Pastor's teaching about our Savior (God). If Christians pay attention to this teaching and put it into action in their lives, they can be said to save themselves (1 Tim 4:16). The complex reality of salvation stems from God's universal will of salvation: It is realized in Christ Jesus; it is expressed in the lives of Christ Jesus' chosen people.

Salvation is not restricted to Christians' modest, just, and pious life in the present age. Salvation is oriented toward the future. If God is our Savior (1:3), Jesus is our hope (1 Tim 1:1). Christians await the blessed hope, the appearance of the glory of our great God and Savior (2:13). They are heirs according to the hope of eternal life (3:7). A baptismal hymn used to explain salvation in Christ Jesus with eternal glory proclaims, "For if we die together, we shall also live together. If we endure, we shall also reign together" (2 Tim. 2:11–12).

Ultimately, the "Savior" title alerts the modern reader to the comprehensive soteriology of the Pastoral Epistles. Their theology is essentially a soteriology, an understanding of salvation. Each of the Pastoral Epistles reminds the hearers that what is said about salvation is a "trustworthy saying" (3:8; 1 Tim. 4:9; 2 Tim. 2:11; see Excursus 1). Soteriology is crucial to the Pastorals' understanding of Christ Jesus. Neither his past nor his future "appearance" (see Excursus 8) can be understood apart from the teaching about our Savior, God.

A Comparative Addendum

The way that the Epistle to Titus uses the title "Savior" is similar to the way that Paul used the title "Lord" (*kyrios*). Not only is "Lord" Paul's favorite christological title; it is also the cipher of much of his theology insofar as it relates to the resurrection, the Lordship of Jesus over believers, and Jesus' future appearance. In the Greco-Roman world, "lord" was a truly evocative—and sometimes provocative—title. Hellenistic Judaism, including its Greek Bible, used the title "Lord" for God. Paul occasionally followed this customary usage. More often he employed the title "Lord" to indicate that Jesus was God's designated agent in doing what God wanted him to do on behalf of the people of God. The Lord Jesus now sits at the right hand of the Father (see Ps. 110:1; Rom. 8:34; 1 Cor. 15:25). As the title "Lord" was used in Hellenistic society of temporal rulers, in Judaism of God, and in Paul of Jesus Christ, God's agent, so too was "Savior" used in Hellenistic society of temporal powers, in Judaism of God, and in the Pastorals of Jesus.

[4] The Pastor's reflection on the significance of Paul's apostolate far exceeds in both length and importance the description of the author found in typical Hellenistic letters. The description appended to the name of the "intended" recipient, an epistolary *intitulatio*, also exceeds in length and importance those found in personal Hellenistic letters, as does the greeting that follows.

The designated recipient is Titus, identified as Paul's "true son according to the common faith" (*gnēsiō teknō kata koinēn pistin*). The Greek word "true" is derived from the root *gen-* and is cognate with a number of words that relate to birth (such as *gennaō, genos*). It means "lawfully begotten" or "legitimate." This classic usage is found in Democritus, Euripides, and many other ancient authors. Hellenistic Jews such as Philo (e.g., *Joseph* 74) and Josephus (*Ant.* 1.16.3 §253) often used the expression in this sense. No ancient source suggests, however, that Titus was Paul's biological son. The qualifying adjective must be taken in the metaphorical sense of "genuine" or "real."

This is in keeping with Jewish concepts of paternity in which the faithful transmission of traditional lore from father to son was the ultimate norm of real paternity (see Gutierrez). According to the rabbis, a father's primary responsibility was the socialization of his son: "The father is bound in respect of his son, to circumcise, redeem, teach him Torah, take a wife for him, and teach him a craft" (*b. Qidd.* 22a). If a man taught the Torah to another's child, it was as if he had begotten that child (see *b. Sanh.* 19b). Through instruction, the child had become a son to him. Paul shared this Jewish understanding of paternity, with one notable difference. The gospel replaced the Torah as the means of generation. Paul is father to those to whom he preached (see 1 Cor. 4:15, 17; Phlm. 10). In 1:4 Titus is identified as Paul's true son insofar as the apostle had instructed him and socialized him into the Christian community by his proclamation of the gospel.

What did the Pastor add to this notion when he qualified Titus's sonship as being "according to the common faith" (*kata koinēn pistin*)? The question ultimately bears on the meaning of the preposition "according to" (*kata*). Of the various ways to understand the preposition, two yield a plausible meaning for the Pastor's phrase. One derives from the use of the preposition to designate a goal or purpose. If this is the Pastor's intended meaning, the phrase could be rendered "for the sake of the common faith." Taken in this sense, the phrase would suggest that Paul has taught the common faith to Titus so that he, in turn, could pass it on (see 1:1). Another understanding of the phrase emerges if the preposition is to be taken as indicative of a norm or standard. In this case the phrase can be rendered "according to the common faith." It would imply that Titus has been engendered by Paul according to the standard of the common faith (see 2 Tim. 2:2).

Both meanings make sense in the context of 1:4. Both enhance the image of Titus that would be in keeping with the rhetorical purpose of the epistolary *intitulatio* of a pseudepigraphic text. The nuances suggested in the translation above would appear to offer the more likely meaning of the Pastor's phrase. The idea that Titus is the authentic son, the real son of Paul, establishes his authority for the legislative text that follows. In using the word "son," the Pastor is not so much concerned with the next generation per se as he is concerned for the authoritative regulation of his community, which belongs to God's chosen people.

The standard by which Titus is described as Paul's son is "the common faith" (*koinēn pistin*). This striking expression designates the norm of faith of God's chosen people. In his description of Paul (1:1–3), the Pastor wrote about "faith." Paul's apostolate, he had said, was "for the sake of the faith" (*kata pistin*, 1:1). He now affirms that Titus is Paul's true son "according to the common faith" (*kata koinēn pistin*, 1:4). The similarity between the two references to faith suggests that the "common faith" is the faith of God's chosen ones whose characteristics and purpose have been described at length in 1:1–3. Its commonality derives from the fact that it is shared among God's chosen people.

Paul used the word "faith" to designate a personal relationship, a relationship of trust and loyalty. Were "faith" to have been used in the Pastor's circles in this way, the expression "common faith" might have suggested that Titus had been engendered by Paul for the sake of the mission of evangelization, that is, for the sake of people's relationship to God. However, in the Pastoral Epistles "faith" usually denotes the reliable content of what is believed (see Excursus 4). Moreover, "chosen ones" suggests a limited group. Thus, the phrase "common faith" might simply focus on the faith of the Pastor's own theological community, without evoking a missionary task.

The third part of the customary salutation in Hellenistic letters (after the author's name and *intitulatio*) was the greeting. Typically it was short and sweet, "rejoice" (*chairein*), to which a health wish was often appended.[16] The apostle Paul's epistolary style employed a longer greeting. The greeting of his first letter was a simple "grace to you and peace" (1 Thess. 1:1). In his later correspondence, Paul expanded the greeting. He added "from God our Father and the Lord Jesus Christ" (Rom. 1:7; 1 Cor. 1:3; 2 Cor. 1:2; Gal. 1:3; Phil. 1:2; Phlm. 3). Paul's epistolary greeting thus became a blessing. This was very appropriate. His letters were read to communities that had gathered to hear the reading of them, presumably celebrating a common meal and recalling what the Lord did on the night before he died (see 1 Cor. 11:17–32).

The Pastor adopted Paul's standard greeting but made significant modifications. Instead of using "our" to nuance "Father," he uses the preposition to qualify "Savior" in the expression "our Savior" (*tou sōtēros hēmōn*), the appositive to "Jesus Christ." The Pastor's focus is soteriological. Earlier, he had identified God as our Savior (v. 3). Now he identifies Jesus Christ as our Savior. God is the Savior whose "executive agent" is Christ Jesus, "our Savior." It is through Christ Jesus that the gifts of salvation,[17] grace and peace, are given to God's people.

The description of Jesus Christ as our Savior has led to the omission of the traditional epistolary designation of Jesus as "Lord." "Jesus Christ our Lord" is the christological title that Paul and his followers generally used in their epistolary greetings. The title "Lord" is central to the development and expression of Paul's Christology. It does not appear in the vocabulary of the Epistle to Titus either as a descriptive epithet for Christ Jesus or as a descriptive epithet or equivalent name for God.

Qualities of an Elder
Titus 1:5–9

Unlike the typical Pauline letter in which some expression of thanksgiving follows immediately after the epistolary salutation (Rom. 1:8; 1 Cor. 1:4; Phil. 1:3; 1 Thess. 1:2; Phlm. 4; see 2 Cor. 1:3; Col. 1:3; 2 Thess. 1:3; 2 Tim. 1:3), the epistle to Titus does not contain a thanksgiving period.[18] Having expressed greetings to Titus, the Pastor immediately proceeds to the purpose of his composition. He portrays Titus as someone who has been charged with responsibility for the good order of the church on the island of Crete.

---

16. See 3 John 2.
17. The word "salvation" (*sōtēria*) does not appear in Titus.
18. 1 Timothy similarly omits the customary thanksgiving period; 2 Timothy does not.

Titus cannot assure the well-being of the church all by himself. He is charged by "Paul" with the task of appointing elders to oversee the church in the several cities in which the church has been established (cf. Acts 20:28). With the aid of some of the typical features of a household code, the Pastor describes the characteristics of a man who deserves to be called an elder. To be an elder is not a matter of having attained a certain age; it is a matter of being respectable, faithful to one's wife, and having raised one's children properly. "Elders" are men who deserve the reputation of being good family men. The elder is not an old man; he is a responsible citizen.

The task of the elders whom Titus is to appoint in the several cities on the island is to be an overseer on the model of a good steward in the household of God (see 1 Cor. 4:1). The steward (*oikonomos*) was generally a slave who had responsibility for overseeing the other slaves in the household. The steward assigned their tasks and coordinated their work so that the entire household functioned effectively. Early Christians came together in the houses of people who effectively served as the patrons of the "house church," the gathering of Christians in their house. The gatherings (*ekklēsia*) came to be described as households (*oikia*); the church was "the household of God" (1 Tim. 3:15).

According to Paul, the primary quality of the good steward is that he be faithful and loyal (1 Cor. 4:2). In 1:5–9 the Pastor spells out in further detail some of the qualities of the good steward. There are some things that he should be and other things that he should not be. He should not be stubborn, hot under the collar, a drunkard, always ready for a fight, or avaricious. On the other hand, the good steward should be hospitable, temperate, just, religious, someone who loves the good, and someone who knows how to stand his ground. Essentially, the good steward of God's household is a man who possesses the classic virtues of prudence, temperance, fortitude, and justice. Hellenistic moralists considered that leaders, in particular, should possess these cardinal virtues. The Pastor adds hospitality and religious devotion to the list.

Hospitality and religiosity are qualities that must be found in someone who is going to be a steward in the household of God. In addition to being a gracious host for the church that would gather in his house, the overseer was expected to welcome traveling missionaries in the manner in which Aquila and Prisca provided accommodation and the possibility of employment for Paul (e.g., Acts 18:1–3). It almost goes without saying that the good steward in the household of God should be a religious person, especially if that person has responsibility for imparting the truth of the gospel message to the faithful and convincing its opponents of their error, the very responsibilities that are assigned to the overseer. In adding to this list of virtues the mention of God's steward and a specific reference to the faithful saying, the Pastor has provided a specifically

Christian aspect to a profile of someone who is not only a good person but is also capable of assuming responsibility within a community.

1:5 For this reason I left you in Crete so that you might set in order what remains to be done and appoint elders in every city as I have commanded you, 6 if anyone is beyond reproach, the husband of one woman, having faithful children who cannot be accused of being wasteful or stubborn. 7 For the overseer should be without reproach as God's steward, not obstinately self-willed, not prone to anger, not addicted to wine, not ready for a fight, not sordidly greedy for gain, 8 but hospitable, loving the good, temperate, just, pious, self-controlled, 9 holding fast to the trustworthy saying according to the teaching, so that he is capable both of exhorting with sound teaching and correcting opponents.[a]

a. A thirteenth-century manuscript in Greek with Latin and Arabic translations (460) adds, "Do not appoint those who have married twice or make them deacons/servants, and do not take wives in a second marriage; let them not come to serve the Deity at the altar. As God's servant reprove the rulers who are unjust judges and robbers and liars and unmerciful." The Greek clause "do not take wives in a second marriage" (*mēde gynaikas echein ek digamias*) is ambiguous. Most probably it enjoins deacons/servants from marrying a woman if her marriage to the deacon were to be her second marriage.

[1:5–6] The tradition of the Pastor's circles is that Titus was assigned to Crete despite the fact that at some point Titus reportedly went to Dalmatia on the Adriatic coast (2 Tim. 4:10). Crete is a relatively large island in the Aegean, some 156 miles from east to west, and, at the widest point, thirty-five miles from north to south. Its ancient civilization dates back to at least the Late Bronze Age. Since the second century B.C.E. a large Jewish population had existed on the island (see Tacitus, *Histories* 5.2).

Titus 1:5 suggests that Paul was on Crete[19] with Titus and that he left Titus behind to attend to the pastoral care of the churches on the island; there is, however, no external evidence to support the idea that Paul had been on Crete, much less that he evangelized its inhabitants. One early church tradition reports that one of the ships used by the Roman centurion Julius to bring Paul to Rome was beset by a severe northeaster as it sailed by Crete (Acts 27:7–20), but this account says nothing about Paul going ashore. At most, Luke's narrative suggests that supplies for the voyage were obtained from the Cretan city of Lasea while the ship was anchored offshore.

Titus's assigned role was to organize the communities of Christians on the island. Given the size of the Jewish population, these communities may have

19. A church dedicated to Paul is located on a hill near the site of the ancient Cretan city of Lasea.

had Jewish Christian foundations (1:10, 14). Titus was to accomplish his task by appointing elders "in every city" or "city by city" (*kata polin*). The expression conveys the impression of a successful Pauline mission to Crete that resulted in the establishment of several different churches on the island. According to 1:5, Paul himself gave Titus the responsibility for the organization of these churches. His oral command (*hōs egō soi dietaxamēn*, with its emphatic *egō*, "I") was confirmed and clarified by means of this epistle (*toutou charin*).

Among Jews, elders were well known and well respected. The Pastor describes the elder whom Titus should appoint as someone who is beyond reproach, is the husband of one woman, has faithful children, and cannot be accused of being profligate or headstrong. For the most part, these qualities and those of 1:7–8 are typical of the virtues that appear on the classic lists of virtues (see p. 55). The terminology is rarely used in the New Testament, except for its use in one or another similar lists of qualities appearing in 1 Timothy (3:2–7, 8, 11, 12; 5:9–16).

Above all, the respected elder must be beyond reproach (*anenklētos*). This quality is a comprehensive virtue. It introduces the list of particular qualities that one expects to find in an elder (see 1 Tim. 3:10, where "beyond reproach" sums up the good qualities of a server). The man who is beyond reproach is a family man, married to only one wife and with children who were reared in the faith. The expectation that a man who is recognized as an elder should have married and raised a family is an implicit rejection of the skewed asceticism that so troubled the Pastor's circles (see 1 Tim. 4:3; cf. 1 Cor. 7:1–7). That men respected as elders within the Jewish community had been married at least once was a matter of their fidelity to Jewish tradition. According to the Torah, "Be fruitful and multiply" were the first words spoken by God to human beings (Gen. 1:28). Among the 247 mandatory commandments that the rabbinic tradition would later extrapolate from the law was the prescription, "You should perpetuate the human race by marrying according to the law."[20] Based on Gen. 1:28 and Deut. 24:1, this commandment incorporated the 212th and 213th mandatory precepts. The requirement that an elder be married just once, apparently implying that the elder not remarry after the death of his spouse (see the discussion on pp. 81–82), runs contrary to Jewish tradition. The requirement may derive from the expectation that leaders of the community, beginning with Titus and Timothy, emulate Paul (see 1 Cor. 7:8).

Married to one wife, the elder should have "faithful children" (*tekna echōn pista*). In ordinary parlance the phrase would generally mean having children who are loyal and faithful. In the Pastor's circles, however, "faith" (*pistis* and its cognates) refers to the Christian faith, the gospel message (see Excursus 4).

20. "Commandments, The 613," *EncJud* 5.770.

Thus, that quality must refer to the rearing of children in the faith (see Eph. 6:4b). As a good Jewish father is one who has taught his son the Torah, so the would-be elder must be someone who has raised his children in the church's faith.

In ordinary society, an indication of well-raised children is that they be neither wasteful nor stubborn or recalcitrant (see Eph. 6:4a; Col. 3:21). The household code of Eph. 5:22–6:9 links together a father's religious and secular responsibilities for his children in a way that is reminiscent of the Pastor's words about the proper rearing of children in 1:6. The Pastor's own description of these properly reared children is *mē en katēgoria asōtias ē anypotakta*, literally, "not in[21] an accusation of wastefulness or being headstrong." No one should be able to point a finger of accusation at the elder's children as being wasteful or headstrong.

In traditional Mediterranean society, material goods were considered to exist in limited quantities. Prodigality was therefore a serious failing, especially when present in a member of the younger generation (see Luke 15:11–32). As the Jewish father was expected to teach his son a trade in the process of bringing him up for life in the world, so a father could be expected to teach his children responsibility with regard to the limited amount of this world's goods. Moreover, the elder's children, reared in the faith and conscientious about the wealth of the world in which they lived, should not be stubborn or headstrong (*anypotakta*). Stubborn and rebellious children are a burden on any family. It was expected that a good father so correct his children that they would not grow up with a stubborn disposition. The translation, "who are not open to any accusation of being wasteful or stubborn," renders the Pastor's grammatically unbalanced phrase in such a way that it indicates what properly raised children should not be.

In this passage, the Pastor has thus far identified for his readers some of the qualities that characterize the person who is known as an elder. He has not yet indicated what role the elder has to play in the community. Verse 7 suggests that the elder is to have the function of oversight (see also v. 9). The good family man has a reputation as an elder; he can serve the community as its overseer (see 1 Tim. 3:2–5).

[7–8] In verse 7 the Pastor says just a word about the function of the "elder" who is to be appointed. He is to be an "overseer" (*ton episkopon*). The overseer appointed by Titus has the responsibility of attending to the administration of the community of believers for which he has been appointed. An "overseer" is to be appointed in each city. The elder and an overseer are one and the same person. The man's status is that of elder; his function is that of overseer. Acts 20:17–38 describes Paul as speaking to a group of elders (v. 17) who have the function of oversight (v. 28) in the community.

---

21. The preposition *en*, used to identify a condition or a state, governs the phrase "accusation of wastefulness."

Paul's farewell discourse uses the image of the shepherd as a metaphor for leadership within the community; the Pastor employs the image of the steward, the household manager (*oikonomos*; see 1 Tim. 3:1–2, 15). Polycarp of Smyrna also adopts the image of the shepherd (see Pol. *Phil.* 6:1) and gives a list of qualities that these elders-shepherds[22] must possess:

> The elders also must be compassionate, merciful towards all, turning back the sheep that are gone astray, visiting all the infirm, not neglecting a widow or an orphan or a poor man; but providing always for that which is honorable in the sight of God and humans, abstaining from all anger, respect of persons, unrighteous judgment, being far from all love of money [*makran . . . pasēs philargyrias*, see 1 Tim. 3:3], not quick to believe anything against anyone, not hasty in judgment (Pol. *Phil.* 6:1).

The way that the Pastor refers to the oversight role of the elder within the household is similar to the way that Epictetus describes the philosopher (*Discourses* 3.22). Speaking of the calling of the philosopher, Epictetus writes, "In a well-ordered house [*en oikia kalōs oikoumenē*] no one comes along and says to himself, 'I ought to be manager of this house [*oikonomou*]'" (3.22.3). For "in this great city, the world . . . there is a Lord of the Mansion [*oikodespotēs*] who assigns each and everything in its place" (*Discourses* 3.22.4). The philosopher is "the scout [*kataskopon*][23] of the gods" (*Discourses* 3.22.69; see 22.24, 38). He is "sent by Zeus to men partly as a messenger in order to show them that in questions of good and evil they have gone astray" (*Discourses* 3.22.23; see 22.26–49).

Epictetus describes some of the things that a philosopher ought not to be: "You must feel no anger, no rage, no envy, no pity; no wench must look fine to you, no petty reputation, no boy-favorite, no little sweet-cake" (*Discourses* 3.22.13). While Epictetus prefers that the philosopher be unmarried because of the burdens of being a husband and father (3.22.71–72), he admits that "there will be nothing to prevent him from both marrying and having children; for his wife will be another person like himself (cf. 3.22.76) . . . and his children will be brought up in the same fashion" (3.22.68)

The parallels between what Epictetus has written about the "scout" (*paraskopos*) and what the Pastor has written about the "overseer" (*episkopos*) are striking. They are all the more striking because Epictetus was a contemporary of the Pastor's. Both Epictetus and Titus were associated with Nicopolis (see commentary on 3:12). A subscription added later to this epistle[24] says that

---

22. Polycarp's linking together of the notion of the elder and the shepherd (see Acts 20:28) is similar to what is said in 1 Pet. 5:1–4, a text that brings together the shepherd's role, the elder, the chief shepherd, and the ministry of oversight.

23. Epictetus uses the verb "to oversee" (*episkopeō*) to describe the philosopher's task (see *Discourses* 3.22.97).

24. A similar subscription is found at the end of 1 Timothy.

it was composed in Nicopolis, a city to which Epictetus had gone as an exile. Epictetus was mostly active in Rome, the presumed provenance of 2 Timothy.

In his description of the philosopher in the *Discourses,* Epictetus mentioned eight things that the philosopher should not be. The Pastor lists only five such negative qualities: obstinately self-willed, prone to anger, addicted to wine, ready for a fight, and sordidly greedy for gain. The elder-overseer should be none of these. The Pastor's short catalog of vices—five was the typical number of vices that appear in some of the earliest catalogs—lists five qualities that no one should have, let alone someone who is in a position of authority.

Like the Pastor, 2 Peter also speaks of those who are self-willed (*authadeis,* 2 Pet. 2:10). Addiction to wine, readiness for a fight, and sordid greed for gain are negative qualities that appear just one other time in the New Testament. Addition to wine and readiness for a fight follow one another on the list of qualifications for the overseer in 1 Tim. 3:3; sordid greed for gain appears on the list of qualifications for the server (1 Tim. 3:8). The latter vice (*aischrokerdē*) was mentioned by the dramatist Euripides (*Andromache* 451) and the historian Herodotus (*Histories* 1.187). "Prone to anger" (*orgilon*) is a word not found elsewhere in the New Testament, but being without anger (*mē orgēn*) is a quality that Epictetus expects of the philosopher (*Discourses* 3.22.13). The Pastor is simply urging that the overseer have none of the negative characteristics that common wisdom identifies as vices.

On the other hand, the overseer should be hospitable, love the good, be temperate, just, pious, and in control. Hellenistic moralists considered that there were four cardinal virtues, hinge virtues from which all others could be derived: prudence, justice, temperance, and fortitude. This concept is usually traced to Plato and Aristotle, but it was common philosophical property by the first century C.E.[25] The Pastor is generally indebted to such traditions, using many of the terms in this catalog of virtues, but he shows no interest in classifying the virtues according to a genealogical scheme as did Philo[26] and many of the philosophers before him.

The Pastor's list begins on a positive note. The overseer should love the stranger (*philo-xenon*) and love the good (*phil-agathon*). Hospitality was greatly appreciated in Mediterranean society. It was an important quality for a household manager, whom Aeschylus calls "the overseer of the house" (*dōmatōn episkopos, Eumenides* 740). Hospitality (see 1 Tim. 3:2; 1 Pet. 4:9) was particularly important in the first-century Christian movement. The open household and a hospitable householder were necessary for the celebration of the Eucharist, the work of catechesis, and the task of evangelization. The love

---

25. See Plato, *Laws* 1.630–31; 12.963–65; Aristotle, *Politics* 7.1.2; and Diogenes Laertius, *Lives of Eminent Philosophers* 3.90–91; 7.92, 102.

26. See *Allegorical Interpretation* 1.63, 65.

of what is good (*philagathon*) is a kind of overarching virtue. The paraenesis of the Pastoral Epistles repeatedly underscores the importance of every good work (1:16; 3:1; 1 Tim. 5:10; 2 Tim. 2:21; 3:17; see 1 Tim. 2:10).

The overseer is to be temperate (*sōphrona*), a virtue constantly promoted within the Pastorals, especially in Titus. Ten of the New Testament's sixteen uses of the root *sōphro(n)-* are found in this corpus, six of them in Titus.[27] In 2:2 the Pastor links temperance with justice and godliness. Temperance is the power to control one's passions. Philo says that "it takes its stand against pleasure, which thinks that it can direct the course of human weakness" (*Allegorical Interpretation* 1.69). Temperance was a virtue to be taught to children, but it was especially important for those who would rule over others. Plato specifically identifies temperance as a quality to be possessed by an overseer (*episkopoi sōphrosynēs, Laws* 8.849a). He taught that a prince must be able to master himself and maintain order and harmony in the community (*Republic* 4.428b–432a; *Laws* 3.697c–e; 6.757a–c).

For the Pastor, the overseer should also be just (*dikaion*; see 1 Tim. 1:9; 2 Tim. 4:8). This virtue is often mentioned in the biblical tradition. To be just is to be in a correct relationship with God and with members of the covenant people. While all people were called to be just, it was imperative that kings and leaders of the people of God possess this virtue (e.g., Ps. 72:1–4). Among Hellenists, for whom justice was one of the cardinal virtues, people whose behavior conformed to custom or law were considered just (Homer, *Odyssey* 6.120). Justice was the virtue of promoting order and harmony among people (Plato, *Republic* 4.443c–e). It included a dimension of fidelity toward the gods. For Josephus, justice had a specifically religious dimension. The good kings of the Deuteronomist's history of Israel were "just and pious." Their justice included faithful fulfillment of God's commandments. In similar fashion, the Pastor says that the overseer must be just (*dikaion*) and pious (*hosion*; see Luke 1:75; Eph. 4:24; 1 Thess. 2:10).[28]

In addition to being temperate, just, and pious, the elder/overseer is expected to be "in control" (*enkratē*). The noun related to this adjective, *enkrateia*, is frequently translated "self-control," specifically connoting control of the appetites, especially the sexual appetite. The Greeks often linked self-control with "temperance." Philo considers self-control to be one of the three fundamental characteristics of statesmanship (see *Joseph* 54). The other two are the art of shepherding (*poimenikon*) and household management (*oikonomikon*).

27. See 1:8; 2:2, 4, 5, 6, 12; 1 Tim. 3:2; 2 Tim. 1:7; cf. Mark 5:15; Luke 8:35; Rom. 12:3; 2 Cor. 5:13; 1 Pet. 4:7.

28. Even as "just" (*dikaios*) and "godly" (*eusebēs*) are linked together in Greek literature, so also "just" (*dikaios*) and "pious" (*hosios*) often appear alongside one another. See Plato, *Euthyphro* 12c–e; *Gorgias* 507b; *Republic* 1.331a; Polybius, *Histories* 22.10.8; Philo, *Moses* 2.108; *Flight* 63; Josephus *Ant.* 8.12.2 §295; 12.2.5. §43.

Barnabas 2:2 links self-control to patience and endurance. Self-control "signifies the free, autonomous, and independent person, who does not allow himself to be tempted or diverted by any allurements" (*EDNT* 1.377). As such, self-control is a quality that befits a person who is going to be a leader. Philo says as much in *Joseph* 55–57. So too does Polycarp, who cites self-control as a quality of a server in the community (Pol. *Phil.* 5:2).

[9] Verse 9 offers additional information about the role of the overseer and identifies a quality that he must possess if he is to fulfill his task. The overseer is a teacher in the community of faith. His responsibility is to exhort the members of the community with sound teaching (see pp. 95–97) and to correct opponents. If he is to do that, he must hang on to the trustworthy saying in accordance with the norm of the community's teaching.

The overseer is to "steadfastly maintain the trustworthy saying" (*antechomenon tou . . . pistou logou*). This is the only time that the expression "trustworthy saying" (see 3:8; 1 Tim. 1:15; 3:1; 4:9; 2 Tim. 1:11; see also Excursus 1) is used in the Pastorals without being joined to a specific formulation of traditional material. The Pastor evokes these traditional formulations in qualifying the "trustworthy saying" as being in accordance with the teaching (*kata tēn didachēn*). The teaching of the community handed down from Paul is the norm of a trustworthy saying, providing it with a hermeneutical key. In the departing Paul's final charge to Timothy, Timothy is told "to encourage [*parakaleson*] with all patience and teaching [*didachē*]" (2 Tim. 4:2).

Epictetus said that the philosopher has a double responsibility with regard to the truth. He must teach it and he must defend it. Similarly, the Pastor says that the overseer has a double responsibility with regard to the faithful word (see 2 Tim. 4:2–3). He is to cling to it so that he is capable of exhorting the faithful and correcting opponents.

He is to exhort the members of the community with "sound teaching," a cipher for the post-Pauline message of the gospel (see 1 Tim. 1:10; 2 Tim. 4:3; see pp. 95–97). The epistle to Titus highlights the beneficial nature of this message more than 1 Timothy does (see Titus 1:13; 2:1, 2, 8). In addition to using the trustworthy word for the salutary purpose of encouraging believers, the overseer is also expected to use it to confront the naysayers. He must disprove and correct those who oppose the sound teaching of the Pauline gospel. The following pericope (1:10–16) provides a description of these opponents and gives further precision to the overseer's responsibility in their regard.

Excursus 10: Church Order

In many Hellenistic letters, as in many contemporary letters, a short statement of the principal purpose of the letter follows almost immediately upon the opening greetings. This would seem to be the case with the Epistle to Titus. After the epistle's very formal presentation of the apostolate of Paul in the guise of an epistolary *intitulatio* and of Titus as "true son according to the common faith," the Pastor recalls the role that has been given to Titus, Paul's protégé and successor: "For this reason I left you in Crete so that you might set in order what remains to be done and appoint elders in every city as I have commanded you" (Titus 1:5). In the Greek text, "set in order" and "appoint" are virtually juxtaposed with one another so that the reader knows that Titus's role is to "set in order and appoint" elders. The appointment of elders is seen as a necessary function of the order that Titus is to establish in the various Christian communities on the island of Crete, an island with a large Jewish population.

Elders

Elders were well known and well respected in Judaism. In his treatise on the *Contemplative Life*, Philo describes the festival gatherings of those who dedicated themselves "to knowledge and the contemplation of the verities of nature, following the truly sacred instructions of the prophet Moses." In the course of his description, Philo explains what being an elder means to the Therapeutae, a community of contemplative Jews in Egypt:

> By senior [*presbyterous*] they [Jews] do not understand the aged and grey headed who are regarded as still mere children if they have only in late years come to love this rule of life but those who from their earliest years have grown to manhood and spent their prime in pursuing the contemplative branch of philosophy, which indeed is the noblest and most god-like part. (*Contemplative Life* 67)

Philo recognizes that an elder is an older man, "the aged and grey headed," as he calls them (see 1 Tim. 5:1), but it is not age alone that gains respect and wins the esteem of people. Elders are revered because of their wisdom and their dedication to understanding the Torah. Philo uses Hellenistic terms to describe this lifelong effort; he describes the study of the Torah as the pursuit of the contemplative branch of philosophy. Elders were the wise men of this Jewish community and were respected as such.

The respect accorded to elders in the Jewish community was an essential element of their ethos and their Jewish heritage. According to Num. 11:16, the Lord said to Moses, "Gather for me seventy of the elders of Israel, whom you know to be the elders of the people and officers over them" (*hoti outoi eis presbyteroi tou laou kai grammateis autōn*). The elder is respected by the people and has authority over them. Texts such as Exod. 3:16; 4:29; 17:5; and 24:1–2, 9–11 underscore the continuing role of the elders associated with Moses. Some of these elders outlived Joshua, Moses' successor (see Josh. 24:31), an indication that the elders continued the leadership role of Moses and Joshua. The Mishnah presents these elders as part of an unbroken chain of tradition that goes from Moses through Joshua to Simeon, the son of Gamaliel, the great first-century C.E. rabbi (see *m.'Abot* 1).

The Synoptic Gospels and Acts, attest to the importance of elders within Jewish communities of first-century Palestine. Elders are frequently mentioned alongside the chief priests or the scribes, or both, as representative of the essential leadership of the community (see, e.g., Matt. 16:21; Luke 9:22; Acts 4:5, 8, 23). The Christian community of Jerusalem had its own group of revered elders (Acts 11:30; 14:23; 15:2, 4, 6, 22, 23; 16:4; 20:17; 21:18). Depicting a decisive moment in the history of early Christianity—the acceptance into fellowship by Jewish Christians of Gentile Christians who do not observe the demands of the law—Luke describes the decision makers as "the apostles and the elders" (Acts 15:4, 22). Within the community, the elders have a leadership role alongside the apostles appointed by Jesus (Luke 6:12–16).

Other late first-century Christian texts also highlight the leadership role of elders within the Christian community (see Jas. 5:14; 1 Pet. 5:1, 5; 2 John 1; 3 John 1). Luke describes Paul as having summoned to Miletus the elders of the church of Ephesus in order to give them final instructions before he was about to leave that area of Asia (Acts 20:17). Writing for the most part to communities of Gentile Christians, the apostle did not explicitly mention the role of the elders, a group particularly respected by Jewish Christians. Some few decades after Paul's death, however, Clement wrote about the elders in the church at Corinth. They were, in Clement's words, "duly appointed" (*tōn kathestamenōn presbyterōn*, *1 Clem.* 54:2; see Titus 1:5). Worthy of honor (*1 Clem.* 1:3) and obedience (*1 Clem.* 57:1), they had a leadership role that was not to be denied (see *1 Clem.* 47:6).

The Epistle to Titus also speaks of the appointment of elders. The epistle says that elders are to be appointed "by city" (*kata polin*), an indication that the people whom "Titus" was to appoint had a role to fulfill in residential communities. The Pastor uses a short catalog of virtues to describe the qualities that one would expect to find in a person whom the community would consider to be an elder (see also Pol. *Phil.* 6:1). An elder was to be beyond reproach, a good husband and father. The function to which respected elders are to be appointed is that of overseer (*episkopon*). Their function is "oversight." The term is derived from the verb *epi-skopeō*, to "look on." The Pastor's use of the term "overseer" in the singular suggests that a singular overseer is to be appointed for each community, supervising each house church. The overseer appears to have had responsibility of attending to the administration of the community of believers for which he was appointed. In this sense, the role is comparable to that of the steward, the *oikonomos*, in the Hellenistic household. Since the Christian community was "God's house" (1 Tim. 3:15), it was appropriate that the chief administrator of the community should also be described as "God's steward" (1:7).

Overseers

The Pastor has chosen a classic term to indicate the role of these community leaders. Homer used the term *episkopos* of people who watch over a ship's cargo (*Odyssey* 8.163). Sophocles (*Antigone* 217) and Plato (*Laws* 8.849a) used the noun "overseer" to speak about people who served as guardians or supervisors. Aristophanes used the term of an intendant, the administrative official sent to a subject state (*Birds* 1022–23). Plato used the term (in a masculine form) in reference to women who served as overseers for young married couples (*Laws* 6.784a), who functioned as overseers during athletic events, or who fed children (*Laws* 7.795d). Given the widespread use of the term "overseer" in Hellenistic times, it is anachronistic to render Titus's use of the term as "bishop," even though the Latin transliteration, *episcopus*, was later used for those who fulfilled the office of bishop in urban churches.

Having identified the role of the elder as that of overseer, a role analogous to that of the steward, the Pastor uses a catalog of vices and a catalog of virtues to spell out what he means by saying that an elder should be beyond reproach (1:7–8). After listing these qualities, including some of the virtues that philosophic moralists considered to be the chief qualities of a good leader, the Pastor identifies the twofold role of the elder/overseer. Speaking from the tradition to which he adheres, the *episkopos* should exhort and encourage the faithful with sound teaching, and should confront and correct those who oppose this teaching.

First Timothy also spells out the qualities that one should expect to find in the overseer (1 Tim. 3:1b–7) but does not identify the overseer as an elder. For the most part, the qualities cited in 1 Timothy are similar to those cited in the Epistle to Titus. As is the case in Titus, the qualities are listed as a combination of vices to be avoided and virtues to be activated. As does the Pastor in Titus, the author of 1 Timothy implies that the role of the overseer is that of managing the house of God but, just as 1 Timothy does not use the notion of elder when speaking about the qualities expected of those who would serve the church community as an overseer, so it has not used the term "steward."

First Timothy has something important to say about elders later on in the epistle. Having addressed another issue of good order in the community, namely, the role and care of widows, the Pastor says, "Let elders who manage well be considered worthy of a double honor, especially those who labor in word and teaching. . . . Do not accept any charge against an elder except on the testimony of two or three witnesses" (1 Tim. 5:17, 19). This two-part exhortation contains something akin to the elders' fundamental bill of rights. Elders have a right to a just wage and judicial equity.

Which elders enjoy these two rights? The Pastor identifies such elders as those "who manage well" (*hoi kalōs proestōtes*). The verb "to manage" is one that the Pastor had used to describe the household responsibilities of overseers and servers (1 Tim. 3:4, 5, 12). It is, however, a term that Paul had used of those who have a special responsibility of administration (1 Thess. 5:12; Rom. 12:8). Centuries before Paul, classical authors such as Aristophanes, Herodotus, Thucydides, and Xenophon used the same word to describe those who had a role of headship or leadership over a group of people. Management is an idea that is as equally applicable to the Christian community as it is to the ordinary household and other communities, large or small.

The Pastor adds another idea to identify further the kind of managers that are worthy of double honor—the respect of the community (see 1 Thess. 5:12) and financial support. The elders/managers who deserve double honor from the community are especially those who labor in word and teaching (1 Tim. 5:17). "To labor" (*hoi kopiōntes*) really means "toil"; its connotation is that of hard work demanding time and energy. Paul used this same word to describe the task of those who had positions of leadership in the community when he urged the Thessalonians to "respect those who labor among you and have charge of you in the Lord" (1 Thess. 5:12). The words that the Pastor uses to describe the task of elders who deserve double honor are the same two verbs, "labor" and "have charge/manage," that Paul used.

The Pastor, however, indicates that the work of these elders/managers is "in word and teaching." Their task is, on the one hand, to profess the prophetic word (i.e., to be God's spokespersons), and to teach, on the other. This latter work entails Christian catechesis: passing on the trustworthy sayings, teaching sound doctrine, and explaining the Scriptures. In fact, the Pastor uses the Scriptures as a warrant for his injunction that double honor be paid to elders who manage well. He follows Paul in citing Deut. 25:4 as a scriptural argument for Christians to provide financial support to their leaders (1 Tim. 5:18; see 1 Cor. 9:9). The Pastor adds to these words of Torah an additional saying: "The worker is worthy of his wages." This adage recalls a logion found in the collection of Jesus' sayings known as Q (see Luke 10:7; Matt. 10:10). The saying about the laborer's being worthy of his wages circulated rather widely in the early churches. Jesus' words were not "Scripture" in the proper sense of the term, but the Pastor was able to use them beside a quotation of Scripture as an argument to urge Christians to provide sufficient support for their elders/managers.

In addition to deserving due respect and sufficient sustenance, elders have a particular right to their good name. In any community, leaders are easily subject to criticism. The Pastor evokes biblical jurisprudence to remind Timothy that a charge should not be brought against an elder unless there are at least two witnesses ready to testify against him (see Deut. 19:15; cf. Matt. 18:16). Leaders of communities within the Pastor's circles may have been subject to criticism and unjust accusation coming from the false teachers who were trying to subvert the house of God (see 2 Tim. 3:6). If such were the case, the Pastor's circles would know that their elders/managers were not to stand accused unless there was at least one corroborating witness. Elders/managers, too, had a right to justice and equity.

Servers

Alongside its exposition of the qualities of an overseer (1 Tim. 3:2–7), 1 Timothy 3 lists the qualities of persons having another role in the church, the role of server (*diakonos*, 1 Tim. 3:8–13; see also Pol. *Phil.* 5:2; Phil. 1:1). To a large extent, the qualities expected of the server are similar to those expected of the overseer. The Pastor summarizes some of these qualities when he says that the server is to be "beyond reproach," using the very same term that was used of the elder/overseer in Titus 1:6–7.

The category of server is rather broad. In 1 Tim. 4:6, Timothy is identified as a good servant of Christ Jesus on the condition that he remain faithful to sound teaching and confront those who reject the message of faith. See also the use of "ministry" (*diakonia*) with regard to Paul in 1 Tim. 1:12 (also 2 Tim. 4:5 and, for Paul himself, 2 Tim. 4:11). Since Timothy is to be regarded as a servant, it is reasonable to assume that the category of servant is also applicable to the overseer. Among the several servers in the house of God, there is one who has the category of oversight.

In this regard, the Pastoral Epistles portray the organization of the Christian community as following the model of the Greco-Roman household. The steward/overseer/elder bears the responsibility for assuring the good order of the household and the collaborative functioning of all the servers. As Titus uses the term "overseer" in the singular number, so 1 Timothy uses the word in the singular. "Servers," however, is in the plural. In the community as in the household, a single individual is the chief administrator.

That the Pastorals follow the Greco-Roman model as closely as they do provides another reason why the reference to "the women" (*gynaikas*) in 1 Tim. 3:11 must be taken as a reference to women who function as people who serve in the house of God. As men who serve well, the women who serve well also procure for themselves a good position insofar as the Christian faith is concerned. As it would be anachronistic to use the title "bishop" for those who served as overseers in the communities for which the Pastoral Epistles were intended, so it would be anachronistic to use the title "deacon" of those male and female servers (see Rom. 16:1) who had other responsibilities in the first-century house of God.

Real Widows

The Pastorals identify the overseer and the servers as having particular roles in the household of God. Concern for the good order of the community is expressed in 1 Timothy and Titus. Each of these epistles uses a household code to speak about the responsibilities and rights of various members of the community (see 1 Tim. 5:1–6:2; Titus 2:2–10). All members of the community must live up to expectations if the community itself is to be well ordered.

First Timothy expresses particular concern for a group of women whom the author identifies as "real widows" (1 Tim. 5:3). These are women beyond the age of childbearing who have been faithful wives, good mothers, and committed Christians and who now have no one but the community to care for them. A roll is to be kept of these widows. Some commentators therefore find it appropriate to speak of an "order of widows." They are a well-identified group within the community and are supported by the community, but their task is different both from the leadership function of the overseer and the role of male and female servers in the community. In their declining years, real widows are expected to continue in prayer and petition (1 Tim. 5:5).

Those Who Need Correction
Titus 1:10–16

After urging Timothy to correct and encourage people, the Pastor provided his readers with a colorful description of those who needed to be corrected (2 Tim. 4:3–4). In Titus 1:10–16 the Pastor gives an equally colorful description of those who stand in need of correction (1:9). The Pastor has added to his acerbic and incriminating description a bit of local color by citing an adage that goes back to Epimenides, the pre-Socratic Cretan poet. Apparently aware of the presence of a Jewish population on the island of Crete, the Pastor describes those who need correction as Jews, people who pursue myths and follow merely human commands. These people claim to know God, he says, but their behavior belies their belief. They are up to no good. In fact, they are incapable of doing any good whatsoever.

> 1:10 For there are many people who are stubborn, idle talkers, and deceivers, especially those from the circumcision. 11 They[a] must be reined in. They subvert whole households, teaching what ought not to be taught for the sake of sordid gain.[b] 12 One of them—their very own spokesperson—said, "Cretans are always liars, evil beasts, lazy gluttons." 13 This assertion is true. Therefore correct them severely, so that they may be sound in faith, 14 not intent on Jewish myths and the commands of people who turn away the truth. 15 Everything is pure for those who are pure; nothing is pure for those who are defiled and nonbelievers. Both their minds and their consciences are defiled. 16 They profess to

know God, but deny (him) by their works. They are^c abominable, disobedient, and unsuitable for every good work.

a. Verses 10–11 are a single sentence in Greek.
b. A thirteenth-century minuscule (No. 460) adds "children who insult and hit their own parents, curb, correct, and admonish them like a father does with his children." See commentary on 1:9.
c. Verse 16 is a single sentence in Greek.

[1:10–13a] The Pastor employs a short catalog of vices to describe those who must be corrected. Those who need correction are said to be stubborn, idle talkers, and deceivers. In addition to not having been brought up well (see commentary on 1:6), they talk loosely and are a bunch of liars. There are many such people, says the Pastor, underscoring the magnitude of Titus's difficult task. They come especially from among the Jews, the people of the circumcision (*hoi ek tēs peritomēs*). This graphic, perhaps demeaning, description has a Pauline ring (see Rom. 4:12; Gal. 2:6). It is difficult to decide for sure whether the Pastor was making an attempt to reflect the situation of the church on the island of Crete (see 1:14), where there were several Jewish colonies, or whether he was attempting to create a measure of Pauline verisimilitude.

One of the issues confronting first-century Christians concerned the circumcision of male Gentile Christians. Were they to be circumcised or not? Paul grappled with the issue in his letters to the Romans and, especially, to the Galatians. The problem was known to Luke, who portrays Paul as having circumcised Timothy, a well-known figure in the Pastor's circles, "because of the Jews who were in those places" (Acts 16:3). Because many Jews lived on Crete, it is possible that there were some Christian Jews or Christians who had previously been Torah-observant synagogue participants who claimed that it was necessary for Gentile Christians to be circumcised in order to be saved. It is also possible that the Pastor, in a manner similar to the description in Acts of the Pauline mission, was merely suggesting that some of the Jews living on Crete were causing problems for Christians. Either scenario is possible.

Using a metaphor taken from the semantic domain of animal husbandry, the Pastor tells Titus that it is his responsibility to curb these troublemakers, presumably by means of the overseers appointed to correct opponents in the several cities of Crete. The troublemakers "must be reined in" (*dei epistomizein*). The verb primarily refers to the reining of horses, but it was used in a metaphorical sense as early as the writings of Aristophanes (*Knights* 845) and Demosthenes (*On Halonnesus* 7.33). The graphic image is consistent with the proverbial description of Cretans as a bunch of wild beasts (1:12).

The troublemakers are portrayed as subverting entire households with regard to their faith (see commentary on 2 Tim 2:18). This description reflects the organization of the early church into household communities, an image that is consistent throughout the Pastoral Epistles. That "whole" (*holous*) households become skewed bespeaks the seriousness of the problem. The issue is that they teach what they ought not to teach (the elliptical *ha mē dei*). Unlike them, Titus and the overseer must be faithful to the "trustworthy saying" according to the Pauline teaching and confront the troublemakers with sound teaching (1:9).

The troublemakers teach things that are not healthy (see 1:13b)—even worse, they do so for sordid gain (see 1 Tim. 6:5). In Greco-Roman society, teachers made their livelihood by being clients of wealthy patrons, working at their own trade, begging for alms, or charging fees for their teaching. The troublemakers seem to have been teaching as they did to make money, *aischrou kerdous charin*, "for the sake of sordid gain." They act from a motive that is unworthy of the community's overseer and teacher (1:7; 1 Tim. 3:8; see 1 Pet. 5:2). Pindar (*Pythian Odes* 3.54) and Greek dramatists (e.g., Sophocles, *Antigone* 222) used the word "gain" (*kerdos*, the Latin *lucrum*) to speak of a desire for economic advantage. The use of *charin* in the sense of "for the sake of" is a classic turn of phrase that the Pastor had employed in 1:5. In stating that the troublemakers taught as they did for the sake of filthy lucre, the Pastor shares Paul's disdain of those who teach for the sake of economic gain (see 1 Thess. 2:5).

The Pastor confirms his assessment that the troublemaking inhabitants of Crete are simply no good by citing an adage that goes back to Epimenides, the saintly seventh-century B.C.E. poet. This native of Crete—the Pastor calls him "their very own spokesperson" (*idios autōn prophētēs*)—said that Cretans are "always liars, evil beasts, lazy gluttons." This demeaning description of the Cretans was proverbial in ancient times. Thus, in his *Hymn to Zeus* (*Hymns* 1.8–9), Callimachus, an early third-century B.C.E. librarian and scholar, wrote "'Cretans are always liars' [*Krētes aei pseustai*]. Yes, O Lord, the Cretans built a tomb for you but you did not die, for you are forever [*essi gar eiei*]." The adage about Cretans being liars derives from a dispute between Thetis and Media over which was the more beautiful. The decision was entrusted to Idomeneus of Crete, who decided on Thetis. In reaction, Media is reported to have said "Cretans are always liars," placing a curse on them so that they would never tell the truth.

The characterization of the Cretans as "evil beasts and lazy gluttons" includes two words, "beasts" (*thēria*) and "gluttons" (*gasteres*, literally, "stomachs") that are not otherwise found in the Pastorals and another word, "lazy" (*argai*, 1 Tim. 5:13) that is used only once. The Pastor's use of such exceptional language is a sign of the proverbial nature of his citation. Its metonymous use of "stomach" to mean glutton is classic. Seventh and sixth-century B.C.E. authors, such as Hesiod and Theognis, used it in this way.

Another popular caricature was that the Cretans were greedy. Their desire for money made them an easy target for those who were recruiting mercenaries (see Livy, *Roman History* 44.45.13). Plutarch capitalized on this legendary greed to write about Aemilius Paulus "playing the Cretan against the Cretans" (*krētizōn pros Krētas, Aemilius Paulus* 23.4).

The Pastor confirms the popular estimation of the Cretans as addicted to various vices by adding his formal testimony, "This assertion is true" (*hē martyria autē estin alēthēs*). His affirmation of the truth of the adage adds a note of irony to Epimenides's characterization of the Cretans as a bunch of liars and to the Pastor's own description of the troublemakers as people who turn away from the truth (1:14).

[13b–14] The Pastor draws an inference from his description of the troublemakers with a resumptive "correct them" (*elenche autous*, see 1:9), to which he adds "severely" (*apotomōs*). Titus must not compromise; the task is urgent. The purpose of his corrective endeavors is that the troublemakers abandon their opposition and open their ears to sound teaching (1:9) so that they can be sound in faith. The contrast with their being attentive to Jewish myths and the human commands of those who reject the truth suggests that Titus is to call his opponents to a kind of conversion.

Continuing his earlier suggestion that the troublemakers are Jews (1:10), the Pastor describes them as being intent on Jewish myths and human commandments. Cretans were noted for their "myths" (*mythois*), a term that Greeks since the time of the poet Pindar had used to designate unreal and fabled stories about the divinities. Strabo contrasts the myths for which the Cretans were famous— at least in his estimation—with "history," his label for the truth (*Geography* 10.3.20; 11.5.3). Philo contrasts myths with "real facts" (*Flight* 121) and the unfeigned truth (*Rewards* 162). He affirms that there is no myth in the words of Moses contained in the Torah (*Giants* 7). "Jewish myths" is a phrase that Jews themselves would never use in reference to their own religious traditions. It is a derogatory remark on the part of the Pastor.

Pindar describes myths as the work of mortals (*Olympian Odes* 1.28–29). The Pastor uses this characterization to describe the human commands (*entolais anthrōpōn*) obeyed by the troublemakers. The expression recalls the biblical expression "human precepts" (*entalmata anthrōpōn*, Isa. 29:13), which first-century Christian scriptural apologetics used to describe Jewish halakah (see Mark 7:6–8). The word "human" (*anthrōpōn*, literally, "of humans") contrasts what is merely human with what is divine.

When the Pastor writes of "Jewish myths and human commands," he is undoubtedly referring to Jewish haggadah and halakah, whose human origins he underscores. To do so, he has used the noun *anthrōpōn* to describe the origin of these stories and precepts. In the Pastor's opinion, such tales and such commands come from people bent on departing from the truth. In no way are such people concerned with attaining the full knowledge of truth (1:1).

[15–16] The Jewish coloring of the Pastor's description continues. He uses the language of ritual purity to describe those who stand in need of correction. His use of antithetical parallelism and chiasm, as well as the contrast between "everything" (*panta*, literally, "all things") and nothing (*ouden*), reinforces the rhetoric of the message. The phrasing is so neatly turned that it would appear that the Pastor has again made use of a kind of proverbial saying—"Everything is pure for those who are pure; nothing is pure for those who are defiled" (*panta kathara tois katharois; tois de memiammenois . . . ouden katharon*).

The traditional nature of this observation is confirmed by the fact that the word "pure" (*katharos*) appears three times in the adage but is not used elsewhere in Titus. Moreover, a passive participial form of the verb "to defile" (*miainō*), a word not used in the Pastorals apart from its two occurrences in 1:15, is used to contrast those who are pure with those who defiled. The adage is similar to sayings found in Luke 11:41 and Rom. 14:20. These sayings pertain to the abolition of traditional purity regulations with regard to the eating of certain foods (see Mark 7:14–19). Food that is created by God for our enjoyment is pure and good (see 1 Tim. 4:4). Only those who are themselves defiled (see Mark 7:20–27) consider some foods to be impure.

The Pastor identifies those who are defiled as nonbelievers, *a-pistoi*, people who have no faith (see 1 Tim. 5:8). The Pastor then proceeds to explain what it means for these people to be defiled and why he can affirm that they have no faith. These people are defiled because both their minds and their consciences are defiled. With this affirmation, the Pastor uses the language of Hellenistic anthropology, rather than Paul's Semitic anthropology, to say that the defiled are totally corrupt. These people lack faith because they profess to know God but their actions prove otherwise. "They deny God[29] by their actions" (*tois de ergois arnountai*).

Using an interpretive triad (see 2:12; 1 Tim. 2:7; 2 Tim. 1:11; 3:11), the Pastor explains why this is so. With regard to "every good work" (*pan ergon agathon*), a cipher for correct behavior (see 3:1; 1 Tim. 2:10; 5:10; 2 Tim. 2:21; 3:17), nonbelievers are "abominable, disobedient, and disreputable." They are "disobedient" (*a-peitheis*) not to their parents (see 2 Tim. 3:2; Rom. 1:30) but to God. This makes them disgusting and abominable (*bdelyktoi*). They are unsuitable (*adokimoi*; see 2 Tim. 3:8) for every good work. Just as Jannes and Jambres were unsuitable, completely unqualified as far as the faith is concerned (2 Tim. 3:8), so the opponents whom Titus must confront lack any capacity whatsoever insofar as correct moral behavior is concerned.

The Christian Household
Titus 2:1–10

Titus 1:9 urges the overseer(s) whom Titus is to appoint in various cities on the island to hold fast the trustworthy saying in order to be able to exhort the community with sound teaching. In this pericope (2:1–10), Titus himself is told to

---

29. This is another instance of the use of ellipsis in the Pastoral Epistles. The verb *arnountai*, "deny," lacks a direct object; "God" (*theon*) must be supplied.

speak on things that are appropriate to sound teaching (see pp. 95–97). Sound teaching is correct doctrine that issues forth in the well-being of the community. To explain the kinds of behavior that should flow from sound teaching, the behavior that contributes to the wholeness of the community, the Pastor employs a common topos of Hellenistic literature, namely, the household code (see 1 Tim. 3:15; see also Excursus 5).

This literary form originated within the traditional discussion on household management (*peri oikonomias*). From the time of ancient discussions of the unwritten laws of popular ethics, a discussion on matters related to the household is found in a wide variety of Hellenistic literature (e.g., Aeschylus, *Suppliant Women* 701–9; [Aristotle], *Rhetoric to Alexander* 1; [Isocrates], *Demonicus* 16; Xenophon, *Memorabilia* 4.4.18–24). Some early examples of the household code may be found in the ethical writings of Aristotle (see *Politics* 1.2.1–2; *Magna Moralia* 1.33.15–18; *Nicomachean Ethics* 8.10.4–6). The typical household code describes relationships among three pairs of reciprocally related social classes in which one group is regarded as superior and the other as inferior.

The discussion of household management continued in philosophic and Hellenistic Jewish writings contemporary with the New Testament (see, among others, Epictetus, *Discourses* 2.10.1–23; Seneca, *Epistle* 94.1; Philo, *Decalogue* 165–67; *Pseudo-Phocylides,* 175–227). Hellenistic Jewish writers such as Philo (*Hypothetica* 7.14) and Josephus (*Against Apion* 2.23–29 §§190–210) used the classic form of the household code to talk about household management. Ephesians 5:21–6:9 and Col. 3:18–4:1 are well-known New Testament examples of the form. Other household codes are found in Titus 3:1–2; 1 Tim. 2:1–2, 8–15; 5:1–8; 6:1–2; 1 Pet. 2:18–25; 3:1–4, 5–7; as well as in *1 Clem.* 1:3; 21:6–8; Ign. *Pol.* 4:1–6:1; *Did.* 4:9–11; and *Barn.* 19:5–7.

The Pastor's household code (2:2–10) belongs to this rich oral and literary tradition on household management. The Pastor writes about senior men, senior women, young women, young men, and slaves. He urges that men and women conduct themselves in such a way that their behavior does not discredit the Christian message. Older women are to train younger women lest the word of God itself be blasphemed or slandered. Titus is to give an example to younger men so that they act with discretion in such a way that the opponents of the community are unable to say anything bad about Christians. Thus, this household code stresses the witness value of the Christian message. The soundness of the message is proclaimed in the lives of all Christians, whether they be male or female, older or younger. The Pastor writes about all four groups, but the emphasis lies on the training of younger women and younger men. This focus is similar to the focus on women and young men in a parallel exhortation found in *1 Clem.* 21:6–8 and is consistent with one of the overarching concerns of the Pastorals, namely, carrying on the message to the next generation.

The Pastor concludes his exhortation with a reflection on the role of slaves. Slavery was a fact of life in the Greco-Roman world. As an institution, it was an integral component of the household and economic structure of the Greco-Roman world. The vast majority of the urban population were slaves. Some slaves were well educated, such as Polybius, Phaedrus, and Epictetus—respectively, a historian, a fabulist, and a philosopher. Many slaves had powerful positions, as did Felix, the former slave who was procurator of Judea, Samaria, Galilee, and Perea at the time of Paul's Caesarean imprisonment (see Acts 23:23–25; cf. Suetonius, *Claudius* 28), and various household managers (*oikonomoi*). The conversion of households to Christianity brought with it the conversion of slaves (1 Cor. 7:21–24; 12:13; Gal. 3:28; Phlm. 10). Although they could not enjoy the status of being free, slaves were able to serve the cause of the gospel by being good slaves. Clement of Rome praised Christians who sold themselves into slavery in order to use the revenue to redeem others or to feed the poor (*1 Clem.* 55:2).

2:1 Say what is appropriate to sound teaching. 2 Older men[a] should be sober, well respected, and temperate. They should be sound in faith, love, and steadfastness. 3 Likewise, older women should be holy and venerable with regard to their state in life, neither slanderers nor addicted to too much wine. They should be teachers of what is good and beautiful 4 so that they can train young women in the feminine virtues: to be devoted wives, devoted mothers, 5 modest, chaste, good homemakers,[b] and subject to their own husbands so that the word of God might not be blasphemed. 6 Similarly, urge young men to act with due discretion. 7 Offer yourself[c] as a model of good works in every regard. With regard to teaching, show integrity, dignity, 8 and a sound and irreproachable message so that an opponent might be put to shame, having nothing bad to say about us. 9 Slaves should be subject to their masters in all things: well pleasing, neither speaking against their masters 10 nor stealing from them but showing complete loyalty to them so that they bring honor in every way to the teaching about our Savior, God.

a. Verses 1–5 are a single sentence in Greek.

b. The majority of minuscules, along with a few majuscules, read *oikourous* rather than *oikourgous*. The former is a common Greek word used to describe the mistress of the house and, contemptuously, a man who hangs around the house. The latter term is found only in the writings of Soranus, a second-century C.E. medical writer. The cognate verb *oikourgeō*, "to manage the household," is used to describe a woman's responsibilities in *1 Clem.* 1:3. Because it is the more difficult reading and is so widely attested in the ancient manuscripts, *oikourgous* is the preferable reading.

c. Verses 6–8 are a single sentence in Greek. A participle, *parechomenos*, qualifies the subject of the verb *parakalei*, "urge." The participle introduces both the notion of Titus as an example and the qualities that he must demonstrate in teaching.

[2:1] The epistle is ostensibly written for Titus (1:4). Its message, however, is for the entire community (3:15c). Thus, Titus is encouraged to pass the word along to various members of the community. He is the *tradens* of the common ethical tradition, providing instruction for five groups in the community: seniors, both male and female, youth, both male and female, and slaves. In this respect, the outline followed by the Pastor is reminiscent of Aristotle's classic formulation of the household code. New Testament household codes generally provide the paraenesis with some form of Christian motivation or a faith-based perspective (see, e.g., Col. 3:18, 20, 22). The Pastor follows this pattern when he says that the ethical tradition that Titus is to pass along is in conformity with "sound teaching" (*tē hygiainousē didaskalia*; see 1:9; 1 Tim. 1:10; 2 Tim. 4:3; cf. 2:8; 1 Tim. 6:3; 2 Tim. 1:13).

[2] The first group to be identified by the Pastor are older men (*presbytas*; see Luke 1:18; Phlm. 9). According to a tradition attributed to Hippocrates, a man is called "an elderly man [*presbytēs*] till fifty-six, up to seven times eight; after that an old man [*gerōn*]." According to this computation, the "older man" would be in his early fifties (see Philo, *Creation* 105; Hippocrates, *De Septimanis* 5[30]). The moral profile that the Pastor outlines for these fifty-year-old men consists of six virtues, arranged as a pair of triads. The first triad is a group of social virtues. Elderly men should be sober (*nēphalious*), well respected (*semnous*), and temperate (*sōphronas*). The second triad is the classic Christian trio of faith, love, and steadfastness (*tē pistei, tē agapē, tē hypomonē*; see 1 Thess. 1:3). These last three nouns are dependent upon the participle "sound" (*hygiainontas*), a buzzword in the Pastor's circles (1:9, 13; 2:1; 1 Tim. 1:10; 6:3; 2 Tim. 1:13; 4:3). Older men are to sound in faith, love, and steadfastness.

The first quality cited in the Pastor's description of what an older man should exemplify is sobriety. Originally used to describe an empty vessel set apart for cultic use, the adjective was used by later authors to designate the virtue of sobriety. "Every evil which has drunkenness as its author," wrote Philo, "has its counterpart in some good which is produced by soberness [*to nēphalion*]. Since then sobriety is a source of the greatest profit to our bodies, to which the use of wine is a natural practice, how much more is it profitable to our souls, which have no relation to any perishable food?" (*Sobriety* 2–3).

The second quality expected of older men is that they be well respected. Spicq notes that "we could translate *semnos* ["well respected"] as 'venerable' or 'very respectable'; seriousness, which excludes eccentricity and peculiarity, is a characteristic of old age" (*TLNT* 3.248). Philo observes, "It is not given to youth but to old age to discern things precious and worthy of reverence [*ta*

---

30. Hippocrates' work is an essay on fevers. In this essay Hippocratus shows his liking for the number seven; there are seven parts of the world, seven parts of the human body, seven ages for human beings, and so forth.

semna], particularly those which are judged, not by unreasoning and deceitful sense but by mind when absolutely pure and unalloyed" (*Eternity of the World* 77). Fourth Maccabees, an apocryphal Jewish work more or less contemporary with the Pastoral Epistles, describes Eleazar, an old man (*presbyta*, 4 Macc. 5:6), who says to Antiochus, his antagonist, "You shall not defile the reverent lips of my old age [*to semnon gērōs stoma*] nor my lifelong service to the Law" (4 Macc. 5:36). This kind of respect is associated with mature years, love of spouse and children, wisdom, seriousness, and dignity (see 1 Tim. 3:8, 11).

The virtue of temperance (*sōphrosynē*) is added to sobriety and venerability on the Pastor's list of qualities that an older man should possess. Hellenists frequently associated the virtue of temperance with venerability (see *MAMA* 8.470.8). The Pastor's community held the virtue of temperance in high regard. One of the four cardinal virtues, it is often mentioned in the Pastoral Epistles.

In addition to being sober, well respected, and temperate, older men are also expected to be sound in faith, love, and steadfastness. Paul identified these three virtues in his first summary of the life of a community of believers (1 Thess. 1:3; see 1 Thess. 5:8). Writing to the Thessalonians, a community that was struggling with issues related to the continuance of life beyond the grave, Paul placed steadfastness in the final, emphatic position on the list. This was to encourage people who might be in danger of being numbered among those who have no hope (1 Thess. 4:13). Writing to a divided community at Corinth, Paul placed love in the final and emphatic position of the triad (1 Cor. 13:13). The earliest description of the Christian life seems to have been simply "faith and love" (see 1 Thess. 3:6; 5:8; Gal. 5:6), summarizing, respectively, the believer's relationship to God and to one another. Paul added "hope" to the two-part depiction in order to respond to the issues at Thessalonica.

The expectation of the coming and revelation of the Lord Jesus Christ is a hallmark of Christian existence. The Pastor's circles spoke about hope when their attention was drawn to the object of their hope. They associated hope (*elpis*) with the appearance of Jesus Christ and with the eternal life that would accrue to them with the appearance of their Savior (1:2; 2:13; 3:7; see 1 Tim. 1:1). They spoke about "steadfastness" (*hypomonē*) when they wanted to underscore the steadfast endurance that characterizes the life of a person who lives in hope— someone like Paul, who longed for the appearance of the Lord (2 Tim. 4:8) but who faced suffering and persecution in the meantime (2 Tim. 3:10–11). Thus, they spoke of "steadfastness" when they used Paul's classic triad to describe the Christian life, just as he had done in 1 Thess. 1:3 (see 2 Tim. 3:10).

[3–5] Having listed the qualities that one should expect to find in the respected older men of the community, the Pastor turns his attention to women. He begins with "older women" (*presbytidas*), presumably women in their early fifties. They are to be "holy and venerable with regard to their state in life" (*en katastēmati hieroprepeis*). This dense phrase—two compound words, one a noun, the other an adjective—employs vocabulary not otherwise used in the Bible but often used in Hellenistic Jewish literature.

Classical writers used "state in life" (*katastēmati*) to refer to a person's state, condition, or demeanor; Hellenistic Jewish authors used this term to refer to behavior or disposition. "The virtuous disposition," wrote the author of the *Letter of Aristeas*, "restrains those who are attracted to the rule of pleasure, and commands them to respect self-control and justice more highly" (*Ep. Arist.* 278; see *Ep. Arist.* 122, 210; *3 Macc* 5:45; Josephus, *Ant.* 15.7.5 §236).

Classical authors used "holy and venerable" (*hieroprepeis*, literally, "fitting for a sacred place or person") in reference to priests and priestesses, religious processions, and the like. Philo used the term to describe the virtuous life of the Essenes; he understands the life that they were attempting to lead as a kind of liturgy in everyday action (see *Every Good Man Is Free* 75). Philo wrote about the dedication of the human faculties, thought, speech, and sense perception to God, calling them "sanctified and holy" (*hieroprepes kai hagion, Heir* 110). Elsewhere Philo wrote that "the mind cleaves to virtue, for it apprehends her loveliness, so pure, so simple, so holy to look upon" (*hieroprepestaton, Abel and Cain* 45). Fourth Maccabees described the eldest of the seven martyred brothers, a great-souled youth and a true son of Abraham (4 Macc. 9:21), as a "saintly youth" (*ho hieroprepēs neanias*, 4 Macc. 9:25).

In similar fashion, the Pastor considers the conduct of older women in the house of God as a kind of living liturgy (see Rom. 12:1). He writes that older men should have a trio of human virtues and the three Christian virtues. Of older women, he simply says that they should be holy and venerable with regard to their state in life. His use of *katastēmati*—a word that the Pastor's society sometimes used for the condition of one's health—to describe their state in life, suggests to his readers that elderly women too should be regarded from the perspective of what is "sound."

As older men were expected to be sober and temperate in addition to being well respected (2:2), so older women were expected to be neither slanderers (*mē diabolous*) nor enslaved to wine (*mē oinō pollō dedoulōmenas*). The malicious people of the final times are "slanderers" (see 2 Tim. 3:3), but the Pastor's circles seem to have seen this particularly as a woman's vice (see 1 Tim. 3:11). On the other hand, men and women are equally prone to the abuse of alcohol. Thus, the Pastor exhorts older men to be sober and temperate (2:2) and servers not to indulge in much wine (1 Tim. 3:8). Older women are urged to be wary of becoming addicted to an excessive amount of wine. The Talmud had much to say about a woman's use of wine (*b. Ketub.* 64b–65a). While poorer women generally did not drink wine, richer women did. For them to drink wine was a sign of their status as being relatively well-to-do (see Valler 77–99).

The Pastor's final word of advice to older women is that they be teachers of what is good and beautiful (*kalodidaskalous*). This new word describes the role of the older woman, who is expected to help younger women become good wives, good mothers, and good housekeepers. Older women are to train younger women in feminine virtues, the domestic virtues that make a woman a good wife, mother, and homemaker (see *1 Clem.* 1:3). The term that the Pastor uses to describe what older women are to do for younger women literally means "make them modest" (*sōphron-izōsin*). "Modesty" was the epitome of feminine virtue in the Hellenistic world (see Collins, *Sexual Ethics,* 159). 1 Heliodorus, for example, said that "modesty is the distinctive virtue of women" *(The Ethiopian Story of Theagenes and Charicleia* 4.8.7). Demosthenes and other ancient sages held that this virtue was especially important for younger women (see Demosthenes, *Against Neaera* 59.114). Thus, when the Pastor urges older women to train younger women in "modesty," he is really encouraging them to teach younger women in such a way that they have all the qualities required of the good wife and homemaker (see 1 Tim. 2:15).

Younger women, specifically, those in their twenties (*tas neas*), are to be devoted wives and mothers, literally, "lovers of their husbands, lovers of their children" (*philandrous einai, philoteknous*). These expressions were well known in the Hellenistic world. An epitaph found on the tomb of a woman who died at about the time that the Pastorals were written says ever so powerfully, yet so simply, "Julius Bassus for Otacilia Polla, his sweetest wife. Loving to her husband and loving to her children [*philandr[ō] kai philoteknē*], she lived with him unblamably [*amemptōs*] for thirty years." Similar words of praise for women are found in a fair number of ancient memorial inscriptions.

Younger women were also expected to be modest (*sōphronas*), chaste (*hagnas*; see 1 Tim. 4:12; 5:2, 22), and good householders (*oikourgous agathas*). The "modest" woman was not merely modest. She also had a well-ordered life, was chaste in her marriage, and was generally considered to be above reproach, a quality reminiscent of the epitaph's "unblamably." The exhortation that young women be chaste is not inappropriate in a community that may have consisted largely of Jewish Christians. For Jews, the Gentiles among whom they lived were considered to be sexual reprobates (see Leviticus 18). Paul, under whose authority the paraenesis of the epistle is promoted, shared this biased view of the sexual life of Gentiles (see Rom. 1:24–27; 1 Cor. 5:1; 1 Thess. 4:5).

In the Hellenistic world, despite the relative emancipation of women vis-à-vis Jewish society, a woman's place was in the home. Thus, the Pastor encourages women to be good homemakers (*oikourgous agathas*). They were also expected "to be subject to their own husbands" (*hypotassomenas tois idiois andrasin*). "Their own" (*idiois*) makes it clear that the Pastor is not talking about the subordination of women to men in general; rather, he speaks of the subordination of women to men within the household (see Eph. 5:22).[31] The Pastor's

31. Using the same expression found in 2:5, the author of Eph. 5:22 has carefully revised the wording of Col. 3:18 so that his readers know that he is talking about domestic order and nothing else.

real concern was with the good order of the household. In the Hellenistic world, men were considered to be the paterfamilias, the unchallenged head of the house. Polycarp does not speak of the submission of wives to their husbands, nor does he distinguish younger women from older women, but his profile of the qualities of the Christian wife is similar to the Pastor's outline. Christian wives, says Polycarp, are "to walk in the faith that has been given to them and in love and purity, cherishing their own husbands [*stergousas tous heautōn andras*] in all truth and loving everyone equally in all chastity [*enkrateia*; see Titus 1:8], and to train their children in the training of the fear of God" (Pol. *Phil.* 4:2).

The Pastor concludes his exhortation on women by giving the reason why young women should act in the way that he has described. He does not want people living outside the house of God to be scandalized by a Christian household. He does not want nonbelievers to look at the way that Christians live their day-to-day lives and come away with the impression that Christians do not know how to live properly by conventional standards (1:5b). If they do, they might well blaspheme, or at least have a very low esteem, of the word of God, the Christian message. With this coda the Pastor reminds his readers that the way they live their ordinary lives bears witness to the truth of the word of God (see 1 Pet. 3:1–2; cf. 1 Pet. 2:15; 1 Cor. 14:23; 1 Thess. 4:12).

[6–8] A "young man" (*neaniskos*) is someone between twenty-one and twenty-eight years of age. Philo writes that a man is "a young man until his whole body has grown, till four times seven; a man [*anēr*] till forty-nine, till seven times seven; an elderly man [*presbytēs*] till fifty-six, till seven times eight; after that an old man [*gerōn*]" (*Creation* 105). The Pastor urges young men to act with due discretion (*sōphronein*). In contrast with this single virtue, Polycarp offers a triad of qualities that one should find in Christian young men (*neōteroi*). They are to be "blameless in everything, caring for purity before everything, and curbing themselves from every evil" (Pol. *Phil.* 6:3).

The Pastor urges older women to train younger women in modesty (*sōphronizōsin*), young women to be modest (*sōphronas*), and young men to act with due discretion (*sōphronein*). Citing Homer as his source, Athenaeus states that moderation is be taught to children as "the virtue that is most appropriate for young people and the first of all virtues, an element of harmony, and productive of good" (*Deipnosophists* 1.8[e]). The virtue of *sōphrosynē* was one of the cardinal virtues (see pp. 324–325), a virtue that both men and women were to have. Philo writes that "reflection on [marriage] should lead both husbands and wives to cherish temperance [*sōphrosynēs*] and domesticity and unanimity" (*Special Laws* 1.138). The virtue relates to character and the conduct of one's life. Ultimately, it is the practical sense of knowing what to do and what to avoid. From the time of Aristotle, however, Hellenists acknowledged that this cardinal virtue was expressed in different ways in the lives of men and in the lives of women (see Aristotle, *Politics* 1.5.8; 3.2.10). Accordingly, the Pastor urges both young women and young men to pursue this virtue, each in the manner appropriate to their social role.

Older women are to instruct younger women in regard to feminine virtues; younger men are to learn the virtue of due discretion by following an example. By their example, virtuous people inspire others to be virtuous. If Titus is to ensure that the younger men in his community act with due discretion, he must provide them with an example for them to imitate. The Pastor urges that Titus himself serve as that model. In every respect he should be an example of proper behavior (*peri panta . . . typon kalōn ergōn*). Not only is Titus required to provide an example of correct behavior to young men; he must also use his teaching office to instruct them in sound teaching.

The Pastor uses the typical language of his circles to describe Titus's twofold responsibility. As a cipher for the Christian life, he uses the expression "good works" (*kalōn ergōn*). For the Christian message he uses the language of "teaching" (*tē didaskalia*) and the metaphor that his circles have borrowed from the domain of health care, that which is "sound" (*hygiē*). "Integrity" should be a characteristic of Titus's teaching. "Integrity" literally means "without decay" (*a-phthoria*). Generally used to describe persons, either physically or morally, "integrity" is an appropriate attribute of "unblemished" and healthy teaching. Another attribute of Titus's teaching is its "dignity" (*semnotēta*), another word that was normally used to describe people (see 1 Tim. 2:2; 3:4). Dignity "suggests grandeur, magnificence, solemnity, a quality that inspires respect, fear, or reverence" (*TLNT* 3.244). Moulton and Milligan suggest that in 2:7 the Pastor is expressing what Latin authors would describe as *gravitas*[32] (MM 4587), a word that evokes seriousness and formality.

A third quality of Titus's teaching is that it should present a sound and irreproachable message (*logon hygiē akatagnōston*). The two adjectives are linked together and form a mixed metaphor. The former, related to the participle (from *hygiainō*) commonly used in the Pastor's circles to describe "sound" teaching (see 1:9; 2:1), belongs to the domain of health. The latter, literally meaning "nothing known against," comes from the language of the courtroom. It describes the innocence of a person who is acquitted of a crime of which he or she has been accused. This is the meaning of the term in its sole occurrence in the Greek Bible. Unfortunate men are said to have been condemned to death "who would have been freed uncondemned [*akatagnōstoi*] if they had pleaded even before Scythians" (2 Macc. 4:47).

With this array of qualities the Pastor has effectively personified the message, "the word" (*logon*), in much the same way that Paul personified love in 1 Cor. 13:4–7. Like that of a mature and healthy person, Titus's message has integrity, dignity, soundness, and an irreproachable character. Concluding his description

---

32. *Gravitas* is used in the Vulgate translation of 2:7.

with a word that has judicial connotations, the Pastor hearkens back to a theme that he had only suggested in 1:9, 13b–14, namely, that Titus's teaching should confront those who had turned from the full knowledge of the truth. It is conceivable that the Pastor who has personified the word has given his own expression to the Pauline idea that it is not human rhetoric but the power of God that provides the force of the Christian message (see 1 Cor. 2:1–5; 1 Thess. 2:13).

The reason why Titus is to persuade young men to follow his exemplary conduct, proclaiming the word in an integral and irreproachable fashion, is that opponents (*ho ex enantias*, literally, "someone from the opposite side") might be put to shame. They will not be able to say about the Christian community anything bad (*phaulon*, a word that the apostle uses as the antithesis to "something good" [*agathon*], in Rom. 9:11 and 2 Cor. 5:10).

[9–10] One of the distinctive features of the household codes in Ephesians and Colossians is that slaves are directly addressed (Eph. 6:5–8; Col. 3:22–25). This is an indication that slaves were integrated into first-century Hellenistic Christian communities. In itself this is not surprising. As Christianity was gaining its foothold in the Greco-Roman world, a majority of the population of urban centers in the Hellenistic world were slaves. The basic unit of the social organization of early Christianity was the household (*oikos, oikia*). Household slaves belonged to the master of the household (*despotēs*). Given the New Testament references to the baptisms of entire households, it is likely that some slaves became believers when their masters did. Other slaves seem to have become believers without their masters' accepting the faith.

Slaves are not directly addressed in 2:9–10; rather, Titus is urged to direct an exhortation to them, an indication that slaves were part of the community for whom the epistle was intended. Slaves are to be subject to their own masters (*doulous idiois despotais hypotassesthai*) just as wives are to be subject to their own husbands (*hypotassomenas tois idiois andrasin*, 2:5). The Pastor adds a qualification to the subjection that slaves owe to their masters: They are to be subject to their masters in all things and in every way (*en pasin*; see Col. 3:22). In reality, their masters are their lords (*kyrioi*). The Pastor's description of the respective responsibilities of both wives and slaves as being "subject"—he uses the verb *hypotassō*—distinguishes the language of his household code from that of the similar codes in Ephesians and Colossians. In those epistles, the verb *hypotassō* is used with regard to wives (Eph. 5:21–22; Col. 3:18); the verb *hypakouō*, "to obey," is used with regard to slaves (Eph. 6:5; Col. 3:22).

In addition to fulfilling their responsibility of obedience to their masters, slaves are urged to please them. All other New Testament uses of "pleasing" (*euarestous*)—with the intensive prefix *eu*, therefore, "well pleasing"—describe the Christian who is to be well pleasing to "God" or to "the Lord" by doing God's will (see Rom. 12:1, 2; 14:18; 2 Cor. 5:9; Phil. 4:18; cf. Eph. 5:10; Col. 3:20; Heb. 13:21). The adjective was commonly used in Hellenistic paraenesis to describe the fundamental attitude of being sensitive to the will of one's master in any situation. The Pastor's use of a word with this connotation to describe the responsibilities of a slave to the master indicates that slaves were regarded as "persons," to use a modern term, rather than as the mere chattel of their masters. They were not only to do what they were told to do; they were expected to look to the fulfillment of their master's will in every regard.

Slaves are not to speak against their masters, nor are they to steal from them. The verb "to speak against" (*anti-legontas*, a participial form in 2:9) often means "to oppose" as it does in 1:9. Opposition may be the connotation of the verb in 2:9, but it is more likely that the Pastor who has already urged Titus to exhort slaves to be fully subject to their masters and pleasing to them is suggesting that Titus tell slaves that they are not to speak against their masters so as to create unrest among the slaves.

Slaves who belong to the community are to be urged not to steal from their masters. "To steal" (*nosphizomenous*) is literally "to set aside," but Hellenists commonly used the verb to describe the unjust appropriation of another's goods by robbery, fraud, or embezzlement. A third-century B.C.E. papyrus describes an oath in which an official swears not to embezzle (*oute nospheioumai*, Flinders Petrie Papyrus III.56b). Philo tells the story of Capito, a poor man who was appointed a tax collector in Judea and became rich by his rapacity (*nosphizetai*, *Gaius* 199). A late second-century C.E. papyrus (*Catalogue of the Greek Papyri in the John Rylands Library* 2, No. 116) describes a woman whose conscience was bothered because she had stolen (*enosphisato*) furniture and stored articles. Were a slave to steal from the master, he or she would violate the loyalty that was expected of slaves. Paul considered that loyalty and trustworthiness (*pistos*) was the primary quality of the slave who served as manager of the household (see 1 Cor. 4:2). The Pastor says that Christian slaves must demonstrate complete loyalty (*pasan pistin . . . agathēn*, literally, "all good faith").

By behaving as they have been exhorted, slaves honor and enhance (*kosmōsin*) the teaching about God our Savior. The Pastor has chosen a verb (*kosmeō*) that literally means "to put in order." The verb was commonly used in the metaphorical sense of beautifying a person or an edifice by adding adornments. In the Hellenistic world, virtues were considered to be a kind of personal adornment. The elderly priest Eleazarus is said to have adorned himself with all life's virtues (see 3 Macc. 6:1). The metaphorical use of the verb was further extended so that by the first century C.E. its meaning was often "to honor." By having a monument erected to Koudan, his mother, a man named Tabeis was able to honor her (see *MAMA* 8, 108). A woman named Lalla honored (*kekosmēkuian*) the virtues of her ancestors by her own exemplary behavior (see Louis Robert, *Hellenica: Receuil d'epigraphic de numismatique et d'antiquités grecques*, vol. 13 [Limoges: Bontemps, 1965] 13, 226).

By being obedient and loyal a slave can bring honor to the teaching about our Savior, God (*tēn didaskalian tēn tou sōtēros hēmōn theou*). The appositive use of "God" to identify the Savior is consistent with the usage of this epistle (see 1:3; 3:4), but a question can be raised with regard to the relationship between "our Savior, God" and "teaching." Do we have here a subjective genitive or an objective genitive? Does the Pastor intend to say that the teaching comes from God? Or does he intend to say that the message is about God? The genitive is clearly a subjective genitive in the Pastor's other uses of the phrase "of our Savior, God" (1:3; 3:4). On the other hand, humans are the subject of the verb *didaskō*, "teach," in the Pastoral Epistles, and Paul frequently adds an objective genitive to "good news" (*euangelion*) or "proclamation" (*kerygma*). On balance, the Pastor's phrase—literally, "the teaching of our Savior, God"— means "teaching about our Savior, God."

During Paul's lifetime, slaves served the gospel by the various tasks that they performed. Chloe's slaves brought news about the situation at Corinth to Paul (1 Cor. 1:11). Onesimus, Philemon's slave, was of service to Paul during the latter's imprisonment (Phlm. 11, 13). Paul accepted the social condition of slaves as a given in the Greco-Roman world. In 1 Cor. 7:21–24 he draws attention to the paradoxical situation of Christian slaves: In the world at large they are slaves; from the perspective of salvation they are freed persons in the Lord.

In 2:10 the Pastor suggests that slaves serve the gospel by the way that they live as slaves. If they are obedient and trustworthy, seeking to please their masters, they bring honor to the teaching about our Savior, Jesus Christ. Bearing witness to the gospel in this way should motivate Christian slaves to be faithful slaves. The Pastor's perspective is reflected in other early Christian literature. Ignatius, for example, wrote Polycarp to "despise not slaves, whether men or women. Yet let not these again be puffed up but let them serve the more faithfully to the glory of God, that they may obtain a better freedom from God" (Ign. *Pol.* 4:3).

Although both wives and slaves had a subordinate social role in the Hellenistic world (see Eph. 5:22–6:9; Col. 3:18–4:1), the Pastor has made it clear that both Christian wives and Christian slaves attest to the claim of the gospel message by the way in which they live. By being a good wife and mother, subject to her husband, a Christian wife prevents the word of God from being spoken about in a derisive fashion. By being an honest and faithful slave, a Christian slave enhances the teaching about our Savior, God. The way that one conducts oneself, appropriate to one's state of life, bears prophetic witness to the gospel message.

This may well be the major point that the Pastor wants his readers to infer from his use of the household code. Everyone in the household has a role to play on behalf of the gospel. By giving the example of himself and his teaching to young men, Titus promotes the gospel message. By their training of younger women, older women enable these younger women to protect the word of God. In this way older women serve God's word. No matter one's situation in life, the proper way that a Christian lives a life that is upright and correct attests to the authenticity of the Christian message.

Salvation
Titus 2:11–14

Having described how people in their various states of life should live as Christians in his Hellenistic world, the Pastor offers a theological reflection on the reason they should do so. He develops the motif of the teaching about our Savior, God, to which believing slaves bear witness by their obedient and loyal service to their masters. Using the technique of ring construction, the Pastor delimits a discrete and tightly knit literary unit (2:11–13). The themes of salvation, God, and appearance highlighted in the Pastor's introductory statement (v. 11) are reprised in verse 13, in which Jesus Christ is identified as our Savior. In retrospect, Jesus Christ is identified as the saving gift of God. The retrospective view deftly created by this literary inclusion (vv. 11, 13) continues in verse 14 in which the salvation effected by Jesus Christ is described in terms that evoke the manumission of slaves and the preparation of a people by means of a ritual lustration. The language evokes ideas that later Christian authors would subsume under the rubrics of redemption and baptism.

The motif of appearance (*epiphaneia*), a key notion in the common Christology of the Pastor's circles (see Excursus 8), receives what may be its defining description in this pericope. The "epiphany" of the Savior is the object of hope; his appearance will occur in the future. The device of inclusion enables the Pastor to place this future epiphany (v. 13) against the horizon of a manifestation that has already occurred (v. 11). People of faith, whose responsibilities have been described in the previous pericope (2:1–10), are people who live between epiphanies. Their existence is defined by a temporal tension. They live as they do in time—one might note the similar importance of the temporal perspective in the Pastor's description of Paul's ministry (1:1–3)—whose horizons extend from the manifestation in the past to the epiphany in the future. Instructed by a teaching that comes from the past, they are to pray for the future. They live their lives, however, "in this age." In this age they are to live modestly, justly, and piously.

The "appearance" pronouncement of verses 11–14 is a mixture of confessional and creedal material blended together into a formal and solemn unit. The Pastor does not describe his exposition as a "trustworthy saying." The failure to do so most likely indicates that the literary unit is his own composition rather than a preformed unit of traditional material (see commentary on 3:4).

2:11 For the saving beneficence of God has appeared to all people, 12 teaching us to deny impiety and worldly passions and to live modestly, justly,
and in godly fashion in the present age, 13 awaiting the blessed hope, that
is, the appearance of the glory of the great God, our Savior, Jesus Christ,

> 14 who gave himself for us,
> to redeem us from all lawlessness
> and purify for himself a chosen people,

eager for good works.

[2:11–13] Capitalizing on the reference to the teaching of our Savior, God,
with which he had concluded the previous pericope, the Pastor explains (see the
explanatory *gar*, "for") why members of the community should live in a way
that responds to Titus's exhortation. His explanation is simple: The saving grace
of God has appeared to all people. The language is intrusive and unusual, but
the Pastor's discourse has moved to another level. Thus far the epistle has made
reference to the grace of God only in its stereotyped epistolary greeting (1:4).
Now the Pastor makes reference to the saving beneficence of God. The "beneficence" or "grace" (*hē charis*) about which he writes is not grace in the Pauline
sense, that is, the grace of God that justifies; rather, the word is to be taken in
its usual Hellenistic sense of "favor" or "beneficence." In the Pastor's world the
granting of favors was often associated with royal "appearances."

The Pastor's expression is unique. The adjective "saving" (*sōtērios*) is used
in no other place in the New Testament. The Pastor's use of the language of
"appearing" is likewise unusual. The verb *epephanē* belongs to the *epiphan-*
word group (see Excursus 8), but it has not previously appeared in this epistle
(see 3:4, which hearkens back to this pericope). The idea of an appearance is an
important notion that the Pastor uses to define his literary unit (see vv. 11, 13).

This kind of language was commonly used in the Pastor's Hellenistic world
to describe the appearance of a god, often Asclepius or Serapion, the god of
healing,[33] or of a divinized emperor. Since gods showed themselves to be sav-
iors in their beneficent interventions in history on behalf of humankind, the religious language that was appropriate to the gods was also used with regard to
emperors who effected a god's beneficence on behalf of their subjects. The
emperor's actions gave expression to or were a manifestation of the saving presence of the gods. Given this cultural usage of the "epiphany" word group, the
Pastor's audience would readily understand what he meant by the appearance
of the saving beneficence of God.

According to the Pastor, this beneficence has been made manifest to all people. The coda "to all people" (*pasin anthrōpois*) may have been confessional

---

33. One might note that the word *sōteria* can be translated either as "healing" or as "salvation."

(see 1 Tim. 2:6); more likely it is polemical. One of the Pastor's concerns arose from the considerable Jewish presence on Crete (see 1:10–11, 13–16; 3:9). It is difficult to know with any certainty whether the Jewish problem that was of such concern to the Pastor derived from synagogal Jews who maintained that salvation was a gift of God to the Jewish nation alone or whether his Jewish problem was akin to that addressed by Paul in his letters to the Romans and the Galatians and by Luke in Acts 15. The Pastor's insistence on the idea that the saving beneficence of God appeared for all people could have countered claims of Jewish exclusivism, whether they were of the synagogal or of the Judaizing-Christian variety.

First Timothy is adamant that salvation is for all people: "There is one God and one intermediary between God and humans, the human being, Christ Jesus, who gave himself as a ransom for all [*hyper pantōn*]" (1 Tim. 2:5–6). Again, the epistle speaks of "the living God who is the Savior of all people [*sōtēr pantōn anthrōpōn*], especially of the faithful" (1 Tim. 4:10; see also 1 Tim. 3:16c–d). Supported by these confessional statements, 1 Timothy reflects its concern for the salvation of all humans in such passages as 1 Tim. 2:1 and 2:4. The concern of 1 Timothy might have been related to a kind of emergent Gnosticism that proclaimed salvation for a privileged few—for example, those who forbade marriage and imposed various dietary laws (1 Tim. 4:3). The Pastor's insistence that God's saving beneficence is for all people reflects concerns similar to those addressed in 1 Tim. 2:4–5, 4:10. First Timothy was ostensibly addressed to Ephesus and Titus to Crete, but a common matrix of the thought is expressed in both missives.

The manifestation of the saving beneficence of God was a personal appearance, the appearance of someone who taught those who accepted his message how they should live. Each of the Synoptic Gospels portrays Jesus as a teacher, using both the verb *didaskein*, "to teach," and the cognate noun *didaskalos*, "teacher" to do so. In each Gospel, Jesus is often addressed as "teacher" (*didaskale*). Mark writes about Jesus teaching but rarely gives the content of that teaching (see Mark 1:21–28). Matthew presents Jesus as a teacher according to the rabbinic pattern, especially in the Sermon on the Mount (Matt. 5:1–8:1). In the Gospel of Luke, Jesus is often presented in the Hellenistic mode of the symposium, teaching both the disciples and other people as they sit at table.

The Pastor uses the verb *paideuō*, "to teach," a word that does not appear in the Synoptic narratives. Etymologically this verb implies the rearing and training of a child (*pais*). In Hellenistic literature its connotations run from training to discipline. The gamut is reflected in the New Testament, where the meaning of the term ranges from instruction (Acts 7:22; 22:3; see also *Herm. Vis.* 3.9.10), through correction (1 Tim. 1:20; 2 Tim. 2:25), to discipline and punishment (1 Cor. 11:32; 2 Cor. 6:9; see also *Herm. Vis.* 2.3.1). Exploiting a passage in Prov. 3:12, the author of Hebrews uses the verb to write about God, as father, disciplining his children (Heb. 12:6, 7, 10).

The Pastor's use of the verb *paideuō* in regard to the saving beneficence of God is similar to that found in the letter of Clement to the Corinthians. In a prayer addressed to the Creator and Overseer of every spirit (*ton pantos pneumatos ktistēn kai episkopon*), Clement writes, "You have chosen from among all people those that love you through Jesus Christ, through whom you instructed [*epaideusas*], sanctified, and honored us" (*1 Clem.* 59:3). Earlier in the same letter, Clement wrote this exhortation: "Let our children share in the instruction that is in Christ [*tēs en Christō paideias*]" (*1 Clem.* 21:8). With the Pastor, Clement shares a Hellenistic view of Jesus, the teacher.

Jesus, the saving beneficence of God, has taught God's people to avoid evil and to do good. The Pastor uses the literary device of antithesis to underscore what it is that members of the community should do. In this age they should live modestly, justly, and in godly fashion; on the other hand, they must avoid impiety and worldly passions.

Impiety (*a-sebeian*) is the total opposite of godliness or piety (*eu-sebeia*), the comprehensive virtue that includes respect for existent values and practices. "Godliness" is a term that sums up what the Pastor's circles considered to be proper behavior (see Excursus 7); they were to avoid its antithesis, "impiety." They were also to shun worldly passions (*kosmikas epithymias*). "Worldly" (see Heb. 9:1) is a pejorative term; it describes the various lusts, among which sexual lust is surely to be included, that are characteristic of this world. The Pastor uses terminology that reflects the Stoic concern that a person not allow himself or herself to become subject to passion. Tenets of Stoic paraenesis were evident in the Pastor's description of the qualities of the overseer (1:8); his teaching on the avoidance of passion belongs to the same current of thought. It may be, however, that the Pastor's rejection of "worldly lusts" reflects that Jewish point of view that abhorred the sexual mores of Gentiles. Paul himself readily characterized Gentile sexual behavior as "lust" (*epithymia*, 1 Thess. 4:5; see also 1 Cor. 5:1).

Believers are to turn from impiety and lust so as to live modestly, justly, and in godly fashion in the present age (*en tō nyn aiōni*). The Pastor does not share Paul's apocalyptic worldview in which "this age" (*ho aiōn houtos*) is an evil age destined to pass away with the coming of the world to come (see Gal. 1:4). For the Pastor, "the present age" (see 1 Tim. 6:17; 2 Tim. 4:10) is the time between the manifestation of God's saving beneficence and the appearance of the Lord and Savior Jesus Christ. Believers live between these two appearances, the two "epiphanies." In this age they are to live modestly, justly, and in godly fashion (*sōphronōs kai dikaiōs kai eusebōs*). Christians ought to be just, that is, they ought to live in right relationship with God and with one another. The Pastor, however, adds to this traditional description of a life correctly lived a pair of adverbs that describe the Hellenistic ideals of his community. Christians are to live modestly (see 2:5–6) and in godly fashion (see 1:1). This particular interpretive triad (see 1:16; 1 Tim. 2:7; 2 Tim. 1:11; 3:11) may have been patterned after the triad in 1 Thess. 2:10, where Paul describes the life of himself and Silvanus in the presence of the Thessalonians as being "pure, upright, and blameless" (*hosiōs kai dikaiōs kai amemptōs*, 1 Thess. 2:10).

In the present age (v. 12), the members of the Pastor's community are to forsake impiety (*a-sebeian*) and live in godly fashion (*eu-sebōs*) while they wait (*prosdechomenoi*). They are people who live in expectation. In his first letter, Paul affirmed that believers are an expectant people. He wrote that we "wait (*anamenein*) for his Son from heaven, whom he raised from the dead—Jesus, who rescues us from the wrath that is coming" (1 Thess. 1:10). When the first Christians gathered together they prayed *marana tha*, "Come, Lord" (1 Cor. 16:22; see Rev. 22:20; *Did.* 10:6).

The Pastor's prospective view uses neither the traditional language of the *marana tha* formula nor the apostle's apocalyptic language. Rather, it speaks of an appearance to come (v. 13) that recalls an appearance in the past (v. 11). Again, the Pastor's community lives between epiphanies. The beneficiary of a saving appearance in the past, the church awaits the appearance of the great God, our Savior, in the future. This appearance is described as a "blessed hope" (*tēn makarian elpida*), which is then explained—the *kai* being epexegetical— as "the appearance of the glory of the great God, our Savior, Jesus Christ." Elsewhere eternal life is identified as the object of hope (1:2; 3:7); now the object of hope is the appearance.

This hope is "blessed." "Blessed" is an attribute of God (see 1 Tim. 1:11; 6:15). God is proclaimed as blessed insofar as he shares his blessedness with others (see pp. 34–35). The salutation of 1 Timothy identified Jesus Christ as our hope (1 Tim. 1:1). These several motifs come together when the Pastor writes about "the appearance of the glory of the great God, our Savior, Jesus Christ" (see pp. 311–314). This appearance is a manifestation of the saving beneficence of God (v. 11). It will bring to closure the present age, in which the Pastor's community lives as a redeemed, purified, and chosen people. This is their condition between the appearances during the present age, when they are to shun impiety, embrace godliness, and be ever eager for good works.

"Glory" is associated with this awaited appearance of Jesus Christ as our God and Savior. The term occurs only this once in the Epistle to Titus. Elsewhere in the Pastorals it appears in doxologies (1 Tim. 1:17; 2 Tim. 4:18), but it is also associated with Jesus Christ (1 Tim. 3:16; 2 Tim. 2:10; see also 1 Tim. 1:11). Apart from such Hellenistic Jewish authors as Philo and Josephus, Hellenistic writers do not use "glory" (*doxa*) with regard to God. They use the term in its ordinary meaning of "opinion," "fame," or "reputation." In the Greek Bible, however, "glory" (*doxa*) is used in translating the Hebrew Bible's *kā-bôd*. This term was used to speak of an impressive manifestation of the presence and activity of the one, invisible, and transcendent God in some sort of sensory experience that could be perceived by humans. Hellenistic Jews followed the Septuagint in using "glory" to designate this divine attribute.

Among New Testament writers, it was Paul who most often spoke of the glory of God. Paul's usage influenced those passages in 1–2 Peter that associate glory with Christ (1 Pet. 5:10; 2 Pet. 1:17) as well as the Pastor, who appropriated Pauline terminology to speak of the future appearance of Jesus Christ in 2:13. For the Jews, with whom he and his community were in dialogue, the "glory" of this appearance would evoke images of the manifestation of Yahweh's glory. The appearance of Jesus Christ as our God and Savior in 2:13 will be a splendid and awesome experience.

[14] With verse 14, the Pastor's language and style changes radically. His complex relative clause reflects Semitic idiom and construction. The first three phrases of the clause offer a christological formula, almost hymnic in its structure, that forms a complete strophe in three parts:

> who gave himself for us (14a)
> to redeem us from all lawlessness (14b)
> and purify for himself a chosen people (14c).

This construction, with the verb found at the beginning of each clause, reflects Semitic style. The two phrases in the *hina* clause ("to"), verses 14b and 14c, reflect the Semitic style of synthetic parallelism. None of the key words in this clause—"redeem," "purify," "lawlessness," "people," and "chosen"—appear elsewhere in the Pastorals, let alone in this epistle. The idiom, as well as the construction, is Semitic.

The Pastor's use of a relative pronoun to bring the hymnic composition into the epistle is similar to the *hos* ("who") with which the christological hymns in 1 Tim. 3:16, Col. 1:15–20, and Phil. 2:6–11 are introduced. In Titus 2:14, 1 Tim. 3:16, and Phil. 2:6, the relative pronoun marks a transition between one form of material and another. In each case the authors, the Pastor and Paul, have apparently inserted material from a preexisting tradition into their text. The careful construction of the strophic form and the singularity of its language identify this material as a preexistent literary unit. Each of these preexistent units offers an interpretation of the death of Jesus Christ in hymnic form. Insofar as these hymnic pieces are interpretive units, their function is similar to that of the interpretive words spoken over the bread and wine in the early Christian liturgical tradition (Mark 14:24; Luke 22:19, 20; John 6:51; 1 Cor. 11:24).

The phrase "who gave himself for us" (*hos edōken heauton hyper hēmōn*) is similar to a phrase found in 1 Tim. 2:6, "who gave himself as a ransom for all." The language is similar to the words of institution in Luke's account of the Last Supper. Apropos the bread, Luke writes, "This is my body, which is given for you" (*to hyper hymōn didomenon*, Luke 22:19). Similar language is found in the creedal or kerygmatic formula that Paul incorporated into the greeting of his letter to the Galatians, "who gave himself [*tou dontos heauton*] for our sins" (Gal. 1:4). The verb "give" (*didōmi*) was often used with a sacrificial connotation, in reference either to an offering (Luke 2:24) or to the self-sacrificial martyrdom of one's own life (see Thucydides, *History* 2.43.2; 1 Macc. 2:50; 6:44; Mark 10:45; Ign. *Smyrn.* 4:2).

With the phrase "for us" (*hyper hēmōn*), the Pastor gives the reason for Jesus Christ's self-sacrifice in death. The formula has a classic ring. Josephus used similar language when he wrote about the death of Judas Maccabbeus "for them" (*hyper autōn, Ant.* 13.1.1 §§1, 6; see *Jewish War* 2.10.5 §201). The Pastor's formula echoes the language of the early Christian dying formula (see Rom. 5:6, 8; 14:15; 1 Cor. 15:3; 2 Cor. 5:14, 15 [2x]; 1 Thess. 5:10; cf. John 11:50, 51; 18:14; Heb. 2:9; 1 Pet. 2:21; 3:18) as well as that of early Christian liturgy, particularly the celebration of the Lord's Supper (see Luke 22:19, 20; 1 Cor. 11:24; cf. Mark 14:24; John 6:51).

The formulaic expression "for us" expresses the vicarious nature of the death of Jesus Christ. The Pastor's hymnic structure unpacks the meaning of the terse formula in a complex purpose clause, "to redeem us from all lawlessness [*lytrō-sētai hēmas apo pasēs anomias*][34] and to purify [*katharisē*] for himself a chosen people." The purpose of the vicarious self-sacrifice of Jesus Christ was to bring about a kind of ritual redemption. The idea of redemption was well known to Paul, who wrote about Christians having been bought and paid for (1 Cor. 6:20; 7:23). The image evoked the manumission of slaves in the Hellenistic world. These slaves were "bought" by means of the offering of the appropriate price to a deity into whose service the freed person entered. Almost 1200 deeds inscribed on temple walls, spanning a three-century period (201 B.C.E.–90 C.E.), attest to the practice of slaves being "sold" to the Pythian Apollos at Delphi. The idea of "redemption" was important in the history of the Jewish people. The notion, including the use of the verb *lytroō*, "to redeem," figured often in their narratives about the Exodus (e.g., Exod. 6:6; 15:13; Deut. 7:6–8; 9:26; 13:5; 15:15; 24:18).

Manumitted slaves fictively entered the service of Apollo. God and our Savior's purpose in redeeming those enslaved to lawlessness was to purify a chosen people for himself. The idea of a chosen people (*laon periousion*) is a biblical one. Exodus 19:5 describes Yahweh as addressing Israel in this fashion: "You shall be my chosen people [*moi laos periousios*] out of all the nations" (= "my treasured possession out of all the peoples," NRSV). The expression "chosen people" occurs five times in the Greek Bible (Exod. 19:5; 23:22; Deut. 7:6; 14:2; 26:18). "Chosen" does not appear in the New Testament except in 2:14; "people" does not appear elsewhere in the Pastorals. In effect, the Pas-

---

34. This is the only mention of "lawlessness" in the Pastorals. The language of "redemption" (see Mark 10:45) appears only here and in 1 Tim. 2:6. The singularity of this language points to the borrowed nature of the hymnic material in 2:14.

tor's use of the classic expression "chosen people" is a sign that he has borrowed material for his hymnic construction. He is clearly evoking the Jewish biblical tradition, as does *1 Clement*, whose final prayer is addressed to God "who chose the Lord Jesus Christ and us through him as a chosen people" (*laon periousion, 1 Clem.* 64:1).

The election of this chosen people is described as a purification. This idea evokes the polemics of 1:15 and a rite of lustration, namely, baptism (see 3:5). Ephesians uses terminology similar to that employed by the Pastor when it describes the church as Christ's chosen bride. Having spoken of Christ as Savior (*Sōtēr*, Eph. 5:23), the author of Ephesians writes that Christ "gave himself up for her [*heauton paredōken hyper autēs*] in order to make her holy by cleansing her with the washing [*katharisas tō loutrō*] of water" (Eph. 5:25–26).

By saying that Jesus Christ has redeemed us and has made us his "chosen people" (see 1:1; 2 Tim. 2:10), the Pastor has clarified the meaning of "our Savior" by means of a pair of juxtaposed images drawn respectively from the religious practices of Hellenism and the Jewish biblical tradition. His soteriology speaks to both the Hellenistic world and the Jewish world.

After his rich soteriological digression the Pastor returns to the familiar concerns of his own circles. They are a redeemed people, a people to be compared with the chosen people of old, but they are not entirely free. They have been vicariously freed from the power of lawlessness so that they might be ready and eager for good works (*zēlōtēn kalōn ergōn*). The readers of the Pastor's missive would recognize in the reference to "good works" a summary description of the life they should lead. As a people redeemed by the Savior Jesus Christ, they are expected to devote themselves eagerly to this new way of life.

Pastoral Exhortation
Titus 2:15–3:3

This pastoral exhortation comes between two "epiphany" passages that contain traditional Christian material (2:11–14; 3:4–7). The paraenetic unit begins with an exhortation to Titus himself. He is to speak to the people about the understanding of salvation that had been developed in the previous pericope (2:11–14), drawing from it an inference that pertains to the behavior of Christians. People may look down upon him for providing them with this challenge, but Titus must not be dissuaded from his task by their attitude toward him.

The paraenetic unit makes use of a catalog of virtues and a catalog of vices neatly arranged in a "now-but once" structure. For the most part, the catalogs make use of the typical language of Hellenistic moralists, but some of the Pastor's own concerns are reflected in the terminology.

2:15 Say[a] these things, exhort, and correct with full authority. Let no one despise you. 3:1 Remind them to be subject to legitimate rulers, obedient, and ready for every good work, 2 to speak evil about no one, to be peaceful, balanced, and showing complete gentleness toward everyone. 3 For at one time we were ignorant, disobedient, going astray, enslaved to various passions and pleasures, living in evil and jealousy, despicable and hateful of one another.

a. In Greek, verse 15 is a single sentence.

[2:15] In verse 15 the Pastor urges Titus to remind the people about the significance of the double epiphany and adds a personal counsel. The Pastor stresses the importance of his teaching with a threefold injunction, one of the many triads characteristic of the style of the Pastorals (see 2:12). The hortatory words "say" (*lalei*), "exhort" (*parakalei*), and "correct" (*elenche*) have already appeared in this epistle (see 1:9, 13; 2:1, 6, 9). The Pastor's triadic expression effectively presents exhortation—pastoral paraenesis—as a kind of two-edged sword. On the one hand, it is a matter of presenting sound teaching so that those who belong to the community remain steadfast in their commitment to the truth. On the other hand, it is a matter of correcting those who have strayed from sound teaching, or have never embraced it, so that they might undergo some kind of conversion experience (see 1:9).

The instruction given to Titus ends on a personal note. He is reminded that he is to speak out "with full authority" (*EDNT* 2.41).[35] This injunction is emphasized with the additional remark, "Let no one despise you." In similar fashion, Paul had encouraged the Christians of Corinth not to look down on Timothy (1 Cor. 16:11). Both expressions suggest that there may have been some reluctance to accept Paul's emissaries and successors. Titus is to have confidence as he fulfills a difficult pastoral role.

[3:1–2] After the summary description of Titus's task and the word of personal encouragement (v. 15), the Pastor gives a detailed analysis of the kind of exhortation that Titus is expected to use in addressing the congregation. Titus is urged to explain to the congregation just what is meant by "good works" (see 3:8). Using five infinitives, the Pastor has constructed a list of seven virtues to illustrate the meaning of the phrase. These infinitives are dependent upon an initial hortatory "remind them" (*hypomimnēske*; see 2 Tim. 2:14). The reminder serves as an indication that Cretan believers were supposed to have been aware of these things even before Titus began his work of pastoral exhortation among them.

Respect for legitimate authority and obedience is cited as the first of the Christian's social responsibilities. The expression "rulers, authorities" (*archais*

35. BAGD 303 and *TDNT* 8.36–37 render the phrase, "with all impressiveness."

exousiais[36]) without any conjunction, seems best rendered by "legitimate rulers," that is, rulers who are able to exercise authority over their subjects. Both words occur in the Pastorals only here. It is not unlikely that the Pastor's words are intended to be a reminder that Christians should avoid any kind of civil disobedience that would render them suspect in the eyes of governmental authorities and perhaps lead to violence or some other form of persecution (see 1 Pet. 2:13–15). First Timothy 2:1–2 urges the members of the community to pray for kings and all people in authority "so that we might live a peaceful and quiet life in all godliness and dignity." Obedience to civil authorities serves to enhance the community in the eyes of those outside, protects them against oppression, and creates the circumstances that enable them to enjoy a certain quality of life.

In addition to their civic responsibilities, Christians must be "ready for every good work" (see 2 Tim. 2:21; 3:17). In contrast, those who have not been purified are unsuitable for every good work (1:16). "Every good work" (*pan ergon agathon*) is the Christian life in its totality. The adjective *pan*, "every," must be taken distributively to include every sort of good work. The Pastor is careful in his description of a total Christian life, for which he uses either the singular *ergon agathon* with the distributive adjective *pan* (1:16; see 1 Tim. 5:10; 2 Tim. 2:21; 3:17) or the plural *kala erga* (2:7, 14; 3:8, 14; see 1 Tim. 5:10, 25; 6:18). "Every good work" and "good works" are synonymous with each other.

The Pastor expands the general exhortation with a series of remarks that indicate that members of the chosen people should have good social graces. They are to speak evil of no one (*mēdena blasphēmein*). In addition, they are to embrace a triad of virtues that are necessary for a good social life; they are to be peaceful, fair, and gentle with regard to everyone. The Pastor's emphasis on "all" and "none" may reflect the paraenetic genre. The genre consists of general exhortations rather than specific directions. Thus, believers are urged to speak maliciously about no one at all, and to be peaceful, balanced, and gentle toward everyone. It may be, however, that "toward everyone" is a salient qualification. The Pastor might have been concerned lest civil authorities (see 1 Tim. 2:1) and outsiders (see 2:5, 10) be excluded from the Christian's social outreach. In any case, the participle *endeiknymenous*, "showing," is taken from the world of rhetoric. Its literal meaning is to "demonstrate," indicating that the fully lived ethical life has a demonstrative appeal. Appropriate social behavior on the part of believers serves as an argument in favor of their faith.

Members of the chosen people are to exclude no one from his or her social-mindedness. Using a familiar triadic mode—the two adjectives and the participle are controlled by the verb "to be" (*einai*)—the Pastor describes the believer's interaction with others as characterized by a calm peacefulness, fairness, and

36. These two words and the verb "be subject to" are found in Rom. 13:1–7, the passage on which the Pastor seems to have relied for the formulation of this exhortation.

gentleness. All three virtues figured in Hellenistic descriptions of life in society: the absence of contentiousness (*amachous*) by Aeschylus, balance (*epieikeis*) by Herodotus, and gentleness (*prauteta*) by Plato and other Greek authors. The first two of these virtues are among those expected to be found in the life of a person who is qualified to serve as an overseer of the house of God (see 1 Tim. 3:3).

[3] By way of further explanation (*gar*) of the kind of life that members of the chosen people are to lead, the Pastor contrasts the way that they are now expected to live (vv. 1–2) with the way that they once lived (*pote*). They have had a conversion experience. The Pastor's use of the "once-now" scheme reflects early Christian usage (once heathen, now illumined or cleansed, in Titus 3:3–7; Rom. 6:17–18; 7:5–6; 11:20–32; Gal. 4:3–9; 1 Cor. 6:9–11; Col. 3:5–10; Eph. 2:1–10, 11–13; 1 Pet. 2:25; 4:3–4; once hidden, now revealed, in Titus 1:2–3; 2 Tim. 1:9–10; Rom. 16:25–27; 1 Cor. 2:7–10a; Col. 1:26–27; Eph. 3:5–6; 8–10; 1 Pet. 1:20; see Bultmann, *The Theology of the New Testament* [London: SCM Press] vol. 1, 1952, 109).

Occasionally this outline is employed in a portrayal of the history of salvation. Once salvation was hidden; now it has been revealed. At other times, the outline is used to contrast humankind under the influence of sin with humankind redeemed. This is the contrast between the "old person" and the "new person." In 1 Tim. 1:12–17 the "once-now" scheme is used to describe Paul's conversion. In Titus 3:1–3 it is used to contrast the life of believers with the life of those who have not yet or will never receive baptismal regeneration (3:3–7). The Pastor's contrasting explanation offers a qualifying nuance to what he has just enjoined upon Titus. Titus is to "remind them" (3:1) of how they should live. He is to remind them of their baptismal catechesis.

As is typical when the "once-now" scheme is used to describe two conditions of a human being, the Pastor employs a catalog of vices to describe what life was like before baptism. His list contains eight vices. The first two, "ignorant" and "disobedient," are expressed in terms that use a privative alpha, *a-noētoi* and *a-peitheis*. Christians were persons who once lacked intelligence and the spirit of obedience (see 1:16). The former description speaks derisively of their former state. While the term "ignorant" may allude to the fact that prior to baptism Christians were ignorant of the message of the gospel ("the full knowledge of truth") and its demands, the term was commonly used to describe someone who was witless, foolish, stupid, and silly.

Their former disobedience contrasts with the obedience (*peitharchein*, 3:1) that is now expected of them. Earlier they were led astray (*planōmenoi*); now they are presumed to be on the right path. The vocabulary that the Pastor uses to identify the third vice on his list reflects the language of Hellenistic moral discourse. "Don't go astray" (*mē planasthe*) was a popular moral exhortation (see Epictetus, *Discourses* 4.6.23; see also 1 Cor. 6:9; 15:33; Gal. 6:7). A popular Stoic proverb spoke of those who had gone astray leading others astray (see 2 Tim. 3:13). One could be led astray by all sorts of things—desire, sensuality, the lure of external things, unclear ideas, and false teaching. According to Plato, someone who goes astray is lacking in purpose and virtue (*phronēsis* and *aretē*; see *Republic* 9.586a). The one who has gone astray simply leads an aimless life.

The Pastor shares with the philosophic moralists of his day the concern that Christians not live a life of sensuality. For the Stoics, the ideal of the moral life was a life without passion (*a-patheia*). Influenced by this view, the Pastor describes the former life of the members of the community as one that was enslaved to passions and various pleasures (*douleuontes epithymiais kai hēdonais*; see 1 Tim. 6:9).

The final phrases of the Pastor's description of the former lifestyle of those who have been purified focus on antisocial behavior in contrast with the list of social graces given in verse 2. The Pastor begins to describe their antisocial conduct with a participial phrase that depicts them having lived in evil and jealousy. The two phrases are arranged in a chiastic structure; encompassing participles embrace a pair of vices. Reflecting his Semitic tradition, Paul commonly described life as a journey, a walk (*peripatein*). The Pastoral Epistles do not use the Pauline expression; rather, the Pastor speaks of life as a passing through (*diagontes*; see 1 Tim. 2:2), a verb used by Herodotus and other Hellenistic authors. As they passed through life prior to their baptism, believers lived a life of evil and jealousy (*en kakia kai phthonō*). Neither term is found on Philo's long list of 146 vices in *Abel and Cain* 32. Such was the wide variety of terms from which Hellenistic authors were able to compile a list of vices.

The Pastor's next two vices, "despicable" (*stygētoi*) and "hating one another" (*misountes allēlous*) likewise make no appearance on Philo's long list. Together the two terms mean "being hated and hateful of others." "Despicable" was used by such classical authors as Aeschylus (*Prometheus* 592), Philo (*Decalogue* 131), Clement (*1 Clem.* 35:6), and Heliodorus (5.29.4) in the sense of hated, abominable, or despicable. Echoing the language of the Pastor's catalog of vices, Clement of Rome described the tormenters of Hananiah, Azariah, and Mishael as "abominable men and full of all wickedness" (*hoi stygētoi kai pasēs kakias plēreis, 1 Clem.* 45:7). To conclude, the Pastor notes that prior to baptism, the members of the community had been hateful to one another (*misountes allēlous*). This is the obvious antithesis of the Christian demand to love one another.

A Baptismal Hymn
Titus 3:4–8a

Having concluded the explanatory exhortation to Titus (2:15–3:3), the Pastor returns to the epiphany motif that was the focus of the preceding pericope (2:11–14). That epiphany period spoke of the purification of the chosen people. This epiphany period returns to the principal theme of the earlier period, the saving appearance of Jesus Christ, our Savior. That pericope made but an allusive reference to baptism by speaking of the purification of the chosen people. This pericope incorporates a traditional baptismal hymn that speaks of the Christian ritual as one of rebirth and renewal.

The vocabulary[37] and rhythm of the hymn indicate that it was a preexistent unit that the Pastor has employed and on which he has already offered a kind of commentary (2:11–14). It is not only the internal evidence of the hymn that suggests that it is borrowed material; the Pastor himself says as much when he qualifies the hymn as "a trustworthy saying." The hymn contains one of the most important statements on the nature of baptism to be found in the New Testament (see Rom. 6:3–11).

The reference in the hymn to the Holy Spirit is one of only two explicit mentions of the Spirit in the Pastoral Epistles (see 2 Tim. 1:14). As did the prior epiphany passage, the hymn situates the existence of the Christian between two appearances of Jesus Christ. Its dominant theme is salvation, effected by Jesus Christ and imparted to Christians in the baptismal ritual. The ritual enables the baptized to be heirs, hoping for eternal life.

4 When appeared the goodness and benevolence
    of our Savior, God,
5 not from works of righteousness
    that we ourselves have done,
but according to his mercy,
    he saved us through the washing of rebirth
and renewal by the Holy Spirit,
    6 which he poured out on us profusely
through Jesus Christ, our Savior,[a]
    7 so that, justified by his grace,
we may become heirs according to the hope of eternal life.

This is a trustworthy saying.

a. In an orthodox reading of this verse, many lectionaries change the reference to "Jesus Christ, our Savior" to read "Jesus Christ, our God" (see 2:13 and Ehrman 87). Similar changes for the sake of presumed orthodoxy are evidenced elsewhere in the manuscript tradition of the Pastoral Epistles.

[3:4–7] Jacques Dupont (108) has described this pericope as a kind of baptismal hymn, with a firm structure and a rhythm that can be appreciated only in

37. Among the words that do not appear elsewhere in the Pastorals are "washing" (*loutrou*), "rebirth" (*palingenesias*), "renewal" (*anakainōseōs*), "pour" (*exechēn*), "profusely" (*plousiōs*), and "heir" (*klēronomoi*). "Mercy" (*eleos*) does not otherwise appear in Titus. Such distinctive vocabulary is compelling evidence of the borrowed nature of the hymn.

Greek. In fact, the editors of the Nestle-Aland edition (27th ed.) of the Greek text have published the pericope in strophic fashion. Dupont observes that the structure of the hymn would be better appreciated if the references to justification were eliminated—"not from works of righteousness that we ourselves have done but" (*ouk ex ergōn tōn en dikaiosynē ha epoiēsamen hēmeis alla*) and "justified by his grace" (*dikaiōthentes tē ekeinou chariti*). These references might be considered as "Pauline" additions to a hymn that was known in the Pastor's circles, just as the words "even death on a cross" (Phil. 2:8) are often considered to be a Pauline addition to a pre-Pauline hymn in Phil. 2:6–11 because they break the metrical symmetry of the hymnic unit.

The first strophe of the hymn (v. 4) echoes 2:11: "For the saving beneficence of God has appeared to all people." Each of the key words of 2:11 recur in 3:4: "saving" (*sōtērios*) in the hymn's "our Savior" (*tou sōtēros hēmōn*), "beneficence" (*hē charis*) in "kindness" (*hē chrēstotēs*), "God" (*tou theou*), "appeared" (*epephanē*), and "people" (*anthrōpois*) in "benevolence" (*philanthrōpia*). It is likely that 3:4–7 was a well-known baptismal hymn and that 2:11 is the Pastor's own composition, inspired by the opening strophe of the hymn.

The hymn proclaims that the goodness and benevolence of our Savior, God (see 1:3; 2:10), have appeared. Neither "goodness" (*chrēstotēs*) nor "benevolence" (*philanthrōpia*) occurs elsewhere in the Pastorals. The former is, nonetheless, a Pauline term (Rom. 2:4; 3:12 [=Ps. 14:3]; 11:22 [2x]; 2 Cor. 6:6; Gal. 5:22; see Eph. 2:7; Col. 3:12); the latter occurs elsewhere in the New Testament only in Acts 28:2. "Goodness" and "benevolence" are, however, a classic pair. Philo writes that the emperor Gaius had once been thought to be "good and benevolent" (*chrēstos kai philanthrōpos, Gaius* 67), showing fairness and fellowship to everyone. He argues with a hypothetical moneylender who outwardly shows goodness and benevolence (*chrēstos kai philanthrōpos, Special Laws* 2.75) while proving to be inhumane (*apanthrōpian*) and brutal in his actions. He characterizes as a false goodness and benevolence (*chrēston kai philanthrōpon, Special Laws* 3.156) a parental or filial piety that leads a father to be punished instead of his son, or a son to be punished instead of his father.

Josephus wrote that Gedaliah, appointed governor over the towns of Judea by the king of Babylon, showed such "goodness and benevolence" (*chrēstotēta kai philanthrōpian, Ant.* 10.9.3 §164) that Johanan and other leaders of the Jews (see Jer. 40:8) experienced a great love for him (*hyperēgapēsan auton*). The physician Galen praised his father because of his benevolence and goodness (*chrēstotaton kai philanthrōpon*).[38] Dio Cassius (ca. 164–229 C.E.) wrote that "a benevolence, a goodness [*philanthrōpia, chrēstotēs*], attentive care for everything

---

38. See Basil Latyschev, *Inscriptiones Antiquae Orae Septentrionalis Ponti Euxini Graecae et Latinae*, 2 vols. 2nd ed. (Hildesheim: Georg Olms, 1965), 39.20–21, pp. 66–69.

that pertains to the public interest" were qualities of the administration of the emperor Pertinax (*Roman History* 73.5.2). The philosopher Onasander wrote that a general should treat with benevolence and goodness (*philanthrōpos kai chrēstos*) cities that open their gates in surrender (see *General* 18.1).

Benevolence was widely viewed as the quintessential quality of a good king. The Rosetta Stone lauds Ptolemy V, a benevolent ruler who had freely given away all the monies that belonged to him (*tais te heautou dynamesis pephilanthrōpēke pasais*, Rosetta Stone 12[39]). The good king is prepared to show clemency (*philanthrōpa*) to the conquered (see Plutarch, *Cicero* 21.4) and to shower benefits (*philanthrōpa*) on the people so that harmony and peace might reign in the kingdom (see the letter of Claudius to the Alexandrians, *P. Lond.* 1912.102). The quality of royal benevolence included the duty not to inflict punishment too readily or to increase people's sufferings (see *Ep. Arist.* 208). Hellenistic papyri offer many examples of petitions addressed to kings or their legates by people who appeal to their benevolence as they ask these royals to intervene in a given situation.[40] Kings who showed benevolence expected that their subjects would show benevolence and love in return (see *Ep. Arist.* 265). Several papyri show that in fact people were thanked for their benevolence (*P. Mich.* 483.3; *P. Oxy.* 3057.8; see *TLNT* 3.445n15).

In sum, manifestations of goodness and benevolence were to be expected when a king, his governor, or his general arrived for a solemn visit to a city. Evidence of such goodness and benevolence manifested that the arriving personage was indeed a Savior (*sōtēr*) or benefactor (*euergetēs*). Since the royal sovereign was often considered to be a representative of the deity—sometimes to the point of being "divinized" himself—these expressions of goodness and benevolence were manifestations of the goodness and benevolence of the gods. Philo attributed benevolence to God, the king of kings, who deigns to visit human beings (*Cherubim* 99). In Philo's view, benevolence is a divine attribute. It belongs to the very nature of God (see *Moses* 1.198). God manifests his benevolence in order to show honor to the ruler that he had appointed.

The first verse of the Pastor's hymn captures this rich Hellenistic image of the formal arrival of an emperor or god. The Hellenistic world associated the benevolence manifested on these solemn occasions with clemency. Philo links both clemency (*epieikeia*, *Moses* 1.198) and tender mercy (*hēmerotēs*, *Cherubim* 99) with the royal and divine attribute of benevolence. In similar fashion the Pastor's baptismal hymn associates the manifestation of God's goodness and benevolence with his mercy (*to autou eleos*, 3:5c). Mercy, a gift of God (see 1 Tim. 1:2; 2 Tim. 1:2, 16, 18), is contrasted with works of righteousness

---

39. See E. A. Wallis Budge, *The Rosetta Stone in the British Museum* (London: Religious Tract Society, 1929), 68.

40. See *P. Oxy.* 2919, 10; *P. Mich.* 529, 13; *P. Sorb.* 53, 6; *P. Thaed.* 22, 11; see *TLNT* 3.444n13.

that we ourselves have done. The emphatic pronoun "we ourselves" (*hēmeis*) highlights the contrast between what we have done and what God manifests.

"Works of righteousness" (*ergōn tōn en dikaiosynē*) has a Pauline ring, but the apostle did not actually use the phrase "in righteousness" (*en dikaiosynē*). Writing about righteousness or justification, Paul occasionally used a prepositional phrase that includes "righteousness" as the object of the preposition, but the preposition is either *eis*, "in," following Gen. 15:6 (LXX; see Rom. 4:3, 5, 9, 22; Gal. 3:6; cf. Rom. 6:16; 10:4, 10), or *dia*, "through," "on account of" (see Rom. 4:13; 5:21; 8:10). The prepositional phrase used by the Pastor is, however, found in four pseudepigraphic epistles, all influenced in some degree by the writings of Paul (Titus 3:5; 2 Tim. 3:16; Eph. 4:24; 2 Pet. 1:1; see Acts 17:31; Rev. 19:11). This nondescript phrase echoes Paul's language but reflects none of the verve of his argument.

The phrase "justified by his grace" (*dikaiōthentes*[41] *tē ekeinou chariti*, 3:7), on the other hand, reflects Paul's thought as it took shape in discussions with those "Judaizers" who troubled Christian communities in Rome and Galatia. Human beings are justified not by their own efforts but by the justifying gift of God.[42] The hymn's double reference to righteousness (vv. 5, 7) captures and emphasizes, by means of its inherent contrast, the apostle's conviction that we are not justified by our own works; rather, we are justified by the saving grace of God. Recollection of this Pauline notion is apropos in a document purportedly intended for Christians living in a society where there were considerable numbers of Jews and the Christian community itself had to deal with various matters pertaining to Judaism (see 1:10, 14–15).

Encompassing as they do the formulaic "according to his mercy" (*kata to autou eleos*), the hymn's two references to righteousness provide a setting for and a Pauline clarification of the notion of the Savior's mercy. In the Hellenistic world, mercy (*eleos*), judgment, and benevolence were qualities that one expected to find in a judge (see Demosthenes, *Against Meidias* 21.100; cf. Plato, *Apology* 34c, 35b). As one might appeal to a sovereign's benevolence, so might one appeal to a judge's mercy (see Plato, *Apology* 34c) and be thankful when mercy was rendered (see *P. Magd.* 18.6). Mercy was apposite to the pursuit of justice (*dikē*).

According to the Hebrew Scriptures (see Num. 14:18; Joel 2:13; Ps. 86:5, 15) and early Christian writings, the mercy of God is a given (see 1 Tim. 1:2

---

41. Anyone who translates New Testament texts inevitably encounters the difficulty that stems from the fact that words with the root *dik-* can be translated in Germanic ("right," "righteous," "made righteous") or Romance ("just," "justify") fashion. For the purposes of the flow of the translation, I have opted to translate the *dikaiosynē* of v. 5 in Germanic fashion, "righteousness," and the *dikaiōthentes* of v. 7 in Romance fashion, "justified." Alternatives respecting the presence of the same root in both Greek words would have been "righteousness," "made righteous" and "justice," "justified."

42. See the discussion in Jas. 2:14–26.

and 2 Tim. 1:2, where "mercy" is juxtaposed with "grace"). The Pastor explains that God's mercy is realized in the salvation that we receive through baptism by the Holy Spirit, with the result that we are justified by grace and become heirs. In the hymn, the Savior's mercy is not only cast in the light of the Pauline understanding of justification, and contrasted with such righteous works as are done by humans; it is also explained in terms of salvation itself. Our Savior, God, motivated by mercy, has saved us (*esōsen hēmas*). The Savior is one from whom salvation is expected; the Savior is also one who has already saved us.

This the Savior has done by means of "the washing of rebirth and renewal by the Holy Spirit" (*dia loutrou palingenesias kai anakainōseōs pneumatos hagiou*). The word "washing" renders a Greek term (*loutron*; see Eph. 5:26) that variously designates a bath, the water with which one bathes, or the act of washing. The act of washing is a common act of human hygiene. From time immemorial, however, washing has served as a ritual action. Ceremonial washings, whether of the whole body or of particular parts of the body, were sometimes a rite of passage, symbolizing the passage from one state in life to another. At other times, ceremonial ablutions symbolized the transition from the secular to the sacred (see *EncRel* 1.9–13). A ritual bathing of the entire body served as an initiation ceremony for Jewish proselytes. In the Eleusinian mysteries, the rite of initiation, held during the February celebrations of the Lesser Mysteries at Agrai, concluded with a ritual washing in which water was poured over the initiate. The ceremonies at Agrai were a prelude to the September celebrations of the Greater Mysteries at Eleusis. Among Christians, bodily immersion into water (baptism) was the rite of entrance into the Christian community.

The ritual bath mentioned in the hymn is one of rebirth and renewal. The term *palingenesia*, "rebirth," from *palin*, "again," and *ginomai*, "to come into being" (*genesis*, "birth," being one of its cognates), occurs elsewhere in the New Testament only in Matt. 19:28. The term was commonly used in the Hellenistic world of a wide range of human or metahuman experiences, including the restoration of health, return from exile, the beginning of a new life, the restoration of souls, new life for a people, and the anticipated restoration of the world.

The *Corpus Hermeticum*, an Alexandrian text written sometime before the end of the third century C.E. and attributed to the "Thrice-Greatest Hermes" (Hermes Trismegistos), says that "no one can be saved before rebirth" (*Corp. Herm.* 13.3). The thirteenth tract of the *Corpus* features a dialogue between Hermes and his son Tat on the subject of being born again. Speaking to his father in a manner that recalls Nicodemus's question to Jesus (John 3:4), Tat inquires about rebirth. He understands rebirth to be accomplished in some physical manner and asks his father about the womb and seed. Hermes responds that these are respectively the wisdom of understanding in silence and the true good, sown in a person by the will of God. The child that results is a different kind of child, "a god and a child of God" (*Corp. Herm.* 13.2). Rebirth enables a person to progress in the moral life, turning from twelve vices—ignorance, grief, incontinence, lust, injustice, greed, deceit, envy, treachery, anger, recklessness, and malice—to the opposite virtues (*Corp. Herm.* 13.7).

Many twentieth-century scholars, particularly those belonging to the history of religions school of New Testament research, attempted to clarify 3:5 in the light of this Hermetic tract. The tract is, however, much later than the Epistle to Titus and lacks any reference to a ritual washing. On the other hand, the late first-century canonical Fourth Gospel features a discourse between Jesus and Nicodemus, a leader of the Pharisees (John 3:3–8), about being "born again" (*gennēthē anōthen*). The Johannine account does not employ the noun "rebirth" (*palingenesia*), as does the *Corpus*, but it does speak about a birth that takes place in water and the Spirit (*gennēthē ex hydatos kai pneumatos*). The substantive similarities between the Johannine text and 3:5d–e—the references to washing, new birth, and the Spirit—suggest that both of these late first-century texts describe the ritual of Christian baptism as bringing about a new life through the power of the Holy Spirit.

The Pastor explains what he means by rebirth by adding "and (an epexegetical *kai*) renewal by the Holy Spirit." The ritual ablution of baptism effects a rebirth that is also a renewal. Elsewhere in the New Testament, the term "renewal" (*anakainōsis*) appears only in Rom. 12:2, the first attested usage of a term that appears only in Christian literature. Apart from these two New Testament passages, the term is found in *Herm. Vis.* 3.8.9, where the female figure speaks to Hermas about "the renewal of your spirits" (*anakainōsis tōn pneumatōn hymōn*). This phrase connotes the conversion that is necessary as the eschaton approaches. Throughout the New Testament, the word "new" (*kainos*) generally has an eschatological connotation.[43] The Pastoral Epistles evoke the eschatological future when they use "epiphany" language to speak of the future appearance of the great God and Savior, Jesus Christ (2:13; see 1 Tim. 6:14; 2 Tim. 4:1, 8).

In his commentary on the opening lines of this hymn (2:11–12), the Pastor explained what baptismal conversion entails. It is a matter of denying impiety and worldly passions. It is living modestly, justly, and piously while we wait in hope for the appearance of the glory of the great God and our Savior (see 2:12–13).

The new life and conversion associated with the baptismal washing result from the working of the Holy Spirit (*pneumatos hagiou*). The Pastoral Epistles do not have a developed pneumatology. It is only here and in 2 Tim. 1:14 that explicit reference is made to the Holy Spirit, the power of God at work. Early Christian tradition, however, generally associates baptism and its effects with the work of the Holy Spirit. The hymn reflects this tradition and its understanding that the Holy Spirit is the eschatological Spirit of God already at work

---

43. See Roy A. Harrisville, *The Concept of Newness in the New Testament* (Minneapolis: Augsburg, 1960).

in the present age. That the Holy Spirit effects a rebirth and a renewal is consistent with the biblical idea that the Spirit of God was at work in the creation of the universe and the creation of humankind (Genesis 1–2). God's eschatological power effects a rebirth and a renewal.

The image of the pouring of water in the baptismal ritual continues to be evoked when the hymn speaks about the gift of the Holy Spirit that God "has profusely poured" (*exechēn*[44] . . . *plousiōs*) out upon us. "Profusely" indicates the abundance and lavishness of God's gift of the Spirit. The idea that Jesus is the mediator of the gift of the Spirit in baptism is traditional (see John 4:10, 14; cf. Matt. 3:11; Mark 1:8; Luke 3:16; John 1:26–27; 20:22–23). The Johannine tradition particularly emphasizes the lavishness of this water gift and its relevance to eternal life (see John 4:14–15).

The New Testament expresses the idea of inheritance that the hymn associates with baptism through various words belonging to the *klēronom-* word group. Among them is the noun *klēronomos*, "heir," used in 3:7. The inheritance motif does not otherwise appear in the Pastoral Epistles, but Paul often wrote about the inheritance, especially in Romans, 1 Corinthians, and Galatians. The idea of an inheritance is often linked, especially in Paul, with the notions of children of God, the Spirit, and baptism (see Rom. 8:14–17). The hymn's idea that those who are justified by grace are heirs is consistent with these Pauline ideas and with the post-Pauline notion that the seal of the promised Holy Spirit is the pledge of our inheritance (Eph. 1:13–14). The very idea of an inheritance is forward looking. An inheritance is something that a person will receive in the future. Baptism is the guarantee that there will be an inheritance in the future. This inheritance is "eternal life," a cipher for eschatological salvation in the Pastor's circles.

[8a] The Pastor places a seal of approval on his version of the baptismal hymn by adding, as a kind of final "amen," the aphorism "This is a trustworthy saying" (*pistos ho logos*; see Excursus 1). This use of his circles' stock phrase (see 1 Tim. 1:15; 3:1; 4:9; 2 Tim. 2:11) affirms that the unit he has just cited has faithfully reproduced the tradition handed down to him.

Final Exhortation
Titus 3:8b–11

Having endorsed the content of the baptismal hymn, the epistle takes a radical stylistic turn as the Pastor adopts the mode of a rhetorical epilogue. Taking a retrospective view, the Pastor proceeds to sum up what he has written thus far,

---

44. The verb is not otherwise used in the Pastorals. In Paul it appears only in a citation of Isa. 59:7 (see Rom. 3:15) and in Rom. 5:5.

giving the reason why he has written as he has. He urges Titus to exhort believers to translate their faith into action. The Pastor, nonetheless, warns Titus not
to give in to any of the things that were troubling his flock. This warning and
the Pastor's emphasis on Titus's obligation to confront those who have strayed
from the truth and healthy behavior confirms that the church for which this epistle was intended was undergoing some difficulty. The Pastor urges that there be
no compromise.

8b I want you to insist on all these things so that those who have come to
believe in God make every effort to choose good works. These are things
that are good and beneficial for human beings; 9 avoid[a] foolish arguments,
genealogies, divisions, and quarrels about the law, because they are useless and stupid. 10 After a first and then a second admonition, avoid the
divisive person, 11 knowing that such a one is perverted, sinful, and self-
condemned.

a. In Greek, verse 9 is an independent sentence. It is, however, so constructed that
"foolish arguments, genealogies, divisions, and quarrels about the law" are juxtaposed
with "things that are good and beneficial for human beings." The contrast between the
two is better rendered in English by means of a compound sentence.

[3:8b–c] The Pastor looks back on the things about which he has written (*peri
toutōn*) and urges Titus to insist (*diabebaiousthai*; see 1 Tim. 1:7) on them. "Insist"
is a common word in Hellenistic paraenesis. Used by Aristotle (*Rhetoric* 2.13.1),
Demosthenes (*On the Treaty with Alexander* 17.30), and Polybius (*Histories*
12.12.6), the verb suggests speaking with confidence and affirming the importance
of what is being said. Titus is to speak in this way so that those who have been
entrusted to his pastoral supervision (see 1:5) might pursue a life of good works.

The apostle frequently describes Christians as "believers," using a present
participle (*pisteuontes*; see 1 Thess. 1:7). The Pastor's phrase uses a perfect participle and cites the object of belief, God (*hoi pepisteukotes theō*). Some translations exploit the perfect tense of the participle so as to imply that Titus's
community consisted largely of Gentiles who had undergone a conversion
experience and now believe in God (NRSV, JB, NEB, and Luther's 1545 Bible).
Other translations exploit the perfect by suggesting continuity in faith (AV, RSV,
RNAB). Some of the translations that attempt to reflect a contemporary idiom
simply render the Greek as "who believe in God" (CEV).

The translation "who have come to believe in God" does not sufficiently
reflect the connotations of "faith" found in the Pastorals. In these writings,
"faith" evokes the content of faith rather than the existential relationship suggested by Paul's use of the term. This nuance is not absent from the Pastor's identification of the members of the community as those who have come to believe
in God. They have come to believe in God as the community understands that

belief in God to be. Jews would have believed in God, but prior to their entrance into the community they would not have believed in God according to the community's understanding of faith in God.

Those who believe in God must be committed to doing "good works," the Pastor's standard description of correct behavior. The verb "make every effort" (*phrontizōsin*; see *TLNT* 3.467–69) is an epistolary term often found in the papyri in both private and official correspondence. It suggests taking something to heart and actively pursuing it until the task is completed, often with the implication that the person has a responsibility to do so. According to the Pastor, the task at hand is a preferential option for good works, an active preference (*proistasthai*) for correct ethical conduct (see 3:14).

The Pastor underscores the importance of his and Titus's exhortation with a simple ethical affirmation: "These are things that are good and beneficial for human beings." Both terms are substantivized adjectives. The Pastor's use of the word "beneficial" (*ōphelima*) adds an element of rhetorical appeal, the argument from advantage, to his observation. The good is to be done because it is advantageous for human beings to do so. The rhetorical argument was often phrased with terms that employ the semantic group developed around the use of the root *ōphel-*, "advantageous" or "beneficial."

[9] As for Titus himself, he is to avoid foolish arguments (*mōras zēteseis*), genealogies (*genealogias*), divisions (*ereis*), and quarrels about the law (*machas nomikas*). The four are linked together with a repeated "and" (*kai*), represented by a comma in the translation, in an exhortation that substantively reappears in 2 Tim. 2:23. Titus and Timothy are urged to be keepers of the peace in their respective communities. Timothy is exhorted to "avoid foolish [*mōras*] and stupid arguments [*zēteseis*], knowing that they produce quarrels [*machas*]." What distinguishes the exhortation addressed to Titus from the one addressed to Timothy is that Titus is also urged to avoid genealogies, divisions, and disputes about the law.

This kind of vocabulary is rarely used in the New Testament. "Genealogies" appears elsewhere only in 1 Tim. 1:4. Plato (*Timaeus* 22a) and Polybius (*Histories* 9.2.1) argue against myths and genealogical lists. The Pastor had expressed a concern lest members of the community become fascinated by Jewish myths (1:14). The kind of genealogies to which he makes reference in 3:9 may well be the kinds of Jewish lists found in the Bible, rabbinic sources, and the Dead Sea Scrolls. The adjective *nomikos*, "about the law," is not used as an adjective in any other New Testament passage.[45] The legal disputes to which the Pastor refers are undoubtedly disputes about the Jewish law (see p. 29).

---

45. A substantivized use of the term ("lawyer") is found in 3:13 and in several passages of the Synoptic Gospels, where it refers to a lawyer who is competent in Jewish law (see Matt. 22:35; Luke 7:30; 10:25; 11:45, 46, 52; 14:3).

"Divisions" is a term used by Paul, generally to designate a vice associated with jealousy (Rom. 13:13; 1 Cor. 3:3; 2 Cor. 12:20; Gal. 5:20; see Rom. 1:29; Phil. 1:15). Only in 1 Cor. 1:11 does Paul use the term to speak of divisions within the community. The presence of "divisions" in the Pastor's list of things to be avoided by Titus suggests that the community might possibly splinter. Titus is urged to make every effort that it not do so. The mention of "divisions" between "genealogies" and "quarrels about the law" may suggest that the precarious situation to which Titus must respond is some kind of fragmentation due to the presence of Jews in his community (1:14–15; 3:5, 7).

The Pastor concluded the hortatory words intended for believers with a reflection on the beneficial nature of good works. He concludes his direct exhortation to Titus with words about the futility of the things that Titus is to avoid. Foolish arguments, genealogies, divisions, and quarrels about the law are simply useless (*an-ōpheleis*, see v. 8) and stupid (*mataioi*). No advantage whatsoever is to be had in pursuing them.

[10–11] Although Titus is to avoid getting involved in quarrels and foolish arguments, he is nonetheless urged to do what he can to bring an errant member of the community to his or her senses and back to the community (see 2 Tim. 2:25–26). If these efforts do not meet with success, Titus is to shun the divisive person. The idea that a recalcitrant person is to be treated as an outcast after a first and second warning is similar to the discipline enjoined by Matt. 18:15–17. The Pastor's language is that of Hellenistic paraenesis. "Admonition," writes the Pseudo-Demetrius, "is the instilling of sense in the person who is being admonished, and teaching him what should and should not be done" (*Epistolary Types* 7).

Titus must admonish the divisive person not once but twice (*mian kai deuteran*). Then he must act. Knowing that the divisive person is perverted and sinful, Titus must stay out of that person's way (*paraitou*; see 1 Tim. 4:7; 5:11; 2 Tim. 2:23). The verb's prefix (*par-*) suggests a nuance of aversion or repudiation. Repudiation may entail the excommunication of the recalcitrant person (see BAGD 616, 1.2.a; Diogenes Laertius, *Lives of Eminent Philosophers* 6.82; Plutarch, "Sayings of Romans: Gaius Caesar" 3, *Moralia* 206A). The Pastor's circles were aware that Paul himself had sometimes favored excommunication as a way of dealing with a recalcitrant sinner (see 1 Tim. 1:18–20; 1 Cor. 5:5).

The person whom Titus is to avoid so radically is described in four ways. He or she is divisive, perverted, sinful, and self-condemned. In Stoic literature, the adjective "divisive" (*hairetikon*) was used of people who caused divisions. Literally meaning "to turn away from" or "to turn inside out," the verb *exestraptai* was used metaphorically to mean "thoroughly confused" or "perverted." The Greek verb "to sin" (*hamartanei*) is rarely used in the Pastorals (only here and in 1 Tim. 5:20). In the Greek Bible, this verb renders the Hebrew *ḥāṭāh*. Both the Greek and the Hebrew literally mean "to miss the mark," but were commonly used in the metaphorical, theological sense of "sin." Hellenists would have understood the term as describing the actions of someone who had done wrong or had failed in his or her purpose.

Finally, the person to be avoided is described as self-condemned, someone who has made a judgment against himself or herself (*ōn autokatakritos*). The adjective was rarely used in Greek. Apart from a single occurrence in a fragment of Philo's *Sacred Parallels*, the term is found only in Christian literature. Since 3:11 may be its earliest occurrence in Greek literature, it may have been the Pastor himself who coined the word.

Final Remarks and Farewell
Titus 3:12–15

The final remarks in the epistle have the form of a kind of travelogue. It was not unusual for Paul to mention his travel plans in his letters. He frequently mentioned his desire to visit those to whom he was writing (Rom. 1:10–11; 15:22–24, 28–29; 1 Cor. 11:34; 16:3; 2 Cor. 1:15–16; 12:20–21; 13:10; Phil. 2:24; 1 Thess. 2:17–18; Phlm. 22). Toward the end of a letter, Paul occasionally entered into some detail about his travel plans (see Rom. 15:22–29; 1 Cor. 16:5–9). The Pastor's mention of a port city and an allusion to the difficulty of winter travel are consistent with the literary genre. The epistle concludes with customary greetings in the first, second, and third persons—all of them tersely stated—but does not have the appended handwritten note found in some of Paul's own letters (see 1 Cor. 16:21; Gal. 6:11; cf. 2 Thess. 3:17).

What is particularly striking about this set of farewell remarks is the mention of Artemas, Tychicus, Zenas, and Apollos. The personal names are an expression of the Pastor's concern for succession in ministry. Artemas and Tychicus are to fill in for Titus, leaving him free to visit Paul. Zenas and Apollos are to be sent to their respective destinations by Titus. Paul effectively delegates to Titus responsibility for sending other delegates on a mission. Thus, Zenas and Apollos are identified as second-generation delegates of the apostle. A plan for succession in ministry has been established.

> 3:12 When I send Artemas or Tychicus to you, make every effort to come to me at Nicopolis, for I have decided to spend the winter there. 13 Get Zenas, the lawyer, and Apollos ready and send them on their way. Make sure[a] that they lack nothing that they need. 14 Let our people learn how to choose good works in situations of urgent need so that they are not ineffective.

15 Everybody with me sends you greetings. Greet those who love us in faith. Grace be with all of you.[b]

a. In Greek, verse 13 is a single sentence.

b. This reading of the epistolary farewell is found in the most ancient manuscripts (P^{61}, $\aleph$) as well as in the Coptic and Armenian versions, but the manuscript tradition attests to no fewer than six other readings of the epistle's final words. The simplest reading is one most likely to have been the source of its variants.

[**3:12**] Paul's ongoing pastoral care of communities that he had evangelized is reflected in his sending of delegates, particularly his trusted coworkers Timothy and Titus, to act in his stead when he himself was not able to visit. He sent Titus and a companion to Corinth (2 Cor. 12:18; see 2 Cor. 7:13; 8:6, 18, 23) and perhaps to Troas (2 Cor. 2:13). He sent Timothy to Corinth (1 Cor. 4:17; 16:10), Thessalonica (1 Thess. 3:2, 6), and probably to Philippi, a place to which Epaphroditus was sent presumably at some other time (Phil. 2:19–30). The deuteropauline Epistle to the Colossians reflects this tradition of Paul's sending delegates on a mission to one or another place by mentioning that Paul sent Tychicus and Onesimus to Colossae (Col. 4:7–9).

Paul's pastoral concern for the churches is also reflected in the tradition that Paul had told Titus to remain in Crete (1:5) and Timothy to remain in Ephesus (1 Tim. 1:3). This tradition attests to the early church's desire for succession in the ministry of the gospel. Another expression of the early church's concern that a community not be without its ministers—and from the Pastor's perspective not without a minister who was familiar with the apostle—is found in verse 12. Paul is described as eagerly desiring to have Titus come to him (3:12). He wants to have him at his side as soon as possible (see 2 Tim. 4:9, 11, 13, 21). To replace Titus on Crete, Paul is sending Artemas or Tychicus. When the replacement arrives, Titus can leave the island and go to meet Paul in the port city of Nicopolis.

The use of personal names in the epistle's final pericope lends a degree of verisimilitude to the entire text. Artemas, like so many other characters in the Pastorals, is not mentioned elsewhere in the New Testament. Tychicus is not mentioned in Paul's own letters but is presented as having been at Paul's side in five of the New Testament's post-Pauline books (see Acts 20:4; Eph. 6:21; Col. 4:7; 2 Tim. 4:12). Here Paul is presented as not having made a decision about which one of these two he should send. Either of them would be able to maintain the Pauline influence on the faith of the islanders during Titus's absence.

Nicopolis, "city of victory," is the name of several imperial settlements that were established to commemorate a military victory. One of the cities named Nicopolis was built on the isthmus of the Bay of Actium, just across from the southern end of the Italian peninsula. The city was established to commemorate the naval victory of Augustus's forces over those of Mark Anthony in 31 B.C.E. Known as Nicopolos in Epirus (see Tacitus, *Annals* 2.53) or Nicopolis of Achaia (see Ptolemy, *Geography* 3.13), the city was a natural site for maritime transportation between Achaia and Italy. As the terminus of a trade route, it became an important commercial center and the site of quadrennial athletic games. Epictetus, the Stoic philosopher, arrived in the city as an exile in 89 C.E. (see Gellius, *Attic Nights* 15.11.5).

This port city was a natural place for a person to pass the winter were he or she intending to take a sea voyage in the early spring when travel conditions became less treacherous than they would be in winter (see 1 Cor. 16:6; Acts 27:9–12). The Achaian port is probably the city that the Pastor had in mind when he composed 3:12. A codicil to the epistle to Titus, first appearing in the sixth-century Codex Coislinianus (H), says that the epistle "was written by Paul the apostle to Titus, the first bishop of the Church of the Cretans upon whom hands had been laid, from Nicopolis of Macedonia." This note appears in most manuscripts of the Byzantine tradition. An eleventh-century minuscule (81) adds to the epistle an alternative form of the note: "Written to Titus from Nicopolis in Crete." Two earlier manuscripts, the fifth-century Codex Alexandrinus and the ninth-century Codex Porphyrianus, append a simple notation, "written from Nicopolis."

Paul often expressed a desire to visit those to whom he was writing. His letters were a substitute for his presence (*par-ousia*). Occasionally Paul gives a reason for why he was not immediately able to make the visit (see Rom. 15:22–29; 1 Cor. 16:5–9; 1 Thess. 2:18). His travelogues expand on his desire to visit those to whom he was writing and to provide substance for his expressed intention. In this epistle's travelogue, however, the fictive Paul expresses no desire to visit Crete or Titus. Rather, he asks that Titus make every effort to come to him (*spoudason elthein*). The real Paul, already deceased, remains absent from the community for whom this text is really intended (see the commentary on the plural number of the final greeting, v. 15c). Paul's protracted absence (*ap-ousia*) is a cover for the pseudepigraphic character of the epistle.

[13–14] No more than Artemas does Zenas appear elsewhere in the New Testament. His name is a contraction of *Zēnodōros*, "gift of Zeus." *Acts of Paul* 3.2 speaks of a man named Zeno as one of the sons of Onesiphoros (see commentary on 2 Tim. 1:16a). As the otherwise unknown Alexander is identified by his coppersmith's trade in 2 Tim. 4:14, so Zenas is identified by his profession. He is a lawyer (*ton nomikon*), but the Pastor does not indicate whether Zenas is versed in Greek, Roman, or Jewish law. According to the Greek menologies, Zenas was the first bishop of Diospolis of Lydda in Palestine. The tradition claims that he wrote a letter to Titus.

In contrast to Zenas, Apollos was a well-known figure in early Christianity. He is mentioned frequently in 1 Corinthians (1 Cor. 1:12; 3:4, 5, 6, 22; 4:6;

16:12), a sign that he was well known in the Achaian area. Acts 18:24–19:1 describes Apollos as an Alexandrian who was well versed in the Scriptures. He was catechized by Aquila and Priscilla and instructed in the ways of the Lord. Paul once tried to send Apollos back to visit the Corinthian community, but Apollos was reluctant to go (1 Cor. 16:12).

Titus is to get Zenas and Apollos prepared for their trip (*spoudaiōs propempson*). The language recalls the language of the previous verse; Titus is to send (*pempō*) delegates and he is to make every effort (*spoudason*) to come. The compound form of the verb in verse 13 connotes both "send on one's way" and "prepare for a journey" by providing money, food, companions, some means of travel, or whatever else is needed for a trip. In the light of the appended clause "make sure that they lack nothing that they need" (*hina mēden autois leipē*), this second nuance must be incorporated into the meaning of the Pastor's *propempson* (see Rom. 15:24; 1 Cor. 16:6, 11; 2 Cor. 1:16). Hence the translation, "Get Zenas . . . and Apollos ready and send them on their way."

In the narrow epistolary context of Titus, the next verse (v. 14) is addressed to Titus as a bit of advice that he should give to Zenas and Apollos as he is about to send them on their way. Christian missionaries should be ready for the hardships that they are bound to face; they must be ready to face these difficulties (*eis tas anankaias chreias*), choosing always to do good deeds no matter what the circumstances. "Good deeds" (*kalōn ergōn*) would be a secularized euphemism for the proclamation of the gospel in word and in work. In this narrow epistolary context, "our people" (*hoi hēmeteroi*) designates Zenas and Apollos.

In the broader context of this pseudepigraphic epistle, Zenas and Apollos belong to the author's narrative plot just as much as do "Paul" and "Titus." Zenas may have been a historical figure whose character has been lost because he is otherwise unknown to us. Both Zenas and the relatively well-known Apollos function in the narrative scene as exemplary figures. The paraenesis of verse 14 thus acquires broader significance. It is an exhortation not only for missionaries but for all of "our people." In fact, the expression "choose good works" (*kalōn ergōn proistasthai*) is found in the Pastor's final exhortation (3:8), where it clearly has a pragmatic, activity-oriented sense.

In the exhortation of 3:8, the good deeds are clearly that—namely, deeds that are beneficial for human beings. The Pastor uses similar language in 3:14 to say that Titus should exhort Zenas and Apollos as he sends them out "so that they are not ineffective (*a-karpoi*, literally, "without fruit")." The early church often used the imagery of growth and fruit (*karpos*) in its kerygmatic discourse. This idiom evoked the positive effect of the proclamation of the gospel (Matt. 13:8; Mark 4:7, 8; Luke 8:8). Matthew and Luke, appropriating Q material, write about "fruit" to describe a person's action (Matt. 3:8, 10; 7:16–20; 12:33; 13:26(?); Luke 3:8–9; 6:43–44; 8:8).

Paul often expressed some concern about the effectiveness of his proclamation of the gospel. He feared that his efforts might prove to be "empty" or "futile" (*kenos*; see 1 Cor. 15:10, 14; Gal. 2:2; Phil. 2:16; 1 Thess. 2:1; 3:5; see 1 Cor. 15:58; 2 Cor. 6:1). Occasionally Paul used agricultural imagery to speak about his ministry (1 Cor. 3:5–9; 9:10–11), but he did not speak of its fruit, nor did he speak about its possible fruitlessness. The language of fruitlessness is the language that the Pastor uses to express Paul's fears about the success of his preaching, his fears that his efforts would be in vain. This expression of concern is ironic; the very existence of post-Pauline texts such as the Epistle to Titus shows that Paul's preaching had *not* been in vain.

[15] Like most of Paul's letters, the Epistle to Titus closes with various greetings. Paul often expressed third person greetings (Rom. 16:21–23; 1 Cor. 16:19–20a; 2 Cor. 13:12b; Phil. 4:21b–22; Phlm. 23–24; see Col. 4:14; 2 Tim. 4:21b). He even sent greetings on behalf of all his Christian siblings (1 Cor. 16:20a; see 2 Tim. 4:21), all the churches (Rom. 16:16b), and all God's holy people (2 Cor. 13:12b; Phil. 4:22). Titus 3:15 says that "everybody with me" (*hoi met'emou pantes*) sends greetings. This unusual formula enhances the epistolary character of the Pastor's text.

Paul often asked that his correspondents convey his best wishes to others. He included second person greetings in his letters to the Romans, Corinthians, Philippians, and Thessalonians (Rom. 16:3–16a; 1 Cor. 16:20b; 2 Cor. 13:12a; Phil. 4:21a; 1 Thess. 5:26; see 2 Tim. 4:19). In verse 15 Titus is asked to convey greetings to "those who love us in faith" (*tous philountas hēmas en pistei*). This unique combination of words underscores the formulaic nature of the expression "in faith" in the Pastoral Epistles.

Hellenistic letters customarily ended with a final greeting, sometimes in the author's own hand. The closing salutation of this epistle, "Grace be with all of you" (*hē charis meta pantōn hymōn*), is one of the shortest in the Pauline corpus (see 1 Tim. 6:21b; Col. 4:18). The finale of Paul's own letters always expanded on the idea of "grace"; he always wrote "the grace of our Lord (or the Lord) Jesus Christ." Sometimes instead of a simple pronoun, "you," Paul mentioned the spirit of those to whom he was writing (Gal. 6:18; Phil. 4:23; Phlm. 25).[46]

The final greeting is a kind of blessing on the gathered assembly. The greeting is in the plural as are the final greetings of 1 and 2 Timothy (1 Tim. 6:21; 2 Tim. 4:22). The plural number of the greeting stands in contrast with the single individual to whom the epistle was presumably addressed, that is, either Titus or Timothy. The final greeting of Titus, unlike the final greetings of the epistles to Timothy, is reinforced by the addition of "all" (*pantōn*): "Grace be with all of you."

---

46. This usage is reflected in two of the variants mentioned on p. 371, note b.

The final section of the Epistle to Titus looks to the future, that is, the missions of Artemis, Tychicus, Zenas, and Apollos, relatively unknown persons who were to continue the mission of the apostle. The pericope concludes with a comprehensive blessing. Those who read the Pastoral Epistles today are well aware that the mission of Paul has indeed been continued by untold numbers of anonymous Christians and that, as a result, the entire church has indeed been blessed.

INDEX OF ANCIENT SOURCES

INDEX OF SUBJECTS